T.R.

T.R.

The Last Romantic

H. W. BRANDS

BasicBooks
A Subsidiary of Perseus Books, L.L.C.

Published by BasicBooks,
A Subsidiary of Perseus Books, L.L.C.

Quotations from the Theodore Roosevelt Collection, Harvard College Library, are by permission of the Houghton Library, Harvard University.

FIRST EDITION

Designed by Charlotte Staub

Library of Congress Cataloging-in-Publication Data

Brands, H. W.
    T.R. : the last romantic / H. W. Brands.
       p.   cm.
    Includes bibliographical references and index.
    ISBN 0-465-06958-4
    1. Roosevelt, Theodore, 1858–1919. 2. Presidents—United States—Biography.
I. Title.
E757.B82   1997
973.91'1'092—dc21   97-21432

97 98 99 00 01   ❖/RRD   10 9 8 7 6 5 4 3 2 1

Brass gift   5/00

CONTENTS

PROLOGUE
July 1918

⌖

He didn't sleep much these days. He never had: Four or five hours a night was all he could stand before the motor inside him made him jump up and start moving again. But in those younger days, sleep—the sleep of the honestly exhausted—had come easily once he *did* get off his feet. Now he was never exhausted, because he was always tired.

His leg—the one he had nearly lost in 1902 after the streetcar accident and that, reinjured, had almost cost him his life in the Amazon a decade later—ached constantly. Gout made every step even more of a trial. The fever he had caught in the jungle—or it might have been the malaria from the Spanish war—washed over him at irregular intervals, lathering him in sweat, then chilling him through, even on these mild summer nights. The eye that had been smashed in that White House spar was now dead to all light; the other eye, never good to begin with, gave out after just a few hours of reading. The ear that had festered so badly in the hospital the previous winter still hurt; it had taken him weeks to regain his equilibrium, and he never did regain all his hearing. He could usually hear the birdsongs through the open windows of the house in the morning or when he sat out on the piazza at dusk, but to the annoyance of one who had delighted in showing off to his birder friends, he could no longer distinguish one species from another as surely as before.

On the other hand, there weren't as many species to distinguish. When his family—his father, mother, brother, and two sisters—had started coming to Oyster Bay, it had been an outpost almost in the wilderness. The train stopped at Syosset, six miles south, and of course there were no automobiles to disrupt the rhythm of the tides, of day and night, of the seasons. But in the half-century since, the village had become a suburb, the thirty miles from Manhattan filled in with factories, shops, houses, schools, restaurants, hotels.

Not even Sagamore had been spared: The cars and delivery trucks came right up to the door. He had resisted this intrusion at first, but ever since Edith's awful fall from her horse, after which he and Archie had flagged down a passing car for an ambulance, he couldn't really condemn this encroachment on his sanctuary.

The place had changed in other ways. The trees had grown up since he had walked this hilltop with Alice Lee and had, with much waving of arms, paced off distances and thrown down rocks here, a hat and coat there, for markers, excitedly sketching the grand house he was going to build for her. Leeholm, it would be called.

Leeholm—it had been many years since he had spoken the original name of the house. And it had been even longer since he had spoken Alice's name. Weeks, sometimes months, now went by without his thinking of her. But now and again something—a certain musty tang in the air off the salt marshes near the sound when the summer breeze shifted to the north; the half-heard notes of a songbird driven farther into the forest by the traffic; the light filtering through the leaves on the road to the village—transported him back to the days when his fondest dream had been to share this house with Alice and his life with hers.

But Alice had never lived here, and for thirty years the house had been Edith's. To be sure, visitors perceived much more of him than of Edith when they walked in the front door. Heads, hides, and antlers from his hunts crowded the walls; swords and flags and other memorabilia of battle filled each corner and cranny. But those who knew Edith recognized her influence. It might have seemed a small matter that she allowed a mounted head behind her own chair in the dining room but not behind his; she refused to have a dead beast staring at her over the soup. Her parlor, to the left of the front door, just off the main hall, was more clearly her domain. Dark leather gave way to sunny satin; the clutter of the rest of the house surrendered to the neatness and control that characterized everything about her: her dress, her handwriting, her approach to household management, her emotions.

He recognized how much he owed to this aspect of Edith's temperament. Without it they might have lost the house. They were quite well off financially now—not rich by the standards of some of their Long Island neighbors but more than comfortable. Yet on a couple of occasions back in the eighties and nineties—after the horrible winter of 1886–87 had killed half his herd in Dakota and destroyed his hopes of becoming a cattle baron, and then again after the Panic of '93 had left them mired in the same depression that was swallowing much of the rest of the country—they had seriously considered giving up the place. Edith had economized: He could still see her in the kitchen mixing her horrible tooth powder of ground cuttlefish bones and alum—anything to save a penny here or there. Thank goodness he had always had strong teeth. He had vaguer recollections of being placed on a stringent allowance, the vagueness no doubt the result of his heedlessly wandering off the allowance at every opportunity. He still had only the faintest idea what ordinary items cost.

Yet in no small part through Edith's determination—and her instinctive appreciation that, given the vagaries of his career, Sagamore Hill was likely to be one of the few constants in their lives and certainly the one place they could truly call home—they had held on to the house. Left to himself, he might have been a gypsy. He had no problem wintering in a tiny cabin in the Badlands, doubling up with Cabot Lodge or Spring Rice in Washington, sleeping in his office at police headquarters in New York or on a train crossing the country. But that was no life for her, and still less was it a life for their children.

The house was important, the geographic focus of their existence, but the children were absolutely vital—the emotional epicenter. To an even greater degree than most men of his prolific era, he believed in large families. Offspring were civilization's duty to posterity and the greatest joy of any man's life. He doted on his children; he spoiled them; he broke the rules of the house with them—and then he left them with their mother while he tore off to work, to Washington, to the West, to war. He sometimes felt guilty for placing his career ahead of them; as elsewhere in his emotional life, guilt wound the spring that drove him so relentlessly. In the case of the children, it surfaced in the intensity of his rambunctiousness with them and in the high—sometimes impossibly high—standards he set for them, by both exhortation and example. Alice responded by rebelling, Ted by breaking down physically, Kermit by fleeing the country. The younger ones—Archie, Ethel, and Quentin—had their own, sometimes more subtle, ways of coping.

Yet in the present hour of national peril, the children—the boys, at least—had rallied to the flag of their country and to their father's ideals. They embraced his romantic concept of life, his belief that physical bravery was the highest virtue and war the ultimate test of bravery. From youth he had held to this view, and in old age he clung to it more tightly than ever.

A man had to cling to something, to some talisman, against the evil, the anarchy, that was all around. "There is not one among us in whom a devil does not dwell," he had written just a year and a half ago. "At some time, on some point, that devil masters each of us." The devil had mastered Elliott, his own brother, his other self as a child. But that was because Elliott had lost his grip and given in to despair. This was the mortal sin: to cease struggling. "It is not having been in the Dark House but having left it that counts."

Yet one never truly left the Dark House, not until death, at any rate. And if one had to die—as everyone did—then there was no better way, no more glorious way, than to go out fighting. This had been his creed; now it was the creed of his four sons.

Until these last few months, though, he had never fully appreciated what this creed cost. He had bared himself to death in the Spanish war and had delighted in doing so. And he had judged that in the act he had proved his prowess and demonstrated his heroism. The reporters who followed him, and the voters who elected him governor six months later, certainly seemed to agree.

But only now did he understand how much harder it was for those who stayed behind. Only now did he appreciate how helpless Edith had felt when he had left her sickbed to indulge his obsession with soldiering. Only now did he realize that it was far more painful to send a loved one into battle than to go oneself.

The pain, the fear, the helplessness—these were the real reasons, far more than the aches of his nearly three-score years, that he wasn't sleeping lately. Fifteen months had passed since the United States had entered the war; finally, after unconscionable delays due to that wretched creature in the White House, American troops were finally coming to grips with the German foe. Partly through their own efforts, partly through his, the boys had gotten themselves precisely where he would have wanted to be: amid the heaviest fighting. Indeed, he would have joined them in France, even at his age and in his condition, had the jealous Wilson not blocked his way.

His pride couldn't have been greater, nor his anxiety. He and Edith hung on the news that came up the drive every day. The mail could be counted on to bring good tidings, for letters revealed that Ted and Kermit and Archie and Quentin were still alive or had been at the time of writing. Telegrams were another matter. If one of the boys had been hurt or killed, he and Edith would learn by cable.

Sometimes the good news came mixed with the bad. Several months ago, Archie had been wounded but had survived and been awarded the Croix de Guerre. His father could hardly contain his admiration for his son; it made him prouder than he had ever felt in his life. Nor could he disguise his relief that Archie would spend the next weeks or months recuperating, out of harm's way.

That Edith shared his feelings, if in different proportions, was a comfort and a source of still more pride. She had never fully understood his preoccupation with heroism and physical bravery; but having learned through bitter experience how closely it was wrapped up with his concept of himself, she accepted it. And she saw enough of the father in the sons to know that it would be worse than useless to stand between them and the front lines, just as it had been worse than useless with him.

Despite her reservations, her heart swelled as much as his when, late at night, just before turning out the lamp, they recounted to each other how Archie had won his decoration. And in their thirty years of marriage he had never seen her so soul-stirringly beautiful as on that day, shortly after the news arrived, when she had silenced the guests at lunch and ordered all the glasses filled. She toasted their hero, and then, with cheeks flushed and eyes glistening, she shattered her goblet on the floor, declaring that lips would never again touch the glass that had been raised to her son's gallantry.

Their hearts had swelled anew just a week ago when word came that Quentin, in the air corps, had shot down his first German air-craft. Quentin's three brothers had engaged the foe; now the youngest lion had been blooded.

His father had ridden in an airplane once, and when he lay awake nights now, waiting for the dawn, or when he watched evening throw its shadows across the sound or gazed absently from his sofa at Edith balancing her books or telling the servants how many places to set at the table, he imagined what Quentin must feel as he flew high above the green meadows of France, with the wind in his face and the smoke and roar of battle far below. It must be glorious. And even more glorious for the dangers Quentin laughed off, as he had always laughed off every care.

Then yesterday morning brought the news that had stopped his heart: Quentin was down behind enemy lines. That was all. No one knew whether he had been killed or maimed or captured or even now was making his way back toward friendly territory.

Theodore had never felt so helpless. There was nothing he could do for Quentin. There was nothing he could do for the other boys. There was nothing he could do for Edith. As much anxiety and heartache as he felt, at least *he* had his faith to cling to: that it was all for a higher and nobler cause. Such faith came harder for her. She knew only that her youngest, her baby—he was only twenty years old—was in dan-ger, maybe dying at that very moment, maybe dead. Her husband's heroic vision was cold comfort to her now.

He sensed the chill in her soul, and it made his vision all the more difficult to hold on to—but all the more necessary.

Part One

PREPARATION

CHAPTER ONE

A Child of the Civil War
1858–65

Like all children, he believed that his home and family occupied the center of the universe; his gradual realization that
they didn't occupy even the center of his native city would be a
primary factor in driving him into public life. To be sure, the
Roosevelts were respected, not least for their long lineage. The
first van Rosenvelt had arrived two centuries earlier from
Holland, at a time when the village of New Amsterdam was still
Dutch. But the quiet village that had greeted old Claes was now
a raucous city, and the solid Dutch burghers, among whom
Claes's descendants had taken their solid place, had been
elbowed aside by the English, the Germans, and lately the Irish.
In the 1850s, New York throbbed with some eight hundred
thousand souls, not counting the additional quarter million in the
separate city of Brooklyn across the East River and the nearly
one hundred thousand in Newark and Jersey City across the
Hudson. Weekly, thousands more poured down the gangplanks
of immigrant ships from Europe. Although New York was by far
the largest city in America and nearly the oldest, the unceasing
torrent of new arrivals gave it a frontier feeling. Nothing lasted;
everything was constantly being remade. "Overturn, overturn,
overturn! is the maxim of New York," complained one lifelong
resident who ached for a modicum of stability. "The very bones
of our ancestors are not permitted to lie quiet a quarter of a century, and one generation of men seem studious to remove all
relics of those who precede them." But most New Yorkers

3

thrived on the changes for the same reason that most Americans cherished the frontier. Henry James had one of his characters in *Washington Square* say that the modest house he and his bride had taken would do for the moment, for they didn't intend to remain there long. "At the end of three or four years, we'll move. That's the way to live in New York—to move every three or four years. Then you'll always get the last thing. It's because the city is growing so quick— you've got to keep up with it. It's going straight up town—that's where New York's going."

What was driving New York uptown was all the immigration downtown. Since Ireland's famine of the 1840s, the largest stream of immigration had come from that hungry isle; the Irish joined an earlier and continuing effusion from the German-speaking lands of central Europe. At first a few of the immigrants sought shelter at the northern edge of the populated districts. Their habits dismayed those who had arrived earlier, causing the editor of the *Evening Post* to harrumph in distaste:

> During the last few years, an immense population of poor Irish and Germans have settled on the vacant lots, between 37th and 50th streets. They have built their own cabins, and live there, the dogs, goats and pigs often all in the same room with the family. Their business is the poorest street or house labor. Picking rags, selling goats' milk, gathering cinders from the ashes to sell to the other poor, cleaning the new houses, working on the docks; and among the Germans, making the wooden splinters for match manufacturers.

But as the moneyed classes fled the crush downtown, they evicted the squatters. These joined the larger number who had crowded into the older districts that the wealthy had left behind, either into their since-partitioned houses or into the newer, even more crowded tenements. Statistics told the tale of the difference between the upper and lower parts of the city. A housing reformer, Samuel Halliday, noted that the two miles of fashionable Fifth Avenue between the parade ground at Washington Square and the reservoir at Forty-second Street provided homes to some 400 families, while a single block of tenements farther south sheltered 700 families, or some 3,500 individuals. At a time when a square mile of London's East End, the neighborhood so wrenchingly portrayed in the novels of Charles Dickens, contained

175,000 inhabitants, New York's Fourth Ward had a population density of 290,000 per square mile. More crowded places on earth existed, but most Americans wouldn't have considered them civilized. Many had similar doubts about the immigrant neighborhoods of lower New York.

The wealthy had another reason for moving uptown besides the breathing room that the new neighborhoods offered. They wanted to get wealthier—to cash in on the boom in real estate prices that the population explosion was driving. Halliday, after enumerating the density of the tenements, offered an explanation for their existence and a warning regarding the prospect of change. "The amount invested in tenant-houses in New York," Halliday said, "together with the enormous percentage which they pay, has created an interest so great that the work of reforming the abuses connected with them will be no child's play." The influx of immigrants generated an insatiable demand for housing, and although the immigrant families couldn't afford to pay much individually, collectively they could pay a great deal. Owners of tenements typically received returns of anywhere from 25 percent to 100 percent per year on their investments, far higher than the rates received by owners of housing rented to middle- and upper-class families. The arithmetic of the situation drove property values up, which in turn drove the more comfortable classes uptown, making many of them rich in the bargain.

The richest of all was John Jacob Astor. At his death in 1848, Astor was one of the wealthiest men in the world, with an estate conservatively valued at $20 million. The rental income alone from his properties topped $200,000 yearly. And yet he still regretted lost opportunities—in particular, the bargains in land he had missed. Asked what he would do differently, he replied, "Could I begin life again, knowing what I now know, and had the money to invest, I would buy every foot of land on the Island of Manhattan."

Theodore Roosevelt's people weren't in the same league as Astor, but they played the same game. In the mid-nineteenth century, Cornelius Van Schaack Roosevelt, Theodore's grandfather, ruled the clan from a brick mansion on Union Square. C.V.S., as the family called him, headed the firm of Roosevelt & Son, founded by his grandfather and father, originally merchandising hardware, more recently providing plate glass to New York's busy builders. The company paid the family's bills and provided employment for the adult sons. But the true source of the family's wealth was real estate, which C.V.S. had cannily collected on the low side of the Panic of 1837. As Manhattan boomed during the middle decades of the century, so did the Roosevelt fortune. During one three-year stretch in the 1840s, Cornelius's worth was estimated to have doubled, and it soon doubled again and then again. An 1868 listing in a nosy magazine placed him among Manhattan's ten genuine millionaires. While he complained of the publicity, he didn't dispute the veracity of the report.

As it lifted the Roosevelts and Astors and others similarly fortunate, the swelling tide of real estate values sifted the city socially, producing two distinct and only occasionally overlapping societies. Theodore Roosevelt was born into one; the other he would come to know professionally. The older wards were home to the poor, some honest, some not. The honest poor included the innumerable peddlers who plied their wares on the ferry landings and in front of the Merchants' Exchange on Wall Street; of these the most visible, or at least the most audible, were the hot-corn girls, whose chant rose above the din of the streets:

> Hot corn! Hot corn!
> Here's your lily-white corn!
> All you that's got money,
> Poor me that's got none—
> Buy my lily-white corn
> And let me go home.

The dishonest poor included the pickpockets, petty thieves, and criminals of somewhat grander ambitions who frequented City Hall Park, lower Broadway, and other less genteel parts of Manhattan. What truly disturbed respectable New Yorkers was not the existence of the criminal element—they had become inured to that—but the esteem in which its leaders were held by so many of the city's inhabitants. One gangster, gunned down in 1855, was given a funeral that featured a full marching band and a procession of thousands of mourners, and attracted scores of thousands of onlookers. Horace Greeley's *Tribune*, expressing the "disgust and contempt" that all public-spirited citizens must share, warned that the circumstances surrounding the slaying evinced a cultural shift of ominous proportions.

A longtime New Yorker, Philip Hone, lamented that "the city is infested by gangs of hardened wretches, born in the haunts of infamy, brought up in taverns." Such persons, said Hone, "patrol the streets making night hideous and insulting to all who are not strong enough to defend themselves." An English visitor remarked, "The practice of carrying concealed arms, in the shape of stilettos for attack, and swordsticks for defense, if illegal, is perfectly common. . . . Terrible outrages and murderous assaults are matters of such nightly occurrence as to be thought hardly worthy of notice."

Not surprisingly, the pervasiveness of crime brought calls for better policing of the city. In 1844 the state legislature ordered the mayor to reorganize and upgrade the city's police force. Mayor James Harper attempted to do so by, among other means, mandating the wearing of uniforms. The policemen, who were accustomed to wearing ordinary clothes with a badge indicating their office, rebelled at the notion of what they derided as livery. Meanwhile, the city's Board of Aldermen, refusing to be overruled by Albany, endorsed a separate reorganization plan, creating a separate police force. For a year the city had two rival police forces, which at one point fought a pitched battle on the steps of City Hall. Finally, in the interest of municipal peace, the aldermen acquiesced in the legislature's plan, and after much persuasion the officers agreed to put on the blue uniforms that became their trademark.

Theodore Roosevelt would grow intimately acquainted with the problems of policing the city when he accepted the post of police commissioner; he would also become acquainted with the corruption that underlay the policing dispute and that generally characterized the government of the city. Corruption in New York took myriad forms. It allowed the city's ten thousand prostitutes, for example, to practice their ostensibly illicit profession usually unmolested. The bolder practitioners, those whom diarist George Templeton Strong called the "noctivagous strumpetocracy," brazenly paraded along Broadway. One client, more appreciative than Strong, described the high-toned streetwalkers: "Their complexions are pure white and red, and their dresses are of the most expensive material, and an ultra-fashionable make. Diamonds and bracelets flash from their bosoms and bare arms, and heavily-wrought India shawls, of that gorgeous scarlet whose beaming hue intoxicates the eye, hang carelessly from their superb shoulders, almost trailing on the walk." Every now and then the police would raid a brothel, to remind its owner why they were being paid off. After one such raid, the *Herald* intoned, "Clerks of respectable mercantile houses were found in this pious place in the embraces of the most depraved and abandoned denizens of the notorious spot. They were compelled to give their names and the names of their employers. They were then suffered to go home, covered with shame and mortification."

Corruption in the city had many other faces. The most familiar watched over the development of public works. Providing the necessities of life to a population that was rapidly approaching one million was a heroic undertaking; one landmark victory came in 1842 with the opening of the Croton water system. Connecting a storage reservoir on the Croton River in upper Westchester County to distribution reservoirs on Forty-second and Eighty-sixth Streets by means of a conduit eight feet in diameter and forty-five miles long, the Croton system brought a flood of fresh water into the city and allowed the city's breathtaking growth to continue unabated. "Nothing is talked of or thought of in New York but Croton water . . ." Philip Hone wrote. "Political spouting has given way to waterspouts, and the free current of water has diverted the attention of the people from the vexed question of the confused state of the national currency. . . . Water! water! is the universal note which is sounded through every part of the city, and infuses joy and exultation into the masses."

Public works necessitated public funding, in the expenditure of which numerous temptations to diversion arose. New York officials were perhaps no more susceptible to temptation than others of their era, but they were demonstrably no less. And none was more human in this regard than William Marcy Tweed, the boss of New York's Democratic Party. Boss Tweed had gifts well suited to an age that lionized schemers and connivers, but where the legal lions did their scheming and conniving in the private sector, Tweed and his Tammany Hall colleagues were more publicly minded. During the 1850s and 1860s, they brought to the government of New York City the same sorts of shenanigans that were cornering markets, watering stocks, and fleecing investors in the corporate world. Their most breathtaking project, the construction of the County Courthouse at City Hall Park, netted the Tweed ring millions of dollars before being revealed in all its grafting glory, and it included such ornaments to civic pride as enough carpet to cover a highway reaching halfway to Albany—paid for but, needless to say, never delivered. Heaping insult atop injury, a special committee appointed to probe the case charged the city more than $18,000 for twelve days' deliberation.

II

Theodore Roosevelt would get to grapple with both the gangsters of the street and the bilkers of the boardroom. But before he did, he had to survive a sheltered youth in the world of upper-class New York. It wasn't easy. By his tenth birthday he had been nearly pampered to death—repeatedly. To be fair to his parents, it wasn't precisely the pampering that carried him to death's doorstep; it was the asthma. But the pampering didn't help, and quite possibly it hurt.

Roosevelt's was a sick family—not dysfunctional but ill. His father died at the age of forty-six from cancer. His mother, never robust, succumbed to typhoid fever at forty-eight. His elder sister, Anna, nicknamed Bamie (short for *bambina* and pronounced "bammie"), suffered from a congenital bone disease that warped her spine and left her partly disabled. His younger sister, Corinne, called Conie, had asthma. His younger brother, Elliott, suffered from emotional illness and perhaps epilepsy, and eventually from chemical dependencies that led to his early death.

But it was Theodore—or Teedie, distinguishing him from his father, also Theodore (often The—pronounced *Thee*, and sometimes so spelled)—who was the frailest. Almost from his birth, on the evening of October 27, 1858, at the family house on East Twentieth Street, the boy suffered from one ailment after another. As an infant he was chronically uncomfortable; when he got old enough to say what was hurting, he described headaches, fevers, stomach pains, intestinal groanings, and as many other maladies as he had names for.

Most serious was his asthma. First appearing not long after he learned to talk, it recurrently seized the child by the bronchi and nearly suffocated him. The illness was only vaguely understood at the time, although an inherited predisposition was suspected, and a connection was recognized between the onset of attacks and various airborne irritants: coal dust (a pervasive problem in an age when coal heated houses, fired factories, and drove trains), powdered horse dung (another problem endemic to city life in the pre-automobile era), pollen, molds, and the like. In addition, asthma researchers noticed an emotional or psychological element in the disease, although what that element was in any particular case remained elusive.

In Teedie's case the attacks came at intervals lasting from several hours to several days or sometimes even weeks. They were terrifying; try as he might to breathe, he couldn't get enough air. He gasped and wheezed and choked, not knowing whether each frantic gasp might be his last. And when the attacks finally eased, he lay sweat-soaked, trembling, and exhausted, torn between relief at having survived and dread at the thought of the next such encounter.

The attacks were equally terrifying for his parents, if in a slightly different way. Helpless to prevent the attacks, neither could they alleviate them. No medications existed to open the swollen air passages. Caffeine sometimes seemed to work; one recommendation was to ply the patient with the blackest, strongest coffee brewable. But equally often the bitter stuff merely made the patient vomit. Nicotine, another stimulant, was also recommended, producing the paradoxical sight of a young child, already strangling on his own breath, trying to smoke a fat cigar. On the other hand, sedatives such as alcohol had their partisans; under this regimen, asthmatic children knocked back shots of whiskey. That all-purpose palliative of the Victorian era—opium— soothed some sufferers. Assorted other remedies, often equally contradictory, testified to the general state of confusion surrounding the condition.

Teedie's parents tried everything they could think of. Nothing worked anywhere near reliably. When the fits came, the only thing they could do was hold him, walk him around, and try to comfort him. Given the slight stature and uncertain constitution of his mother, this chore fell to his father, the more as Teedie grew older. As a result, the boy came to associate the attacks—unconsciously, to be sure— with an opportunity to receive his father's undivided attention. Teedie's father was hardly a cold or remote figure to his children, but he was a busy man who spent the great majority of his waking hours away from home. Moreover, Teedie had three siblings who also competed for their father's attention. Quite possibly it didn't escape Teedie's notice that their father particularly doted on Bamie, who had the bone disease. In any event, it definitely didn't escape his notice that during his attacks he became the center of his father's world. Bamie could wait; Elliott and Conie could wait; his mother could wait; his father's outside activities could wait. His father would pick him up in strong, reassuring arms. Fresh air sometimes seemed to afford relief: often at night his father would bundle him in blankets and take him for a fast ride through the darkened streets of Manhattan—a thrill the young child could appreciate as the siege of his pulmonary system gradually lifted.

All of which is not to imply that Teedie's asthma was anything but a real disease or was merely in his head. It most definitely was in his lungs. Yet many diseases have psychological components, asthma among them. And as distressing as the physical manifestations of the attacks were, some of the emotional consequences could be distinctly rewarding. It isn't surprising that they occurred as often as they did.

III

Teedie would have idolized his father even without the asthma. The elder Theodore Roosevelt was an easy man for his children to idolize. He was a large, powerful figure with a broad forehead, strong brow and nose, full bristling beard, and sparkling blue eyes that revealed beneath the distinguished demeanor a soul that had never lost the joyfulness of youth. Theodore was the youngest of grandfather C.V.S.'s five surviving offspring—all boys (a sixth boy died as a baby). As children, the group—Silas Weir, James Alfred, Cornelius Jr., Robert Barnhill, and Theodore—made quite an impression on polite New York society. The neighbors spoke of "that lovely Mrs. Roosevelt" and her "five horrid boys." James took most after their father in temperament and interests, and it was to James that Cornelius handed direction of the family's business affairs, including management of the Broadway Improvement Association, the corporate entity that controlled the family's property holdings. Robert, the maverick of the bunch, went into politics (discreetly allowing his given middle name to be corrupted to Barnwell, which he considered less likely to afford an opening to slander-minded opponents who might liken a Barnhill to a manure pile). Setting something of a precedent for his nephew, Robert campaigned to recapture New York politics from the machinations of the Tweed ring. He also established another family precedent by making the conservation of natural resources a priority. His efforts at saving the shad run on the Hudson River brought him international attention; when the British minister in Washington requested information on the subject, Secretary of State Hamilton Fish, who presumably chose words on this subject with care, directed him to Robert Roosevelt as "the Father of all the fishes."

Theodore joined brother James in the family business. But he never warmed to it the way James did. He had neither passion nor flair for commerce and found the whole thing rather a bore. His blood might have been stirred by the thought of helping to build the great metropolis, of providing, literally, windows on the world to the thousands of the present and the millions of the future. But it didn't. Neither did he conceive of money-making as the test of a man's mettle in the dawning age of industry.

Yet if Theodore fell short in the art of making money, he knew well enough how to spend it. He had an eye for the finer things in life. He kept himself impeccably attired, partly to befit his station in society but also, apparently, to offset his childhood experience as the last of five boys and the recipient of the others' hand-me-downs. Once, overhearing his mother say, for what seemed the thousandth time, "These were Robert's, but will be a good change for Theodore," he objected vociferously that he was "tired of changes." As an adult he bought only the best clothing. He was an accomplished horseman and kept the most handsome mounts; when he took his family out for a drive, his coach and team—not to mention his fast driving—made onlookers turn and stare. The house on Twentieth Street that all his children were born in was a wedding gift from his father; while it wasn't especially imposing or luxurious, Theodore never stinted on its operation and maintenance.

Theodore's generous ways extended well beyond his family circle. He was a pioneer of a new class in America: committed and essentially full-time philanthropists. Charity had existed from time out of mind, of course, but in America during the nineteenth century it became organized as never before—at a time, not coincidentally, when most other areas of life were becoming similarly organized, and when poverty was becoming increasingly entrenched and visible. Theodore Roosevelt Sr. once remarked that he possessed a "troublesome conscience"; that conscience inspired him to activities that he found far more engrossing, and rewarding, than peddling plate glass. He helped found the Children's Aid Society and the State Charities Aid Association. He spearheaded a drive to establish the Newsboys' Lodging House, a shelter for Ragged Dicks who had pluck but not so much luck; most Sunday evenings were spent with the newsboys, inquiring after their activities and dreams, and sharing some of his own.

A special project was the New York Orthopedic Hospital. Bamie's affliction attuned her father to the sufferings of similarly stricken children, and it acquainted him with New York's leading doctors in the field. He initially tried to talk his friends and business associates into backing a state-of-the-art orthopedic hospital, but they claimed other causes as reason to decline. So one spring afternoon he held a small party at the family house, to all appearances a strictly social gathering. When the guests, representing New York's most prominent and affluent families, arrived, he had several poor children in need of orthopedic treatment brought in and introduced to the guests. The effect was exactly as he had hoped. Mrs. John Jacob Astor turned to him and declared, "Theodore, you are right; these children must be restored and made into active citizens again, and I for one will help you in your work." Mrs. Astor's pledge precipitated others, and by afternoon's end enough money had been raised to get the orthopedic hospital up and running.

This event and others like it won Theodore a reputation as an irresistible solicitor for worthy causes. Friends and business acquaintances came to recognize a characteristic gleam in his eye; most would surrender without a fight, asking merely, "How much this time, Theodore?"

Theodore put his fund-raising skills to work for the Union during the Civil War. Not long after the fighting began, he journeyed to Washington to lobby for legislation to guarantee that the families of the men under arms would not suffer unnecessarily from their absence. He pressed for a bill that would facilitate the voluntary allotment of part of each soldier's pay to his family. The measure struck most of the legislators as patriotic and reasonable, and it passed without difficulty. After it did, Theodore accepted an unpaid appointment as one of New York's allotment commissioners. In this capacity he traveled from camp to camp, encouraging the troops to earmark a set portion each month for their loved ones at home. He proved as adept at opening the soldiers' pay envelopes as he was at prying money loose from the likes of the widow Astor. "The men looked as hard as I have often seen such men look in our Mission neighborhood," he wrote home on New Year's Day, 1862, "but after a little talking and explaining my object and reminding them of those they had left behind them, one after another put down his name, and from this company alone, they allotted, while I was there, $600.00. . . . One man, after putting down five dollars a month, said suddenly, 'My old woman has always been good to me, and if you please, change it to ten.' In a moment, half a dozen others followed his example and doubled their allotments."

IV

Teedie, at age four, was too young to appreciate such stories. But the Civil War came home to him in other ways. The conflict convulsed New York City. Most of the city's immigrants had little understanding of the constitutional arguments behind the campaign to suppress secession, and they had even less sympathy for the slaves the war eventually was intended to free. Least of all did they warm to the idea of conscription, which President Lincoln turned to after his calls for voluntary enlistments fell shy of his armies' needs. During the summer of 1863, antipathy to the draft combined with the numerous other volatile ingredients of working-class life in the city to produce an explosion that rocked the Union as unnervingly as any detonations on the field of formal battle.

The draft riots—an outbreak of urban warfare, really—began when a company of volunteer firemen, who had expected that their traditional exemption from militia duty would carry over to exemption from the draft, learned otherwise, and attacked and set fire to the office where the local draft lottery was being held. Overpowering the police on the scene, they quickly grew intoxicated on their success, as well as on the liquor they liberated from local saloons, and they roamed the streets looking for more trouble. Meanwhile, the draft-office fire touched off blazes in nearby buildings; as the inhabitants of those buildings fled for their lives, looters raced the flames to snatch up unguarded valuables. Denunciations of Lincoln gave way to demands for vengeance against local symbols of support for the war. One man who had the misfortune of resembling Horace Greeley was beaten nearly to death; the house of a friend of Greeley, where the pro-war editor had stayed during a recent illness, was sacked.

African-Americans, angrily blamed for the war, came under violent assault as well. A British military officer, lately arrived from the Pennsylvania front where he had been observing operations, was surprised to see a mayhem-minded mob chasing a black man down the street. "Never having been in New York before," the officer recorded, "and being totally ignorant of the state of feeling with regard to negroes, I inquired of a by-stander what the negro had done that they should want to kill him? He replied civilly enough—'Oh, sir, they hate them here, they are the innocent cause of all these troubles.'" Blacks were dragged from streetcars and beaten; their houses were looted; an orphanage for black children was torched, and when firemen came to put out the flames, the hoses were cut and the hydrants sabotaged. A black sailor from a ship anchored at the foot of Leroy Street unluckily chose the beginning of the riot to go ashore looking for groceries. While asking directions, he was set upon and mortally stabbed and stoned.

For nearly a week the rioting raged out of control. The political and racial antagonisms melded into a form of class warfare. Employers with hard reputations had their buildings destroyed; fashionable shops were ransacked and the goods carried off. Well-dressed gentlemen weren't safe on the street, liable to be singled out and beaten as "three-hundred-dollar men"—three hundred dollars being the price of exemption from the draft. When the police failed to quell the destruction, army troops were rushed to the city. The first units had to fight their way through barricades and over downed telegraph poles, returning fusillades from armed rioters.

Ultimately, the weight of the government's military force wore down the rioters, who in any event were exhausted from days and nights of drinking, arson, assault, looting and shooting. By the time more than 4,000 army troops had arrived, order had nearly been restored. A renewed flutter of fear followed news of a mutiny of some 350 recruits on Riker's Island, who seized and imprisoned their officers. But when the ranking naval officer in the area threatened to bombard the mutineers' position, they surrendered, and the riot gradually sputtered out. The toll of the week of violence reached more than one hundred dead—early exaggerations placed the number at more than one thousand—hundreds more wounded, and tens of millions of dollars of property damaged or destroyed.

Teedie knew nothing directly of the riot. The family was vacationing at the seashore, where, with many of their class, they waited out the violence. Many, but not all: One Colonel O'Brien, a friend and neighbor, was torn to pieces by a mob while defending his home and family from the rioters. The Gramercy Park–Madison Square neighborhood where Teedie habitually played became the scene of a pitched battle when soldiers attempted to retrieve some weapons stolen from the local armory and cached at the Union Steam & Iron Works on Second Avenue, just blocks from the Roosevelt house.

Teedie's elders shuddered at the shocking demonstration of the fragility of the social order. His grandmother observed, "I really do not wonder that the poor mechanics oppose conscription. It certainly favors the rich at the expense of the poor."

Grandmamma Bulloch had special reason for sympathizing with the opposition to the draft. A Georgia native, she naturally believed in the justice of the cause of the Confederacy. More to the point for Teedie, so did her daughter, the boy's mother. Martha Bulloch Roosevelt had married Theodore Roosevelt in 1853. The marriage appeared a good match—the handsome, wealthy New York businessman of fine family and standing, and the charming, gracious southern belle of even more distinguished lineage if somewhat less distinguished present fortune. Although Theodore at once took Mittie, as she was called, back to New York, her mother and sister, Anna, visited frequently and for extended periods, and as a result the southern influence was pervasive at Teedie's house.

Upon the outbreak of the war, a psychological fault line opened, running right through the center of the household. On one side were Theodore and, for the most part, the children, particularly Teedie. On the other were the Bulloch women. Unbeknownst to the neighbors, and evidently even to Theodore, the ladies spent many afternoons putting together relief packets for relatives and friends back home. These were shipped to the Bahamas and then by blockade-runner to Georgia.

Teedie couldn't understand the causes of the war between the states, but he could feel the strain it produced in his family. He knew that his mother and aunt and grandmother were silently pulling for the South, while his father and nearly everyone else he knew were rooting for the North. Already Teedie was strongly identifying with his father; consequently, he, too, desired a Union triumph. With the fierceness that would mark his feelings throughout his life, he hoped and prayed for the success of the Blue. His aunt recalled an evening when, in her presence, he concluded his bedtime prayers with a request that the Almighty "grind the southern troops to powder."

When the Almighty—in league with General Grant—did just that, Teedie cheered the victory as loudly as anyone. Mittie and her sister and mother were unsurprisingly subdued. Theodore Sr. was relieved more than anything else—relieved that the side of justice had won and that his family might be made emotionally whole again. One reservation spoiled his enjoyment of the victory: a nagging feeling that he had done less than his duty. In deference to Mittie's wishes that he not take up arms against her brothers and cousins, Theodore stuck to his allotment activities and repeatedly ignored Lincoln's calls for soldiers. He hired a substitute from among the many thousands of recent immigrants whose ardor to fight was probably no greater than his but whose ability to pay was indubitably less. This maneuver was perfectly legal, and it raised few eyebrows among Theodore's friends and associates, many of whom availed themselves of the same opportunity. And indeed most of those spent the war in activities less worthy than his. A convincing case could be made that Theodore served the Union far better by ensuring the well-being of soldiers' wives and children than he would have by toting a gun or some general's field glasses.

But persuasive though these arguments might have been, they didn't convince Theodore himself. As the war progressed and as more and more men on both sides fell, he came increasingly to believe that he should have heeded the martial call rather than the marital. According to his daughter Bamie, who as the eldest had the deepest insight into her parents, he "always afterward felt that he done a very wrong thing" in not ignoring every other sentiment and joining the fighting forces.

CHAPTER TWO

Foreign Ventures
1865–73

In time the younger Theodore Roosevelt would be troubled by his father's failure to serve. His sister Conie attributed much of her brother's later obsession with war to a desire to compensate for their father's deficiency in this regard. But at seven Teedie was too busy being impressed by those of his relations who did serve. The most conspicuous family heroes hailed from his mother's side. The Bullochs fought under the wrong flag, of course, but they did so with conspicuous gallantry. Several Bullochs served in the Confederate army; one uncle, James Bulloch, was an admiral in the Confederate navy who carried out secret assignments for Jefferson Davis in Europe. The most important of these was the construction of the famous raider *Alabama.* Bulloch arranged with a Liverpool shipbuilder to construct a vessel Bulloch called the *Erica,* ostensibly a merchantman. The ruse didn't fool anyone for long, however, and Charles Francis Adams, Lincoln's ambassador in London, complained that the construction of what clearly was destined to be a Confederate warship violated Britain's avowed neutrality in the war and constituted an unfriendly act. The consequences could be most grave. British leaders, under pressure from British arms-makers and, in any event, not particularly solicitous of Washington's good wishes, tugged their chins and shuffled their papers for many months, until the ship was nearly completed. In July 1862, Bulloch took the unfinished vessel on what was billed as a sea trial; for cover he invited along dozens of English notables and their wives. But as the liquor ran out and the day waned, he politely asked his guests to step aboard a tender, which carried them back to harbor. He sailed the *Erica* to the Azores, where it was quickly rerigged as a warship and rechristened the *Alabama*.

The vessel went on to a brilliantly deadly career of destruction against Union commerce. With a crew that included another Roosevelt uncle, the teenager Irvine Bulloch, it ranged the Atlantic and Indian Oceans in search of Yankee merchantmen. In two years it captured or sank more than sixty vessels and became the target itself of a Union search-and-destroy operation that covered nearly half the world's oceans. Finally, in June 1864, the Union warship *Kearsage* cornered the *Alabama* in the English Channel. A savage fight followed, with the *Kearsage* eventually getting the better of the engagement. According to Bulloch family lore, Irvine Bulloch fired the Confederate raider's final shots before abandoning ship with the captain. They were picked up by a British pleasure boat, whose owner had polled his children whether they would rather attend church that Sunday morning or witness the battle; God lost in a unanimous vote. The yacht carried the two Confederates off safely to Southampton.

Lacking any comparable war stories on his father's side, the young Theodore Roosevelt latched on to the exploits of his uncles. He memorized every detail of the *Alabama*'s voyages and doubtless imagined himself firing those final defiant shots. The impression lasted a lifetime; in adulthood he recounted the tale with relish, especially on campaign swings through the old Confederacy. A Washington reporter noted wryly: "One would suppose that the President, himself, fired the last two shots from the *Alabama* instead of his uncle. Mr. Roosevelt's relationship with a Confederate officer is accepted as practically equal with having fought for the cause, himself."

Roosevelt's retellings aside, the story of the *Alabama* would have melted into memory after the war, along with most other such stories, if not for the fact that it became the focus of acrimonious wrangling between the governments of the United States and Britain. Ambassador Adams's protests had been followed by claims by the United States against Britain for the damage the *Alabama* and other British-built Confederate raiders had done to the Union cause. Figures in the billions were thrown about as fair compensation by such hardliners as Charles Sumner, the chairman of the Senate Foreign Relations Committee; some in Washington were willing to annex Canada and call it even.

London indignantly rejected the American claims. It was all a matter of politics, the British said, and very low politics at that—although considering the caliber of people in the Grant administration and the Reconstruction Congress, one could hardly expect better. One British diplomat suggested that something more was involved. Senator Sumner's love life—or, rather, the lack of it—was to blame. The senator "was fool enough some year or so ago to marry a young and pretty widow," the envoy explained to his superiors in the British Foreign Office. "She found that he was not gifted with 'full powers' and has left him. . . . He therefore makes up by vigour of tongue for his want of capacity in other organs." The British refused to accept responsibility for even the so-called direct damages; the indirect claims were utterly out of the question.

II

The diplomatic echoes of the *Alabama*'s guns were reverberating over the Atlantic when Teedie got a chance to meet the uncles who started the whole dispute. In 1869, Theodore and Mittie decided to take the family to Europe. Bamie was fourteen, Teedie ten, Elliott nine, and Conie seven. All were old enough, their parents judged, to benefit culturally from the experience. An additional consideration prompted the journey: They hoped the ocean voyage and the change of environment would ease Teedie's asthma. Grandfather C.V.S. penned a rhyme for the boy upon the family's departure:

> We shall all gladly see you back
> Again at your home,
> And hope that sickness may no more
> Compel your feet to roam.

Teedie was less than delighted to leave his familiar haunts. He cried in the carriage all the way from the house to the dock, not really knowing where they were going or understanding quite why. He had never been on shipboard before; curiosity competed with anxiety at the size, noise, and strangeness of everything about the steam liner. The anxiety won out: In a diary begun for the voyage he declared himself "so, so homesick." He also fell horribly seasick, which doubled both his homesickness and the inexplicability of the journey. If travel was supposed to make you feel better, why did he wish he were dead?

Relief appeared in the form of the mouth of the Mersey on the ninth day. The ship docked at Liverpool; before Teedie could reacquire his land legs, he was introduced to his famous uncles. James and Irvine Bulloch, like many former Confederates, had taken up residence in England after the war while awaiting pardons back home; until then they supported themselves and their families by brokering cotton. The elder uncle, James, cut the more imposing figure, with luxurious whiskers, eyes that had stared far to sea for many years—he had served in the U.S. Navy before taking up with the Confederacy— and a bearing that betold his admiral's rank. At the same time his reputation benefited, in the estimate of the young Roosevelts, from the aura of mystery that always surrounds secret agents. Irvine, the younger uncle, was the firebrand of the two. After fighting to the bitter end on the *Alabama,* he had soon found another ship on which to make war on the Yankees: the raider *Shenandoah,* which scourged Union whalers in the Pacific. In his early twenties when young Theodore met him, he seemed incomparably older and more experienced than his years.

For two weeks, while Mittie caught up with her brothers, the children got to know Liverpool and their Bulloch relations. Teedie wasn't impressed with the city. "Liverpool is a verry funny place," he wrote to Edith Carow, a friend of the three younger Roosevelt children. "The names of the streets are verry funny also." As for the Bullochs, they were nice but overly affectionate. "I do not think you would like them so much because they kiss so much," he told Edith.

Kisses or not, Teedie couldn't help being enamored of his dashing uncles. It was probably at this time that the seeds of fascination with the sea and ships were planted in Roosevelt's mind; these seeds would mature in later years into a preoccupation with sea power. (Something must have done it besides the joy of the bounding main, whose bounding habitually rendered Roosevelt as incapacitatingly ill as on his first voyage.) Perhaps, too, meeting his hero uncles made him wonder why his own father hadn't done anything so daring.

But for all the aura that surrounded his uncles, the boy didn't forget which side they had fought on. A journal entry for May 27, 1869, recorded a run-in at play with a friend of his cousins: "Met Jeff Davises son and some sharp words ensued."

Leaving Liverpool, the family headed south. From the first, Teedie found grand touring trying. "We went to York 8 hours in the cars!!!" he complained. "I did not like it. We were verry dirty when we got there. I saw the cathedral but was so tired I did not stay to see it all."

From York they made their way to London, partly to view the city but largely to have a lung specialist inspect Teedie. The physician's findings were both reassuring and puzzling. He could find nothing wrong with Teedie's lungs, which meant, at the same time, that he had no explanation for the attacks. With the best doctors in the world unable to make sense of his malady, still less could Teedie. "A little while ago I was threatened with an atack of asthma," he wrote Edith Carow on July 10. "A doctor was sent for, who sent me to the coast where I got the original disease. Father explained this and he said that my disease had changed its character and so off we went."

The coast was no cure. Neither was anything else. "I was sick with asthma and did not sleep at all after quarter past two," Teedie noted on September 24. Two days later he wrote, "I was sick of the Asthma last night. I sat up for 4 successive hours and Papa made me smoke a cigar." Two weeks after this he wrote that he was "verry sick last night." A couple of days later: "I had a miserable night." Another three days after this: "I was rubbed so hard on the chest this morning that the blood came out."

Nor was it only the asthma that prostrated him. He complained of toothaches and headaches and intestinal problems, some of which may well have been compounded by the tobacco and coffee he ingested for his asthma. Entry after entry in his journal recorded how he had been up all night or laid low most of the day. The other members of the family occasionally came down with one thing or another; this was only to be expected on a long journey far from home. Possibly some of his siblings' sickness owed to emulation of Teedie, who instantly became the center of attention when his attacks hit. More revealingly than he may have known, he recounted a bout suffered by his sister: "Conie was sick but her sickness always decreased when mama was out of the room and she could not be peted." For Teedie, it was usually his father who came to the rescue. His father sat up with him, medicated him, took him for rides away from the stuffy hotels and dirty downtowns. "As I was not well Papa and I went to Voslaver in the country," he wrote in October, after they had reached Austria.

Fortunately for all concerned, he wasn't sick the entire time. The family covered an ambitious amount of ground. From Britain they crossed the Continent to Switzerland. Long walks in the Alps elevated Teedie's spirits. Following a trek he estimated at nineteen miles (almost certainly an exaggeration), he declared with modest pride, "I have had a good day." After another outing he boasted that he alone had been able to keep up with his father. "Papa and I walked most . . ." he said. "I had a splendid day." In Italy they ascended Mount Vesuvius. "We came to a small hole through which we saw a red flame inside the mountain. I put my alpine stock in it and it caught fire right away."

The cultural benefits of the tour proved less than Theodore and Mittie had hoped. Bamie, not surprisingly, got the most out of the museums and cathedrals and ruins, nearly as much as her parents. As Corinne later recalled, "My older sister, though not quite fifteen, was so unusually mature and intelligent that she shared their enjoyment, but the journey was of rather mitigated pleasure to the three 'little ones,' who much preferred the nursery at 28 East 20th Street, or their free summer activities in wood and field, to the picture-galleries and museums, or even to the wonderful Swiss mountains where they had to be so carefully guarded." The younger three ("we 3," Teedie called them) had more fun playing games in the houses and hotels where they stayed. Evidently their parents humored them in their amusements. At their very first stop, Teedie noted, "We ran about and once when we jumped on a wall it nearly broke." Elsewhere they tormented the help. "We played in the house, threw paper balls at the waiter and chambermaid and rushed around upstairs and downstairs to dodge them." On another occasion: "We 3 children all dressed up in towels, wrappers, went about the house attacking all the chambermaids."

In at least one respect the trip was more eye-opening than the elder Theodore thought appropriate. Christmas 1869 found the Roosevelts in Rome, where in their hotel they attempted to recapture what they could of the Christmases the children had known in New York. Of course the Italian Christmas was far more Catholic than anything the

Dutch Reformed Roosevelts celebrated at home. On one of his outings a curious Teedie encountered a priest, an American visiting the
Vatican, who invited him to come to a pair of lectures at a nearby hall.
"Papa would not let me go to either," Teedie recorded. Curious or
not, Teedie was clearly skeptical of the miracle stories retailed on the
Italian streets. After a visit to Naples, where a church boasted a con-
gealed clump of matter claimed to be some blood of Christ, and which
was said to liquefy once a year when the parishioners prayed particularly hard, Teedie wrote, "If you were to doubt the pretended miracle
the priest would nearly kill you."

Through the winter and early spring the touring continued. Across
Austria and Prussia, and France again, the family took in far more
than the younger children could absorb. The little ones counted the
days until they could return to America. "We want to get home,"
Teedie had written Edith as early as January, and the sentiment
strengthened with each passing week. Finally, after visiting once more
with the Bullochs, they boarded ship for the States. Teedie's entry for
May 25, 1870, summarized his feelings: "New York!!! Hip! Hurrah!"

III

Reflecting in maturity on this first venture overseas, Theodore
Roosevelt realized he had simply been too young to appreciate what
he was seeing. "I do not think I gained anything from this particular
trip abroad," he wrote. "I cordially hated it." Speaking for himself
and his younger siblings, he added, "Our one desire was to get back to
America, and we regarded Europe with the most ignorant chauvinism
and contempt."

Roosevelt wasn't one to mince words, even when they needed minc-
ing, as for him they often did. In this case he may not have appreciated the cultural icons to which he was introduced, but he did
imbibe something that proved more important to him personally.
His hikes through the Alps, on the days when his afflictions allowed,
awakened in him a sense of physical achievement that would transform his life. He had played outdoors at home, of course, especially
during summers when the family escaped the city for the Hudson

Valley or the seashore, but he had never played in such inspiring surroundings as the Swiss and Austrian Alps. Frail as he was, he discovered that if he really tried, he could just about keep up with his father.
For an eleven-year-old—he celebrated his eleventh birthday in
Cologne, in a snowstorm—this was heady stuff.

He wasn't the only one to notice the change. His father, too, by a
combination of consultation with experts, reading, personal observation, and common sense, discovered the efficacy of outdoor exercise in
alleviating the ailments that beset his boy. This discovery gave rise to
what became the most enduring and potent piece of the Roosevelt legend. As his sister recalled, their father one day summoned Teedie and
said, "Theodore, you have the mind but you have not the body, and
without the help of the body the mind cannot go as far as it should.
You must make your body. It is hard drudgery to make one's body,
but I know you will do it." The young boy, adoring his father and naturally craving his approval, responded to the challenge. "I'll make my
body," he vowed.

So began a course of physical exercise that continued for the rest of
Roosevelt's life. He lifted weights, practiced gymnastics on equipment
set up in a specially remodeled room in the house on Twentieth Street,
took lessons in wrestling, rode horseback, hiked, climbed, swam,
rowed, and generally engaged in just about every form of physical
activity imaginable, in hot weather and cold, rain and shine, days and
sometimes far into the night.

To the extent all the exercise had an effect on his asthma, the effect
may have been as much psychological as strictly physiological. In syn-
dromes such as asthma, where psychological elements play a significant role, a fundamental first step in recovery can be the patient's consciously taking charge of his condition. Until Teedie determined to
"make his body," the disease had been in control. Now he would be in
control. Not perfectly, to be sure, nor always—the bronchial passages
wouldn't always get the message from the mind. But as Theodore
made his regimen of exercise and fresh air a regular part of his life, his
physical condition began to improve.

In fact, his asthma might well have cured itself on its own. Children
often grow out of asthma as they get older. It is entirely possible that
all of Roosevelt's exercising and carrying on had little effect on his

asthma. Yet even if that were so, the lesson he learned—and this was the real insight of his father in putting the challenge to his son—went far beyond mere physical health. Roosevelt learned that he didn't have to accept whatever life happened to throw his way. He didn't have to live within his limitations but rather should strive to push those boundaries back. As lessons go, it was pretty prosaic; at the same time, it's one many people never master.

IV

This lesson wasn't all Roosevelt got out of a sickly childhood. He got something else that ultimately had an equally profound influence on his later life, namely, a love of literature and learning. When ill health kept him from the rambunctious adventures of other boys, Teedie found diversion in books. He never attended school except for a brief and unsatisfactory experiment with a small private school a few blocks from his house; instead, he was tutored at home, in large part by his aunt Anna. She delighted the children with tales of the Old South, including the Brer Rabbit stories later made famous by Joel Chandler Harris. From her tales to those of books was a small step, and Teedie soon found a way to escape the confines of poor health into the most exotic and exciting worlds far away. The family subscribed to *Our Young Folks*—"which I then believed," Roosevelt remarked decades later, "to be the very best magazine in the world, a belief, I may add, which I have kept to this day unchanged." The issues were full of such stories of battles against natural and human odds as "Cast Away in the Cold" and "Grandfather's Struggle for a Homestead." The mature Roosevelt described these and others like them as "first-class, good healthy stories, interesting in the first place, and in the next place teaching manliness, decency, and good conduct." He wasn't embarrassed to add that he liked the girls' stories too.

The more adventurous and heroic his books, the better. He found the first, island-bound part of *Robinson Crusoe* tame; the second part, where the hero takes on the wolves of the Pyrenees and wanders about the Far East, was much more to his taste. He lost himself in

Longfellow's "Saga of King Olaf," which introduced him to the Vikings and their mythic world of warfare and discovery.

These romantic tales provided models for emulation. As an adult, Roosevelt remarked on how different he had been as a child. "The saying that the child is the father to the man may be taken in a sense almost the reverse of that usually given to it. The child is father to the man in the sense that his individuality is separate from the individuality of the grown-up into which he turns." Roosevelt's version, applied to people at large, is basically wrong: For most people there is an essential continuity from childhood to adulthood. The fact that Roosevelt believed his assertion true of himself—a judgment less true than he thought—is significant, for it indicates the degree to which he deliberately and consciously threw off the feeble young child he was and refashioned himself into something different.

Roosevelt ascribed a good part of his transformation to the direct influence of the people around him, especially his father. But he also credited the vicarious influence of those he read and heard about. "I was nervous and timid. Yet from reading of the people I admired—ranging from the soldiers of Valley Forge, and Morgan's riflemen, to the heroes of my favorite stories—and from hearing of the feats of my Southern forefathers and kinsfolk"—not least the Bulloch uncles—"and from knowing my father, I felt a great admiration for men who were fearless and who could hold their own in the world, and I had a great desire to be like them."

This romantic view of the world would shape Roosevelt's entire life. Repeatedly, and in diverse circumstances, he cast himself as the romantic hero, battling natural and human odds in pursuit of noble and glorious goals. Struggle was the essence of life; where circumstances of themselves didn't afford sufficient struggle, he sought out the additional struggle of contrived tests of physical and moral strength. Not for him the muddy reality of confused motives and compromised conclusions; Roosevelt, with most romantics, cleaved life conceptually into camps of good and evil. Few of his contemporaries saw so clearly as he what should be done in any given situation, and consequently few could apply such force to accomplish their aims. If the actual world was rarely as simple as he conceived it, he refused to be bothered by the discrepancy.

V

Roosevelt learned to find romance in the most unlikely places. One day he was walking up Broadway not far from the house. He regularly made this trip: His mother often sent him to a produce market to purchase strawberries for the family's breakfast. He hadn't yet discovered the charm in the lives of ordinary people, and he probably didn't see the businessmen in the cabs hurrying south toward the financial district or notice the delivery men dodging him on their way in and out of the buildings along the sidewalk. He might have heard the cries of the newsboys hawking the latest headlines, but that was because his father had made a special project of the newsboys, sharing Sunday suppers with them (his treat) and otherwise assisting the more promising to get a foot up onto the ladder of life. But it was equally likely that Teedie's head was down and his mind lost in a tale of Nordic adventure.

Yet something unusual snapped him back to the Broadway sidewalk. There, laid out on a slab of wood next to the curb, as for a funeral or an Eskimo's feast, was a sleek and shiny—albeit quite dead—seal. Teedie knew of seals, sea lions, and walruses from his stories, but he had never expected to run into one around the corner from his house. He circled the creature, sniffed it, poked it. After several minutes he continued on his way, but he couldn't get it out of his mind.

The next morning he returned and was delighted to find it still there, in only slightly diminished majesty. By now he determined to find out all he could about it. Where had it come from? The harbor, he was told. How long was it? How big around? Measure it yourself, sonny. What did it eat? Little boys—ha, ha, ha!—how should I know? Fish, I guess. Teedie went back the next day and the day after that. As the seal's flesh started going the way of all flesh, he talked the owner into letting him have the skull, which he proudly carted home.

Teedie never forgot this first eyeball-to-eyeball encounter with a denizen of the vasty deep. Forty years later he could still declare that "that seal filled me with every possible feeling of romance and adventure."

In so doing it inspired the lad to commence a career in zoology. He supplemented his sidewalk research with bookish investigations; soon he was writing and lecturing on his scientific findings. His maiden paper, a largely derivative description of the seal, was followed by a truly pioneering treatise on a previously overlooked insect species, the "foregoing ant." So-called—and only by the slightly confused young naturalist—from a passage in a well-thumbed natural history book in which the author referred to an ant previously mentioned ("the foregoing ant"), the insect appeared in no other of Roosevelt's reference texts, and he accordingly deemed it quite special. The family elders did, too, albeit for a different reason, as they listened with suppressed smiles to the budding scientist announce his discovery.

Roosevelt couldn't get enough of natural history. At the age of nine he wrote a letter describing his collection of mice to his sister, then visiting Georgia with their mother. "I have got four mice," he related, "two white skinned, red eyed velvety creatures, very tame for I let them run all over me, they trie to get down the back of my neck and under my vest, and two brown skined, black eyed, soft as the others but wilder. Lordy and Rosa are the names of the white mice, which are male and female. I keep them in different cages." Appended was a sketch of the two cages. To his mother he wrote of his excitement on hearing that she had received flowers from friends. "I could revel in the buggie ones." Reports of the southern fauna fascinated him even more. "I jumped with delight when I found you had heard a mockingbird. Get some of its feathers if you can."

As he grew older and grew into his routine of outdoor exercise, the field study of natural history provided a double benefit: While exercising his mind, it also exercised his body. When the family summered along the Hudson or at the coast, he would devote countless hours to collecting samples of this species or that. No nest was too high or tide-pool too treacherous; indeed, the more remote or inaccessible a given niche, the more likely it was to harbor an unusual prize, and the greater the challenge to his strength of body and character.

VI

Sometimes challenges came looking for him. The summer before his fourteenth birthday, traveling to Maine to meet friends for a camping trip, he ran into two boys about his own age. They were bored and so decided to have some fun. They teased him, taunted him, provoked him, circling this way and that, challenging him to defend himself. At first he tried to ignore their provocations, recognizing that he was substantially outweighed by each, not to mention outnumbered by the two together. But as the treatment continued he grew more and more frustrated until tears of anger began to fill his eyes and he could stand it no longer. Disregarding the possibility of bodily peril, he threw himself upon his tormentors.

But it was his psyche rather than his body that proved to be in danger, for to his immense mortification the two boys handled him as an adult might handle an unruly child, rendering his attack utterly ineffectual without hurting him in the slightest.

He retired in shame. Yet the experience extended his education—his moral education at once, his physical education subsequently. During the rest of the stagecoach ride, sitting in his corner in grim silence, he determined never to be placed in such a predicament again. At the first opportunity he asked his father if he might begin boxing lessons. Theodore Sr., without learning the details behind the request but perhaps guessing, readily assented.

Teedie's teacher, a former prizefighter named John Long, conducted a school for such boys as Roosevelt. Teedie was an enthusiastic but untalented pupil; by his own admission, it was years before he made any noticeable improvement. Yet he stuck to his pugilistic studies, and when he finally won a couple of bouts against two "reedy striplings who were even worse than I was" and received a pewter mug as prize, it became one of his most cherished possessions.

About the same time, Teedie learned to shoot. This might have been a logical step from boxing if the purpose of the shooting had been self-defense. In fact, people of the Roosevelts' class rarely required firearms to defend their persons and property from assault—although, given New York's crime rate, one could never be too sure. Rather, the shooting was for sport—skeet, birds, bigger game—which was an activity very much in keeping with Teedie's station-to-be in society.

More to the immediate point, shooting was an essential part of the study of natural history as it was then commonly practiced. In those days of relatively abundant nature, the ornithologists' primary tool was a shotgun, and collecting specimens was often indistinguishable from hunting. Not unusually for males of his own species, Roosevelt identified hunting with manliness, and from the time he received his first gun—a double-barreled shotgun—at fourteen, he was inordinately fond of chasing down and killing wild animals. Throughout his life he regularly escaped into the woods of Maine, the prairies of the Midwest, the badlands of Dakota, the mountains of Wyoming, the cane breaks of Louisiana, or the savannah of Africa to see how many wild things he could kill. He would as soon talk hunting as politics, and he had far greater respect for a woodsman than for any mere legislator or jurist. In his pursuit of science he simultaneously developed an image of himself as a hunter; and, significantly for a naturalist, he had scant taste for botany. What couldn't put up a fight, or at least a flight, didn't interest him. Roosevelt's scientific ventures were exercises in self-improvement but also in self-esteem.

VII

For such reasons, among others, Roosevelt found a second journey across the Atlantic, beginning in October 1872, far more satisfactory than his first. The trip started badly again: On the voyage from New York he was miserably ill and kept almost exclusively to his stateroom. But then things perked up. In Liverpool the family once more was met by the Bullochs; once more Teedie had the opportunity to admire his gallant uncles (and dodge his kissing aunts). Although his seasickness had precluded a pelagic extrapolation of his scientific studies, no sooner did he land on solid ground than he was back at his work. He procured various birds and small animals on which to practice his preservation techniques. The whole business made a mess and a stink, but the other members of the family had learned to humor the boy and largely ignored the feathers and carcasses that littered the bathrooms and kitchens of the hotels they visited. The proprietors of England's chemical shops had a harder time understanding this queer American youth; for his part, he thought it quite odd that they should insist on guarantees that he wasn't bent on murder or suicide with the arsenic he required to keep his specimens from rotting.

After two weeks in England the clan headed for the mainland.

Teedie hoped he had left his mal de mer in the Irish Sea, but the Channel crossing undid him. "I gave up all the meals of the day before," he noted delicately in his journal. (During this journey he showed the first signs of an emerging literary style; as with many writers before and after, the practice of keeping a journal greatly improved his command of the language.) They crossed the Low Countries to Germany before doubling back through Paris on the way to Italy. The boy's opinion of foreigners hadn't risen much from his previous trip. He constantly remarked the woeful standards of hygiene in the cities they visited, and following an excursion into the markets of Bologna, he commented matter-of-factly, "As usual everybody combines to cheat you."

The principal goal of this journey was the Near East, especially Egypt. After an uneventful crossing of the Mediterranean—the weather was fair and the sea calm, to the relief of Teedie's stomach—the Roosevelt party reached Alexandria at the end of November. Teedie's books had transported him to the land of the pharaohs before; to be there in person was enough to inspire the teenage journalist to emulate the breathless prose of those volumes. "At eight o'clock we arrived in sight of Alexandria. How I gazed on it! It was Egypt, the land of my dreams; Egypt the most ancient of all countries! A land that was old when Rome was bright, was old when Babylon was in its glory, was old when Troy was taken! It was a sight to awaken a thousand thoughts, and it did." Up close, the reality was even more exotic than the literary view. When the ship pulled into the harbor, it was immediately surrounded by Arab boatmen "in all stages of picturesque dress and undress." The trip from the dock to the hotel was still more striking. "I shall never forget that drive. On all sides were screaming Arabs, shouting Dragomen, shrieking donkey boys and braying donkeys, and in fact the only quiet creatures were the dogs (large, fox like creatures with erect ears and of a yellow colour), which seemed the laziest animals in creation and also the most cowardly, for I observed a dozen run away from a scotch terrier."

The following days brought excursions into the bazaar for taxidermic and other supplies. Teedie delighted to discover that he could bargain the merchants down to half their asking price; goods that were, by American standards, cheap enough at the start ended up seeming a downright steal. At the beginning of December the party moved on to

Cairo. They climbed the Great Pyramid with the help of Egyptian guides who boosted them over the big stones. The experience again ignited his literary imagination. "To look out on the desert," he declared, "gives one some what the same feeling as to look out over the ocean or over one of the North American Prairies." As it involved the prairies, this passage really was a work of his literary imagination, for he had never seen them.

Hiring a boat, the family pushed up the Nile. For all the ancient glories of Egypt, if the children had any doubts regarding the contemporary political and economic pecking order in the world, these were erased by their three-month voyage aboard their *dahabeah*. When the wind blew from the north, the *fellahin* guiding their vessel put out the sails and they moved slowly up against the current, but when the wind died or shifted to the south, the crew had to pound the footpath and haul the boat upstream by main muscle and sweat. On board, meanwhile, the rich Americans took their ease. Mittie lounged, the children frolicked or engaged in lessons in French led by Bamie, and Theodore Sr. read or kept up his correspondence.

Teedie spent little time reflecting on how the wheel of history had brought ancient Egypt—in the 1870s a province of the Ottoman empire—and the upstart republic on the Atlantic's western shore into their present configuration; he was too busy with his investigations into natural history. During this trip his obsession was ornithology; on December 13 he killed his first African bird. "I was proportionately delighted," he noted. Killing the local avifauna quickly became a habit, which his father encouraged by presenting him with a fine breech-loading shotgun for Christmas. Teedie could hardly contain his excitement. "He was perfectly delighted," Theodore Sr. wrote in a letter. "It was entirely unexpected to him, although he had been shooting with it as mine." The gun occasioned some concern among family members and others encountered on excursions ashore. The very picture of the distracted scientist, not to mention the careless adolescent, and perpetually preoccupied with bagging another specimen, Teedie paid little attention to the possibility of accidental discharge. His sister Corinne remembered "the excitement, and, be it confessed, anxiety and fear inspired in the hearts of the four young college men who, on another dahabeah, accompanied us on the Nile, when the ardent young sportsman, mounted on an uncontrollable donkey, would ride unexpectedly into their midst, his gun slung across his shoulders in such a way as to render its proximity distinctly dangerous as he bumped absent-mindedly against them."

Teedie had the time of his young life. "I think I have never enjoyed myself so much as in this month," he wrote to his aunt Anna halfway through the river trip. The hunting was the most fun. "I have had great enjoyment from the shooting here, as I have procured between one and two hundred skins." Explaining that he never went ashore without his gun, except on Sundays, he related proudly, "The largest bird I have yet killed is a Crane which I shot as it rose from a lagoon near Thebes." Yet he didn't want his aunt to think that bagging birds was the whole of the journey. "We had those splendid and grand old ruins to see, and one of them will stock you with thoughts for a month. The temple that I enjoyed most was Karnak. We saw it by moonlight. I was never impressed by anything so much. To wander among those great columns under the same moon that had looked down on them for thousands of years was awe-inspiring; it gave rise to thoughts of the ineffable, the unutterable; thoughts which you cannot express, which cannot be uttered, which cannot be answered until after The Great Sleep." Between the birds and the temples, Teedie had eyes for little else, although once again he couldn't help commenting on the clothing of the Egyptians along the route: "I may as well mention that the dress of the inhabitants up to ten years of age is nothing. After that they put on a shirt descended from some remote ancestor, and never take it off till the day of their death."

Theodore's and Mittie's hopes that the children would gain some cultural sophistication from the journey were more fully realized this time than last. Teedie, at any rate, became a connoisseur of ancient art, in his own eyes if not those of others more knowledgeable. "Visited the Tombs of Reni Hassan," he commented on February 12. "Interesting in subject but not in execution." But then he immediately turned to a topic of more pressing moment: "Killed an owl and a kestrel."

While entrancingly exotic to the children, the Nile journey was not especially unusual for Americans of the Roosevelts' class. The college men—Harvard, to be precise—who accompanied them were a constant reminder of home; another brush with the familiar was a run-in with Ralph Waldo Emerson, undertaking a similar voyage. Theodore introduced the children to the New England sage, who struck Corinne as past his prime. Recalling his "lovely smile, somewhat vacant," she afterward related an anecdote about the venerable transcendentalist: "It was at this time that the story was told in connection with Mr. Emerson that some sentimental person said: 'How wonderful to think of Emerson looking at the Sphinx! What a message the Sphinx must have had for Emerson.' Whereupon an irreverent wit replied: 'The only message the Sphinx could possibly have had for Emerson must have been 'You're another.'" Corinne added her own comment: "I can quite understand now, remembering the mystic, dreamy face of the old philosopher, how this witticism came about."

The desert air agreed with Teedie, as Theodore and Mittie had hoped. Except for a few mild attacks, his asthma went into remission. Equally encouraging, the youth suddenly started to sprout. Within weeks his clothes became too small, and when the family got back to Cairo, he had to have new ones made. "But there was one set of clothes too good to throw away," he remembered afterward, "which we kept for a 'change,' and which was known as my 'Smike suit,' because it left my wrists and ankles as bare as those of poor Smike himself."

Following their return downriver, the family set off for Syria and Palestine. The big thrill of this part of the journey was the opportunity for long rides on horseback across the desert. "The horses are all very good and I have the best of the lot," Teedie boasted at Ramallah. "I have named him Grant. He has some Arab blood in him"—doubtless an understatement, considering where they were—"and is very swift, pretty and spirited." In a letter to Edith Carow, he wrote, "We were out on horseback for several hours of each day, and as I like riding ever so much, and as the Syrian horses are very good, we had a splendid time." He hunted birds and small game such as rabbits, but on one occasion he tried for a larger prize. After stumbling upon a pack of jackals devouring a goat, he and his guide put them to flight, then followed on horses as fast as they could go. For miles they trailed their quarry over ridge and ravine. At one point he thought he had one of the jackals cornered, but with a sudden bound it darted away into ground where the horse couldn't follow. Despite this culminating disappointment, the chase was by far the most exciting adventure he'd had to date, and the taste got in his blood.

In Jerusalem, which was much smaller than he had anticipated, he visited the holy places of the three religions of the Book. While he demonstrated an appropriate, though hardly undue, respect for the sites associated with the life of Jesus, he was more skeptical regarding some aspects of Jewish tradition. A visit to the Wailing Wall prompted him to declare, "Many of the women were in earnest, but most of the men were evidently shamming." The Mosque of Omar was sufficiently intriguing that he remarked, without editorializing, "At one place we saw a stone with three and a half nails in it. When these nails fall out the world will come to an end. Fifteen and a half have fallen out already." The Jordan River was disappointing—"what we should call a rather small creek in America."

A trek across the desert brought them to another impressive sight, at Baalbek. Teedie's journal recorded his reaction as well as his ongoing efforts to endanger the local bird species: "The ruins are, with the exception of Karnak, the grandest and most magnificent I have ever seen, and they gave me the same feeling as to contemplate the mighty temples of Thebes. I killed a yellow throated finch, a lark and a gardel in the afternoon." Damascus was a picturesque treat. At the Dead Sea he attempted to refute the conventional wisdom that nothing living could sink therein; he gave up shortly before being pickled.

The family stopped briefly at Beirut, then part of Syria, and made the acquaintance of some members of the American community there. One of their hosts, a Dr. Bliss, taught school to Arab and foreign students. Years afterward Bliss liked to show his pupils a photograph taken at the time of the Roosevelts' visit. Teedie shared the back of a big white donkey with two of the Bliss boys. "That middle boy is now president of the United States," Bliss would say before adding even more proudly: "The rear boy is now president of the Syrian Protestant College." On one occasion an irreverent, nationalistically minded Lebanese student broke in, "Yes, and that donkey is now the Waly of Beirut."

At the Syrian coast the family boarded a steamer for the Greek isles. En route, Teedie branched out into ichthyology, persuading the crew to catch as many varieties of fish as they could, which he then eviscerated and stuffed. Athens was nice, but the grace of its temples didn't impress the children as much as the grandeur of Egypt's monuments had. On April 11 they reached Constantinople. The ancient city lived up to its reputation as the crossroads of the Near East, arousing the curiosity of the adolescent Teedie in more ways than one. "There was a strange medly of costumes. Greeks in white tunics or short skirts, Turks in baggy trousers, and short jacket, Arabs in loose flowing garments, Europeans and Americans in their regular tight-fitting clothes, and Circassian ladies of the harem who so far as I could see were very beautiful."

A dutiful round of the tourist sights of Constantinople followed. After six months of constant traveling, the children were getting tired, as Teedie's ever-terser journal entries indicated. Then came another voyage by steamer, this across the Black Sea, with more seasickness. Landing briefly, they transferred to a riverboat for a cruise up the Danube. They traveled alternately by boat and train to Belgrade, Pest, and finally Vienna.

In certain respects the whole journey thus far had been a long way round to Vienna, where Theodore Sr. was to serve as American commissioner at an international commercial exposition. Consequently, the children were able to catch their breath for a few weeks while he went about his business. Teedie required the least time of the four to recuperate. After all the hunting, riding, and camping out in the desert, he was feeling stronger and fitter than ever, and he filled his days with further investigations into ornithology and the art of taxidermy. Yet finally even these grew tiresome. "The last few weeks have been spent in the most dreary monotony," he exaggerated in the manner of adolescents. More accurately, he added, "If I stayed here much longer I should spend all my money on books and birds 'pour passer le temps.'"

VIII

Thus it was to his relief that the family departed Vienna in mid-May for Prussia. The plan was for Theodore to return to America, Mittie and Bamie to travel on to Paris and various spas, and the three young children to spend the summer with families in Dresden. In September, Mittie and Bamie would return east and fetch the children before heading home.

Preoccupied as he was with natural history, Teedie paid little attention at this time to current politics. If he had, he might have realized that Prussia in the early 1870s was one of the most dynamic countries in the world—and potentially one of the most enthralling for a fourteen-year-old boy with manliness on the mind. Two years earlier the Prussian army had smashed France in the Franco-Prussian War, creating the modern German empire. This development was arguably the most important event in world politics during Theodore Roosevelt's lifetime; Roosevelt would spend much of his presidency coping with the consequences of this crowning—but internationally destabilizing—achievement of the Iron Chancellor, Otto von Bismarck. In 1873 the Germans were already feeling full of themselves, and none more than the Prussians, who considered themselves the quintessential Germans. And among the Prussians, none considered themselves more the representatives of the Prussian tradition of strength and physical valor—or at least acted as though they did, which to a young and impressionable visitor from America amounted to the same thing— than the brash young students of the Prussian dueling societies.

Roosevelt enjoyed extended contact with two such characters during his sojourn in Dresden. The American consul there had arranged for Teedie and Elliott to stay with the Minkwitz family, and for Conie to live with a family nearby. Herr Doktor Minkwitz was city counselor of Dresden and a member of the Reichstag, a man of liberal persuasions who had taken part in the uprising of 1848 and served a prison sentence for his pains. Frau Minkwitz and four daughters lived at home; the eldest daughter assumed the task of teaching the guests German and instructing them in mathematics.

But it was the Minkwitz boys—young men, rather—who had the greatest impact on Roosevelt. Students at the University of Leipzig, they belonged to dueling societies there and had acquired appropriate scars and nicknames. Ulrich went by "Der Rothe Herzog," or the Red Duke, while Oswald had been dubbed "Herr Nasehorn," or Sir Rhinoceros, because the tip of his nose had been sliced off in a duel and sewn back on slightly askew. The impression made by these two on a boy like Roosevelt, now a few years into his campaign of physical self-improvement, must have been dramatic. He never took up dueling, which in America died about the same time as the Confederacy (although a remnant lived on in the American West, where Roosevelt would encounter it and nearly indulge), but the physical and moral prowess the dueling culture embodied was something he forever admired.

Not that his hosts left much time for idle admiration. With Prussian thoroughness they kept Teedie, Elliott, and Corinne, who joined her brothers under the Minkwitz roof after coming down with a acute case of homesickness, hard at work on their studies. Lessons filled most of each day: up at six-thirty, to the books by seven-thirty, a brief break at nine, more study until twelve-thirty, lunch and still more study until three. From three to eight their time was largely their own, to explore the city or, in Teedie's case, to kill or purchase and then dissect and catalog the local birds and minor beasts. From eight to ten, two more hours with the books.

The children's free time also included meetings of something they called the Dresden Literary American Club. The charter members of this organization were the three Roosevelts and two cousins, likewise staying in the city; the group was as much an exercise in expatriate solidarity as anything else, but at times it lived up to its literary pretensions. Teedie's contributions tended to the scientific; even when he turned to fiction, in a short story entitled "Mrs. Field Mouse's Dinner Party," the dramatis personae were all creatures he had lately skinned, pinned (in the case of the insects), or tried to.

Teedie's intellect thrived on the demanding schedule. He had never studied so diligently, but he thought the rewards matched his efforts. "I really feel that I am making considerable progress," he wrote.

His body, however, didn't quite match the demands he placed on it. After his nearly asthma-free time in the desert, the old affliction returned. "Excuse my writing, the asthma has made my hand tremble awfully," he explained to his father in one letter home. Another letter revealed complications from other maladies. "Picture to yourself an antiquated woodchuck," he wrote his mother, "with his cheeks filled with nuts, his face well-oiled, his voice hoarse from gargling and a cloth resembling in texture and cleanliness a second-hand dust man's castoff stocking around his head; picture to yourself that, I say, and you will have a good likeness of your hopeful offspring while suffering from an attack of the mumps."

Mittie was sufficiently alarmed by her son's condition, as well as by an outbreak of cholera in Dresden, to carry the children off to Switzerland for much of the month of August. Teedie's state improved somewhat, and the cholera ran its course; at the end of the month Mittie returned the children to the Minkwitzes.

IX

The five months in Dresden came at just the right moment for Teedie. As the oldest of the three younger children (five, counting the cousins), he assumed the role of clan chief. Elliott was more facile and clever; he and cousin Johnnie Elliot were the "wits" of the group, according to Corinne. But Teedie was the "ringleader"—by age, naturally, but also by moral force. Although Corinne idolized her eldest brother, Elliott could have done without some of Teedie's endless self-improvement. "Suddenly an idea has got hold of Teedie," Elliott complained in a letter home, "that we did not know enough German for the time we have been here, so he has asked Miss Anna to give him larger lessons and of course I could not be left behind so we are working harder than ever in our lives."

The younger children looked to Teedie for reassurance when home felt far off and Germany strange and disconcerting. A particularly frightening thunderstorm one night had even the Minkwitz adults hiding under the covers. Elliott and Corinne were comforted by their brother's nonchalance. "Teedie woke up only for one minute," an impressed Elliott reported to their parents, "turned over and said, 'Oh—it's raining and my hedgehog will be all spoiled'" (a freshly skinned specimen was curing on a string outside the window). Teedie quickly went back to sleep, letting his brother and sister know that it was all right for them to do the same.

With his father an ocean and half a continent away, Teedie didn't have him to fall back on when his asthma flared; to whatever extent his attacks had been a way of gaining his father's attention, they no longer served. They still gained his mother's attention, but to Teedie that had never been the same thing. (That the attacks continued simply underlined that they had physical causes as well as psychological.)

Despite his medical setbacks, his bodybuilding and pugilistic campaign continued. With ongoing encouragement from his father, who donated boxing gloves to the children's club, Teedie sparred almost daily with his brother and Johnnie Elliot. In mid-June he sent his father a report from ringside:

> The boxing gloves are a source of great amusement to us. Whenever Johnie comes to see us we have an hours boxing or so. Each round takes one or two minutes.
>
> The best round yet was one yesterday between Johnie and I. I shall describe it briefly. After some striking and warding, I got Johnie into a corner, when he sprung out. We each warded off a right hand blow and brough[t] in a left hander. His took effect behind my ear, and for a minute I saw stars and reeled back to the centre of the room, while Johnie had had his nose and upper lip mashed together and been driven back against the door. I was so weak however that I was driven across the room, simply warding off blows, but I almost disabled his left arm, and drove him back to the middle where some sharp boxing occurred. I got in one on his forehead which raised a bump, but my eye was made black and blue. At this minute "Up" was called and we had to separate. . . . If you offered rewards for bloody noses you would spend a fortune on me alone. All send love.

When they tired of boxing, they wrestled. The American boys wrestled each other and sometimes the Minkwitz sons; Teedie reported proudly that he had often defeated the younger son, despite the three-year difference in their ages. In less combative moments he swam in the Elbe River and rowed on a pond in a park in the city.

Clearly evident in Teedie at this time was a trait that would distinguish him as an adult: an ability to make the most of his circumstances. Another youngster might have been discouraged by the frequent physical relapses despite all his efforts at conditioning. Teedie learned to take the bad with the good, minimizing the former and emphasizing the latter. A note to Bamie shortly before the three children departed Dresden for home captured the man that was beginning to emerge from the boy.

> My dear darling Bamie,—
>
> I wrote a letter on the receipt of yours, but Corinne lost it and so I write this. Health; good. Lesson; good. Play hours; bad. Appetite; good. Accounts; good. Clothes; greasy. Shoes; holey. Hair; more "a-la-Mop" than ever. Nails; dirty, in consequence of having an ink bottle upset over them. Library; beautiful. Museum; so so. Club; splendid. Our journey home from Samadan [in Switzerland] was beautiful, except for

the fact that we lost our keys but even this incident was not without its pleasing side. I reasoned philosophically on the subject; I said, "Well, everything is for the best. For example, if I cannot use my toothbrush tonight, at least, I cannot forget it tomorrow morning. Ditto with comb and night shirt."

Psychological and emotional maturity aside, Teedie gained important insights into Germany and the German people while in Dresden. He became passably proficient in German, and he acquired a lifelong love of German poetry, especially the epics. More important for his career as a statesman was what he learned about the German character. "I gained an impression of the German people which I never got over," he explained later. "From that time to this it would have been quite impossible to make me feel that the Germans were really foreigners." (Significantly, he wrote these words prior to the outbreak of World War I, which would change his mind about many things German.) No one who lived among them could help respecting the German people, he contended. "The affection, the *Gemütlichkeit* (a quality which cannot be exactly expressed by any single English word), the capacity for hard work, the sense of duty, the delight in studying literature and science, the pride in the new Germany, the more than kind and friendly interest in three strange children—all these manifestations of the German character and of German family life made a subconscious impression upon me which I did not in the least define at the time, but which is very vivid still forty years later."

CHAPTER THREE

Oyster Bay
1873–76

Roosevelt had just turned fifteen when he and his mother and siblings arrived back in New York from Germany in the autumn of 1873. In early adolescence he was a bundle of contradictory traits. Still subject to bouts of asthma and other ailments, he was a body-builder and all-around enthusiast of physical fitness. Bookish and a budding writer, he lived for the outdoors, for the chase and the kill. Sheltered from social intercourse with almost everyone outside his family sphere, he had ranged widely across the Western world and seen nearly everything thought important by his generation of Americans. Adolescence is an age of contradictions, but even by the standards of fifteen-year-olds, Theodore Roosevelt was a study in contrasts.

Mittie and the Roosevelt children returned to a neighborhood different from than the one they had left. During the two decades since Theodore Sr. and Mittie had taken up housekeeping at the residence on Twentieth Street, the center of fashionable gravity in the city had continued to migrate north. For a time the old money had resisted the migration, but property values downtown continued to rise until even the old money couldn't afford not to move. The Theodore Roosevelts, trading uptown in the early 1870s to a new house at 6 West Fifty-seventh Street, were in good company.

Life in Manhattan has always held its excitements, but in the 1870s the middle part of the island produced peculiar thrills. Compared to the lower reaches, the newly settled portions required considerable cosmetic work before they were habitable. In another time or culture, the builders might have worked around the rocky outcrops and bluffs, but with the can-do spirit that marked post–Civil War America—and armed, in the really up-to-date cases, with the recently introduced dynamite (the profits from which would enable inventor Alfred Nobel to fund the peace prize that Roosevelt would win in 1906)—the builders blasted their way through the most obstinate outcroppings. Residents eventually became accustomed to the regular roar of explosions that broke the rock into pieces the Irish laborers could manhandle, but they never quite got used to the granite missiles that occasional overly ambitious detonations produced. One miscalculation sent a four-hundred-pounder skyward above the house of Dr. William Moffatt; on its return flight it crashed through the roof and several ceilings and floors before coming to rest suspended above the street-level parlor. The *Herald* reported an incident in which a flying stone nearly decapitated a young woman; the paper added, "Another piece, weighing about 500 pounds, fell upon the roof of a house occupied by Mr. McDowell, tearing away everything before it, until it reached the ground floor. Another piece, about 700 pounds in weight, flew into the air, and coming in contact with the chimney of a small dwelling, tore it away. The devastation here ended."

The timidity of Teedie's younger years had largely disappeared by now, evaporated by age, by the amelioration of his assorted ailments, by the responsibility he experienced in Germany, and by the self-confidence engendered by his continuing program of physical self-improvement. As a result he was able to enjoy the entertainment that all the destructive construction in the new neighborhood afforded—entertainment that would have been lost on him a few years before, and still was on most of his elders.

Even more entertaining, if rather less exciting, was Central Park, just around the corner and two blocks away. The city had purchased the land for the park in 1856. Work began the following year, partly to provide paychecks for the thousands of unskilled laborers displaced by the panic of 1857. Gradually, under the guidance and according to the vision of Frederick Law Olmsted, the rugged tract became the gem of the city. Yet enough of its wilderness character remained for it to provide an outlet for the naturalist in Theodore, and if, over time, it attracted more people and fewer species of plants and animals, it still afforded opportunities almost at the Roosevelt front door for hiking, riding, skating, and assorted other athletic endeavors. As had become his habit, Theodore took full advantage—to the point, as he reported after one cold afternoon on the ice, of "falling on my head and being senseless for several hours."

II

More fun still than the wild patches of Central Park were the open reaches at the shore of Long Island Sound. The family had spent previous summers—those not passed in Europe—at a variety of locations within weekend-commuting distance of Manhattan. Mittie and the children escaped the heat, and the dirt that wafted in through necessarily open windows, soiling the furniture and the linen, triggering Teedie's and Corinne's asthma, and choking and irritating everyone. They left the city as well to flee the summertime diseases—polio, cholera, typhus, smallpox, and the like—that made urban living a risky affair even for the well-to-do and the otherwise healthy. Meanwhile, Theodore Sr. could maintain a presence in his office and keep track of his eleemosynary efforts.

But none of the summer camps proved attractive enough to inspire continuing loyalty until the elder Theodore decided in the summer of 1874 to join the colony his father and brothers had established at Oyster Bay. The sleepy community on the north shore of Long Island, about thirty miles from Manhattan, was reached from the city by boat, typically, or by a combination of ferry, train, and carriage. The completion of the Brooklyn Bridge, recently begun, would eliminate the ferry ride for those who came by land but not the required carriage journey from the train station at Syosset, some six miles inland from Oyster Bay.

Corinne remembered the times at Oyster Bay, shared among the three younger children and numerous cousins, as akin to a wonderful dream. "During those years," she wrote, "when Theodore was fifteen, sixteen, and seventeen, every special delight seems connected with Oyster Bay. We took long rides on horseback through the lanes then so seemingly remote, so far from the thought of the broad highways which now are traversed by thousands of motors"—she was writing in the mid-1920s—"but were then the scenes of picnics and every imaginable spree."

Perhaps because he was older, Oyster Bay made no such halcyonic impression on Theodore; his autobiography hardly mentions the summers spent there. All the same, he seems to have enjoyed himself well enough. He certainly had the opportunity to engage in the kinds of activities he enjoyed. Oyster Bay was a community where teenagers and even younger children could roam freely and unsupervised. They walked everywhere—to the village, where they would run into the children of other vacationing families; to the waterfront, to watch the oystermen land the day's catch; to Syosset, to see who was arriving on the afternoon train; along tracks well beaten and paths newly blazed through the forest and across the salt marshes. Theodore had often counted the miles to measure his exercise; here the miles mounted without being summed. The sheltered waters of the sound were ideal for swimming; if Oyster Bay and neighboring Cold Spring Harbor seemed chilly to some, to Roosevelt they were invitingly bracing. Many of the children and adults sailed regularly; Theodore preferred to row, which got him where he wanted to go more reliably than the wind would and built up his arms, shoulders, and back in the bargain. A sandy bluff overlooking the sound made an agreeably exhausting hill to climb—or a fortress to assault if one's imagination turned to battle, as Theodore's often did. From the summit the youngsters raced back down at top speed, competing to see who could reach the bottom first without tumbling head over heels.

Theodore liked to record his physical progress. In the summer of 1875 he commenced a "sporting calendar," a journal annotating his athletic and associated achievements. He measured himself (literally) and tabulated the results: height, five feet eight inches; weight, 124 pounds; chest, thirty-four inches; calf, twelve and one-half inches; shoulders, forty-one inches; arm at rest, nine and three-quarter inches; arm flexed, ten and one-half inches—in short, a scrawny seventeen-year-old with no muscles to speak of. His journal also described how he had run a hundred-yard race in thirteen seconds, beating his cousin West; he likewise triumphed in the running long jump, covering eleven feet five inches. He probably didn't realize how pitiful this latter effort was since his journal invariably indicated that he won the competitions he inflicted on Elliott and his cousins.

Winning is important to most adolescent boys, but it was especially important to Theodore Roosevelt. Until lately, he had generally been the loser in his athletic contests with his principal partner, the healthier and better-coordinated Elliott. (Boxing, where the willingness to absorb punishment could compensate for lack of other gifts, was a significant exception.) To lose to an older brother is galling enough, as any younger brother can attest, but to lose to a *younger* brother is far worse, flying in the face of the natural order. This was the position Theodore had typically found himself in, and it was a position he spent much of their lives together trying to reverse.

When he wasn't running and jumping, he was often hunting and collecting. A stage driver who carried the Roosevelts from the railhead to the village recalled of young Theodore: "He had queer things alive in his pockets." But his pockets didn't hold the birds that had become his passion since his first shoots in Egypt. Oyster Bay and its environs afforded nearly unmatched opportunities to pursue ornithological research, comprising marsh, woodland, seashore, and the assorted feathered fauna thereof. Roosevelt took full advantage, heading out almost daily with loaded gun and empty game bag, and returning with empty gun and full bag. After one outing he informed Bamie, "At present I am writing in a rather smelly room, as the fresh skins of six night herons are reposing on the table beside me; the said night herons being the product of yesterdays expedition to Loyd's (how do you spell the name?) neck." He didn't explain why six herons were necessary; a person not as caught up in the thrill of the kill might have contented himself with one or two. Roosevelt himself later obliquely admitted that he might have overdone things in his pursuit of science. "I worked with greater industry than either intelligence or success," he said, "and made very few additions to the sum of human knowledge." He continued, however, with more than a hint of scientific pride in the enthusiastic young man he had been: "But to this day certain obscure ornithological publications may be found in which are recorded such items as, for instance, that on one occasion a fish-crow, and on another an Ipswich sparrow, were obtained by one Theodore Roosevelt, Jr., at Oyster Bay, on the shore of Long Island Sound."

III

One reason the Oyster Bay years seemed less carefree to Theodore than to Corinne was that for him they included some serious studying, and in subjects he found less congenial than natural history. Theodore Sr. and Mittie hadn't planned for young Theodore not to attend school; if it weren't for his uncertain health, he probably would have gone off to boarding school at some point. But until about his sixteenth year he never seemed up to the rigors of boarding school life, and his education took place at home. Theodore Sr. intermittently insisted on speaking French at dinner; Theodore Jr. cooperated but without enthusiasm. "We have to talk french all the time at table," he complained. "It does sound so funny." Aunt Anna tutored the children when they were young; as they grew older, professional tutors were engaged. And of course the foreign travels added to the children's store of knowledge.

The consequences of this style of education—which was by no means unheard of for children of the Roosevelts' class, even healthy ones—were mixed. On the positive side, it prevented Roosevelt from developing the idea (so common among schoolchildren, despite the best efforts of generations of educational reformers) that learning is somehow divorced from real life. For Roosevelt, learning—whether by reading, writing, stalking specimens, or stuffing them—was coexistent with life. He read constantly. He later confessed (or perhaps boasted), "With me, reading is a disease." Arthur Cutler, who acted as Roosevelt's tutor during the Oyster Bay period, commented, "The young man never seemed to know what idleness was, and every leisure moment would find the last novel, some English classic or some abstruse book on natural history in his hands." This refusal to allow a moment to pass without being turned to intellectual or other benefit persisted throughout his life.

The most obvious drawback to the home schooling Roosevelt received was uneven coverage of the various areas of human knowledge. An intellectual inventory of the fifteen-year-old's mind showed him to be solid in geography (largely from all his travels) and history (unsurprising for an avid reader), strong in the natural sciences (natu-

rally) and modern languages (especially French—he got over his dinner table distaste—and German), but deficient in mathematics and
classical languages. In short, Roosevelt was competent where his own
experience and inclinations had taken him, but suspect elsewhere.

By this time his health was coming around, and Theodore Sr. and
Mittie decided that the boy should plan on college—Harvard, specifically. They arranged with Arthur Cutler, a recent Harvard graduate
and subsequently founder of the Cutler School of New York, to devise
a program of work that would lead Theodore to the successful completion of the Harvard entrance examinations. Much of the work
took place at Oyster Bay, and the rest at the family's new house on
Fifty-seventh Street. As with nearly everything else, Theodore threw
himself into his studies, grinding away for as much as eight hours a
day during the winter in New York, somewhat less during the warm
months at Oyster Bay. In contrast to most of his previous experience
of learning, a good part of this was drudgery, for it included what others considered important rather than what he himself selected. The
classical languages at least had the advantage of opening a door to the
heroic stories of Homer and Virgil; mathematics was never anything
but a chore.

IV

The drudgery was relieved by that reliable diversion of most
teenage boys—girls. Like many other adolescents, Roosevelt didn't
quite know what to do with girls, but there they were, and they
increasingly caught his attention. He kept no diary during this period;
unlike the months abroad, when there was always time to fill in hotels
and on trains, he was too busy to stop, reflect, and recount his days'
activities. Nor did he write many letters during the Oyster Bay years,
for the obvious reason that most of the people he might have written
were within speaking distance. Consequently, it is impossible to read
his thoughts regarding the opposite sex. Indications are that he viewed
them with the same combination of attraction and impatience with
which most young men—not to say men generally—view members of
the opposite sex.

It wasn't long ago that he had displayed the typical boy's attitude toward the social niceties. "We have to go to dancing school," he moaned to his aunt. "I do not like it much." Matters of appearance and general presentability received scant attention. Bathing was optional, more dependent on proximity to a cove or stream than to a bathtub. As a result he often smelled of sweat or, more distinctively, dead animals and the arsenic he used to preserve them.

But now he took care about such things. After being a guest at a wedding, he remarked to his mother that one of the other guests—a woman—had complimented him. "She evidently had a great deal of discrimination," he said with tongue only slightly in cheek. And now he happily engaged in dances and other forms of mixed gatherings. "Saturday evening we had our little dinner party," he recounted in a letter, "the boys being from 15 to 18 and the girls from 14 to 17 years old. . . . I took in Annie Murray, and Fanny Smith sat on the other side of me." Annie Murray clearly caught his eye; on another occasion he wrote, "Friday night I went to the Bodens, dancing the German with Annie Murray; who gave a picnic on Saturday which I also attended. I enjoyed both intensely—and Annie Murray is a very nice girl, besides being very pretty. Ahem!" But perhaps Annie Murray didn't reciprocate—either that or he simply enjoyed playing the field, for a short while later he was talking about someone else. "In the evening I rowed over to Laurelton and after tea took Miss Nelly Smith out in my boat. The moonlight was beautiful and we took a lovely long row so that I did not get back home 'till eleven o'clock."

At other moments, when his liaisons proved less than satisfactory, he entertained doubts about the whole idea of love. With other males from time out of mind, he swore off such silliness for himself and derided it in others. "The 19th Streets have lately been seized with the idea that Mary Hale and a poor little she-trottling (I think Helen is her name) have fallen deeply in love with Frank," he related to Bamie. "Why should the elder members of that family always try to impress the younger ones with the idea that they are great 'catches' and beaux?" He went on to say that having had a "fling" with the ladies in question, he preferred the company of his male friends.

Although Roosevelt evidently had no favorite at this time, one young lady seems to have had her eye on him. Edith Carow was the daughter of Charles and Gertrude Carow, whose house occupied a lot adjacent to Grandfather Cornelius's property on Union Square. The Carows were longtime friends of Theodore Sr. and Mittie, and their children naturally inherited the habit. Edith Carow and Corinne Roosevelt, born less than two months apart, were playmates from before they could talk and remained fast friends through childhood and adolescence. Although the Carows summered at the New Jersey shore rather than Long Island, Edith visited Oyster Bay regularly and was considered part of the summer crowd there.

Three years younger than Theodore, Edith habitually hovered beneath his attention. She was intelligent and not unattractive, but at the moment she was too young and too familiar for him to consider seriously. To the extent he considered her at all, she was primarily his kid sister's friend. Yet he didn't ignore her entirely. She accompanied him on outings in his rowboat; gamer than other girls, or at least more willing to put up with his gaminess and other peculiarities, she earned the honor of having his rowboat named after her. On the other hand, it may not have been such an honor after all, for the christening was followed shortly by a request that she fashion a flag "for your name-sake." Surviving records do not indicate whether she complied; in light of their later history, one guesses that she did.

V

A more important figure in Roosevelt's life at the time was Arthur Cutler. Cutler's primary qualification as Theodore's tutor—beyond general intelligence and upstanding moral character—was that he had personally experienced the Harvard examination process and knew what his charge should expect. Cutler set the course of study, and Theodore followed it. Daily they labored at mathematics and the classical languages. The Greek and Latin still came easier than the geometry; both came harder than the various other subjects with which Cutler rounded out the curriculum.

Through the winter of 1874 and the spring of 1875, Roosevelt kept at his work. He grew increasingly nervous as an initial moment of truth approached. "How horribly near the examinations seem!" he lamented in late June. But the work paid off. "Is it not splendid about my examinations?" he wrote Bamie at the end of July. "I passed well on all the eight subjects I tried." Buoyed by these good results, he plunged into a final year of preparation. In February 1876 he wrote to Anna Minkwitz, now Anna Fisher, his Dresden tutor: "This winter I am studying quite hard."

He stuck with the routine for several months more; by the summer of 1876 he had cleared the final hurdles. Harvard indicated it would be pleased for the young man to enroll with the class of 1880.

CHAPTER FOUR

Anxious Underclassman
1876–77

"When I arrived here on Wednesday night," Roosevelt informed his mother from Cambridge in late September 1876, "I found a fire burning in the grate, and the room looking just as cosy and comfortable as it could look." The room in question occupied the northeast corner of the second floor of a boardinghouse owned by a Mrs. Richardson at 16 Winthrop Street. The address was by no means the most convenient or prestigious in Cambridge; most boys preferred to live in Harvard Yard, the center of campus a few blocks north. But when Bamie, in her long-standing role as second mother (and sometimes second father) to the younger three, had come to Cambridge that summer seeking a place for Theodore, only ground-floor lodgings were left in the Yard, and she judged these too likely to aggravate his asthma. As it was, an exerciser like himself certainly didn't begrudge the five-minute walk to classes; and he positively appreciated that another five-minute walk, this time south, carried him to the banks of the Charles River, with its opportunities for rowing, swimming, and skating.

The room itself couldn't have looked like much when Bamie first saw it. Necessarily for New England, it had a fireplace, one that could burn either short sticks of wood or, more commonly, coal. Four large windows afforded light for reading and a view of passersby. Patterned paper covered the walls from wooden baseboard to matching crown molding. A somewhat clashing pattern of flowers adorned the student-resistant (but evidently not student-proof) carpet, which was reinforced before the stone hearth by a throw rug cut from the same cloth. A gas chandelier would light the room during those long New England evenings when Theodore would be bent close to his books, seated either at the writing table in the center of the room or in the rocker in front of the fire.

But Bamie saw possibilities, and she was confident she could make it feel like home. Actually, with Theodore this wasn't hard, for he had already begun to collect assorted items that, transported from Fifty-seventh Street, could give any room a familiar feel. He would want his crossed daggers over the fireplace, his framed prints and portraits on the walls, his stuffed birds atop a bookcase—of which, considering his appetite for reading, he would need at least two or three. He'd require some pillows for the chaise longue in the corner, and one or more of his fur rugs. Curtains would set off the windows and hold in the heat at night.

Theodore was no connoisseur of interior design, but he appreciated Bamie's efforts on his behalf. "Everything is really beautiful," he told her even before the bulk of the collectibles arrived. Of course, almost anything would have looked attractive to him just then. The trappings of the room were less important than the fact that it was his—his first home away from home (and, although he couldn't know for certain yet, his principal residence for the next four years). As he stood in front of the fire that September night, a month before his eighteenth birthday, and shook the early autumn chill from his bones, he surveyed his domain and decided that it was good.

II

The Harvard to which Roosevelt presented himself was in the throes of remaking itself—as, more slowly, were several other venerable institutions of higher learning in America. The leaders of such established schools as Harvard, Yale, and Columbia, inspired by innovations made at newcomers like Johns Hopkins, Cornell, and later Stanford, pursued what they liked to call the "university idea"—a hazy notion that varied from one commencement speaker or essay writer to the next but that generally comprised a diversified curriculum, graduate study, and an emphasis on faculty research. The pursuit came harder at first for Harvard, the oldest of the old schools, than for some of the others, and the appointment in 1869 of Charles Eliot as president precipitated a near mutiny among the mossbacks on the faculty. Eliot might have seemed an unlikely revolutionary to those familiar with his antecedents, which were entirely in keeping with the pedigreed standards of Harvard and upper-class Boston. He was the scion of an established Harvard family—to be precise, the grandson of the benefactor of the Eliot professorship of Greek language and literature, the son of a former Harvard treasurer, the first cousin of a member of the board that appointed him, the nephew of two faculty members, and the possessor of numerous other ties to the institution, including, of course, a Harvard degree. But he was also an abrasive sort, and during an earlier stint at the university he had gotten on the wrong side of both the student body, whose members thought him a prig and a pain, and influential professors, including the formidable Louis Agassiz, who was instrumental in having him passed over for a permanent post in 1863, with the result that Eliot had to leave.

His absence proved to be temporary. When an 1868 resignation compelled the board of overseers to go looking for a new president, Eliot wasn't their first choice, but Charles Francis Adams diplomatically declined their offer, and Eliot was the second choice, although by no means a unanimous one. Young (thirty-five years old), energetic, and self-confident (except for a lifelong sensitivity regarding a large birthmark on his right cheek, which caused him to insist, when posing for photographs, on showing only his left profile), Eliot immediately set about shaking up the university. He rejected the notion that college ought to be the preserve of the well-to-do; while allowing that "the community does not owe superior education to all children, but only to the elite," he significantly qualified this by adding that "the process of preparing to enter college under the difficulties which poverty entails is just such a test of worthiness as is needed." He aimed to overturn the principle of a one-size-fits-all curriculum for undergraduates, arguing that the young worthies he had in mind should decide on their own what they needed to learn. "A well-instructed youth of eighteen," he insisted, "can select for himself—not for any other boy, or for the fictitious universal boy, but for himself alone—a better course of study than any college faculty, or any wise man who does not know him and his ancestors and his previous life, can possibly select for him." To the obvious objection that, in fact, most eighteen-year-olds were not so well instructed, he rejoined that the old-fashioned required curriculum was at least equally lost on them. Eliot endorsed entirely the comment of one of his supporters: "In vain was the dunce Hellenized, in vain the drone Latinized." Or, as he put it himself, "It really does not make much difference what these unawakened minds dawdle with."

Theodore Roosevelt probably was fortunate in having little direct dealing with Eliot; the Harvard president intimidated many a more worldly youth than the youngster from Oyster Bay. In fact, Eliot had direct dealings with very few undergraduates. They saw him stride purposefully across the Yard and at a distance at the requisite official functions, but for the most part he inhabited a world distinct from theirs.

All the same, Eliot's world had a decided impact on theirs. His inauguration of the elective system and his emphasis on science and research altered Harvard beyond recognition. Students now carried more responsibility for their education; rather than merely learning what they were told, they were expected to become active partners in designing their programs of study. The elective system placed even more pressure on the faculty. Instructors formerly had taught captive audiences that were forced to accept the good with the bad. Now students could choose, and they flocked to some instructors while shunning others. Theodore Roosevelt's future friend and ally Henry Cabot Lodge taught a course in American history that was tedious in the extreme; when students were emancipated, Lodge watched his enrollment plunge from fifty to three. So did Eliot: Lodge was let to understand that he had a brighter future making history than teaching it. He duly transferred to the Massachusetts department of practical politics.

Eliot's emphasis on research prodded the faculty toward the cutting edge of scholarship, which at this time was slicing science and other disciplines into finer and finer specialties and subspecialties. The German model of study, which emphasized total mastery of a single area of knowledge, dictated this narrow specialization; so did the explosion of scientific knowledge that characterized the nineteenth century. It had been possible for Isaac Newton's mind to span natural science during the late seventeenth century; two hundred years later not even a Newton could have known all there was to know in all the branches his old interests had divided into. Simultaneously with specialization, a hierarchy was developing among specialties. The observational sciences were losing ground to the experimental sciences; laboratory work, with its replicability and presumed rigor, increasingly replaced messy and often inherently irreproducible fieldwork.

The Harvard faculty didn't take kindly to the new president's approach; the student body took less kindly still. Eliot wanted to weed out those thoughtless or supercilious young men who deemed college simply a stepping-stone to some comfortable position already reserved for them, but by the time of Theodore Roosevelt's matriculation, the weeds still had the edge on the gardener. Indifference was the attitude of choice among the undergraduates. One of Roosevelt's classmates captured the campus spirit in a verse.

> We ask but time to drift,
> We deem it narrow-minded to excel.
> We call the man fanatic who applies
> His life to one grand purpose till he dies.
> Enthusiasm sees one side, one fact;
> We try to see all sides but do not act. . . .
> We long to sit with newspapers unfurled,
> Indifferent spectators of the world.

Other contemporary observers described a "repression or even disdain of enthusiasm" and an "emulation of highbred cynicism and arrogant coolness." The socially correct form of personal locomotion was the "Harvard swing," a slouching shamble; the approved manner of speech was the "Harvard drawl," a mumble verging on a yawn.

Dominating the social life of the campus were the sons of Boston's upper crust. Although Eliot was reaching out to other parts of the country, a majority of the student body hailed from the neighborhood of Boston. Roosevelt, from New York, was one of the more distant recruits. The Brahmin boys had the advantages of wealth in many but not all cases; of long-standing ties to Harvard and its traditions, dating in some instances to the seventeenth century; of preexisting connections among themselves, affording an edge in setting campus standards; of proximity to home and its conveniences, including that perennial need of young adult males, personal transportation; and of a head start regarding that even more perennial need of young men, young women.

III

Such an atmosphere could hardly have been less congenial to an individual of Roosevelt's upbringing. Of course, any college would have strained his powers of adjustment. Roosevelt had passed essentially all of his nearly eighteen years sheltered in the bosom of his family. Whether wintering in Manhattan, summering in the Hudson Valley or Oyster Bay, touring Europe or cruising the Nile, the boy had been surrounded by siblings and cousins. Even his sojourn in Dresden, which was his great adventure in independence to date, had featured Elliott in the next bed, Corinne in the next room, his cousins in the next block, and his mother on call. By eighteen most boys had been exposed to the social tests of at least the classroom and the school yard. Roosevelt hadn't. Nor had his recurrent ill health contributed to his social development, and his passion for books and dead birds merely made matters worse. Even Corinne, who never could find a negative word to say about her famous brother, implicitly conceded his interpersonal immaturity at this point by remarking that Elliott was "more naturally a social leader" than Theodore. As a result of all this, Theodore spent most of his first two years at Harvard anxiously assessing how he fit in and measured up.

The effort to find his footing showed in his first few letters home. Roosevelt initially liked the food at the college commons, describing it as "very fair," but within a week he had changed his mind. "As I am decidedly discontented with the food at Commons," he wrote, "I am going to join a table with some of the Boston men." Although college dining halls are notorious for putting on a good show for new arrivals and then reverting to less appetizing fare, one can't help suspecting that the food had less to do with Roosevelt's dining decision than the company: If the "Boston men" decreed the Commons too common, Roosevelt would, too. Another week later he confirmed his newly refined tastes: "I am very glad that I joined the table I am now at, as the food at Commons is getting gradually uneatable; almost all the fellows I know are leaving it."

The influence of his new acquaintances extended to his lodgings. The room that had seemed so satisfactory at first soon slipped into disrepute. He was tactful but clear in a letter to Bamie, his personal decorator. "Do you think it possible to express on my bookcase, pictures etc. now?" he requested. "My room, in spite of the swell curtains and paper, looks awfully bare, while all the other boys have theirs' completely fixed. If it is perfectly convenient"—a recurring phrase he appears to have picked up since his arrival in Cambridge— "I should like the above mentioned articles together with any stray ornaments I may happen to possess, and as many of my scientific and poetical books as you can collect, as soon as possible."

As for those new acquaintances themselves, they included sons of some of Boston's most respected families. Henry Shaw would become a Boston banker, Arthur Hooper, a Boston lawyer, George Peters, a Boston businessman. Others of his table would find fame or fortune farther south: William Andrews as a justice of the New York supreme court (appointed by Roosevelt) and John Lamson as vice president of New York Security and Trust. Despite the social connections of his new friends, Roosevelt reckoned it appropriate to testify to his parents of their good character. His father had warned him about the vices of tobacco and alcohol; Roosevelt wrote reassuringly that "out of the eleven other boys at the table where I am, no less than seven do not smoke and four drink nothing stronger than beer." Whether Theodore Sr. and Mittie were in fact reassured by this statement—the obvious implication of which was that several of their son's friends did smoke and a majority knocked back the hard stuff—they kept their concerns on this point to themselves. Doubtless they put more store in Theodore's comment that "I do not find it nearly so hard as I expected not to drink and smoke."

Yet even Roosevelt himself sometimes wondered just what he knew about his classmates. They seemed respectable enough, but who could say for certain? Thus he felt on firmer ground when he met someone of known antecedents. In October he wrote to his mother, "I have become acquainted with a very nice fellow named Townsend, from Albany. He is a cousin of Mr. Thayers. It is really a relief to find someone whom I know something about, as I have not the slightest idea about the families of most of my 'friends.'"

With the majority of his classmates—and to a greater degree than many of them—Roosevelt was impressed by the athletic and otherwise-physical standouts in his class. Basking in a bit of reflected glory, he described some of his "chief friends" to Corinne. "Tom Nickerson is the one who started our table. He is quite handsome with a truly remarkable black moustache. At first he gives one the impression of being effeminate, but is not a bit so in reality, being one of our best football players." The biggest man on campus during Roosevelt's time was Robert Bacon, who captained the football team, took top track honors, captured the heavyweight boxing crown and pulled an oar on the crew. And was good-looking and congenial to boot: "Bob Bacon is the handsomest man in the class and is as pleasant as he is handsome." (Roosevelt's admiration for Bacon persisted; as president he would appoint Bacon assistant secretary of state and, briefly, secretary of state.)

In November, Roosevelt joined a large crowd of Harvard students who traveled to New Haven for the second annual Harvard-Yale football game. The expedition was fun, even if the outcome of the game was disappointing. "I am sorry to say we were beaten, principally because our opponents played very foul." The trip was also enlightening, with Roosevelt's commentary indicating that he was becoming imbued with the true Harvard spirit. "I am very glad I am not a Yale freshman; the hazing there is pretty bad. The fellows too seem to be a much more scrubby set than ours."

Roosevelt would have given an arm to make the football team, but he had neither the size nor the athletic ability for it. At eighteen he was still slight, slow afoot, and rather uncoordinated. His eyesight was poor; although partially corrected by glasses, these couldn't be worn in games. His myopia wouldn't have been a disqualifying problem in close-contact sports like football, but it rendered such intensively hand-eye activities as baseball out of the question.

Yet what Roosevelt lacked in coordination he made up in determination, and all the hours and miles he had invested in walking, rowing, and riding had given him stamina. One of the class stalwarts, Richard Welling, described an encounter with Roosevelt. Welling had agreed to go skating with him one afternoon; having seen Roosevelt at the college gymnasium and deeming him "verily a youth in the kindergarten stage of physical development," he expected a light workout on the ice. He first suspected something more when they got to the pond and discovered that the ice was rough and the surface unprotected from the arctic wind. Roosevelt nonetheless tore out onto the pond and seemed to be having the time of his life. "When any sane man would have voted to go home, as the afternoon's sport was clearly a flop," Welling remembered, "Roosevelt was exclaiming, 'Isn't this bully!'— and the harder it blew and the worse we skated, the more often I had to hear 'Isn't this bully!'" Though Welling wanted to leave, he refused to be the first to call it quits. Roosevelt, meanwhile, continued to enjoy himself immensely, apparently oblivious to his companion's discomfort. Only when it grew too dark to see did Roosevelt suggest that they head home. Welling thought that if there had been a moon, Roosevelt might have wanted to skate until midnight.

IV

Roosevelt's determination stood him well in the classroom. Prior to college neither he nor his parents had any good gauge as to the precise nature of his intelligence. He was no idiot, to be sure. He had developed a facility for reading and writing, chiefly because of his large appetite for books and, to a lesser extent, the letter- and journal-writing habit he practiced overseas. Although he complained of how long it took him to compose letters and the like, one wouldn't have known it from reading them. In the fundamental literacy skills he was ahead of most of his peers. He had a good memory for particular kinds of information: the poems that impressed him with their epic themes or their swinging meter, the Latin and common names of the birds he collected, along with the time, place, and circumstances of their collection. In other words, like most people, he remembered those things that engaged his interest.

Unlike most people, Roosevelt seems to have had something of a photographic memory. Especially later in his life (when, admittedly, people were likelier to believe extraordinary things about him), friends noticed his ability to recite long passages from books he had read. Regarding one such instance, Roosevelt explained, "I remembered a book that I had read some time ago, and as I talked the pages of the book came before my eyes, and it seemed as though I were able to read the things therein contained."

The undergraduate Roosevelt could be intellectually diligent—although again with most noticeable effect in those areas he considered important. While he accepted the notion that learning was valuable for its own sake, he reserved the right to judge some kinds of learning more valuable than others.

On the other hand, he was not brilliant. Most people aren't—even most of those people who make an intellectual mark on the world. Indeed, one of the secrets of Roosevelt's success in life—of both his intellectual accomplishments and of his political triumphs—was his recognition that lack of brilliance is rarely a disqualification for anything. Where others allowed themselves to be deterred from acting by a recognition that someone else might be better qualified, Roosevelt plunged ahead and let the results of his actions speak for themselves.

These marks of the mature Roosevelt were just beginning to emerge during his first year at Harvard. While he didn't disgrace himself in the classroom, neither, on the whole, did he cut much of a swath. "I think I am getting along all right in all," he told his father after a month of classes, a characterization that was accurate enough. His first-year course work consisted of Greek composition and translation, Latin composition and translation, classical literature, German, mathematics, physics, and chemistry. The inclusion of German and the two science courses reflected the changes Charles Eliot had made since his arrival seven years before, when French had been required and students didn't start science until their second year. In one respect Roosevelt was fortunate in having arrived after Eliot. He got to apply the knowledge of German he had gained in Dresden and through his reading of the German sagas; in fact, German was by far his best subject. He made a 92 for the year, while in no other course did he score above the seventies. He continued to struggle with Latin and especially Greek; these courses brought his lowest marks, a 73 and a dismal 58, respectively. Mathematics was also difficult. Although the course was labeled "advanced" and indeed was advanced by comparison to the pre-Eliot freshman course, it consisted of trigonometry and analytical geometry, material typically taught in high school a century later. Nonetheless, Roosevelt had to scramble to keep up. After a month in Cambridge he told his mother to expect fewer letters: "I only write on Sundays now as my work is beginning to press a little on me, one of my Mathematics especially being very hard." A strong finish allowed him to salvage a 75 for the year. Classical literature came easier, not least on account of his solid reading habits, although his grade for the year—a 77—hardly revealed the fact.

One would have thought Roosevelt would particularly have benefited from Eliot's reforms regarding the science courses freshmen could take. Oddly, he didn't—or, rather, he benefited in an unexpected and negative way. The possibility of studying science early had been one of the attractions of Harvard, since it would give him an opportunity to do soon what he liked best. He even toyed with the idea of making science his career.

In this last matter he received some unanticipated encouragement from his father. Since childhood Roosevelt had casually expected to go into the family business, if perhaps only in the perfunctory way Theodore Sr. had. Initially, it seems, Theodore Sr. held similar expectations. But the excitement with which the young boy commenced his scientific researches and the assiduousness with which the adolescent continued them caused his father to reconsider. Maybe the lad wasn't meant for business after all. Moreover, the business was beginning to look as though it might not be meant for the lad.

The Panic of 1873 and the continuing fright that followed had strangled new construction in New York and driven Roosevelt & Son out of plate glass. The family was far from destitute—perhaps a little illiquid, but the real estate that undergirded the Roosevelt lifestyle remained intact. All the same, things were slow at the office, and with several cousins coming of age in the next several years, there was no point in bringing the reluctant aboard.

Accordingly, Theodore Sr. broached with his son the possibility of a career in science. Such a career wouldn't return much money; the father said he was willing to help out. Characteristically, however, he couched his offer as an admonition. "He told me that if I wished to become a scientific man I could do so," Roosevelt remembered. "He explained that I must be sure that I really intensely desired to do scientific work, because if I went into it I must make it a serious career; that he had made enough money to enable me to take up such a career and do non-remunerative work of value *if I intended to do the very best work there was in me;* but that I must not dream of taking it up as a dilettante." Roosevelt also recalled a Micawberesque formula his father had referred to: "If I was not going to earn money, I must even things up by not spending it. As he expressed it, I had to keep the fraction constant, and if I was not able to increase the numerator, then I must reduce the denominator."

With this paternal blessing, Roosevelt prepared to devote himself to a life of science. But before long the prospect began to pale, when he discovered that the kind of science he had his heart set on wasn't the kind of science his Harvard mentors favored. As he explained, "At that time Harvard, and I suppose our other colleges, utterly ignored the possibilities of the faunal naturalist, the outdoor naturalist and observer of nature. They treated biology as purely a science of the laboratory and the microscope, a science whose adherents were to spend their time in the study of minute forms of marine life, or else in section-cutting and the study of the tissues of the higher organisms under the microscope." Roosevelt acknowledged that the reforms Eliot had put in place were warranted, but he thought that in the case of natural history the reformers had gone too far. "The sound revolt against superficiality of study had been carried to an extreme; thoroughness in minutiae as the only end of study had been erected into a fetich. There was a total failure to understand the great variety of kinds of work that could be done by naturalists, including what could be done by outdoor naturalists."

But outdoor work was precisely what had drawn Roosevelt to science, and being informed that it wasn't real science put him off. Gradually—he required some time to determine whether the mismatch between science and himself was his fault or science's—he surrendered the idea of making science a career. "I had no more desire or ability to be a microscopist and section-cutter than to be a mathematician"— which for him was definitely out of the question. "Accordingly I abandoned all thought of becoming a scientist."

V

It was just as well that Roosevelt discovered that a scientific career didn't suit him before actually embarking on one. Eliot would have said that such self-discovery was precisely what his elective system was designed to evoke. In Roosevelt's case, however, it left him somewhat at a loss as to what to do. He continued to study science, not least because his natural history courses were the ones in which he made his best grades. Yet he began to consider other options.

Meanwhile, his social career began to unfold. He attended theatrical performances in Boston with friends and got up a whist club. He found an occasional kindred spirit regarding his view of natural history. "Harry Minot was speaking to me the other day about our making a collecting trip in the White Mountains together next summer," he informed Corinne. "I think it would be good fun." He attended dancing classes, which he found "quite pleasant." A forty-eight-hour furlough home for Thanksgiving was followed by preparations for a longer visit over Christmas. Saying that he hoped to entertain some of his new friends during the holidays, he declared, "I should like a party very much, if it is perfectly convenient." The party was duly held and proved a signal success. "A delightful Christmas experience" was how Corinne remembered it. "The New York girls"—herself among them—"and the Boston boys fraternized to their hearts' content." Another party, this hosted by Roosevelt's aunt, Anna Bulloch Gracie, was fully as fun. Roosevelt squired Edith Carow around; she "looked as pretty as a picture and was very sweet." Edith and his other old flame, Annie Murray, made a very favorable impression on his college chums, who judged the two the "prettiest" girls they had met, as he told Corinne—who might not have been entirely happy to hear it, as he ought to have guessed. This judgment caused him to look on Edith and Annie with newly appreciative eyes. "My two weeks have been as pleasant as they could be," he told Elliott by way of summary, "and have been spent in a perfect round of gaiety."

Although admitting to a fleeting case of homesickness upon his return to Cambridge, he quickly got back into a social mood. "I have been having a pretty gay time during the last week," he wrote in mid-January to Bamie. "It is very funny to keep meeting people whose sisters and brothers I have heard of through you (such as Miss Whitney, Miss Revere and Miss Lindsay). Some of the girls are very sweet and bright, and a few are very pretty." He quickly added, however: "'Still Oh Anneth I remain Faithful to Thee!' (The proper name in the above beautiful rhapsody is a compound of Annie and Edith)."

The following few weeks brought exams, but they hardly cut into Roosevelt's socializing. Early in February he wrote, "On Wednesday evening Harry Jackson gave a large sleighing party. This was great fun, for there were forty girls and fellows, and two matrons in one huge sleigh. We sang songs for a great part of the time, as we soon left Boston, and were dragged by our eight horses rapidly through a great many of the pretty little towns which form the suburbs of Boston. One of the girls, by name Miss Wheelwright, looked quite like Edith—only not nearly as pretty as her Ladyship: who when she dresses well and don't frizzle her hair is a very pretty girl." The singing and subsequent carrying on lasted late. "We came home from our sleighride about nine and then danced till after twelve. I led the German with Harry Jackson's cousin, Miss Andrews. After the party Bob Bacon, Arthur Hooper, myself and some others came out in a small sleigh to Cambridge, making the night hideous with our songs."

Nor was that the end of the week's festivities. "On Saturday I went, with Minot Weld, to an Assembly (a juvenile one I mean) at Brookline, where I danced with Miss Fisk. This was a very swell affair there being about sixty couples in the room. As I knew a good many of the girls, from having met them out before, I enjoyed myself very much. I was introduced to a Miss Richardson, the prettiest girl I have seen for a long while." Unfortunately this Miss Richardson was not very talkative, which made conversation somewhat strained. Roosevelt couldn't help tossing off an obiter dictum: "Her brother is in my class, and (although very bright) is not a particularly favourable specimen of humanity."

VI

As this last comment revealed, Roosevelt was developing a tendency toward snap judgments of people he met. In his letters and in his diary he rarely exhibited ambivalence. His physical eyesight may have been blurred, but not his moral eyesight, which cast his contemporaries into sharp reliefs of black and white, good and bad. This would become a lifelong trait.

Later, people would display equally decided opinions about him. But at this stage he wasn't a big enough fish to attract much notice, and nearly all the surviving recollections of him are of the (often far) ex post facto variety and hence are colored by the recognition he subsequently achieved. One of his teenage flames, for example, remembered saying that he would some day be president, but she didn't put this memory to paper for others to read until long after he had become president. This doesn't make her statement false, merely unreliable for the biographer. Other impressions of Roosevelt fall into the same category. One has Roosevelt entering Charles Eliot's office and, somewhat flustered, blurting out, "Mr. Eliot, I am President Roosevelt." A classmate recalled him speaking up so much that their teacher had to reprimand him: "Now look here, Roosevelt, let me talk. I'm running this course."

In such cases the biographer seeks patterns, and the pattern that emerges most clearly is a general impression of Roosevelt as eccentric. Reports circulated among those who knew him that he kept snakes, lizards, and other vile creatures in his room; Robert Bacon, for one, was said for this reason to have given Roosevelt's room a wide berth. Charles Washburn was struck by Roosevelt's odd eating habits: He ate chicken "as though he wanted to grind the bones." As late as their senior year, William Thayer couldn't make up his mind about this unusual fellow. "I recall, still," Thayer wrote four decades later, "looking hard at him with an eager, inquisitive look and saying to myself, 'I wonder whether he is the real thing, or only the bundle of eccentricities which he appears.'"

VII

One eccentricity few could miss was Roosevelt's continuing obsession with exercise and physical prowess. All young men feel the need to prove themselves physically, but few carry it as far as Roosevelt did. Barred from the major sports by his lack of size and strength, not to mention talent, he concentrated on those activities that had weight divisions, particularly boxing and wrestling. In the former he had by now the advantage of several years of experience. Not long after his arrival in Cambridge he wrote home for some equipment he had left behind: "Please send on my best pair of boxing gloves—I think they have green wrist bands." Later, describing a typical day to his mother and father, he explained how he studied and attended classes until noon when he broke for exercise. "I go over to the gymnasium, where I have a set-to with the gloves with 'General' Lister, the boxing master—for I am training to box among the lightweights in the approaching match for the championship of Harvard."

In this same letter he went on to describe a food fight at lunch by the boys in "an obstreperously joyful condition." Later, on the way back to his rooms, he ran into two of the stalwarts of the class playing catch with a baseball. Typically, he stayed on the sidelines, watching, until a wayward toss broke a window and ended the session. "We abruptly separated."

Whatever they did or didn't do for his self-esteem, Roosevelt's athletic endeavors continued to fortify his constitution. During his freshman year his health was better than it had ever been in his life. His asthma flared only a couple of times, and in the late winter he caught the measles. Occasional letters make passing reference to some sensitivity of his eyes. "I do not go often to the Theatre, as I don't care for it, and it might hurt my eyes" went one such (rather puzzling) missive. But compared to the chronic afflictions he had lived with for years, these were almost nothing.

The New England winter constrained his outdoor exercises, limiting them to walking and skating. As the summer drew near, however, the opportunity for roaming the woods arose again. As per their earlier plan, he and Harry Minot took off shortly after classes let out in June for an excursion in the Adirondacks. Minot was a good match for Roosevelt; besides being a keen woodsman, he knew almost as much about birds in general and even more about the avifauna peculiar to that particular stretch of the Northeast. Roosevelt and Minot collaborated during this expedition to produce "The Summer Birds of the Adirondacks in Franklin County, N.Y.," a catalog that they paid to have printed. As Roosevelt explained in an introductory note, "The following catalogue (written in the mountains) is based upon observations made in August, 1874, August, 1875, and June 22d to July 9th, 1877, especially about the Saint Regis Lakes, Mr. Minot having been with me, only during the last week of June. Each of us has used his initials in making a statement which the other has not verified."

From the Adirondacks, Roosevelt headed south to Oyster Bay,

where he quickly fell into his former routine. "Am leading the most thoroughly out of door life," he noted in his diary in mid-July. "Riding and walking every day and rowing in my little boat almost as often." If anything, his adventures were more ambitious than ever. One August day Roosevelt set out with cousin Johnnie Elliot for Whitestone, more than twenty miles away. Returning the next day, the pair ran into a squall and several times their boat nearly capsized. They didn't reach the safety of home until after midnight. Roosevelt loved every minute.

He also loved the chance for some more armed science on the old turf. "I shot several cross bills in the woods," he informed Harry Minot. "A woodcock was shot near Paul Smiths; none of the inhabitants knew what it was, or had ever seen another. The blackbirds we saw were not the Scolecophagus but the females of Quisqualus purpureus. I found several colonies of this bird widely separated from one another, and shot both male and female specimens."

VIII

The return to Oyster Bay also occasioned a renewed opportunity to see old friends, including Edith Carow. Edith had joined Theodore Sr. and the other three Roosevelt children on a visit to Cambridge in May. They got a chance to observe young Theodore's situation at college as well as to meet more of his classmates. Edith had a delightful time. "I enjoyed to the utmost every minute of my stay," she wrote by way of thanks. As she had at Christmas, Edith made a favorable impression on Roosevelt's friends and, partly through them, on him. "I don't think I ever saw Edith looking prettier," he told Corinne a few days after the visitors left. "Everyone, and especially Harry Chapin and Minot Weld admired her little Ladyship intensely, and she behaved as sweetly as she looked." He closed with a request: "When you write to Edith tell her I enjoyed her visit very much indeed."

In August, Edith made her regular trip to Oyster Bay. She and the numerous Roosevelts, including Theodore, engaged in their habitual activities—rowing by sunlight and moonlight, walking in the woods, climbing Cooper's Bluff, reading poetry. Theodore was less boisterous than in former days; as a college man he had his dignity to consider.

Even so, away from the pressure of his peers, he could relax in a way that was impossible in Cambridge.

Though appreciative of Edith, Roosevelt wasn't oblivious to the charms of other young ladies. A late-summer flirtation blossomed in September after Edith had left and just before Roosevelt was to return to Cambridge. A Miss Boden who was staying across the bay had caught his eye. Undeterred by the distance that separated them, he arranged to meet her, and one morning set out at five o'clock for the long row over to her house. He arrived at eight, but deeming this too early to ring the bell, he lay down on a rock for a nap. When he awoke some time later, he discovered that his boat had drifted out into the sound. Not wishing to soak his clothes, he removed them and went swimming after the boat, which he retrieved with some difficulty. He rowed back to the dock near her house. Here he thought to let the air dry him off before putting his clothes back on. But all the rowing and swimming had tired him out, and he fell asleep once more. And again the waves carried the unsecured boat away from the shore—but this time with his clothes. While pondering his predicament, he heard the voices of his young lady friend and a female companion coming down to the dock to greet him. Utterly embarrassed, he cowered under the dock, motionless, silent, and shivering. The two girls waited and waited, growing increasingly impatient at the suitor who never appeared. Finally, they returned to her house, leaving the mortified young man to slip stealthily into the water in search of the missing boat and clothes. Luckily, he found the wayward vessel, saving himself additional discomfiture. The next time he visited, he traveled overland.

IX

Roosevelt's summer of 1877 flashed by, as college summers do, and within the week of wishing Miss Boden farewell he was back in Cambridge. He returned to the same quarters he had occupied the previous year, although now, knowing what the accepted style was, he got them decorated right sooner. A few weeks into his second year he sent a note of thanks and approval to Bamie: "I had Harry Chapin in here the other day to look at the new bookcase (which makes the room just perfection) and after he had examined it he exclaimed 'Jove! Your family do act squarely by you!' And I most heartily agree with him."

Predictably, he felt more comfortable socially this second time around. Not the new kid or the outsider anymore, he had a circle of friends he could be himself with. These didn't include the stars of the class, who still couldn't quite fathom this unusual New Yorker if they noticed him at all; rather, they were individuals whose eclectic tastes ran closer to his. "My respect for the mental qualities of my classmates has much increased lately . . ." he told Corinne, "as they now no longer seem to think it necessary to confine their conversation exclusively to athletic subjects. I was especially struck by this the other night, when, after a couple of hours spent in boxing and wrestling with Arthur Hooper and Ralph Ellis, it was proposed to finish the evening by reading aloud from Tennyson, and we became so interested in 'In Memoriam' that it was past one o'clock when we separated." A few weeks later he described another such soiree. "Some of the boys came down to my room and we had a literary coffee party. They became finally interested in Edgar Poe—probably because they could not understand him."

His classes, which now included natural history, were more congenial the second time around as well. "The work is much pleasanter than last year," he recorded during his first month back. "I like the Zoological courses very much." A week later he remarked, "One of my studies (French) is extremely difficult, but I get along pretty fairly in the others, while my anatomical course is extremely interesting." Though it made no particular impression on him at the time, the instructor of this anatomy class—actually, vertebrate biology—was William James.

His grades reflected his greater interest in his courses. Except for an abysmal 51 in French literature (just two points from failing) and a 69 in composition (in which he had to write six themes on assigned topics), his marks were all in the honors range (which started at 70 for electives and 75 for required courses). Two German classes were his easiest: He breezed through German scientific prose with a 92 and German composition with a 96. William James gave him a 79 in vertebrate biology, and he made an 89 in elementary botany. In Anglo-American constitutional history he scored 87, and in rhetoric, 94.

X

In the same letter in which he told Bamie about his anatomy class, Roosevelt remarked that he would shortly be starting to teach his Sunday school class again. Prior to entering Harvard, he had conducted a "mission class" in New York; in the fall of his freshman year he took charge of a Sunday class for children of the Episcopal Christ Church in Cambridge. Occasionally this commitment cut into his social life: When his friends stayed away from Cambridge for a weekend, he had to return Sunday morning to teach his class. But following his father's example, he considered it his duty to give back something of what he had been blessed with, and he came to enjoy the experience. "I am beginning to get very much interested in my scholars," he told Corinne, "especially in one who is a very orderly & bright little fellow—two qualities which I have not usually found combined."

Roosevelt's religiosity was subdued and orthodox. He had acquired the habit of going to church in childhood when Theodore Sr. had made a point of honoring the Sabbath wherever the family found itself—at home in Manhattan, at Oyster Bay, or traveling in Europe or the Near East. Theodore Sr. wasn't a fanatical sabbatarian; if a train ride on Sunday was the only reasonable way to get where they wanted to go when they needed to get there, then travel they did and made no fuss. But even on such days he led the family in Bible readings and prayer. The habit impressed the children, especially Theodore, who more than the rest identified with their father.

Roosevelt's moral code was also orthodox, although a bit strait-laced for some of his college friends. On Roosevelt's leaving for college, his father had admonished him: "Take care of your morals first, your health next and finally your studies." Roosevelt did his best to heed this advice. Even if his asthma and his desire to attain top physical condition hadn't advised against it, he probably wouldn't have smoked; to him smoking was a vice, albeit a minor one. Likewise, immoderate consumption of alcohol. He wasn't a teetotaler and certainly not a prohibitionist, but nonetheless he drank sparingly. He considered gambling a waste of money and especially time; although he wasn't stingy with his purse, he was tight with his time.

Sex was something to be reserved for marriage. Social conventions of Roosevelt's college days were designed to keep young men and women from opportunities of intimate liaisons; in Roosevelt's case the conventions were unnecessary. With Victorian propriety he insisted on "purity" in himself and any potential intended. While some of his classmates celebrated their weekends by taking in the lower forms of theater and dance, leading one Boston paper to complain that "seeing the world meant, to them, gazing with watery eyes upon half-clad ballet girls and burlesque actresses, and hovering about them, later, like flies about a carcass," Roosevelt told Bamie that his idea of a good time was "decidedly different." He heard that one of the cousins had married such an entertainer; he immediately registered his disgust: "Cornelius has distinguished himself by marrying a French actress! He is a disgrace to the family—the vulgar brute." Roosevelt prided himself on his superiority in such matters. Weighing his own marriage prospects, he reflected, "Thank Heaven, I am at least perfectly pure."

Of course, morality meant more than missing out on sexual adventures or forgoing strong drink and tobacco. For Roosevelt, integrity was the thing, defined to mean living the kind of life he wouldn't mind owning up to—especially to his father. Compared to many other young people, Roosevelt had an easy time determining the difference between right and wrong. All he had to ask himself, regarding some action, was whether he would be proud for his father to know he had done it. At this stage of his life the choices he faced were relatively straightforward, and he rarely had much difficulty deciding what his father would have had him do. The decisions would get harder later; occasionally even he would confess to being at a loss. But for now the choices seemed stark, and, the master of his will, he generally chose the one he knew to be right.

While Roosevelt's moral code didn't appeal to some of his peers, it suited his own temperament well enough. He rarely spoke about an afterlife; he accepted that moral behavior was the best guarantor of happiness here below. And he certainly seemed happy. Repeatedly he commented on how happy he was. Two days after his eighteenth birthday, in October 1876, he told his mother, "It seems perfectly wonderful, in looking back over my eighteen years of existence, to see how I have literally never spent an unhappy day, unless by my own fault!" Coming from one who had spent very many days ill or otherwise confined to quarters, this was a remarkable statement.

CHAPTER FIVE

A Man of His Own
1877–78

By all evidence, the Theodore Roosevelt of his first two years at Harvard was oblivious to the larger political events that swirled around the communities of Cambridge and Oyster Bay and the country as a whole. The Panic of 1873 and the ensuing depression had forced his family's firm out of a principal part of its longtime trade, but it rated only the most oblique mention in his letters. He seems not to have noticed the disputed presidential election of 1876, which returned the Republicans to the White House but terminated Reconstruction in the South. The biggest story of the summer of 1877—the labor violence that wrenched much of the nation—seems to have escaped him entirely.

That violence was hard to miss. One epicenter was western Pennsylvania, where June 21, 1877, the day on which Roosevelt was happily packing to leave Cambridge for his bird-collecting expedition in the Adirondacks, was known ever after as "the day of the rope." On that day Pennsylvania authorities hanged ten men for committing or inciting violence in the anthracite coal region of the state. The hangings marked the culmination of a government offensive against assertive labor unionists in the coalfields, epitomized by the radical "Molly Maguires." Opinions differed as to where justice in the coalfields lay—with the miners or with management and the powers-that-were. But both sides and nearly all observers were shocked at the degree of violence, legal and otherwise, that the dispute provoked.

Yet the killings in the coalfields were almost immediately overshadowed by the violence in another industry. Less than a month after hanging day in Pennsylvania, firemen and brakemen on the Baltimore & Ohio Railroad walked off the job in Martinsburg, West Virginia. Like the coal miners, the railworkers were protesting wage cuts, which, like the cuts in the coal industry, were a response to the economic depression. The mayor of Martinsburg intended to stifle the strike by seizing the instigators, but his efforts failed when the police, many of whom had friends or relatives among the railworkers, refused to follow his arrest orders. As the news of the strikers' success in Martinsburg spread along the B & O, so did the strike itself. It then jumped the tracks on to the Erie and thence to the Pennsylvania, the nation's largest railroad. Eventually, the effects of the strike reached from coast to coast, from the New York Central to the Central Pacific.

As in the coal strike, the political authorities portrayed the rail strike as a communist-inspired insurrection, a charge originating in memories of the Paris Commune of just seven years earlier and made more credible by the recent violence in the coalfields. Governors of the affected states called out the militia to suppress the strike. When the state troops couldn't accomplish this goal, federal troops were sent in by President Hayes, whose recent victory procession to Washington had been sponsored by the Penn, with him riding in the special car of Penn president Thomas Scott. The regulars finally snuffed out the strike, but not before more than a hundred people had died and tens of millions of dollars in property in more than a dozen states had gone up in flames.

II

The battles in the coalfields didn't keep Theodore Roosevelt from keeping cozy in Cambridge, and the railroad stoppage didn't stop him from reaching Oyster Bay; neither development, as far as can be ascertained, intersected his field of activity or even his awareness. (As president he would become intensely interested in both industries.) His letters and diaries reveal almost nothing of the world beyond his narrow personal realm and, of course, the realm of his books. It is unclear if he ever read a newspaper during this period.

This isn't especially surprising, considering his class and upbringing. In the age of the spoilsmen, politics was a low profession to those of breeding and inherited money. Occasionally, one encountered the political classes, just as one encountered muddy streets. At such times there was nothing to do but step carefully and try to avoid getting too dirty. Yet one didn't choose to consort with politicians any more than one went strolling through the slop. God had given the better classes horses and carriages for a reason.

Sometimes, however, politics simply insisted. Theodore Roosevelt, Sr., had served his country, politically if not militarily, during the Civil War; a decade later he again answered a call to public service. This latter summons also came from a Republican president, in this case Rutherford Hayes, who, despite the post-election horse-trading that won him his office, had resolved to clean up as much of the Augean stables of national politics as possible. Not everyone took Hayes seriously, partly because of that recent horse-trading, partly because it was hard not to smirk at a man who indulged the prohibitionist fancies of his wife—"Lemonade Lucy," she was called—by striking everything stronger from the beverage list at state dinners.

Among those who had trouble with Hayes's reformist notions was Roscoe Conkling, the formidable Republican senator from New York. Conkling was a large and physically powerful man; a contemporary described him as being of "commanding, even magnificent presence, six feet three inches tall, with regular features, lofty forehead, and piercing eyes—blond and gigantic as a viking." He was also a party man, first and last, but after the fashion of the times, for he felt obliged to defend the Republican organization not merely against the expected depredations of the Democrats but also against the insidious assaults of reformist Republicans. "Parties are not built up by deportment, or by ladies' magazines, or gush," he declared; and he swore defiance at those who thought otherwise. This opinion had led him to try to stymie the deal that won Hayes the presidency. He preferred the Democrat Samuel Tilden, a person he could openly oppose, to the Republican Hayes, whom he would be expected to accommodate. Put otherwise, a Democratic president wouldn't threaten Conkling's livelihood and power as chief of the New York Republican machine, while a Republican president would.

And did. No sooner had Hayes been inaugurated than he fired a warning shot in Conkling's direction. He announced his support—

which included the patronage and other perquisites of the presidency—for an anti-Conkling faction in the New York Republican Party. Principal among the targets of the reformers, besides Conkling, who for the moment was out of reach, was Chester Arthur, a Conkling colleague and the collector of customs at the port of New York. Arthur's job was an executive appointment and well within the president's reach.

Conkling responded with a sulfurous assault on the reformers at a party convention in Rochester in the early autumn. He lashed them as "the man milliners"—homosexuals, and so understood—"the dilettanti and carpet knights of politics. . . . Their stock in trade is rancid, canting self-righteousness. They are wolves in sheep's clothing. Their real object is office and plunder. When Dr. Johnson defined patriotism as the last refuge of a scoundrel, he was unconscious of the then undeveloped capabilities and uses of the word 'Reform!'"

George William Curtis, leader of the Republican reformers, was used to Conkling's vituperation, but even he thought the old boss had outdone himself. Afterward, Curtis remarked that he couldn't rid his mind of the image of "that man glaring at me in a fury of hate, and storming out of his foolish blackguardism." Curtis added, "No one can imagine the Mephistophelean leer and spite."

Theodore Roosevelt, Sr., came close to imagining them. In October 1877, President Hayes sent Roosevelt's name to the Senate as the replacement for Arthur as customs collector at New York. Although Conkling had nothing particularly personal against Roosevelt, he couldn't abide what he considered the hypocrisy of Hayes, whom he regularly referred to as "His Fraudulency," and he wasn't about to roll over while his man Arthur was rolled out of office. Consequently, Conkling began scorching the earth around the Roosevelt nomination. He branded it a breach of senatorial courtesy—the time-encrusted tradition by which senators could preemptively veto nominations to posts in their home states. On this ground alone Conkling could expect to rally the support of many senators, even among those not otherwise disposed to back him against the president. He went on to declare Hayes's action an outrage against the principle of party rule, which he deemed democracy at its working best.

Theodore Roosevelt, Sr., through no fault of his own, found himself in the thick of an intra-Republican battle royal. His nomination became a cause célèbre in New York politics and then in national politics. No one seriously questioned his capacity for the customs collectorship—which didn't really require much capacity—or, even less, his integrity. All this was beside the point. In fact, as Conkling mustered the troops of opposition, it increasingly appeared that the nomination had been less an honest effort by Hayes to install Roosevelt than a device to draw Conkling and the Republican regulars into the open. It worked, but it also left Roosevelt exposed and vulnerable. By December his nomination was obviously doomed. In the crucial ballot, the Senate rejected Roosevelt by a vote of 31 to 25.

Unlike his son in later years, Theodore Sr. didn't thrive on political combat; indeed, just the opposite. The strain of the autumn took a physical toll. Those who knew him saw him age before their eyes, as vague digestive distress developed into intestinal blockage. At times it was very painful, but although he and his doctors gradually realized that something was gravely amiss, he did his best to hide the diagnosis from his children.

The younger Theodore, living away from home at college, was kept almost completely in the dark. As the Christmas holidays approached, he looked forward to a romp with the family. He wrote to his father in early December: "I am anticipating the most glorious fun during the holidays." When word arrived that his father was feeling poorly again, he grew somewhat more worried but attributed the decline to the unfavorable outcome of the collectorship battle. "I am very uneasy about Father," he told Bamie in mid-December. "Does the Doctor think it anything serious? I think that a travelling trip would be the best thing for him; he always has too much work on hand." He deemed it unfair that his father should fall ill just as he, the son, was leaving his own childhood maladies behind. But, on the other hand, perhaps that was a blessing, for it would allow the son to look after the father as the father so long had looked after the son. "Thank fortune, my own health is excellent, and so, when I get home, I can with a clear conscience give him a rowing up for not taking better care of himself." Roosevelt continued, "The trouble is the dear old fellow never does think of himself in anything." He concluded on a note that revealed a suspicion, perhaps unconscious, of imminent mortality: "We have been very fortunate, Bamie, in having a father whom we can love and respect more than any man in the world."

Theodore Sr.'s condition fluctuated by the day. "Dear Father very sick," Roosevelt recorded in his diary on December 21. Two days later he wrote, "Father very much better." And on Christmas Day: "Father seems much brighter." The Christmas entry added cheerily, "Received a double barreled shot gun."

This was the last gift his father gave him in life—unless one counts the concealment of the ultimate stages of his illness. Reassured that the worst was past, Roosevelt returned to Cambridge. His father didn't want to disrupt his studies, which were going so well this year. In any event there was nothing the son or anyone else could do about the situation. Perhaps the elder Theodore didn't desire for his son to see him at his worst. By now there was no keeping the truth from those at home. The tumor, for such it was, caused him excruciating pain and prevented him from eating. Corinne later described the "frightful suffering" and "constant agony" of the patient; Elliott recounted that their father was "mad with pain." The younger son afterward added, "Oh, my God, my father, what agonies you suffered."

At the last moment the family sent a telegram to Cambridge telling Theodore to catch the next train to New York. He arrived hours too late. Theodore Sr. had died, just before midnight on February 9, 1878.

III

The death of his father had a profound effect on Roosevelt, some of it immediate, some slower-acting. It appears to have confirmed his opinion—unformed and uninformed as it currently was—that politics was the preserve of opportunists and scoundrels. The customs house conflict may or may not have hastened Theodore Sr.'s death, but Theodore Jr. would have had to be a saint or an expert oncologist not to have concluded that it had. If politics could kill a man as strong and as good as his father, it must be a foul practice indeed.

At the same time, and somewhat contradictorily—but such is often the nature of the wisdom imparted by life's transforming moments— his father's death may well have heightened his appreciation of the value of a life spent in public service. By the time Roosevelt arrived in New York just after his father's death, crowds were already beginning to gather for the funeral vigil. In those crowds Manhattan's wealthiest and most favored stood beside some of the city' poorest and most despised. Family friends shared their grief and fond recollections with those who had benefited from Theodore Sr.'s charitable activities. Newsboys and men who had been newsboys but moved on to better things stood silently with bowed heads, recalling Sundays past that he had shared with them, and would no more. Parents of children who had been patients in the Orthopedic Hospital pointed out the window where lay the man who had helped make the young ones' healing possible.

The local papers registered their praise and gratitude for a life well lived. In an age of cynicism and self-centeredness, this one man had given much of himself to others; in a city that often seemed heartless, this great heart had made life a bit more humane. Theodore Roosevelt, Sr., was one of New York's finest citizens, and the city would sorely miss him.

This outpouring of thanks and respect opened the younger Theodore's eyes. He had always known that his father was a fine man, but he hadn't realized the extent to which other people thought so, too. "It is lovely to see how widely known and respected my dear Father was," he told his mother. At a time of life when he was deciding on a career, the example of public service provided by his father, and the appreciation of that service by the leaders of the community, made a career along similar lines more attractive than it had seemed before.

Other effects of his father's untimely death went deeper into Roosevelt's psyche. His father's death signaled the end of the world as he had known it. A thick black swath of ink canceled his diary for the day of his father's passing; only the words "My dear Father. Born Sept. 23 1831" alleviated the barrenness of the page. Three days later, following the funeral, the son summoned the strength to reflect provisionally on what had happened.

> He has just been buried. I shall never forget these terrible three days; the hideous suspense of the ride on; the dull, inert sorrow, during which I felt as if I had been stunned, or as if part of my life had been taken away; and the two moments of sharp, bitter agony, when I kissed the dear, dead face and realized that he would never again on this earth speak to me or greet me with his loving smile, and then when I heard

the sound of the first clod dropping on the coffin holding the one I loved dearest on earth. He looked so calm and sweet. I feel that if it were not for the certainty that, as he himself has so often said, he is not dead but gone before, I should almost perish. With the help of my God I will try to lead such a life as he would have wished.

His father's death was indeed the most painful blow the nineteen-year-old had ever had to deal with. Aside from his asthma, he had managed to avoid many of the worries and cares that typically afflict children growing up. His material wants were generously provided for; spending nearly all of his pre-college years in the circle of family, he didn't even confront the emotional distress of having to make new friends at school. And significantly, when the terror of asthma did threaten this secure world, it was his father whose strong arms had cradled the frail and frightened boy and walked him about the house, had wrapped him in blankets and taken him out into the fresh night air. Theodore's deepest memories were of his father sheltering him from harm. For his mother—retiring, almost an invalid—he felt the expected tenderness; she was, he wrote in his autobiography, "a sweet, gracious, beautiful Southern woman." But that was about all she was to him; the autobiography quickly passes on to other members of the Bulloch clan. About his father, however, Roosevelt's memoir goes on for pages and pages, recounting the powerful impressions the father made on the boy. It describes waiting for Theodore Sr. to come home in the afternoon, competing for the spot on the sofa next to him, receiving the little trinkets he fished from his pockets while getting undressed, thrilling at the fast rides in the father's phaeton, receiving a pony of the children's own, trembling at incurring his displeasure for childhood malfeasances. And, for all the details, the son's feelings toward the father are summarized in a sentence: "My father, Theodore Roosevelt, was the best man I ever knew."

He had not been perfect; there was that failure to fight for the Union. Perhaps in some unconscious way the younger Theodore, by his later actions, would try to remedy that single deficiency in the elder Theodore. But at nineteen the son was old enough to see that no one was perfect, and that the father came as close to perfection as anyone the son was likely to encounter.

The father's death broke a bond that was unusual for its strength and intimacy. "I hardly know a boy who is on as intimate and affectionate terms with his family as I am," Roosevelt had written to his mother a month after leaving home for college. At about the same time he told his father, "I do not think there is a fellow in College who has a family that love him as much as you all do me, and I am sure that there is no one who has a Father who is also his best and most intimate friend, as you are mine."

The loss of his father was a double blow: It simultaneously deprived Roosevelt of the one he considered his closest friend. "It is almost impossible to realize I shall never see Father again," Roosevelt wrote Henry Minot on February 20. "These last few days seem like a hideous dream. Father had always been so much with me that it seems as if part of my life had been taken away."

Indeed, a part of Roosevelt's life had been taken away, but not only the part he thought. His father's premature death robbed Roosevelt of the opportunity to make one of the most important transitions in a young man's life: of learning to deal with his father on adult terms, as an equal. However revered parents may be, children eventually come to recognize that they are just ordinary people, with the same cares, fears, and troubles as anyone else, including the children. For many children this recognition can require the better part of their lives; sometimes it doesn't happen until the parents become old and weak and dependent on the children, as the children were once dependent on them. For some children it never happens. But for most, it provides an opportunity for insight into the parents, into the children themselves, and into the human condition generally. In learning that their parents can be tested and tempted, frightened and confused, they learn to accept life's limitations and ambiguities. They become more forgiving of weakness in others and in themselves; they become more fully human.

Roosevelt, by losing his father at nineteen, missed this opportunity. Roosevelt still idealized his father, and this ideal image became frozen in time. (Significantly, so would another central image in his life—that of his first wife.) This freezing of his father's image suspended part of Roosevelt's maturation process. Roosevelt would never have the opportunity to deal with his father as an equal. For his whole life, his father would walk somewhere ahead and above him, encouraging him to be better, stronger, and wiser than he was.

Far worse things can happen to a young man than to have a personal model of near perfection to emulate, even if the model is unrealistic. The world would improve significantly if more people had such models. And in any event, it would be a mistake to make too much of this. No one's childhood is perfect; everyone misses something. In the nineteenth century, even in the social class the Roosevelts inhabited, the loss of a parent during youth was hardly unusual. To say that Roosevelt was deprived of a crucial aspect of growing up isn't to say that he was uniquely flawed—except in the sense that all of us are flawed, each uniquely.

Yet it does help to explain certain aspects of Roosevelt's character. Already inclined to a romantic view of life, he had that inclination strengthened by what amounted to the canonization of his own private patron saint. Like a medieval knight who held before him an idealized image of his lady fair and slew dragons in the quest for her love, Roosevelt held before himself the idealized image of his father and strove just as hard in pursuit of his father's posthumous blessing. Young people naturally tend to interpret the world in absolute terms of right and wrong, good and evil, but most eventually grow out of this simplistic version and come to appreciate the complications and confusions of the world as it actually is. Roosevelt never quite made the transition; he remained in most respects a moral absolutist until the day he died.

IV

Theodore Sr.'s death had another, and related, effect on his son: It ushered in a period of intense emotionalism. The younger Theodore had always been a sentimentalist; no one who didn't harbor a sentimental streak could be so swept up in the romantic tales he loved. This showed as well in the homesickness he felt when traveling or away at college. But his father's death opened floodgates of emotion. For weeks and months he poured his feelings out across the pages of his diary until the volume for 1878 began to read like the script of a grand, if rather repetitious, tragedy. "It seems impossible to realize I shall never see him again; he is such a living memory." "Every now and then it seems to me like a hideous dream." "Oh, my father! what loving, living memories you have left in my heart!" "Have been thinking about Father all the evening; have had a good square break down and feel much the better for it." "Looking back on his life, it seems as if mine must be such a weak useless one in comparison." "It is just one month since the blackest day of my life." "Have been thinking over the many, many lovely memories I have of him; had another square break down." "It has been a most fortunate thing for me that I have had so much to do that I have not had much time to think." "It is really wonderful, what sweet, unselfish letters the dear ones at home send me. It seems so strange never to write to him." "Looked over his sweet, affectionate letters. They will always be to me a talisman against evil." "Have been reading one of his favourite chapters, John XIV." "Sometimes when I think of my terrible loss it seems as if my heart would break; he shared all my joys, and in sharing doubled them, and soothed all the few sorrows I ever had." "He was as pure and unselfish as he was wise and good." "Have been writing to the dear ones at home; and thinking of the dear one to whom I shall never write again." "I realize now that the days of unalloyed happiness are now over forever." "I remember so well how, years ago, when I was a very weak, asthmatic child, he used to walk up and down with me in his arms for hours together night after night; and oh how my heart pains me when I think that I never was able to do anything for him during his last illness!" "I really think that I would at any moment have died to save him pain." "O, Father, Father: how bitterly I miss you, mourn you and long for you."

Through his sorrow, Roosevelt discerned his duty. He must bear up under this trial and conduct himself as his father would have wished. "It seems brutal to go about my ordinary occupations," he told himself four weeks after the dark day, "but I must keep employed." It wasn't easy to carry on, even when effort yielded success. "Am working away pretty hard," he wrote at the beginning of May. "But I do not care so much for my marks now; what I most valued them for was his pride in them." Though the ways of Providence were mysterious, wisdom consisted in accepting them. "If I had very much time to think I believe I should almost go crazy; but I think I can really and humbly say 'Thy will be done.'" A June sermon brought solace and insight: "Christianity gives us, on this earth, rest in trouble, not from trouble." The pain never quite disappeared, but its legacy was a new sense of direction. "Oh, Father, my Father, no words can tell how I shall miss your counsel and advice! However for the next two years my duty is clear—to study well and live like a brave Christian gentleman."

Without questioning the sincerity of these sentiments, it is hard to read them—and the many more like them—without perceiving a certain sense of melodrama in their author. Roosevelt gives the impression of having been swept up in one of the heroic stories he favored. This isn't especially surprising. He was a young man without any previous experience of such tragic loss; literature, which had long been his window on life, afforded the next closest thing. Roosevelt's heroes knew how to comport themselves in the face of tragedy; knowing them, Roosevelt knew how he should act.

V

At least partly for this reason, the several months after his father's death witnessed the beginning of a remarkable blossoming of Roosevelt's personality. The awkward, uncertain youth matured into a self-confident, if still quirky, young adult. Some of the blossoming would have occurred in any event: Teenagers invariably become adults. But Roosevelt matured particularly rapidly. As the man of the family he felt a new responsibility for his mother and siblings. Certain personalities are bent low by responsibility, especially that which is unexpected or premature; Roosevelt always thrived on responsibility, and did so now. In point of fact, for the time being he didn't have to do much as the family's eldest male; it was mostly an honorary position. But all the same, it lent seriousness to his outlook on life.

His schoolwork continued to go well, partly because redoubled diligence in studying fit his conception of how to carry on in the face of tragedy and partly because he was simply getting the hang of what his instructors required. Although his natural history courses weren't all that he had hoped, the subject still interested him, as his grades showed. His German classes were easy, and his constitutional history class was a pleasant surprise.

At least as important, his circle of friends filled in supportively around him. "All of the boys have been very kind and considerate," he told his mother in late February. "Harry Shaw has just paid me a really sweet visit. It is needless to say that old Hal Minot has acted like a trump. Minot Weld and Arthur Hooper each wanted me to spend Sunday with him, but I preferred not to go. Charley Washburn has been very sympathetic also."

With the growing sense of responsibility came a new financial independence. Not long after the funeral, Uncle James Roosevelt took his nephew aside and explained that his portion of his father's estate would yield him an income of about $8,000 annually. This was a handsome, indeed extravagant, sum, particularly for an unattached young man not yet twenty years old. (Translated to terms of the 1990s, it was worth well over $100,000). Until this time Roosevelt had never had to do without, but in entertaining friends, planning vacation trips, and engaging in the myriad other activities on which young people spend money, he had always been dependent on his father. He would report that he was keeping within his allowance or that he would need a little extra to tide him over to the end of the term. Now he was a man of independent means.

And he played the part. Taking after his father, he treated himself to the finest suits, shoes, hats, gloves, and other items of apparel and adornment. He bought generous, even lavish, gifts for friends. He traveled where and when he wanted. Unusually among Harvard students, during his senior year he kept his own horse and buggy. He stinted not at all in throwing parties and arranging other amusements for himself and his college mates. The most exclusive clubs opened their doors to him. He had always considered himself a gentleman, and now he could live like one—or better.

VI

Yet Roosevelt could never be merely a gentleman. Where was the romance in that? Where the challenge? Even as he grew into the style of life his inheritance allowed, he sought new ways to test his strength, his physical skills, his courage. Indeed, his sudden wealth enabled him to devise tests more challenging and, if overcome successfully, more rewarding than any to date.

One such test took place during the summer of 1878, between his sophomore and junior years of college. Following the recommendation of his old tutor, Arthur Cutler, Roosevelt traveled to Maine for a hunting expedition. His host would be William Sewall, a lumberman who supplemented his income by guiding hunters from a base at the woodland hamlet of Island Falls. Merely getting to Island Falls took some doing: The nearest railroad station lay thirty-five miles distant, leaving visitors to traverse the final stretch by buckboard. To Theodore Roosevelt, of course, this merely enhanced the appeal of the place, and when he arrived on the evening of September 7, he was ready for a fine time.

Most of Sewall's clients came to Maine for a vacation, ranging out daily from his cabin at Island Falls but enjoying the comforts of a roof overhead and dry sheets and blankets at night. Having heard from Cutler of Roosevelt's youthful illnesses, Sewall evidently expected this sheltered Manhattanite to follow the script. He later recalled his first impression of Roosevelt as "a thin, pale youngster with bad eyes and a weak heart." Sewall certainly didn't expect the kind of nonstop activity Roosevelt insisted on, starting the day after his arrival. Canoeing was followed by tramping through the woods, which in turn was followed by more canoeing and more tramping, with shooting, fishing, climbing, swimming, chopping, skinning, and cooking interspersed. It was hard to tell which activity Roosevelt enjoyed the most; his diary recorded the miles covered by boat and foot as faithfully as it did each day's bag and creel. He and Sewall lived off the land, bivouacking in the bush, bathing in rivers, sleeping on boughs of pine and fir. Autumn rains soaked them; the wind off the river and lake chilled them to the bone. Sewall, for whom roughing it was no novelty, could have done without the drenching and freezing, but it simply intensified the fun for Roosevelt.

After some initial puzzlement at what this city boy was trying to prove, Sewall discovered that he rather liked the lad. One couldn't fault his enthusiasm; unlike many of Sewall's other customers, he carried his own weight and more, and conditions that would have had the others asking for their money back only made Roosevelt happier than ever.

As for Roosevelt, he took to Bill Sewall at once. Here was a man who had mastered all the outdoor arts that for years had entranced

Roosevelt. When the boy had read of strong, brave men meeting the wilderness on its own terms and conquering it, and had dreamed of becoming such a person, Bill Sewall was the type he had envisioned. If Roosevelt had ever wondered whether the rugged and the refined could coexist—beyond books, in real life, perhaps his own—Bill Sewall demonstrated that they could, for to his mastery of the wilderness Sewall added a sensitive appreciation of literature, particularly the kind Roosevelt loved. They swapped verses from Longfellow on the trail, and traded tales from Walter Scott over the campfire. As if to complete the character of this Acadian alter ego, Sewall, like Roosevelt, had had to overcome youthful sickness. At thirty-three, Sewall was halfway between the older brother Roosevelt never had and the father he had just lost.

The hunting on this trip was poor, partly because Roosevelt missed many shots he should have hit. "I don't think I have ever made as many consecutive bad shots as I have this week," he jotted in his journal of the trip. "I am disgusted with myself." But not really. On the contrary, in fact: He was absolutely thrilled at his ability simply to keep pace with this professional woodsman mile for mile. Hunting was but the excuse, and if the game failed, nothing much was lost. "Today I took a thirty-mile tramp through the woods with Sewall, keeping near the Mattawamkeag river most of the time. Except for half an hour for lunch we were on the go steadily from 8 A.M. till 7 P.M. I got but four shots and saw no game whatever during the last twenty miles, but enjoyed the walk greatly." On another day he again had "wonderfully bad luck" shooting, but again delighted in the cross-country tramping with Sewall. He summarized the whole expedition: "A great success."

This first visit to Island Falls inaugurated a lifelong friendship between Roosevelt and Sewall. Roosevelt's instant admiration for Sewall would broaden into comradeship and affection in the coming years. Sewall would serve as a sounding board for Roosevelt for nearly four decades; Roosevelt would consider Sewall's voice and judgment to be those of the ordinary man, unspoiled but hardly uninformed. Moreover, Sewall would provide Roosevelt with an important emotional bulwark at certain critical periods of his life.

In one sense that was what he provided on this first encounter. Roosevelt's Island Falls trip served as an emotional coming-out after his father's death. With his father gone, the son had to become a man of his own. To Roosevelt, no better test of manhood existed than the test of the outdoors. Luck brought him an almost mythological figure to test himself against. He passed the test, if not brilliantly—that was why he was upset about missing those shots, not because he brought home fewer trophies—at least substantially. When he returned to college, he carried the quiet knowledge that he had accomplished something that 90 percent of his classmates couldn't conceive of doing—keeping up with Bill Sewall. After Island Falls, anything Cambridge could throw at him would be child's play.

VII

As it turned out, Cambridge threw garlands. His junior year started with unaccustomed success with his friends and classmates. "Funnily enough," he wrote ten days after arriving straight from Maine, "I have enjoyed quite a burst of popularity since I came back, having been elected into several clubs." The A.D. and the Porcellian clubs vied for his favor; after promising the former, he changed his mind and chose the latter. The decision caused him some anguish—but not too much. He had never been in such demand before, and subsequently he was relieved that "the A.D. men have behaved like trumps" upon being let down. Perhaps significantly, the A.D. was Bob Bacon's club, and Bacon remained the class standout. Though Roosevelt continued to consort with Bacon on occasion, he felt sufficiently sure of himself to strike deliberately out in a different direction. He was also selected for Hasty Pudding and, not surprisingly, the Natural History Society. Other organizations—rifle club, art club, and glee club—occupied additional slices of his time.

What, precisely, accounted for this sudden social success is difficult to ascertain; it was probably a combination of things. The laudatory press coverage following his father's death and the overall honor shown the deceased certainly had cast the son in the favorable light of his father's reflection. His enhanced income, which allowed a more sociable lifestyle, couldn't have hurt.

But more than anything it was Roosevelt's growing self-confidence.

In two years of college he had discovered that he could hold his own in the classroom; some students stood ahead of him, but they were mostly drudges who took no time for other activities. He was still no athlete but was growing stronger all the time, and as his recent trip to Island Falls had demonstrated, for stamina and determination he could keep up with the best. His health was sounder than ever, as, again, his recent expedition had demonstrated. The simple fact was that after almost twenty years of leaning on his father, physically and emotionally, he was learning to stand on his own. Moments of sorrow recurred, but the bitter, lost feelings that had followed the death were gone; the disorientation and the emptiness had been replaced by a positive desire of emulation and a sense of direction.

As a result, the traits that had been evident to his family all along, and subsequently to a small cluster of friends, gradually grew apparent to larger groups. Although he took his work—scientific, literary, and academic—seriously enough, he possessed a sufficient sense of the absurd to keep from taking himself too seriously. He recognized his own idiosyncrasies, including his preoccupation with physical accomplishment, and generally was able to laugh about them. He now had sufficient physical energy for anything anyone could propose, whether a morning hike, an afternoon gallop or boxing match, an evening sleigh ride, or a late-night literary argument. Most of all he displayed an enthusiasm for life—for people, for action, for thought, for debate—that was hard to resist. There wasn't much that didn't interest him; rarely did he meet someone he didn't have something in common with.

Energy and enthusiasm couldn't conquer all. The platform of the public speaker, for example, remained foreign territory. William Thayer recalled the 1879 annual dinner of the campus newspaper, the *Crimson,* at which Roosevelt, representing another paper, the *Advocate,* was invited to speak. Thayer remembered that Roosevelt had "difficulty in enunciating clearly or even in running off his words smoothly." This difficulty intensified the harder Roosevelt tried. "At times he could hardly get them out at all, and then he would rush on for a few sentences, as skaters redouble their pace over thin ice." Roosevelt, essaying a bit of humor that turned out to be unintentionally apposite, told the story of two stammerers, one of whom, after numerous false starts and backtrackings, and with enormous and evidently painful effort, managed to blurt out to the other that he ought to go see Dr. So-and-so. "He c-c-c-cured me" was the punch line.

Though he did better in the classroom than during his first two years, he still had to apply himself dutifully. "My studies do not come very well this year," he told his mother in October, "as I have to work nearly as hard on Saturday as on any other day—that is, seven or eight hours." Yet such was his temperament that two of his most challenging courses, metaphysics and philosophy, were the two he found most stimulating. The former was actually a course in Greek philosophy, the latter an examination of the principles of political economy. Significantly for his future, he found that he preferred these courses to his former favorites. "They are even more interesting than my Natural History courses; and all the more so, from the fact that I radically disagree on many points with the men whose books we are reading." Laissez-faire was the watchword in political economy at Harvard; Roosevelt was already finding himself at odds with this devil-take-the-hindmost philosophy of social organization. His German class was dull but not especially difficult; Italian was promising.

Despite the slow start, Roosevelt's junior year turned out to be his best academically so far. Aside from a dreary 60 in forensics and a respectable 76 in a theme-writing class, all his grades were in the 80s and 90s. In zoology he made a 97. Whatever else he may have learned in the classroom and the library, he was definitely learning the value of hard work.

At first the press of studies constrained his exercise routine, which didn't bother him overly much since he felt he could coast on the workout he had gotten in Maine. But as the effect of that trip wore off and as he sorted out his studying schedule, he found time for exercise, as he eventually found time for everything he judged worthwhile. "I have hitherto relied chiefly on walking," he wrote in the second week of October, "but today I have regularly begun sparring. I have practised a good deal with my rifle, walking to and from the range which is nearly three miles off." Doubtless his shooting sessions were a reaction to his embarrassment with the gun with Sewall. His improvement was spotty. "My scores have been fair, although not very good."

Roosevelt's boxing career climaxed in a fight that produced another piece of what became the Roosevelt legend. In March of his junior year he competed in the lightweight division of the college tournament. The crowd was in a spirited mood and noisy, so noisy, the story goes, that Roosevelt's opponent missed hearing the call ending one of the rounds. Roosevelt heard it and dropped his guard. The oblivious opponent landed a shot to Roosevelt's nose, which burst into a spray of blood. The crowd cried foul and demanded that the offender be penalized. Roosevelt, stung but understanding what had happened, raised his arm for silence.

"It's all right," he proclaimed. "He didn't hear." Then he strode over to his foe and shook his hand.

Curiously, the reporter covering the bout for the *Boston Globe* didn't mention this noteworthy feature of the fight in his article, although he did find space to recount that when Roosevelt's opponent delivered another heavy blow, one so punishing that he felt obliged to beg Roosevelt's pardon, Roosevelt responded, "Don't mention it."

Whatever this omission says about the veracity of the remembered details of the incident, the fact that they were remembered the way they were is meaningful. As the years passed, people forgot who won the fight (it wasn't Roosevelt); all they remembered—or thought they did—was the grand gesture.

CHAPTER SIX

First Love
1878–81

B ut of all Roosevelt's successes of the autumn of 1878, none compared with falling in love for the first time. Roosevelt's new friends included Richard Saltonstall, the son of Mrs. and Mrs. Leverett Saltonstall of Boston. Dick Saltonstall habitually brought friends to the family home on Chestnut Hill. One attraction was the Saltonstall hospitality; another was the Saltonstall girls and their various female friends and relations. On a visit in October, Roosevelt met Dick Saltonstall's cousin and next-door neighbor, Alice Lee.

Seventeen years old in the autumn of 1878, Alice Lee was a girl to break a boy's heart. She was tall and athletic, with wide, pale blue-gray eyes, long golden curls, a pert, slightly upturned nose, a dainty mouth, and a bright, ready smile (friends and relatives called her "Sunshine"). By now Roosevelt had been introduced to a sizable segment of the eligible young ladies of Boston and New York; more than a few had intrigued him with face, form, or spirit. But none captivated him so quickly, and certainly not so completely, as Alice Lee. He had only just gotten to know Dick Saltonstall well; now he insisted on being a regular guest at Chestnut Hill. "This afternoon, immediately after dinner," he informed Corinne in early November, "Minot and I are going to drive over to Dick Saltonstall's, where we shall go out walking with Miss Rose Saltonstall and Miss Alice Lee and drive home by moonlight after tea." His enchantment with Alice—"a very sweet pretty girl," in his diary—was sufficient to make him reorder his priorities; even certain habits adhered to religiously now had to be altered. "I am going to cut Sunday School today, for the second time this year," he explained discreetly, "but when the weather is so beautiful as this I like every now and then to spend Sunday with a friend."

During November and early December, Roosevelt found every opportunity to visit the Saltonstalls. Walks about the neighborhood of Chestnut Hill with Alice and rides into town filled weekend afternoons and evenings. On one occasion he, Alice, and Rose sat for photographs; on December 6 he wrote to Alice: "I have been anxiously expecting a letter from you and Rose for the last two or three days, but none has come. You must not forget our tintype spree." With the required decorum but with a meaning Alice couldn't have overlooked, he added, "Tell Rose that I never passed a pleasanter Thanksgiving than at her house." He signed the note: "Your Fellow-conspirator."

Doubtless he was encouraged by Alice's reply. "We have by no means forgotten our little spree," she assured him. But parental considerations precluded repeating the adventure. "As neither of our Mothers like us to go in town on Saturdays if we can possibly help it, we think it had better be put off until the Spring when dancing school is done." Alice entered into Roosevelt's conspiratorial spirit. "Remember," she cautioned, "you said that you would not show this note."

For some months Roosevelt attempted to maintain the appearance of simple friendship with Alice. Stories later sprouted that he had determined almost at first sight to win her; one version related by Mrs. Robert Bacon had him pointing to Alice in a crowd and declaring, "See that girl? I am going to marry her. She won't have me, but I am going to have her." Roosevelt himself claimed in his diary, many months after the fact, that on Thanksgiving 1878 he had vowed to win Alice's heart. Certainly he had his hopes, perhaps even from their first meeting, but through the winter and spring of 1878–79 he held them to himself. Alice was coy enough to keep him guessing as to her feelings, and until the two of them came to some firmer understanding, he didn't want to risk the embarrassment of a public rejection. He went out of his way to include other girls in his activities. Rose Saltonstall served especially well as romantic cover, living right next door to Alice. Rose joined them on various ventures; whenever he bought Alice a gift, he bought one for Rose as well. Considering his generous ways, this practice grew expensive. At one point he noted in his diary, "Those two young ladies have cost me over $150 so far."

Yet his feelings toward Rose were encapsulated in a confidential remark to Bamie; Rose, he said, "isn't a bit pretty but just as sweet and jolly as she can be."

Beyond his bank account, his love affair also ate into his time. Every weekend took him to Chestnut Hill, and many weekdays as well. It was during this period that he brought his horse from home, the more swiftly to reach his love. "It was the one thing wanting for perfect enjoyment," he commented. Indeed, he enjoyed himself too much: Within less than a month he had ridden the poor beast lame. While it recuperated, he made the six-mile trek from Cambridge on foot, which consumed even more time, although it gave him a better workout.

II

Efforts to be with Alice filled most of his spare hours, and his thoughts when he couldn't join her in person. Unable to attend a certain party at Chestnut Hill, he sent flowers instead. Alice replied with thanks, with a report on the success of the festivities, and with a welcome sentiment: "I only regret that you were not there with us to enjoy it."

Enamored though he was of Alice, he didn't entirely neglect his other interests. In March 1879, during a break from classes, he returned to Island Falls and Bill Sewall's camp. Winter had distilled the essence of the north woods, rendering the region more remote than ever and the test of the woodsman's mettle more demanding. A fellow caught out might easily freeze in temperatures that plunged well below zero; even more dangerous were the relatively warm days that turned falling snow to rain and soaked the unwary or unprepared, hastening hypothermia.

Wrapped warmly in his usual enthusiasm, in his obsession to prove his strength and endurance, and now in his infatuation with Alice, Roosevelt ignored the hazards. He donned snowshoes for the first time and set out after caribou. He tracked one all day, and night found him and Will Dow, Sewall's nephew, far from camp, with no blankets and just the food in their pockets. So they sat up all night, stoking a blazing fire. "Pretty uncomfortable," Roosevelt conceded. The chase resumed at daybreak, but the caribou, having apparently gotten a better rest than Roosevelt and Dow, managed to escape. Other creatures, including a deer, a lynx, a fox, a raccoon, and a porcupine, didn't.

Roosevelt's first experience of winter in the woods mesmerized him. "I have never seen a grander or more beautiful sight than the northern woods in winter," he wrote. "The evergreens laden with snow make the most beautiful contrast of green and white, and when it freezes after a rain all the trees look as though they were made of crystal. The snow under foot being about three feet deep, and drifting to twice that depth in places, completely changes the aspect of things." The human inhabitants of the forest were equally intriguing—a whole race of Bill Sewalls, if perhaps less refined. "I like the lumbermen very much, and get on capitally with them—great, rough, hospitable fellows. I am great friends with one in especial, Charley Brown."

As usual, Roosevelt enjoyed himself immensely. "I have never passed a pleasanter two weeks," he declared. And the beneficial effects of the expedition would linger. "I have got enough health to last me till next summer."

III

Fortified by his reconnection to the primitive, Roosevelt resumed his pursuit of Alice. He grew increasingly confident, enough so that his feelings began to appear in his letters. Writing from Chestnut Hill in mid-April, he told Bamie, "Harry Shaw came over in the afternoon, and Rose and he, and Alice and I took a long walk. I like the two girls more and more every day—especially pretty Alice." If Alice sometimes still played hard to get, at least he was making headway with her family. "All the family are just lovely to me." A week later Roosevelt reported to his mother that he was gainfully employing his horse, now recovered from its earlier injury. "I have ridden him every day last week, and of course my rides ended up quite often at Chestnut Hill."

Sometime about the close of his junior year Roosevelt apparently proposed marriage to Alice. She didn't say yes; in his state of mind an affirmative answer would have had him turning cartwheels, at least in his diary, which reveals no such feats. But neither, evidently, did she say no, for through the summer of 1879 he pursued her as ardently as ever. The chase nearly caused him to cancel another scheduled trip to Island Falls. "I am going to Maine this evening," he told Corinne, "which shows the greatest resolution on my part, for it has been awfully hard to resist going down to the Glades for a few days. To tell the truth, the only reason I resisted was because it was perfectly impossible to communicate with Sewall, the telegraph not going to Island Falls. Even as it was, Alice was so bewitchingly pretty, and the Saltonstalls were so very cordial, that I came near to going in spite of everything."

Love transformed Theodore Roosevelt. Besides making him wish he didn't have to go hunting, it caused him—also uncharacteristically—to slack off intellectually. In the wake of his father's death he had set himself a rigorous academic schedule for his junior year, doubtless partly to bury his grief in books; but after he met Alice, he decided that he shouldn't study so hard, and from nine courses in his junior year he cut back to five for his senior year. Nor did he devote himself even to these few. His grades tumbled from his junior year, to 91 and 89 in his natural history courses, and the 60s and 70s in his other courses. During every other period of his life, Roosevelt was an incessant improver, not least in matters of the mind; during his senior year in college, he took a vacation.

Moreover, while most of his life he was impatient with, not to say scornful of, dandies, with those who placed style over substance, in his pursuit of Alice he was the dandiest man on campus. "Saturday morning I rode over (very swell, with hunting crop and beaver) to Chestnut Hill," he bragged to Corinne after a typical visit to his love. In the summer of 1879 he spent weeks training his horse Lightfoot to pull a "dogcart," the most fashionable form of transportation for young gents. When the animal and kit arrived in Cambridge, he declared, "The senior year has opened most auspiciously. The cart and horse, with whip, rug &c, came to hand in fine condition, and I really think I have as swell a turnout as any man." The dogcart made Roosevelt conspicuous; at the time he was the only undergraduate on campus who had one. Owen Wister, later a friend but then not even an acquaintance, jibed the dandy who drove it, adding new words to a popular song:

Each lucid ray
Has gone away,
And so we'd better part.
Just like, by Jove,
The cove who drove
His doggy Tilbury cart.
Awful tart,
And awful smart,
With waxed mustache and hair in curls;
Brand new hat,
Likewise cravat,
To call upon the dear little girls.

When performed, this ditty brought down the house—much to Roosevelt's chagrin. On another occasion Roosevelt's new stylishness caused him to get testy with his own mother, who had neglected to ensure the arrival of an essential item. "Please send my silk hat at once," he scolded her. "Why has it not come before?"

Though Alice was certainly the focus of Roosevelt's attentions, she didn't quite monopolize them. Perhaps partly as payback for her coyness but also, almost certainly, because he simply got swept up in the role of bachelor blade, he ran rounds of socializing that would have made the liveliest fellow weary. "Pretty Annie Murray" remained an interest, as did Helen White, "one of my old flames." Margie Tuckerman, Fanny Smith, and Edith Carow were "looking very prettily" during a visit home in April 1879. Edith in particular was "just the same sweet little flirt as ever." Nana Rotch received individualized instruction from Roosevelt in the five-step waltz; on another occasion he had "an extremely jolly time" with Miss Rotch and the two Lane sisters. Lulu Lane was "too pretty for anything." An afternoon at the Whitney house caused Roosevelt to remark, "Miss Bessie I like more and more." He treated Emily Swan, "one of the prettiest girls in Oyster Bay, and one of the most charming," to tennis and rides in his rowboat.

Roosevelt's busy social schedule got him into trouble now and then. He found himself briefly on the wrong side of Bessie Whitney. "It appears that she and Nana Rotch had compared notes and come to the conclusion that I was a 'gay deceiver'!" In this instance Roosevelt was unrepentant. "I had great fun teasing pretty Bessie about having called me a flirt."

But occasionally even he had to concede that he got carried away. After Alice took offense at some rather egregious flirtation with Nana Rotch, in Alice's very presence, Roosevelt was suitably humbled. "My conscience reproaches me," he admitted.

Roosevelt was blessed with the joy of living; throughout his life he found pleasure—albeit an often frantic pleasure—in nearly everything he did. But this period really did mark his salad season. "Truly these are the golden years of my life," he declared not long after getting to know Alice. He wondered if he would ever be really unhappy. "In spite of the great sorrow—the greatest which could ever have befallen me—I have been very happy these last six months." Holidays brought opportunities for hiking and hunting about Oyster Bay. After one twelve-hour tramp with neither food nor rest, he remarked, "I am tired out, but I have never had a more glorious day; the weather was beautiful (clear, cold & still), the sport splendid & I shot very well. 6 quail 8 rabbit 1 squirrel." The trips to Maine brought similar satisfaction, intensified. Socially, he couldn't ask for greater success: The young men liked him, as did the young ladies. "What a royally good time I am having," he declared. "I can't conceive of a fellow possibly enjoying himself more." He told his mother, "I am leading the most luxurious life imaginable." A week later he added, "I doubt if I shall ever enjoy myself so much again. I have done well in my studies"—this was before his senior slump—"and I have had a most royally good time with the [Porcellian] Club, my horse, and above all the sweet, pretty girls at Chestnut Hill &c."

IV

Roosevelt's golden days grew only more golden. The late summer of 1879 brought the expedition to Maine he almost canceled in favor of visiting Alice; Maine, in turn, brought another chance to rub shoulders with the honest folks of the frontier. "I don't know a better or more intelligent race of men than these shrewd, plucky, honest Yankees—all of them hunters, lumbermen or small farmers." Maine also brought more opportunities to reflect on his wonderful life. "Tired out, & wet through, hungry & cold—but having a lovely time," he noted, following one long session in the woods. To his mother he reported afterward that though the physical labor of the expedition was "very severe," he had enjoyed the trip "exceedingly." In his diary he mused: "My life has such absurd contrasts. At one time I live in the height of luxury; and then for a month will undergo really severe toil and hardship—and I enjoy both extremes almost equally." The wilderness had its usual tonic effects on his health. "Am feeling strong as a bull. By Jove, it sometimes seems as if I were having too happy a time to have it last. I enjoy every minute I live, almost."

The autumn slipped by in a whirl of weekends at Chestnut Hill, parties at the Porcellian, rides in the dogcart, and the odd hour studying. He continued to see other girls, but Alice commanded his special affection, as she and everyone else increasingly realized. Thanksgiving found Roosevelt at the Saltonstalls', along with Alice's family. The weekend, which included rides with Alice, went wonderfully. "The horse, harness, cart and robes all looked beautifully and I was exceedingly proud of the whole turn out, and especially of my pretty companion." Over Christmas, Alice visited New York with her sister and cousins. "It is perfectly lovely having the dear, sweet Chestnut Hillers with us;—and so natural."

Alice's evident warmth emboldened Roosevelt to press his suit more forcefully again. In late January he once more asked him to marry her. This time, to his rapturous delight, she consented. His diary for the day recorded the emotions that overwhelmed him.

> At last everything is settled; but it seems impossible to realize it. I am so happy that I dare not trust in my own happiness. I drove over to the Lees determined to make an end of things at last; it was nearly eight months since I had first proposed to her, and I had been nearly crazy during the past year; and after much pleading my own sweet, pretty darling consented to be my wife. Oh, how bewitchingly pretty she looked! If loving her with my whole heart and soul can make her happy, she shall be happy; a year ago last Thanksgiving I made a vow that win her I would if it were possible; and now that I have done so, the aim of my whole life shall be to make her happy, and to shield her and guard her from every trial; and, oh, how I shall cherish my sweet queen! How she, so pure and sweet and beautiful, can think of marrying me I can not understand, but I praise and thank God it is so.

Screwing up his courage to demand an answer evidently had taxed even Roosevelt's joie de vivre. With touchingly typical melodrama— typical of both Roosevelt individually and lovers as a class—he explained to himself: "When I look back at the last four months and realize the tortures I have been through it seems like a dream; I have hardly had one good nights rest; and night after night I have not even gone to bed. I have been pretty nearly crazy, over my wayward, wilful darling. But I do not think any outsider suspected it; I have not writ-ten a word about it in my diary since a year ago last Thanksgiving. It was a real case of love at first sight—and my first love too." Now that Alice had agreed to be his, his mind could rest—but not entirely. "I am so happy, that I hardly dare trust in my own happiness."

The official announcement of the engagement followed a few weeks later, giving Roosevelt time to buy a ring and the families to make the necessary preparations. Roosevelt's mother and siblings came to Boston, where they were treated to a gala dinner by the Lees. A party with Roosevelt's friends ensued; he stayed up the whole night, put his family on the train for New York the next day, then rejoined Alice and her relatives before returning to Cambridge for a further blowout with the boys.

While Roosevelt's family and nearly all his friends were pleased at his good fortune, one who wasn't was Edith Carow. For years Edith had cherished the thought that she was the girl closest to Theodore's heart; until he met Alice she may have been right—although being closest didn't make her particularly close. She afterward claimed that he had proposed to her before putting the question to Alice but that she had turned him down. While no contemporary evidence confirms this claim, some historians have suggested that a vaguely described quarrel during Edith's 1878 visit to Oyster Bay evidenced her refusal. If Roosevelt did indeed propose at that time, one would have to won-der how seriously to take such an offer, given that she had just turned seventeen, while he wasn't yet twenty, had two years left of college, and had no idea what he was going to do with himself after college. Indeed, one version of the story explains that Edith's family vetoed any engagement because of her youth. (Other versions have Edith's grandfather worrying about a—nonexistent—history of scrofula in the Roosevelt family, and Theodore's father complaining—more accurately—of Edith's father being a lush.)

Some variant of Edith's story may be true, but she may also have remembered things in a way that spared her feelings. For however close she and Theodore had been as children and adolescents, once he fell head over heels for Alice, any romantic thoughts he might have had for her disappeared. She knew it, and the knowledge had to hurt.

V

In the flush of his now openly reciprocated and soon to be requited love, the end of Roosevelt's college career approached. Class work was all but forgotten; he could concentrate only on his darling. "My own, sunny faced Queen," he wrote Alice, "I don't think you are ever absent ten minutes from my thoughts." What book work did take place came at the convenience of his betrothed. He described a typical day:

> Alice studied and practised music a couple of hours, while I pumped the water up and studied. Then we played tennis; then she sewed while I read Prescott's Conquest of Peru aloud. In the afternoon I took my sweet, sunny faced darling for a three hour ride in my dog-cart, all round the country, way up to Dedham and the Blue Hills. After tea, I read aloud to Bella and Georgie, romped with them, and told them stories—the other girls all coming in as auditors. Played whist till nine o'clock; then spent an hour alone with my sweet queen. This is a fair sample of my days; and no wonder I am supremely happy.

Roosevelt managed to rationalize his academic indolence. "Since I have been engaged I have studied very little, and cut most of my recitations; and intend so to continue during the balance of my college course. I have always studied well in college, so I can afford to cut now." The concluding part of Roosevelt's rationalization contained an early mention of a new plan for post-college endeavors: "It is my last holiday, as I shall study law next year, and must there do my best, and work hard for my own little wife."

As his college years ran out, Roosevelt turned reflective. A little over two years before, his father had died. At that time his world had crashed down around him. But against all odds—or so it seemed then—the period since had proved to be the most successful and happiest of his life.

> I have certainly lived like a prince for my last two years in college. I have had just as much money as I could spend; belonged to the Porcellian Club; have had some capital hunting trips; my life has been varied; I have kept a good horse and cart; I have had half a dozen good and true friends in college, and several very pleasant families outside; a lovely home; I have had but little work, only enough to give me an occupation; and to crown all—infinitely above everything else put together—I have won the sweetest of girls for my wife. No man ever had so pleasant a college course.

In later life Roosevelt would assert that he didn't get as much out of college as he should have. From the perspective of fifty-five, that may have been true. At twenty he thought differently. To ask for more than he had gotten would have seemed to be tempting fate.

VI

The summer after graduation was filled with plans for the wedding, scheduled for October. As per tradition, the major portion of the planning fell to Alice and her family; Roosevelt found himself at loose ends. He returned to Oyster Bay, but the old activities had lost their tang while he was apart from his love. "I miss Alice too much to care so much as I used to for things." Alice felt the same way. "I love you with my whole heart," she wrote, "and you are always in my thoughts."

Hoping for diversion, he planned a hunting trip with his younger brother. After spending seventeen years rarely out of sight of each other, Theodore and Elliott had grown somewhat apart of late. Theodore Sr. and Mittie at first had thought Elliott would follow his brother to Harvard and had included him in the tutoring sessions led by Arthur Cutler. But Elliott lacked Theodore's drive—doubtless partly as a younger-sibling reaction to an overachieving older brother—and found other matters more interesting than his lessons. He also began to show symptoms of a worrying emotional or neurological disturbance.

He grew nervous easily, fretting over whether he would amount to anything in life, and suffered debilitating headaches and occasional seizures. "I jump involuntarily at the smallest sound and have a perpetual headache," he confided to his brother, adding that he was "nearly always in low spirits."

Theodore Sr. and Mittie consulted various doctors, who could find no organic cause, and tried various remedies, including a special holiday for Elliott in England. Nothing worked for long. In 1875 they sent him to join a cousin at boarding school in New Hampshire. He applied himself as well as he could, but the symptoms only intensified, and after a few months Theodore was sent to bring his brother home. At this point his parents decided that what Elliott needed was fresh air and exercise. They arranged for him to live with a friend in Texas, where he spent days on end riding the prairies and shooting game animals large and small. His physical symptoms improved somewhat, but not his self-esteem. With his brother making steady progress at college, Elliott saw himself falling further behind. "I feel well enough to study and instead here I am spending all your money," he apologized to his father.

Not unusually for brothers, even as Elliott envied Theodore's scholastic achievements, Theodore envied Elliott's experience and prowess as a hunter. And during the summer before his wedding, Theodore sought to measure himself against Elliott in this regard. In August they left New York by train for Chicago, which would serve as their jumping-off point for excursions into the open reaches of the West. Unlike Theodore's trips to Maine, which had a predetermined destination, a guide, and an at-least-implicit itinerary, this one was haphazard and open-ended—very much a boys' month out. They spent a day touring Chicago before hooking up with a man who owned a farm in upstate Illinois; for a suitable remuneration they could hunt on his fields.

Theodore's previous weeks, spent with Alice, had included a round of generalized gastrointestinal disturbances that Roosevelt diagnosed as cholera morbus. "Very embarrassing for a lover, isn't it?" he wrote, "so unromantic, you know; suggestive of too much unripe fruit." The journey out west afforded an opportunity to get the bad air out of his system. It also seems to have been, in Roosevelt's estimate, something of a shakedown cruise prior to marriage. Not long before he left

Harvard, a college physical examination revealed an irregular heart-beat. The examining physician had no way of knowing whether this was a temporary anomaly or a chronic condition, but he ventured that Roosevelt probably ought to eliminate his more strenuous activities. As Roosevelt recounted the conversation almost forty years later, he answered: "Doctor, I am going to do all the things you tell me not to do. If I've got to live the sort of life you have described, I don't care how short it is." And so off he went hunting, to kill or be killed.

He was encouraged from the start. "We have had three days good shooting, and I feel twice the man for it already," he declared on August 22.

Roosevelt may or may not have realized before he got there that the West of western Illinois was hardly the unsettled frontier; it was farm country, fully, if not densely, inhabited. Whatever his expectations, he found the inhabitants almost as fascinating as the lumberjacks of Maine. "The farm people are pretty rough, but I like them very much; like all rural Americans they are intensely independent." His temporary housemates included "a canny, shrewd Scotchman; a great, strong, jovial, blundering Irish boy; a quiet, intelligent yankee; a reformed desperado (he's very silent but when we can get him to talk his reminiscences are very interesting—and startling); a good natured German boor who is delighted to find we understand and can speak 'hochdeutch,'" and two women: "a clumsy, giggling, pretty Irish girl, and a hard-featured backwoods woman who sings methodist hymns and swears like a trooper on occasions." He and Elliott were fitting right in with the locals—especially Elliott. "We are dressed about as badly as mortals could be, with our cropped heads, unshaven faces, dirty gray shirts, still dirtier yellow trowsers and cowhide boots; moreover we can shoot as well as they can (or at least Elliott can) and can stand as much fatigue." On Sunday, taking the day off from hunting, he and Elliott decided to organize the house into an appropriate observance. "We got this motley crew together to sing hymns; thanks to Elliott it was a great success. It was all I could do to keep a sober face when I saw him singing from the same book with the much-flattered Mrs. Rudolf and Miss Costigan."

Notwithstanding the picturesqueness of the people, the game proved disappointing, and after several days Theodore and Elliott returned to Chicago. A second foray carried them into Iowa. The game was better than in Illinois, the company less intriguing, and Theodore's health worse. His asthma flared up—perhaps from the autumn pollens blowing across the prairie—and his stomach growled and fulminated. Ignoring these distractions, Theodore kept a daily record of whether he or Elliott had killed more game. Elliott was the sharper shot, both from his experience in Texas and because he could see better than the myopic Theodore. But this simply gave Theodore greater pleasure when he bested him. Meanwhile, Theodore broke both of his guns, was bitten by a snake, and was pitched from a wagon onto his head when the vehicle hit a hole. But as usual he didn't complain; on the contrary, he had "very good fun."

Elliott, although a happy hunter, wasn't as excited as Theodore about roughing it for roughing's sake. Other things being equal, he preferred the comforts of civilization. As Theodore explained to Corinne when they returned again to Chicago:

> Elliott revels in the change to civilization—and epicurean pleasures. As soon as we got here he took some ale to get the dust out of his throat; then a milkpunch because he was thirsty; a mint julep because it was hot; a brandy smash "to keep the cold out of his stomach"; and then sherry and bitters to give him an appetite. He took a very simple dinner—soup, fish, salmi de grouse, sweetbread, mutton, venison, corn, macaroni, various vegetables and some puddings and pies, together with beer, later claret and in the evening shandigaff. I confined myself to roast beef and potatoes; when I took a second help he marvelled at my appetite—and at bed time wondered why in thunder he felt "stuffy" and I didn't.

The day would come when Elliott's affinity for alcohol wasn't at all amusing, but on this trip it didn't worry his brother. Theodore went on to say that Elliott's "good living" had gone to his head, launching him into some rambling and largely incoherent disquisitions on a variety of topics—"the Infinity of the Infinite, the Sunday School system and the planet Mars—together with some irrelevant [!] remarks about Texan 'Jack Rabbits' which are apparently about as large as good sized cows."

A third venture out from Chicago took them as close to the real frontier as they would get on this trip. Their cousin Jack Elliott had moved to Moorhead, Minnesota, on the Red River just east of Dakota Territory. This was plains country, the first time Theodore or Elliott had seen what still was sometimes called the Great American Desert. Not many years before, they could have expected to spot buffalo, but all they encountered now was more birds. Theodore carefully tallied the bag, noting with quiet satisfaction a total for the trip of 203 for him, 201 for Elliott. A recurrence of asthma and stomach troubles didn't keep him from tramping scores of miles, getting lost in a squall, nearly freezing to death in an early norther, and having to sleep out tentless and provisionless—in other words, having a thoroughly enjoyable time.

VII

Except for missing Alice, that is. This trip had been even harder to undertake than his venture to Maine the previous summer. Alice had never been more affectionate. "I do miss you so very much Teddy," she wrote before he left. "I do not know what I shall do when you go out West for six weeks." He replied that he would miss her terribly, too; but he gallantly told her to have a good time while he was gone and not to worry about his being jealous. "The more attention you have the better pleased I'll be," he declared, perhaps stretching a point.

The six weeks seemed an age. "The trip has been great fun; but how glad I am it is over and I am to see Alice!" he penned on the way back east. It was difficult to tell if absence had made his heart grow fonder, so enraptured had he been before going; but now he certainly gushed as purplely as any lover approaching the altar. "She is so pure and holy that it almost seems profanation to touch her, no matter how gently and tenderly; and yet when we are alone I can not bear her to be a minute out of my arms. . . . My happiness now is almost too great." A week later he added, "I am living in a dream of delight with my darling, my true-love."

He must have been in a dreamy state when he hit the jewelry stores in New York and walked away with $2,500 worth of brooches, necklaces, and other ornaments for his sweetheart. "What a very extravagant boy you are, Teddy," Alice remarked. The bill, if not Alice's reaction, snapped him out of his reverie long enough to promise to watch his wallet after the wedding. "I have been spending money like water these last two years, but shall economise after I am married." (Alice and Theodore weren't the only ones struck by his rate of spending. Uncle James, the custodian of Roosevelt's inheritance, cast a quizzical glance at his nephew's habits. "I'm in frightful disgrace with Uncle Jim, on account of my expenditures—which certainly have been heavy," Theodore confided to Elliott.)

Roosevelt experienced the normal bridegroom's jitters. He worried that he wouldn't live up to his darling's expectations, going so far as to question whether it wouldn't have been better if they had never met. "It almost frightens me," he moaned in his diary, "in spite of my own happiness, to think that perhaps I may not make her happy." But he would certainly do his best, inspired by his overwhelming love. "I shall try very hard," he promised her, "to be as unselfish and sunny tempered as you are, and I shall save you from every care I can."

Alice reassured him. "My own dearest Teddy . . ." she wrote in early October: "How I wish it was three weeks from to-day our wedding day." Her heart was as full as his. "I just long to be with you all the time and never separate from you." She gently scolded him for his doubts. "Teddykins I know that you can make me happy and you must never think it would have been better for me, if we had never met; I should die without you now Teddy and there is not another man I ever could have loved in this world."

Finally the great day arrived. October 27, Roosevelt's twenty-second birthday, dawned bright; by noon the autumn sun had the male members of the wedding party—including Elliott as best man—wishing they could doff their coats. As soon as the vows were exchanged at the Brookline Unitarian Church, they did just that. Dancing and eating filled the afternoon, and by all accounts the guests had a merry time— even Edith Carow, or so she said many years afterward to her daughter, who reported her mother's claim to have "danced the soles off her shoes."

The newlyweds retired to Springfield, Massachusetts, for their wedding night, and the following day traveled on to Oyster Bay, which Mittie and the rest of the family had kindly vacated. For two weeks Theodore and Alice enjoyed what he described as "the most absolutely ideal time." "We breakfast at ten, dine at two, and take tea at seven. . . . In the morning we go out driving in the buggy, behind

Lightfoot, who is in splendid trim. In the afternoon we play tennis or walk in Fleets woods. In the evening I read aloud—Pickwick Papers, Quentin Durward or Keats poems." Alice was even more enchanting as a wife than as a fiancée. "It is impossible to describe the lovely, little teasing ways of my bright, bewitching darling; I can imagine no picture so pretty as her sweet self, seated behind the tea things in the daintiest little pink and gray morning dress, while, in my silk jacket and slippers, I sit at the other end of the table." Greater delight defied imagination. "I doubt if there was ever a happier honeymoon than ours has been." The world had vanished; only Alice remained. "I am living in dreamland; how I wish it could last forever."

VIII

It couldn't, of course. The immediate reason was Roosevelt's desire to return to law classes. In early October he had enrolled at Columbia Law School, as planned since the previous spring. And as he had promised himself then, he studied hard. Faithfully each morning he walked the three miles from the family house on Fifty-seventh Street, where he and Alice had temporarily moved in on the third floor, to the law school downtown at 8 Great Jones Street (it would shortly relocate to midtown with the rest of the Columbia campus, before the entire college headed up to Morningside Heights in the 1890s). The case method of legal education had yet to reach Columbia, where the faculty instead expounded the general principles and philosophy of law. Instruction included a great deal of rote dictation: Professors, clutching their yellowing and tattered notes, read lectures to a roomful (a stuffy roomful, in this converted old house) of students who faithfully transcribed these pearls of wisdom into their own bound, lined notebooks.

Roosevelt's course commenced at the fountainhead: "Blackstone Oct 7th," he began on the first page of his first notebook. "Law; ambiguous. . . ." Roosevelt raced to keep up with Professor Theodore Dwight's gloss on the commentaries by the great philosopher of law. "Moral laws can be brought under domain of jurisprudence. Sovereign power = power able to carry out commands of society = essential element."

Roosevelt's law school notebooks contain almost nothing of his own impressions of what he was hearing. He had never been quick with a pencil; one senses it was all he could do to maintain pace with the lecturer. Yet in light of his overall outlook on life, one can imagine what might have been going through his head. "We are concerned with question of what law is; not what it ought to be," he wrote on that first day; if this didn't immediately raise doubts in his mind regarding the enterprise of law, it would soon enough. Moralist that Roosevelt was, and activist that he became, he couldn't accept such an agnostic view. The law was made for man, not man for the law.

The second day afforded a certain reassurance. "In U.S. supreme power is in people; and some of it is parcelled out to Congress, some to states, and the residuary still remains with the people, in the shape of the constitution." Which meant that if something was wrong with the law as enacted by Congress or the states, the people could effect a remedy. What Roosevelt made of this concept during the autumn of 1880 is unclear; he would make a great deal of it later. So also with another paraphrase from Blackstone during that initial week: "Law implies authority and sanction. International law depends upon universal consent of various nations, so progress is slow." A willingness to apply sanctions in international affairs and an acceptance that progress would necessarily be slow underpinned his foreign policy as president.

Professor Dwight went on to explain the evolution of the common law over the centuries. The subject matter was compelling enough, but Roosevelt almost certainly raised an eyebrow (he may well have raised his hand, too, and challenged Dwight) at the statement that "common law is from time to time announced by judges and by a legal fiction is presumed to have been already known on the principle that the law is a science and the new rule is a deduction from principles previously known." Understanding the principles of modern science, even if he didn't agree with all of modern scientific practice, Roosevelt could tell that legal "science" wasn't real science.

The common law touched all forms of social intercourse, from the nature of citizenship and political allegiance (a matter that would exercise Roosevelt greatly during World War I) to the legal grounds for divorce (which did not include "habitual drunkenness" but did include "actual violence . . . or reasonable apprehension of such violence," points that would be critical in his dealings with Elliott).

By all indications Roosevelt was a dedicated student. He actively engaged in discussions when Dwight and the other professors put down their notes and solicited student responses. Some of his classmates thought he talked too much; one fellow student sharply recalled "the pertinacity with which he interrupted the kindly Dwight." Roosevelt certainly took pains with his notes, filling as many as twenty-three pages at a sitting. When necessity kept him away from the lecture hall—as during the three weeks for his wedding and honeymoon—he made certain to borrow a classmate's notes and copy them into his own notebook.

IX

Assiduous though he was in the classroom, Roosevelt didn't allow the law to monopolize his time. On any given day, a morning of lectures might be followed by lunch with friends or a visit to the Astor Library (conveniently just around the corner and up Lafayette Place from the law school) to read the recent journals or do some research for a naval history of the War of 1812 he had begun in college. The late afternoon would find him once more at home, squeezing in an hour of writing on his naval history before preparing to sit down to dinner or to go out for the evening.

During the late autumn and early winter of 1880, he and Alice dined out nearly every night. The social season was just beginning, and all their relatives and friends wanted to inspect these latest additions to the mid-Manhattan circle. Roosevelt reestablished links suspended during his Cambridge years and established new ones; Alice tied into Theodore's circle and started one of her own. When they didn't go out, they had friends in. "The other night we had a grand dinner here," Roosevelt told Elliott in a typical remark of early December.

Married life suited Roosevelt splendidly. On December 31 he reflected on his good fortune: "Thus ends by far the happiest year I have ever spent, for in this year I have won the fairest and purest and sweetest of women for my wife. I never conceived it possible that there could be such a bright, sunny, unselfish girl. I can never express how I love her; and if I should love her as much and as tenderly it would not be nearly as much as she deserves; I never can understand how I won her!"

The following months only intensified his infatuation. When Alice visited her parents in March, he sent love letters to Chestnut Hill after her. "I have had no one to jog my arm and make me blot the paper while I was writing," he lamented. "It always made me feel rather bad-tempered, but I loved it all the same. I feel dreadfully lonely going to bed without you." Several days later he added, "There is no pretty, sleepy little rosebud face to kiss and love when I wake in the morning; nor any sweet, loving heart to whom I can confide all the little joys and pains of the day." Alice grew slightly spoiled by the constant attention from home; one day when he had had time to jot only a card rather than a full letter, she complained: "I do wish you would write me a little longer letter, as I am so home sick for you that I should like to hear a little more what you are doing."

The winter passed quickly. Law lectures and historical research and writing filled Roosevelt's days; parties, balls, the theater, and sleigh rides filled his nights. Law school had the distinct advantage over college of not requiring the students to take regular examinations. Students would be tested at the end of the two-year term, but until then their progress was their own concern. Roosevelt had mastered the art of cramming in college; he would worry about the exams when the time came.

In the spring of 1881 his class commenced studying corporate law. Roosevelt continued to attend lectures religiously, and he filled his notebook (volume four by now) with page after page on the ownership and use of property in society. Some of what he learned seems— from his later actions—to have stayed with him. In the matter of when a person might be justified in taking action that incidentally destroyed or diminished the value of another's property (as in tearing down a building to prevent a fire from spreading), he noted: "It is not necessary that property of one who acts should be in danger; it is enough that general good is in danger." Roosevelt probably didn't recall these precise lines when, as president, he imposed regulations that diminished the value of certain corporate property (he didn't reread them from his notebooks, which he bequeathed to a classmate when he dropped out of law school). But the idea of safeguarding the general good certainly stuck.

Yet on the whole he found corporate law rather off-putting. "The *caveat emptor* side of the law, like the *caveat emptor* side of business, seemed to me repellent," he wrote later. "It did not make for fair social dealing." Nor did it make for gripping study. Roosevelt's notes for this period display a decided distraction. He experiments with handwriting styles: now large and bold, now compact and tidy, now slanted backward, now forward again. More than once he writes "May" for the current month rather than "March."

X

May indeed was on his mind, for as the end of the semester approached, he laid plans for a proper honeymoon, something more extended and elaborate than the fortnight of the previous autumn. During the second week of May he and Alice set sail for Europe. Roosevelt experienced mixed feelings about discovering someone who handled the sea even less well than he did. Alice was agonizingly ill for most of the crossing. "We had a beautiful passage; very nearly as gay as a funeral," he explained to Alice's sister, Rose.

> If ever a person heartily enjoyed a sea trip, Alice did. She enjoyed it so much that she stayed in bed about all the time; the stewardess and myself being her devoted attendants. I fed her every blessed meal she ate; and held her head when, about 20 minutes later, the meal came gal-lopping up into the outer world again. I only rebelled once; that was when she requested me to wear a mustard plaster first, to see if it hurt. About every half hour during the night I turned out to superintend mat-ters while Alice went through a kind of stomachic earthquake. After each one of these internal convulsions Alice would conclude she was going to die, and we would have a mental circus for a few minutes; finally after I had implored, prayed and sworn with equal fervency she would again compose herself for a few minutes. . . . Alice was really awfully sick.

Even Roosevelt's energy occasionally flagged in his new capacity as nurse. "Confound a European trip, say I! I haven't been at all sick but tired out by taking care of her."

Despite his and Alice's recurrent doubts, the passage eventually ended, and on solid ground once more her stomach settled and their spirits revived. "Alice is the best travelling companion I have ever known," he declared four days after landing at Queenstown. This trip showed Roosevelt sights he hadn't seen before or was too young to appreciate. The Irish countryside joined physical charm to what he called "a terrible under-stratum of wretchedness." The most beautiful mountains overshadowed windowless hovels, clinging desperately to their single potato patches, their lone oat fields, and their skinny cows. On a boat ride, their oarsmen were "stout, merry, regularly Irish, fellows"; aboard a carriage they passed a man lying on the road, "insensible from sheer hunger." This last scene stirred Roosevelt's conscience. He instructed some peasants nearby to wake and feed the man, and he gave him ten shillings.

From Dublin they traversed the Irish Sea to Liverpool. They visited with Uncle James and Uncle Irvine, who encouraged Roosevelt in his naval history. This time Alice had to endure the kissing cousins, too. "There was but one thing that marred our visit," Roosevelt informed his mother. "That was the everlasting slobbering (there is no other word for it) of the younger Bullochs. I really like Jimmie, and all the others too; but the kissing was simply disgusting."

In London they linked up with some of Roosevelt's college friends for dinner, theater, and museum-going. He tried to get access to British documents relating to his historical study but found that few were available for examination—by him, at any rate.

On this third visit to England, Roosevelt felt quite at home, so much so that when he and Alice crossed the Channel to France, he wrote, "The two innocents are now on foreign soil." By all appearances Alice didn't especially enjoy this part of the trip. While defending her as "an excellent traveler," he also described her as "austere" and explained, "When I reach a station I leave her in a chair with the parcels, and there she stays, round eyed and solemn, but perfectly happy, till I have extricated my luggage, had it put on a hack and arranged everything." Nor did she get on with the natives. "Alice resents it as an impertinence if she is addressed in any language but English."

The high point of the Continent for Roosevelt, emotionally and geographically, was Switzerland, where he climbed that country's most challenging peaks. He obviously recalled his outings here with his father when he had just begun to emerge from his shell of sickness. The memory of what he had then accomplished—and probably the presence of Alice—pushed him to attempt more adventurous climbs. He tackled the Jungfrau first, with the assistance of a pair of hired guides. The two-day journey, with the intervening night spent in a climber's cabin high on the mountainside, tested his stamina and conditioning more than his skill or nerve. The descent especially was "great fun."

The Matterhorn posed a greater test. Unconquered until sixteen years earlier, the crag above Zermatt had claimed dozens of lives during the decades in which people had been driven to try to reach its summit. After the Whymper expedition succeeded in 1865, the route was rendered considerably less perilous by the installation of cables and the training of guides who knew the safest way up and down. In the 1880s the mountain was a regular stop for climbers, not to mention a major draw for the local economy.

Roosevelt couldn't resist the challenge. He wasn't a real climber but believed that the Matterhorn might make him one. "I was anxious to go up it because it is reputed very difficult and a man who has been up it can fairly claim to have taken his degree as, at any rate, a subordinate kind of mountaineer." Patriotic considerations counted as well. "There were some English climbers there," he confided to Bill Sewall, "and one of the chief reasons I made the ascent was to show them that a Yankee could climb just as well as they could."

Roosevelt again secured the services of guides and commenced the two-day journey. The first day lasted from nine in the morning until six in the evening; the night was spent in a hut dug into the mountain face, its floor covered with ice that never melted. Several hours in such a location gave the climber a chance to ponder what he had taken on. "The mountain is so steep that snow will not remain on the crumbling, jagged rocks, and possesses a certain sombre interest from the number of people that have lost their lives on it. Accidents, however, are generally due either to rashness, or else to a combination of timidity and fatigue; a fairly hardy man, cautious but not cowardly, with good guides, has little to fear. Still, there is enough peril to make it exciting, and the work is very laborious being as much with the hands as the feet, and (very unlike the Jungrau) as hard coming down as going up."

The next morning he and the guides set out before four in order to be off the mountain before the summer sun softened the ice and made the footing more treacherous than it already was. On the way up they were greeted by "a most glorious sunrise which crowned the countless snow peaks and billowy, white clouds with a strange crimson irridescence." By seven they had reached the summit. After a few minutes to rest and savor their triumph, the party headed down. By lunchtime they were at the base of the peak. "We then literally ran down the foot hills to Zermatt, reaching it at half past three." The climb had been wearing. "It was like going up and down enormous stairs on your hands and knees for nine hours. . . . It had been excessively laborious and during the journey I was nearer giving out than on the Jungfrau." But a warm bath and a cup of tea—joined to the knowledge of having earned his crampons on Europe's premier mountain—had him fresh as ever by dinner.

From Switzerland they traveled down the Rhine. "The scenery was lovely," he recorded, "but no more so than the Hudson except for the castles. These 'robber knight' castles are so close together that I always wonder where there was room for the other people whom the Robber Knights robbed." Ireland had stirred Roosevelt's conscience regarding the poor; the Rhine country stirred it again. "The Age of Chivalry was lovely for the knights; but it must have at times been inexpressibly gloomy for the gentlemen who had to occasionally act in the capacity of daily bread for their betters. It is like the purely traditional 'Merry England' of the Stuarts; where the merriment existed only for the Stuarts, who were about the worst dynasty that ever sat on a throne." In Cologne he made a contact he hoped would be valuable: an American naval officer, a Commodore Baldwin, who "may do me a good turn at the Navy Department, in getting me access to records for that favourite chateau-en-espagne of mine, the Naval History."

In this letter to Bamie, Roosevelt revealed a rare moment of frustration regarding his history project, and of a larger self-doubt. "I have plenty of information now, but I can't get it into words; I am afraid it is too big a task for me. I wonder if I won't find everything in life too big for my abilities."

Yet it was only a moment. "Well, time will tell," he declared in passing on to another topic. "Alice having just killed a flea is eying with horror what she calls 'his little giblets.'"

The Rhine carried them to the Low Countries. They haunted Holland's museums, where Roosevelt found the secular subjects, especially those depicting ordinary lives—"how the people of those times lived and made merry and died"—far more engaging than the innumerable pictures of saints and madonnas. "I have really tried to like the Holy pictures but I can't." (In an earlier letter he had put the matter more strongly: "I never have sympathized with the mediaeval idea of saint—an abject, whiney-looking specimen, with a straw hat instead of a halo. Thank heavens, they were all martyred.")

From Holland they returned to France. Now Alice got to call the tune for a change. "Our stay in Paris was mainly devoted to the intricacies of dress buying." Yet he did manage to fit in a visit to the tomb of Napoleon. The famous general's final resting place moved him deeply. "I do not think there is a more impressive sepulchre on earth than that tomb; it is grandly simple. I am not very easily awestruck, but it certainly gave me a solemn feeling to look at the plain, red stone bier which contained what had once been the mightiest conqueror the world ever saw." Roosevelt's reverence for the soldier overshadowed his reservations regarding the rest of Napoleon's life. "He was a great fighter, at least, though otherwise I suppose an almost unmixed evil. Hannibal alone is his equal in military genius; and Caesar in cruel power and ambition. What a child such a mere butcher as Tamerlane, Genghis Khan or Attila would have been in his hands!"

Roosevelt's respect for Napoleon didn't diminish his attachment to those things that made his own country different from France, England, Germany, and all the other places he and Alice visited. On their return to London he wrote to Bill Sewall: "This summer I have passed travelling through Europe, and though I have enjoyed it greatly, yet the more I see, the better satisfied I am that I am an American; free born and free bred, where I acknowledge no man as my superior, except for his own worth, or as my inferior, except for his own demerit."

The travelers passed through London on their way back to Liverpool and another visit with the Bullochs, who gave him another nudge to finish his naval history. Roosevelt in turn encouraged Uncle Jimmie to put his recollections of the Civil War to paper. The conversations with his uncles aggravated again that small sore spot in

Roosevelt's memory of his father, as he implicitly acknowledged: "Of course, had I been old enough, I would have served on the Northern side."

XI

On return to New York, Roosevelt followed his uncles' advice and pushed his naval history through to the end. Owen Wister left a picture of the author at work:

> He finished his Naval History of the War of 1812 mostly standing on one leg at the bookcases in his New York house, the other leg crossed behind, toe touching the floor, heedless of dinner engagements and the flight of time. A slide drew out from the bookcase. On this he had open the leading authorities on navigation, of which he knew nothing. He knew that when a ship's course was one way, with the wind another, the ship had to sail at angles, and this was called tacking or beating. By exhaustive study and drawing of models, he pertinaciously got it all right, whatever of it came into the naval engagements he was writing about.
>
> His wife used to look in at his oblivious back, and exclaim in a plaintive drawl: "We're dining out in twenty minutes, and Teedy's drawing little ships!"
>
> Then there would be a scurry, and he would cut himself shaving, and it wouldn't stop bleeding, and they would have to surround him and take measures to save his collar from getting stained.

The book's prose was robust, with masts crashing to decks, yards being blown away, hulls catching fire and burning to the waterline; yet for a war story it was surprisingly bloodless. The author meticulously calculated casualties but rarely invested his numbers with human form and pain. Roosevelt's was a story of war as gallantry and heroism, not mutilated corpses and screaming seamen. It was a story of war by one who obviously had never witnessed or experienced the real thing.

Roosevelt's opinions were as robust as his prose. He derided the conclusions of a disagreeing author as "nonsense"; another's judgments were "utterly without foundation." The reader quickly ascertained that for Roosevelt the primary purpose of history was didactic. The author drew a number of morals from his story. One was that patriotism and courage could carry the day even in the face of overwhelming odds. "It must be but a poor-spirited American whose veins do not tingle with pride when he reads of the cruises and fights of the sea-captains, and their grim prowess, which kept the old Yankee flag floating over the waters of the Atlantic for three years, in the teeth of the mightiest naval power the world has ever seen." Another lesson, more pertinent for the present, was the need for naval readiness. Americans had allowed their fleet to deteriorate shamefully since the War of 1812. If they didn't repair this deficiency, they would be unworthy heirs to that heroic generation. Roosevelt repeated the adage: "There is only success for those who know how to prepare it."

Part Two

ENGAGEMENT

CHAPTER SEVEN

Crashing the Party
1881–83

To outward appearances, Roosevelt was the soul of respectability during his first year after college. Devoted husband, sober student of the law, serious scholar, patriotic writer—he was all of these, and a fully vested member of the New York gentry to boot. He might dress rough while hunting on the prairies, but in his native habitat of midtown Manhattan or on the grand tour of Europe he was unmistakably of the finest stratum of the upper crust.

Yet this dignified exterior concealed a dark secret. By day and most evenings he adhered to the rules and expectations of his class, but one night a month, later more frequently, he consorted with characters of dubious morals and indubitably shady reputations. He led a double life; in short, he entered politics.

The portal to this nether realm was Morton Hall, a grimy, smelly clubhouse above a saloon on Fifty-ninth Street. The hall was a short walk from his home, but it might just as well have been a world away. The men—women weren't welcome and didn't come—who crowded into Morton Hall, filling its air with cigar smoke, its floor with ashes, and its spittoons (alternatively, the floor) with tobacco juice, were of a kind Roosevelt hadn't consorted with to date. They were professionals and businessmen, but of a distinctive caste. Their profession was people and their business was winning public office. Their work was keenly competitive: Those with the gift succeeded and prospered; those without fell by the side.

Joseph Murray had the gift. Irish by birth, Murray had fled his hungry homeland as a toddler during the potato famine, wrapped in his mother's love but little else; he grew up, as he liked to say, "a barefoot boy on First Avenue." Bare knuckles soon supplemented bare feet, and quick wits complemented both. By the age of fifteen he had developed a following among the young toughs of the East Side. He joined the Union army for the bounty that Abe Lincoln offered; in the bargain he bolstered his reputation as a fighter and a fellow who knew his way about the world.

The politicos of Tammany Hall were always on the lookout for such up-and-comers, and before long they were courting him. He didn't resist. In an era when each party set up a booth at the precinct's polling place on election days and passed out the party's straight ticket to approaching voters, Murray and his gang were assigned the job of beating up the Republican representative early election morning, smashing his booth for kindling, and casting his ballots to the wind. For their efforts the boys received walking-around money; Murray got more regular compensation.

Murray might have remained a faithful Democrat had Tammany's local leader not grown forgetful of his roots and especially of those whose diligent work had made his success possible. In a word, he didn't hold up his end of the bargain. Murray paid little heed to election laws and other formalities, but he insisted on fair dealing man to man and took this neglect as a personal affront. He decided to hit Tammany where it hurt—in the ballot box. Without informing his erstwhile patron that he had experienced a change of political heart, he secretly instructed the lads that on the next election day they would do to the Democrats what they had formerly done to the Republicans. The result was an astonishing turnaround—probably even more astonishing to the Republicans, who carried a district in which they had been lucky to leave the single digits of the vote percentage, than to the Democrats, who for all their anger at least could figure out whence their defeat arose.

As soon as the Republicans got over their amazement and began looking into the cause of their triumph, they invited Murray to join their organization. To cement his new affiliation they offered him a job in the local post office. Murray subsequently became a loyal Republican and a stout defender of the party of the Union. The party served him well in turn: Unusual for a postal worker, he managed to afford a spirited racing trotter—"Alice Lane"—and rig in which he took new recruits to the party out for rides.

II

Roosevelt was one such recruit. Roosevelt's interest in politics awakened slowly. In college he had participated in the occasional rally, but more out of social solidarity with his chums than as a matter of conviction. He stole time from his first honeymoon, at Oyster Bay, to vote for James Garfield for president, but his darling bride held far more fascination for him. On his second honeymoon, in Europe, he reacted with dismay to the news of the attempt on Garfield's life. "Just heard of Garfields assassination," he wrote on July 5, 1881. "A frightful calamity for America." In fact, Garfield wasn't yet dead, as a second report made clear. But damage had been done to the country just the same. "This means work in the future for all men who wish their country well."

The son of Theodore Roosevelt, Sr., couldn't help counting himself among that group, and he gradually determined to take up that work—although partly, at first, from lack of any attractive alternative. Law lost its appeal the further he got into it. "Some of the teaching of the law-books and of the classroom seemed to me to be against justice," he said afterward. Moreover, many of the big corporate lawyers, those who dominated the profession and largely set its code of ethics, adhered to standards that couldn't bear moral scrutiny. Roosevelt still considered law good training for the mind; it required one to draw distinctions ("Idiot has congenital trouble. Lunatic has been rational," he wrote during one dictation) and thus honed abilities that would prove useful in any kind of debate. But less and less did law interest him as a career.

Literature remained a possibility. He enjoyed writing and, judging from the reception of his first book, showed promise. Yet even the most optimistic scenario promised meager remuneration from his literary endeavors. While this didn't disqualify writing as a career, neither did it particularly recommend it. Roosevelt wasn't wealthy enough to be immune to monetary considerations. A more serious drawback of writing was that it was too solitary a vocation. As he had discovered in college, he liked being around people. Writers, as writers, spend their hours alone.

It was Roosevelt's gregariousness as much as anything else that had led him up Fifty-ninth Street to Morton Hall. What he found there intrigued him in the same way that the loggers of Maine and the immigrants of Illinois had intrigued him. Roosevelt understood that politics in the Gilded Age was a hard and sometimes bruising game, just as life on the frontier was hard and often bruising. Precisely because it was, it was a challenge. Where others of his class wanted to have as little as possible to do with the iron-knuckled types who ran the machines that ran the cities and the states, Roosevelt couldn't keep away. (By contrast, his cousin Emlen Roosevelt, who accompanied him on some early visits to Morton Hall, subsequently grew disgusted and stayed home.) For several years Roosevelt had felt compelled to test his body against every challenge he could think of; the Matterhorn was his most recent conquest. Now, in climbing the dim stairway to Morton Hall, he was testing himself in another way: He was testing his savvy, his intelligence, and his character. He later explained his thinking:

> The men I knew best were the men in the clubs of social pretension and the men of cultivated taste and easy life. When I began to make inquiries as to the whereabouts of the local Republican association and the means of joining it, these men—and the big business men and lawyers also—laughed at me, and told me that politics were "low"; that the organizations were not controlled by "gentlemen"; that I would find them run by saloon-keepers, horse-car conductors, and the like, and not by men with any of whom I would come in contact outside; and, moreover, they assured me that the men I met would be rough and brutal and unpleasant to deal with. I answered that if this were so it merely meant that the people I knew did not belong to the governing class, and that the other people did—and that I intended to be one of the governing class; that if they proved too hard-bit for me I supposed I would have to quit, but that I certainly would not quit until I had made the effort and found out whether I really was too weak to hold my own in the rough and tumble.

Roosevelt chose to try his hand with the Republican members of and aspirants to the governing class, in preference to the Democrats.

In New York City the Democrats were the party of Tammany Hall and the Tweed Ring; this circumstance by itself nearly disqualified them for Roosevelt. More damning still, they were the party of disunion and bloody rebellion. In later years, largely as the result of efforts by reformers after Roosevelt's mind, political parties would be recognized for the quasi-official organizations they were, but in the early postwar decades they remained the equivalent of private clubs, writing their own rules and controlling their own membership. Each district had its own party chapter or association. Morton Hall was the headquarters of the Twenty-first District Republican Association; on its wall hung a framed picture of Ulysses S. Grant.

The members of the Twenty-first Association initially eyed Roosevelt with some suspicion, being as skeptical of his type as his type generally were of them. But he comported himself harmlessly enough, and beneath the fancy clothes and eyeglasses he seemed a regular fellow. At least he made the effort to come to the meetings, which was more than could be said for most of the silk-stocking set.

Joe Murray observed Roosevelt for some months, then decided to try him out. Murray wanted to make a challenge for the leadership of the Twenty-first District, currently headed by Jake Hess. The occasion for the challenge was an upcoming election for representative from the district to the state assembly; Hess had selected his candidate for the Republican nomination, and Murray wanted to put up another. Roosevelt seemed a likely choice. His family name was known and respected, and the Columbia crowd he currently associated with might otherwise be hard to reach. "I thought I would interest the football team of Columbia, the baseball team, and the other different athletes connected with the College, together with the professors," Murray remarked later. The question was: Would Roosevelt be willing to run?

Roosevelt, surprised at the speed with which his political career was commencing, hesitated. He realized that he was a piece in the larger contest between Murray and Hess, but he decided that if he was in for a dime, he might as well be in for a dollar. He accepted Murray's offer. (It hadn't escaped Murray that Roosevelt could easily afford the dollars required for the filing fee and other expenses of a race.)

Murray had laid his plans carefully and in the crucial caucus dealt Hess a stinging defeat. Roosevelt, just turning twenty-three, became the Republican nominee for the lower house of the legislature.

The nomination shocked Roosevelt's relatives as much as it surprised him. Uncle Jim Roosevelt registered grave disapproval, as did various cousins. But other acquaintances expressed support. "Most of my friends are standing by me like trumps," he commented.

Still new to the game of politics, Roosevelt proceeded to wage a staidly unimaginative campaign. A form letter went out to all the voters of the Twenty-first District:

> Dear Sir:
>
> Having been nominated as a candidate for member of Assembly for this District, I would esteem it a compliment if you honor me with your vote and personal influence on Election Day.
>
> > Very respectfully,
> > Theodore Roosevelt

The flyer offered voters no reasons why they should lend their support, providing neither background about the candidate and his views nor promises as to what he intended to accomplish if elected. An ordinary voter might have been forgiven for wondering at the presumption of one who hoped to be elected on his name alone.

Murray and Jake Hess—the latter conceding his defeat with good grace and committed to Republican solidarity—improved Roosevelt's election chances by mobilizing the party machinery. For the benefits of the district's bluebloods, they solicited endorsements of the nominee from the Fifth Avenue crowd. Such notables as Joseph Choate and Elihu Root signed a statement affirming their appreciation of Roosevelt's "high character and standing in the community" and their confidence in his "honesty and integrity." He was, they declared, "eminently qualified to represent the District in the Assembly."

To persuade other influential groups in the district, Murray and Hess designed a more personal appeal. A few days before the election they took Roosevelt on a tour of the saloon row on Sixth Avenue. The saloon owners formed a crucial constituency, having a sizable portion of the working classes by the throat, so to speak. At the first stop on this walking tour, Roosevelt's handlers introduced the proprietor to the nominee. This owner, a man named Fisher, struck Roosevelt as somewhat importunate: He said he expected the candidate to treat the liquor business fairly. Roosevelt, annoyed at Fisher's tone of voice, replied that he would treat the interests of all his constituents fairly. Fisher, getting more specific, asserted that liquor licenses were too expensive.

"What is the license fee?" inquired the obviously unprepared candidate.

"We have got to pay two hundred dollars," said Fisher.

"Two hundred dollars?" replied Roosevelt. "That isn't half enough! It ought to be one thousand dollars."

Murray and Hess had expected a certain naïveté in their candidate but nothing so obviously counterproductive as this. They hustled him out the door, deciding on the run to keep Roosevelt away from the saloons. "That was the first and last visit," Murray recollected.

Otherwise the campaign went well, and election day brought Roosevelt victory. He hadn't won many real contests in his life and was understandably pleased. Yet the triumph hardly convinced him to make politics a career. Replying to a friend who had heard secondhand of his entry into politics, and who had expressed concern, Roosevelt wrote, "Too True! Too True! I have become a 'political hack.' Finding it would not interfere much with my law I accepted the nomination to the assembly, and was elected by 1500 majority, heading the ticket by 600 votes. But don't think I am going to go into politics after this year, for I am not."

III

These were famous last words—or they would be by the time Roosevelt grew famous. Though he didn't quite realize it at the time, he had just embarked on his life's work. With a brief exception, precipitated by extraordinary personal circumstances, he would remain in politics for the rest of his life. To be sure, he would simultaneously pursue other interests, so when he averred, as he did in his memoirs, that no man should make politics his complete career—that "it is a dreadful misfortune for a man to grow to feel that his whole livelihood and whole happiness depend upon his staying in office"—he wasn't being hypocritical. In his case, having an inheritance to fall back on didn't hurt, either. All the same, from the time he entered the New York legislature in January 1882 until his death, politics was the primary occupation of his life.

As the youngest member of the assembly and, while not its wealthiest, at least from the wealthiest district, Roosevelt drew dubious and often derisive comments from his colleagues, a working majority of whom were pretty sure they didn't like this college boy from Manhattan. Isaac Hunt remembered him as "a society man and a dude." Hunt described an early appearance by Roosevelt at a committee meeting:

> All of a sudden the door opened and in rushed Mr. Roosevelt. He made his way up and sat right down in front of the chairman of the conference. He had on an enormous overcoat and had a silk hat in his hand. As soon as opportunity was given, he addressed the chairman and he pulled off his overcoat and he was in full dress. He had been to a dinner. He had on his eyeglasses and his gold fob. His hair was parted in the middle and he addressed the chairman in the vernacular of the FFV's of New York. We almost shouted with laughter to think that the most veritable representative of the New York dude had come to the Chamber.

Another assemblyman remembered Roosevelt as being off-puttingly full of himself. John Milholland visited Roosevelt's Albany office and was impressed by a tiger skin displayed there. Roosevelt explained that his brother Elliott had shot the animal on a hunting expedition. "That's his game," he continued, "but I brought down some pretty good game recently. My brother got this tiger, but I got Jake Hess."

Roosevelt returned the skepticism, not to say distrust, of his new colleagues. Not long after taking up a post on the Committee on Affairs of Cities, he sketched his committee-mates, beginning with the Democrats:

> The chairman is an Irishman named Murphy, Colonel in the Civil War, a Fenian; he is a tall, stout man with a swollen red face, a black moustache, and a ludicrously dignified manner; always wears a frock coat (very shiney) and has had a long experience in politics—so that, to undoubted pluck and a certain knowledge of parliamentary forms, he adds a great deal of stupidity and a decided looseness of ideas as regards the 8th Commandment. Next comes John Shanley of Brooklyn, an Irishman, but born in America; much shrewder than Murphy and easier to get along with, being more Americanized but fully as dishonest; then comes MacDonough, an American-born Irishman from Albany; Higgins, a vicious little, Celtic nonentity from Buffaloe; Gideon, a Jew from New York who has been a bailiff and is now a liquor seller; Dimonn, a country Democrat, who is either dumb or an

idiot—probably both; and, as the last of the Democrats, a Tammany Hall gentleman named MacManus, a huge, fleshy, unutterably coarse and low brute, who was formerly a prize fighter, at present keeps a low drinking and dancing saloon, and is more than suspected of having begun his life as a pick pocket.

Roosevelt granted that some of his fellow Republicans were "bad enough." He declared—to himself—that one G.O.P. colleague had the same idea of public office "that a vulture has of a dead sheep," while the intellectual capacity of another Republican "about equals that of an average balloon."

But the Democrats were far worse. And the Irish were the dregs of the bottom-scum. "They are a stupid, sodden vicious lot, most of them being equally deficient in brains and virtue." As mostly immigrants or the sons of immigrants, they were so many walking arguments for immigration restriction. "The average catholic Irishman of the first generation as represented in this Assembly, is a low, venal, corrupt and unintelligent brute."

If the situation hadn't been so disgraceful, Roosevelt judged, it would have been funny. Sometimes it was anyway. One Tammany loyalist named Bogan, "a little celtic liquor seller, about five feet high, with an enormous stomach, and a face like a bull frog," was the perpetrator of an especially inane dialogue with the assembly clerk—an exchange Roosevelt recorded in his journal, complete with brogue. The assembly had not yet adopted rules, and the clerk presided.

BOGAN. "Mr. Clur-rk!"
CLERK. "The gentleman from New York, Mr. Bogan."
BOGAN. "I rise to a pint of ardther (order) under the rules!"
CLERK. "There are no rules."
BOGAN. "Thin I objict to thim!"
CLERK. "There are no rules to object to."
BOGAN (meditatively). "Indade! That's quare, now. (brightening up, as he sees a way out of the difficulty) Viry will! Thin I move that they be amended till there ar-r-r!" (smiles complacently on the applauding audience, proudly conscious that he has at last solved an abstruse point of parliamentary practice).

While Roosevelt continued being contemptuous of nearly all the Democrats and a good portion of the Republicans, he gradually warmed to a select group of the latter and an even more select group of the former. His closest friend and ally in the legislature was William O'Neill, an upstate Republican and small-business man. Thirty years later Roosevelt recalled O'Neill fondly: "In most other countries two men of as different antecedents, ancestry, and surroundings as Billy O'Neill and I would have had far more difficulty in coming together," he wrote. "I came from the biggest city in America and from the wealthiest ward of that city, and he from a backwoods county where he kept a store at a crossroads." Roosevelt didn't explicitly say that Billy O'Neill reminded him of Bill Sewall, but Roosevelt's partiality toward simple, straightforward men of the backcountry, and his identification with the values of such men, was plainly evident in his assessment of both O'Neill and Sewall. He went on: "In all the unimportant things we seemed far apart. But in all the important things we were close together. We looked at all questions from substantially the same view-point, and we stood shoulder to shoulder in every legislative fight during those three years." Like Sewall, O'Neill had used his time in the wilderness well. "He had thought much on political problems; he admired Alexander Hamilton as much as I did, being a strong believer in a powerful national government; and we both of us differed from Alexander Hamilton in being stout adherents of Abraham Lincoln's views wherever the rights of the people were concerned." When Roosevelt looked at O'Neill, as when he looked at Sewall, he saw what he himself might have been had life's dice rolled differently. "Fortune favored me, whereas her hand was heavy against Billy O'Neill. All his life he had to strive hard to wring his bread from harsh surroundings and a reluctant fate; if fate had been a little kinder, I believe he would have had a great political career; and he would have done good service for the country in any position in which he might have been put."

Another Roosevelt ally in the assembly was Michael Costello. A native Irishman sent to Albany as a Tammany Democrat, Mike Costello grew disenchanted as he discovered that Tammany's practices fell considerably short of the ideals Tammany speakers embraced on the Fourth of July and other patriotic occasions. He carved out a niche for himself that was independent of the Democratic leadership, much as Roosevelt was doing on the Republican side. "He and I worked hand in hand with equal indifference to our local machines,"

Roosevelt boasted—but not inaccurately. In Costello's case, independence would shortly cost him his position. Roosevelt learned from his friend's experience.

IV

Roosevelt brought to his legislative work his penchant for perceiving reality in crisp terms of right and wrong, good and evil. Where others saw the legislative process as a means for effecting compromise among groups with comparably legitimate interests, Roosevelt looked on it as an arena of combat. In theory he could sometimes accept that reasonable people might differ with him, but in the heat of battle his toleration usually withered. Honest, brave men agreed with him; those who disagreed were, by his definition, cowardly and corrupt.

Roosevelt probably overestimated the cowardice of his colleagues but not their corruption. A journalist who covered Albany during the 1870s and 1880s recalled the "evil and heart-sickening days" when corruption "swept in a black tide through the Legislature, a cesspool of manifold iniquity." This observer continued: "On its foul edge stood all the forces of evil in our society, like the demons in Dante's Fifth Chasm, fishing out one venal legislator after another, as Graffiacane 'hooked out Ciampola's pitchy locks and haled him up to open gaze so that he seemed an otter,' sleek, shining, and shameless. So I had seen legislators fished for, caught and exposed, in my work as an Albany correspondent."

The most formidable of the corruptionists were the "Black Horse Cavalry," party hacks and legislative opportunists who made a habit and a business of trading political favors for pecuniary ones. Sometimes the political favors consisted of positive legislation designed to benefit deep-pocketed constituents, particularly corporate owners and managers. Equally often the favors were of the negative variety: votes against legislation that would harm corporate or other well-heeled interests. In the latter case, the dusky dragoons would introduce blackmail bills, having no desire to see the bills approved but rather intending to be paid off for orphaning their own measures.

The possibilities were endless, and the political cover the process afforded was quite effective in concealing the true motives of legislators from public scrutiny. The worst grafters could be found introducing the most stringent anticorporate regulatory schemes, only to abandon them in committee when the required contributions came in. At other times the same legislators could give the most impassioned speeches against obviously crooked bills, and then, after similar reconsideration by the corporations, attach cosmetically appealing but essentially meaningless amendments and vote in favor.

This conscious confusion of motives became apparent in one of the first fights Roosevelt waged in the legislature—a fight, moreover, that threw him into the middle of one of the great stock-jobbing schemes of the era. For years reformers and other ostensible guardians of the public welfare had been trying to get the corporations that operated elevated trains in New York City to pay higher taxes and charge lower fares. But the elevated train companies had friends in the right places who beat back the challenges. The issue gained immediacy during the summer of 1881 when certain speculators commenced a deliberate— or so it seemed to most observers—and successful campaign of rumor and innuendo to drive down the stock price of the Manhattan Elevated, the foremost of the carriers. That the bad-mouthing of the Manhattan was most marked in the *New York World*, recently acquired by the most infamous of the industrial empire builders, Jay Gould, seemed entirely uncoincidental to Gould's many critics.

That the plunge of the Manhattan's price was followed by the sudden purchase by Gould of enough shares to control the corporation and that news of this purchase was followed in turn by a rapid doubling of the stock price appeared to clinch the case for corrupt collusion. The editors of the *New York Times* had no doubt what had happened: Of Gould's latest coup the paper declared, "There is no more disgraceful chapter in the history of stock-jobbing." Disgraceful or otherwise, Gould's takeover of the Manhattan enhanced his position as one of the most powerful men in America. He already controlled the Missouri Pacific Railroad and the Western Union telegraph company (which latter control, according to his critics, allowed him to read his competitors' cables); with the Manhattan he now had a stranglehold on a major piece of the nation's transportation and communication network.

Gould often adopted the public-be-damned attitude that typified corporate management during the 1880s—and that increasingly infuriated Roosevelt—but in this instance he appreciated the value of avoiding additional bad press. Rather than fight openly for a reduction in the tax burden on the Manhattan (and other elevated railroads), he and his platoon of legal advisers engaged in a covert operation. They arranged for their Albany allies to amend an unrelated and otherwise innocuous bill so that it remitted one-third of the taxes paid by the elevated lines. The plan was for the amended bill to be reported at the end of the session, amid the usual eleventh-hour confusion, and be passed without anyone's noticing anything amiss.

Such might have happened had Mike Costello not thought to check on the bill as it made its way from the assembly to the senate. Costello caught a whiff of palm grease and alerted Roosevelt. When the bill came back to the assembly, the black cavalrymen were out in force, prepared to pass the amended measure before anyone could come to the defense of the public. At the head of the black brigade was a man known equally for his mastery of parliamentary procedure and his lack of scruples. This speaker pro tem bided his time until Costello and Roosevelt stepped out of the chamber, then hurriedly ordered the bill read and brought to a vote. Costello chanced to hear what was happening from the next room and immediately returned to mount a filibuster. The speaker slammed down his gavel, and again and again, declaring the upstart out of order and demanding that he be still. When Costello refused, the speaker ordered the sergeant at arms to arrest him and haul him away.

Just as that officer was complying, Roosevelt raced into the chamber and took up where Costello was being compelled to leave off. The speaker now turned his vehemence on Roosevelt, and bedlam ensued. In the middle of all the confusion, the speaker declared that the measure had passed and would be sent to the governor.

Yet Gould's goons hadn't won after all. The attention the riot in the assembly attracted swung the light of public scrutiny around to the tax-remittance bill, which shriveled under the glare. Several timid assemblymen changed their minds and backed a motion to reconsider; although this failed of the necessary two-thirds, it encouraged the governor to refuse to sign the bill.

The brawl over the train tax made Costello and Roosevelt instantly famous. The fame did Tammany Democrat Costello no good, and he was forced out of the assembly at the next election. But it brought Roosevelt, the reform-minded Republican, kudos as a valiant fighter for the public against the machines and the political status quo. One editor asked for a copy of the speech Roosevelt had made against the bill. Roosevelt replied that he had no copy, having spoken off the cuff. But he took the opportunity to reiterate his case against the bill and those who voted for it, and the editor obligingly printed the reiteration. "It is sheer nonsense for any man to pretend that he voted on the bill without being fully aware of its character," Roosevelt insisted. "It was put through under the gag law of the previous question, which cut off all debate, and which was of itself enough to excite the suspicions of any man of reasonable intelligence. Then, when my turn came to vote, I spoke with the greatest emphasis, stating and showing beyond doubt that the bill was a steal, and the motives of its supporters dishonest." In the end, honesty had prevailed, but barely.

V

Roosevelt won additional headlines when he personally attacked one of the principals in Gould's seizure of the Manhattan Elevated. The takeover couldn't have succeeded without the favorable attention of Judge Theodore Westbrook, who had made crucial rulings on the solvency of critical components of the deal. As it turned out, at the height of the battle for the Manhattan, Judge Westbrook had sent a letter to a lawyer closely associated with Gould, recommending a certain course of action in the Manhattan case and saying, "I can see with Mr. Gould's great interests how such an act by him to save the property would be a good financial operation as one affecting all his interests." Westbrook went on with a promise: "To accomplish this result I am willing to go to the very verge of financial discretion."

An air of irregularity had wafted around Westbrook for some time, and his role in the Manhattan takeover seemed to confirm what many people had already concluded about his lack of integrity. A substantial number of Roosevelt's colleagues, wise in the ways of the world, expected no better and greeted the reports of Westbrook's impropriety with a collective shrug. But not Roosevelt. With the full indignation of his twenty-three years, he insisted on a probe into the behavior of Judge Westbrook. He detailed the allegations at length, weighed the prima facie evidence, and concluded: "We have a right to demand that our judiciary should be kept beyond reproach."

Roosevelt was immensely pleased with the response to his call for an investigation, and with himself. "I have drawn blood," he crowed to Alice. Recounting his speech, he explained, "It is rather the hit of the season so far, and I think I have made a success of it. Letters and telegrams of congratulations come pouring in on me from all quarters."

Editorial writers—those that weren't in the pay of Gould and the grafters, at any rate—cheered him on. They relished the image of the slight young David taking on the Goliath of corporate-political corruption, armed with nothing more than the sling of his lone voice and the stones of righteousness (and, admittedly, a rather stylish turnout). The *New York Times* applauded the novice legislator: "Mr. Roosevelt has a most refreshing habit of calling men and things by their right names, and in these days of judicial, ecclesiastical, and journalistic subserviency to the robber-barons of the Street [Wall Street], it needs some little courage in any public man to characterize them and their acts in fitting terms." The *New York Sun* said of Roosevelt's speech: "It was delivered with deliberation and measured emphasis, and his charges were made with a boldness that was almost scathing." *Harper's Weekly,* edited by Republican reformer George Curtis, praised the courage of the freshman lawmaker: "It is with the greatest satisfaction that those who are interested in good government see a young man in the Legislature who, like Mr. Roosevelt, does not know the meaning of fear, and to whom the bluster and bravado of party and political bullies are as absolutely indifferent as the blowing of the wind."

Predictably, Gould's *World* denounced Roosevelt and dismissed his charges as grandstanding: "The son of Mr. Theodore Roosevelt ought to have learned, even at this early period of his life, the difference between a call for a legislative committee of inquiry and a stump speech. Why not allow Mr. Roosevelt to impeach the judge at once, try him and convict him? Why irritate an estimable youth into making a spectacle of himself to no purpose?"

Less predictably, Roosevelt received similar advice from an individual not so obviously interested in the Manhattan case. This person was a partner in a prominent law firm and an old friend of the family. He invited Roosevelt to lunch one day, evidently to gauge just what the young man intended to do in the legislature and with his life. As Roosevelt related the experience afterward:

> I believe he had a genuine personal liking for me. He explained that I had done well in the legislature; that it was a good thing to have made the "reform play," that I had shown that I possessed ability such as would make me useful in the right kind of law office or business concern; but that I must not overplay my hand; that I had gone far enough, and that now was the time to leave politics and identify myself with the right kind of people, the people who would always in the long run control others and obtain the real rewards which were worth having. I asked him if that meant that I was to yield to the ring in politics. He answered somewhat impatiently that I was entirely mistaken (as in fact I was) about there being merely a political ring, of the kind of which the papers were fond of talking; that the "ring," if it could be called such—that is, the inner circle—included certain big business men, and the politicians, lawyers, and judges who were in alliance with and to a certain extent dependent upon them, and that the successful man had to win his success by the backing of the same forces, whether in law, business, or politics.

Roosevelt later claimed that this conversation afforded him his first glimpse of the interlocking directorate of business and political power in America. Yet at the time it was merely a glimpse, and with the impetuosity of youth he threw himself against that portion of the ring he could hope to get a handle on. He fought off repeated efforts by the leadership of the assembly to prevent a vote on his resolution for an investigation, believing that if he could force his colleagues to take public positions on the matter, most would feel obliged to go along. He eventually succeeded, and his belief proved out. The vote on his resolution was 104 in favor and only 6 against.

The guardians of the status quo were hardly vanquished, however. The committee assigned to investigate Judge Westbrook's behavior returned a divided verdict. A majority of the members settled for a reprimand and a caution against the appearance of impropriety; the minority called for impeachment.

Roosevelt kept a tactically low profile during most of the deliberations, although certain statements by Westbrook provoked him beyond the bounds of reticence. The judge cited as evidence of the rectitude of his actions that all parties to the affair were satisfied and none had appealed his decision to a higher court. Of course they were satisfied, Roosevelt retorted. That was precisely the problem. "'Every party to the action is satisfied.' But the great mass of people who were not parties to the action, but who suffered by it, are not satisfied. The people have not appealed for the very good reason that their representatives, by whom alone they could appeal, have betrayed them." The judge had complained that he was being attacked for the sin of saving vast interests. "He did save vast interests; he saved them from being taken out of the hands of men who had acquired them by an unscrupulous swindle, and from being restored to their lawful owners."

While the committee conducted its investigation, Gould's agents commenced an investigation of their own: of Roosevelt. Private detectives painstakingly scrutinized his career for cracks in his armor of apparent integrity. One of his colleagues in the legislature later recollected wonderingly that he had survived the scrutiny, so close and malevolent was it. "How that man ever ran the gauntlet and they did not get the goods on him is more than I know." Another colleague couldn't see any mystery in the matter at all. "They could not get him because there wasn't anything to get."

In one instance at least during the Westbrook affair, those whose toes Roosevelt was treading on prepared to try more direct persuasion. Walking home one night in New York, he encountered a woman who inexplicably collapsed on the pavement in front of him. Gentleman that he was, he tended to her needs and called a cab to take her to her home. He thought nothing of the occurrence until she insisted that she would not be all right unless he escorted her. This aroused his suspicion, and he refused. Instead, while paying her cab fare in advance, he made a mental note of the address. As soon as the vehicle pulled away, he summoned a private detective he knew; this man hastened to the address and discovered that several tough-looking characters were lying in wait there.

The knowledge that he was a marked man increased Roosevelt's conviction that he was doing the right thing, but it didn't do anything to get Westbrook impeached. When the diverging majority and minority reports were read to the assembly, Roosevelt immediately moved to accept the minority report. Many years later, after the heat from the fight had long dissipated, he conceded that there might have been some merit in the majority opinion. "I was by no means certain that the judge himself was corrupt," he wrote in his memoirs. "He may have been; but I am inclined to think that, aside from his being a man of coarse moral fibre, the trouble lay chiefly in the fact that he had a genuine—if I had not so often seen it, I would say a wholly inexplicable—reverence for the possessor of a great fortune as such. He sincerely believed that business was the end of existence, and that judge and legislator alike should do whatever was necessary to favor it; and the bigger the business the more he desired to favor it."

The Roosevelt of 1882 wasn't bothered by such ambivalence, however: "I cannot believe that the Judge had any but corrupt motives in acting as he did in this case," he declaimed to the assembly. "He was in corrupt collusion with Jay Gould." The evidence of the investigation allowed no room for doubt. "There cannot be the slightest question that Judge Westbrook ought to be impeached." The truth was plain as day; the only question was whether the legislature would yield to it. "You cannot by your votes clear the Judge. He stands condemned by his own acts in the eyes of all honest people. All you can do is shame yourselves and give him a brief extension of his dishonored career. You cannot cleanse the leper. Beware lest you taint yourselves with his leprosy."

Roosevelt's vehemence availed little. The assembly ignored his motion and opted instead for the majority report by a margin of 77 to 35. Yet Roosevelt was righter than he knew in predicting that a failure to impeach would extend the judge's career only briefly. A few weeks later, amid reports that new evidence was being unearthed regarding his role in the Gould railroad heist, he was found dead in his hotel room in Troy. Circumstances suggested suicide, although no coroner confirmed the suggestion. ("He really got what he deserved," commented a hard-hearted reporter, who added: "And his death must come to us all as a lesson.")

VI

The Westbrook affair, after Roosevelt's tangle with Gould, earned him the support of many of his formerly skeptical colleagues. "He won his spurs in that fight," Isaac Hunt asserted. Hunt, among many, watched Roosevelt blossom in the legislature.

> He made me think of a growing child. You know you take a child and in a day or two their whole character will change. They will take on new strength and new ideas, and you can see them going right up the ladder. He would leave Albany Friday afternoon and he would come back Monday night and you could see changes that had taken place in him. New ideas had taken possession of him. He would run up against somebody and he got a new perspective in regard to matters.... He took on strength just like that.

Hunt added an impression of Roosevelt as he entered the rooming house where he often stayed while in Albany: "He would come into that house like a thunder bolt. He would swing the door open and he would be half way up the stairs before that door would come together again with a bang. Such a super-abundance of animal life was hardly ever condensed in a human life."

Roosevelt's energy compensated for certain other shortcomings. For someone who hoped to make a name in public office, he remained a distinctly unimpressive speaker. Roosevelt recognized his deficiency in this regard. Of an early effort he conceded, "It really was not much of a speech." For a time he memorized his addresses but then came to appreciate the drawbacks of this approach. He wrote his mother of a certain address he had given in which he hadn't forgotten a single line: "But I doubt if it really pays to learn a speech by heart; for I felt just like a schoolboy reciting his piece." He went on: "Besides I do not speak enough from the chest, so my voice is not as powerful as it ought to be."

Lack of power wasn't the only problem. As his friends had noticed in college, words came out of his mouth with some difficulty. "He was not a fluent speaker," recalled Isaac Hunt. "He never was. He spoke as if he had an impediment in his speech, sort of as if he was tongue-tied." Eventually Americans would get used to Roosevelt's clipped style of speech, which would become something of a trademark. But no one would ever characterize his style as smooth or pleasing. "I always think of a man biting tenpenny nails when I think of Roosevelt making a speech," journalist George Spinney remembered.

Yet as with all of his shortcomings, Roosevelt considered his lack of fluency a challenge to be overcome, and by the time the legislature adjourned in June 1882, he had reason to feel pleased with himself. Reformist papers continued to praise him; his friends and fellow Republicans held a dinner in his honor at Delmonico's. The evening's toast—"To Young New York"—could hardly have identified the young new champion of honest dealing more directly.

VII

After the whirlwind of the winter and spring, summer slowed the pace a bit and allowed the hero to put his personal life back in order. It did require a little reordering. A leisurely first year of marriage had given way to the helter-skelter of activity upon his entry into politics. He still missed Alice when she was gone, but he valued the extra time her absences gave him to do all he had committed to. "I am really glad you are away now," he wrote frankly during the autumn of 1881, "for I am so busy that I could not be any company atall for you." Yet when time allowed, he could be as affectionate as ever. "I so longed for you when I received your darling letter that I could hardly contain my desire to see you. . . . I care for nothing whatever else but you. I wish for nothing but to have you to love and cherish all the days of my life."

While the legislature was in session he had commuted weekly between the capital and the metropolis. Alice often accompanied him to Albany; this kept them together but often left her at loose ends. Not surprisingly, she looked forward to the legislature's adjournment.

June and July brought a long visit to Alice's family in Boston, with stops before and after at Oyster Bay. In September, Theodore and Alice joined Mittie, Corinne, and her recently acquired husband, Douglas Robinson, on a trip through the Catskills. The journey was principally for pleasure, and it served well enough. "Every day we play tennis and croquet," Roosevelt recorded, "and then we men go off for a long ride, and all of us go driving in the afternoon, generally in the democrat. In the evening the rest of the men smoke while I play whist with Mother, Alice and Pussy [Corinne]."

The other purpose of the trip was reconnaissance. Roosevelt found his first taste of politics enticing, and he thought about moving closer to Albany. Although the capital city itself held few attractions, the hinterland offered possibilities. Alice had been a good sport about shuttling up and down the Hudson, but if he made a career of politics, he would have to do better by her. A farm in the Washington Irving country might be just what was required. And at the same time that it afforded a home base for political activities, it could function as a retreat for his writing. Douglas Robinson had such a farm; Roosevelt and Alice could be his and Corinne's neighbors.

On the other hand, despite the favorable response to his first session in the legislature, Roosevelt wasn't yet sure that politics was truly his calling. If anything, his experience in Albany had reinforced his notions about politics being the refuge of scoundrels and other lowlifes; exceptions like Mike Costello and Billy O'Neill merely proved the rule. Whether there were enough exceptions to make a career in politics worthwhile was an open question.

As for literature, his *Naval War of 1812* wasn't exactly drawing crowds to the bookstores. Initial reviews were favorable but unenthusiastic, and sales weren't likely to supplant his inheritance. Although a writing career could be respectable enough, it didn't seem quite the thing for a young man brimming with energy, with a decidedly combative streak, and with a desire (albeit not entirely recognized yet) to make a mark on the world. Writing as a sideline would be fine but not as a primary occupation.

Roosevelt acknowledged his perplexity. "I hardly know what to do about taking a place up here," he told Bamie. "It would be lovely to have a farm, and fortunately Alice seems enchanted with the country. The only, or at least the chief, drawback is the distance from New York. Still, if I were perfectly certain that I would go on in politics and literature I should buy the farm without hesitation; but I consider the chances strongly favorable to my getting out of both—and if I intend to follow law or business I ought to stay in New York."

Law did remain a live option even if it wasn't kicking very vigorously of late. The opening of the legislative session in January had required his dropping out of Columbia; now he sought to recover the lost ground. "I have decided to study law in [Cousin] John's office during three or four days a week for the rest of the summer," he told his mother in July. And indeed he did dive into the cases recorded in his cousin's law library. Come autumn he would return to Columbia or continue by the reading route.

Business couldn't be dismissed entirely, either. Uncle Jim would certainly give him a try if he wanted a chance in the family firm. If he chose instead to strike out on his own, his inheritance would provide some start-up cash or the wherewithal to purchase an interest in an existing enterprise—perhaps a publishing house, which would work double duty as a source of income and an outlet for whatever further writing he did.

VIII

Yet politics had its claws in Roosevelt. His showing at Albany had made him the New York Republicans' hottest property in years, and they—at least those who shared his reform sentiments—weren't about to let him go. Not that he struggled to escape. Roosevelt craved excitement, and neither law nor business nor anything else on his horizon promised half the excitement of battling the bad men bent on subverting democracy to their corrupt and selfish ends. During the summer, away from the fray, he might reflect on the merits of a more staid and stable vocation; but come October and his return to the realm of Tammany and Morton halls, the pull of political combat drew him in once more. He hadn't been back in Manhattan two weeks before he was helping to organize the City Reform Club, a group designed to remedy what he called "the deplorable lack of interest in the political questions of the day among respectable, well-educated men—young men especially." By the end of October he had accepted renomination to the assembly.

This acceptance marked Roosevelt's first serious career move. When he had thrown his hat into the ring the previous year, it wasn't really his hat but a bowler borrowed from Joe Murray. Now he tossed in his own silk homburg. However unsavory and untalented he deemed some of his colleagues in the legislature, he couldn't deny that the political fisticuffs were the most fun he'd had since he first learned to fire a gun. On the evidence of one term he could hold his own with these bark-on types, and he took pleasure and pride in the fact. At the same time he could tell himself that a life in politics served the public good, and on those days when the admonitory shade of Theodore Sr. was hovering especially close, this argument may have been the more persuasive.

Yet despite his initial successes, Roosevelt's timing looked bad. Chester Arthur, a man of merits even his friends often had trouble discerning, became president after Garfield's assassination, and the Republican Party was in greater disarray than ever. Meanwhile, New York Democrats were falling into line behind Grover Cleveland. The recently elected reform mayor of Buffalo rated the label "ugly honest"; he was so upstanding that he alienated even his friends. New York voters, accustomed to a Democratic diet of Tammany venality, were thrilled at the change, and in the autumn elections swept Cleveland into the governor's mansion and a large majority of Democrats into the legislature.

Roosevelt bucked the Democratic tide, however. "All Hail, fellow survivor of the Democratic Deluge!" he wrote to Billy O'Neill, who did, too. "Down here such voting was never seen before. I carried my Assembly district by 2200 majority, the Republican Congressman by 700, and the Democratic Governor carried it by 1800 the other way!" Though pleased at the fact and size of his victory, Roosevelt had few illusions that he and his party mates would be able to accomplish much. "As far as I can judge the next House will contain a rare nest of scoundrels, and we Republicans will be in such a hopeless minority that I do not see very clearly what we can accomplish, even in checking bad legislation." But Roosevelt didn't discourage easily. "We will do our best," he promised.

Roosevelt's strong victory, following his inspiring performance the previous spring, made him a likely candidate to lead the Republicans in the assembly. Never one to hide his light under a bushel, he launched a bid for the Republican nomination for speaker—although he preferred to contend that he did so by default. He told one of his colleagues, in soliciting his vote against the candidate of the old guard: "I went in as nobody else seemed inclined to make the fight."

In immediate, practical terms, the nomination meant nothing. The two-to-one majority of Democrats in the assembly guaranteed that their nominee would win the speakership. Roosevelt was battling for a symbol without substance. Yet battle he did. "The fight is a very hot one," he reported to Alice from Albany. "My chances of winning seem about even, but the result is impossible to foresee." That Roosevelt understood his situation was plainly evinced by his next sentence: "I trust and hope that Chapin will get the Democratic nomination and the election."

Roosevelt's Republican rivals understood the situation as well as he did, and it was this fact that gave him his opening. The regulars had no reason to fight over an honorific. Let the young whippersnapper have his day and his say, they reasoned. Maybe he would talk himself to death.

Whatever the mix of motives, Roosevelt carried the nomination. As expected, he then lost to the Democratic nominee (Alfred Chapin, as Roosevelt hoped). Roosevelt ended up with no more power than before, but the recognition by his colleagues—however insincere some of them may have been—made a nice feather in that silk homburg.

IX

As a leader of the reform Republicans, Roosevelt should have sought common ground with Governor Cleveland, the leader of the reform Democrats. He eventually found himself on such ground, but he got there by accident and with a minimum of good grace. It wouldn't be the last time Roosevelt resisted someone who should have been an ally. Even at this early date he showed the egotism that would chronically compel him to denigrate almost anyone who competed with him for the limelight.

The 1883 legislative session brought its regular crop of "strike" bills, as pieces of extortionate legislation were called. The most striking this time around was a measure mandating reduction of fares on New York's elevated railways from ten cents to a nickel. Roosevelt waffled philosophically about the bill. On one hand, he sympathized with the train riders, most of whom needed the nickel far more than Jay Gould and the railroad monopolists did. On the other hand, he was enough of a Republican to worry about the precedent of such intrusion by government into private business. To confuse matters more, he knew that most supporters of the bill weren't real reformers but blackmailers hoping to be paid off for not voting the reduction; he hesitated to join such company. As things turned out, Gould and his operatives refused to meet the terms of the strikers, who brought a majority for the nickel fare. Roosevelt, weighing the various aspects of the situation, voted with the majority.

Cleveland, however, vetoed the bill. The governor approached the bill from the same direction as Roosevelt, albeit from a different party, but his calculation came out negative for the measure. He judged the bill unconstitutionally meddlesome into the private sector. Out-Republicaning Roosevelt, he threw his considerable weight against the bill.

This didn't end the matter, for the supporters had sufficient votes to override the governor's veto. Yet Cleveland's forceful veto message caused a few of the supporters to reassess their ayes. Among these was Roosevelt, who discovered himself in the uncomfortable position of having to take lessons in principle from someone else—and a Democrat to boot.

Roosevelt manfully admitted his mistake. "I have to say with shame that when I voted for this bill, I did not act as I think I ought to have acted, and as I generally have acted on the floor of this House. For the only time that I ever voted here otherwise than in the way I thought I honestly ought to, I did on that occasion. I have to confess that I weakly yielded, partly in a vindictive spirit toward the infernal thieves and conscienceless swindlers who have had the elevated railroad in charge, and partly to the popular voice of New York."

A more temperate individual than Roosevelt would have stopped there. A shrewder politician would have capitalized on his forced retreat to reach out to his rivals, to cast himself as a conciliator, to parlay his position as minority leader into indispensability to a Democratic administration often at odds with its own regulars. But Roosevelt was neither temperate nor shrewd. He was convinced that most of those who differed with him did so out of the meanest motives. "All the small curs—whether on the floor of the house or in the newspapers—are now howling at me," he told Alice. "And the hardest thing to stand is the complacent pity of the shallow demagogues who delight to see a better man than themselves stumble, or seem to stumble."

Roosevelt lashed out publicly at the small curs—and many other people besides—a few days later. The occasion for what was one of the most ill-considered speeches of his career was the failure of the full house to support a motion by the committee on privileges and elections to award a contested seat to Henry Sprague, one of Roosevelt's Republican allies. As a member of the committee, Roosevelt had seen evidence that convinced him of the validity of Sprague's claim; a 7 to 2 majority, including most of the Democrats on the committee, agreed. But the full assembly rejected the committee's advice and turned Sprague out.

Roosevelt couldn't contain his outrage at this blatant jobbery. "It would be farcical for me to waste my time any longer by remaining on the Committee of Privileges and Elections," he declared in highest dudgeon, "and I herewith tender my resignation from that committee." He castigated "the shameless partisanship and gross disregard of all right and reason" of the assembly Democrats in ousting Sprague, and he asserted that it was "simple folly" for anyone to try to act honestly and objectively in the face of such "blind and bitter partisanship." The future would surely bring more of the same from the Democratic majority, which had manifested clearly "that it is not going to pay the faintest earthly attention to justice or reason, that, with its narrow, purblind policy, it is going to grasp at once at the thing that is nearest to it, to try and put its fingers on what little amount of patronage and upon what little hold of office it can get, without reference to the justice of the case and without reference to the future effect upon itself." Some dozen Democrats had rebuffed their party's leadership and voted on the merits of the present case; to these Roosevelt granted the respect due "honest and manly men." But they were far too few. "Exactly as ten men could not have saved the 'cities of the plains,' so these twelve men will not save the Sodom and Gomorrah of the Democracy. The small leaven of righteousness that is within it will not be able to leaven the whole sodden lump of the Democracy."

Roosevelt's outburst brought him attention, but not the kind he wanted. Most veteran observers of the legislature accepted as part of the practice of majority rule the kind of stiff-arming that had thrown Sprague to the sidelines. The Democrats had run as Democrats and won; was it surprising that they now were acting like Democrats? Only a fool or an utter utopian would think otherwise. Moreover, regardless of Roosevelt's view of the Democrats' handling of the affair, it was exceedingly imprudent—not to mention downright offensive—to liken the Democracy to Sodom and Gomorrah. With the Democrats in the majority, it was the task of the Republicans—and, a fortiori, the leader of the Republicans—to make the best of being a minority. It was particularly foolish of Roosevelt to burn his bridges to the reform wing of the Democratic Party. Just a week earlier he had made what amounted to common cause with Governor Cleveland. Now, in denouncing the Democrats as a group, he was spitting in Cleveland's face.

Roosevelt's holier-than-thou attitude prompted one New York editor to jibe, "There is an increasing suspicion that Mr. Roosevelt keeps a pulpit concealed on his person." Another metropolitan daily called him "silly and sullen and naughty" for taking the position that if he couldn't have things his own way, he wouldn't play the game. This same paper reported that "when young Mr. Roosevelt finished his affecting oration, the House was in tears—of uncontrollable laughter." An Albany editor chaffed him for his habit of holding that all virtue rested with his side and all vice with the other. "Such a habit shows flippancy, prejudice and want of patriotism, as well as of execrable ignorance." This editor went on to advise: "Let him content himself with a becoming espousal of his own views and avoid patronizing those who agree with him and abusing those who do not. His limitations make him look ridiculous in both roles."

Such criticism would have stung anyone, and it certainly stung a self-important young man propelled too quickly to a position of leadership. Roosevelt later admitted that he had let success go to his head. He summarized his early political career to his son:

> Immediately after leaving college I went to the legislature. I was the youngest man there, and I rose like a rocket. I was re-elected next year by an enormous majority in a time when the republican party as a whole met with great disaster; and the republican minority in the house, although I was the youngest member, nominated me for speaker, that is, made me the leader of the minority. I immediately proceeded to lose my perspective, also [this "also" was a reference to an analogous setback to Ted]. Unfortunately, I did not recover it as early as you have done in this case, and the result was that I came an awful cropper and had to pick myself up after learning by bitter experience the lesson that I was not all-important and that I had to take account of many different elements in life.

Another ten years later he again looked back on this early period and elaborated on what this lesson implied:

Like most young men in politics, I went through various oscillations of feeling before I "found myself." At one period I became so impressed with the virtue of complete independence that I proceeded to act on each case purely as I personally viewed it, without paying any heed to the principles and prejudices of others. The result was that I speedily and deservedly lost all power of accomplishing anything at all; and I thereby learned the invaluable lesson that in the practical activities of life no man can render the highest service unless he can act in combination with his fellows, which means a certain amount of give and take between him and them.

Roosevelt also learned that the stump wasn't the same thing as the confessional and that though mea culpas may soothe the soul, they win few votes. His acknowledgment to the assembly of moral failure made him sound preachy, needlessly offending those who, in good faith, had sided with him the first time, without gaining him compensating favor from those who had sided against him. Meanwhile, both sides could, by quoting selectively, condemn him out of his own mouth. He would make mistakes again, but rarely would he own up to them, and almost never in public.

X

When the legislature adjourned in early May, Roosevelt couldn't get out of town fast enough. Summer brought its customary escape to Oyster Bay, where he and Alice walked some acreage he had recently purchased on a hill between the bay and adjacent Cold Spring Harbor, and envisioned the house they would build there. In June they again visited the Catskills. The decision to buy land on Long Island had also been a decision not to buy upstate; consequently, this time they were merely vacationers and not potential residents. Roosevelt found the traveling itself diverting enough, particularly the climb up Overlook Mountain, the steepness of which gave him an excuse to get out of the carriage and walk—while Alice rode and got sick from the swaying and jolting.

Their destination, a health resort, proved rather less satisfactory, to him if not to Alice. He arrived feeling fit and strong, but the director and custodians of the spa, aided by a patented elixir, quickly cured him.

> Under the direction of the heavily jowled idiot of a medical man to whose tender mercies Doctor Polk has intrusted me, I am rapidly relapsing. I don't so much mind drinking the stuff—you can get an idea of the taste by steeping a box of sulphur matches in dish water and drinking the delectable compound from an old kerosene oil can—and at first the boiling baths were pleasant; but, for the first time in my life I came within an ace of fainting when I got out of the bath this morning. I have a bad headache, a general feeling of lassitude, and am bored out of my life by having nothing whatever to do, and being placed in that quintessence of abomination, a large summer hotel at a watering place for underbred and overdressed girls, fat old female scandal mongers, and a select collection of assorted cripples and consumptives.

The resort didn't improve with time. "This place is monotonous enough to give an angel the blues," he wrote a week later. But Alice liked it, and he was willing to humor her.

All the while, however, he was plotting his escape. During the previous year he had encountered a naval officer named Gorringe, who had read Roosevelt's naval history and shared his views on the need for modernizing the American navy. They also shared an interest in hunting, and at one point Gorringe had recommended Dakota Territory as a splendid place to spend a few weeks shooting. The town of Little Missouri, on the river of the same name, would provide a good jumping-off point. The two men made plans to travel west together during the summer of 1883 and chase buffalo, antelope, and deer.

As matters transpired, other demands kept Gorringe from going, but at the beginning of September, Roosevelt took a train from New York to Chicago, then another across Illinois and Minnesota to Dakota. This was farther west than he had ever been, and with each mile past the 100th meridian he felt more in touch with the frontier. Bismarck struck him as "a typical frontier town of the northwest; go-ahead, prosperous, and unfinished." He continued on past Bismarck until, in the middle of the night, in the middle of a broad but steep-sided valley not far from the Dakota-Wyoming line, he got off the train.

Little Missouri wasn't much to look at even after day broke. Originally a hunter's camp at the edge of the Badlands, it had skulked around the fringes of civilization and the law. The arrival of the Northern Pacific in the 1870s had discomfited some of those inhabitants who had hoped never to see a sheriff's star again; others greeted the railroad with the same developmentalist mentality that settled the rest of the West. By 1883 a newspaper in the nearby (as distances on the frontier went; actually more than a hundred miles away) community of Dickinson described Little Missouri as positively vibrant.

> This town, situated in Pyramid Park on the banks of the Little Missouri River and surrounded by the Bad Lands with their fine scenery, is, at the present time, one of the most prosperous and rapidly growing towns along the line of the Northern Pacific. New buildings of every description are going up as fast as a large force of carpenters can do the work and an air of business and enterprise is apparent that would do honor to many an older town.

Little Missouri was riding one of the recurrent waves of boosterism that swept across the American West during the late nineteenth and early twentieth centuries; this particular swell was driven by the growing appetite of American cities for beef. A decade before, the northern plains had still been the domain of the buffalo and of the Indians who lived off the great herds. But the arrival of the rails from the East had doomed both. Hunters massacred the buffalo by the millions, depriving the Indians of sustenance; the U.S. cavalry, despite such momentary setbacks as Custer's defeat at the Little Bighorn, conducted mopping-up operations.

The blotting-out of the buffalo culture opened the plains to substitutes; the likeliest candidate was the cattle culture that was being transplanted north from the Texas borderlands. Only during the construction of the transcontinental railroads, and then largely by accident, did anyone discover that the southern-bred longhorns could survive the northern winters; this discovery, combined with the subsequent clearing of the buffalo herds, triggered a cattle rush to the oceans of grass in the North. Although the profits weren't so spectacular as those that attended gold and silver rushes, they were sufficient to excite the dollar lust of a variety of investors, and they drew capital from all over the world.

The largest portion of the foreign investment came from Britain, but in the case of Little Missouri the principal investor was Antoine de

Vallombrosa, the Marquis de Mores, a distant relative of former French kings. De Mores suffered from the chronic affliction of superfluous aristocracy: too much money and too little sense. Had he lived seven hundred years earlier, in the twelfth century, he probably would have sailed off to the Holy Land to reconquer Jerusalem; in the seventeenth century he would have taken up sugar-growing in the Caribbean. Now he was going to forge a bovine empire on America's last frontier.

Just a year older than Roosevelt, de Mores arrived in Little Missouri just a few months before him, in the spring of 1883. Having heard of the unparalleled opportunities awaiting investors of vision, he determined to corner the market in livestock that traveled the Northern Pacific east. He would slaughter and pack the meat, saving the freight charges to Chicago that the animals on the hoof incurred; passing his savings on to customers, he would multiply the millions he was prepared to sink into his project.

The scheme was absurd—but no more absurd than others that were making their authors rich all across the frontier and, indeed, throughout the booming American economy. And de Mores had one crucial advantage over most other dollar dreamers: deep pockets. The initial and unavoidable reverses that ruined many grand but undercapitalized projects would scarcely deflect de Mores's program. He spoke of many millions of dollars at his disposal; no one in Little Missouri was in a position to corroborate such sums, but he certainly spent like a multimillionaire. He established the Northern Pacific Refrigerator Car Company; when some potential competitors in Little Missouri refused to come to terms with him, he purchased several square miles of land on the opposite bank of the river and founded a rival community, Medora. Perhaps he would have done so anyway: His wife liked the idea of a town named after her—but no more than he liked the opportunity to play the feudal baron.

Medora remained in its infancy—a collection of tents, some small and hastily thrown together wooden structures, and a few half-finished buildings that might be impressive if ever completed—when Roosevelt arrived in early September. He knew next to nothing of its brief history and no more about its future prospects. What he saw when he woke up the next morning hardly inspired optimism. "It is a very desolate place," he informed Alice: "high, barren hills, scantily clad with coarse grass, and here and there in sheltered places a few stunted cotton wood trees; 'wash-outs,' deepening at times into great canyons, and steep cliffs of the most curious formation abounding everywhere."

But Roosevelt hadn't come for the scenery; he had come for the hunting. His primary goal was to add to his life list of animal trophies. He had never killed or even pursued anything as large and imposing as a buffalo, and, consequently, he had hardly finished breakfast before he began inquiring about buffalo guides. Gorringe had told him to look up a man named Moore who could find him someone reliable. Moore ran a hotel in Little Missouri and was usually outsiders' first contact; his son managed a store and knew everyone in town. The younger Moore recommended Joe Ferris, an employee who moonlighted as a guide. Ferris wasn't impressed with Roosevelt on first sight. Eastern dudes were common enough of late in these parts, but this one, with his pince-nez spectacles, his side-whiskers, his high-pitched voice, his abrupt gestures, and his unsettling intensity, seemed stranger than most. Ferris could easily imagine having to carry this one home on his back, fish him out of a stream, or rescue him from a dozen other self-inflicted mishaps. But the fellow offered hard money, and Ferris could always use the cash, so he consented to become his guide.

Although there weren't any buffalo left around Little Missouri, there might be a few upstream—which was to say, south. Moore and Ferris knew a man who had a place some forty miles south of town; the hunters could use that as their base of operations. Roosevelt and Ferris set out after reinforcing Roosevelt's arsenal with a borrowed buffalo gun and a replacement hammer for the Winchester rifle he had brought. The deeper they penetrated into the Badlands, the more striking the region seemed. Roosevelt described the "frightful ground" over which they rode. "There is very little water, and what there is, is so bitter as to be almost a poison, and nearly undrinkable; it is so alkaline that the very cow's milk tastes of it."

They reached the cabin of Gregor Lang late the following evening. Though the journey had been tiring, Roosevelt found his host, a Scottish immigrant, eager to talk, and the two stayed up past midnight discussing cattle ranching, hunting, politics, foreign affairs, and the human condition generally. At some point in the conversation this evening or one of the following, Lang let slip that he was the last of fifteen children in his family. Roosevelt thought this was marvelous. "I want to congratulate you, Mr. Lang," he declared (in the recollection of Lang's son, Lincoln, who was even more intrigued than his father by this unique guest and who lay in his bunk eavesdropping). "The first essential of progress is the perpetuation of the human race and I admire the men who are not afraid to propagate their kind as far as they may." Roosevelt also congratulated his host for naming his son after the Great Emancipator; when Gregor Lang related that the christening had caused a near mutiny in the family, he congratulated him a third time.

After talking until two, Roosevelt was up at dawn. The sky had lowered over the Badlands, and a steady rain was falling. Ferris suggested waiting out the weather, but Roosevelt, despite his regard for Lang's conversational skills, insisted on venturing forth. The buffalo had better judgment than the hunters—or at least than Roosevelt—and stayed well out of sight. All day Ferris kept hoping Roosevelt would realize the futility of the quest, but the damp and the mud, and the treacherous footing the latter produced, merely heightened Roosevelt's enjoyment. They spotted a deer, and Roosevelt got off a shot from two hundred yards but missed. Buffalo were nowhere to be found.

The next day brought more of the same. So did the day after and the day after that and the day after that. "I have been out a week now, nearly," he wrote Alice, "and though it is a good game country, yet, by Jove, my usual bad luck in hunting has followed." Envisioning their future home at Oyster Bay, he lamented, "I havn't killed anything, and am afraid the hall will have to go without horns for this trip at least."

Despite the lack of success, Roosevelt didn't for a moment consider calling off the hunt. Joe Ferris wished he would. Lincoln Lang afterward recalled Roosevelt's effect on his guide: "He nearly killed poor Joe. He would not stop for anything." Roosevelt couldn't see why he should. "I am now feeling very well," he wrote Alice, "and am enjoying the life very much."

During the evenings Roosevelt continued to talk cattle and ranching with Gregor Lang. Whether he was mining his host for information or employing him as a sounding board for his own ideas was a

matter of perspective: Roosevelt had a tendency to dominate any conversation he got into, and his questions, such as they were, frequently
took the form of statements his interlocutors were free to dispute—
just as he felt free to dispute theirs. Especially later in life, it was not
uncommon for Roosevelt to take up a discussion with an expert on
some subject and within minutes be explaining to that expert how
things stood in his field of expertise. Some observers interpreted this
as intellectual arrogance; Roosevelt saw it as the most efficient way of
testing his ideas.

During the course of his talks with Lang, Roosevelt crystallized the
idea that he wanted to become a cattle rancher. Not full time; he
would have partners who would handle the operation when he wasn't
around. But state politics in New York was a decidedly part-time
affair, with legislative sessions lasting less than six months. And the
cattle frontier, after the arrival of the railroad, was only a couple of
days' train ride from the East. Moreover, Roosevelt was bitten by the
same bug—or perhaps a smaller cousin—that injected dreams of
empire into the Marquis de Mores. Blessed with youth, energy, ambition, and the ready cash of his inheritance, Roosevelt wanted to take a
gamble on this last frontier. Who knew? Maybe if things went well
he'd eventually move to the West. The most recent political season
had demonstrated that what went up also came down. New York
wasn't the only place to practice politics. To be sure, Alice might
require some convincing to come west, but with the train and all, she
could travel frequently back to Boston and the East.

Roosevelt initially approached Gregor Lang to go in with him. "I
have definitely decided to invest, Mr. Lang," he told his host. "Will
you take a herd of cattle from me to run on shares or under some
other arrangement to be determined between us?"

Gregor Lang had overcome the initial puzzlement that Roosevelt
induced in most people and, as most people did, had grown to like
this unusual fellow. Yet he already had a contract with another man.

"That is exceedingly kind of you, Mr. Roosevelt," he replied. "And
I am more than sorry that I cannot see my way clear to accept, but
Pender is depending on me to carry this undertaking through and I do
not feel that I can disappoint him."

Lang's response disappointed Roosevelt even as it enhanced his respect for his host. So he asked him if he could recommend anyone else. Lang replied that Sylvane Ferris, the brother of Roosevelt's guide, and Bill Merrifield were reliable, resourceful men. When Roosevelt expressed interest, Lang sent his son Lincoln with the message that this easterner wanted to do business.

Awaiting a reply, Roosevelt resumed the hunt. Two days more of frustration—fun, by Roosevelt's estimate—followed. When Roosevelt and Ferris returned to Lang's cabin on the second day, Sylvane Ferris and Merrifield were there. Roosevelt pitched the project to them. They, too, had contractual obligations, managing a small cattle herd for an absentee owner. When they explained their situation, he offered to buy them out: contract, cattle, and kit. They said they'd have to go to Minnesota to talk to their employer, but they liked the idea.

They liked it even more when Roosevelt pulled out a checkbook and scribbled off a draft for fourteen thousand dollars. This was to cover their expenses, to buy a few hundred cattle beyond the 150 they were already managing, and generally to get the operation going. They were flabbergasted at Roosevelt's dash and decisiveness—and at his trusting nature. When they asked if he wanted a receipt, he replied that if he didn't trust them—whom he had known a total of several hours—he wouldn't be going into business with them. Decades afterward, Merrifield still wondered at the event. "We were sitting on a log up at what we called Cannonball Creek. He handed us a check for fourteen thousand dollars, handed it right over to us on a verbal contract. He didn't have a scratch of a pen for it." To which Sylvane Ferris added, "All the security he had for his money was our honesty."

After his two prospective partners set off, Roosevelt went back to his hunting. Finally, the weather broke for the better, and with it his hunting fortunes. Spotting a buffalo upwind, he and Joe Ferris tethered their horses and pursued it afoot. When they drew close enough for a shot, Ferris instructed Roosevelt to aim for a point just behind the beast's shoulder. Roosevelt got off one shot, then two more as the bull ran away up the far side of a ravine. Roosevelt and Ferris followed, uncertain whether the bullets had found the mark. But when they crossed the ridge top they discovered the buffalo lying on its side, "dead as Methusalem's cat," in Ferris's words.

If Roosevelt had been having fun before this, bagging a buffalo made him positively delirious. He whooped and shouted and danced a victory jig around his prize. "I never saw anyone so enthused in my life," Ferris recollected. Ferris had killed plenty of buffalo in his day, but even he was touched by Roosevelt's excitement. "By golly, I was enthused myself and for more reasons than one. I was plumb tired out, and, besides, he was so eager to shoot his first buffalo that it somehow got into my blood; and I wanted to see him kill his first one as badly as he wanted to kill it." Roosevelt had that effect on people. That he paid Ferris a hundred-dollar bonus on the spot didn't diminish the effect.

Roosevelt couldn't wait to tell Alice the wonderful news. "Hurrah!" he scrawled. "The luck has turned at last. I will bring you home the head of a great buffalo bull." A few days later he added, "This has been by all odds the pleasantest and most successful trip I have ever made. . . . Of course I am dirty—in fact I have not taken off my clothes for two weeks, not even at night, except for one bath in the river—but I sleep, eat and work as I never could do in ten years time in the city."

Roosevelt went on to tell Alice of his decision to invest in cattle. Doubtless anticipating skepticism—if not horror—he took pains to justify his action and put the best face on it: "The more I have looked into the matter—weighing and balancing everything, pro and con, as carefully as I knew how—the more convinced I became that there was a great chance to make a great deal of money, very safely, in the cattle business. Accordingly I have decided to go into it, very cautiously at first, and, if I come out well the first year, much more heavily as time comes on." Roosevelt conceded that no investment was foolproof. "Of course it may turn out to be a failure." But he didn't think it would, and in any case he was hedging his bet. "Even if it does I have made my arrangements so that I do not believe I will lose the money I put in." The beauty of the scheme was that it would solve the problem of how to make money while leaving him free to pursue politics or the literary life. More cautious minds might think he was risking too much. "Neither Uncle Jim, nor I am afraid, even Uncle Jimmie, will approve of the step I have taken." But he was going to do it anyway—subject, of course, to her approval. "My own darling, everything will be made secondary to your happiness, you may be sure."

Roosevelt left the Badlands feeling better, physically and emotionally, than he had ever felt in his life. He had once more proven himself in the field, and he had made additional progress toward figuring out what to do with his life.

His optimism was palpable and persuasive. As Roosevelt said farewell to the Langs and rode off for the railhead, Gregor Lang told his son, "There goes the most remarkable man I ever met. Unless I am badly mistaken the world is due to hear from him one of these days."

CHAPTER EIGHT

The Light That Failed
1883–86

Roosevelt had reason beyond those he told Gregor Lang for wanting to acquire a stake in the West; this same reason encouraged him to take extra care to soft-pedal to Alice the commitment and risk of his ranching venture. Namely, Alice was expecting a child.

When she discovered in July 1883 that she was pregnant, Roosevelt was predictably thrilled. As his remarks to Gregor Lang indicated, Roosevelt fully endorsed the traditional American ideal of large families. He believed that procreation was one of the highest of human obligations as well as a patriotic duty in a competitive world of expanding populations. And, theory aside, he simply thought children and family life were God's great blessings to humanity. The arrival of even a niece, nephew, or cousin excited him. "I could not write you a decent letter at first," he informed his cousin John and Nannie Roosevelt on learning of the birth of their child. "I was so 'knocked up' by the glorious news." Evidently Roosevelt and Alice had attempted to have children more or less from the start of their marriage, for when a couple of years passed with no luck in the matter, she consulted a physician. According to family tradition (handed down on the female side), Alice underwent some kind of surgery designed to facilitate conception. Perhaps the surgery succeeded; perhaps she would have conceived anyway. But the end result was that she learned she would bear a child sometime in February 1884.

Alice had long fussed over Theodore ("You must not dirty your new clothes or bite your handkerchiefs," she scolded in a typical note); now he had an excuse to fuss over her. He attended to her faithfully during the early autumn in Manhattan; when he returned to

Albany after reelection, he wrote regularly, sometimes twice a day, and with the greatest affection. "Darling Wifie," he called her as he kept her up on his affairs in the legislature. He characteristically closed: "How I long to get back to my own sweetest little wife!" Following weekends at home, he departed with growing regret. "How I did hate to leave my bright, sunny little love yesterday afternoon!" he avowed. "I love you and long for you all the time, and oh so tenderly; doubly tenderly now, my sweetest little wife. I just long for Friday evening when I shall be with you again." Alice suffered the usual pains and discomforts of pregnancy; he did his best to ease them when he was with her and offered moral support when he was away. "I wish I could be with you to rub you when you get 'crampy.'"

Roosevelt became concerned when Alice fell sick just as her due date drew nigh. The nature of her illness was hard to pinpoint, but Alice's doctor didn't deem it cause for alarm, especially since the baby wasn't in any apparent hurry to enter the world. "I don't think you need feel worried about my being sick," Alice wrote on Monday, February 11, "as the Dr told me this afternoon that I would not need my nurse before Thursday. I am feeling well tonight."

Alice was well enough to worry more about Theodore's mother than about herself. Mittie had contracted something virulent and wasn't improving. "Her fever is still very high and the Dr is rather afraid of typhoid," Alice said. If it was indeed typhoid, there was nothing to do but pray for the best. The doctor reassured Alice, who reassured Roosevelt, that typhoid wasn't contagious, at least not under the present circumstances. Alice promised to write the next day to keep Roosevelt apprised of the situation. She closed with a sentiment universal among women in late pregnancy: "I wish I could have my little new baby soon."

She got her wish the following day. At 8:30 on the evening of Tuesday, February 12, she was delivered of a girl weighing somewhat more than eight pounds. Roosevelt's aunt Anna assisted the doctor; on receiving the baby from the physician, she remarked, "You ought to have been a boy." Alice overheard the comment and defended her offspring: "I love a little girl."

The happy news was quickly telegraphed to Albany. Roosevelt was delighted. He accepted the congratulations of his friends in the assembly and passed out cigars. He tidied up some immediate business and prepared to head south to be with his wife and daughter.

But before he could leave, a second telegram arrived. Alice had taken a sudden turn for the worse. He must come home without the slightest additional delay.

Roosevelt habitually used his time on trains reading; now all he could do was stare out the window, silently berating the engineer for not opening the throttle more, begrudging each stop, and wondering if this trip would end like his emergency journey home from Cambridge just six years before. He finally reached Manhattan late on Wednesday, February 13; he leaped from the platform into a carriage and urged the driver to fly to the house on Fifty-seventh Street.

He was met at the door by Elliott. His younger brother was ashen with anxiety and fatigue; he declared, "There is a curse on this house." The curse was a double one. Mittie was burning up with the fever of typhoid, and there was nothing the doctors or anyone else could do. Alice was battling what the doctors described vaguely as Bright's disease, a kind of kidney failure. Quite likely Alice was suffering from undiagnosed preeclampsia, a hypertensive condition frequently associated with first pregnancies, that, if untreated, can wreak havoc on the kidneys.

Roosevelt spent the next sixteen hours at one bedside or the other. His heart drew him toward Alice, but his mother seemed to be slipping faster. And indeed she went first, succumbing in the darkest predawn hours of Thursday, February 14. Sleepless, Roosevelt climbed the stairs once more to Alice's bedside. His vigil there was longer but no more availing. In the early afternoon of the same day, Alice breathed her last.

The stunned, disoriented sensation he had felt upon his father's death now returned. He summoned the energy to inscribe a thick black X in his diary for February 14, followed by the single sentence: "The light has gone out of my life." Otherwise he was dazed and inconsolable. The double funeral brought out New York's most respected families, along with more recent acquaintances of Roosevelt's political career. But he hardly heard what anyone said; he scarcely knew what he himself did.

After the funeral he composed an epitaph for his bride.

Alice Hathaway Lee. Born at Chestnut Hill, July 29th 1861. I saw
her first on Oct [blank] 1878; I wooed her for over a year before I won
her; we were betrothed on Jan. 25 1880, and it was announced on Feb
16th; on Oct 27th of the same year we were married; we spent three
years of happiness greater and more unalloyed than I have ever known
fall to the lot of others; on Feb 12th 1884 her baby was born, and on
Feb 14th she died in my arms, as my mother had died in the same
house, on the same day, but a few hours previously. On Feb 16th they
were buried together in Greenwood.

He concluded: "For joy or for sorrow my life has now been lived
out."

II

As this last sentence suggested, Roosevelt believed he was simultaneously writing an epitaph to his own emotional life. To lose a spouse
is always hard; to lose a young wife in childbirth is harder still. For
Roosevelt it was even harder than that, since he lost his mother at the
same time.

But in certain respects it may have been the loss of his father, six
years earlier, that now made Alice's death so unbearable. Theodore
Sr.'s death had devastated Roosevelt briefly, depriving him of his role
model and confidant, but it hadn't crippled him emotionally. Although
Roosevelt withdrew from some of his social activities for a while, he
still found solace in the other members of his family, who felt the same
loss and could share his grief, and in friends, who lent emotional support even in the cases where entire empathy was impossible.

As a result, Roosevelt had remained very much alive emotionally.
Indeed, it was probably no coincidence that he fell so madly in love
with Alice just months after his father's death. To be sure, she had
charms that had nothing to do with Theodore Sr., but a reading of
Roosevelt's diary and correspondence suggests that, in addition to her
unique attractions, she served as an emotional replacement for his
father, a repository for the deep feelings that moved Roosevelt's
romantic, emotional soul. Like many people in love, Roosevelt wasn't

simply in love with his darling; he was also in love with the idea of being in love.

He had always been emotional, but he hadn't always known how to deal with his emotions. Literature was one acceptable avenue. Adventure tales appealed to his yearning for heroism, to his desire to feel himself striving toward great goals. His father's death had provided a different sort of outlet for his feelings. It was entirely proper, noble, and manly to mourn his father. And for month after month he did, pouring out his emotions in his diary and in letters to his family— even after he had resumed what to all outward appearances was his normal routine at college. Needless to say, his courtship of Alice was an appropriate channel for his emotions, and he really let the feelings flow. Even a reader thoroughly taken by the idea of romantic love can't help wishing, upon perusing his diary and letters for the months of his betrothal to Alice, that once in a while he'd cut the gush.

Then Alice died—suddenly, shockingly, just as his father had died— and all at once a part of Roosevelt's emotional life closed down. His first great loss had caused him to look elsewhere for the emotional sustenance he required, and he had found Alice. But now Alice had been torn from him, and he wasn't going to risk a third such loss. Better to keep those emotions locked tightly away. Soon after the funeral he deliberately distanced himself from everything having to do with Alice. He gave his favorite photograph of Alice—taken when she was fourteen—to his aunt Anna; he couldn't bear even to carry her picture. He refused to speak of Alice to anyone—a silence he maintained, with very rare exceptions, for the rest of his life.

Most tellingly, considering the importance he invested in family and children, he all but abandoned the daughter Alice had borne him. It may have meant nothing when he wrote in his epitaph to Alice that on February 12 "her baby" was born, rather than "our baby," but he certainly acted as though little Alice didn't belong to him. He placed the baby in the care of his sister Bamie and for the first few years of her life had next to nothing to do with her besides paying Bamie child support. Even afterward he never warmed to her the way he did to his other children.

The impact of Alice's death was obvious even to casual acquaintances. "He was a changed man," remarked Isaac Hunt, recalling Roosevelt's return to Albany after the funeral. "From that time on there was a sadness about his face that he never had before." Looking hard, Hunt detected the same "indomitable spirit" as earlier. "However, he never manifested it. He did not want anybody to talk to him about it, and did not want anybody to sympathize with him. It was a grief that he had in his soul."

And there it stayed. When Alice entered Roosevelt's life in 1878, she brought out an emotional side to his personality that had been latent and rudimentary until then. He fell helplessly in love with her, and although the first flush of infatuation eventually wore off, he remained smitten. When she died, he didn't simply put away his feelings for her; he walled off a wing of the emotional house in which he lived. He would marry again and become devoted to his second wife. He would overflow with paternal feelings for his children. But he would never again visit that part of his personality where he had courted Alice.

Paradoxically, perhaps—but such is the romantic temperament— Roosevelt's denial of the possibility of love, his denial of the emotional side of his personality, fit neatly into his romantic conception of life. After Alice's death, he vowed never to love again, to remain true to her memory, to hold the love he had shared with her and keep it pure and unsullied by other loves. Literature holds no more romantic character than the hero who cherishes the thought of his departed love until he is reunited with her after his own death. It was a role that appealed enormously to Roosevelt.

III

As he had after the death of his father, Roosevelt buried his sorrow in his work. Two days after the double funeral he wrote to a friend, "I shall come back to my work at once; there is now nothing left for me except to try to so live as not to dishonor the memory of those I loved who have gone before me."

It took an effort—and would have even without his personal tragedy. His reelection in November had been comfortable enough, although after the bad press he had received the previous spring, his margin of victory was much smaller than the year before, in an election that saw a stunning swing back to the Republicans. His relative weakness, and the fact that the leadership of a legislative majority meant more than the leadership of a minority, caused the old guard to mount an effort to depose Roosevelt from the top G.O.P. post in the assembly. Roosevelt campaigned hard to keep his job. He lobbied wavering members, traveled to their home towns, promised the vigorous kind of leadership they could be proud of, and constructed what he hoped would be a winning coalition. But his efforts fell short, and he landed with a thump.

Yet he did what he could with what he had. He investigated labor conditions in cigar-making; appalled at what he discovered, he backed a bill to outlaw sweatshop cigars. In no small part because of his efforts, the bill passed and Cleveland signed it. Unfortunately, the New York Court of Appeals, operating under the code of laissez-faire that eventually would provoke Roosevelt to some of his most controversial progressive proposals, invalidated the measure.

Meanwhile, he pursued another, separate investigation. Having introduced a bill to centralize authority in New York City in the office of the mayor, with the goal of making the municipal government more accountable, he sought to lay bare the corruption that made such a change in the charter necessary. The bosses, as expected, bent every effort to blunt the probe: delaying, complaining, obfuscating, prevaricating. Determinedly, Roosevelt kept after them, generating thousands of pages of testimony in hearings held over two months. A final roadblock—whether engineered by the bosses or merely the result of a bad staffing decision—arose when the counsel for the committee submitted a draft report that fell far short of what Roosevelt and the other committee members judged to be fair and necessary. With the final report due in less than forty-eight hours, the committee decided that Roosevelt must write it himself.

Better therapy for a grieving man couldn't have been prescribed. Rather than face another long night wrestling with his memories of Alice, he barricaded himself in his office with his notes, with the testimony of the investigation, with various reference materials, and with a supply of ink and paper, and began to write. He wrote past midnight, through the small hours of the morning, and on until dawn. He broke briefly for breakfast, then returned to his writing. When the assembly commenced business for the day, he carried his materials to his desk in the chamber. He stopped occasionally to address a comment to the house, only to take his seat again immediately and resume writing. There was no opportunity for revision; as he completed writing the pages, they were torn from his hand and sent off to the typesetter. Finally, he put down his pen, exhausted but done. The bound version soon returned from the printer. The committee examined it, found it satisfactory, and approved it just under the deadline.

IV

The political high point of Roosevelt's year was the 1884 Republican national convention. The party approached the presidential election of that year in two columns. One faction, the "Stalwarts," wanted to stick with Arthur; although it was hard to argue that Arthur was presidential, he was president, which was even better. The other faction, the "Half-breeds," plumped for James Blaine of Maine, a man of captivating presence and undeniable ability but also of dubious, or at least widely doubted, integrity. Roosevelt was hard-pressed to choose. He disliked Blaine for his dishonesty, yet liked still less Arthur and the swarm the president attracted—a swarm that included Roscoe Conkling. Whether Roosevelt drew a conscious connection between the Arthur-Conkling cabal and the death of his father is unknown; nothing in his diary or surviving letters reveals that he did. Yet Roosevelt made unquestionably clear that he couldn't stand the Stalwarts.

With a small but significant company of Republican reformers, Roosevelt initially backed Senator George Edmunds. Actually, although Edmunds was a good man and might have made a decent president, Roosevelt's backing was less an endorsement of the Vermont lawmaker than a rebuke to the party regulars in Albany. When the Republicans met at Utica in late April to select delegates to the national convention, Roosevelt cannily employed Edmunds's candidacy to manipulate the balance between the Arthurians and the Blainesmen. With neither side willing to grant the victory to the other, the convention chose four at-large delegates to the national convention, in addition to those committed to the front-runners. Roosevelt headed the uncommitted slate.

Roosevelt relished his victory, modest as it was. According to at least one recollection, after he gained his seat at the national convention, he turned to Warner Miller, a Blainesman and one of those behind Roosevelt's defeat for the speakership the previous December and now a U.S. senator, and shook his fist, saying, "There! We beat you for what you did last year!"

At the same time, Roosevelt suffered no illusions that he had won anything more than he had. "The result of the Utica convention was largely an accident," he wrote to Henry Cabot Lodge, a casual acquaintance from Boston who was becoming a political ally. "Chance threw in our way an opportunity such as will never occur again; and I determined to use it for every ounce it was worth."

During the next month Roosevelt labored to strengthen the independents' position at the national convention. He bad-mouthed Blaine to such editors as would listen; simultaneously, he tried to keep Arthur from forging ahead. When he heard that the delegates from Massachusetts were leaning toward the president, he dashed off a warning to Cabot Lodge: "For Heaven's sake don't let the Massachusetts delegation commit any such act of suicidal folly as (from panic merely) supporting Arthur would be." He judged Blaine "the most dangerous man" and decried his "decidedly mottled record"; on the other hand, Arthur was "the very weakest candidate we could nominate." Winning wasn't everything, but it wasn't nothing—and with Arthur, it wouldn't happen. "Arthur could not carry New York, Ohio or Indiana; he would be beaten out of sight."

At the beginning of June, Roosevelt and thousands of other Republicans traveled to Chicago for their quadrennial conclave. Despite the advantages of incumbency, a distinctly funereal atmosphere pervaded the convention hall and spread to the hotel corridors and suites where the real business of the party was conducted. (The atmosphere would have been even more funereal if the conventioneers had known what Arthur knew but wasn't telling: that he was dying. This went far toward explaining why he wasn't campaigning as hard as he might have.) The party regulars recognized, though most weren't prepared to admit, that political success is often self-limiting. In feeding at the public trough, certain of the victors invariably hog more than their share, creating dissension in the ruling coalition.

Meanwhile, defeat and hunger create cohesion among the outs, fostering a unity sufficiently lasting to get them back into office. By 1884 the cycle of swilling, on the Republican side, and deprivation, on the Democratic, had reached the point where it took no genius to forecast that the Republicans would splinter while the Democrats would rally around a single candidate. A few diehards hoped to coax one more victory out of the old formula of the bloody shirt and the feed bag; against the odds, they had managed to do so in the two most recent presidential contests. But this only lengthened the odds against a third such stroke.

For their part, Roosevelt and his fellow independents hoped against hope to head off the inevitable by reforming the party from within. They saw that Arthur had no chance to win the general election, and Blaine almost as little. A reform nominee, one unsullied by the corruption that blighted all the regulars—a nominee like Senator Edmunds—would demonstrate the party's devotion to integrity and principle. Of course, in their candid moments, Roosevelt and the reformers admitted that such a man as Edmunds stood next to no chance of becoming the nominee—machines weren't machines for nothing. But the independents had to make the effort if only to distance themselves from the debacle to follow.

Roosevelt certainly did his best to distance himself. When, as part of the opening business, Lodge placed the name of Thomas Lynch, an anti-machine man from Mississippi, in nomination for temporary chairman of the convention, Roosevelt immediately leaped onto a chair and seconded the nomination. From that moment until the final vote he never stopped expounding principles, stalking delegates, plotting strategy, answering reporters, and broadly making his presence felt.

His heroics were futile. Blaine led Arthur on the first ballot, followed by Edmunds and sundry lesser candidates who divided up the remaining votes. On the second and third ballots those remaining votes leaked toward Blaine, who went over the top on the fourth ballot.

The result disappointed Roosevelt even if it didn't surprise him. "The fight has been fought and lost," he told Bamie. "And moreover our defeat is an overwhelming rout. Of all the men presented to the convention as presidential candidates, I consider Blaine as by far the most objectionable, because his personal honesty, as well as his faith-fulness as a public servant, are both open to question." There was no gainsaying, however, that Blaine was the choice of the convention—which was a sobering thought. "That such should be the fact speaks badly for the intelligence of the mass of my party, as well as for their sensitiveness to the honesty and uprightness of a public official, and bodes no good for the future of the nation." It was enough to make Roosevelt wonder—not for the last time—about democracy. "It may be that 'the voice of the people is the voice of God' in fifty-one cases out of a hundred; but in the remaining forty-nine it is quite as likely to be the voice of the devil, or, what is still worse, the voice of a fool."

Roosevelt defended his support of Edmunds as consistent with the judgment of the best element of the party. "It included all the men of the broadest culture and highest character that there were in the con-vention; all those who were prominent in the professions or eminent as private citizens; and it included almost all the 'plain people,' the farmers and others, who were above average, who were possessed of a keen sense of personal and official honesty, and who were accustomed to think for themselves."

If Roosevelt's allies were of the angels, his opponents—Blaine's backers—were a decidedly different sort.

> Their ranks included many scoundrels, adroit and clever, who intend to further their own ends by supporting the popular candidate, or who know Mr. Blaine so well that they expect under him to be able to develop their schemes to the fullest extent; but for the most part these Republicans were good, ordinary men, who do not do very much think-ing, who are pretty honest themselves, but who are callous to any but very flagrant wrongdoing in others, unless it is brought home to them most forcibly, who "don't think Blaine any worse than the rest of them," and who are captivated by the man's force, originality and bril-liant demagoguery.

The convention marked Roosevelt's first personal exposure to national politics, and many of the people he encountered impressed him greatly. The nominating speech for Edmunds, delivered by John Long, the Massachusetts governor (and later Roosevelt's boss at the Navy Department), was "the most masterly and scholarly effort I have ever listened to." The lead speech for Blaine was even more pow-erful, in a different way:

Blaine was nominated by Judge West, the blind orator of Ohio. It was a most impressive scene. The speaker, a feeble old man of shrunk but gigantic frame, stood looking with his sightless eyes towards the vast throng that filled the huge hall. As he became excited his voice rang like a trumpet, and the audience became worked up to a condition of absolutely uncontrollable excitement and enthusiasm. For a quarter of an hour at a time they cheered and shouted so that the brass bands could not be heard at all, and we were nearly deafened by the noise.

Although his candidate had ultimately lost, Roosevelt took pride in his own role in Chicago. Referring to Blaine, he told Bamie, "About all the work in the convention that was done against him was done by Cabot Lodge and myself, who pulled together and went in for all we were worth. We achieved a victory in getting up a combination to beat the Blaine nominee for temporary chairman. . . . To do this needed a mixture of skill, boldness and energy, and we were up all night in arranging our forces so as to get the different factions to come in to line together to defeat the common foe." This victory hadn't been achieved easily. "Many of our men were very timid; so we finally took the matter into our own hands and forced the fighting, when of course our allies had to come into line behind us."

The strategy called for Roosevelt to give a short speech, which, he boasted, "was listened to very attentively and was very well received by the delegates, as well as the outsiders." Impressed by his own performance, he added, "It was the first time I had ever had the chance of speaking to ten thousand people assembled together." In this spirit, he asked Bamie to look into getting copies of the New York papers—the *Times, Sun,* and *Post,* in particular—for the week of the convention. "I would like to see them."

V

Roosevelt might have clipped the papers himself except that he was headed in the opposite direction. Even while the Blainesmen were toasting their triumph, he boarded a train for Dakota. Within twenty-four hours he was in Little Missouri.

It doubtless was meaningful that after having closed his diary on the day of Alice's burial with the words "For joy or for sorrow my life has now been lived out," and having made no more entries during the next four months, Roosevelt reopened his journal on June 9. "Arrived at my cattle ranch (Chimney Butte Ranch) on the Little Missouri." Roosevelt's late winter and spring had been filled with political activity, but nothing that registered emotionally. Only after he reached the frontier—at a time, perhaps not coincidentally, when wildflowers sprayed the prairies with color and the new shoots of the cottonwoods greened the bottoms of the coulees—did he come alive again. What his long-term plans were when he reached the ranch, or whether he had any, is unclear. He definitely didn't intend to return to the New York legislature in the autumn. His political life in the assembly was too closely connected in memory to his married life with Alice; he had never known Albany without her. She had been at his side when he entered politics; she had endured the monotony of too many hotel nights and train days; she had shared his satisfaction when he smote the bosses and his frustration when they outmaneuvered him. He might eventually return to the scene of those fights, but not before time had eased the ache of her loss.

Something else was involved in Roosevelt's decision to leave the assembly. After his taste of national politics—of devising strategy with Lodge and others from different states, of taking on the party heavyweights at the Republican convention—Roosevelt was reluctant to return to the lighter division in Albany. It had been good training, but after a few rounds against the big boys in Chicago, he was ready to move up a division or two.

When his next bout would occur was an entirely open question. For the present, ranching would be his principal occupation. "I have been having a glorious time here, and am well hardened now," he wrote to Bamie after a week at the Chimney Butte. "I have just come in from spending thirteen hours in the saddle. For every day I have been here I have had my hands full. First and foremost, the cattle have done well, and I regard the outlook for making the business a success as being very hopeful. This winter I lost about twenty-five head from wolves, cold, etc., the others are in admirable shape, and I have about a hundred and fifty-five calves. I shall put on a thousand more cattle and shall make it my regular business."

The ranch life certainly agreed with him. "I have never been in better health than on this trip. I am in the saddle all day long either taking part in the round-up of the cattle, or else hunting antelope." The surroundings were magnificent. "The country is growing on me, more and more; it has a curious, fantastic beauty of its own." He was taking full advantage of it. "As I own six or eight horses I have a fresh one every day, and ride on a lope all day long." Such a life could cure anyone of cares and afflictions. "How sound I do sleep at night now!"

In late June he took off on a solitary jaunt across the prairie. "For the last week I have been fulfilling a boyhood ambition of mine—that is, I have been playing at frontier hunter in good earnest, having been off entirely alone, with my horse and rifle, on the prairie." As usual, he was testing himself. He explained to Bamie: "I wanted to see if I could not do perfectly well without a guide, and I succeeded beyond my expectations." Although the hunting left something to be desired—he had missed many shots—the experience was especially soothing to the soul. "I felt as absolutely free as a man could feel; as you know I do not mind loneliness; and I enjoyed the trip to the utmost." The weather was as gorgeous as the scenery. "Every night I would lie wrapped up in my blanket looking at the stars till I fell asleep, in the cool air. The country has widely different aspects in different places; one day I would canter hour after hour over the level green grass, or through miles of wild rose thickets, all in bloom; on the next I would be amidst the savage desolation of the Bad Lands, with their dreary plateaus, fantastically shaped buttes and deep, winding canyons."

Fortified by this experience, Roosevelt embarked on a more ambitious hunting trip: to the Big Horn Mountains of Wyoming. He had never skimped when outfitting himself for hunting—or anything else, for that matter—and he didn't skimp now. His hunting costume couldn't help causing snickers along the Little Missouri. "I wear a sombrero, silk neckerchief, fringed buckskin shirt, sealskin chaparajos or riding trousers; alligator hide boots." Being well accoutered gave him a feeling of confidence. He added, "With my pearl hilted revolver and beautifully finished Winchester rifle, I shall feel able to face anything." Bill Merrifield came along as guide, fellow hunter, and companion, while "an old french halfbreed named Lebo" drove the supply wagon, cooked the meals, and managed camp. The wagon carried several changes of Roosevelt's clothing, including foul-weather gear; generous quantities of flour, bacon, beans, coffee, sugar, and salt (though a sartorialist, Roosevelt was no epicure); a modest supply of brandy and "cholera mixture"; five guns, and seventeen hundred rounds of ammunition. Two horses pulled the wagon; four ponies took turns carrying the hunters.

The party scouted its way into Montana, making anywhere from zero to thirty miles per day, depending on the weather, the "wheeling" (ease of travel of the wagon), and the game. From the start Roosevelt was enamored of the company he was keeping. "Lebo is a chatty, tough old plainsman, full of expedients, and ready with the wits and hands," he wrote. "Merrifield is a good looking fellow, who shoots and rides beautifully; a reckless, self confident man." A few days later they encountered a cowboy from whom Roosevelt purchased a horse to supplement their remuda; they followed him to his ranch and met his fellows. "Cowboys are a jolly set; picturesque, with broad hats, loosely knotted neckerchiefs, flannel shirts, leather chaparajos."

Late summer on the plains brought a breathtaking array of weather. Most days were hot and dry, but the sky could change in a minute. When it did, simple survival supplanted other considerations. "One day we rode through a driving rain storm, at one time developing into a regular hurricane of hail and wind, which nearly upset the wagon, drove the ponies almost frantic and forced us to huddle in a gully for protection. The rain lasted all night and we slept in the wagon, pretty wet and not very comfortable. Another time a sharp gale of wind and rain struck us in the middle of the night, as we were lying out in the open (we have no tent) and we shivered under our wet blankets till morning."

Roosevelt and Merrifield shot all kinds of birds and small mammals, but the climax of the trip came when Roosevelt got his first grizzly.

> I saw Merrifield, who was directly ahead of me, sink suddenly to his knees and turn half round, his face fairly ablaze with excitement. Cocking my rifle and stepping quickly forward, I found myself face to face with the great bear, who was less than twenty-five feet off, not eight steps. He had been roused from his sleep by our approach: he sat up in his lair, and turned his huge head slowly towards us. At that distance and in such a place it was very necessary to kill or disable him at the first fire; doubtless my face was pretty white, but the blue barrel was

steady as a rock as I glanced along it until I could see the top of the bead fairly between his two sinister looking eyes; as I pulled the trigger I jumped aside out of the smoke, to be ready if he charged; but it was needless, for the great brute was struggling in the death agony, and, as you will see when I bring home his skin, the bullet hole in his skull was as exactly between his eyes as if I had measured the distance with a carpenter's rule.

In this letter to Bamie, Roosevelt acknowledged the therapeutic purpose—and effect—of the trip: "I have had good sport; and enough excitement and fatigue to prevent over much thought; and moreover I have at last been able to sleep well at night." Yet he recognized that the effect couldn't last forever. "Unless I was bear hunting all the time I am afraid I should soon get as restless with this life as with the life at home."

VI

Restless he was, and he had no sooner returned to the Chimney Butte than he boarded a train for the East. By now the 1884 presidential campaign was setting new standards for scurrility. The Democrats lambasted the Republican candidate's character; a common jingle ran: "Blaine, Blaine, James G. Blaine, continental liar from the state of Maine." When the Republicans delighted to discover that Democratic candidate Grover Cleveland had fathered a child out of wedlock, they returned a taunt of their own: "Ma, ma, where's my pa?"

The principal uncertainty in the campaign was the effect of the bolt of a sizable minority of Republicans unhappy with Blaine's nomination. These mugwumps (so called, as wags had it, because their mugs were on one side of the fence and their wumps on the other) included many people Roosevelt had collaborated with in supporting George Edmunds. Not surprisingly, the mugwumps urged Roosevelt to join them.

If Roosevelt's decision on seeking reelection to the New York assembly in 1882 had been his first career move, his decision on the Blaine nomination in 1884 was his second. He had fled the Chicago convention in such haste not simply because he wanted to kill antelope and bears but because he needed time to think about what he should do. His instinctive reaction was to continue opposing Blaine. Just hours after Blaine's selection he told a comrade at the convention, Horace White, that any proper Democratic nomination should have the support of honest Republicans; he made clear that he included Cleveland in this characterization.

But he soon changed his mind. Within ten days he was telling Cabot Lodge to "keep on good terms with the machine, and put in every ounce to win." He couched his reasoning in terms of Lodge's political career, but certain of his remarks might as easily have applied to his own: "I am very anxious you should take no steps hastily, for I do not know a man in the country whose future I regard as so promising as is yours; and I would not for anything have you do a single thing that could hurt it, unless it was a question of principle, when of course I should not advise you to hesitate for a moment."

Roosevelt's actions soon revealed that he didn't consider the Cleveland-Blaine contest a matter of principle. As much as he had blasted Blaine, now he attacked Cleveland. "Certainly the Independents have little cause to congratulate themselves on a candidate of Cleveland's moral character," he told Lodge. He added that the New York governor's veto of a recent reform bill was "inexcusable."

Yet try as he might, he couldn't work up any enthusiasm for Blaine. Announcing to a reporter that he intended to vote Republican in November, he launched into a Hamlet-like soliloquy on the alternatives confronting a person such as himself. "A man cannot act both without and within the party; he can do either, but he cannot possibly do both. Each course has its advantages, and each has its disadvantages, and one cannot take the advantages or the disadvantages separately." Grasping at a military metaphor, he went on: "It is impossible to combine the functions of a guerilla chief with those of a colonel in the regular army; one has greater independence of action, the other is able to make what action he does take vastly more effective. In certain contingencies the one can do most good, in certain contingencies the other; but there is no use in accepting a commission and then trying to play the game out on a lone hand."

Roosevelt didn't deny having opposed Blaine; he was proud of the fight he had made. But he pointed out that he couldn't have fought as effectively as he had if he had not been known as a solid party man.

He had been defeated in a fair fight and would abide by the party's decision. "I did my best and got beaten; and I propose to stand by the result." He reaffirmed his attachment to the party: "I am by inheritance and by education a Republican; whatever good I have been able to accomplish in public life has been accomplished through the Republican party; I have acted with it in the past, and wish to act with it in the future."

Roosevelt's retreat enraged the mugwumps. One, Henry Lee (who happened to be Alice's uncle), muttered to Owen Wister: "As for Cabot Lodge, nobody's surprised at him; but you can tell that young whipper-snapper in New York from me that his independence was the only thing in him we cared for, and if he has gone back on that, we don't care to hear any more about him."

Roosevelt responded defensively. "Most of my friends seem surprised to find that I have not developed hoofs and horns," he told Lodge. Having learned the hard way that repentance in politics rarely paid, he now exhibited the corollary: When attacked, hit back. "I have replied with vivacity or ferocity, according to the circumstances of the case." E. L. Godkin and Arthur Sedgwick of the *Evening Post* had taken Roosevelt to task for abandoning his principles; he told Lodge he had asked a mutual friend to relay the message that "they were suffering just at present from a species of moral myopia, complicated with intellectual strabismus."

When Horace White published his account of Roosevelt's late-convention statement in favor of Cleveland, Roosevelt vehemently denied making any such statement—and then eviscerated his denial by explaining that even if he had, he had done so in the passion of the moment and shouldn't be held accountable. "At midnight, two hours after the convention had adjourned, when I was savagely indignant at our defeat, and heated and excited with the sharpness of the struggle, I certainly felt bitterly angry at the result, and so expressed myself in private conversation. . . . But I fully realized that I did not wish to commit myself in the excitement of the moment, and therefore positively refused to say anything in public or to any newspaper until I had carefully considered the matter."

For a time Roosevelt considered retreating to Dakota for the duration of the campaign. But his combative spirit wouldn't let him be content bearding grizzlies in their dens; he had to go after Democrats and mugwumps as well. October found him addressing the Young Republican Club of Brooklyn—chosen for the speech because, as he put it, its members were men "who have won for themselves so honorable a name for their upright and fearless independence, and who have yet had the good sense to show that, though Independents, they are emphatically and distinctly Republicans, and that they mean to reform and not to destroy the party to which they belong."

VII

Roosevelt took to the stump several more times. He never found anything good to say about Blaine, so he concentrated on speaking ill of Cleveland and the Democrats, whom he likened to murderers, armed robbers, and burglars. He went to Massachusetts to campaign for Cabot Lodge, who was running for Congress. Lodge was a safe choice for Roosevelt: a Republican in good standing, yet one of independent mind and reformist persuasion.

And also one destined to lose. On election day Lodge ran second by a hair—as, by a larger margin, did Blaine. The presidential result divided the Republicans even more deeply than the contest had, with the regulars not illogically laying the blame at the feet of the mugwumps. Roosevelt had spent the weeks just before the election reattaching himself to the regulars, and now he spent the week after the election reaffirming that reattachment. "Here everything is at sixes and sevens," he told Lodge from New York. "I shall be happy if we get clear without bloodshed; thanks to the cursed pharisaical fools and knaves who have betrayed us."

Roosevelt went on to say that he was retiring from political life, in all likelihood permanently. "I have not believed and do not believe that I shall ever be likely to come back into political life; we fought a good winning fight when our friends the Independents were backing us; and we have both of us, when circumstances turned them against us, fought the losing fight grimly out to the end." Roosevelt looked backed phlegmatically on the chapter just finished. "Blaine's nomination meant to me pretty sure political death if I supported him; this I realized entirely, and went in with my eyes open. I have won again and again; finally chance placed me where I was sure to lose whatever I did; and I will balance the last against the first. I have stood a great deal; and now that the throw has been against me, I shall certainly not complain."

Roosevelt may actually have believed that his political career was over; but if he did, this merely showed how little he knew himself. For Roosevelt—hardly alone among men of action—self-knowledge was an elusive commodity. He was better at doing things than understanding why he did them.

Yet a certain self-knowledge slipped in the back door, and the agent of the surreptitious entry was Cabot Lodge. For Roosevelt, Lodge served as an alter ego, but one step ahead of him on life's path. Eight years older, Lodge for much of their two careers was where Roosevelt was aiming to be. Lodge won a national political reputation before Roosevelt; his literary career, as a nationalist historian of the United States, similarly set a standard for Roosevelt to try to match. In certain respects Lodge became the older brother that Roosevelt never had. In other respects he was the confidant that Theodore Sr. had been. From the moment the two men commenced collaboration in the spring of 1884, and continuing for most of the thirty-five years until Roosevelt's death, they carried on a regular and frequent correspondence. In this correspondence Roosevelt revealed much about his hopes, fears, ambitions, and dreams. Often the revelations appeared between the lines, but in such cases the lines were usually generously spaced.

Thus when Roosevelt, following the November 1884 election, counseled Lodge to interpret his loss as a setback rather than a defeat, he could have been speaking about himself. "Of course there seems to be no use saying anything in the way of consolation," Roosevelt wrote, revealing precisely how he would have felt under the same circumstances. "And probably you feel as if your career had ended"— again, just what Roosevelt was feeling. However: "That is not so: you have certainly received a severe blow; but you would be astonished to know the hold you have on the party at large; not a man I know in New York have I seen (Republicans I mean, of course) who does not feel the most bitter indignation at your defeat." This didn't apply to Roosevelt directly, but he hoped something like it did. "They will never forget you and come back in time you must and will."

VIII

So would Roosevelt, as he must have hoped, regardless of what he was saying. Yet, impetuous though he was, he understood that he must bide his time patiently until his next political opportunity. With Roosevelt, patience never implied inactivity, merely a change of venue. In this case he returned to Dakota, where his empire in miniature was under construction. Since his initial meeting with Bill Merrifield and Sylvane Ferris in the cabin of Gregor Lang in September 1883, he had increased his play in the cattle business. Merrifield and Ferris had succeeded in breaking their previous contract, and they soon went to work for Roosevelt. They lived at the Chimney Butte ranch and tended the initial herd through the winter of 1883–84. Aiming to expand operations by at least another thousand head, Roosevelt cast about for a second property to acquire. Opportunity brought the Elkhorn ranch, some forty miles north—that is, down the Little Missouri—from the Chimney Butte.

The new property required new hands, and Roosevelt thought of Bill Sewall of Maine. His old hunting guide wasn't conspicuously unhappy at Island Falls, and Roosevelt recognized that he'd have to make him an attractive offer. He began by sending Sewall a check for three thousand dollars to pay off his mortgage, thus freeing him to leave Maine. Then he described the essentials of the proposition: "I have arranged matters in the west, have found a good place for a ranch, and have purchased a hundred head of cattle, for you to start with." Finally, the challenge:

> If you are afraid of hard work and privation do not come west. If you expect to make a fortune in a year or two, do not come west. If you will give up under temporary discouragements, do not come west. If on the other hand you are willing to work hard, especially the first year; if you realize that for a couple of years you can not expect to make much more than you are now making; and if you also know that at the end of that time you will be in the receipt of about a thousand dollars for the third year, with an unlimited rise ahead of you and a future as bright as you yourself choose to make it; then come.

Sewall did come, bringing his nephew Wilmot Dow; both were eventually joined by their wives. The Maine woods were a rather different ecosystem than the northern Great Plains, and the two men required time to discover their niche. Dow noted dubiously that the only real riding he had done had been on logs floating down rivers; half-broken broncos were a new challenge. Without casting doubt on Roosevelt's respect for the character and abilities of Sewall and Dow, one can't help wondering if their very lack of expertise at the tasks of ranching encouraged Roosevelt to invite them west. He had never considered himself an especially good rider even on the trained and familiar mounts of the East; on the wild ponies of Dakota he was a genuine greenhorn. His partners Merrifield and Ferris got a good laugh out of their boss's equine difficulties. Ferris, especially, prided himself on being able to ride anything on four legs; when some cantankerous animal would refuse to yield to Roosevelt, Ferris would climb aboard and bring it under control, usually with a comment like, "Why, there's nothing the matter with this horse; he's a plumb gentle horse." Roosevelt took the ribbing good-naturedly—not that he had much choice—but it must have occurred to him that it would be nice not to be the only novice on the Little Missouri. As always, Roosevelt measured himself against his comrades; he wasn't the kind to accept lightly always coming up short.

Yet even if Sewall and Dow weren't much on horseback, they had other gifts. They swung mighty axes, a skill that they soon turned to good use. Roosevelt's purchase of the Chimney Butte ranch brought him title to the herd and presumptive grazing rights; the house and outbuildings still belonged to Merrifield and the Ferris brothers. Consequently, Roosevelt chose to establish his headquarters on the Elkhorn. The cabin there was hardly adequate for one man let alone three men and two women, so he set Sewall and Dow to work building a new house. The construction material was cottonwood logs from the trees that grew in the river bottom. Compared to wrestling horses and cows, this was recreation for the Mainers. Roosevelt lent a hand, but his efforts provided moral support rather than much substantive assistance. Roosevelt told a story on himself of a neighbor asking Dow how the tree-falling was going. Dow, not realizing that Roosevelt was within earshot, replied, "Well, Bill cut down fifty-three, I cut down forty-nine, and the boss, he beavered down seventeen." Dow's verbs were well chosen: A woodsman cut trees cleanly and efficiently; an amateur generated a pile of chips that would have embarrassed a beaver.

During that first winter, the time of year when the herds needed little tending, the Elkhorn ranch house went up. It was a large, rambling structure with kitchen, dining area, quarters for the Sewalls and Dows, and a bedroom and study for Roosevelt. In time he brought out a bathtub, rocking chair, desk, books, and sundry other artifacts of civilization. The veranda provided a view out across the river to the hills beyond. Occasionally, Roosevelt shot dinner from his front porch, but most of the time he contented himself with watching the cattle, admiring the scenery and the wildlife, and merely being master of his small slice of the West. In winter, roaring fires kept the cabin warm—if not all the rooms, at least those closest to the hearths and stoves. Although the wildlife was scarcer during the winter, the landscape was more open, the light sharper, and the vista grander than ever. Then Roosevelt could particularly relish his role in helping tame the West.

Except that he never spent much of the winter in Dakota. Even that first year he left after scarcely a month back, returning to New York before Christmas and remaining there for three months. The fact of the matter was that Roosevelt never became more than a part-time rancher. He made a point of participating in the exciting and challenging activities of cowboy life: the cattle drives, the roundups, the branding. But the boring parts—riding the line looking for strays, repairing tack and fences, waiting for the weather to warm up—which composed most of the cowboys' weeks and years, he generally left to Merrifield, Ferris, Sewall, and Dow. Like the gentleman he was, he would either go off on a hunting expedition or return to his home in the East.

In certain respects Roosevelt must have seemed to his Dakota neighbors almost as aristocratic as the Marquis de Mores. For both, ranching was a hobby rather than the serious business it was to most of the ranchers. On the other hand, like every other hobby Roosevelt engaged in, he threw himself into this one. At roundup time he rode as long and as hard as anyone, never shrinking from his turn on the night picket or complaining when storms and stampedes kept him in the saddle for thirty or forty hours at a stretch. He never impressed any of the real cowboys with his talents at riding, roping, or branding, but they all came to respect his tenacity and courage.

He had sufficient opportunity to demonstrate these qualities. The country around Little Missouri in the mid–1880s was a relatively lawless land on a day-to-day basis. The closest sheriff was responsible for a territory the size of Connecticut, and the nearest federal marshal had his hands full keeping order in his home base of Deadwood, the rowdy mining camp two hundred miles to the south. Justice was therefore an ad hoc affair. A man who insisted on his rights, reasonably construed, usually went unmolested after a test or two to confirm that he really did insist. The meek, on the other hand, while they might inherit the earth, wouldn't find their inheritance in western Dakota.

And earth—or land, rather—was precisely the source of most disputes in that vicinity. Though still a frontier territory, Dakota was filling up fast, not with people yet but with cattle, and anyone could see that the region could support only so many cattle. The early settlers worried that newcomers would crowd the range, doing harm to all. Accordingly the old-timers often tried to discourage the arrivistes.

In 1884, Roosevelt found himself squarely in the latter category, and he became the object of attempted discouragement. Sewall and Dow had barely begun chopping logs for the house at the Elkhorn before they received a visit from a party of men associated with de Mores. The leader of the group was a reputed killer named Paddock, hired for the purpose precisely on account of his reputation. Paddock warned Sewall—Dow being briefly absent—that he should tell their boss his cattle were trespassing on range that by rights belonged to the marquis. Roosevelt might purchase grazing rights for a substantial sum; otherwise, he must clear out.

This exchange occurred while Roosevelt was off hunting grizzlies; as soon as Sewall gave him the message on his return, he decided to confront the issue directly. Paddock had been bragging about town that he was going to shoot the dude from New York the first chance he got. Roosevelt calculated that the roughneck couldn't be more dangerous than a grizzly, and after checking his rifle and revolver to make sure they were still in working order, he rode to Paddock's place at the edge of town. He hammered on the door of the cabin and demanded that the occupant come out. He said he had heard that Paddock was threatening gunplay; well, he was ready for the shooting to start. Paddock, who evidently had hoped that threats would suffice to scare the newcomer off, didn't want to tangle with this well-armed and obviously determined fellow. He explained that there had been a misunderstanding; he had been misquoted.

Paddock didn't bother Roosevelt after that, and as word of the incident passed around the small community, few of its other inhabitants did, either. Occasionally, however, someone dropped in who didn't know about the new man and mistook his unusual appearance for weakness or lack of resolve. One such incident gave rise to another bit of Roosevelt lore, recounted in various versions over the years by people who were there, who had it from someone who was there, or who imagined they had been there. The ruffian in question, several shots of cheap whiskey beyond best behavior, spied Roosevelt one night in a bar. "Four-eyes!" he roared. Smitten by his own cleverness, he repeated the epithet and declaimed to all present that "Four-eyes" was going to treat the house. Roosevelt initially attempted to laugh off the affront as the drunken inanity it was, but the bully persisted. Roosevelt recalled:

> He stood leaning over me, a gun in each hand, using very foul language. He was foolish to stand so near, and, moreover, his heels were close together, so that his position was unstable. Accordingly, in response to his reiterated command that I should set up the drinks, I said: "Well, if I've got to, I've got to," and rose, looking past him. As I rose, I struck quick and hard with my right just to one side of the point of his jaw, hitting with my left as I straightened out, and then again with my right. He fired the guns, but I do not know whether this was merely a convulsive action of his hands or whether he was trying to shoot at me. When he went down he struck the corner of the bar with his head. It was not a case in which one could afford to take chances, and if he had moved I was about to drop on his ribs with my knees; but he was senseless.

Roosevelt learned the value of soft talk combined with strong action in this incident; he also learned to stay out of saloons and barrooms, and made such avoidance a regular practice.

On another occasion he had to confront a scoundrel who challenged him in a different way. Mike Finnegan had a bad reputation, even for the Badlands, and one March day, following an afternoon of alcoholic high jinks in town, he and two friends took Roosevelt's rowboat for a ride down the Little Missouri. The boat itself wasn't worth much trouble, but Roosevelt had his reputation to consider, and summoning Sewall and Dow, he determined to set off in pursuit of his property and those responsible for its removal. To lend an air of official respectability to the chase, he had himself named a deputy sheriff.

A stretch of foul weather—"furious blizzard," in his diary—and the need to build a new vessel gave the thieves a substantial head start. But after several days on the water, Roosevelt and his companions hove within sight of the rowboat-rustlers' camp. They quickly got the drop on the lone man there, who told them that the other two were out finding dinner. Keeping a sharp eye and a rifle on the man, the posse took cover to await the return of the others. Their capture occasioned no more resistance, though substantially more sputtering and swearing, than the first man's. Roosevelt chuckled in his diary over the thieves' "absolute surprise" at being captured so far from the scene of such a small crime.

Had he been less attached to the forms of justice than he was, Roosevelt might have administered punishment on the spot, as others in that part of the world often did. He would have spared himself considerable trouble if he had done so. As it was, he now had to escort the prisoners the hundred miles to Dickinson. The first part of the journey was by the river, but ice kept blocking the way, and eventually Roosevelt left Sewall and Dow with the boats and struck out overland. He hired a wagon, and while the three prisoners rode, he walked behind, his Winchester at the ready. With no one to share the watch—and with the weather so cold he couldn't in conscience bind the prisoners lest their limbs freeze—he stayed up at night; to keep himself awake he read *Anna Karenina*.

"I was glad enough to give them up to the Sheriff this morning," he wrote Corinne from Dickinson, "for I was pretty well done out with the work, the lack of sleep and the strain of the constant watchfulness." Yet as with most things he did, this effort produced its own recompense. After visiting a doctor for treatment of his sore feet, he pronounced himself "brown and as tough as a pine knot" and feeling "equal to anything."

IX

His memory of the frontier code of justice would color Roosevelt's approach to international affairs, which were, in their own way, as lawless and anarchic as the affairs of the wild West. His Dakota days influenced his approach to domestic politics as well. Among other things, ranching made Roosevelt into a conservationist. As his tangle with Paddock demonstrated, the potential for overstocking the range weighed constantly on the minds of the ranchers of the plains. Had Roosevelt been content to run only those cattle that came with the Chimney Butte and Elkhorn ranches, no one would have bothered him; but when he moved to multiply their numbers by five or ten times, importing a thousand new head, the neighbors had to complain. Their complaints carried no force of law, however, because none of the complainants owned the land in question. (This was why de Mores and Paddock resorted to attempted intimidation.) With minor exceptions, all grazed their herds on public land, to which no one west of Washington held legal title. On the open range it was first come, first served, a principle that invited abuse. Without putting the matter in so many words, all involved understood that they faced the dilemma of the commons, where each individual's pursuit of self-interest, in the form of grass for more of his cattle, threatened the ruin of all, in the form of degradation of the range and a massive dying off. Only by some concerted action, some self-denying compact, could the community avert the disaster.

Roosevelt addressed this issue not long after facing Paddock down. In other parts of the cattle country, ranchers had formed stockmen's associations to deal with overgrazing and other shared concerns; on his return to Dakota following the 1884 elections, Roosevelt set about creating just such an organization for the Little Missouri region. For weeks he rode from ranch to ranch talking up the need for a cattlemen's group. His canvassing paid off, and in mid-December the first meeting of the Little Missouri Stockmen's Association convened at Roberts Hall in Medora. As instigator, Roosevelt brought the meeting to order; the ranchers in attendance, who included the most influential men of the area, immediately made him president and charged him with writing a constitution for the organization. The charter members discussed such issues as cattle rustling and disease, the protocol for branding strays, and the necessity for improving the herds by importing breeding bulls. As recounted in the *Bad Lands Cowboy*, a recently established local paper, "the utmost harmony and unanimity prevailed." All attending appeared well pleased with their two hours' work and agreed to meet again in April.

Roosevelt's education as a conservationist continued during the following months. The day after the stockmen's meeting he left Medora for his wintering grounds in the East. While there, besides drafting the association's constitution, he wrote an account of his hunting expeditions on the plains and in the mountains. Compared to his *Naval History,* this kind of writing required little effort or thought, consisting chiefly of personal observations supplemented by a modest amount of research in similar writings by other hunter types. *Hunting Trips of a Ranchman,* as he called the book, began with a scene-setting chapter on the Badlands. Roosevelt waxed descriptive and at times poetic about the Dakota countryside ("In the early spring, when the young blades first sprout, the land looks green and bright; but during the rest of the year there is no such appearance of freshness, for the short bunch-grass is almost brown, and the gray-green sage-bush, bitter and withered-looking, abounds everywhere, and gives a peculiarly barren aspect to the landscape"), about ranch life ("The charm of ranch life comes in its freedom and the vigorous open-air existence it forces a man to lead"), about the cowboys ("Sinewy, hardy, self-reliant, their life forces them to be both daring and adventurous, and the passing over their heads of a few years leaves printed on their faces certain lines which tell of dangers quietly confronted and hardships uncomplainingly endured"), and about numerous other people, places, and events he had encountered. Roosevelt was sufficiently authoritative in tone and sufficiently imprecise in detail that the casual reader might easily have mistaken him for a veteran of many years on the plains rather than a tyro whose total time on the frontier amounted to several months.

Yet that tone, if not entirely earned, gave the story an undeniable robustness and charm. So did Roosevelt's handling of his own exploits. He made himself the hero of the tale, but a hero with endearing imperfections. He recited his failures—clumsy chases, missed shots—as well as his successes. In the final chapter he related his encounter with "Old Ephraim," the anthropomorphized grizzly bear. He tossed off an aside, given without authority, that the popular impression that the species derived its name from its grizzled color was wrong. "The name of this bear has reference to its character and not to its color, and should, I suppose, be properly spelt grisly." He added with studied matter-of-factness that in hunting grizzlies steady hands counted for less than steady nerves. "A bear's brain is about the size of a pint bottle; and any one can hit a pint bottle offhand at thirty or forty feet." Without carrying on about the matter, Roosevelt gave the reader enough information to realize that thirty or forty feet was dangerously—indeed almost foolishly—close to such a formidable beast. By way of justification he cited a Viking saying (doubtless remembered from one of his childhood sagas): "If you go in close enough your sword will be long enough."

Roosevelt's book entered a publishing field crowded with similar accounts of frontier adventures. While some other authors had to hunt for publishers with almost the same tenacity as they pursued the big game of the mountains, Roosevelt avoided the problem by the neat expedient of having purchased an interest in a publishing house. In 1884, before leaving New York for the West, he signed a partnership contract with G. P. Putnam's Sons, the house that had issued his *Naval History.* His twenty-thousand-dollar investment guaranteed him a share of the firm's profits for three years—and presumably a home for whatever books he authored during that time.

His new book had a small first run of five hundred copies and drew modest notice. Yet among those who noticed was the editor of *Forest and Stream* magazine. George Grinnell gave the book a vigorous review, liking the project as a whole but taking exception to some of Roosevelt's flimsier generalizations regarding certain game animals and the conditions of their lives. Roosevelt responded to the review with a visit to the New York offices of *Forest and Stream,* where he began a series of conversations with Grinnell. At first he defended his interpretations, but as he recognized Grinnell's greater experience and authority as a hunter and observer of nature, he dropped his guard and commenced picking Grinnell's brain. Grinnell was older than Roosevelt and had been traveling in the West longer; he knew that the hunting that so thrilled Roosevelt in the mid–1880s was a thin remnant of what it had been merely a decade before when the game had been far more plentiful. In these conversations Grinnell helped convince Roosevelt—who didn't need much convincing—of the need for measures to protect the game species from further destruction and eventual extinction.

With the zeal of the new convert and with the same brashness that had impelled him to organize a stockmen's association in his first season as a rancher, Roosevelt badgered his friends about helping him start a conservation club. They required longer to respond than the ranchers, but the following year he opened his house to the charter meeting of the Boone & Crockett Club. A principal purpose of the club, manifested in various activities over subsequent decades, was the conservation of large game animals and their habitat.

X

Shortly after completing the manuscript of *Hunting Trips,* Roosevelt returned to Dakota. Having renewed his acquaintance with Cabot Lodge during the winter, he kept his Massachusetts friend apprised of his adventures on the frontier. "Tomorrow I start for the roundup," he wrote on May 15. "And I have just come in from taking a thousand head of cattle up on the trail. The weather was very bad and I had my hands full, working night and day, and being able to take off my clothes but once during the week I was out." A postscript apologized for illegibility: "Writ in a cowcamp; I fear that my calligraphy harmonizes with the environment."

Roosevelt couldn't well boast of his accomplishments as a cowboy to the likes of Merrifield and Ferris, who wouldn't have been impressed, so he boasted to Lodge. "I have been three weeks on the roundup," he wrote three weeks later, "and have worked as hard as any of the cowboys; but I have enjoyed it greatly. Yesterday I was eighteen hours in the saddle—from 4 A.M. to 10 P.M.—having a half hour each for dinner and tea. I can now do cowboy work pretty well."

Roosevelt's correspondence with Lodge covered more than his saddle sores; it also served as a link to the political world he had ostensibly left behind. Roosevelt regularly remarked on political developments back across the Missouri. In March 1885 he described the current situation in national politics as "the Apotheosis of the Unknown" but granted that with a couple of exceptions President Cleveland's cabinet choices were "respectable." He went on to reassure Lodge that the two of them had done the honorable thing the previous autumn by sticking with their party even when their friends and allies urged them to make a break. "If our consciences would have permitted it I have not the slightest doubt that by bolting we could have done an immense amount for ourselves, and would have won a commanding position—at the cost, perfectly trivial in true Mugwump eyes, of black treachery to all our warmest and truest supporters and also at the cost of stultifying ourselves as regards all of our previous declaration in respect to the Democracy."

At some level of Roosevelt's intelligence, conscious or otherwise, he must have recognized the nonsensical nature of the major part of this statement. Sticking with the Republicans was patently a tactic of expediency, not principle, however much Roosevelt might protest to the contrary. To have bolted would have left him a man without a party. The Democrats would never have accepted one who had said so many nasty things about them, and the Republicans would never have trusted him again—as they never again trusted the mugwumps. Roosevelt figured this out during his cooling-off period after the Chicago convention, which was why he had swallowed his words and backed Blaine.

Yet once again Roosevelt demonstrated his ability to convince himself that the expedient thing was the principled thing. In many other people this would have appeared as hypocrisy, which is precisely how his critics interpreted it in him. But hypocrisy implies a self-knowledge that Roosevelt lacked. In his case, self-delusion was a more accurate description of his mental state.

Events soon suggested that Roosevelt hadn't done himself much harm at all by remaining faithful to the Republicans. Although small game by national political standards, he was a prize specimen by the standards of the Dakota frontier. He had hardly arrived in Little Missouri before Dakotans with big plans began boosting him for Congress once Dakota received statehood. Since that happy day was still a distance off (it actually arrived in 1889), Roosevelt could be flattered without committing himself.

In the spring of 1885 some reformist Republicans from back home sounded him out about a return to New York politics. For a man who had all but announced his permanent retirement six months earlier, he replied in a surprisingly available, if somewhat coy, tone. "I really have not given a single thought to my taking a place on the state ticket this fall," he answered one confidential query. "I shall let you know at once if such an idea enters my head; but I don't think it at all probable unless for some reason it should seem best to outsiders."

This enigmatic reply didn't elicit a groundswell of enthusiasm for a draft-Roosevelt movement, but neither did it rule out a return to the state of his birth in the profession of his first choosing. Within two weeks he received an offer of an appointive position in the administration of New York City, as president of the Board of Health under Mayor William Grace. He hesitated briefly before turning it down. A man might do good work in such a post, but it wasn't quite what he had in mind after his taste of the national limelight in Chicago.

His New York admirers were persistent, however. Several months later Grace again dangled the health-board job before him. Again he was tempted; again he temporized. Before he made a final decision, another opportunity arose. Respectable Republicans, including Elihu Root, forwarded his name as a candidate to succeed Grace. The offer of the party's nomination was an honor of sorts, but only of sorts. The Democrats had already fielded a strong candidate, Abram Hewitt, a businessman with the backing of Tammany but also of much of the city's commercial community. Radical reformer Henry George had announced as an independent; he would appeal to many of the mugwumps. Reckoning the odds against Republican success, Root himself had already refused the nomination.

But Roosevelt accepted. Party loyalty figured in his decision, as, no doubt, did an understanding that while a couple of refusals might make him more attractive to political suitors, if he kept saying no much longer, he would wind up an old maid. "I took the nomination with extreme reluctance," he told Fanny Smith, his college friend, who had written inquiringly, "and only because the prominent party men fairly implored me." He understood what he was getting into. "There is no chance of success"—although he took care to add, "This you must be sure not to breathe as coming from me." After all, if there had been a chance of success, Root or someone else would have grabbed the nomination before it ever came his way. "The best I can hope for is to make a decent run."

In fact, he made more than a decent run. He hurled himself into the contest against Hewitt and George with as much energy and determination as he had recently been throwing himself at cattle and bears. His blood rose as he mounted the stump once more, and, egotist that he was, he found it far more satisfying to be battling on his own behalf than for someone else. At Cooper Union he pounded one fist into another as he declaimed to the packed house, "There is need of reform, radical reform, in the City Hall." At this a man in the audience shouted, "That's what we want." Roosevelt replied, louder than before, "That's what you'll get." To another gathering he reaffirmed his Republican regularity but averred that it would not cause him to overlook any wrongdoing. Getting carried away in the heat of the moment, he promised, "Though I am a strong party man, if I find a corrupt public official, if he were the most prominent politician in the Republican party, I would take off his head."

But the circumstantial handicaps were too great. He ran third in the three-way race, albeit a respectable third. As was becoming his habit, he read malevolence and baseness into the motives of those who opposed him. "I have made a rattling canvass, with heavy inroads on the Democratic vote," he told Lodge. "But the 'timid good' are for Hewitt. Godkin, White and various others of the 'better element' have acted with unscrupulous meanness and a low, partisan dishonesty which would disgrace the veriest machine heelers."

Insightful Roosevelt watchers interpreted the result of the election, after the obvious gusto with which he fought the campaign, less as a defeat than as a sign that the cowboy might be soon hanging up his spurs. Had they read his mail they would have felt their interpretation confirmed. Roosevelt told Lodge that he wasn't through with his enemies. "May Providence in due season give me a chance to get even with some of them!"

CHAPTER NINE

From the Little Missouri
to the Potomac
1886–89

There was another sign pointing in the same direction, for those in a position to read it. After a season in the wilderness, love once more had entered Theodore Roosevelt's life.

It caught him quite by surprise—unlike the first time. Falling in love at twenty hadn't been a question of whether but of who; if Alice hadn't stolen his heart, someone else would have—Annie Murray or Nana Rotch or Bessie Whitney or Fanny Smith or someone else. The loss of his father had primed him to form a deep emotional attachment to someone; his personality and prospects made him a very eligible young man; and the circumstances of his social life placed him in nearly constant contact with young ladies likewise eligible.

The second time around was different. Alice's death had been even less expected than his father's, and the blow had sent him reeling once more. It left him hesitant and apprehensive about forming other such close attachments; with life so uncertain, how could one risk that kind of pain again? Alice's death also left him torn and confused about his rights and responsibilities, emotional and otherwise. His abandonment of baby Alice certainly preyed on his mind. He could rationalize leaving her with her aunt, contending that his busy life afforded him little time for tending to a small child, that the Dakota frontier was no place for an infant, that Bamie could provide Alice a far more stable and nurturing environment than he could, that in any case he was furnishing financial support for the baby.

These were all valid reasons, but they don't account for the extent of his lack of interest in the child. He almost never spoke of her in his

193

letters; aside from perfunctory visits to Bamie's home in Manhattan and one trip to Boston to let her grandparents see her, he made next to no effort to include her in his life. Quite evidently—and not unnaturally—he couldn't think of her without thinking of her mother, especially since there was a growing physical resemblance between mother and daughter. Roosevelt was still actively suppressing his memories of the elder Alice (as he ever would); this almost required that he avoid the younger Alice. At some level he probably blamed baby Alice for her mother's death. Consciously, of course, he would have resisted any such bald formulation: Alice's death had been bad luck and perhaps God's will but not little Alice's fault. Yet at a deep emotional level he understood that if not for the baby, the mother wouldn't have died.

One shouldn't place too much weight on this kind of reasoning if only because in those days death in childbirth was much more common than it would be a century later. It was a fact of life that required no elaborate explanation. At the same time, though, Roosevelt's aloofness, almost repulsion, from his only child does require explanation, and this seems as likely as any.

Whatever the explanation, Roosevelt did display strange and dysfunctional behavior around little Alice. The most striking example was his refusal to tell the girl anything about her mother. "He never ever mentioned my mother to me," Alice recalled many years later. "He never even said her name, or that I had a different mother [from Roosevelt's other children]." Alice added, with an emotion the years had hardly diminished, that her father's actions in this regard were "absolutely wrong." So complete was Roosevelt's denial of the elder Alice that he refused to call the baby by her given first name. Rather than "Alice," he referred to her as "Baby Lee."

Roosevelt's pathological reticence had unfortunate effects on Alice that would manifest themselves as she grew up; it also had unhappy consequences for Roosevelt himself. In contrast to his time of mourning for his father, when he poured out his feelings in his diary and in his letters, and was surrounded by friends and family, his mourning for Alice was barren and incomplete. He shut up and shut off those feelings, speaking and writing almost nothing of them. Instead, he channeled his emotional energy into politics in Albany and Chicago, and subsequently into hunting and ranching in Dakota. But politics and ranching were poor substitutes for honestly confronting his feelings, and although time diminished the pain, the emotional wound, like a broken bone unset, was never allowed to heal completely.

Denying his emotions didn't make Roosevelt less emotional, of course, nor did the suspension of close emotional attachments make such attachments less necessary to his psychological well-being. Consequently, when the opportunity arose for forming another such attachment, he leaped at the opportunity with an alacrity that astonished himself and those who knew him best.

The circumstances surrounding Roosevelt's courtship of Edith Carow are shrouded in mystery. Some of the mist was his doing, some hers. "I utterly disbelieve in and disapprove of second marriages," Roosevelt told Bamie even after his own was imminent. "I have always considered that they argued weakness in a man's character." He especially disbelieved in second marriages so soon after the death of the first spouse—divorce being essentially out of the question. For Roosevelt, weakness of character was the cardinal sin, the source of all evil. To see such weakness in himself was mortifying. He certainly wasn't about to broadcast the occasion of his mortification, and so he kept his courtship of Edith as quiet as possible.

Edith had different reasons for obscuring the circumstances of her coming together with Roosevelt. She confronted the perennial problem of the second wife, intensified by the particulars of her special case. She couldn't help feeling that she was Theodore's second choice. She had been as eligible as Alice and apparently as interested in him, but he had chosen Alice for reasons that were as obvious to Edith as to anyone else. Alice was prettier and had a sunnier personality; her charms were those that would win any young man's heart. Edith had her gifts, but they weren't of that romantic sort—as evidenced by the fact that she remained unmarried in 1886, a veritable spinster at the age of twenty-five.

Not only that but Alice's death enshrined her memory for Roosevelt. Alice would never grow old; she would always be twenty-three; she would forever be Theodore's blooming bride. Edith was already older than Alice would ever be, nor was she as fair. She would grow older and less fair. Edith might help Theodore mend a heart broken by death, but she could never claim the heart as it had been before its breaking.

Eventually Edith would spin a web of concealment around the circumstances of her early relationship with Theodore. She would have had to be more than human not to want to put the best face on ambiguous circumstances—to protect the feelings of her and Theodore's children if not just her own. An era that insisted on lifelong commitments disposed her to present theirs as a love that was not merely a replacement for a lost love but one ordained from youth and destined to defeat the diversions and distractions thrown in its way.

The reticence and obfuscation of the principals makes it impossible to reconstruct the romance in any detail, but its general outlines are clear enough. From a few months before meeting Alice in the autumn of 1878 until about two years after her death, Roosevelt saw little of Edith Carow and communicated with her hardly at all. In 1886, revealing the news of his engagement to Edith to a surprised Bamie, Roosevelt referred to a falling-out that they had had: "Eight years ago she and I had very intimate relations; one day there came a break for we both of us had, and I suppose have, tempers that were far from being of the best. To no soul now living have either of us ever since spoken a word of this." What the break involved, Roosevelt never said; as noted earlier, Edith afterward asserted that he had proposed marriage and she declined. Again as noted, this seems improbable, for his diary, which he was keeping religiously at the time, records not a hint of anything so serious.

More likely Edith and Theodore got into a row during the summer of 1878 about one thing or another of merely modest significance; this then escalated—both of them indeed possessing the tempers he spoke of and a reluctance to disengage from a tussle—with the exchange of sharp words and mutual avowals to have nothing to do with each other. By the time they cooled off, Roosevelt was back at Harvard, swept up in the social whirl of his junior year. He often confessed that he hardly had time to think about his dear, recently departed father; still less did he pine for a difficult girl he still often looked on as his younger sister's friend. Then he met Alice, who quickly banished any remaining thoughts of Edith from his mind. Edith, on the other hand, being more attuned to emotional nuance than he and in any case having less on her social calendar, may well have brooded over the break and invested it with more importance than he did. But because she was also proud and reserved, she, too, said nothing about it.

Had Alice lived, that would have been the end of that. For a period after Alice's death Roosevelt seems to have avoided Edith, or perhaps she avoided him. He remembered her for her moodiness, and amid his other emotional troubles he probably preferred not to have to deal with her. He may have expected her to make some sharp remark about his ranching venture. Most of his other acquaintances thought he was at least mildly unhinged in sinking so much of his inheritance in the cattle business; he didn't need to have Edith add her criticism. As for her, she had no desire to be thrown into contact with the man who had spurned her for another woman—however she may have been reconstructing events in her mind.

And then, apparently quite by accident, they bumped into each other at Bamie's house in September 1885. They spoke briefly. He found her more agreeable than he remembered; doubtless several years had matured and mellowed the teenager he had known. She had always been old for her age; the adult that had been trapped inside the child had now come into her own. The years had also improved her appearance: Her squarish face with the strong jaw, which had seemed simply plain among the coquettes who caught the eye of the college boys, had acquired a handsomeness that suited her sober personality.

As for Roosevelt, besides being a recognized political figure and a published author, he, too, was better looking than he had been. She had known him as a skinny, frail youth; now he was robust and brimming with energy, hardened and bronzed after a spring and summer in the Badlands, and carried himself with the self-assurance he always derived from recent acts of physical prowess. A reporter for the *Bismarck Tribune* caught Roosevelt on the train crossing Dakota east. "You've never talked with Theodore Roosevelt?" the reporter asked rhetorically. "Well, if you've ever met a bright, eager, impulsive and positive young man with a square, plump face, a mustache that looks as though it had suffered from drought, two pearly rows that glitter when he speaks and blue, laughing eyes that squint with emphasis, you can rest assured that he is Theodore Roosevelt, the famous young New York reformer and millionaire Dakota ranchman."

He and Edith agreed to meet again. What went through their minds during the initial phase of their reacquaintance can only be imagined, as neither left a record. A young, healthy, formerly married man like Roosevelt must have longed for female companionship. Where many of his associates in Dakota alleviated such longing with specialists in the ancient art, he was too fastidious and too attached to conventional morality. Moreover, for all his love of travel and adventure, Roosevelt acutely appreciated the satisfactions of home. At nine he had gotten homesick on leaving for Europe; at fourteen he sought to re-create the conditions of home in the Dresden Literary American Club; his college diary recorded his pangs of homesickness almost every time he returned to Cambridge. Since Alice's death, he hadn't really had a home. The big family house on Fifty-seventh Street had been sold shortly after the funeral of Alice and Mittie; Roosevelt stayed at Bamie's house on Madison Avenue during his visits to the East. The house at Oyster Bay that he had designed with Alice remained unoccupied; whether he would ever take possession seemed an open question. Edith, with all her connections to his childhood and youth, must have reminded him of home. Being with Edith resurrected the hopes of a normal family life such as he had shared with Alice but then put away in his closet of broken dreams.

Roosevelt's company doubtless rekindled Edith's dreams as well. Some of those dreams apparently pertained specifically to him, some generically to the kind of home and family to which most young women of her generation aspired. Edith didn't need the remarks of relatives as candid as herself to know that she wasn't getting any younger—nor was she getting any more comfortable financially. Indeed, at the time she encountered Roosevelt again she was in the process of planning a move to Europe with her mother and sister; the move was precipitated by recently straitened finances and was intended to lead to a lengthy sojourn in some comparatively inexpensive but not unfashionable country like Italy. Finally, finances aside, Edith recognized the potential for an intellectual compatibility with Roosevelt that she found in few other men.

During the late autumn of 1885 Roosevelt accompanied Edith to various events around New York. He invited her to a ball that he threw after an annual Long Island fox hunt; the ball, held at the house at Oyster Bay, doubled as something of a trial housewarming for what he had decided to call Sagamore Hill, after an aboriginal notable of the vicinity. (The name he had first thought of—Leeholm—was abandoned with all his other memories of Alice.) The day found Roosevelt in fine spirits; he broke his arm in a fall halfway through the chase but persevered to get in on the kill. Only then did he consent to have the injury examined; in a splint and sling he joined the festivities that evening, whisking Edith and several other women by turns about the dance floor in a dizzy one-armed waltz.

(Little Alice—almost three—recalled this moment of her father's triumph vividly but in a decidedly different light. "One of my earliest memories of my father was his coming back from hunting with a broken arm and a bloody nose. I started screaming at this apparition and he started shaking me to shut me up, which only made me scream more. So he shook more." Alice appended a commentary: "It was a theme which was to be repeated, with variations, in later years.")

That winter Roosevelt and Edith were spotted regularly around New York. The gossips twitted, but those who knew the pair best suspected nothing more serious than friendship. Roosevelt couldn't get over the idea that a second romantic involvement somehow diminished his love for Alice and especially that such involvement less than two years after her death verged on the scandalous. His diary for that winter included numerous entries consisting of the single initial "E"— these in striking contrast to his effusive entries during his courtship of Alice. Edith was content to accede to his desire for discretion; she had no more inclination than he to court allegations of unseemliness.

Yet sometime during the winter of 1885–86 they decided to wed as soon as seemed decent. Until then they would go about their affairs much as before. She would sail for Europe as planned, to help her mother and sister get settled. He would return to Dakota and his ranches.

After their parting, they wrote to each other regularly. Of the dozens of letters they exchanged, only one survives, from Edith to Theodore, written in June 1886. This one reveals two distinguishing facets of her personality: her intellectual self-assurance and her emotional insecurity. In a long paragraph she defends her enjoyment of *The Arabian Nights* against his criticism of its low moral tone; elsewhere she mocks Browning's poetry as incomprehensible, encourages Roosevelt to work on his Spanish, and derides a singer she has seen at the London opera (and who happened to be a Roosevelt relative by marriage) as "middle aged, ugly and uninteresting with not enough voice to redeem his bad acting." She adds that "his one idea of making love is to seize the prima donna's arm and shake her, violently."

This provides her a segue into the more intimate part of her letter, for she immediately continues: "I am so glad it is not your way." After a remark about all the interesting people she has seen on the street, she goes on to say, "You may not believe it, but I never used to think much about my looks if I knew my dress was all right; now I do care about being pretty for you, and every girl I see I think 'I wonder if I am as pretty as she is,' or 'At any rate I am not quite as ugly as that girl.'" Later she declares, "You know I love you very much and would do anything in the world to please you. I wish I could be sure my letters sound as much like myself as yours do like you; or that they are what you like. You know all about me darling. I never could have loved anyone else. I love you with all the passion of a girl who has never loved before, and please be patient with me when I cannot put my heart on paper." In closing she responds to a comment by him evidently wondering whether his love of nature isn't too sentimental. "I do not think you sentimental in the least to love nature; please love me too and believe I think of you all the time and want so much to see you."

His impending marriage to Edith doubtless influenced Roosevelt's decision to make the mayoral race that fall. He could hardly ask her to take up residence in Dakota; she would go crazy there—just as he would go crazy spending all his time in New York without the outdoor activities that ameliorated what he called "my usual restless, caged wolf feeling." No, the frontier was not a place for a cultivated, intellectually discriminating woman like Edith. Besides, however attractive he found the frontier, it wasn't home—especially now that he had a house of his own in the village the Roosevelts had made their own since his youth. When he told Bamie in June 1886 that "if I did not miss all at home so much, and also my beautiful house, I should say that this free open air life, without any worry, was perfection," he was stating a very large *if*. Much of Edith's attractiveness was her connection, in his memory and imagination, to home. In marrying Edith he was going home; it was only fitting that he do so in reality as well.

The thrill of the election fight in the fall of 1886 clinched his decision to return to the East. Although he lost, he had acquitted himself well and made plain that he was still a force to contend with in New York politics. Ranching might remain a hobby, but his heart and his home were in New York.

Even so, he hadn't overcome his ambivalence about remarrying. A notice in the society section of the *New York Times* announcing his engagement to Edith had surprised his friends and outraged Corinne and Bamie, who evidently then forced the paper to retract what they believed was an unfounded piece of presumption. Roosevelt felt compelled to write Bamie to say that while he was "savagely irritated" at the printing of the notice, the substance of the report was true. He pleaded uncertainty as to the date of the wedding in explaining why he hadn't told his own sisters. He said he didn't like the idea of second marriages now any more than he ever had; they betrayed a flawed moral character. "You could not reproach me one half as bitterly for my inconstancy and unfaithfulness, as I reproach myself." In a remarkable statement for one as outwardly orthodox as he, he declared, "Were I sure there were a heaven my one prayer would be I might never go there, lest I should meet those I loved on earth who are dead." Assuming that Bamie would condemn him, he continued, "No matter what your judgement about myself I shall most assuredly enter no plea against it."

In fact, it probably wasn't Bamie's censure he worried about so much as implicit condemnation by their dead father. Roosevelt's rule of morality was to live as his father would have lived; and he couldn't conceive that Theodore Sr. would have been so faithless to Mittie as to marry someone else in the event of her untimely death. When he spoke of wanting to avoid heaven so as not to have to face his loved ones, he almost certainly was thinking of his father—more than, for instance, of Alice. Alice represented love and sweetness and beauty; his father, love and justice.

Inconstancy aside, Roosevelt was also embarrassed at having deceived Bamie and Corinne. Corinne found the news that her brother and her childhood friend were to be married "all too incomprehensible." Once she got over the initial shock, she recognized that she could hardly object to the match even though there had always existed an unspoken competition between her and Edith for Teedie's favor, and, indeed, she later told Alice that she knew Edith would now come between her and her brother.

Bamie was no less shocked and upset than Corinne. In a strange sort of Victorian way, Bamie had come to see herself as the next thing to Theodore's wife. She had long looked after his domestic needs; now she was raising his child. Her devotion to her brother bordered on the passionate. In a letter to Edith, Bamie admitted candidly, "Theodore is the only person who had the power except Father, who possessed it in a different way, of making me almost worship him." Bamie would still worship Theodore, but henceforth his emotions would be wrapped up in Edith. It was a hard thing to accept.

Yet the truly wrenching issue for Bamie was Baby Lee. Bamie was thirty-one, with no real husband and scant prospects of one, and therefore there was little likelihood that she would have children of her own. Little Alice was almost certainly the closest she would come to having a child, and having tended the baby literally since birth, she naturally had become quite attached to her. Now, not only was she losing Theodore to another woman, she stood every chance of losing little Alice. Theodore tried to soften the blow by denying that it need occur: "If you wish to you shall keep Baby Lee, I of course paying the expense." But Bamie would have had to be far less acute than she was not to guess that once her brother got settled in a proper home with a wife and probably other children, his reviving paternal feelings would overpower whatever sense of obligation he had to her regarding the baby.

Even at this late date, Roosevelt wasn't ready to come completely clean. In this letter to Bamie he said he would write Corinne and Douglas, Elliott and his wife Anna (they had married shortly before Alice Lee's death), and Aunt Annie and Uncle Jimmie. (Interestingly, he didn't include his uncle James Roosevelt or anyone else on his father's side of the family.) Beyond these, however, the veil of secrecy must be maintained. "No other person is to be told a word about it." Moreover, he would go out of his way, literally, to avoid Alice's family. "As I do not care to see Rosy Lee I shall return about Oct. 6, '86."

Roosevelt had to fend off reports of the wedding plans throughout the mayoral campaign; only after the votes had been counted did he make the news public. A measure of his continuing sensitivity on the subject was the fact that the announcement came on November 8 when he was already two days at sea on his way to London to join Edith.

Roosevelt's relations and friends wished him well once they got over their amazement at this sudden turn of events. Bamie wrote Edith a warm letter of congratulations, expressing satisfaction that her brother had found a woman worthy of his love. "I would never say or write this except to you, but it is very restful to feel how you care for him and how happy he is in his devotion to you." The general judgment—hardly novel in an age that believed that men and women ought to be married—was that the match made sense for both parties. Roosevelt's cousin West, the one over whom he had shaken his head as being hopelessly in love (with the woman to whom he was now happily married), sent best wishes. "I am really more than pleased," he declared. "I had hoped that you would marry." West, who of course had known Edith for years, went on to offer an astute forecast: "You will be a better man because you will have a fuller life. You are marrying a woman who can enter into your plans and who can appreciate your aims, and you have the best earnest of real happiness in that. You are marrying one who will love you—that is best of all."

II

The thrill of the election campaign had gone far to distract Roosevelt from the tugs of conscience he felt regarding a second marriage; a new form of excitement that awaited him in England erased most of the rest. On the crossing he met Cecil Spring Rice, a British diplomat almost exactly his age. Spring Rice came from the class in England that was the analogue of Roosevelt's class in America, with the difference that in England that comfortable, respectable class doubled as the governing class. Spring Rice found Roosevelt as fascinating as most of Roosevelt's acquaintances did; in Spring Rice's case the fascination was augmented by the belief, which would become common among Roosevelt's foreign acquaintances, that he was a kind of American archetype, combining in his person the bumptiousness of New York, the cultivation of Cambridge (the copy, not the original), and the self-reliance of the western frontier.

On Roosevelt's arrival in England, he was shown off to Spring Rice's circle of friends, who found him as exotically intriguing as Spring Rice did. Even while affecting a certain patriotic disdain of British customs and mores, Roosevelt had the time of his life. He couldn't wait to tell Cabot Lodge all about it. "I have had very good fun here," he wrote ten days after landing. "I brought no letters and wrote no one that I was coming, holding myself stiffly aloof; and perhaps in consequence, I have been treated like a prince. I have been put down at the Athenaeum and the other swell clubs, have been dined and lunched every day, and have had countless invitations to go down into the country and hunt or shoot." Roosevelt rattled off the names of some of England's best-connected public and literary figures to whom he had been introduced. He relayed greetings from James Bryce, who had been "especially complimentary" about Lodge's recent work on Alexander Hamilton. Lord North had been very pleasant; also Lord Carnarvon. English fox hunting was quite different from the stateside version. "There was infinitely more head work needed by the men and more cleverness by the horses, but there was not any of our high jumping or breakneck galloping."

Almost as an afterthought to his account of social triumphs, Roosevelt added, "I am to be married on Dec. 2d. Edith sends her warmest remembrance to you and Nannie, and says that you two at any rate must try to like her."

On the appointed day, Spring Rice stood for Roosevelt as best man while Edith's sister Emily seconded the bride. The newlyweds left London for the Continent; Roosevelt took care to cross as little as possible the path of his earlier European tour with Alice. Though enamored enough of Edith, he lacked the intoxicated feeling of his first honeymoon, and so he didn't take it amiss when Edith's sister and mother joined them for part of the trip. Quite the contrary, in fact, for it freed him up to work on a series of articles he had arranged to write for *Century* magazine on ranch life in the West.

III

The articles were of more than literary interest to Roosevelt; they were also a source of income. During this period he began to feel the pinch of strained finances. Roosevelt had about as much sense for business as his father, which was why Theodore Sr. had asked his brother James to keep watch over the boy. But Roosevelt was as headstrong with his money as with everything else, and he invested where he chose. His publishing gambit had occasioned avuncular groaning but nowhere near as much as his Dakota fling, which drank more money each month. The biggest expense was purchasing cattle, but the new ranch house and the outbuildings at the Elkhorn also needed paying for, as did supplies and labor of various sorts—not to mention Roosevelt's Dakota-based hunting expeditions. By the end of 1886 he had poured eighty thousand dollars into the Badlands. As yet he had received next to nothing in return except for some antlers for his hall-way and the material for a book and some articles. Nor did he seem likely to receive much return in the near future. Beef prices were low during the summer and fall of 1886 despite a drought that seared the northern plains. Actually, the drought was partly responsible for the low prices, as ranchers decided to thin their herds rather than have to buy winter feed for them. But in addition to driving down present prices, the drought promised hard times ahead.

So discouraging were the prospects that Bill Sewall and Will Dow decided to up stakes and return to Maine. Sewall, as practical as Roosevelt was visionary, had had some doubts about the range-cattle business in Dakota from the start, but he was sufficiently taken with Roosevelt to place his skepticism on the shelf and give ranching a try. Besides, Roosevelt had guaranteed him against any loss. He and Dow would share profits with Roosevelt, but the boss would stand the losses alone. The arrangement had seemed satisfactory as long as there was a reasonable hope of profits after a fair amount of time, but in the autumn of 1886 profits looked further off than ever. Sewall couldn't conscientiously keep running through Roosevelt's inheritance. As he laconically put it, "I never wanted to fool away anybody else's money." Besides, his wife had recently given birth to a son—as, coincidentally, had Dow's wife. They had to think of their children. If there was a future for Medora and the surrounding region, the kids might grow up with the country. But if not—as appeared increasingly likely—this was no place to be. Better to go back to Maine, to country and people they knew. And so they did. After arranging to consolidate the Elkhorn herd with that of the Chimney Butte, they settled accounts with Roosevelt and departed at the end of September.

Losing Sewall and Dow only underlined Roosevelt's financial prob-lems. Beyond the dubiousness of his Dakota venture, Sagamore Hill was turning out to be expensive to operate, what with the cost of house servants, stable boys, groundskeepers, and the rest. Even though the house was nearly new, maintenance and necessary improvements were a constant drain. The house was cold and drafty when the north winds whipped off Long Island Sound; Edith decided they needed a backup furnace. The estimate for installation was $315. "Although it is a lot of money," she told her husband, "you should consider well before deciding not to have it done, for since we hope to keep this house for our home, it will never be thoroughly comfortable without the second furnace."

In fact, between the heating bills and all the rest, Roosevelt at one point strongly considered relinquishing the house. Perhaps recalling the conversation with his father in which the elder man declared that if one's income were modest, then one's expenses must be modest, too, Roosevelt weighed closing up or renting out Sagamore Hill and spending a couple of years in Dakota.

Edith shuddered at the thought. Sagamore had its chilly spots, and especially in the early days she must have felt sometimes that it was still Leeholm—Alice's house rather than her own. But as much as she tried to share her husband's enthusiasms, the idea of living in a log cabin hundreds of miles from anything that passed for civilization was more than she could bear. The house on the hill above Oyster Bay might be drafty, but compared to Dakota it seemed downright snug.

IV

Events beyond Edith's control—and beyond Theodore's and anyone else's—soon ruled out the Dakota option. The winter of 1886–87 was delightful in Italy; from Florence, Roosevelt wrote of the "idyllic" time he and Edith were having. That same season was anything but idyllic on the northern Great Plains. Winter started early and lasted long. According to the old-timers—a relative term in that recently settled region—winter typically began in December. Snow frequently fell before then but rarely amounted to much and generally melted before the real cold hit. This winter was different. Eyewitnesses recalled that a bright haze replaced the customarily crystalline sky. Although they didn't know it, the haze resulted from a layer of ice crystals held high

in the atmosphere by strong winds. The first snow commenced falling
in early November, but unlike the usual autumn snowfalls, which
were marked by wet, sticky flakes and temperatures just below freezing, this one arrived as a full-blown blizzard. Within hours of the initial flakes, the mercury had plummeted to some seventy degrees below
freezing, and the gale-force wind drove dry, icy snow shards before it,
scouring the plains, filling the draws, and burying cattle, horses, and
anything else that couldn't find shelter. Even those creatures that did
find shelter, including humans, didn't escape the storm's fury, for by
the next morning many were completely drifted in, entombed in their
cabins or, in the case of the rare lucky livestock, barns.

Arriving early as it did, this first storm caught most of the region
unprepared for winter. Humans had yet to purchase seasonal supplies;
livestock had yet to put on their winter coats. The beasts were particularly endangered by the early storm. On account of the drought that
summer, the herds were already gaunt and weakened before winter
even began. And the pastures were overgrazed, reflecting both the
hard season and the overstocking that had occurred during the previous several years—overstocking to which Roosevelt had contributed
his full share.

Had the winter of 1886–87 included its normal warm spells
between cold snaps, the herds would have had opportunities to
bounce back. But the warm western chinook was kept at bay for a full
four months by a jet stream that funneled the roaring northers direct
from the arctic onto the plains. When the snow stopped falling, the
wind recycled the flakes that already blanketed the ground, whirling
the dry powder into ever deeper drifts, then tearing those drifts down
and relocating them like dunes on a sandy sea.

Fortunate folks waited out the weather indoors. Those who had to
venture abroad risked disorientation and death in their own yards—
blinded, bewildered, and finally frozen between their back doors and
their barns.

Most of the stock were without recourse or hope. Recent additions
to herds fared the worst, not knowing how to paw through the snow to
the dried but nutritious grass that lay beneath. These were the first
to freeze, with their internal furnaces robbed of fuel. But as one snow-
fall succeeded another and the drifts deepened in the coulees and other
places where the animals sought relief from the deadly wind, even the

natives succumbed. Those that stayed in the draws were paralyzed in place as hard ice crystals drifted four feet, eight feet, twelve feet deep. Those that struck out for the open plains where the snow blew away as fast as it fell found fodder for a time, but by Christmas they had eaten through most of the little that the drought had spared.

As the cold and snow continued unrelieved through January and February, the people of the plains realized that a fifth horseman of the apocalypse had descended upon them. But only when the cold lifted were they able to survey the full extent of the destruction. The news arrived in a fashion none had anticipated—on the breath of what they all had been waiting and praying for. Lincoln Lang remembered that awful spring. "In the latter part of March," he wrote, "came the Chinook wind, harbinger of spring, releasing for the first time the iron grip that had been upon us. At last, it seemed, the wrath of Nature had been appeased." The melting wind did its work well—dreadfully well.

A few days later such a grim freshet was pouring down the river valley as no man had ever seen before or ever would again. For days on end, tearing down with the grinding ice cakes, went Death's cattle roundup of the upper Little Missouri country. In countless valleys, gulches, washouts and coulees, the animals had vainly sought shelter from the relentless "Northern Furies" on their trail. Now, their carcasses were being spewed forth in untold thousands by the rushing waters, to be carried away on the crest of the foaming, turgid flood rushing down the valley.

With them went our hopes. One had only to stand by the river bank for a few minutes and watch the grim procession ceaselessly going down, to realize in full the depth of the tragedy that had been enacted within the past few months.

V

In Europe, Roosevelt caught intimations of the disaster that had struck the plains, but details were impossible to obtain from such a distance. The closer he got to Dakota, the more doleful grew the news.

Upon his return to New York at the end of March, he wrote Bill Sewall. "You were mighty lucky to leave when you did," he said. "This spring I should have had to rustle pretty hard to pay your fare back." He went on: "By all accounts the loss among the cattle has been terrible. About the only comfort I have out of it is that at any rate you and Wilmot are all right."

This comfort didn't stretch very far once Roosevelt saw the damage for himself. "I am bluer than indigo about the cattle," he confided to Bamie shortly after reaching his ranch. "It is even worse than I feared." Sewall had been right: This was no country for cattle, at least not the way Roosevelt and most other ranchers had been running them. Many of his neighbors were ruined, and he himself was in serious straits. "I wish I was sure I would lose no more than half the money ($80,000) I invested out here," he told Bamie. "I am planning how to get out of it."

Unfortunately, much of the population of Dakota had the same idea, which made getting out appear as expensive as getting in had been. If he sold soon, he'd surely take a shellacking. On the other hand, if he held on awhile, prices might improve, and he wouldn't lose quite so much. Besides, it cut against his grain to deal with a setback by turning tail. No one had ever said making money as a rancher would be easy. It certainly wasn't. But by itself it was no reason to give up trying.

There was another reason for trying to hold on. Roosevelt simply liked to think of himself as a ranchman, a man of the West. The West was the American land of myth; his stake in the West afforded him a role in his own private romance—which was, at the same time, the national romance. He might return to the East to live and work, but he wanted to keep one foot, or at least a couple of toes, in the West.

So he hung on to his ranch. He no longer dreamed of being a cattle baron, and he sunk no more money into the business beyond what was absolutely necessary. Had he possessed the financial acumen and nerve of his grandfather, he might have seized the opportunity of the cattle crash to snatch up some bargains, just as old Cornelius had plunged into the Manhattan property market after the Panic of 1837 and grown rich on the rebound. The disaster of 1886–87 didn't kill cattle ranching on the plains; it merely forced a rethinking of premises. Ranchers discovered the hard way that cattle couldn't survive winters consistently on their own. They weren't simply buffalo with long horns and short hair. They had to be fed. This meant that ranchers had to grow hay for winter feed. Some ranchers had irregularly harvested wild grass for hay, but most relied on hay on the stalk: the dead grass cured in the autumn winds. (One reason for the cattle famine of 1886–87 was that the early snow had kept much of the grass from curing on the stalk and also kept those ranchers who had intended to cut wild hay from getting their harvest in.)

Running cattle on the public domain was one thing; growing crops like hay was something else. The hay fields had to be fenced to keep cattle off during the growing season; fencing implied an exclusive claim that could be defended in the long run only by purchasing the land.

This realization was what transformed the cattle industry on the plains. There was money to be made in cattle, but it wasn't to be made on a whim or a lark. It required a substantial investment of money and time—more than Theodore Roosevelt's eighty thousand dollars and four months a year. Those who weathered the winter of 1886–87 and eventually came out ahead would be those who bought land, fenced it, built barns, drilled wells, raised hay, cut and stored it, imported better breeds, and did the thousand things that separated successful farmers—and businessmen—from those who failed. Theodore Roosevelt lacked the necessary dedication, perseverance, and attention to detail. Roosevelt did well to play ranchman for a few weeks at a time; he didn't have it in him to hold the pose for several years.

VI

The only pose Roosevelt could hold for that long was politician. And the only reason he could hold it was that it wasn't a pose. Bill Sewall's parting words when he left Medora for Maine were that Roosevelt ought to go into politics, because good men were needed in that line. Sewall added a prediction: "If you do go into politics and live, your chance to be President is good." Sewall had seen the kind of recklessness Roosevelt equated with courage, which was why he inserted the condition about living into his forecast. It was a fair bet that Roosevelt would get thrown from a horse onto his head, be mauled by a grizzly bear, freeze in a blizzard, stop a bullet fired by a drunken rowdy, or die any one of several other deaths before reaching the constitutional threshold of thirty-five. But if his luck held, he had as good a chance as anyone of making it to the top of the ladder.

Yet making it to the top required getting back on a lower rung, and in the spring of 1887 that presented problems. The onetime boy wonder of New York state politics was neither a boy nor a wonder anymore. Eccentricities and enthusiasms excusable in a novice fresh out of college were harder to forgive in a man who had been around awhile. Roosevelt at twenty-eight had lost much of the perceived quirkiness of his youth, partly because he actually had moved toward conventionality—he no longer made quite such a fetish of physical exercise, for example—and partly because people had gotten used to his idiosyncrasies. But he still was far from the ordinary pol—who didn't run cattle in Dakota or chase mountain sheep about the Rockies. And his enthusiasms, if less violently expressed than before, were evident to anyone who got within range of his personality. Though his two most recent, if unsuccessful, ventures into politics—the Blaine campaign of 1884 and the mayoral race of 1886—showed a commendable party-mindedness, he still struck doubt into the heart of Republican regulars. They weren't exactly lining up to offer him plums of office.

With ranching behind him and politics still some distance ahead, he returned to writing. Through Cabot Lodge he got a contract from the publishing house of Houghton Mifflin for a biography of Thomas Hart Benton, the Missouri senator and apostle of western expansion. The book was to fill a place in a series on American statesman; its audience would be readers broadly interested in American history. The tone should be lively and opinionated.

Roosevelt was the right author for opinion, and the general nature of the project fit well with his migratory lifestyle. The research materials he required were modest in scope and size, and could be transported easily enough, including to the Elkhorn ranch. He commenced the writing early in 1886 in New York, carried the manuscript and such books and documents as supported the writing to Dakota for the spring roundup, and completed the first draft there during the summer. Like most authors he had his moments of doubt. "I feel a little appalled over the Benton," he confided to Lodge early in the writing. "I have not the slightest idea whether I shall make a flat failure of it or not." Six weeks later he reported, "I have written the first chapter of the Benton; so at any rate I have made a start. Writing is horribly hard work to me; and I make slow progress. I have got some good ideas in the first chapter, but I am not sure they are worked up rightly; my style is very rough and I do not like a certain lack of sequitur that I do not seem able to get rid of."

Roosevelt's complaints to Lodge suggested a literary inferiority complex vis-à-vis his friend. Lodge already had a reputation as a polished historian, and his style was indeed more elegant than Roosevelt's. Lodge also had a way of making things look easy—much in the way things that older brothers do generally look to their younger brothers. Graceful phrases flowed from his pen, while Roosevelt struggled to get his words lined up right.

Moreover, various objective logistical factors made Lodge's work much easier than Roosevelt's. In Boston, Lodge had access to Harvard's library; in Washington, to the Library of Congress. The Medora Public Library didn't quite measure up. Roosevelt repeatedly requested research help from Lodge. "I wonder if your friendship will stand a very serious strain," he inquired from Dakota in June 1886. "I have pretty nearly finished Benton, mainly evolving him from my inner consciousness; but when he leaves the Senate in 1850 I have nothing whatever to go by; and, being by nature both a timid and, on occasions, by choice a truthful man, I would prefer to have some foundation of fact, no matter how slender, on which to build the airy and arabesque superstructure of my fancy—especially as I am writing a history." Roosevelt asked if Lodge knew of anyone who could act as a research assistant and dig up the necessary information. "I hate to trouble you; don't do it if it is any bother; but the Bad Lands have much fewer books than Boston has." After Lodge obliged by sending the material himself—apparently along with some expressed reservations about Roosevelt's mode of historical composition—Roosevelt responded, "You are an old trump. The information is just what I want." He added, "Seriously, and joking aside, of course I shall not send the manuscript to Morse [his editor at Houghton Mifflin] until I have carefully gone over it in New York or Boston; but I wanted to get it so far done that a week's hard work when I get East near the Public Libraries would finish it."

In fact, the ever impatient Roosevelt didn't wait for his return east. After Lodge sent him some books that allowed him to check names, dates, and other vital information, he called this checking sufficient and packed the manuscript off from Medora to the publisher—but not without some residual trepidation. "I sent the Benton ms. on to Morse yesterday," he informed Lodge in the second week of August. "I hope it is decent, but lately I have been troubled with dreadful misgivings." Ten days later he registered a few more, these also peculiar to his isolated situation. "I couldn't insure the Benton in the express office here, so I sent it on trust; I haven't heard whether it turned up safely or not; I hope so for I would not rewrite it for a good deal."

Roosevelt didn't have to rewrite the book—indeed, he rarely rewrote anything. The perfectionism required of a diligent reviser was foreign to Roosevelt's nature; he was much too eager to get done and get on to the next project. The Benton bundle arrived safely at Houghton Mifflin, and after the usual editorial tinkering appeared in print at the beginning of 1887.

The book bore the distinctive stamp of its author. Roosevelt portrayed his subject as a giant—a flawed giant but a giant all the same. "He was a faithful friend and a bitter foe; he was vain, proud, utterly fearless, and quite unable to comprehend such emotions as are expressed by the terms despondency and yielding." Benton wasn't a great orator or writer, or even an original thinker. But his energy and industry, his indomitable will and fortitude, gave him an influence that surpassed nearly all of his contemporaries. "He was very courteous, except when provoked; his courage was proof against all fear, and he shrank from no contest, personal or political. He was sometimes narrow-minded, and always wilful and passionate; but he was honest and truthful. At all times and in all places he held every good gift he had completely at the service of the American Federal Union."

The book broke no new historical ground, but it was a rousing read—snappier than the exhaustive Naval War of 1812 and more compelling than the pleasant but pointless accounts of his hunting expeditions. Here Roosevelt had a protagonist who was larger than life to begin with, who could bear the burden of didacticism (not to mention authorial identification) that Roosevelt placed upon him. It was debatable whether readers learned more about Benton or Roosevelt, but either way they spent several hours with an engaging personality.

The book received favorable notices, even—to Roosevelt's "utter surprise," as he put it to Lodge—in the mugwumpish *Nation*. (Preparing himself for the worst, he had predicted, "Of course from its very nature if it attracts criticism at all it will be savagely attacked. It was not written to please those political and literary hermaphrodites the mugwumps.") *The Nation*'s anonymous reviewer did think the author a bit quick to judgment, saying he came close to being the "hanging judge" of American history. And he found disturbing the bellicose character of Roosevelt's comments on the expansionism that Benton championed. "There is a stain of blood and iron, muscular Christianity minus the Christian part, in the author's philosophy of civilization." The reviewer went on, with prescient hopefulness: "If Mr. Roosevelt shall be an active American statesman thirty years hence, we trust he will recast more than one sentence in his chapter on the 'Boundary Troubles with England,' when a longer life shall have shown him the boundless evils entailed by war."

The response to the Benton book encouraged Roosevelt to accept his publisher's invitation to do another volume in the same series, this on Gouverneur Morris. The work that resulted had a smoother finish than the Benton biography, reflecting its composition chiefly in the composed conditions of Oyster Bay rather than the catch-as-catch-can atmosphere of the Little Missouri. But it lacked the verve of the Benton book. Despite the New York roots of Morris, and certain other parallels to his own life, Roosevelt didn't identify with Morris as he had with Benton. "The work was not as congenial to me as the Life of Benton," he remarked the day after sending the manuscript to Houghton Mifflin. "I don't know whether I have done well or not. However I think I struck one or two good ideas. I laid into him savagely for his conduct in 1812–15 [a Federalist, Morris had opposed the war against Britain]; when, I am sorry to say, some of my worthy forefathers still continued much of the same mind with him."

His unsatisfactory experience with Morris, after the fun he had had with Benton, inspired Roosevelt to plan a far more ambitious project. "I should like to write some book that would really take rank as in the very first class," he told an old acquaintance from Albany, before adding, "But I suppose this is a mere dream." Yet Roosevelt wasn't one to let dreams go lightly unaddressed, and he commenced to outline what he called his "magnum opus." The work would be a multivolume history of the exploration and settlement of the West. His recent biographies had been written in months; this would take years. Those books had been based on other authors' efforts; this would rely on original sources. Those had been written for amateur historians; this would satisfy specialists. Those had reflected certain facets of the American experience; this would capture the essence, the central theme.

And this, like the Benton book, would allow him to relive the most romantic era of American history—the era of conquest and settlement, of life to the hilt and battle to the death, of courage and daring and strength. At a time when the frontier was fast closing on America as a nation, and when his own frontier, after the Dakota debacle, was closing on him personally, his literary expedition to the West of history would enable him to transcend the limitations of mundane life. His identification with his subjects was deliberate and avowed. "For a number of years I spent most of my time on the frontier, and lived and worked like any other frontiersman," he explained in the preface to the first volume. To be sure, Dakota differed from the Allegheny upcountry that formed the setting for Roosevelt's big book. "Yet the points of resemblance were far more numerous and striking. We guarded our herds of branded cattle and shaggy horses, hunted bear, bison, elk, and deer, established civil government, and put down evil-doers, white and red, on the banks of the Little Missouri, and among the wooded, precipitous foot-hills of the Bighorn, exactly as did the pioneers who a hundred years previously built their log cabins beside the Kentucky or in the valleys of the Great Smokies. The men who have shared in the fast-vanishing frontier life of the present feel a peculiar sympathy with the already long-vanished frontier of the past."

VII

Shortly after their return from Europe in the spring of 1887, Roosevelt and Edith moved into Sagamore Hill. The house was huge—twenty-two rooms—and mostly empty. Bamie had stayed there off and on, but she and little Alice hardly filled the place. Readying it for regular occupation required considerable work. The heavy lifting was done by hired hands and servants, of course, but executive decisions on such matters as where to put this elk head and that bear skin, this sideboard and that étagère, this volume of Ovid and those of Walter Scott couldn't be delegated. If Edith had perhaps once worried about the house being haunted by the ghost of Alice, by the time Theodore got through filling it with his books, trophies, and other memorabilia, there was hardly room for the living, let alone the dead.

The house filled up more, and Edith's fears eased additionally, when she gave birth to a son in September. The child was duly christened Theodore, as much for Roosevelt's father as for himself. Roosevelt was proud of both mother and son. "Edith is getting on very well," he told Bamie several hours after the delivery. "She was extremely plucky all through. The boy is a fine little fellow about 8½ pounds." A few days later he added, "I am very glad our house has an heir at last!"

Though actually his second child, Theodore Jr. introduced Roosevelt to full-time fatherhood. Little Alice, now three, had come to live with her father and stepmother in the spring, but had stayed only briefly before being sent to Boston to visit her grandparents. She was back by the time her brother arrived, and wasn't impressed. "My little brother's a howling polly parrot," she declared—accurately, as her father acknowledged to Corinne. He appended his own observation: "His eyes work with the irregular independence apparently characteristic of extreme juvenescence. It is lovely to see Edie with him. Alice watches him, especially when he 'eats Mama' as she calls it, with absorbed interest; Edith seems able to nurse him magnificently."

The family remained at Oyster Bay until January when they migrated to Bamie's house on Madison Avenue, which was otherwise vacant while she traveled in Europe. In March a late blizzard, the worst in a century, brought Manhattan to a halt—all Manhattan but Roosevelt, who breasted the drifts and declared the experience "great fun." Edith thought rather less of being cooped up in someone else's house, and she longed to get back to her own. Accordingly, almost before the snow had been shoveled from the sidewalks, they returned to Oyster Bay.

By now little Ted was mobile, frequently finding his way into the study where his father was busy with his book on the West. "I have not the least idea whether it will be worth anything or not," he told Lodge, but he was enjoying the writing. He talked Edith into taking up tennis, while he added polo to his list of outdoor pursuits. He attacked the pitch with the gusto he brought to everything; during one spirited contest he rode headlong into his brother Elliott's horse and was tossed violently to the turf and knocked unconscious. His head didn't clear for an hour, and he was not fully himself again until several days later.

The concussion had a more serious, secondary effect—or so Roosevelt interpreted matters. Several weeks earlier, Edith had discovered she was pregnant again. The pregnancy appeared to be going smoothly; on July 8, Roosevelt remarked to Bamie how well Edith looked. But ten days after his polo accident she suffered a miscarriage. Roosevelt blamed the former for the latter. "The mischief of course came from my infernal tumble at the polo match," he told Bamie. "The tumble was nothing in itself; I have had twenty worse; but it looked bad, because I was knocked perfectly limp and senseless, and though I was all right in an hour, the mischief had been done to Edith, though we did not know it for over a week."

Roosevelt probably misdiagnosed the cause of the miscarriage. Edith wasn't such a delicate flower as to wilt at the sight of a dazed husband, and having known Roosevelt for twenty-five years, she was fully aware of the kinds of collisions and other accidents he regularly survived.

But whatever its cause, the miscarriage cast a momentary shadow across the best summer that Roosevelt had spent since Alice's death. Marriage suited him as well the second time around as the first, if perhaps not as giddily. Fatherhood was growing on him. Little Alice was "too sweet and good for anything," he wrote Bamie two days before Edith's miscarriage. "As for Ted, he crawls everywhere, does his best to stand and talk—but fails—and is too merry and happy for anything. I go in to play with them every morning; they are certainly the dearest children imaginable."

VIII

As shadows almost always did for him, that cast by the miscarriage soon lifted. Or perhaps it was more accurate to say that he got out

from under the shadow—by running away. He put aside any notion—
if it even occurred to him—that Edith might need his emotional support, and within two weeks he was off on a hunting trip to the
Kootenay country of the Idaho-British Columbia border. "We will
take canoes, and then go in on foot, with indians to pack our goods,"
he wrote from Chicago. The trip, to last some six weeks, was already
well begun. "West [the cousin] and I have started off in fine feather."

They almost didn't return in such fine feather—or at all. "It was
an awful hard trip," recollected the guide, Jack Willis. At one point
he was leading Roosevelt across a rock face high above a narrow
defile. Willis hesitated, realizing the risks involved in the traverse.
"If we fall and break a leg, Mr. Roosevelt," he said (politely employing the first person plural but meaning the second person singular),
"I could not get you out; I would have to kill you." And though that
might be the end of the matter for Roosevelt, it wouldn't be for
Willis. "You know there'd likely be trouble for me making people
understand that shooting you was the best thing to do for you."
Roosevelt, relying on his abbreviated education in the law and
impatient to get on with the pursuit of the escaping beast that had
rendered the crossing necessary, promised to sign a statement exon-
erating Willis. Whether this statement would be thrown up from the
bottom of the ravine or left pinned to his shirt, Roosevelt didn't say.
But Willis, satisfied, didn't insist on knowing, and across they went,
without mishap.

IX

Roosevelt returned in time for the 1888 national campaign, into
which he threw himself with his accustomed verve. Edith joined him
for a swing across the upper Midwest, from Detroit to St. Paul, and
then again east by a more southerly route. The whole experience was
"immense fun." It was even better than hunting in that his quarry got
to shoot back. Shortly after the election he wrote Cecil Spring Rice: "I
am now recuperating from the Presidential campaign—our quadrennial Presidential riot being an interesting and exciting, but somewhat

exhausting, pastime. I always genuinely enjoy it and act as target and marksman alternately with immense zest; but it is a trifle wearing."

The campaign was even more wearing on Republican nominee Benjamin Harrison, who lost the popular vote to incumbent Cleveland but carried the electoral college and hence the election. The exhausted winner thanked Providence for his victory. "Providence hadn't a damn thing to do with it," retorted Matthew Quay, his campaign manager, who knew more about how politics in the Gilded Age really worked. Harrison had campaigned on a promise of appointing only the best and most qualified men to government offices but soon discovered how little freedom he had in the matter. "When I came into power," he later was reported to have said, "I found that the party managers had taken it all to themselves. I could not name my own Cabinet. They had sold out every place to pay the election expenses."

Although he never would have put it so, Roosevelt hoped he had purchased at least a minor office with his lively campaigning. His friends offered help. Cabot Lodge, now a member of Congress, recommended Roosevelt's appointment as assistant secretary of state. This would have made Roosevelt half of an odd couple, for the top job in the State Department was being held for James Blaine in recognition of the old charmer's last-minute round of stem-winders on Harrison's behalf. Roosevelt, of course, had backed Blaine in 1884 but only after doing his best to deny him the nomination. Doubtless the two good party men could have submerged their differences in the common cause, but Harrison—perhaps encouraged by Blaine, perhaps simply feeling that Roosevelt's services to the party didn't rate such recompense—passed him over for the State Department assistantship.

"You are certainly the most loyal friend that ever breathed," Roosevelt wrote Lodge upon learning that the latter was acting as his patron in Washington. At the moment of writing, Harrison's gaze had just landed elsewhere regarding the State Department post. Roosevelt seemed of two minds on the subject, although it wasn't difficult to tell which of the two was the stronger. "I would have particularly liked to have been in Washington, in an official position, while you were in Congress," he told Lodge. "We would have had a very good time; and so I would have been glad to have been appointed. But aside from this feeling—and of course the pleasure one feels in having one's services recognized—it is a good deal better to stay where I am. I would like above all things to go into politics; but in this part of the State that seems impossible, especially with such a number of very wealthy competitors. So I have made up my mind that I will go in especially for literature, simply taking the part in politics that a decent man should."

Roosevelt may have guessed more than he was letting on. In this letter he proceeded to congratulate Lodge on a new method Lodge had been promoting for selecting postmasters—the most numerous beneficiaries of the spoils system. In the campaign Roosevelt had hit hard on the need for reducing patronage; he did so again, in public statements and in private correspondence. He invited Lodge to dinner, along with such other influentials as Thomas Reed of Maine, one of the most respected and feared legislators in the country, one whom Roosevelt had enthusiastically endorsed in the campaign and who now might speak for Roosevelt. "Do come," he urged Lodge. "I want to see and talk with you dreadfully. I do hope the president will appoint good civil service commissioners."

Meanwhile, Lodge was intimating that Roosevelt wasn't entirely out of the running for a job. "I had a little talk with the President about you and he spoke very pleasantly," Lodge wrote at the end of March. "But he is a reserved person. I met Reed today. He said he had been waiting to see me because he wanted to talk to the President about you and said all kinds of pleasant things. . . . He is a loyal friend and as true as steel." Lodge reported that he had been in touch with Walker Blaine, James's son, who in turn had contacted former secretary of state and continuing party powerhouse William Evarts. "Blaine told me that Evarts had spoken to him about you saying you should have handsome recognition and be brought into public life again."

Knowing that his friends were still pulling for him and knowing that the civil service posts were open, Roosevelt evidently thought it wouldn't hurt to reemphasize his interest in that ever-vital subject. He did, as before; and it didn't: In April, Harrison announced his selection of Theodore Roosevelt as one of three members of the federal Civil Service Commission.

X

Irony was generally lost on Roosevelt and almost always when it touched his own actions. He apparently didn't think it odd that he should receive a job to diminish patronage and clean up the spoils system as a reward for his good work on behalf of the party. It was precisely this lack of irony or even self-reflection that so infuriated those mugwumps and others who called him a hypocrite (and whom he in turn lambasted as hypocrites for thinking him one). To the extent that he reflected on the subject at all, he simply took the view that in the real world one plays by the rules as they exist in order to get to a position where it is possible to change them. Taking the civil service post fell into this category.

The job itself was no great prize. The pay was poor, a mere $3,500 a year. The position was as thankless as any in the government. According to their job description, the commissioners were essentially expected to antagonize nearly the whole federal workforce: to utterly alienate those who lost their jobs to civil service reform (along with their wives, children, parents, friends, pastors, and creditors), and to unnerve those who survived each round of reform but worried about the next. The patronage system also created a class of upset losers, of course, but for every loser there was a winner who felt a warm glow toward his benefactor at payday and election time. Civil service reform created no comparable good feelings, since persons who got jobs under the new merit system felt the jobs were something they had earned on merit, not the gift of a patron. Nor could Roosevelt even expect much publicly displayed gratitude from the politicians in whose name he dismantled the spoils system. He was their lightning rod, a convenient deflector of the dissatisfaction of those who lost jobs or failed to gain jobs they had set their hearts on. It didn't take a genius to guess that a civil service commissioner might not have much of a future in politics. But Roosevelt wasn't in a position to be choosy.

Besides, the job description of civil service commissioner was sufficiently imprecise that an ambitious man might make as little or as much of the post as he saw fit. Roosevelt soon demonstrated that he was an ambitious man and that he intended to make much of his job.

Indeed, he didn't even wait to start his job before he began weighing in—on, of all things for a person bound for the civil service, foreign policy. During the late 1880s the United States, Germany, and Britain squabbled intermittently over control of the archipelago of Samoa. Expansionists in each country wanted a piece of that South Pacific outpost; but while the British were willing to share, the Germans were acting exclusively possessive. By the spring of 1889 the issue had become a rallying point for nationalistic types like Roosevelt. In his articles and other writings, Roosevelt tried to alert his countrymen to the need for strong defenses and an assertive policy overseas; now he hoped that the Samoan contretemps would aid in the educational process. At the height of the crisis he wrote Spring Rice: "Just at present our statesmen seem inclined to abandon the tail of the [British] lion, and instead are plucking vigorously at the caudal feathers of that delightful war-fowl, the German eagle—a cousin of our own bald-headed bird of prey. Frankly, I don't know that I should be sorry to see a bit of a spar with Germany; the burning of New York and a few other seacoast cities would be a good object lesson on the need of an adequate system of coast defences." Other consequences of a conflict would be equally edifying. "I think it would have a good effect on our large German population to force them to an ostentatiously patriotic display of anger against Germany; besides, while we would have to take some awful blows at first, I think in the end we would worry the Kaiser a little."

Some awful blows did indeed resolve the crisis, but they were the hammerings of a hurricane that swept Samoa nearly off the atlases of the great powers and raised serious reservations regarding its potential as a safe harbor. After they located most of the pieces of the squadrons that lately had postured so menacingly, the three governments agreed to a three-way condominium. Roosevelt was deprived of his spar by the same winds that stripped the warships of theirs.

But he soon found and created opportunities for confrontation of a different sort. He had been in his office at the Civil Service Commission only days when he began trampling on sensitive toes. Harrison's postmaster general, John Wanamaker, was one of those who had purchased their positions through the time-proven method of giving lots of money to the president's election campaign.

Wanamaker was, to put matters kindly, no great friend of civil service reform. What was the use of being postmaster general, he thought, if he couldn't reward his friends with jobs?

Roosevelt ran headlong into Wanamaker. In June 1889 he and fellow commissioner Hugh Thompson undertook an inspection tour that carried them across much of the Midwest. Post offices headed their itinerary; they sought to determine whether local postmasters were behaving according to the Pendleton Act, the landmark civil service law of 1883. They quickly discovered that many of the objects of their investigation couldn't even spell Pendleton, let alone implement it. Other illegalities, from minor peccadilloes to major grafting, were rife as well.

Roosevelt and the commission had no power beyond that of revealing wrongdoing; it was up to the president to accept their recommendations that wrongdoers be removed. When those slated for removal were Democrats—for example, the postmaster at Milwaukee, whom Roosevelt labeled "about as thorough paced a scoundrel as I ever saw—an oily-Gammon, church-going specimen"—White House acceptance came comparatively easy. But when the searchlight of scrutiny fell on Republicans, Roosevelt often found himself fighting Wanamaker. The postmaster general was "as outrageously disagreeable as he could possibly be," Roosevelt reported to Lodge. Speaking for himself and his fellow commissioners, Roosevelt said, "We have done our best to get on smoothly with him; but he is an ill-conditioned creature." A few days later Roosevelt told Lodge, "I mean to avoid a quarrel with him, both for the sake of the reform and of the party; but every now and them he intrudes too much, and I have to hit him a clip."

Complain though he might, this kind of righteous struggle appealed immensely to Roosevelt. It was what had brought him into politics in the first place, what had hooked him on politics, and what would keep him politically active for the rest of his life. He loved to be able to relate, as he did to Lodge, how he had held staunch for his principles in the councils of power.

> I have made this Commission a living force, and in consequence the outcry among the spoilsmen has become furious; it has evidently frightened both the President and Halford [Harrison's secretary] a little. They have shown symptoms of telling me that the law should be rigidly

enforced where people will stand it, and gingerly handled elsewhere. But I answered militantly; that as long as I was responsible the law should be enforced up to the handle every where; fearlessly and honestly. I am a great believer in practical politics; but when my duty is to enforce a law, that law is surely going to be enforced, without fear or favor. I am perfectly willing to be turned out—or legislated out—but while in I mean business.

A short while later he told Francis Parkman, the historian, that he expected to spend more time writing in the future. "Literature must be my mistress perforce, for though I really enjoy politics I appreciate perfectly the exceedingly short nature of my tenure. I much prefer to really accomplish something good in public life, no matter at what cost of enmity from even my political friends than to enjoy a longer term of service, fettered by endless fear, always trying to compromise, and doing nothing in the end." Roosevelt was having such fun that he decided—as he almost invariably did—that an earlier disappointment had been for the best. "How fortunate it is that I did not get the Assistant Secy'ship of State! I could have done nothing there; whereas now I have been a real force, and think I have helped the cause of good government and of the party."

With every chance, Roosevelt preached the gospel of good government as manifested in the merit system. He constantly tilted against those who resented and rejected civil service reform for being an un-American infringement on democracy. This turned things precisely on their head, he rebutted. It was the spoils system that was undemocratic. "The spoils system means the establishing and perpetuation of a grasping and ignorant oligarchy." The merit system, on the contrary, was "essentially democratic and essentially American, and in line with the utterances and deeds of our forefathers of the days of Washington and Madison."

Roosevelt amplified his message with stories from his days in the New York assembly, when he had been investigating problems of spoilsmanship. One applicant for a position on the police force of New York City, asked why he should receive the job, replied that he had a grievous drinking problem that made him unfit for any other work. A second individual, a Republican like Roosevelt, wrote on behalf of a friend. This friend had offered to pay the writer $200 if he could get him a police job, and the writer thought Roosevelt surely would want that money to go to a Republican rather than someone else, likely a Democrat. A third individual, a county clerk, was queried by the investigative committee—perfunctorily, the committee thought—whether he attended to his official duties. "Yes," came the reply, "when they don't interfere with my political duties."

A typical complaint against the merit system was that it was "Chinese." Such complainers knew enough of China to know that it had a system of competitive examinations for government positions, and enough of the American political mind to know that few insults slapped so stingingly as the label "Chinese." Roosevelt ridiculed any man who likened China's overgrown and ossified system to America's modern and efficient efforts to employ examinations to weed out the incompetent. "As well might he inveigh against our alphabet because the Chinese have long had a cumbersome alphabet of their own, or against the use of gunpowder because it was first used in China, or decline to carry a Winchester rifle because jingals have long been known in the East."

To those who fretted that the merit system rewarded boys fresh from school at the expense of men with experience of the world, Roosevelt answered that such was simply not the case. The average age of successful candidates for basic positions such as letter carrier was twenty-eight. "The boy fresh from school evidently stands less chance than the man who has left his school-days at least ten years behind him."

Roosevelt was willing to grant the good intentions, if misguidedness, of some of the critics of the merit system, but for those partisan and otherwise interested objectors who knew better, he had only scorn. He decried the "utter recklessness" of editors and party hacks—"whether Democratic, Republican or Independent"—who sapped confidence in public honesty by denigrating reform. After this brief but commendable display of bipartisan (or perhaps tripartisan) indignation, Roosevelt went on to say that the problem manifested itself most acutely in the South—needless to say, not a Republican stronghold. Southerners showed little interest in and less knowledge about the workings of the federal government; many of them simply assumed that any civil service system administered by northern Republicans would work to their detriment. Roosevelt went on to say with some pride that he and his fellow commissioners were changing this misperception. During a recent three-month period the commission drew more southern candidates into the examination system than had entered in any three years previously.

Roosevelt encountered certain slights of civil service reform repeatedly; but some slanders stood out, and in doing so demanded detailed and specific rebuttal. One critic, a semi-anonymous "W.H.S.," had written to a Cincinnati paper leveling a variety of allegations against the merit system. Included in his complaints was a list of questions said to have been asked of candidates in Indianapolis on a recent examination for letter carriers. The list was riddled with inaccuracies and outright fabrications, Roosevelt retorted. Did anyone really believe that postal carriers were expected to know the distance from the earth to Mars? Other questions claimed to have been asked were only slightly less ludicrous but equally figments of fevered—or malicious—imaginations: the surface area of Lake Michigan, the name of the only county in New York not served by a railroad, the highest mountain peak in the United States. Roosevelt didn't deny that occasional slips occurred in writing and administering examinations. Now and then, perhaps, a question appropriate to one position appeared on an examination for another. A person applying for appointment as an astronomer might well be asked the distance from the earth to Mars—but that was something such a person ought to know. A geographer or cartographer employed by the government should know what the highest peak in the country was. No right-minded person could complain of such expectations. Indeed, taxpayers were completely justified in expecting competence in the people they hired. "Our examinations are, as a whole, eminently common sense and practical."

XI

A decade later Roosevelt would mount a more visible pulpit for his preachments, but for the moment the Civil Service Commission served quite well. He became the spokesman of the Republicans on the subject of good government—a position that had its advantages but also its drawbacks. While he liked to be on the side of right and justice and all that, he didn't like everybody who occupied that side, or claimed to. To his dismay he found that he had become something of a hero to the mugwumps. Roosevelt was no more immune to praise than others; in many ways he was less. But mugwump approval wouldn't benefit him in the circles to which he aspired. "I have been seriously annoyed at the mugwump praises," he told Lodge, "for fear they would discredit me with well-meaning but narrow Republicans, and for the last week my party friends in Washington have evidently felt a little shakey." Yet despite his uneasiness about their praise, he hesitated to attack the mugwumps publicly since their backing served the cause of civil service reform. All the same, he had no compunctions about encouraging others to batter them. "Show the great harm they do by pretending to be independent, and foully slandering decent men in a spirit of shameless partisanship . . ." he urged Lodge. "My hands are tied by my position here; otherwise I should be at their throats in a moment."

Roosevelt's visibility was enhanced by his travels across the country for the commission; in each city he visited he formed new contacts, made new acquaintances, created new alliances. Long before he left the commission he was well known to good-government reformers—to those who would form the core of the Progressive movement—throughout the country.

But the key to his elevated stature was his relocation to Washington. For the first three generations after being carved out from the forest on the banks of the Potomac, the capital city had been a novelty within a novelty, an experiment within an experiment: a custom-built city at the heart of a de novo polity. Until the 1860s, Washington had remained something of an outpost, a winter camp where part-time politicians gathered to debate and occasionally legislate regarding those relatively few subjects that fell beyond the purview of the states. Summers, all persons who could would flee to parts more equable, which included nearly every place else in the country. Washington might be the political capital of the American republic, but collectively the state capitals counted for more. Meanwhile, New York was the nation's financial capital and Boston its cultural capital, if it could be said to have a cultural capital.

The Civil War changed things. Unintentionally—at least not according to the intentions of anyone before the war started—but decisively and irretrievably, the war altered the political geography of the nation. Washington, the headquarters of the commander in chief, became the hub of wartime operations; and as the war grew into a political revolution, it became the cockpit of that revolution. The Union overthrew the states, and the federal government transformed itself into the locus of ultimate power within the nation as a whole. Supplicants, complainants, and anyone else with something to say or wish for about how things were or ought to be, now gravitated to Washington before their state capitals. The federal government expanded greatly during the Civil War—partly as a result of the insurrectionary emergency and partly as a result of the Republican takeover, which brought to power people convinced of the possibilities of beneficent cooperation between business and government. Federal underwriting of railroads was the most visible form of this cooperation, but it extended into all manner of economic enterprises, from mining and commercial farming, via variants on the (Republican) homestead law, to tariff-protected (and usually Republican-owned) manufacturing.

Theodore Roosevelt was heir to this tradition of big-government Republicanism, and he took his first steps toward claiming the legacy when he moved to Washington in the spring of 1889. Edith and the children remained at Sagamore Hill, she being pregnant again; after the arrival of the new baby they would join him in Washington. For the time being he occupied a room in Cabot and Nannie Lodge's house.

Roosevelt's neighbors in Washington were mostly politicians, but the infrequent literatus leavened the dough. Or, in the case of the gloomy Henry Adams, weighed it down. Adams, like everyone else, originally went to Washington for political reasons, in his case as secretary to his diplomat father, Charles Francis Adams. Unlike nearly everyone else, he returned to Washington (after a frustrating stint teaching history to Roosevelt's classmates at Harvard) for personal reasons. With longtime friend John Hay—the two built matching mansions on Lafayette Square, across the park from the White House—he watched what he took to be the decline of American civilization under the spoilsmen. He founded a microcolony of letters among the unread; it consisted chiefly of himself and Hay, the coauthor of a lengthy life of Lincoln, and George Bancroft, the historian and occasional diplomat. Seasonal migrants such as Lodge brought news of the outside world.

By the time of Roosevelt's arrival, Washington offered a semblance of real life. "Slowly, a certain society had built itself up about the Government," Adams wrote. "Houses had been opened and there was much dining; much calling; much leaving of cards." It wasn't

New York or Boston or Philadelphia in terms of the trappings of civilization, but as it had never been until recently, it was the home of the governing class and therefore was where Roosevelt wanted to be.

XII

In Washington, Roosevelt learned to cultivate the nation's most powerful politicians. He already had a speaking and corresponding acquaintance with Tom Reed of Maine, who became Speaker of the House in 1889. Reed was perhaps the most remarkable political figure of the era; had he possessed the popular touch of a McKinley or especially a Roosevelt, he might have become president, possibly a great one. In an era when physical weight connoted moral substance, when gravity implied gravitas, Reed filled the role—and then some. Well over six feet tall, he carried close to three hundred pounds on his imposing frame. He was better educated and better read than almost anyone else in Congress, probably including even Cabot Lodge, who never tired of being known as the "scholar-in-politics." Reed's personal library comprised several thousand volumes, many in languages other than English. He kept a daily diary in French, perhaps partly to foil prying eyes but mostly to keep fresh in a language he spoke fluently. His tastes in literature were even broader than Roosevelt's, ranging from philosophy and law to economics and history. Apart from his political influence, he made a brilliant dinner guest and conversationalist, as Roosevelt had already discovered.

But it was as a debater and parliamentarian that Reed excelled. Roosevelt, who was never particularly quick on his feet either in the ring or on the platform, could only watch with awe as Reed spitted opponents and barbecued them. Of two colleagues in the House of Representatives, Reed once observed, "They never open their mouths without subtracting from the sum of human knowledge." When a long-winded legislator, noted for eschewing the single word whenever several would suffice, remarked of a rival, "There he sits, dumb, mute and silent," Reed added, in his down east drawl, "He ain't saying a word, either." Another silver-throated warbler who made every speech sound like a funeral oration was declaiming one day when

Reed turned to Joseph Cannon and said, "Joe, were you acquainted with the deceased?" An effusively patriotic appeal on behalf of a measure to indemnify individuals for war-related damages elicited the withering rejoinder: "You may bring together Bunker Hill and Yorktown, Massachusetts and Virginia, and tie them together with all the flowers of rhetoric that ever bloomed since the Garden of Eden, but you cannot change the plain, historic fact that no nation on earth was ever so imbecile and idiotic as to establish a principle that would more nearly bankrupt its treasury after victory than after defeat." Joe Cannon, himself not exactly tongue-tied, said, "I have never heard my distinguished friend from Maine take the floor upon any subject but that I did not feel sometimes regretful that I could not crystallize an idea, if I had one, as he does, roll it up with my hands into proper shape and hurl it at the head of my opponent." Cabot Lodge, another who knew a thing or two about the subject, said simply that Reed was "the finest, the most effective debater that I have ever seen or heard."

During the Fifty-first Congress, which convened in 1889, Reed engineered a coup d'état in parliamentary procedure in the House of Representatives. Following endorsement by Roosevelt, Lodge, and others more influential, the Maine legislator narrowly defeated William McKinley for the post of Speaker, and he set at once to streamlining the operation of the lower chamber. His most dramatic and controversial blow was to terminate an illogical but time-encrusted practice that allowed members physically present to plead parliamentary absence at the time of quorum calls and thus block action on objectionable bills. The Democrats sputtered and raged at Reed's action, challenging him all the way to the Supreme Court, which sided with him. Throughout the uproar he retained his sense of humor. He paid his opponents the courtesy of keeping them informed of Republican strategy, as when he sent a note to Tennessee Democrat Benton McMillin: "Mack, here is an outrage McKinley, Cannon, and myself are about to perpetrate. You will have time to prepare your screams and usual denunciations."

Roosevelt lacked Reed's raspy wit, but he thoroughly appreciated the Speaker's feel for power and its uses. From the sidelines Roosevelt cheered his party colleague for frustrating their foes and rescuing government from the obstructionists. "Beyond question," he told a gathering of New York Republicans, in the presence of honored guest Reed, "the historian who in the future shall write a history of representative government through a legislative assembly will have to credit Speaker Reed and the Republican majority of the Fifty-first Congress with having achieved one of the greatest victories for the cause which has ever been achieved."

Roosevelt had a harder time warming to another key figure of the Fifty-first Congress, William McKinley. Part of the problem was a mismatch of personalities. McKinley was as self-effacing as Roosevelt was assertive, as cautious as Roosevelt was reckless, as reflective and questioning as Roosevelt was sure of himself. McKinley hailed from that cradle of presidents, Ohio. It was as an Ohio congressman that he first attracted the attention of Republican leaders. When the Republican convention of 1888 deadlocked before nominating Harrison, someone forwarded McKinley as a tie-breaker behind whom the various factions could unite. But McKinley declined the honor, refusing to put himself ahead of John Sherman, his senior in the Ohio senatorial delegation. Many party members shook their heads at this strange behavior, labeling McKinley as too humble to ever amount to anything in national affairs. One who didn't was Marcus Hanna, an Ohio businessman who, having earned all the money he needed, was turning to politics. Hanna valued loyalty, not least for its scarcity among the people he customarily consorted with, and he kept an eye on McKinley.

Although McKinley lost the contest for the speakership in 1889 to Reed, he made his mark on that legislative session, most particularly by sponsoring a tariff modification that subsequently bore his name. Roosevelt, unusually for a Republican, had little interest in the tariff; throughout his political career his lack of business sense showed in his disregard for and confusion about some basic economic issues. Yet like many other people he slowly came to recognize McKinley's virtues. "I have the very highest regard for Major McKinley," he said. "I look upon him as possibly some day a presidential candidate."

XIII

Politics preoccupied Roosevelt—in the capital city this was inevitable—but he didn't neglect his literary endeavors. He remained fascinated by the subject of his study of the West; his fascination inspired additional digging in published and unpublished sources. The more he delved, the more he discovered and the more fascinated he became; the more fascinated he became, the longer the narrative grew. The publisher, Putnam, decided to put out two volumes of *The Winning of the West* in 1889, with the rest to follow in due course.

The approach and style of writing fell into what was becoming Roosevelt's signature mode—heroically nationalist, but not unthinkingly so. Roosevelt placed the colonization of the early West in the context of the broader movements of that time and the periods before and after. "During the past three centuries," he stated stoutly, "the spread of the English-speaking peoples over the world's waste spaces has been not only the most striking feature in the world's history, but also the event of all others most far-reaching in its effects and its importance." Some of the pioneers appreciated their place in this grand scheme. Daniel Boone, for instance, said he was "ordained of God to settle the wilderness." Others had no inkling of a higher calling but simply followed their interests and their inclinations—which, as fate decreed, were those of civilization as a whole. Although many of the backwoodsmen were rough characters and fearsome foes, they were spared that complete consciencelessness that distinguished the aboriginal Indians:

> Not only were the Indians very terrible in battle, but they were cruel beyond all belief in victory; and the gloomy annals of border warfare are stained with their darkest hues because it was a war in which helpless women and children suffered the same hideous fate that so often befell their husbands and fathers. . . . It was a war waged by savages against armed settlers, whose families followed them into the wilderness. Such war is inevitably bloody and cruel; but the inhuman love of cruelty for cruelty's sake, which marks the red Indian above all other savages, rendered these wars more terrible than any others.

Roosevelt wrote history in order to instruct and guide; his work was timely by design. In this case his account of the Indian wars of a century before had particular application to current politics. Two years earlier, Congress had passed the Dawes Act, which attempted to force the Indian tribes to accept white ways by parceling out to individual Indians the heretofore commonly held reservation lands.

Although a majority of Congress and almost certainly of the American public supported this policy, a nascent school of Indian apologetics was developing, pointing out that the U.S. government had generally played less than fair with the Indians. Roosevelt didn't deny that expedience rather than strict integrity had sometimes marked the actions of the government, but he had no doubt that such expedience was in a good cause—namely, the expansion of American civilization. He was fully aware that his harsh historical treatment of the Indians would afford moral aid and comfort to those individuals and groups committed to harsh current treatment of the tribes. Indeed, lest there be any thought that the intervening decades might have softened what he saw as the savage heart, he appended a footnote from his own experience of the northwestern frontier:

> Any one who has ever been in an encampment of wild Indians, and has had the misfortune to witness the delight the children take in torturing little animals, will admit that the Indian's love of cruelty for cruelty's sake cannot possibly be exaggerated. The young are so trained that when old they shall find their keenest pleasure in inflicting pain in its most appalling form. Among the most brutal white borderers a man would be instantly lynched if he practised on any creature the fiendish torture which in an Indian camp either attracts no notice at all, or else excites merely laughter.

Roosevelt's book was too long—even though his tale wasn't half told (he would give up after seven more years and two more volumes, when the demands of politics became too great). It lacked the subtlety and nuance that were absent from all his writings (and speeches and most of his actions). Its ethnocentrism and moral self-assurance likewise were typical of the author (not to say of the age).

But it was an undeniably gripping story, and even if one disagreed with the author's judgments, there was never any doubt what those judgments were. The book filled an historical niche—to bursting—and confirmed Roosevelt as both an intellect and a personality to contend with.

The work received good reviews. A long, unsigned piece in the *Atlantic Monthly* applauded Roosevelt's broad and diligent research. "Few writers of American history have covered a wider or better field of research, or are more in sympathy with the best modern method of studying history from original sources," the reviewer declared. This reviewer, apparently a professional historian, also praised Roosevelt's style and approach: "His style is natural, simple, and picturesque, without any attempt at fine writing, and he does not hesitate to use Western words which have not yet found a place in the dictionary. . . . He has struck out fresh and original thoughts, has opened new lines of investigation, and has written paragraphs, and some chapters, of singular felicity." The reviewer chided Roosevelt for certain hasty judgments, believing that such judgments reflected carelessness in composition. "No man, whatever may be his ability or industry—even if he be a ranchman—can write history in its best form on horseback. . . . Mr. Roosevelt, in making so good a work, has clearly shown that he could make a better one, if he would take more time in doing it." The reviewer quibbled with a few of Roosevelt's interpretations and corrected a handful of errors. But the overall tone was positive and respectful, and the reviewer forecast that the book would find "many appreciative readers."

XIV

If Roosevelt was looking for an indication that he was being accepted into the guild of serious historians, this was about as straightforward a sign as he could expect. Whatever his political destiny, a future in literature didn't appear out of the question. He was slowly building a reputation as a writer; it would not be overly optimistic for him to hope that sales would follow.

Such thoughts were heartening and especially timely, in that his family was growing again. Not long after the book came out, Edith delivered their second child, his third.

Edith had spent the summer of 1889 at Oyster Bay growing large— and lonely. Roosevelt's work kept him busy through June and July; only occasionally did he take time to get home. At the beginning of August he headed west for his annual hunting holiday, which lasted until the end of the month. "Do be very careful," Edith wrote. "I try not to worry about you, but it is hard, & though of course as you have been away so much I am accustomed to not seeing you in the house, still it has been a hopeless kind of summer to look back on, & all I can think of are the times you have been here."

Yet Roosevelt would have his holiday, regardless of Edith's sentiments. "By Jupiter, I feel well," he wrote Lodge from Montana. "I have had a hard but a very successful trip—moose, bear, elk, etc.; one bear nearly got me—and never was in better condition." Roosevelt also managed to fit in some politicking on the way, with gratifying success. "They have all received me like a prince here in Helena; I wish to Heaven I could take off my coat and go into the campaign for the next three weeks; I get along pretty well with a Rocky Mountain audience."

Roosevelt was back at his desk in Washington a little over a month later when he received an emergency telegram from Oyster Bay. Perhaps he briefly relived the terrible moments when the wire had summoned him from Cambridge and Albany to New York. But this message reported that Edith had been delivered several weeks early of a baby boy. He raced north, making the final leg by a special train from Long Island City, hired impetuously when he learned that the last scheduled train had already left. Edith was mildly aghast at the extravagance, though pleased at the gesture; the newest family member, christened Kermit from Edith's side of the family, howled his approval, or disapproval—it was hard to tell.

At the end of the year the family moved into rented quarters on Jefferson Place in northwest Washington. The expense of maintaining two households strained the budget, but Edith had had enough of single parenting. So had the children, she decided. "Alice needs someone to laugh and romp with her instead of a sober and staid person like me," she told her husband.

The move to Washington at the end of 1889 allowed Roosevelt to romp with the children more regularly. By diminishing the number of trips he took up north, it also afforded him greater opportunity to romp with some of the nation's leading political figures. If they occasionally acted like children too, that came with the neighborhood.

CHAPTER TEN

Strategic Alliances
1890–95

"My dear Captain Mahan," Roosevelt wrote to the author of a book he happened across in the summer of 1890: "During the last two days I have spent half my time, busy as I am, in reading your book; and that I found it interesting is shown by the fact that having taken it up I have gone straight through and finished it." Roosevelt's tastes in books were as decided as his tastes in everything else, but even for him he registered strong approval. "I can say with perfect sincerity that I think it very much the clearest and most instructive general work of the kind with which I am acquainted. It is a very good book—admirable; and I am greatly in error if it does not become a naval classic."

Alfred Thayer Mahan was an intellectual among military men, in the same way that Roosevelt was an intellectual among politicians. Neither man was a true intellectual, interested in ideas for the sake of ideas; rather, each man valued ideas for the influence they could exert on current affairs. Mahan taught history at the recently established Naval War College in Newport, Rhode Island. Roosevelt had visited the college in the summer of 1888 at the invitation of its founder, Rear Admiral Stephen Luce, who knew Roosevelt's book on the naval war of 1812 and bet on its author as an up-and-coming political figure and potential patron of the college. Roosevelt spoke to the faculty and students on aspects of the material covered in his book; he also met Mahan.

At that time Mahan was polishing a set of lectures on naval power in history. He had received encouragement—in the form of research assistance and time off from teaching—from Luce, who was still having to defend the existence of the war college and to justify its appropriations. Mahan's project would demonstrate the significance of sea power in history and, indirectly, the significance of a naval war college in the United States.

It was this collection of lectures, revised and published as *The Influence of Sea Power upon History, 1660–1783,* that so impressed Roosevelt in 1890. The book appealed to Roosevelt in his capacity both as a student of naval history and as an advocate of a larger and more powerful American navy. "Captain Mahan shows very clearly the practical importance of the study of naval history in the past to those who wish to estimate and use aright the navies of the present," Roosevelt asserted in a feature review in *Atlantic Monthly.* "He dwells on the fact that not only are the great principles of strategy much the same as they ever were, but that also many of the underlying principles of the tactics of the past are applicable to the tactics of the present; or, at least, that the tacticians of to-day can with advantage study the battles of the past." As a naval historian, Roosevelt appreciated Mahan's analysis of tactics; he also appreciated the advantage in historical exposition an officer with experience at sea and under fire (during the Civil War) had over armchair admirals like himself. Roosevelt was even more impressed with Mahan's analysis of strategy. "Hitherto," Roosevelt declared, "historians of naval matters, at least so far as English and American writers are concerned, have completely ignored the general strategic bearing of the struggles which they chronicle; they have been for the most part mere annalists, who limited themselves to describing the actual battles and the forces on each side." (Whether Roosevelt included himself in this blanket indictment or slipped himself through the loophole left by "for the most part" was unclear.)

Roosevelt gently critiqued Mahan's accounts of sundry battles of the seventeenth and eighteenth centuries; he roundly applauded the points of the author's volume that had what Roosevelt called "a very important bearing on our present condition." Among these was a refutation of the quaint and distinctively American notion that in wartime the country could rely on privateers to provide the needed naval punch. Mahan showed "very clearly" that privateers, however useful, could never be more than a secondary factor in fighting a war to a successful finish. Mahan also demonstrated the need for forward naval bases, located near the enemy's lines of commerce, and stronger coastal defenses. Both of these required extensive preparation in peacetime; they couldn't be cobbled together after the fighting began. "There is a loose popular idea," Roosevelt scoffed, "that we could defend ourselves by some kind of patent method, invented on the spur of the moment. This is sheer folly."

What America really needed was a stronger navy. "Our ships should be the best of their kind—this is the first desideratum," Roosevelt declared. "But, in addition, there should be plenty of them. We need a large navy, composed not merely of cruisers, but containing also a full proportion of powerful battleships, able to meet those of any other nation." At a time when public officials found funds to spend on all manner of other things, priorities had to be kept straight. "It is not economy—it is niggardly and foolish short-sightedness—to cramp our naval expenditures, while squandering money right and left on everything else, from pensions to public buildings."

Roosevelt's discovery of Mahan helped launch the latter on a brilliant career as the founding member of a tribe that would proliferate in America during the century ahead: the defense intellectuals. Well before World War I, Mahan's corpus became required reading in admiralties and war colleges the world over for the eminently practical reason that Mahan said more gracefully and, with the support of history, more convincingly what the denizens of those niches had been saying themselves—namely, that they needed more, newer, and bigger vessels.

Roosevelt linked up with Mahan for much the same reason, as well as from professional admiration for a fellow naval historian. Roosevelt grabbed each new title that Mahan turned out during the 1890s; his subsequent reviews were nearly as enthusiastic as the first.

The relationship was symbiotic. Mahan benefited from the favorable publicity, Roosevelt from the reflection of that publicity and from the approval Mahan in turn showed for Roosevelt's literary and political efforts. Their joint cause of naval preparedness and of what they—along with Cabot Lodge, the third musketeer of American expansion—came to call the "large policy" of American assertiveness abroad benefited from the mutual reinforcement and congratulation. And as the cause advanced, so did the careers of those who advanced it.

II

Yet in the first years of the 1890s it wasn't at all clear that Roosevelt's career was going anywhere interesting or important. As he had recognized when he took the civil service post, the victories that he managed to achieve were hardly the sort to endear him to the party regulars who appeared to hold his fate in their hands. Republican enthusiasm—what there was of it—for civil service reform was primarily rhetorical. Whatever they might say about the spoils system when the Democrats held the gift basket, the Republicans understood human nature well enough to realize that gifts were the glue that held the party together, and they were in no hurry to supply the solvent. Roosevelt was caught in a debilitating bind: Success in his job would anger those who might otherwise have rewarded a competent and ambitious young man, while failure (besides being unacceptable to him personally) would brand him as ineffectual. The only people who really appreciated Roosevelt's efforts on behalf of good government were the mugwumps, who were in no position to return the favor and whom he continued to despise.

Not that the Republicans, even those who applauded his work, were particularly well positioned at the moment. The 1890 congressional elections witnessed a serious backlash against the Republican assertiveness of the Fifty-first Congress. William McKinley was retired to Ohio and Reed lost the speakership as the party was battered in ignominious defeat.

"I have felt too down hearted over the election to write you since," Roosevelt told Lodge a week after the polling. "And besides there seemed really nothing to say." With many others, especially those like himself who had few close ties to big business, Roosevelt blamed McKinley's tariff measure. "The overwhelming nature of the disaster is due entirely to the McKinley bill; as you know I never liked that measure." The future appeared bleak. "The Democratic majority will run wild." Their leaders would have "a fine time keeping pace with the capers of the [Farmers'] Alliance men of the West and Southwest."

The 1890 election combined with the generally unsatisfactory nature of his civil service job to cast a pall of uncertainty over Roosevelt. From one day to the next he didn't know what he ought to do with himself. He couldn't decide whether it would be better to be fired or to stay on with the commission. Staying on provided the obvious advantage of a steady, if meager, paycheck and a continuing reason to remain in Washington, near the center of national power. But staying on merely delayed the inevitable moment when the president—perhaps Harrison, perhaps a Democratic successor—would demand the head of the man who stood between all those deserving applicants and their careers as public servants. It might be better to grab the future by the lapels—to resign and devote himself entirely to writing. His books weren't making him rich, but neither were they simply anchoring his publisher's warehouse against high winds. He could certainly use the time to complete *The Winning of the West;* at the rate he was currently progressing, even the new West would be but a vague memory by the time he had done with the old one. His publisher—family friend and business partner George Haven Putnam—was politely importuning him to finish the book.

Roosevelt had complicated matters for himself by agreeing, before the civil service appointment came up, to write a history of New York City. This volume would be part of a series on historic American cities and towns edited by Professor E. A. Freeman, an English academic. (That Lodge was doing Boston had encouraged Roosevelt to accept the New York assignment.) Although the book would be brief and based mostly on published accounts, and therefore wouldn't take a great deal of time once he got down to it, he couldn't seem to get started. "It has been weighing over me like a nightmare for the past eighteen months," he told Putnam early in 1890. He added, by way of assuring Putnam that the West remained his top priority: "I was led into the Freeman matter in a moment of weakness, not at the time understanding the consequences of my promise, and now I cannot honorably back out." He explained how difficult it was to get any serious writing done while devoting his daytime hours to the public's business; he concluded in a handwritten postscript to the typed letter: "I half wish I was out of this Civil Service Commission work, for I can't do satisfactorily with the *Winning of the West* until I am; but I suppose I really ought to stand by it for at least a couple of years."

But standing by it grew increasingly difficult. Following the 1890 Republican beating, Harrison was in no position to alienate any of the few survivors. He became even less interested than before in civil service matters. Roosevelt privately railed against "the little runt of a President" and complained: "He has never given us one ounce of real backing. He won't see us, or consider any method for improving the service, even when it in no way touches a politician. It is horribly disheartening to work under such a Chief."

The mugwumps still liked Roosevelt, but their applause was simply another evil omen. "As for their praise of me, it is I am sorry to say a measure and sign of the fact that my career is over, and that though as I firmly believe I have done a good work—the best work I could do—yet that in doing it I have spent and exhausted my influence with the party and country. I am at the end of my career, such as it is."

For all his discouragement, Roosevelt remained philosophical. Harrison might be ignoring him, but that wasn't all to the bad. "The very fact that he takes so little interest gives me a free hand to do some things." Besides, a man accomplished what he could, not necessarily what he would. "I know well that in life one must do the best one can with the implements at hand, and not bemoan the lack of ideal ones."

III

Whether or not the civil service job led anywhere, at least it allowed him to widen and deepen his circle of friends. He got to know Spring Rice better than ever; during summers when Edith and the children had moved back to Long Island, Roosevelt shared digs with "Springy." Through Spring Rice, he took up with the British minister in Washington, Julian Pauncefote. His English connections also included a renewed acquaintance with James Bryce, the author of the already influential *American Commonwealth* and later British ambassador to the United States; when Bryce visited America in August 1890, Roosevelt escorted him around Washington. "Each morning I breakfasted alone with him and his wife—a bright, pleasant woman," Roosevelt reported, with satisfaction. "One day we lunched in the Speaker's [Reed's] room." On another day Roosevelt hosted a dinner for Bryce and several Republican leaders, including Reed, McKinley, and Joseph Cannon. "They are an able set of men, and Bryce thoroughly appreciated them," Roosevelt said. "He grasped at once the distinction between these men who *do* things, and the others who only think or talk about how they ought to be done." In the latter category

Roosevelt classed the mugwumps, against whom he warned Bryce. "He ended his letter of thanks, when he left, 'I won't let myself be captured by excessive mugwumpery after your warnings.'" Pleased with himself, Roosevelt told Lodge, "So you see I did good missionary work."

Some months later Roosevelt reported another social and political triumph.

On Wednesday and Thursday evenings of this week I gave two dinners, assisted by Springy, with nice colored Millie as cook and waitress. First dinner. Guests, the British Minister [Pauncefote] and the Secretary of War [Redfield Proctor]. Bill of fare, crabs, chicken and rice, cherries, claret and tea. (Neither guest died; and I think Proctor, who is a good native American, hungered for pie, in addition.) Springy nervous and fidgety; I, with my best air of oriental courtesy, and a tendency to orate only held in check by the memory of my wife [Edith was at Oyster Bay] and intimate friend [Lodge]. 2nd Dinner. Guests, the Secretary of the Navy [B. F. Tracy] and the British Minister, who was laboriously polite and good but somewhat heavy in grappling with the novelty of the situation. Bill of fare, chops and rice, *paté de foie gras,* raspberries, claret and tea. (Guests still survive.) Springy still nervous. Tracy in great form, very amusing and entertaining.

I'll bet they were dinners new to Sir Julian's experience, but both the Secretaries enjoyed them.

Roosevelt did, too, needless to say. As much as anything it was this sort of opportunity to mingle with the powerful that kept him in Washington. Civil service reform might not win him many friends, but as a base for networking the commission had real advantages. Come what may, he could look on his time spent there as an investment in his future. Since he had already lost a large part of the money he had available to invest, time was about all he had to work with.

IV

Of course, staying in Washington kept Roosevelt away from his family. For much of each year, after they made their annual migration back to Sagamore Hill, he lived apart from Edith and the children. He missed out on some important moments—first steps, first tumbles, first sentences. Edith was growing used to his absences, but she couldn't help wishing he were around more. "Come home just as soon as you can," she wrote in one letter. "Please think of me all the time," in another. "The children want you so much," in a third.

In the late summer of 1890 he attempted modestly to make up for his absences. He didn't cancel his annual trip to the West, but he did take Edith along—together with Bamie, Corinne and Douglas Robinson, and Lodge's teenage son "Bay." Acting as tour guide, he showed off Medora and its picturesque characters, including Bill Merrifield and the Ferris brothers; the Badlands and the Elkhorn ranch; and the various locales of some of his frontier exploits. They all then proceeded by train farther west to the Yellowstone country of Wyoming, where they visited the nation's first national park, now eighteen years old. A pack trip along the continental divide, amid the dazzling weather of early September, revealed the wonders of the region: the boiling springs, the booming geysers, the thundering falls, the iridescent mud pools—not to mention the Rocky Mountain flora and fauna. Although one of the geysers spooked Edith's horse, which threw her to the ground, she thrived on the journey and on her husband's attention. "I have rarely seen Edith enjoy anything more than she did the six days at my ranch, and the trip through the Yellowstone Park," Roosevelt wrote to his mother-in-law. "And she looks just as well and young and pretty and happy as she did four years ago when I married her—indeed I sometimes almost think she looks if possible even sweeter and prettier."

This same letter revealed some of Roosevelt's ambivalence about his relationship with his children. Ostensibly a report to a grandmother living abroad, it doubled obliquely as a report on the state of his own feelings.

> The children are darlings. Alice has grown more and more affectionate, and is devoted to, and worshipped by, both the boys; Kermie holds out his little arms to her whenever she comes near, and she really takes care of him like a little mother. Ted eyes him with some suspicion; and when I take the wee fellow up in my arms Ted clings tightly to one of my legs, so that I can hardly walk.

Kermie crawls with the utmost rapidity; and when he is getting towards some forbidden spot and we call to him to stop Ted always joins in officiously and overtaking the small yellow-haired wanderer seizes him with his chubby hands round the neck and trys to drag him back—while the enraged Kermie endeavors to retaliate. Kermie is a darling little fellow, so soft and sweet.

As for blessed Ted he is just as much of a comfort as he ever was. I think he really loves me, and after I come back from an absence he greets me with wild enthusiasm, due however, I fear, in great part to knowledge that I am sure to have a large paper bundle of toys—which produces the query of "Fats in de bag," while he dances like an expectant little bear.

When I come in to afternoon tea he and Alice sidle hastily round to my chair, knowing that I will surreptitiously give them all the icing off the cake, if I can get Edith's attention attracted elsewhere; and every evening I have a wild romp with them, usually assuming the role of "a very big bear" while they are either little bears, or "a raccoon and a badger, papa." Ted has a most warm, tender, loving little heart; but I think he is a manly little fellow too. In fact I take the utmost possible enjoyment out of my three children; and so does Edith.

One can easily picture Roosevelt as the oft-absent father who somewhat guiltily ensures his children's affection by spoiling them when he arrives. "I think he really loves me," he says of Ted, not quite sure, and suspecting that the child's affection has been purchased by the goodies he brings home. He conspires with them against their mother; he romps with them in the evening as their playmate. He acts more like an uncle or a grandparent than like a father; and perhaps he feels that way.

V

Another family matter caused Roosevelt even greater concern at this time than the ambiguities of his relations with his children. Brother Elliott was in a sad state. While Theodore had been making his brilliant start in New York state politics during the early 1880s, Elliott had continued to flounder. Following Theodore and Alice's wedding, he had headed across the Atlantic for a grand tour of

England and the Continent, and then a hunting extravaganza in the Indian subcontinent. He shot elephants and tigers (including the one that had graced Theodore's office in Albany), and fell into the luxurious but essentially aimless existence of the British colonial ruling class. He also contracted some kind of recurrent fever, against which he liberally medicated himself with various kinds of liquor.

He returned home via China in time for his sister Corinne's wedding to Douglas Robinson, and shortly thereafter fell in love himself. His darling was Anna Hall, a New York society beauty whose life was as aimless as his, although, being a woman, her aimlessness occasioned less comment. When the romance turned serious and an engagement was announced, family members hoped the marriage would settle Elliott down. "I think the dear old boy has won a lovely girl for his wife," Theodore told Corinne before he got to know Anna well; to their mother he declared, "I honestly believe it to be a great thing for Nell to marry and settle down with a definite purpose in life."

Unfortunately, married life did not settle Elliott down. Anna simply provided further excuse to indulge his addiction to the endless round of parties, hunts, races, and dances; and the emotional demands of marriage made those distractions more appealing. "I do hate his Hempstead life," Theodore told Bamie. "I don't know whether he could get along without the excitement now, but it certainly is unhealthy, and it leads to nothing." Perhaps because he appreciated the stabilizing effect of Edith's steady personality on his own life, Theodore increasingly blamed Anna for not supplying the same to Elliott's. "Anna, sweet though she is, is an impossible person to deal with. Her totally frivolous life has, as was inevitable, eaten into her character like an acid." In another letter, in which he again referred to "darling Anna," he condemned her "thoroughly Chinese moral and mental perspective."

But it wasn't just the lifestyle that Elliott was addicted to. His alcoholism was increasingly apparent, and following a riding accident in which his leg was badly broken and then so badly set that it had to be broken again, he apparently became addicted to the opiates he took for the pain. His addictions exacerbated his low self-esteem and what clearly was a grave condition of depression. He grew unpredictable— at times still the charming old Nell, at other times a sullen, slovenly, resentful wretch. He doted on his daughter Eleanor, then abandoned her and her younger brother Elliott Jr. and Anna for weeks at a time. Theodore, Bamie, and Corinne came to dread his approach.

After Theodore and Edith moved to Washington, the burden of dealing with Elliott fell on Bamie. "I hate to think of you in your time of worry and real anguish over Elliott," Theodore wrote Bamie during the spring of 1890, "and to be able to be of no possible assistance myself. Edith and I talk over it all the while. It is a perfect nightmare." Theodore wrote his brother periodically, remonstrating with him to pull himself together. "But of course it will do no good," he mused. The only thing that would do any good, he concluded, was for Elliott to seek competent professional help. "Elliott must be put under some good man, and then sent off on a sea voyage, or made to do whatever else he is told." The advice about the sea voyage was partly for Elliott's benefit—to dry him out and to get him away from the evil influences that had brought him to such a state. It was also for Theodore's own benefit and that of the rest of the family. As Theodore explained to Bamie: "Half measures simply put off the day, make the case more hopeless, and render the chance of public scandal greater."

The chance of scandal appeared to diminish when Elliott took Anna and the two children to Europe in the summer of 1890. Perhaps he hoped that by leaving behind the familiar sources of his temptation, he could more easily get a grip on himself; perhaps he simply didn't want to have to face the spoken and unspoken reprimands of family and friends. Things got no better, however—only worse. He ran through money faster than ever, and in his frustration he often threatened and sometimes inflicted violence on Anna, now pregnant again. In late 1890, Anna wrote to Bamie, asking her to come and keep her company during her pregnancy. Bamie did more than that. On arrival in Austria she half-shamed, half-dragged Elliott to a sanitarium, where she also rented a room for herself to keep guard over her younger brother. The treatment gradually took hold; by April 1891, Elliott's doctors and Bamie agreed that he might leave the center. She escorted him to Paris, where in June he greeted the birth of his and Anna's third child.

But developments back home pretty well ruined this otherwise promising turn. Some months earlier a young woman who had been one of Elliott and Anna's servants and was now pregnant claimed that Elliott was the father of the child she was carrying. Although Theodore hoped this Katy Mann was lying, he feared she wasn't, and he realized that if her claim was true, it could destroy the family name forever—and certainly would do nothing good for the political career of one who made such a fetish of character and integrity. "The last hideous revelation hangs over me like a nightmare," he told Bamie. During the first half of 1891 he vacillated between believing Katy Mann's assertions and Elliott's denials. In March he wrote Bamie, "From what you say Katy Mann's story must be true." Yet, still hoping to salvage some respect for Elliott, he added, "Of course he was insane when he did it." In the next two months he rethought the matter. "We believe Elliott innocent," he declared.

At this point, however, innocence alone wasn't sufficient to avert the scandal that Theodore feared. Katy Mann was threatening a lawsuit. "We regard it as mere blackmail," he told Bamie, "but remember what a hideous tale of his life we should have to testify to if put on the stand." For one of the few times ever, Theodore found himself morally at a loss as to what to do. "I hate the idea of the public scandal; and yet I never believe in yielding a handsbreadth to a case of simple blackmail. . . . I am at my wits' end to know what to advise."

In the end he advised discretion and gained Elliott's approval to try to arrange a quiet settlement. Theodore's relief was palpable. "How glad I am that I got his authorization to compromise the Katy Mann affair!" he declared. Yet Katy Mann wasn't to be bought off easily or cheaply. Her price astounded Theodore even as it killed any hopes of a quick disposal of the matter. "K.M. has demanded so huge a sum— $10,000.00—that negotiations are at a standstill," he reported to Bamie in July. For that kind of money she was going to have to provide some very convincing evidence that Elliott was indeed the father.

She did, in the form of the baby. Theodore hired a detective experienced in such matters, who pronounced the unwelcome verdict. "Cosgrove has seen the baby," Theodore relayed to Bamie. "He went over to Brooklyn believing the case one of mere blackmail; he came back convinced from the likeness that K.M.'s story is true. It is his business to be an expert in likenesses."

In the face of this opinion, Theodore, Bamie, and Corinne agreed to settle. The amount they consented to pay remains unclear, as does the portion of the payment that survived the grasp of Katy Mann's lawyers. Theodore never met or acknowledged the child in question, his nephew Elliott Roosevelt Mann, although Douglas Robinson did, and years later some correspondence passed between the child—then an adult—and Theodore's niece (and the nephew's half-sister), Eleanor Roosevelt.

The narrow avoidance of scandal in the paternity case exhausted Roosevelt's patience and sympathy toward his brother. From this point his letters became filled with angry denunciations. He urged Bamie to confront Elliott: "Tell him that he is either responsible or irresponsible. If irresponsible then he must go where he can be cured; if irresponsible he is simply a selfish, brutal and vicious criminal." Ten days later he declared: "He is evidently a maniac, morally no less than mentally." Lest there be any question, he added in this same letter that his brother was "a dangerous maniac." Another three days later he asserted, "If he is not utterly irresponsible then his moral condition is one of hideous depravity." Elliott could do nothing right, in Theodore's eyes; even correspondence that appeared more or less normal was turned against him. "This morning I had a dreadful letter from Elliott. The horrible part is it is quite a sane letter, but with a hideous lack of moral sensibility about it. It is all horrible beyond belief."

Theodore evidently believed that Elliott's particular brand of depravity was hereditary, for he went to great lengths to keep his brother from having any more children. "I regard it as little short of criminal for Anna to continue to live with him and bear his children," he told Bamie in March 1891. Nor did he think Anna's views carried any weight in the matter. "Anna has no *right* to live with him henceforth." He reiterated this theme during the last months of Anna's pregnancy. "It is no less criminal than foolish for her to go on living with him." The birth of Anna and Elliott's child simply confirmed his judgment. "It is dreadful to think of the inheritance the poor little baby may have in him," he wrote, before repeating what he had said earlier: "I regard it as criminal for her to have any more children by Elliott."

To prevent this happening, as well as to forestall further scandals and the final squandering of Elliott's share of the family fortune, Theodore and Bamie initiated legal efforts to have Elliott declared insane. From Paris, Elliott defended his sanity, and the quarrel spilled into the open, to Theodore and everyone else's dismay. The New York court hearing the insanity pleadings appointed a committee to weigh the merits of the matter, raising the likelihood that all the details of Elliott's sad and irresponsible history would be laid out for the whole world to observe.

The very thought appalled Theodore. For some months he had been pondering whether to go to Europe himself to have things out with Elliott, but he wanted to be sure his actions would be definitive. "I come on but one condition," he told Bamie in June. "I come to settle the thing once for all." By the end of the year he concluded he had no choice, and off he went to Paris.

Elliott was alternately belligerent and plaintive; Theodore was stern. In certain respects the confrontation represented the climax of the sibling rivalry that had long created tension between the two. Theodore interpreted it so, at any rate, for when he persuaded Elliott to give up a large part of his money and to separate from Anna— although without being declared insane—he commenced his report to Bamie with the single word, "Won!" He went on to recount the victory: "I had been perfectly quiet, but absolutely unwavering and resolute with him; and he now surrendered completely, and was utterly broken, submissive and repentant." The terms of the surrender specified that Elliott would sign over two-thirds of his property to Anna and enter a rehabilitation program in the United States. Until he demonstrated his worthiness to reenter the family circle, he would live apart from Anna and the children. Theodore was magnanimous in victory: "I then instantly changed my whole manner, and treated him with the utmost love and tenderness." For his part, Elliott promised to do all he could to win back his brother and family's respect. Theodore couldn't help being moved; he described Elliott's words and demeanor as "terribly touching." All the same, he wasn't going to get carried away. "How long it will last of course no one can say."

VI

Roosevelt's own money troubles made him especially sensitive to Elliott's squandering of his inheritance. Elliott was throwing his money away on what Theodore, even at his most generous—which in such instances wasn't generous at all—could only consider debauchery. Theodore, by contrast, had lost much of his own money in a far better cause in Dakota. But the end result was the same.

Roosevelt's expenses escalated in August 1891 with the arrival of a new baby, Edith's first girl. Ethel was a healthy, solid lass, so sturdy that her father, with scant sensitivity to how she might feel about it later, took to calling her "Elephant Johnny." Although the six of them still rattled around in the house at Sagamore Hill, the quarters they occupied in Washington were becoming cramped—all the more since the rented home in the capital lacked the surrounding open acreage that made Oyster Bay ideal for the older children, who already were showing some of their father's famous energy. Accordingly, when Edith and the children joined Theodore in Washington at the end of the year, all moved into a larger house on Jefferson Place, not far from their previous home.

But a bigger house and more and bigger children cost more money. "My darling," Edith wrote in a note typical of the period. "This will be a depressing letter all about bills." She enumerated the damage, then asked, "How many of them do you think you can pay?" She constantly sought means to trim inessential outlays. She placed Roosevelt on an allowance and scanned the monthly bills for possible economies. At one point she asked him if he might consider resigning from the Harvard Club to save the dues.

Yet there was only so much she could accomplish. Roosevelt considered it necessary to entertain, and if the dinners they gave weren't sumptuous, neither were they niggardly. Certain habits of his died hard—or not at all. A few weeks after Ethel's birth, at a time when Edith was doing her best to stretch their income across their expenditures, Roosevelt headed west for a six-week hunting trip.

Bad news in the spring of 1892 brought some good news: The death of a Carow uncle promised a bequest that would ease the budgetary burden. When the estate was settled, Edith received an annual income of some twelve hundred dollars—not enough to banish financial worries but sufficient to keep them at arm's length.

For his part, Roosevelt sought to supplement his income as a civil servant with continued literary efforts. He plugged away at volumes three and four of *The Winning of the West,* but that work still went slowly, requiring the sustained periods of attention he rarely found. He had an easier time managing short pieces—reviews and essays that, earning him little money immediately, increased his visibility and reputation as a man of letters and might pay off in the longer term.

VII

In the short term, Roosevelt was better known as a Republican attack dog. Even those party leaders who opposed his assaults on the spoils system applauded his assaults on the party's foes, and at each election they turned him loose to chew on the Democrats. Roosevelt relished the work: He thrived on being the center of attention at campaign rallies, and he loved the warm moral glow that came with castigating the villainy of the party of Jefferson and the rebellion. He also appreciated that, for all his efforts on behalf of civil service reform, the higher appointments went to those who had contributed to the party's victories. Wealthy men contributed money; lacking ready cash, he had only his strong voice and his robust rectitude.

The approach of the election of 1892 brought Roosevelt up to peak form. A recent run-in between the U.S. Navy and some Chilean vessels had prompted a war-warning by the Harrison administration, an action many Democrats labeled overwrought and reckless. Roosevelt publicly defended his chief to the hilt. "It is safe to state in the most sweeping terms possible that throughout the controversy with Chile the United States was absolutely in the right and Chile absolutely in the wrong." Democratic critics of the president were equally wrong, treating the Chilean challenge "in a spirit of the grossest partisanship, and with the most contemptible lack of all true American feeling."

In the late summer of 1892, Roosevelt followed an inspection trip of Indian reservations and schools with a campaign swing across the West on behalf of Harrison and against third-time candidate Grover Cleveland. The response was gratifying. "In Deadwood [South Dakota] I was enthusiastically received, and opened the Republican campaign by speaking to a really large audience in the fearful local opera house," he told Lodge.

The Republicans needed the help in the West. A tide of rural radicalism was rising on the plains and prairies; just that summer the northern and southern wings of the Farmers' Alliance had linked arms in the Populist Party. "The Farmers' Alliance is giving our people serious concern in Kansas, Nebraska and South Dakota," Roosevelt recorded. In Illinois and Wisconsin, German immigrants who until recently had been staunch Republicans were similarly succumbing to the Populist message. Roosevelt judged this prima facie evidence of the folly of unrestricted immigration. He said he felt like "making a crusade" against the Germans of the upper Midwest to pound some sense into their Teutonic heads. "I wish the cholera would result in a permanent quarantine against most immigrants!"

As election day neared, the race was too close to call. The voters in many areas were holding back. "There is astonishingly little excitement over the President contest," Roosevelt noted with some puzzlement. "The country as a whole feels reasonably content, and very sure that both Harrison and Cleavland are pretty good men, and that we are safe with either." To Lodge he remarked, "I don't know what to say. We have an excellent fighting chance; but I think the odds are a little against us. [Democratic boss David B.] Hill and Tammany seem to be pulling straight for Cleveland in New York; and it would be comic, were it not outrageous, to see how anxious the mugwumps are to let them have everything, if they'll only help Cleveland." Wisconsin and Illinois looked very bad. "The movement among the Lutheran and Catholic Germans against us is most formidable; and it means a landslide, unless the latent Americanism in native Democrats is awakened—and though this may be, I hardly dare hope for it." The Populists were rampaging on the plains, but Roosevelt caught a glimmer of a chance there, saying, "The old party feeling is strong, even among the German Lutherans and the wild Farmers' Alliance cranks."

Although a Republican victory would better serve his own interests, Roosevelt was candid enough to recognize that a Democratic triumph wouldn't necessarily kill the cause of civil service reform. He wrote Lodge from his desk in Washington,

> Frankly, I think the record pretty bad for both Cleveland and Harrison, and it is rather Walrus and Carpenter work choosing between the records of the two parties, as far as civil service reform is concerned. In the classified service Cleveland made more extensions than Harrison; but on the other hand Tracy has made an admirable start in the Navy Yards—but it is only a start, not permanent, and can not be until put under us. Cleveland had a much worse Commission; but Harrison has not sustained his Commission at all. . . . So I really think it about a stand off here.

If Cleveland got elected, Roosevelt could pretty well count on losing his job, but he had already survived longer than he had expected, and four years of making enemies was probably enough.

VIII

Cleveland did indeed get elected, but Roosevelt, against odds, kept his job. That he did surprised him initially. Not long after the election he wrote a friend, "When I leave on March 5 . . ." as though there was no doubt about the matter. Within a few more weeks, however, he was beginning to think perhaps his time hadn't yet come. After all, it made good political sense for Cleveland to retain him, at least for a while. The whole idea of the civil service system was to push partisanship off the table. If Cleveland, who stood on principle until it nearly collapsed under his weight, removed Roosevelt at once, the removal would smack resoundingly of the old spoils sport. Besides, by law at least one of the three commissioners had to be of the minority party, and Roosevelt's recurrent run-ins with Wanamaker and the ringleaders of the Republicans indicated that, on civil service matters at any rate, he was as good—which was to say, as bad—a Republican as the Democrats were going to get. Roosevelt himself claimed "the profound gratification of knowing that there is no man more bitterly disliked by many of the men in my own party"; this wasn't exactly a secret.

Roosevelt made sure it didn't become one during the first months of 1893. For all his brave talk of a brief career in Washington, untempered by fear of being fired, he had grown quite comfortable in his position in the capital. He had made influential friends, and although the Republican Party had lost the last two elections, the wheel would keep turning, and his friends would eventually return to office. His closest friend—Cabot Lodge—had survived the party's latest loss and come out stronger than ever: In January 1893 the Massachusetts legislature elected him to the Senate. Roosevelt delighted in plotting strategy with Lodge and excoriating their mutual foes; he would miss this fun if he left Washington.

Accordingly, Roosevelt discreetly lobbied to stay on. He swallowed his distaste for the mugwumpish record of Carl Schurz and wrote him a cordial letter. Schurz, who had close ties to the Cleveland camp, had indicated an interest in discussing the civil service with Roosevelt. "I am very anxious to see you about civil service matters myself," Roosevelt replied. "I need not say that I am always anxious to see you on other matters likewise." Later in this letter Roosevelt resorted to flattery: "By the way, I can never help regretting that you would not do the Lincoln for the Statesmen series. It ought to have been a crowning piece of what really on the whole is a pretty good series. We do want a comparatively short biography of Lincoln written by a master hand. I think your sketch of Lincoln is by far the best thing that has ever been published about him." Regarding the present business, Roosevelt said he had contemplated calling on the president-elect but had decided that this would be an unwarrantable intrusion on a very busy man. Perhaps Mr. Schurz would have a moment? "I should like to see you who stand so close to him and to tell you exactly how the civil service question appears to me here." When Schurz answered that Roosevelt should go see Cleveland, Roosevelt countered: "I should rather communicate with Mr. Cleavland through you; can I not see you first?" Perhaps he could visit Mr. Schurz on the way to the White House. "If I could see you first I should be very glad; say earlier on the same day I saw Mr. Cleavland." (Roosevelt may have divined that writing to "Mr. Cleavland" to request an interview wouldn't be a good idea for one in charge of examining, among other things, the spelling skills of applicants to the civil service.)

Roosevelt's persistence paid off, and, as he obviously hoped, Schurz accompanied him to his session with Cleveland. Roosevelt pitched his case for keeping the civil service above partisanship; Cleveland, who could do political sums as well as Roosevelt, likewise came to the conclusion that retaining Roosevelt would be of benefit to both of them and perhaps to the country at large. He told Roosevelt he wanted him to stay.

Roosevelt never liked thinking of himself as a supplicant. And sure enough, he soon began talking as though in remaining at his civil service post he was doing Cleveland a favor. One can imagine Carl Schurz's reaction to a letter in which Roosevelt pronounced,

> I will stay if he wishes it, provided, always, that he has a good commission. It would be folly for me to try to accomplish anything as a

Republican fighting Democratic colleagues over the actions of Democratic spoilsmen under a Democratic administration. I don't mean folly for my own fortunes, because they would not be affected by it. On the contrary, I would gain credit rather than otherwise; but I mean that it would not benefit the reform nor the administration. I do hope that he gets a first-class commission, and if he does I care very little whether he retains me or not.

Yet, as Roosevelt's lobbying on his own behalf made evident, he did indeed care whether Cleveland kept him on. After nearly a decade as a faithful party man, Roosevelt was beginning to discover the limits of partisanship. At twenty-three he had thought he could remake the Republican Party in his own image; for three years he engendered distrust in the party regulars by his irregular ways. After the 1884 convention, however, he had sought to mend fences, campaigning for party candidates and hewing to the party line. And what had it earned him? A chance to play sacrificial lamb in the 1886 New York mayor's race and a lousy job overseeing exams for prospective postmasters. The simple fact was that the Republican Party wasn't going to be reformed. The entrenched interests—from the ward heelers in the districts to the bosses of the boardrooms—had too much at stake in the status quo to let the likes of Roosevelt overturn it.

As much as it galled him, Roosevelt had to realize that the mugwumps were his natural constituency. His was a moralistic temperament that desired clean contrasts; so did the mugwumps'. He liked to think of himself as one who refused to compromise on matters of principle; the mugwumps made a fetish of noncompromise. Though he never seems to have put the matter in quite such terms, in his honest hours he must have had a harder time seeing his father—his moral guide in such matters—seated next to James Blaine or John Wanamaker than allied to Carl Schurz.

By the mid–1890s, as Roosevelt's hopes of a political career in the Republican camp withered, his bitter partisanship showed signs of wearing thin, too. He began to look on the mugwumps and even reform Democrats with greater sympathy. Schurz wasn't such a bad fellow, and a man could work with Cleveland, if matters came to that. At thirty-five, Roosevelt was hearing the first distant strains of the trumpet that would call him out of the party of his youth and onto the Lord's ramparts at Armageddon.

IX

Politics apart, Roosevelt had reason to want to hang on to his job at the civil service commission. During the spring of 1893 the American economy plunged through a crust of foreign investment into the sinkhole of depression. Since the onset of industrialization in the early nineteenth century, American business had been subject to cycles of boom and bust, advance and retreat; but the extent and severity of the bust of the 1890s stunned even those who had lived through several rounds of the economic cycle. "Men died like flies under the strain," wrote Henry Adams, who himself woke one day to find himself crushed under debts he hadn't known he had. The situation was the more stressful for being mystifyingly automatic. "The more he saw of it," said Adams of himself in his archly analytical third-person voice, "the less he understood it. He was quite sure that nobody understood it much better. Blindly some very powerful energy was at work, doing something that nobody wanted done."

The depression didn't hammer Roosevelt quite so hard as Adams; Uncle James had found safer havens for the Roosevelt fortune than the Adamses' financial adviser had for theirs. But neither did the depression do Roosevelt and Edith's financial circumstances any good. Compounding their distress was their discovery that their financial counselor—brother-in-law Douglas Robinson—had made a large error. "Even my Micawber-like temperament has been unable to withstand a shock it received this week," Roosevelt confided to Bamie a few days before Christmas 1893. "Douglas blandly wrote me that there had been a mistake as to my income and expenditure, and that I was $2,500 behind!" Until this point he and Edith—especially Edith—had been scrimping here and trimming there; now they must redouble their efforts, with no guarantee of success. "We are going to do everything possible to cut down expenses this year; if we again run behind I see nothing to do save to leave Sagamore." Should they survive the next twelve or twenty-four months, the longer term looked hardly better, for then the children would begin to require education. "The trouble is that my career has been a very pleasant, honorable and a useful career for a man of means; but not the right career for a man without the means." Roosevelt told Bamie he would try to remain at the Civil Service Commission for another winter, at which time volumes three and four of his *Winning of the West* would be coming out. "I am all at sea as to what I shall do afterwards."

As usual, however, Roosevelt's response to financial distress was more rhetorical than real. He might talk of selling Sagamore—and indeed did peel off a parcel of the outlying property to Uncle James—but he changed his style of living scarcely at all. Upon receiving a stenographer's bill for one hundred dollars, he assured Edith that the total "horrified" him, but there is little evidence that he cut back significantly on stenography. He and Edith continued to maintain the two homes. They continued to entertain. If they didn't travel as extensively as they might have, that owed as much to the demands of his work and the responsibilities of parenthood as to anything else.

In the spring of 1893 they did undertake one noteworthy trip, to Chicago to see the grand world's fair. The Columbian Exposition, as it was called, celebrated the four-hundredth anniversary of the discovery of the New World by Europeans; it also celebrated America's coming of age as an industrial power. The technological marvels of the era and of the era to come—the works of Westinghouse and Edison, of Krupp and Carnegie—were on display. Electricity turned night into day on the Midway Plaisance. A huge mechanical wheel designed by the Frenchman Ferris lifted fairgoers high above the grounds to where they could see steamships arriving from over the lake horizon to the east, and the frontier vanishing over the prairie horizon to the west.

Frederick Jackson Turner came to the fair; it was here that he unveiled what would become the most influential interpretation in the history of American history. Little Egypt came to the fair; the famous belly dancer attracted considerably more attention than Turner with her own interpretation of the essential elements of the human condition. The exalted and noble came to the fair: President Cleveland opened the exhibition, assisted by the Spanish infante and a few heirs of Columbus himself. The low and mean came to the fair: pickpockets, card sharks, con men, and garden-variety thieves. The city's saloons and brothels did a booming business, kicking tips to the cops to look away while the fairgoers frolicked.

Roosevelt missed Turner, who arrived later in the summer; he spurned Little Egypt and of course the mansions of ill repute. But he was impressed all the same. Since his first visit with Elliott the summer after college, he had been to Chicago numerous times, and so before the fair opened, he questioned whether it would be worth another, special trip. Ten days in May 1893 dispelled his doubts. "Indeed Chicago was worthwhile," he told James Brander Matthews, the editor of *Atlantic Monthly*, by now a friend and one who had already been to the fair.

> The buildings make, I verily believe, the most beautiful architectural exhibit the world has ever seen. If they were only permanent! That south lagoon, with the peristyle cutting it off from the lake, the great terraces, the grandeur and beauty of the huge white buildings, the statue, the fine fountains, the dome of the administration building, the bridges guarded by the colossal animals—well, there is simply nothing to say about it. And the landscape effects are so wonderful. In the fine-arts building, by the way, did you not like the "Death arresting the hand of the sculptor," and the "Peace Sign," the quiet pose of the naked warrior on the naked horse?

X

Chicago may have reminded Roosevelt of those carefree days with Elliott. They were gone forever, and Elliott himself was going fast. During several months after being exiled to Illinois for treatment of his addictions, Elliott showed improvement. Perhaps the fear of forever losing his family and all he had grown up with strengthened his resolve. The improvement, in turn, occasioned efforts by Corinne, the most sympathetic of his three siblings, on his behalf. At her request Douglas Robinson found him a job in the Robinson family business in Virginia. The post was safely away from Anna and the children, who were in New York; it was also under the watchful eye of people who could report on Elliott's progress or otherwise.

For a time he continued to improve, apparently drying out. But in December 1892 tragedy found an unexpected opening. Anna died suddenly of diphtheria. The death seemed to cut the rope Elliott was clinging to, and within weeks he was drinking as heavily as ever. His condition spiraled downward and inward through the spring of 1893, aggravated in May by another untimely and shocking death, of his son and namesake. Elliott moved back to New York and resumed his old habits, seeking solace in drink and in the arms of one Mrs. Evans.

Theodore was now at a total loss as to what to do about his brother. After insisting on Elliott's exile from his family, Theodore had been willing to let Anna and the children be the incentive for his brother's improvement. But now that incentive had essentially evaporated. Although Corinne again pleaded sympathy, Theodore thought such emotions wasted. "I do wish Corinne could get a little of my hard heart about Elliott," he told Bamie. "She can do, and ought to do, nothing for him. He can't be helped, and he must simply be let go his own gait." Elliott had recently injured himself again. "While drunk he drove into a lamp post and went out on his head." The whole situation made Theodore reflect on the caprice of fate. "Poor fellow! if only he could have died instead of Anna!"

Edith, not surprisingly, worried more about Theodore than about Elliott. Already the Roosevelt name had been soiled by Elliott's dissipation; she feared worse to come. "Elliott has sunk to the lowest depths," she informed her mother. "Consorts with the vilest women and Theodore, Bamie and Douglas receive horrid anonymous letters about his life. I live in constant dread of some scandal of his attaching itself to Theodore."

During the summer of 1894, Elliott completed his self-destruction. Two weeks after his drunken carriage wreck, a fatal attack of delirium tremens set in. He thrashed about and tried to hurl himself out a window in a mad attempt to flee the monsters that had him at last. Finally he collapsed in a convulsive fit and expired.

Roosevelt felt torn by this final stage of his brother's demise. According to Corinne, he was "more overcome than I have ever seen him—cried like a child for a long time." The death was a tragedy, of course, but also a blessing. "He would have been in a straight jacket had he lived forty-eight hours longer," Theodore told Bamie. Death afforded Elliott a release he had been unable to find in his alcohol, his opiates, and his mistresses. It also afforded Theodore a release from his anger and his lifelong rivalry with Elliott. "When dead the poor fellow looked very peaceful, and so like his old, generous, gallant self of fifteen years ago. The horror, and the terrible mixture of sadness and grotesque, grim evil continued to the very end; and the dreadful flashes of his old sweetness, which made it all even more hopeless. I

suppose he has been doomed from the beginning; the absolute contradiction of all his actions, and of all his moral even more than his mental qualities, is utterly impossible to explain." Sympathy had been
scarce in Roosevelt's tone toward Elliott of late, but now it returned.
"For the last few days he had felt the awful night closing in on him; he
would not let us come to his house, or part with the woman [Mrs.
Evans], nor cease drinking for a moment, but he wandered ceaselessly
everywhere, never still, and he wrote again and again to us all, sending
to me two telegrams and three notes. He was like some stricken,
hunted creature; and indeed he was hunted by the most terrible
demons that ever entered into man's body and soul."

Yet Roosevelt's sympathy didn't extend to permission for Elliott to
be buried beside Anna. "I promptly vetoed this hideous plan," he
explained to Bamie. Instead he insisted that Elliott be laid to rest at
Greenwood "beside those who are associated with only his sweet
innocent youth, when no more loyal, generous, brave, disinterested
fellow lived."

The weeks after the funeral, however, brought reminders of the
more recent, more complicated times. Mrs. Evans demanded $1,250
to cover expenses related to Elliott's last days; when she didn't receive
satisfaction, she started waving a loaded revolver about. She was paci-
fied with difficulty and with a promise by the executors of the estate
that Theodore and Corinne would pay her—which Theodore indignantly refused to do. Katy Mann visited Douglas Robinson with child
in tow, reiterating her claim that the child was Elliott's. On hearing of
the visit, Theodore mused, "I have no idea whether it was or not; she
was a bad woman, but her story may have been partly true. But we
can not know. Well, it is over now; it is fortunate it is over and we
need only think of his bright youth."

XI

To Roosevelt's thinking, Elliott's disintegration represented the triumph of moral anarchy, which was why it disturbed him so. If Elliott,
the person once closest to him, could harbor the demons that
destroyed him, was anyone safe? Yet instead of dealing directly with

this fundamental question, Roosevelt preferred to suppress it and pretend that, for him at any rate, it didn't exist. That it did, despite his denials, was indicated by the fact that throughout his adult life the merest mention of anarchy—personal or social—frightened him and consequently inspired his wrath.

At times during the 1880s and 1890s anarchy seemed to be abroad in the land. To many observers the 1886 riot and bombing in Haymarket Square in Chicago appeared to presage general upheaval. Roosevelt reacted with utter contempt for the motives and objectives of the demonstrators. "My men here are hardworking, labouring men, who work longer hours for no greater wages than many of the strikers," he wrote Bamie from Dakota. "But they are Americans through and through; I believe nothing would give them greater pleasure than a chance with their rifles at one of the mobs. When we get the papers, especially in relation to the dynamite business they become more furiously angry and excited than I do. I wish I had them with me, and a fair show at ten times our number of rioters; my men shoot well and fear very little."

The specter of anarchy didn't diminish during the next several years. The industrial antagonisms that had spawned the Molly Maguires in the 1870s and the Haymarket bombing festered into the 1890s. An 1892 strike at the Carnegie steel works outside of Pittsburgh produced a pitched battle between the workers and the Pinkertons employed by Carnegie to break the strike and the steel union. The panic of 1893 added to the strains on both management and labor across the corporate spectrum, causing the former to slash wages and the latter to slash back where possible. The most spectacular strike of the decade erupted outward from Pullman, Illinois, in 1894 after George Pullman, president of the Pullman Palace Car Company and de facto dictator of the town that bore his name, ordered deep cuts in wages while holding the line on the rents of workers' homes.

At this stage of his political and intellectual development, Roosevelt still equated labor action with anarchy, and he had no more sympathy for the railroad strikers than he had had for the Haymarket men. "We have come out of the strike very well," he wrote in late July, following a decision by Cleveland and Attorney General Richard Olney to employ federal troops to break the strike. "Cleavland did excellent, so did Olney, and my friend Senator Davis of Minnesota [who had backed Cleveland against strong pro-labor sentiment in his home state] best of all." Roosevelt wasn't put off by the use of soldiers against American citizens; on the contrary, he thought such action was one test of the usefulness of the army. During the next several years Roosevelt would come to scorn Edward Atkinson, an unusual individual who combined business experience (he was a well-known industrialist) with a moral and visceral aversion to imperialism and war. Atkinson recently had written an essay characterizing America's regular army as useless; Roosevelt mentioned the essay in a letter to Lodge and commented indignantly, "And this less than two months after the Chicago strike." Roosevelt added, "I must go for that prattling creature soon; I mean just to dress him down incidentally in the course of an article."

XII

Roosevelt's publisher Haven Putnam preferred that the author leave Atkinson—and articles, for that matter—for later and concentrate on finishing the third volume of *The Winning of the West*. After many more distractions and interruptions, Roosevelt finally did during the summer of 1894. The book was published at the beginning of 1895; the first reviews followed shortly.

The one that particularly caught Roosevelt's attention appeared in *The Nation*. That journal's anonymous reviewer praised Roosevelt for a trailblazing work that joined diligent research to historical insight. The reviewer appreciated Roosevelt's personal experience of life on the frontier and seconded Roosevelt's judgment that the settling of the West was best understood as a phase in the general movement of civilization.

The reviewer did register a few complaints. Roosevelt spent too much time on battles between settlers and Indians, and not enough on the development of frontier society and the frontier economy. His treatment of some important land companies was "superficial at best." The book showed less polish than it ought; in places it was marred by "imperfect proof-reading, loose citation of authorities, and occasional whipping together of material." At times Roosevelt took an overly romantic view of his subject; at other times he succumbed to "a certain smartness of generalization which is not entirely free from the appearance of a homily."

The review closed with a barbed commendation: "We should be thankful to Mr. Roosevelt for the valuable work which he has done, while not shutting our eyes to the fact that the study of the early stages of the spread of democracy over the virgin soil of this continent is far from being exhausted."

This last comment became clearer when Roosevelt learned the identity of the reviewer. Frederick Jackson Turner naturally thought there remained much virgin soil to be tilled, since he was in the middle of a very long furrow of his own. Roosevelt discovered Turner's identity upon writing him a "Dear Sir" letter, care of *The Nation,* requesting more information about a particular archive the reviewer had alluded to. Roosevelt also employed the opportunity to defend himself against a couple of the criticisms in the review, but in an amicable tone that invited an amicable response.

When Turner responded to the invitation in a similar tone, Roosevelt initiated a friendship. Several months earlier he had written Turner for a copy of his paper on the significance of the frontier, saying, "I think you have struck some first class ideas, and have put into definite shape a good deal of thought which has been floating around rather loosely." He added that he hoped to incorporate some of Turner's ideas in his third volume on the West.

Now he reintroduced himself. "It was a great pleasure to find that you were my reviewer," he said. "I can assure you that I am not at all sensitive to intelligent criticism, and I entirely agree with you as to there being new fields for research in Western history upon which I haven't even touched." He still took exception to certain of Turner's interpretations—regarding the unity of the West, for example, which Turner considered more cohesive than Roosevelt did. But in disagreeing, again he did so agreeably, and he invited further conversation, which did indeed ensue.

XIII

Roosevelt's literary humility contrasted starkly with his political arrogance. As a historian he accepted, almost meekly, criticism of a kind that would have set his blood boiling as a politician. To some extent this owed to his awareness that as an historian he was an amateur in a field increasingly claimed by professionals. Other people, such as Turner, really did know more about the subject than he did. Humility was entirely appropriate.

At the same time, Roosevelt's modesty betrayed an uncanny—and perhaps partly unconscious—capacity to cultivate people who could advance his career. He cultivated Turner much as he had cultivated Francis Parkman and Mahan and even Lodge. There was nothing cynical about this; being a gregarious person of broad interests, he could find something to like in almost anyone. And other people could usually find something to like in the interested, intelligent person he was. His allies usually became his friends. But the fact was that Roosevelt repeatedly managed to ingratiate himself with individuals who could do his career some good. And they often did, at one stage or other.

His political career certainly could have used a good turn in the mid–1890s. Roosevelt had thought Cleveland would be no worse on civil service than Harrison; he soon decided he was no better. The evil genius in the Democratic administration, according to Roosevelt's interpretation, was Treasury Secretary John Carlisle, who kept not only the nation's financial accounts but Cleveland's political ones. For this reason Carlisle opposed civil service reform, which would deprive the president of an essential tool to pay the administration's debts. Roosevelt's ire under Harrison, especially at postmaster Wanamaker, had been somewhat ameliorated by their shared Republicanism; his righteous wrath at Democrat Carlisle knew no such countervailing influence, and he could work himself into a frenzy over the treasury secretary without the slightest pang of partisan conscience. "Not even Wanamaker was a meaner, smaller cur than Carlisle," he spluttered. "He is dishonest, untruthful and cowardly."

And Carlisle was simply the worst apple in a bad barrel. "In fact (but this is not for publication)," Roosevelt continued to Bamie, with unnecessary caution: "Cleavland's second administration is a lamentable falling off from the first; and the Democrats have given an exhibition of fairly colossal incompetence. If I read the signs aright they will meet with humiliating disaster next fall."

Roosevelt's was a common feeling among Republicans. William McKinley, currently governor of Ohio, toured the country on behalf of Republican candidates—and of himself, thinking ahead to 1896.

He succeeded in both respects, bringing out the voters with a folksy but sincere style and ringing up chits cashable two years hence. Tom Reed of Maine examined the entrails of a sacrificial offering and predicted, "The Democratic mortality will be so great next fall that their dead will be buried in trenches and marked 'Unknown.'"

This possibility caused Roosevelt to reconsider his position and prospects once again. If the Democrats indeed were doomed, now might be a prudent time to abandon ship. He would distance himself from the debacle and would gain the opportunity to fire a few rounds at his recent allies himself. Staying at his civil service post for part of an opposition administration could be justified as high-minded; staying too long would smack of party disloyalty. A Republican successor to Cleveland would have difficulty rewarding one who had stuck beyond necessity with the Democratic administration—and who had, on that account, been silent on the important partisan issues.

On the other hand, leaving Washington wouldn't be easy, for the same reasons as before. "Washington is just a big village, but it is a very pleasant big village," Roosevelt explained to Bamie. "Edith and I meet just the people we like to see. This winter we have had a most pleasant time, socially and officially." He and Edith dined out or had guests in for dinner five or six nights a week; the company was important and engaging. "The people we meet are mostly those who stand high in the political world, and who are therefore interested in the same subjects that interest us; while there are enough also who are men of letters or of science to give a pleasant and needed variety." It was most rewarding to be in close contact with people "from whom one really gets something; people from all over the Union, with different pasts and varying interests, trained, able, powerful men, though often narrow minded enough."

Such company shouldn't be abandoned lightly, and so Roosevelt weighed his options carefully. In the late summer of 1894 a group of reformist Republicans approached him about making another run for mayor of New York. An independent organization, styled the Group of Seventy, had nominated William Strong, an honest but politically inexperienced businessman who was campaigning on a platform to clean up the corruption at city hall. The Republicans struggled to find a candidate who could appeal to the same good-government constituency as Strong. Someone suggested Roosevelt's name to Thomas

Platt, the reigning kingmaker of New York Republican politics; Platt allowed himself to be persuaded.

Roosevelt had reservations about working with Platt, largely because of the boss's ill repute in the circles Roosevelt favored. He told Lodge:

> It is curious to see how bitter the anti-Platt feeling is. It is not so much anything that Platt does, but the fact that he is unwise enough to say things attacking reformers, and making a show of bossism, which sets many people against him. The professional reformers in the city are loudest against him, but they are not really the ones that hurt. It is the farmers in the country and the men in the small cities, who have a vague idea that they want to be against him because he is a boss, and who have a queer distrust of the machine, so often irrational, which is, I am inclined to think, a real marked attribute of the Republican party.

Partly on account of his misgivings about Platt, but mostly because of the opposition of Edith, who had grown attached to their social set in Washington and who didn't want him to give up a paying job for the vagaries of elective politics, Roosevelt declined the offer of the nomination.

XIV

Within weeks he was berating himself for doing so, for the simple reason that he began to realize he might have won. The thought galled him no end. Looking at his life, Roosevelt could find little to show for his thirty-five years. He was an abject failure at the one business venture to which he had devoted any energy: his cattle ranch. His political career, after a fast start, had fizzled; to the extent that anyone even knew what a civil service commissioner did, the post appeared a cross between a schoolmarm and a street sweeper. It was enough to make one despair of the whole idea of public office. "High attainments in this country," he wrote one aspiring public servant, "have far greater reward in private than in public employment." As for his books, they appealed to a small circle of history buffs and cognoscenti—but what was writing about history compared to making history? Where the romance and the heroism?

Things might have been worse, of course. He had only to consider Elliott's sad fate to see what could befall a man. Elliott had begun with such promise and ended so ignominiously. And yet the lesson for Roosevelt of Elliott's demise wasn't that life was capricious but that the struggle against despair must never end. Elliott had been lost because he hadn't found anything truly grand to strive for. If the darkness could swallow Elliott, it might swallow anyone, but only if one ceased to strive.

Roosevelt couldn't complain about his marriage. If not for Edith and her ability to manage money, he might have lost the house at Sagamore. If not for Edith, he wouldn't have had his children—obviously not the younger ones, and even Alice would probably still be with Bamie. If not for Edith, his social circle in Washington would be sparer and less rewarding. If not for Edith . . .

If not for Edith he might be mayor of New York. Almost as soon as Roosevelt said no to the offer of the Republican nomination, he recognized that he had underestimated the height of the reformist wave cresting across his home city. Strong's candidacy lived up to the candidate's name, and as the election approached he looked increasingly like a winner.

Roosevelt was certain he could have beaten Strong, and with each passing day the knowledge gnawed at him. "The last four weeks, ever since I decided not to run, have been pretty bitter ones for me," he told Lodge. "I would literally have given my right arm to have made the race, win or lose. It was the one golden chance, which never returns." The more he thought about it, the more he appreciated what a coup it would have been to leap from the Civil Service Commission to the mayor's mansion in New York. The timing would have been perfect. Tammany had never been weaker, as a result of recent revelations of more spectacular corruption than usual. Roosevelt had spent five-and-a-half years administering good government to the nation as a whole; now he could have come triumphantly back home. In those days there was no such thing as an essentially national political candidate; a man had to have a solid base in his home town and state in order to make any mark in national affairs. If Roosevelt still aspired to a political career—and he did, particularly during campaign seasons— he needed to cultivate voters in New York. The more he thought about the opportunity just lost, the more it angered him.

And the more he blamed Edith—or, rather, the more he blamed himself for listening to Edith. "At the time, with Edith feeling as intensely as she did, I did not see how I could well go in," he confided to Lodge. But now he saw that he was wrong. "I have grown to feel more and more that in this instance I should have gone counter to her wishes and made the race anyhow." Roosevelt granted that the fault was his. "I should have realized that she could not see the matter as it really was, or realize my feelings." But the end result was the same.

If Roosevelt was bitter, Edith was distraught. Their eight years of marriage had been comparatively calm until now. Theodore's one career move during that time—to Washington and the Civil Service Commission—had come when the family was still small and easily transported. Most other decisions had been domestic—to lease this house or that, to spend more or less time in Oyster Bay or Washington—and Theodore had been happy enough to defer to her wishes. Family crises had been about other people, principally Elliott.

But this was a crisis about Theodore and Edith, and the old insecurity rushed back. "He never should have married me," she told Bamie, "and then he would have been free to make his own course." She confessed that she hadn't fully understood either Theodore's desire for the mayoralty or the terms on which the nomination was offered. "If I knew what I do now I should have thrown all my influence in the scale with Corinne's and helped instead of hindering him."

It only aggravated her wound that Theodore disappeared to Dakota after declining the nomination. She knew he was brooding over his missed opportunity, and she imagined the worst. She resolved never again to make the mistake she had just made. She would keep her opinion on such matters to herself. "This is a lesson that will last my life," she told Bamie: "never to give it for it is utterly worthless when given, worse than that in this case for it has helped to spoil some years of a life which I would have given my own for."

XV

The crisis gradually passed. Bamie took Edith and the children to Vermont for a vacation, and Theodore, returning home from the

West, began to see reason for hope that he wouldn't languish on the Civil Service Commission forever. After Strong did indeed win, Roosevelt quietly let it be known that he wouldn't necessarily reject an appointive post in the new mayor's administration. Advocates of good government must put their shoulders to the wheel together to ensure that the will of the voters, so clearly expressed in the recent election, not be frustrated by rearguard action by the blackguard interests.

Yet he wasn't going to take just any position; he had his dignity to consider. After more than half a decade in the national spotlight, whatever role he assumed on the New York stage would have to be a principal one. In early December, Strong offered him appointment as commissioner of street cleaning. If the job had had a more illustrious title, he might have accepted. As it was, he nearly did. "I was very strongly tempted to take it," he told Carl Schurz. But after agonizing over the pros and cons, he said no. The reason he gave was that his civil service work wasn't quite finished.

> My New York friends, rather to my amusement, all took the ground that the work of cleaning the streets of New York was practically necessary, and that this work here at Washington was merely "academic," and of very little consequence comparatively. But as I told them this is all nonsense. In the last six years we have added 25,000 employees to the classified service. In a few cases the changes have been merely nominal, but in the bulk the change is real and permanent. In another year I will have put this business in position so that I can leave it with a clear conscience, but I do not want to spend six years' faithful work at a thing and then leave it, for another work, with the ends all loose, and just when I could tie these ends up by staying a twelvemonth longer.

To Jacob Riis, the crusading journalist, author of *How the Other Half Lives,* and a man who would join him in campaigns against corruption, Roosevelt wrote, "I should have been delighted to smash up the corrupt contractors and to have tried to put the street cleaning commissioner's force absolutely out of the domain of politics; but with the actual work of cleaning the streets, dumping the garbage, etc., I wasn't familiar. It was out of my line, and, moreover, I didn't feel that I could leave this work here—in which I believe with all my heart and soul—for at least a year to come, and so I had to refuse."

There was something to Roosevelt's reasoning, but much was rationalization. This became apparent just a few months later when he accepted a better offer from Strong. For years the New York Police Department had been the object of efforts at reform; lately these had been spearheaded by Dr. Charles Parkhurst, the hellfire-and-damnation pastor of the Madison Square Presbyterian Church, who made it his personal mission to stamp out vice in New York, including that part overlooked or abetted by the police. Roosevelt supported police reform, if not everything else Parkhurst stood for, and in conversation with friends indicated that he could see himself as a member of the commission that supervised the police department. Some of these friends, as Roosevelt well knew, had close connections to Mayor Strong. Nonetheless, Roosevelt claimed to be taken aback when one such friend, Lemuel Quigg, passed his remarks on to Strong. "Your letter was a great surprise to me," he told Quigg. "It had not occurred to me that you would really press my name upon the mayor." Though obviously interested, Roosevelt felt obliged to disclaim any unseemly desire for the post. "I think I had better not take the position. A year hence I would like to take an active part in the presidential campaign, and I could not well do that as Police Commissioner, and until a year hence I really ought to be here to complete some work I am at now." Lest Quigg think him ungrateful, Roosevelt added, "I am greatly touched by your thinking of me."

Almost before the words were out of his pen, Roosevelt got nervous that he might have been too coy. And when he didn't hear anything from Strong in the next several days, he thought he had missed his opportunity again. "I do not know that there is much need of discussing the matter now," he moaned to Lodge, "for I suppose the Mayor has settled on somebody else. A week ago he would have offered it to me if I had been willing to take it."

On the other hand, maybe a glimmer remained. And maybe Lodge, now the distinguished senator, could be of help. Roosevelt asked Lodge to talk to Strong, as well as to Douglas Robinson, who had his own connections to city government. Yet obvious as his desire for the police job was, Roosevelt couldn't bring himself to admit that he really wanted it. "The average New Yorker of course wishes me to take it very much," he asserted. "I don't feel much like it myself, but of course I realize that it is a different kind of position from that of Street Cleaning Commissioner, and one I could perhaps afford to be identified with." Roosevelt concluded, inconclusively, "You know as well as I do, and indeed I think you feel as much as I do, the arguments for and against my being Police Commissioner. You are on the ground, and do talk it over with Douglas and the Mayor; it is an important thing for me and if I ought to take it I must do so soon. It is very puzzling!"

It became less puzzling after Lodge made the requested calls: Strong offered Roosevelt the job. Roosevelt quickly accepted. In a letter to Bamie he laid out his thinking: "I hated to leave Washington, for I love the life." The new job would be harder and more time-consuming than the old one. "I will hardly be able to keep on with my literary matters." In addition, it might well prove even more thankless than the civil service post. "It is a position in which it is absolutely impossible to do what will be expected of me; the conditions will not admit it. I must make up my mind to much criticism and disappointment." Then again, he said (updating his own recent forecasts to the contrary), he had just about completed his work in Washington. "I am nearly through what I can do here; and this is a good way of leaving a position which I greatly like but which I do not wish permanently to retain."

It was time to return home. "I think it a good thing to be definitely identified with my city once more. I would like to do my share in governing the city after our great victory; and so far as may be I would like once more to have my voice in political matters." There were no guarantees; a man had to act in the face of uncertainty. "It was a rather close decision; but on the whole I felt I ought to go, though it is 'taking chances.'"

CHAPTER ELEVEN

On the Beat
1895–96

As much as Edith initially had resisted the move from Washington, Roosevelt's return to New York politics simplified their life. No longer would they—meaning Edith, mostly—have to arrange the annual migrations from Long Island to Washington and back. There would still be the moves from Sagamore Hill to Manhattan, to the house on Madison Avenue, but that was a much easier expedition. Moreover, Edith wouldn't have to deal with the lengthy summer absences of her husband; now that the train ran clear to Oyster Bay, it was possible for him to commute into town daily to work.

The children needed their father more than ever. They were getting bigger, and there were more of them. Alice was eleven, as headstrong as always, if perhaps ever so slightly more gracious in insisting on having her way. Ted was seven, Kermit five, and Ethel three. The newest arrival was Archie, born in April 1894 and named for Archibald Bulloch, Theodore's great-great-grandfather, who had been Georgia's governor ("president," to be precise) during the American Revolution. Theodore's researches into the Revolutionary period had reminded him of his familial connection to that heroic age, and he had been eager for the opportunity to attach his famous ancestor's name to a son.

In light of his growing family, another advantage of Roosevelt's new job was that it paid better than the Civil Service Commission; he would now receive six thousand dollars per year. This advantage was partially offset, however, by the crimp his new responsibilities would put in his literary career and the income his books and articles brought in. Unlike the civil service job, the police post was full-time and then some. Crime never slept in the big city, nor the temptation to police corruption that made much of the crime possible. Consequently, a police commissioner could never sleep, either (and on some nights Roosevelt really didn't).

As anyone who knew Roosevelt would have guessed, he took police graft personally. It offended his sense of justice and propriety—and even patriotism, since he saw it as un-American. And once he accepted the job, it challenged his personal honor. The police department became his department, the police officers his men. Who tampered with the department or the officers affronted him personally. It didn't require Roosevelt long to reconceive his responsibility as that of a military commander. The men in blue were his troops; the enemy was the army of grand criminals and petty crooks who swarmed the city, abetted by the guerrilla forces of those who turned coat in the service of corruption and the many more who tolerated corruption as the price of doing business in the city.

Getting a late start at his post—Strong's administration was months old and corruption in New York decades, if not centuries, old—Roosevelt hurled himself into it with his customary abandon. He left home early in the morning, riding a bicycle to the train station, and came home late at night; many nights, after the family moved to Oyster Bay for the summer, he did not come home at all but stayed in town. The law that created the police commission specified four commissioners, two Republicans and two Democrats; these four would select one of their own to be president of the commission. By force of personality, and because none of the other commissioners wanted the job as much as he did, he quickly gained election.

The reason no one else wanted the job was that the president's powers were essentially no greater than the other commissioners', but his visibility and political exposure were. The president served as spokesman and defender of the police board's mission. In this regard the post suited Roosevelt perfectly. It was a great improvement, for example, over his civil service job, which, despite allowing him to take the side of justice and reform and responsibility, had dealt in pretty dull issues when one came right down to it. Who got the job of postmaster in Pittsburgh and clerk in Des Moines meant something to those individuals and presumably their families and friends, but it wasn't quite the item for stirring the collective soul of the citizenry.

By contrast, everyone had a stake in the behavior of the police. New York City in the 1890s was, if anything, more frightening than it had been at the time of Roosevelt's birth. Lower Manhattan—including the districts abandoned by the Roosevelts and their neighbors in their dollar-driven flight uptown—had evolved into a universe of different worlds inhabited by the hundreds of thousands of immigrants who flooded annually through Ellis Island. Little Italy, Poletown, Jewtown, Chinatown, Germantown, and similar enclaves of newcomers from Greece, Bohemia, Hungary, Ukraine, and as many other homelands as people could escape made much of Manhattan foreign soil even to—especially to—a native like Roosevelt.

Roosevelt's guide through this exotic terrain was the same one who had guided tens of thousands of other Americans equally in need of an introduction to these strange communities in their midst. Jacob Riis shocked and illuminated with his 1890 *How the Other Half Lives,* a graphic portrayal of life in the city's worst slums. Not long after the book's publication, Roosevelt had called on Riis to commend the author for his fine investigative work—the book was "both an enlightenment and an inspiration for which I could never be too grateful," Roosevelt wrote later—and to express a desire to do whatever he could to rectify the disgraceful social wrongs the book described. Riis thought Mayor Strong's offer of the street-cleaning post fit this description and told Roosevelt so; disappointed when Roosevelt declined, he was delighted when the civil service commissioner became president of the police board.

The two made a well-matched set. Riis was the pathologist who could locate and diagnose the malignancies of the city, and Roosevelt was the surgeon who would cut them out. The metaphor was doubly apt, for Roosevelt's position as president of the police commission also made him a member of the city's health board, which had special concern for the abysmal living conditions that Riis portrayed with pen and camera. "In both positions," Roosevelt wrote afterward, "I felt that with Jacob Riis's guidance I would be able to put a goodly number of his principles into actual effect. He and I looked at life and its problems from substantially the same standpoint. Our ideals and principles and purposes, and our beliefs as to the methods necessary to realize them, were alike."

They were also unusual—at least among those inured to New York ways. While corruption in New York City politics in the 1890s lacked the virtuoso character of the glory days of Boss Tweed, it was epidemic and entrenched. The chief of Tammany Hall was Richard Croker, a comparatively cultivated man for one of his calling and who indeed did feel as though managing the affairs of the Democratic Party of New York was a calling. "In Tammany Hall there is no discrimination against citizens on account of race or religion," Croker told a skeptical reporter. "We meet on the common ground of one common citizenship. We know no difference of Catholic or Protestant, of Irishman, German or American. Everyone is welcome amongst us who is true to the city and true to the party." Did Tammany sometimes get down in the gutter? Croker didn't deny it. On the contrary, he defended it, for the gutter was where many thousands of people lived—and where the blue-blooded, self-styled reformers were quite happy to leave them. Far from being a blight, Tammany was a beacon to the nation. "It is of the people, created for the people, controlled by the people—the purest and strongest outcome of the working of democratic government under modern conditions."

Lately Croker's message had fallen on ears attuned to a different message; Mayor Strong's election signaled one of New York City voters' recurrent fits of disgust at machine politics. Yet though Tammany might be tossed out of city hall, undoing years of machine handiwork presented a more formidable challenge. The police board, for example, was an invitation to obstruction. Its mandated makeup of two Republicans and two Democrats ostensibly ensured nonpartisan (or at least bipartisan) behavior in the commissioners; in fact, it more often guaranteed inaction. The mayor appointed the commissioners but could not remove them, except with the concurrence of the governor, who in the case of the Democratic incumbent, a protégé of boss David Hill, concurred with the mayor on precious little. The commission in turn appointed a police chief, but he could not be removed except after a thorough hearing subject to judicial review. Likewise, the commission appointed patrolmen, but they, too, had rights of review that made their dismissal difficult if not impossible.

To his horror, Roosevelt learned that even this dismal situation might soon be made worse. As he arrived in his office at 300 Mulberry

Street, the New York legislature was considering a bill that would have shifted such power as the police commission possessed to a single police chief. During his days in the New York assembly, Roosevelt had advocated a similar measure as necessary to effective police reform, but that was before he had been named one of the commissioners. Now he publicly described the bill in question as "hopelessly vicious" and "obviously drawn to perpetuate the worst and most corrupt abuses that have flourished in this department." More to the point, it would reduce the commission to a "nullity." Approval would be "an act of scandalous iniquity."

To Roosevelt's gratification, Mayor Strong agreed with his assessment, in general terms if not in particulars of language. Following passage by the legislature, Strong vetoed the bill. At least partly because of the publicity generated by Roosevelt's violent denunciation, the legislature declined to override, and the measure mercifully expired.

Having survived this preemptive strike, Roosevelt counterattacked. He initially targeted Thomas Byrnes, the longtime police chief who had risen from the detective division, where he had nabbed record numbers of criminals and compiled, according to entirely believable reports, intriguing dossiers on many influential individuals who remained unindicted as yet. By the mid–1890s Byrnes was a wealthy and powerful individual. As with many politicians, not only in New York, the two attributes reinforced each other. When investigations into police impropriety revealed that Byrnes had amassed a fortune of more than three hundred thousand dollars, he indignantly denied any wrongdoing; he explained that he had simply acted on the advice of Jay Gould and other Wall Street friends to make some successful investments.

Had Byrnes determined to fight for his job, he could have made Roosevelt's professional life unendurable and certainly unfruitful. But apparently he figured that he would rather retire in peace than spend his time fending off as feisty a character as Roosevelt, and he quietly cleaned out his desk and left.

At about the same time another department fixture, Inspector Alexander Williams, affectionately known as the "Clubber" for his skillful use of the baton in maintaining order, encouraging confessions, and generally promoting respect for the law, decided to join Byrnes in retirement. It was the Clubber who was said to have offered the gem of jurisprudence dear to generations of patrolmen: "There is more law at the end of a policeman's night stick than in any ruling of the U.S. Supreme Court." Roosevelt didn't entirely disagree, but neither did he complain when Williams chose to do his philosophizing elsewhere.

"I am getting the police department under control," Roosevelt boasted to Bamie at the beginning of June. "I forced Byrnes and Williams out, and now hold undisputed sway." Roosevelt's three fellow commissioners—Republican Frederick Grant (son of the late general and president) and Democrats Avery Andrews and Andrew Parker—might have taken exception to this statement, since their votes counted as much as his. Eventually they *would* take exception, but for now they were willing to let Roosevelt lead. Roosevelt judged Parker the most capable of the three. "My queer, strong, able colleague Parker is far and away the most positive character with whom I have ever worked on a commission," he said. "If he and I get at odds we shall have a battle royal; but I think we can pull together." Grant and Andrews, though not as gifted, also did "excellent work"—by which Roosevelt meant that they stood aside and let him run the show.

II

Roosevelt adopted a decidedly interventionist style of leadership for the police department. After the example of Riis, he took to prowling the streets of the city at night. One of his first sorties commenced at 2 A.M. on June 7, following a festive evening at the Union League Club. The commissioner excused himself to his friends, then slipped out onto Fifth Avenue. As the night was warm, he didn't really need his coat and hat, but they served as his disguise, so he kept them on, pushing his collar up and pulling his brim down. He loitered for a moment, looking as suspicious as many of those his patrolmen were supposed to be on the lookout for; he was met shortly by Riis, who, wearing his usual grubby attire and sunglasses, looked even more suspicious than Roosevelt.

The two headed east on Forty-second Street, then turned south on Third Avenue. Riis had a whole itinerary planned: down First, Second,

and Third Avenues to the neighborhood of Bellevue Hospital, and
from there to the Bowery. But they hadn't gone a block before they discovered matters that demanded the commissioner's attention. Two
roundsmen passed by, entirely engrossed in a conversation and utterly
oblivious to all else. Roosevelt momentarily considered halting them
and asking what was so interesting that they were ignoring their duties,
but he decided at this early stage of the outing not to blow his cover.

Farther on they met a waiter carrying a trayful of food and muttering to himself. "Where in blazes does that copper sleep?" he said,
obviously seeking a patrolman who obviously made a habit of sleeping on the beat. The sleeper was nowhere to be found. A few blocks
farther still, another snoozing patrolman was all too easily found—
perched atop a buttertub and snoring so loudly that he nearly woke
the whole neighborhood. Yet another patrolman was merely
glimpsed, engaged with a prostitute, before he disappeared.

When Roosevelt finally ran into a policeman who wasn't patently
derelict in his duty, he discovered that the man was on the wrong beat.
"What are you doing here?" he demanded.

The patrolman, thinking his interrogator an ordinary civilian,
replied sarcastically, "Why, I'm standing, of course."

Roosevelt asked his post number.

"Seventeen," he lied.

Roosevelt ordered him—and various of the other slackers and miscreants he encountered that night—to appear at headquarters at half
past nine the next morning. He himself arrived a little after seven, following a few more hours on the street. When the chagrinned patrolmen trailed in, he rebuked them roundly; yet, tempering justice with
mercy, he decided to let them off with a warning.

Roosevelt's subsequent dispensation of justice was often sterner,
but not always. On one occasion a policeman with a history of infrac-
tions was ordered before the commissioner to answer for his latest, a
potentially career-ending slip. This individual had little to say in his
defense; instead he relied on the eleven children he brought with him.
He introduced each of the little ones to Roosevelt and then related the
sad tale of his wife's recent death. "What, no mother?" inquired
Roosevelt. "All these children? Go, then, and don't go wrong again."
The patrolman expressed suitable humility and gratitude, and went
out to return the children to their real parents.

The police board president was willing to swerve from strict impartiality in other good causes as well. A New Haven citizens' organization tried to get the high-profile police commissioner to visit their town and share his experience of civic reform. Roosevelt begged off, pleading the pressure of his official duties. The director of the New Haven group persisted, this time sending Roosevelt's invitation on the stationery of the Yale Football Association, of which the director happened to be president. This caught Roosevelt's eye; the police commissioner inquired if the New Haven man knew of any way to procure tickets to an upcoming Yale-Princeton game. The tickets arrived shortly on Roosevelt's desk. Roosevelt responded by return mail, "Tickets received. By George, you are a trump. When do you want that speech?"

III

Roosevelt's early accomplishments as head of the police commission included some very practical measures. Pedestrians thanked him for clearing the sidewalks of packing crates. Though illegal, the practice of leaving the crates on the sidewalk had become epidemic, saving shopkeepers and warehouse owners the cost of storing the boxes or disposing of them but pushing pedestrians out into the street. Roosevelt took the position that what was illegal ought to be stopped, and the crates soon disappeared.

Roosevelt was also instrumental in putting the police force on wheels—bicycle wheels, that is. During the mid–1890s a veritable craze for bicycles swept America; between two and four million bicyclists took to the roads and streets of the nation. They became an important political presence, lobbying for better roads over which to roll their two-wheeled steeds. They also became something of a nuisance. Stretches of Manhattan's thoroughfares were soon drag strips for the velocipedes, which could move considerably faster than any policeman on foot. This fact had not escaped the notice of state-of-the-art thieves, who saw the bicycle as a promising getaway vehicle.

Roosevelt had already taken to wheels in the vicinity of Oyster Bay; now he embraced the new technology for the police department. He and his fellow commissioners initially authorized an experimental plan to put a few patrolmen on bicycles; when the experiment proved successful, the bicycle squad was expanded. Within its first year the squad made more than a thousand arrests.

IV

But it was Roosevelt's midnight rambles that garnered the most attention. Roosevelt thought they were "great fun"; the press thought they made great copy. The New York papers couldn't resist Roosevelt. The editorialists didn't all care for his methods or even his aims, but the reporters loved the copy he generated with his combative mien, his self-righteous rhetoric, and his flair for the dramatic. The 1890s witnessed some brass-knuckled battles among New York's press barons; expensive new machinery lowered the per-copy cost of newspapers even as it raised overall costs, driving the publishers to desperate attempts to boost circulation and thereby advertising revenues. In slow seasons the press lords weren't above manufacturing sensational stories; such would push the United States toward war against Spain in 1898.

Roosevelt saved the publishers wear on the imagination with his one-man crusade against corruption in law enforcement. "A Bagdad Night," blared the *Commercial Advertiser* after one of Roosevelt's undercover jaunts. "Roosevelt in the Role of Haroun Alraschid. Police Caught Napping. None Knew the Commissioner: All Were Insolent." The *World* rhapsodized, only half in jest: "Sing, heavenly Muse, the sad dejection of our poor policemen. We have a real Police Commissioner. His name is Theodore Roosevelt. His teeth are big and white, his eyes are small and piercing, his voice is rasping. He makes our policemen feel as the little froggies did when the stork came to rule them. His heart is full of reform, and a policeman, in full uniform, with helmet, revolver and night club, is no more to him than a plain, every day human being."

It was during this period that Roosevelt's personal appearance grew into a trademark. On warm days he would wear a black silk sash instead of a vest, and a pink shirt with tassels that hung down to his knees. Never had such style occupied Mulberry Street.

But the permanent features of Roosevelt's physiognomy made a more lasting impression. One reporter was quite taken with his ears and voice, although the contrast he drew between the commissioner's equipment for hearing and that for speaking was at least partly metaphorical. Calling Roosevelt's ear "probably the smallest ear on any full-grown man in New York," the newsman remarked, "If a small ear, a wonderfully small ear, means anything, Mr. Roosevelt's ear means a lot." As for the voice, that was something else again. "It is an exasperating voice, a sharp voice, a rasping voice. It is a voice that comes from the tips of the teeth and seems to say in its tones, 'What do you amount to anyway?'"

Yet rasping voices and small ears didn't make for striking caricatures, and soon the cartoonists settled on Roosevelt's teeth and eyeglasses as his defining features. Before long these alone identified the police commissioner to newspaper readers—and to wayward patrolmen, according to reports. The story went around that the flash of teeth in the night was enough to scare the most corrupt copper back to good behavior. One cartoonist gained immortality by depicting a poor patrolman being chastened into eternal sobriety by the sight of an oversized pair of eyeglasses advertising an optician's shop, hanging just above an enormous pair of dentures making known the proximity of a dentist.

Other accounts were probably less fanciful. One described an outing on which Roosevelt discovered a policeman drinking beer on duty, at the door of a saloon. The officer spied Roosevelt approaching, tossed his beer glass through the saloon door, and bolted in the opposite direction. Roosevelt had never been swift afoot, even in college when he weighed 135 pounds; now, much closer to 200, he was slower still. But evidently this wasn't the patrolman's first encounter with a beer stein, and his waddle was no match for Roosevelt's gallop. The commissioner collared the misguided man shortly before the latter—and perhaps the former, who wasn't getting his usual exercise these busy days—collapsed of a heart attack.

On another occasion Roosevelt was said to have interrupted a conversation between a night patrolman and a lady of the evening, a conversation that appeared to be going in a direction other than arrest. Roosevelt confronted the policeman and demanded, "Officer, is this the way you attend to your duty, talking to women?"

"What are you looking for—trouble?" the officer retorted, not recognizing Roosevelt. "You see that street?" He pointed down Third Avenue. "Now, run along there or I'll fan you, and I'll fan you hard." He turned to his friend. "Will I fan him, Mame?"

Mame thought he would, but Roosevelt didn't. "Oh, no, Officer," he declared. "You will neither fan me hard nor easy. I am Police Commissioner Roosevelt." As this sank in, he gave the order: "Instead of fanning anybody, you report at Headquarters at 9:30 o'clock."

V

Life as president of the police board wasn't always such a lark. Roosevelt quickly discovered that cleaning up the Augean stables of the New York Police Department made civil service reform seem like merely changing the paper in the cage of one of the mice he had kept as a boy. At the heart of the problem was an entrenched habit of selective enforcement of the law, with the selection depending on the political pull and economic enticements at the command of the lawbreakers. And at the heart of the habit of selective enforcement were some laws that many New Yorkers found conspicuously uncongenial.

The most obvious of these was the Sunday closing law, which forbade saloons to operate on Sundays. The law was a sop to the prohibitionists, but equally it was a device by which cynical pols and shrewd crooks (two classes being not mutually exclusive) could leech a living off the body politic and economic. Political favors averted the gaze of policemen from a saloon's side door that swung on a Sunday afternoon; blackmail payments accomplished similar results. The failure of either the political or the financial payoffs to arrive on schedule could bring down the heavy arm of the law, which seemed all the heavier when it didn't descend on the saloon next door that delivered the goods to the powers-that-were and consequently was allowed to deliver the drinks to the customers-that-would-be.

In the process the entire police force was compromised. The sizable minority on the take cast suspicion over even the honest, with the result that the latter's efforts at impartial enforcement were often interpreted as some particularly devious device for individual enrichment or advance.

Roosevelt decided that in order to restore the police department to a place of public respect, he needed to tackle the Sunday closing law. Although he—along with much of the citizenry of New York—had serious reservations about the wisdom of the law, he determined that while the law remained on the books, he must enforce it. To fail to do so would invite the continued corruption and demoralization of the department. And he would enforce the law absolutely impartially. There would be no nod to political influence and certainly no concession to blackmail.

"I do not deal with sentiment," he announced in an early statement to the press. "I deal with the law. How I might act as a legislator or what kind of legislation I should advise has no bearing on my conduct as an executive officer charged with administering the law." There had been campaigns in the past to enforce the Sunday law, but they had failed for lack of persistence. The solution was to stay the course. "I shall try to procure the enforcement of the Sunday Closing Law, not by spurts, but with steadily increasing rigor." Success was not guaranteed, but effort was. "If it proves impossible to enforce it, it will only be after the experiment of breaking many a captain of the police in the endeavor to secure the enforcement has first been tried."

Roosevelt rejected the argument raised by opponents that the law could not be enforced—and probably should not be—because public sentiment was against it. Public sentiment, he pointed out, working through the political process, had passed the law. This was the public sentiment he, as an officer of the law, had sworn to uphold.

Besides, selective enforcement was the engine of corruption. "To allow a lax enforcement of the law means to allow it to be enforced just so far as individual members of the police force are willing to wink at its evasion." There would be no winking on his watch. "The law will be enforced rigidly in the interest of every honest saloonkeeper, and in the interest of honesty in the management of the police force."

There was a broader point at issue. "Law-abiding citizens are rarely blackmailed. The chief chance for blackmail, with all its frightful attendant demoralization, arises from having a law which is not strictly enforced, which certain people are allowed to violate with impunity for corrupt reasons, while other offenders who lack their political influence are mercilessly harassed." This was unfair and imprudent. It must stop, and would. "Woe be to the policeman who exposes himself to the taint of corruption."

Some of the sager heads in New York politics counseled Roosevelt not to tie himself to the mast of the Sunday closing law. In certain respects the predicament of the police commissioner was similar to that of the civil service commissioner, only worse. Vigor in disrupting the saloons' Sunday services would make Roosevelt out to be the enemy of all those working stiffs who wanted a brew with the boys on their one day off. Needless to say, if the Sabbath pint hadn't been popular, the idea of a ban never would have occurred to anyone.

Yet Roosevelt wasn't about to follow such advice. To tolerate the status quo was, to his mind, utterly out of the question. The police department had become rotten with graft, and if he didn't start chopping away the rot, no one would.

Roosevelt's difficulty was a Democratic delight. Tammany Hall saw the saloon campaign as its salvation, its return ticket from exile. David Hill took his stand with the common man against the Harvard dandy—who with his silk sash and tassels was almost as dandified in appearance now as when he had entered the assembly in Albany.

Hill lashed Roosevelt for picking on honest beer-drinkers, who, he said, had no choice but to imbibe their humble beverage at the corner saloon, while the police commissioner and his friends frequented private clubs that kept commoners at a distance and served champagne with breakfast, lunch, and dinner.

Briefly, Roosevelt maintained an air of nonpartisan impartiality in the squall he had stirred up, much as he had done throughout his stay in Washington. But the politics of New York were considerably less genteel than politics in the national capital, and once the coats came off Roosevelt's opponents, he quickly doffed his jacket, folded his sash, tightened his braces, and returned every blow. "The position of Senator Hill and the Tammany leaders," he declared, "when reduced to its simplest terms, is merely the expression of the conviction that it does not pay to be honest. They believe that advocacy of lawbreaking is a good card before the people."

Roosevelt deemed it especially ironic—nay, cynical—that Hill was attacking the police board for enforcing a law that had been "put on the statute-book but three years ago by his legislature and his governor (for he owned them both)." Roosevelt continued, "This is of course a mere frank avowal that Senator Hill and the Democratic leaders who think with him believe that a majority in the State can be built up out of the combined votes of the dishonest men, the stupid men, the timid weaklings, and the men who put appetite above principle—who declare, in the language of Scripture, that their god is their belly, and who rank every consideration of honor, justice, and public morality below the gratification of their desire to drink beer at times when it is prohibited by law." Needless to say, such men would not dictate terms of law enforcement in New York City—not while Theodore Roosevelt had anything to do with the matter.

VI

By his own testimony, Roosevelt had never worked harder than during his first months on the job with the police board. He himself didn't mind, saying he found the work "absorbingly interesting." On those days that started at Sagamore Hill, he disappeared at dawn, coasting silently down the drive on his bicycle (the one form of exercise he could fit in besides stalking the Manhattan streets late at night), and didn't arrive back, blowing and sweating from the effort of climbing back up from the village, until just before a late supper, when he came home at all.

The children had much to do and for the most part missed their father only notionally, but Edith could have stood more attention and companionship. The strain of bearing four children and, more important, rearing five was beginning to tell. Although most of her health problems were minor and merely annoying, recurrent migraines periodically laid her low. They also increased her desire to see her husband. "I was so overjoyed when I found your letter here . . ." she wrote plaintively during one of his many absences. "I needed consolation badly for I waked this morning with a bad head ache."

The spring and summer of 1896 added to her burdens. At the end of April word arrived from Italy that her mother had died. The relationship between mother and daughter had often been difficult, but the loss came as a blow nonetheless. It was followed by the return to America of Edith's sister Emily, who spent the next six months at Sagamore. Emily took after her mother, and so the proximity, while welcome in certain respects, was wearing in others.

The big family news of the summer was Bamie's engagement. Theodore's elder sister had been spending most of her time in London lately, tending to matters of family and friends; there she had met William Cowles, the naval attaché to the American embassy. He was forty-nine and divorced; she was forty and never married. The engagement stunned nearly all who knew Bamie and had expected her to live out her life as an old maid—although, with both the prospective bride and groom approaching an age when the relative weight of physical and other charms was tilting in the direction of the latter, Theodore and Edith could see why Bamie would seem a good match. They knew Cowles only casually but thought his selection of a wife spoke well for his discernment.

The pressure on Theodore of the work of the police board and the demands on Edith of the five children prevented their attending the London wedding. But they deputized Corinne and Douglas to represent the family and pitched in on a joint wedding gift.

For obvious reasons, Bamie's marriage continued the distancing between Theodore and his sister that had begun with his own wedding to Edith. He had had a special and intimate confidante for these eight years; now she had one of her own. Although they still corresponded regularly, and even though Theodore and Edith warmed readily enough to Will, the expansion of the triangle to a quadrilateral inevitably diminished the intensity of the sibling bond further.

Yet enough of it remained on Bamie's side that if Will Cowles had been the jealous type, he might easily have resented his wife's continuing attachment to her brother. Bamie was fond enough of her husband, and she grew fonder over the years, but "Mr. Bearo," as she liked to call him, lacked the native inquisitiveness, the zest for life, and the ceaseless drive that made Theodore such a compelling figure to so many people. Bamie shared these traits, if perhaps in different proportions, and although she identified herself as an "anti-suffragist," she was nearly as enthralled as he was with public affairs. Like many women of her era, she lived vicariously through a man; in her case the man was not her husband.

VII

Besides keeping him away from home, Roosevelt's preoccupation with his police work worried some of his friends. Cabot Lodge thought he was overdoing it. "He looks very well," Lodge reported to Bamie, "but yet I am anxious about him, not from physical but from mental signs. He seems overstrained & overwrought—that wonderful spring and interest in all sorts of things is much lowered. He is not depressed but is fearfully overworked & insists on writing history & doing all sorts of things he has no need to do. He has that morbid idée fixe that he cannot leave his work for a moment else the world should stop."

Lodge had sufficient faith in his friend's resilience to realize that the spring would return to his step and the zing to his curiosity, but he wondered whether Roosevelt might be getting too entangled in what, in the grand scale of things, were rather parochial matters. Lodge had counted on Roosevelt to help him transform the Republican Party into an instrument for the assertion of the "large policy" they favored. By his books, essays, and reviews, Roosevelt had earned a modest reputation as a spokesman for this assertive nationalism. Now Roosevelt himself admitted that he had next to no time for writing, which was why he had to work so hard to squeeze it in, and Lodge couldn't help fearing the loss of a valuable ally.

Roosevelt reassured him. "You need not have the slightest fear about my losing my interest in National Politics," he averred. Though he was up to his ears at present, such a state wouldn't last forever. "For the next six months I am going to be absorbed in the work here and under a terrific strain." But things would ease after that. "In a couple of years or less I shall have finished the work here for which I am specially fitted, and in which I take a special interest." Then, with the department in good running order, he would be ready to move on. In the meantime, he would keep in touch. "I shall not neglect the political side, you may be sure."

Lodge needed allies at this time especially, for he was heading an effort to force an ambitious interpretation of American national interests upon the Cleveland administration. This particular occasion involved an unlikely run-in with Britain over some obscure territory in the jungles of South America. The quarrel arose in secondhand fashion, out of a dispute between Venezuela and Britain regarding the boundary between that South American republic and the neighboring British colony of Guiana. The two territories abutted somewhere in the watershed of the Orinoco River, but for decades no one had bothered to determine just where the abutment occurred, for the good reason that a definitive survey and conclusive negotiations would have cost more than the region in question was thought to be worth. This all changed in the 1880s when a lucky prospector discovered gold. The Venezuelans immediately envisioned an easy end to their poverty; the British, though considerably richer, demonstrated the possessiveness that had made them rich. Although no one knew the size of the gold deposits, uncertain reports and vaguer rumors made them sound immense (and indeed the largest gold nugget ever wrestled from the earth, a relative boulder weighing forty-two pounds, came from the Orinoco fields).

The boundary dispute might have remained a spat between Britain and Venezuela had a shrewd publicist cleverly hired by the Venezuelan government not cast the quarrel in terms of hemispheric solidarity and American prestige. William Scruggs printed a pamphlet entitled *British Aggressions in Venezuela, or the Monroe Doctrine on Trial* and circulated it among American influentials. Lodge picked up on the Monroe Doctrine theme and mounted his own offensive. In a breathtaking article in *North American Review,* Lodge expanded the doctrine beyond anything James Monroe (or his ghostwriter John Quincy Adams) would have recognized, insisting that the United States must defend the supremacy of the doctrine—which was to say, the supremacy of the United States in the Western Hemisphere—"peaceably if we can, forcibly if we must."

"I have just read your article; and it is admirable," Roosevelt congratulated Lodge. Roosevelt especially applauded Lodge's explication of Britain's misdeeds in the Venezuela matter, and he fully concurred with his friend's forthright admonition to the president and the nation. "If only our people will heed it!"

To the surprise of Lodge and Roosevelt, the Cleveland administration did heed the Republican senator's advice. The Democrats in the executive branch had been hammered once too often on international affairs, and with the depression bleeding them domestically, they decided they couldn't stand any more pounding. It so happened that

Richard Olney had just transferred from the Justice Department to the State Department, and he quickly adapted the no-nonsense approach he had taken toward the railroad strikers to foreign affairs. He drafted a stiff note to London asserting American hegemony in the Western Hemisphere and telling Britain in no uncertain terms to butt out. Cleveland was taken slightly aback at the boldness of what he called Olney's "twenty-inch gun," but upon reflection the president decided he liked it and sent it off.

Roosevelt was delighted at the Democrats' unaccustomed truculence. "I am very much pleased with the President's or rather with Olney's message," Roosevelt wrote Lodge. "I think the immense majority of our people will back him. I earnestly hope he will receive full support from both houses of Congress." Roosevelt clapped Lodge on the back for having so much to do with this sudden stiffening of Cleveland's spine. "This is a most remarkable vindication of your attitude last Spring." The mugwumps worried that things would get out of hand and war might ensue; Roosevelt worried just the opposite. "I do hope there will not be any back down among our people. Let the fight come if it must; I don't care whether our sea coast cities are bombarded or not; we would take Canada."

The prospect of war had always thrilled Roosevelt, and it did now. "If it wasn't wrong I should say that personally I would rather welcome a foreign war!" he told Bamie. To Lodge he expressed dismay at those who appeared frightened by the looming thunderclouds. "The antics of the bankers, brokers and anglomaniacs generally are humiliating to a degree." The men of commerce feared that a war would disrupt trade and hurt their profits; Roosevelt interpreted this fear as an extension of the (Democratic) doctrine of free trade. "Thank God I am not a free-trader. In this country pernicious indulgence in the doctrine of free trade seems inevitably to produce fatty degeneration of the moral fibre." Nor did the pacifists lack moral fibre alone; they were also deficient in common sense. "Our peace at any price men, if they only knew it, are rendering war more likely, because they will encourage England to persist; in the long run this means a fight. Personally I rather hope the fight will come soon. The clamor of the peace faction has convinced me that this country needs a war."

And if war should come, Roosevelt would race to the front. "If there is a muss I shall try to have a hand in it myself!" he told Will

Cowles. Of course, Roosevelt had no special qualifications for military service, but a war would expand opportunities for all sorts of people. "They'll have to employ a lot of men just as green as I am even for the conquest of Canada; our regular army isn't big enough."

Roosevelt undertook to buck up those faint hearts who preferred talking to fighting. On discovering that the disease of moderation had infected his alma mater, he sent a scorching letter to the Harvard *Crimson* defending Lodge's extravagant construction of the Monroe Doctrine. He denounced as intellectual descendants of the traitorous Federalists of the War of 1812 (who similarly had nested in the northeastern corner of the country) those people who now advocated a "spiritless submission to improper English demands." The self-styled peace-seekers might succeed momentarily but only at ultimate expense. "By a combination of indifference on the part of most of our people, a spirit of eager servility toward England in another smaller portion, and a base desire to avoid the slightest financial loss even at the cost of the loss of national honor by yet another portion, we may be led into a course of action which will for the moment avoid trouble by the simple process of a tame submission to wrong." But this answer was no answer at all. It would only invite a repetition of the wrong. More to the point, it would traduce American honor. The patriotic reply—the correct reply—to Britain's demands was a stout insistence on American rights. Congressional appropriations for construction of a "first-class Navy" would emphasize the point.

VIII

After the big buildup, Roosevelt was acutely disappointed when the war clouds scudded by without a single thunderbolt crashing to earth. The British, who were busying bullying the Boers in South Africa, confronting the French in Central Africa, and antagonizing the Germans in East Africa and much of the rest of the world, calculated that the Yanks would make better friends than enemies. They offered to arbitrate the Venezuela dispute. The Cleveland administration, which found the heady excitement of war-threatening more congenial than the grim business of war-making, accepted the offer.

Political reckoning motivated Cleveland as much in the de-escalation of the Venezuela dispute as it had in the escalation. Twisting the lion's tail might have made good politics in 1895, but sticking America's head in the lion's mouth didn't seem so smart as the 1896 elections approached. The Republicans had been sweaty with anticipation since their big victory of 1894, aiming to add the presidency to their control of Congress. The Democrats had to worry not just about the G.O.P. but about the Populists. Some Democratic strategists said the Populist wave had washed about as high as it was going to; others, without disagreeing, noted that this afforded scant solace, since on its way back out to sea the wave was carrying half the Democratic Party with it.

By this time the defining issues of national politics had reduced to the currency question, and the currency question had reduced to free silver. The Populists demanded the unlimited coinage of silver at a ratio to gold of 16 to 1; this would cure the malady of falling prices that had afflicted farmers for a generation, a malady that had grown more virulent than ever during the present depression. But silver was more than an economic issue; it also represented, in the eyes of its advocates, a blow for the people against the plutocrats, for traditional American values ("the dollar of our daddies," the silverites called the silver coin) against the encroachments of high finance and high living, for the country against the city, for the true Christian religion against irreligion and counterfeits like Judaism (the Jewish moneylender was a fixture in Populist demonology), for America against foreigners (British speculators were another mainstay; the Rothschilds did double duty as both Jews and foreigners). There was truth in the silverites' stories; there was also a great deal of nonsense. The nonsense allowed their opponents to ridicule the silverites and dismiss their arguments without taking on the truth.

Theodore Roosevelt fastened on the nonsense. By the autumn of 1895, Roosevelt's enthusiasm for police reform had started to wane. He had expected to make enemies with his campaign against Sunday saloons, but he hadn't realized quite how few friends he would win. In July he wrote Lodge: "The outcry against me at the moment is tremendous. The *World, Herald, Sun, Journal* and *Advertiser* are shrieking with rage; and the *Staats-Zeitung* is fairly epileptic." Certain other papers supported him, but they often did so warily, with frequent glances over their shoulders at their readers and advertisers.

Roosevelt bravely added, "However, I don't care a snap of my finger; my position is impregnable; and I am going to fight no matter what the opposition is."

Roosevelt's position may have been impregnable, but, to extend his military metaphor, that didn't do him much good, since he was attacking rather than defending. And in fact his opponents soon found ways around the fortress he was erecting on Mulberry Street. The Sunday laws forbade saloons from serving alcohol but exempted restaurants; accordingly, once it appeared that Roosevelt was going to persist in his crusade against tippling on the Sabbath, the saloons took to serving meals with their beer. When an understanding judge upheld one establishment's claim that a single pretzel spread over a dozen beers constituted a meal, others rapidly followed suit.

In this case the joke was on Roosevelt; another way around the Sunday law was less funny. A second loophole exempted hotels, presumably on grounds that out-of-staters shouldn't be subjected to New York's peculiar habits. Many saloons therefore reconstituted themselves as hotels, renting out a few rooms above the main body of the premises. Since these weren't honest hotels, they attracted few honest guests; instead they catered to those who preferred to rent beds by the hour. To his dismay Roosevelt discovered that by trying to stamp out the small vice of Sunday imbibing, he had contributed to the larger one of prostitution.

Roosevelt liked to think that the silent majority, at least of Republicans, supported him. "I have undoubtedly strengthened myself with the rank and file of our party," he told Lodge in August. But even this dubious assumption, which was as impossible to prove as to disprove in those pre-polling days, offered meager encouragement for someone who didn't intend to remain police commissioner for the rest of his life. "I have administered this office so far with what I may call marked success," he said in another charitable estimate, "but I have done so by incurring bitter enmity. I have not in any way increased my grip on the party machinery. In other words, my victory here does not leave me with any opening. It leads nowhere." Two weeks later he again assessed his prospects within the party and came to the same conclusion. "It would be self-deception if I thought I had gained a permanent position, or opened any future career." He didn't regret taking his present job or pursuing the policies he had, but he couldn't see that they would do him personally any good. "The chance for future political preference for me is just about such a chance as that of lightning striking."

Roosevelt's central political problem was that he had incurred the wrath of the head man of New York Republican politics, Tom Platt. Boss Platt's position on the Sunday issue was much the same as Tammany's, and he found Roosevelt's imperious rectitude both annoying and inconvenient. At first Platt and the regular Republican leadership conspicuously withheld approval of Roosevelt's campaign against the Sunday saloons; later, in the name of the common man and to prevent Tammany from monopolizing the issue, they openly opposed the police commissioner's actions. Roosevelt could hardly claim betrayal, since Platt and the G.O.P. panjandrums had never made any pretense of liking or backing him, but this hardly eased his indignation. "Nothing ever done by Tammany or by the Southern Democrats in the way of fraudulent management of primaries and of stuffing and padding the district associations, has surpassed what Platt has been doing recently," Roosevelt complained to Lodge. He went on to condemn Platt's "utter unscrupulousness and cynical indifference to the wellfare of the party, unless it redounds to his own personal benefit," and he warned that Platt's selfishness might damage the party's interests in the upcoming elections.

It might also put Roosevelt out of a job. Platt's control of the state party machinery afforded him the opportunity to close down Roosevelt's anti-saloon campaign by closing down the police commission. The boss proposed to do just that, although he paid Roosevelt the courtesy of advance notice. In January 1896 he invited Roosevelt to a meeting. Roosevelt was surprised to find Platt cultivated and easy to deal with. (Others found likewise; hence Platt's sobriquet, "Easy Boss.") "We got along very well, in an entirely pleasant and cold-blooded manner," Roosevelt remarked. "They intend to legislate me out in about 60 days; and are confident they can do it—sure of it in fact." Roosevelt thought it would take a little longer; he gave himself until April before his job vanished. But he didn't doubt that Platt could ultimately do what he said.

For all his frustration with Platt, Roosevelt refused to denounce the boss openly. From the perspective of the police commission, Platt was as great an obstacle as Senator Hill and the Democrats, but Roosevelt reserved his public wrath for them. He had been a party man his whole political career, and despite some recent wavering, he chose to remain one.

IX

Beyond his attachment to the principles of Republicanism, Roosevelt had a specific design in not breaking with Platt and the Republican leadership. After a decade during which his political career seemed to be going nowhere, Roosevelt anticipated a Republican victory in 1896 as his potential salvation. Some Republican was nearly certain to win, and Roosevelt intended to ensure that he shared the spoils of victory. He intimated at this calculation in a letter to Lodge, explaining why he wouldn't get into a public fight with Platt. "I shall not break with the party; the Presidential contest is too important." He didn't have to tell Lodge that it was as important to him personally as to the party.

In early 1896, Roosevelt and Edith visited Lodge and Nannie in Washington, and were reminded how enjoyable the capital could be. "We are having just the loveliest time imaginable," he explained to Bamie. "Every one is doing everything possible for us; and we are fairly revelling in the congenial surroundings—so much more congenial than New York on its social side!" He sorely missed the old gang. "There is no society in New York which makes up in any way for the circle of friends whom I found so congenial here."

Roosevelt initially hoped to hitch a ride back to Washington with Tom Reed. Since the late 1880s, Roosevelt had never stopped cultivating Reed personally or touting him publicly. By all evidence, Reed appreciated Roosevelt's gifts, and he couldn't help appreciating Roosevelt's loyalty. A President Reed would certainly rescue Roosevelt from the limbo of New York municipal politics and get his career on track again. With Lodge and others, Roosevelt conspired and schemed for Reed, who himself was engaged in some manful maneuvering. "I have seen a good deal of Reed," Roosevelt told Bamie. "The weight of the struggle is very evident in his face, and I can see how hard it is. The presidency is a great prize! And there is a bitter fight for it."

Of course, no one loved a fight better than Roosevelt, but in this case the contest was beyond his power to decide. Reed had faithful friends, such as Roosevelt, but he also had enemies, including those many people who had felt the sting of his wit. Besides, the party leaders recognized what a risk they would be taking entrusting the nomination to one as intelligent and openly intellectual as Reed. Not even Jefferson had kept a diary in French. Voters would have a hard time feeling comfortable with Reed, and the 1896 election—coming after the financial panic and amid the ongoing depression and related social turmoil—was certain to be about comfort and reassurance. Moreover, James Blaine's long career as a bridesmaid had demonstrated Maine's lack of pulling power. Reed didn't originate it, but he would have appreciated the sour adage that as Maine goes, so goes Vermont.

William McKinley, on the other hand, was from Ohio, that forest of presidential timber, and he was as comfortable as an old shoe. He was smart enough, although nowhere near as quick as Reed, but he had the good sense to keep his brains to himself. McKinley's strength lay in his temperament, which inspired confidence and affection. The individual most inspired was Mark Hanna. The Ohio businessman-turning-politician made McKinley a personal project; he helped McKinley gain the Ohio governorship and quietly orchestrated McKinley's collecting of commitments toward the presidency.

By the time the Republicans gathered in St. Louis in June 1896, the McKinley forces were too well organized to be turned back. Reed reluctantly recognized this, as did other, lesser challengers. The only real question for the convention was what the party's platform should look like, and in particular what position the party should take regarding the currency. The Democrats were threatening to snatch silver from the Populists, and in doing so promised to snatch many of the Populists' voters. The Republicans might disdain silver as the snake oil of the Know-Nothings, but they couldn't ignore the large number of voters who looked with favor on a loosening of the currency. Some Republican strategists, including those who hoped to halt an incipient bolt by the Rocky Mountain wing of the party, sought a middle ground on the issue, somewhere to the right of the 16-to-1-ers, to be sure, but perhaps not entirely unyielding against bimetallism. Yet the party's business backers insisted on the staunchest endorsement of the gold standard. Anything less, they said, would undermine the investor confidence that was necessary to restore prosperity to the land.

Amid the high-stakes hammering on the currency plank, Roosevelt had no opportunity to get in a whack. But Lodge did, or tried to. Lodge had opposed McKinley even more vigorously than Roosevelt had; the senator had told his friend, "It will be a great misfortune to have McKinley nominated, a much wider misfortune than anything else." But the misfortune had happened, and now Lodge attempted to make the best of it. He drafted a statement affirming gold and went to see Hanna in his hotel room. "Mr. Hanna," he said with all the gravity and authority he could muster, "I insist on a positive declaration for a gold-standard plank in the platform."

Lodge was less well known than he evidently thought, for Hanna replied, "Who in hell are you?"

"Senator Henry Cabot Lodge of Massachusetts."

"Well, Senator Henry Cabot Lodge of Massachusetts, you can go plumb to hell. You have nothing to say about it."

"All right, sir; I will make my fight on the floor of the convention."

"I don't care a damn where you make your fight."

The plank Hanna and the Republican bosses fashioned, after Lodge had been shown the door, and that the convention accepted was a wonder of electoral workmanship. It affirmed the existing gold standard, thereby reassuring the business classes, without completely closing the door on bimetallism as long as such a monetary two-step was accomplished in the company of other advanced nations. Given that the trend in international affairs was in precisely the opposite direction and that Britain, the acknowledged leader in such affairs, was undivorceably wedded to the gold standard, the dance floor in question promised to be bare for a long time.

X

Although he had preferred Reed, Roosevelt, like Lodge, had little trouble accepting McKinley. Nor did he have any difficulty convincing himself that the election of William Jennings Bryan, the Democratic candidate, would inaugurate anarchy and the dissolution of the American republic.

Apart from this conviction, Roosevelt recognized that while men with much money might purchase stateroom passage on the S.S. *McKinley,* persons such as himself would have to work their way aboard. He started at once to do just that, savaging the Democrats more intemperately than ever before. He blasted Bryan for plotting to take money out of the wallets of honest workers. The silverites pretended that only the bankers and big-money men would suffer in the event the currency was devalued; Roosevelt didn't defend such people, who could certainly defend themselves. "There are in this country but a very small number of great capitalists," he explained. "I am not concerned for them." Instead he was concerned "for the great body of the people," those who toiled hard, saving for the future. The short dollar the Democrats demanded would short precisely such honest folk.

Roosevelt made much of Bryan's double nomination—by the Populists as well as the Democrats—and of the fact that the two parties had nominated different men for vice president. Indeed, he devoted an entire article in the *Review of Reviews* to the otherwise unlikely subject of the vice presidency. (At this point he could have had almost no idea that what he was saying might apply to himself.) He offered an historical reminder of how the original provision for choosing a vice president had led to the disastrous pairing of Jefferson with Adams and how the framers and their immediate heirs had soon seen fit to alter their handiwork to prevent a recurrence of such an unsettling circumstance. The goal was to give voters a fair idea of what they were voting for and to prevent the possibility of a sudden shift in policy as the result of the unforeseen death of the president. The Republicans had hewed to this principle, in the present case by nominating two men—McKinley and Garret Hobart—whose views on all important matters were essentially identical. But what was one to make of Mr. Bryan and his running mates? Indeed, how would voters know which running mate—Democrat Arthur Sewall or Populist Thomas Watson—they would be getting? Both men joined Bryan in supporting silver, but beyond that they could hardly be more different. Sewall was a capitalist. "He is a well-to-do man. Indeed, in many communities [if not Roosevelt's New York] he would be called a rich man. He is a banker, a railroad man, a shipbuilder, and has been successful in business." In brief, he was precisely the kind of man the Populists, and many Democrats, including Bryan, regularly railed against. As for Watson, "whose enemies now call him a Georgia cracker"—saving Roosevelt the trouble—he was like Bryan only more so. "In the language of mathematicians Mr. Watson merely represents Mr. Bryan raised several powers." Again slapping Watson second-handedly, Roosevelt remarked, "Someone has said that Mr. Watson, like Mr. Tillman [Pitchfork Ben Tillman of South Carolina], is an embodied retribution on the South for having failed to educate the cracker, the poor white who would give him his strength." Roosevelt conceded that it would ill behoove any city dweller from the North— "especially any dweller in the city of Tammany [Democratic Tammany, readers would recall]"—to reproach the South for having failed to educate anyone. But Watson played peculiarly on the weaknesses of poor southern whites.

Roosevelt slashed Watson's supporters, nearly all of whom were also Bryan's supporters, in a nasty, sneering verbal offensive.

> They distrust anything they cannot understand; and as they understand but little this opens a very wide field for distrust. They are apt to be emotionally religious. If not, they are then at least atheists of an archaic type. Refinement and comfort they are apt to consider quite as objectionable as immorality. That a man should change his clothes in the evening, that he should dine at any other hour than noon, impress these good people as being symptoms of depravity instead of merely trivial. A taste for learning and cultivated friends, and a tendency to bathe frequently, cause them the deepest suspicion. A well-to-do man they regard with jealous distrust, and if they cannot be well-to-do themelves, at least they hope to make matters uncomfortable for those that are. They possess many strong, rugged virtues, but they are quite impossible politically, because they confound the essentials and the non-essentials, and though they often make war on vice, they rather prefer making war upon prosperity and refinement.

Roosevelt might have had more to say about the working-class whites of the South but for the fact these very people, a few generations removed, were the heroes of his *Winning of the West*. Whether he recognized the irony of his present situation is impossible to say; he didn't mention it.

As the campaign wore on, Roosevelt's attacks on the Democrats and other challengers of the status quo became still more violent. He compared McKinley's opponents to the leaders of the French Revolution. "Messrs. Bryan, Altgeld, Tillman, Debs, Coxey, and the rest have not the power to rival the deeds of Marat, Barrere, and Robespierre, but they are strikingly like the leaders of the Terror of France in mental and moral attitude, plus an added touch of the grotesque rising from the utter folly as well as the base dishonesty of their trying to play such a role in such a country as ours." Of Bryan in particular he declared: "His utterances grow wilder and wilder, until they can only be described as the ravings of a man whose folly even surpasses his capacity for harm. . . . We hang our heads as Americans for the disgrace that has befallen this country in the nomination of such a man for such an office by one of the two great parties of the land." Despairing of victory through an approach to the better angels of the American electorate, Bryan, Roosevelt alleged, had turned to summoning their demons.

> Mr. Bryan is appealing more and more openly to the base malig-
> nancy and hatred of those demagogues who strive to lead laboring men
> to ruin, in order to wreak their vengeance on the thrifty and well-to-do.
> He advocates principles sufficiently silly and wicked to make them fit
> well in the mouth of the anarchist leader. For the government of
> Washington and Lincoln, for the system of orderly liberty bequeathed
> to us by our forefathers, he would substitute a red welter of lawlessness
> as fantastic and as vicious as the dream of a European communist. . . .
> Instead of a government of the people, for the people, and by the peo-
> ple, which we now have, Mr. Bryan would substitute a government of
> the mob.

XI

Roosevelt's flame-throwing was accurate in one regard: As the election drew nigh, Bryan grew more frantic in his appeals for votes. The man whose friends called him the Great Commoner conducted a campaign that would have staggered most other politicians. He toured the country by train, speaking early in market towns, late at whistle stops, and at all times and locations in between. He shook the hard, calloused hands of farmers and the dainty, gloved hands of schoolmarms; he kissed babies and ate pie with grandmothers; he preached, promised, cajoled, instructed, and implored. He would have appeared more desperate than he already did if he hadn't so obviously thrived on contact with the masses of ordinary souls who looked to him to ease the troubles of their lives.

By contrast to Bryan's prairie whirlwind, McKinley's campaign was a mild Ohio zephyr. The Republican nominee stayed at home, on his front porch with his mother and invalid wife. Mark Hanna and McKinley's other handlers made sure their man didn't want for exposure: In conjunction with friendly railroad companies (which was to say, all the railroad companies) they arranged for cut-rate excursions to McKinley's hometown of Canton by scores of thousands of Republican enthusiasts. The orchestration was sufficiently adept that McKinley saw nearly as many people as Bryan—or, rather, they saw him—but he looked far more presidential in doing so.

McKinley's better logistics were supplemented by a larger campaign fund. Hanna brought the efficiencies of modern business techniques to McKinley's campaign. Like a manufacturer sizing up the market for a new product, Hanna carefully estimated how much various industries and individual companies could afford to spend toward McKinley's election. Hanna didn't call the object of his solicitations protection money, but when he—and floggers like Roosevelt—described the dire fate awaiting the country in the event of a Bryan victory—it required little imagination on the part of those solicited to feel that they were indeed purchasing protection.

And they passed the message along. Suppliers received orders for purchases conditioned on a McKinley victory: If Bryan won, the orders would be automatically cancelled. Workers received similar warnings: Pay envelopes contained notices that in the event of Bryan's election the workers would be laid off. The campaign of economic and psychological warfare grew so intense that Bryan took the extreme step of telling supporters that they needn't reveal their preference for him if it threatened their jobs.

Hanna arranged an eleventh hour rally on Wall Street to cement McKinley's lead. Stockbrokers, bank clerks, lawyers, and executives marched for McKinley. The demonstration confirmed much of what Bryan and the Democrats had been saying: that McKinley was the candidate of the rich and powerful.

But he was also the candidate of the rank and file, particularly in the industrial cities of the East and the Ohio Valley. Factory workers, shopkeepers, miners, artisans, and most others who lived outside the depressed farming districts of the plains and the South voted their lunch buckets. In a sectional tally the likes of which hadn't been seen since 1860, McKinley carried the day by a wide but troubling margin.

CHAPTER TWELVE

The Cockpit of Empire
1896–98

"You may easily imagine our relief over the election," Roosevelt told Bamie shortly after the results of the polling came in. The stakes, he said, had been higher than many people realized. "It was the greatest crisis in our national fate, save only the Civil War." But right had emerged victorious. "And I am more than glad I was able to do my part in the contest."

For a person who studied history professionally, Roosevelt curiously lacked perspective on current events. The election of 1896 was hardly as critical as the election of 1800, for example, which had demonstrated that the ruling party in America would relinquish power peacefully. Yet Roosevelt would never concede that anything having to do with Democratic idol Jefferson was a turning point in American history. And besides, even more than most historians, Roosevelt went hunting in the past for trophies that would impress the present. Thus, while he often lacked historical perspective on the present, he never lacked presentist perspective on the past.

What Roosevelt really meant was that the election of 1896 was critical to him. He appreciated that his days on the police board were numbered, and if he didn't find another position quickly, he'd be in a worse fix than during his final days on the Civil Service Commission when he thought he had missed the last train to any chance of career success.

Besides, the police job had become well-nigh impossible. "I have to contend with the hostility of Tammany, and the almost equal hostility of the Republican machine," he told Bamie. "I have to contend with the folly of the reformers and the indifference of decent citizens; above all I have to contend with the singularly foolish law under which we administer the Department. . . . Add to this a hostile legislature, a bitterly antagonistic press, an unscrupulous scoundrel as comptroller, quite shameless if he can only hamper us." If he were going to achieve any success in life, it wouldn't be on the police board.

Roosevelt's recognition of his dismal prospects, combined with his compulsion to win at least some small slice of greatness, had prompted his descent into scurrility during the late campaign. Of course, like most successful politicians, he possessed the gift of being able to believe the nasty things he found it convenient to say about his opponents—a happy circumstance that made his attacks all the more effective.

Now, following McKinley's victory, he had every reason to hope for deliverance. He wouldn't be in the first round of those rewarded, being neither a longtime supporter of McKinley nor a heavy contributor to Hanna's kitty. But a second-round spot—an appointment at the level of assistant secretary of one of the major cabinet departments—was a reasonable prospect.

The votes were still being tallied when Roosevelt began calculating how to make it a sure thing. He pondered traveling to Canton to talk to the president-elect. Many other people would be going, and he didn't want to be forgotten. But he had already been to Canton once, just weeks earlier when he and Lodge took time out from campaigning to visit McKinley, and he didn't like to seem importunate. "I don't wish to go to Canton unless McKinley sends for me," he explained to a friend who was recommending that he do just that. "He already knows me, and does not need to find out anything by personal investigation. Moreover, I don't wish to appear as a supplicant, for I am not a supplicant."

But of course he was; he simply deemed it prudent to leave the direct pleading on his behalf to others. Lodge was his point man. As a friend, Lodge wanted to find Roosevelt a job that matched his talents and at least approached his ambition. As the leading legislative exponent of an aggressively expansionist policy, Lodge wanted to place an ally in the executive branch. McKinley was known for his aversion to adventurism, and under the influence of cautious businessmen like Hanna he could hardly be expected to change his thinking without

encouragement. Roosevelt could provide some of that encouragement, serving as an agitator behind the administration's lines.

This was precisely what worried McKinley. Lodge didn't have
Roosevelt's qualms about traveling to Canton. As a distinguished
member of the Senate and a figure of standing in certain segments of
the party, he would meet McKinley on relatively equal footing—or at
least footing far surer than Roosevelt's. Indeed, when Lodge went to
Canton, much of his discussion with the president-elect involved matters of high policy: Hawaii, Cuba, and world affairs generally.

But he didn't forget his friend. McKinley was interested and
encouraging. "He spoke of you with great regard for your character
and your services and he would like to have you in Washington,"
Lodge related to Roosevelt. A position in the Navy Department was
mentioned.

Yet one thing troubled the president-elect. "The only question he
asked me was this, which I give you: 'I hope he has no preconceived
plans which he would wish to drive through the moment he got in.'"

Lodge told Roosevelt that he had reassured McKinley. "I replied
that he need not give himself the slightest uneasiness on that score,
that I knew your views about the Navy, and they were only to push on
the policies which had been in operation for the last two or three
administrations."

The discussion subsequently turned to other matters, yet before
leaving, Lodge again mentioned Roosevelt's name. "I have no right to
ask a personal favor of you," he said to McKinley, "but I do ask for
Roosevelt as the one personal favor." The president-elect responded in
what Lodge interpreted as a positive manner. Lodge conceded in his
letter to Roosevelt that nothing could be counted on until the appointments were officially offered, but optimism was in order. "One thing
is certain. The matter is thoroughly in McKinley's mind. He is not
going to forget it and, although I am not over sanguine about such
things, I believe we shall succeed."

McKinley's well-founded reservations about Roosevelt's impetuosity aside, the president-elect had several items to weigh before offering
him an appointment. Of these, the heaviest was the opinion of Tom
Platt. The New York Republican boss could be a powerful ally to
McKinley or a powerful foe. Moreover, as he was again a senator
from the Empire State, senatorial courtesy required consulting him

regarding an important appointment of a fellow New Yorker. Roosevelt's differences with Platt were a matter of common knowledge, and though the two men papered them over in public, McKinley didn't wish to start off his administration by antagonizing Platt through the selection of someone he couldn't abide.

On the other hand, Platt had reasons for wanting to see Roosevelt take a job with the McKinley administration. The most compelling of these was that it would gracefully relieve him of his Rooseveltian burden in New York. Roosevelt's hard line as police commissioner had cost the Republicans ground in their continuing conflict with Tammany, and Platt naturally wanted to recapture as much as possible. As he later recollected: "My thoughts and expressions ran about like this: I do not particularly like Theodore. He has been a disturbing element in every situation to which he has been a party. I have no reason to believe the leopard changes his spots. But he is not essentially harmful and can probably do less harm to the organization as Assistant Secretary of the Navy than in any other office that can be named."

Although Platt was willing to assent to a Roosevelt appointment, he wouldn't have gotten to where he was without working all the angles of every political issue, and he determined to extract payment for his approval. For three months he kept Roosevelt on tenterhooks, leaning this way and then that. He told Lodge that while he was most anxious to oblige his fellow senator in any way he could, he worried that Roosevelt intended to make war on him from a new position in the Navy Department. When Lodge expressed surprise that such a thought should occur to Platt, that the Navy Department had nothing to do with the interests of the New York Republican organization, Platt responded that it did indeed. The Brooklyn navy yard was an important source of employment. Lodge rejoined that he didn't think the navy yard would pose any problems. In relating this conversation to Roosevelt, Lodge did his best to preempt such problems. "It is really to my mind not a matter of any consequence," he said. "The questions in the Navy Department with which you will be called to deal will be the big questions of naval policy." The Brooklyn yard wasn't something to get excited about. It certainly wasn't something to jeopardize a plum appointment over.

"Of course I should not go into the Department to make war upon

Platt," Roosevelt reassured Lodge, as though the thought had never crossed his mind. A few days later, at Platt's invitation, Roosevelt paid a call on the boss to convey the same message personally. The meeting went well; Roosevelt found Platt "exceedingly polite." Shortly after this, Roosevelt pointedly declined an invitation to speak on behalf of Joseph Choate, one of his earliest sponsors in politics, who now was fighting for Platt's Senate seat. In recounting the event to Lodge, Roosevelt rationalized his decision: "I refused to speak at the Choate meeting; of course if I have to declare, I shall be for Choate against Platt, for the feeling about Platt is ugly; but it is a futile and useless fight"—when had Roosevelt ever admitted long odds as just grounds for staying out of a fight?—"and as I have my hands full of fights which are neither futile nor useless, I do not care to be dragged into this."

Having reassured himself about Roosevelt, Platt went on to secure a guarantee from McKinley that a Roosevelt appointment wouldn't be charged against the New York machine's quota of election spoils. This wasn't an unreasonable demand, since by no stretch of the imagination could Roosevelt be considered a Platt man. But it demonstrated the attention to detail that made Platt a master of his game, and when it was satisfied, Platt dropped his last opposition to Roosevelt's appointment.

Roosevelt also required the approval of John Long, the new navy secretary. Like McKinley a man of equable temperament and a preference for composed circumstances, Long likewise fretted that Roosevelt would be overly rambunctious as a subordinate. Roosevelt sought to assuage this concern. Through Lodge he promised Long he would be a model subaltern. "I want him to understand that I know enough to go into this position, if I am offered it, with my eyes open, and shall work hard, and shall stay at Washington, hot weather or any other weather"—this referred to Washington's habit of emptying out during the dog days of summer—"whenever he wants me to stay there, and go wherever he sends me, and my aim should be solely to make his administration a success."

Roosevelt's promises didn't immediately dispel the doubts of Long and McKinley, and for two weeks more his appointment dangled uncertainly. One day he felt elation at the thought of returning to Washington in a responsible position; the next day his stomach tightened at the thought of being jobless and politically unemployable.

Finally, on April 6, the blessed word came through. Roosevelt immediately wired Lodge: "Sinbad has evidently landed the old man of the sea."

The "evidently" reflected the requirement for the Senate to confirm his appointment. And as he told Bamie a bit melodramatically, the Senate was a place "where I have very bitter enemies." But notwithstanding this last hurdle (which turned out to be no barrier at all), he allowed himself to feel satisfied. "I was even more pleased than I was astonished at the appointment; for I had come to look upon it as very improbable. McKinley rather distrusted me, and Platt actively hated me."

His ticket to Washington arrived not a moment too soon. Clearing off his desk at the police commission, he told a friend, "I am very glad to get out of this place; for I have done all that could be done, and now the situation has become literally intolerable." He concluded wryly, "Now that I am going, all the good people are utterly cast down, and can not say enough of my virtues!"

II

Roosevelt's appointment to the Navy Department may have been a critical career move, but it disrupted his family life again. Edith and the children had settled into their Oyster Bay–Manhattan routine and were thriving on it. In a letter to Cecil Spring Rice, Roosevelt sketched his wife and the young ones:

> I have never seen her so well as she was this winter, in looks, in health, in spirits and everything. Alice is taller than she is now, and has become a very sweet girl indeed. Ted is an excessively active and normally grimy small boy of nine. He is devoted to Kipling's stories and poems, and has learned to swim, ride and chop quite well. He and Kermit go to the Cove School, where they are taught by the daughter of Captain Nelse Hawkshurst, one of the old-time baymen. Ethel is a cunning, chubby, sturdy little thing of five, and Archie is just three, and is treated by the entire family as a play-toy. I can't say much for either his temper or his intelligence; but he is very bright and cunning, and we love him dearly.

At the time his Navy Department job came through, the annual family migration to Sagamore Hill was about to commence. Roosevelt at first believed he would be able to get his work done in Washington during busy weeks and have weekends to enjoy at Oyster Bay. But he soon decided that the department couldn't be without him. Late in April he took thirty-six hours off during a weekend when Secretary Long was also gone; in his absence some minor affairs came up that consequently weren't attended to until Monday morning. Embarrassed, he apologized to Long and promised to prevent a recurrence: "Never again shall I leave this city when you are not here, unless you expressly order me to. I told Mrs. Roosevelt that I guessed I should have to give up even the thing I care for most—seeing her and the children at all until next fall when they come on here; this because I don't wish again to be away when there is the slightest chance that anything may turn up."

Roosevelt accordingly looked for rental housing; in the meantime he stayed once more with Cabot and Nannie Lodge. It was just like old times. He and Lodge conspired over dinner and on lengthy walks through Rock Creek Park, plotting how they would compel the country to recognize the wisdom of their "large policy." Roosevelt regularly consorted with Henry and Brooks Adams. The latter, dubbed "Herodotus" by friends for the sweep of his historical vision, recently displayed in *The Law of Civilization and Decay*, simultaneously intrigued and dismayed Roosevelt. "I think the trouble is largely that his mind is a little unhinged," he told Spring Rice. "All his thoughts show extraordinary intellectual and literary dishonesty; but I don't think it is due to moral shortcomings. I think it really is the fact that he isn't quite straight in the head." The other Adams—"Adams not Herodotus," Roosevelt called Henry—was as engaging in his dismal way as ever. "He is having a delightful time here, and simply revelling in gloom over the appalling social and civic disasters which he sees impending." Nannie Lodge was her ever-charming self. "She has had great fun recently with the amiable Walter Berry, whom we have christened 'the ball of worsted,' because he is such a nice thing for a kitten to play with. The suggestion implied in the name made Cabot a little suspicious at first, but not for long, as he now rates the good Walter at his proper level of harmlessness."

Roosevelt also conspired with A. T. Mahan. The conditions of the conspiracy were evident in the preface to a letter he sent to Mahan two weeks after entering the Navy Department. "This letter must, of course, be considered as entirely confidential," Roosevelt wrote, "because in my position I am merely carrying out the policy of the Secretary and the President." Roosevelt knew he could count on Mahan to keep mum about their exchanges, for he knew that their perceptions on foreign policy ran closely parallel. "As regards Hawaii I take your views absolutely, as indeed I do on foreign policy generally. If I had my way we would annex those islands tomorrow. If that is impossible I would establish a protectorate over them." President Cleveland had committed a "colossal crime" by failing to take the islands in 1893 when they had first become available, and "we should be guilty of aiding him after the fact if we do not reverse what he did."

Roosevelt reported that Lodge had been working on McKinley along these lines; for his own part he was equally active. "I have been getting matters in shape on the Pacific coast just as fast as I have been allowed." Time was of the essence. "I am fully alive to the danger from Japan"—Tokyo was full of itself following its thrashing of China in the Sino-Japanese War, and remained concerned about the condition of Japanese workers in Hawaii. Japan's admiralty had contracted with British shipbuilders for some new warships; delivery of a pair of powerful vessels was to be taken any day. "My own belief is that we should act instantly before the two new Japanese warships leave England. I would send the *Oregon,* and, if necessary, also the *Monterey* (either with a deck load of coal or accompanied by a coaling ship) to Hawaii, and would hoist our flag over the island, leaving all details for after action." There was hardly a moment to lose. "Even a fortnight may make a difference." But swift success would reward swift action. "With Hawaii once in our hands most of the danger of friction would disappear."

The Pacific, large as it was, couldn't contain the whole of Roosevelt's strategic vision. "I believe we should build the Nicaraguan canal at once," he declared. Difficulties with Spain in the West Indies cried out for stern measures. "Until we definitely turn Spain out of those islands (and if I had my way that would be done tomorrow), we will always be menaced by trouble there." Complemented by acquisi-

tion of the Danish West Indies, the ejection of Spain from Cuba and
Puerto Rico would "serve notice that no strong European power, and
especially not Germany, should be allowed to gain a foothold by sup-
planting some weak European power." Roosevelt averred that he did
not fear Britain, whose fleet was the most powerful in the world; he
calculated, "Canada is a hostage for her good behavior." But the other
powers might be more reckless. For such as these, a broad increase in
American naval strength would serve as a valuable warning. "We
should build a dozen new battleships."

Rather ambitiously for an assistant secretary, Roosevelt even pressed
his views upon the president. Within a week of winning access to the
charts in the map room of the Navy Department, Roosevelt began
pushing ships this way and that across the paper oceans. On April 22
he warned the president that naval intelligence had reported that the
Japanese had just dispatched a cruiser, the *Naniwa,* to the vicinity of
Hawaii; the United States ought to respond. With an attention to detail
that must have impressed McKinley, Roosevelt laid out the president's
options. "There are [sic] at Hawaii now the protected cruiser
Philadelphia, which is just about the strength of the *Naniwa,* but as her
bottom is foul she is probably not quite so swift; and, moreover, she
has no torpedoes, while the Japanese vessel has. There is also an old
boat—the *Marion*—armed mostly with smooth bore muzzle loaders,
and quite unfit for conflict with any modern warship." This in contrast
to the vessels of Japan's fleet, which was "an efficient fighting navy."

American strength in Hawaiian waters could be augmented by sending the gunboat *Bennington,* currently on its way to San Francisco; but
Roosevelt's preference was the battleship *Oregon.* Her commander
was "thoroughly acquainted with the harbor and the island," and the
charts showed that there was enough water in the harbor to accomo-
date her. "She would be an overmatch for half the entire Japanese
Navy, although they have two battleships of the same class now on
the point of completion."

Four days later Roosevelt was counseling the president again. This
time the area of concern was the eastern Mediterranean, where a war
between Greece and Turkey was disrupting trade and threatening
some minor American interests. The question had arisen whether the
United States ought to weigh in by sending a battleship. Roosevelt
cautioned against: "It seems to me inadvisable to send a battleship to

the Mediterranean unless we intend to make a demonstration in force, in which case we should send certainly three or four armored vessels, and not one." In fact, he argued, circumstances nearer at hand dictated holding America's best ships closer to home. "We should keep the battleships on our own coast, and in readiness for action should any complications arise in Cuba."

III

Roosevelt worked hard during the summer of 1897 to ensure that complications did arise in Cuba. For two years, nationalist rebels in that island had contested Spain's colonial control, waging a war for independence intended to accomplish what an earlier effort, the Ten Years' War of 1868–1878, had not. American sympathies lay almost exclusively with the rebels. America's anticolonial tradition inclined Americans toward independence for Cuba, and American distaste for Spain—monarchical, Catholic, decadent Spain—slanted in the same direction. Moreover, the rebels had mastered the art of propaganda, establishing a public relations office in New York and disseminating stories favorable to their cause and unfavorable to Spain's. In this endeavor they received priceless support from the American yellow press, which played the plight of suffering Cuba for all it was worth— not least in terms of increased circulation.

By the summer of 1897 the situation in Cuba had reached an impasse. The rebels had resorted to a guerrilla war against the Spanish authorities and their loyalist allies; the Spanish and the loyalists were responding with reprisals and counterinsurgency campaigns. Between them, the two sides were laying waste to much of the Cuban countryside. Cuba's *campesinos,* who mostly wanted to be left alone to go about their already difficult business of making a living, got caught in the crossfire, damned by the rebels when they didn't provide sufficient aid and comfort, punished by the authorities when they did—or were even suspected of doing so. After standard antiguerrilla tactics stalled, the Spanish inaugurated a policy of *reconcentrado,* designed to deny the countryside to the rebels. Peasants were driven into camps where they were kept under strict surveillance; anyone who remained outside the camps was presumed to be a rebel and was subject to summary arrest or execution. Under the best of circumstances the policy would have guaranteed the alienation of much of the populace; no one likes being uprooted and relocated at the point of a gun, and farmers, whose living depends on access to the soil, dislike uprooting most of all. The circumstances obtaining in Cuba in the middle of a civil war were far from the best, and the *reconcentrado* policy soon degenerated into a catalog of tropical horrors. Food failed at the camps, water went bad, sanitation was ignored. Diseases such as cholera raged through the crowded quarters, killing by the scores and then the hundreds, starting with the weak and already ailing but soon assaulting those who had arrived healthy.

Theodore Roosevelt could have cared less about the Cubans, but not much less. They were suffering, to be sure, but so were a great many people around the world. The Cubans' ordeal didn't especially ennoble them, and it certainly didn't qualify them for independence. "I doubt whether the Cubans would do very well in the line of self-government," he remarked. But they could hardly do worse in running Cuba than the Spanish. "Anything would be better than continuance of Spanish rule."

Roosevelt saw the strife in Cuba as an opportunity for an assertion of American power. Cuban independence might be a by-product of such assertion, but it wouldn't be the primary objective. Even before McKinley's inauguration, Roosevelt confided to Bamie, "I am a quietly rampant 'Cuba Libre' man." The United States should flex its muscles and eject Spain; at the same time it would put the other powers on notice regarding American intentions in the hemisphere. "I believe that Cleveland ought now to recognize Cuba's independence and interfere, sending our fleet promptly to Havana. There would not in my opinion be very serious fighting; and what loss we encountered would be thrice over repaid by the ultimate results of our action."

IV

Roosevelt had been itching for war for years; now that he was in a position to help make it happen, he could hardly contain himself. The

summer and autumn of 1897 were the most exciting and satisfying
stretch of his career so far. He had sometimes worked harder as police
commissioner, but in that job about three-quarters of his energy went
to merely holding the line, to keeping corruptionists and other evildo-
ers at bay; positive progress came painfully slowly when it came it all.
At the Navy Department, by contrast, the scope for real accomplishment was far greater. Congress, of course, placed a check on what he
could do, as did Secretary Long and President McKinley. But Congress
concerned itself with the navy only intermittently and, for the most
part, through the appropriations process. Roosevelt talked up the need
for more money at every opportunity, and while he never thought the
navy received enough, he could live with his budgets. As for the president and the secretary, they seemed to have gotten over their initial
mistrust of him. McKinley consulted him regularly, and Long evidenced sufficient confidence—and sufficiently uncertain health—to
spend substantial periods away from the department, leaving
Roosevelt in charge as acting secretary.

It was chiefly in Roosevelt had the run of the place from late July to late September
1897. He couldn't have asked for more. "Long is just a dear,"
Roosevelt told Lodge in September. "He has wanted me to act entirely
independently while he was away, and to decide all these things
myself, even where I have written him that I was going to decide them
in a way that I doubted whether he would altogether like."
Roosevelt's unaccustomed autonomy occasionally made him nervous:
He wasn't always sure when to act on his own and when to refer to
the secretary. "However, on the whole I think he has been satisfied
with these two months during which I have had charge of the
Department."

It was chiefly in Roosevelt's capacity as acting secretary that he had
dealings with McKinley. The president was far less bellicose than
Roosevelt, yet he appreciated the benefits of having a war hawk at the
Navy Department in the event conflict did arise. And in the meantime
it didn't hurt the administration's image either at home or abroad for
someone like Roosevelt to be ringing the tocsin for military readiness;
such statements from Roosevelt made McKinley appear the more reasonable and statesmanlike by comparison.

During spare moments that summer, Roosevelt compiled a pamphlet of quotations from American presidents citing the need for a

strong navy; on release, the pamphlet attracted attention as suggesting a rift within the administration between the bumptious assistant navy secretary and his less militant superiors. Roosevelt half-expected a dressing-down from McKinley. But nothing of the sort occurred. "He had previously told me that he hadn't had time to read the pamphlet when it came, but seeing how much attention it attracted in the newspapers he had afterwards read every word of it, and was exceedingly glad that I had put it out."

Roosevelt was equally gratified at the president's reaction to a stiff address he had given regarding Japan. "Somewhat to my astonishment he also said that I was quite right in my speech to the Naval Militia, in which I mentioned Japan; that it was only the headlines that were wrong; and, in fact, generally expressed great satisfaction with what I had done, especially during the last seven weeks that I have been in charge of the Department." Roosevelt added the caveat: "Of course the President is a bit of a jollier." But on the whole he really did appear pleased. "I think his words did represent a substratum of satisfaction."

Satisfaction didn't necessarily imply agreement. McKinley was more clever than he was generally credited with being—by Roosevelt among others. The president refused to take the lead in agitating for overseas adventures; he left such agitation to the likes of Roosevelt. Yet neither would he rule out intervention in places like Cuba. A shrewd political diplomat, he would wait for public opinion to build behind intervention—or for it to dissipate. Meanwhile, he would appear the lover of peace, the good cop to Roosevelt's bad cop.

Such a political style was entirely foreign to Roosevelt, who at this stage of his career still made a habit of grabbing the horns of every bull he could reach. Roosevelt had difficulty interpreting McKinley. "He is evidently by no means sure that we shall not have trouble with either Spain or Japan," Roosevelt remarked rather confusingly. Yet the assistant secretary was confident that if circumstances forced the president's hand, he would meet the challenge. "I think he could be depended upon to deal thoroughly and well with any difficulty that arises."

Roosevelt undertook to instruct McKinley in what the navy could do in emergencies—and what it could not do. He explained that the fleet could be primed for action at any particular day and hour but that it couldn't be kept on constant alert without reducing overall effectiveness. "We can get ready for any time set us, just as you can get horses ready for any particular time; but you can't keep horses ready minute after minute for 24 hours and have them worth much at the end of the period." Roosevelt promised that should a war break out, the navy would be in the best shape the appropriated means would allow. To Roosevelt's pleasure, McKinley indicated that the department ought to keep on building up the fleet, laying keels for everything from battleships to torpedo boats.

Roosevelt took the opportunity of this session with the president to volunteer that in the event of war with Spain, he would resign his post at the Navy Department in order to join the fighting. McKinley thereupon queried what Mrs. Roosevelt thought of this plan. Roosevelt said she wouldn't like it, but he added that he wouldn't consult her. McKinley laughed and said that if by any chance war did arise, he would do all he could to see that Roosevelt got his chance to serve. This pleased Roosevelt the more. "Altogether I had a very satisfactory talk," he related to Lodge.

At another of Roosevelt's sessions with the president, the acting secretary handed the commander in chief a plan for action against Spain. As Roosevelt described the exchange: "I gave him a paper showing exactly where all our ships are, and I also sketched in outline what I thought ought to be done if things looked menacing about Spain, urging the necessity of taking an immediate and prompt initiative if we wished to avoid the chance of some serious trouble, and of the Japs chipping in." Roosevelt advocated gathering the main body of the American fleet at Key West just in advance of a war declaration; if this were done, the vessels could be on the Cuban coast within forty-eight hours after the war officially commenced. At the same time the navy could assemble a task force of four fast cruisers, which could harass the Spanish coast until some battleships were able to leave the Caribbean and join them there. Meanwhile, the U.S. Asiatic squadron would blockade Manila and if possible capture that Spanish colonial position. Wandering a bit beyond his naval portfolio, Roosevelt also urged the immediate dispatch of an expeditionary force of ground troops to Cuba. If such a force were sent, the war probably wouldn't last six weeks. On the other hand, tardiness would be costly. "If we hesitate and let the Spaniards take the initiative, they could give us great temporary annoyance by sending a squadron off our coast, not to speak of the fact that if they were given time, when once it was evident that war had to come, there would be plenty of German and English, and possibly French, officers instructing them how to lay mines and use torpedoes for the defense of the Cuban ports. Besides, we would have the Japs on our backs."

Roosevelt generally returned from his White House briefings hopeful that he had moved McKinley toward war; but when succeeding days saw no action, he slumped toward discouragement. McKinley kept avowing the need for a peaceful resolution of the troubles in Cuba. Roosevelt wished otherwise, believing that the United States needed to wave the flag on the end of a bloody bayonet. Morosely, he told Lodge in late September, "I haven't the slightest idea that there will be a war."

V

But there must be war. American honor required it. So did Roosevelt's conception of himself. Since he had learned to read his hero tales as a boy, since he had memorized the *Saga of King Olaf* (an epic he already was committing to the memory of his own boys), since he had learned of the Civil War exploits of his dashing Bulloch uncles, since he had first flinched on discovering how his father had failed in that regard—in short, for the great majority of his thirty-nine years, Roosevelt's fundamental outlook on life had been pointing toward war. His romantic sense had shown him how to deal with the great tragedies of his life—his father's death and Alice's—but the bravery of fortitude that those deaths had elicited paled in his mind next to the physical bravery required by battle. Perhaps he recalled his father's challenge to the eleven-year-old to make his body—but, more fundamentally, to confront and overcome his fears. Perhaps he felt in some way that by testing and proving himself under fire he could erase that one blemish on his father's escutcheon. Perhaps—and his later actions would lend weight to this argument—some part of him harbored a death wish. He had long identified with the heroes of his romances; what was more heroic than death in battle?

Whatever the precise mix of motives, Roosevelt certainly banged the drums of war during this period. In June he addressed the Naval

War College, Mahan's institution, and reminded the gathered officers of the glory and necessity of the warrior code. "If we forget that in the last resort we can only secure peace by being ready and willing to fight for it, we may some day have bitter cause to realize that a rich nation which is slothful, timid, or unwieldy is an easy prey for any people which still retains those most valuable of all qualities, the soldierly virtues." A really great people, proud and high-spirited, would gladly face every disaster of war rather than meekly accept the base prosperity that was purchased at the price of national honor. "All the great masterful races have been fighting races, and the minute that a race loses the hard fighting virtues, then, no matter what else it may retain, no matter how skilled in commerce and finance, in science or art, it has lost its right to stand as the equal of the best." Nothing could compensate for a lack of courage. "Cowardice in a race, as in an individual, is the unpardonable sin."

Given the current position of the president, Roosevelt couldn't come right out and demand immediate war with Spain; instead he stressed readiness for war. But this served his rhetorical purpose almost as well. "We ask for a great navy, partly because we think that the possession of such a navy is the surest guaranty of peace, and partly because we feel that no national life is worth having if the nation is not willing, when the need shall arise, to stake everything on the supreme arbitrament of war, and to pour out its blood, its treasure, and tears like water rather than submit to the loss of honor and renown." Did opinions differ on appropriate occasions of war? Let the nation enlist with the brave. "Better a thousand times err on the side of overreadiness to fight, than to err on the side of tame submission to injury, or cold-blooded indifference to the misery of the oppressed." For it was in the heat of battle that nations and individuals earned their right to glory. "No triumph of peace is quite so great as the supreme triumphs of war."

VI

As acting navy secretary—"hot-weather secretary," he called himself—Roosevelt got his first whiff of real power. It wasn't quite a taste, merely a whiff, but even the vapors made him giddy. The giddiness was most apparent in a letter to Cecil Spring Rice in which Roosevelt elaborated a philosophy of global relations that drew together several ideas, some that had been delineated explicitly in his published writings, some that had been implicit, and some that seemed to come straight off the top of his head. The result was a curious conglomeration of realism, racialism, and romanticism—one that would mark his own foreign policy within fewer years than he could imagine.

Spring Rice had raised the issue of Russia and how the Western powers ought to treat the czar and his domain. Roosevelt thought the Russian question hinged on the German question. And the German question was worrisome. Roosevelt said he wasn't sure he respected the "little Kaiser," Wilhelm II. "But in his colonial plans I think he is entirely right from the standpoint of the German race. International law, and above all interracial law"—whatever that was—"are still in a fluid condition, and two nations with violently conflicting interests may each be entirely right from its own standpoint. If I were a German I should want the German race to expand." There were but two places fit for such expansion—southern Africa and temperate South America. "Therefore, as a German I should be delighted to upset the English in South Africa, and to defy the Americans and their Monroe Doctrine in South America." Of course it was in the nature— in the blood—of the English and the Americans to oppose such German expansion for precisely such racial reasons as were impelling the Germans to expand. "As an Englishman, I should seize the first opportunity to crush the German Navy and the German commercial marine out of existence, and take possession of both the German and Portuguese possessions in South Africa, leaving the Boers absolutely isolated. As an American I should advocate—and as a matter of fact do advocate—keeping our Navy at a pitch that will enable us to interfere promptly if Germany ventures to touch a foot of American soil." Such a course needn't be justified by elaborate explanation. "I would not go into the abstract rights or wrongs of it; I would simply say that we did not intend to have the Germans on this continent [meaning North and South America together], excepting as immigrants whose children would become Americans of one sort or another, and if Germany intended to extend her empire here she would have to whip us first."

Roosevelt confided doubts to Spring Rice that either of their governments possessed the nerve to pursue such policies. But that was their weakness, not their wisdom. "I am absolutely sure that it is the proper course to follow." And he was no less sure for the fact that the German course was the right one for Germany. "I should adopt it without in the least feeling that the Germans who advocated German colonial expansion were doing anything save what was right and proper from the standpoint of their own people. Nations may, and often must, have conflicting interests, and in the present age patriotism stands a good deal ahead of cosmopolitanism."

As opposed as American (and English) policies ought to be to German, Roosevelt reckoned—with a prescience that vaulted across two world wars and a couple of revolutions—that the real enemy over the long term was Russia. At the moment the United States and Russia got on well enough. "But Russians and Americans, in their individual capacity, have nothing whatever in common." The Russians were a powerful, yet powerfully flawed, people—not unlike the Americans. "I look upon them as a people to whom we can give points, and a beating: a people with a great future as we have, but a people with poisons working in it, as other poisons, of similar character on the whole, work in us." The poisoning process was more recently evident in America, but it promised to be more profound in Russia. "She may put off the day of reckoning; but she cannot ultimately avert it, and instead of occasionally having to go through what Kansas has gone through with the populists she will sometime experience a red terror which will make the French Revolution pale."

Roosevelt was almost as hard on American civilization as on Russian. "We are barbarians of a certain kind," he told Spring Rice. "And what is most unpleasant we are barbarians with a certain middle-class Philistine quality of ugliness and pettiness, raw conceit and raw sensitiveness. Where we get highly civilized, as in the northeast, we seem to become civilized in an unoriginal and ineffective way, and tend to die out." All the same, at the history-determining moment of truth the barbarians of the West would hold their own against the barbarians of the East. "Though the people of the English-speaking races may have to divide the future with the Slav, yet they will get rather more than their fair share."

VII

When he wasn't grandly theorizing with Spring Rice or prodding the president toward war, Roosevelt devoted hours—and hours, and more hours—to mundane but essential matters of administration. "I have been flying about the country inspecting the Naval Militia," he told a friend in August between such flights. There were new keels to be fitted to vessels that rolled excessively in heavy seas, dry docks to be enlarged to handle bigger bottoms, steelmakers to be jawboned into curbing cost overruns on armor plating, able officers to be promoted and incompetents to be canned, budgets to be drawn up and defended. There was no rest from morning till night. "I belong to the laboring classes and the eight hour law does not apply to me."

Roosevelt's principal reward came as knowledge that America's fighting capacity was increasing by the month; a smaller but no less personally satisfying part was an opportunity to play sailor for three days in September 1897. "I never enjoyed or profited by anything more than I did my three days with the fleet," Roosevelt wrote Long. For one thing—and no slight thing, considering Roosevelt's history of seasickness—the water off Hampton Roads was smooth and calm during that week. (This exercise was as much a public relations affair as a real shakedown; the officers in charge of scheduling knew enough to pick a time when the weather was likely to be good.) "Think of it," Roosevelt told Lodge, "on the Atlantic Ocean, out of sight of land, going out to dinner to a battleship in evening dress without an overcoat!" Roosevelt observed the operation of the different kinds of gun turrets—hydraulic, pneumatic, steam, and electric. He felt the concussion of the monster battleship guns during target practice and verified directly something he had known before only academically. "I was aboard the *Iowa* and the *Puritan* throughout their practice under service conditions at the targets," he recorded, "and was able to satisfy myself definitely of the great superiority of the battleship as a gun platform." He took part in nighttime drills when the flash of the guns lit the sea from horizon to horizon. He rubbed shoulders with the fighting men who commanded these vessels. "I saw the maneuvers of the squadron as a whole, and met every captain and went over with him, on the ground"—so to speak—"what was needed."

Roosevelt saw the September maneuvers as a learning experience for the American people as well as for himself. He took care to publicize the exercises as favorably as possible. He closely vetted the two reporters he allowed aboard with him, making sure that neither worked for the New York *World* or *Journal*, two papers that "try in every way to discredit the Navy by fake stories," he explained. He also brought along artist, friend, and fellow frontier buff Frederic Remington. "I wish I were with you out among the sage brush, the great brittle cottonwoods, and the sharply-channeled, barren buttes," he told Remington shortly after returning to harbor. "But I am very glad at any rate to have had you along with the squadron; and I can't help looking upon you as an ally from henceforth on in trying to make the American people see the beauty and the majesty of our ships, and the heroic quality which lurks somewhere in all those who man and handle them."

In time Roosevelt would evince a rare virtuosity at news management and image making; for now he had to content himself with a modest public relations victory. The coverage was indeed favorable, but he wished for more. "Oh, Lord! if only the people who are ignorant about our Navy could see those great warships in all their majesty and beauty, and could realize how well they are handled, and how well fitted to uphold the honor of America, I don't think we would encounter such opposition in building up the Navy to its proper standard."

VIII

Or, perhaps, in employing the fleet against Spain. During the last months of 1897 and the first of 1898, the McKinley administration swung around to Roosevelt's way of thinking on the Cuban question, but slowly and grudgingly. The American economy had begun to climb out of its three-year depression at about the time of McKinley's inauguration; though hardly a tool of Wall Street, McKinley was a Republican, and when the business interests of the country registered concern that a foreign war would short-circuit the recovery, he had to listen. Promisingly for the president and for the Cuban people, in

October 1897 a new cabinet in Madrid announced a new policy for Cuba, one that would guarantee humane treatment of the innocent and lead to greater Cuban autonomy. Soon thereafter Madrid confirmed its fresh approach by canceling the *reconcentrado* policy and ordering the recall of its instigator, General Valeriano Weyler.

This announcement appeared a triumph for McKinley, who had demanded amelioration of such a sort. Unfortunately, the rickety government in Madrid found pledges concerning Cuba easier to make than to keep, and the announced reforms retreated before a wave of loyalist rioting in Havana. Then the Spanish minister in Washington dropped a brick on his government's foot by letting an indiscreet letter fall into the hands of a friend of the insurgency. In this letter Enrique Dupuy de Lome described McKinley as "weak and a bidder for the admiration of the crowd, besides being a would-be politician who tries to leave a door open behind himself while keeping on good terms with the jingoes of his party." When leaked to the anti-Spanish press in America, the de Lome letter triggered an explosion of outrage over this incredible insult to the American president—despite the fact that McKinley's domestic opponents characterized him in language far less flattering at least twice weekly.

But it was another explosion—a real one—that finally brought on the war. The rioting in Havana prompted the American consul there to request the protection of an American warship. McKinley resisted the request for a time, not wishing to provoke worse violence. But eventually he changed his mind and asked permission of the Spanish government to allow the U.S.S. *Maine* to visit Havana. As a sign of the intended nonthreatening nature of the visit, he invited reciprocal visits by Spanish vessels to American ports. Madrid, eager to defuse the recent tensions, granted permission for the *Maine* to enter Havana's harbor, and in the first week of February 1898 the vessel, one of the navy's best midsized battleships, steamed in. For several days an air of cautious expectation hung over the city. Locals visited the waterfront to see the sleek steel warship; American sailors ventured ashore in search of their usual forms of recreation.

On the evening of February 15, however, the party came to an abrupt end. A horrifying explosion shattered the sultry air, tearing the ship's hull to shreds and throwing huge chunks of wreckage high and far out across the bay. By the time the smoke cleared and the bubbles ceased breaking the surface of the black water, only the central mast and a portion of the twisted superstructure remained in view. The rest of the recently proud vessel lay on the floor of the harbor, along with more than 250 American bodies, less those that had been atomized in the explosion or blasted clear of the wreckage.

IX

If Roosevelt thought he had been busy before, the destruction of the *Maine* sent him, and the rest of the Navy Department, into a frenzy. He had followed the maneuvering between Madrid and the McKinley administration with mounting exasperation. Each week that passed put off the war he coveted, and he didn't think it could be postponed indefinitely without being missed entirely. At times the thought made him "bitterly angry"; at times it drove him nearly to despair. "I am afraid that our hopes as to the Spanish business are a dream," he moaned. But then he brightened. "I doubt if those Spaniards can really pacify Cuba, and if the insurrection goes on much longer I don't see how we can help interfering."

What Roosevelt wanted was war—if not with Spain, then with some other country. Indeed, because Spain was weak and decadent, Germany would make a worthier opponent. Unfortunately an occasion for war with Germany wasn't presenting itself; America would have to be settle for what it got. As he outfitted the *Maine* some weeks prior to its ill-fated voyage, he mused, "I wish there was a chance that the *Maine* was going to be used against some foreign power; by preference Germany—but I am not particular, and I'd take even Spain if nothing better offered."

The onset of the rioting in Havana had raised Roosevelt's hopes that indefinite peace might be averted, and he began laying serious plans for war. In a memo to Long he advocated measures to enhance American readiness for war and to maximize success when war came. The current practice of dispatching small cruisers and gunboats to foreign waters singly or in small numbers ought to be suspended; if war broke out, these minor vessels could be snatched up by an enemy very quickly, to the damage and especially the humiliation of the United

States. Concentration of forces was the key. American ships in the Atlantic and near Pacific should be massed for a blockade of Cuba; those in the Far East should be readied for a strike against Spain's forces in the Philippines. Beyond these obvious moves, Roosevelt restated the case for a "flying squadron" that would attack Spanish shipping at and around Barcelona. Such an action would demoralize the Spanish and compel them to keep the main body of their fleet in home waters. But regardless of the precise steps taken, the essential thing was to be ready to take them. "In short, when the war comes it should come finally on our initiative, and after we have had time to prepare."

During the subsequent weeks Roosevelt continued agitating for war. "I have been hoping and working ardently to bring about our interference in Cuba," he told German friend Speck von Sternberg. At a minimum, a war would be educational. "If we could get the seven Spanish ironclads together against our seven seagoing ironclads on this coast we would have a pretty good fight; and I think more could be learned from it than from the Yalu"—referring to the Yalu River battle between Japan's and China's armored vessels during the Sino-Japanese War. Dishearteningly, however, Americans didn't want to be educated. "It is very difficult to make this nation wake up. . . . I sometimes question whether anything but a great military disaster will ever make us feel our responsibilities and our possible dangers."

Until the explosion of the *Maine,* Roosevelt's remained a minority viewpoint, but that tragedy transformed political opinion in the United States. Those already favoring intervention shouted louder than ever for Spanish blood. "Remember the *Maine*! To Hell with Spain!" set the tone for numerous headlines distinguishable from one another principally by type size and number of capitals and exclamation points. Opponents of intervention were rendered temporarily speechless, branded as cowards or worse for abetting this assault on American life and honor. Many of those on the fence were blown into the war camp by the force of the explosion.

The day after the disaster Roosevelt opined to Long that it might well be impossible ever to determine definitively whether the explosion was accidental or deliberate. But he was inclined to believe it was the latter, if only because of the improbability of such a close coincidence between the ship's arrival in Cuba and its destruction "by an accident such as has never before happened." (To a friend Roosevelt was more forthright: "The *Maine* was sunk by an act of dirty treachery on the part of the Spaniards I believe.") Regardless of who or what had done the vile deed, however, it behooved the Navy Department to prepare for what might follow. The stakes were both political and strategic. "If ever [by] some such incident as the de Lome affair, or this destruction of the *Maine,* war should suddenly arise, the Navy Department would have to bear the full brunt of the displeasure of Congress and the country if it were not ready. It would in all probability take two or three weeks to get ready vessels laid up in reserve, and these two or three weeks would represent the golden time for striking a paralyzing blow at the outset of the war."

Roosevelt assigned himself the task of preparing the paralyzing blow. The Navy Department had been working around the clock since the *Maine* disaster, and by Friday, February 25, Long—still not entirely recovered from the maladies that had kept him away from the office so long the previous summer—was exhausted. Fortunately, the approaching weekend promised a slight lull, and Long felt he could afford to leave the office early. Roosevelt, ever solicitous of his boss's health, bade him good day and sweet dreams.

Then he flew into action. First he sent a message to Lodge, who had been working for war in the Senate as assiduously as Roosevelt had been working in the administration. Lodge lacked Roosevelt's logistical expertise in naval matters, but he could provide moral support, which he did as the assistant secretary raced about the department checking the cable traffic here, poring over the maps there, analyzing fuel stocks, tallying up ammunition supplies, assessing the quality of commanders of each squadron and task group, forecasting the need for enlistments.

Soon he began scribbling orders, dashing them off on slips of paper that he gave to department clerks for coding and immediate dispatch around the globe. On his authority as acting secretary, he repositioned American warships in the Atlantic and Pacific. He ordered enough coal and ammunition to get a war well started. He directed the transfer of guns from the navy yard at Washington to New York. He placed docked ships on alert with instructions to make ready to sail on a moment's notice. He even sent a message to Capitol Hill, requesting special wartime legislation from Congress.

The most portentous directive of all was a cable to Commodore

George Dewey, the commander of the American Asiatic squadron, based in Japan.

> Secret and confidential. Order the squadron except Monocacy to Hongkong. Keep full of coal. In the event of declaration of war Spain, your duty will be to see that the Spanish squadron does not leave the Asiatic coast, and then offensive operations in Philippine Islands. Keep Olympia until further orders.

X

Roosevelt departed the office that day well pleased with himself. Leonard Wood, an army surgeon, a fellow war hawk, and soon to be Roosevelt's superior officer, afterward recalled that they had arranged to meet for a walk the next day. Wood waited for Roosevelt at the appointed hour.

> Suddenly I saw him trotting around the court from Connecticut Avenue to my house at 2000 R Street, with a broad smile on his face. As I met him at the door he said: "Well, I have had my chance, Leonard, and I have taken advantage of it. Yesterday afternoon the Secretary of the Navy left me as acting secretary. He has gone to take a short and much-needed rest, and I have done what I thought ought to be done. I have placed various ships in commission with orders to be ready for sea at once. I have given large orders for the purchase and shipment of coal. I have assembled supplies and forwarded munitions. In other words, I have done everything I can to get the navy ready.

Perhaps reflecting on the magnitude of his afternoon's work, Roosevelt added, "I may not be supported, but I have done what I know to be right; some day they will understand."

Secretary Long also was impressed, albeit not quite so favorably, with what his subordinate had wrought. Long had learned to appreciate Roosevelt's energy. "He was heart and soul in his work," he wrote later. To be sure, the secretary could have stood seeing fewer of the lengthy memos his assistant made a habit of circulating. "His typewriters had no rest." But on the whole Roosevelt was a positive influence in the department. "He was especially stimulating to the younger officers who gathered about him and made his office as busy as a hive."

That office had been a bit too busy these last twenty-four hours, Long thought on discovering what Roosevelt had done during his afternoon in charge. "I find that Roosevelt, in his precipitate way, has come very near causing more of an explosion than happened to the *Maine*. . . . The very devil seemed to possess him." Long noted wryly that the navy had no means to move all the ammunition Roosevelt had ordered or sufficient space to store it. Guns he had requisitioned from warehouses in Washington would now sit in the open at New York, exposed to the rain and snow. "He has gone at things like a bull in a china shop." Long added, with uncharacteristic acerbity, that Roosevelt had been not only rash but discourteous in that all his arm-waving and order-sending implied serious laxity on the (real) secretary's part. "It shows how the best fellow in the world—and with splendid capacities—is worse than no use if he lack a cool head and careful discretion."

Yet Long survived his exasperation, and for the most part he let Roosevelt's orders stand—including, most significantly, the directive to Dewey to neutralize the Spanish fleet at Manila. This wasn't something Roosevelt had conjured up on the spur of the secretary's absence; rather, it reflected the sober thinking of many in the Navy Department regarding appropriate strategy in the event of war. But sober or rash, Roosevelt's orders on that particular day had the effect of pushing the country closer to war—precisely as he intended.

Although McKinley still held out against the war fever, Roosevelt was confident his resistance would give way soon. "The President will not make war, and will keep out of it if he possibly can," Roosevelt told his brother-in-law. "Nevertheless, with so much loose powder round, a coal may hop into it at any moment." The report of the president's special committee investigating the *Maine* sinking would be appearing shortly. "If it says the explosion was due to outside work, it will be very hard to hold the country."

McKinley was a good sport about the free advice he was receiving. Leonard Wood, whose patients included President McKinley, visited the White House almost daily; McKinley regularly queried, with a rather resigned smile, "Have you and Theodore declared war yet?" To which Wood regularly answered, "No, Mr. President, but we think that you should."

Events soon forced McKinley to agree. The investigative committee did indeed pronounce that the explosion that killed all the American sailors had originated outside the *Maine*'s hull. In other words, it was an act of sabotage. The report didn't explicitly finger Spain as the saboteur but left readers to draw their own conclusions. (A later investigation, conducted after the passions of the moment had cooled, seconded the external-explosion opinion. A still later one, informed by different passions, disputed it.)

McKinley remained skeptical about the wisdom of war, but even he could no longer resist the rising tide for belligerence. A mild man, he had never expected to be burned in effigy as he now was. Nor had one who was proud to be addressed as "Major," his rank in the Union army, ever expected to be called a traitor to the American nation as he now also was. Editorialists ranted for vengeance; enraged senators and congressmen threatened to declare war even without the president's request.

Roosevelt took the opportunity to try to push the president over the edge. "Of course I cannot speak in public," Roosevelt told William Cowles, "but I have advised the President in the presence of his Cabinet, as well as Judge Day and Senator Hanna, as strongly as I knew how, to settle this matter instantly by armed intervention; and I told the President in the plainest language that no other course was compatible with our national honor, or with the claims of humanity on behalf of the wretched women and children of Cuba."

Finally McKinley surrendered. He handed Madrid an ultimatum of several points, summing to a simple demand: Cuban independence.

The Spanish government still dithered and dodged. If it refused the American ultimatum, it faced war with the United States. If it accepted, it faced a revolt at home. Preferring to keep its enemies at arm's—and ocean's—length, it refused.

On April 11, McKinley asked Congress for authorization to employ American military force in Cuba. "In the name of humanity," he said, "in the name of civilization, in behalf of endangered American interests which give us the right and the duty to speak and to act, the war in Cuba must stop." To stop the war, the United States must take up the sword.

This didn't quite settle the issue. Congress had to debate the president's request. Roosevelt, having helped get the country to the brink of war, now had to endure a week of legislative posturing and pontificating. And while the lawmakers jabbered, he thought he detected backsliding in McKinley. "The President still feebly is painfully trying for peace," he scribbled in his diary. "His weakness and vacillation are even more ludicrous than painful." The uncertainty was unbearable. "I don't think anybody knows anything," he grumbled angrily. "We don't even know whether we are going to have war or peace."

But war it was. Congress approved the president's request, prompting Spain to break relations and declare war. Congress responded in kind.

Part Three

FULFILLMENT

CHAPTER THIRTEEN

The Hero in His Element
1898

With the United States going to war, Theodore Roosevelt had to go to war, too. There was never any doubt that he would serve, although there was plenty of reason for him not to. As his friends and relatives pointed out, he could do far greater good for the country in Washington than in Cuba. Hundreds—nay, thousands—of men were better qualified to march into battle and trade lead with the Spaniards; the country had but one assistant navy secretary, and he was needed at his desk. As gently as they could, Lodge, Douglas Robinson, and several others reminded Roosevelt that he was nearly forty, that he had never served in the military (three years of very part-time duty in the New York militia hardly qualified), that he wasn't in the physical condition he once had been in, that if he did enlist he would probably end up guarding some fort in Florida, that however well his bravery might protect him from Spanish bullet or bayonet, bravery was no protection against malaria or typhoid.

Roosevelt conceded these objections, but still he had to go. Without putting it so directly even to himself, he was going not for the country's sake but for his own. After all the noise he had made over the years and especially recently about the glories of war and the need to back words with weapons, he couldn't possibly do otherwise. "It does not seem to me that it would be honorable for a man who has consistently advocated a warlike policy not to be willing himself to bear the brunt of carrying out that policy," he told Douglas Robinson. "I have a horror of people who bark but don't bite." To Bill Sewall, who similarly counseled against going to war, he replied, "I thank you for your advice, old man, but it seems to me that if I can go I better had. My work here has been the work of preparing the tools. They are prepared; and now the work must lie with those who use them. . . . I would like to be one of those who use the tools." Roosevelt reckoned that that while Secretary Long had been willing to listen to him during peacetime, once the guns started firing, other voices would carry more weight than his. "My usefulness will largely disappear in time of war, for it is conditioned mainly upon the fact that in time of peace the military advisers of the Secretary cannot speak to him as they ought to and will speak in time of war. . . . In time of war the military advisers will promptly come to the front." Roosevelt went on to say that his primary accomplishments at the Navy Department had occurred during moments when he got to be the acting secretary; now and for the duration Long would certainly stick close to his desk.

Roosevelt explained that he had considered the matter carefully. "I can assure you that I am quite disinterested in this," he told a friend. "I am not acting in a spirit of recklessness or levity, or purely for my own selfish enjoyment. I don't want to be shot at any more than anyone else does; still less to die of yellow fever. I am altogether too fond of my wife and children, and enjoy the good things of this life too much to wish lightly to hazard their loss, or to go away from my family." But the call of duty was simply too strong. "It may be that I am mistaken, but I can assure you that I am acting conscientiously, after having weighed the matter very carefully in all its bearings."

Although Roosevelt didn't mention it, the parallel between his own situation and that of his father during the Civil War certainly occurred to him. At that time Mittie's reservations had prevented Theodore Sr. from doing what he himself later, and his son after him, conceived to be his duty. The son wasn't about to let the reservations of friends or family get between him and his duty now. He may or may not have had to work hard to convince himself that he would be of greater use at the fighting front than in Washington—a conclusion that was as spurious as it was strained. But such arguments were beside the point, just as the similar argument—also true—that Theodore Sr. did more good as allotment commissioner than he would have done in the line of fire had been beside the point in assuaging his father's uneasy conscience. "I suppose, at bottom, I was merely following my instinct instead of my reason," he conceded a few months after the fact.

Instinct it was, but acquired instinct. Ever since his father had challenged him to remake himself, Roosevelt had sought out every form of physical and moral test he could imagine or devise. His all-day hikes, his forty-mile excursions in his rowboat, his tramps with Sewall through frozen Maine, his grizzly hunts with Bill Merrifield in Wyoming, his climb up the Matterhorn, his headlong style of polo, his tennis matches with Spring Rice and others, his decision to enter politics against the advice of friends and family—these were simply variations on the theme of testing his mettle, of determining whether he measured up. Now the ultimate test—war—was at hand, and there wasn't a possibility in the world he would let it slip. "It was my one chance," he explained years later, "to do something for my country and for my family and my one chance to cut my little notch on the stick that stands as a measuring rod in every family. I know now that I would have turned from my wife's deathbed to answer that call."

II

He did something very close to that. The previous November Edith had delivered a fourth son, christened Quentin after Edith's paternal grandfather. Postpartum troubles developed, initially diagnosed as grippe but subsequently revealed to be an abdominal infection. For weeks she suffered from fever, pain, and related secondary symptoms. "Edith's eyes trouble her," Roosevelt told her sister at the beginning of March. "She can write only postal cards, and ought not to write those" (which was why Roosevelt, who wrote Emily Carow only when necessary, was standing in). One doctor after another puzzled over her condition and prescribed treatments, none of which did much to alleviate her affliction.

Finally, Roosevelt summoned an internist from Johns Hopkins, reputed to be the best in the world. This doctor diagnosed an abscess and prescribed its removal. Roosevelt feared complications from surgery, which in those days was a hazardous undertaking in the best of circumstances, but after gathering additional opinions, he consented. "The doctors came and found a condition of things which demanded immediate action," he explained to Bamie. "Accordingly they operated on her; it was a large abscess, in the psoas muscle, reaching down to the pelvis. Everything went well; but of course it was a severe operation; and her convalescence may be a matter of months. She is now well over the effects of the ether and the shock; but of course exceedingly weak. She behaved heroically; quiet, and even laughing, while I held her hand until the ghastly preparations had been made."

Edith's heroism underwent a different kind of test the following month when her husband announced that he was off to war. She remained postoperatively weak; the thought of trying to take care of her large family and the house by herself must nearly have occasioned a relapse. Beyond this immediate concern was the larger, deeper worry that he would be killed. How would she manage without him? How would she raise their children without a father?

Edith was particularly concerned about young Ted. For some time the ten-year-old boy had complained of recurrent headaches and what seemed to be a form of nervous prostration. A series of doctors had an even harder time diagnosing his troubles than her own doctors had with hers. "We have been very much worried over the little fellow," Roosevelt told his sister-in-law, "for the doctors are utterly unable to find out the ultimate cause of the trouble." Eventually one physician, a family friend and likely for that reason more insightful than the others, agreed with Edith's private estimate that Ted was overwrought from trying to live up to his father's excessive expectations, spoken and unspoken.

Roosevelt was embarrassed at this opinion but recognized the truth in it. He promised to go easier on the boy. "I shall give plain proof of great weakness of character by reading your letter to Mrs. Roosevelt, who is now well enough to feel the emotions of triumph," he wrote to the doctor who identified the problem. "Hereafter I shall never press Ted either in body or mind. The fact is that the little fellow, who is particularly dear to me, has bidden fair to be all the things I would like to have been and wasn't, and it has been a great temptation to push him." Partly because of Edith's illness, partly from a hope that a change of scenery would do him good, and partly to be examined by this doctor, Ted had been sent to stay with Bamie in New York (along with Alice, who was entirely too unruly for a convalescent household and who, in any event, had a standing invitation from her former surrogate mother to return if things got difficult with her father and step-mother). Roosevelt continued, "My purpose is to keep him in New York just as long as you think it well for him and as my sister is willing to have him. I feel sure you are doing exactly the right thing for him."

Perhaps Edith estimated that having Theodore away for a while would make life easier for Ted; certainly she realized—not least after the unhappy experience of persuading him to forgo the New York mayor's race—that it would be worse than useless to try to keep her husband home from the war for which he had been preparing in one way or another since childhood. So, setting aside her own worries, she gave him her blessing. He appreciated the gesture and the love it evinced. "I can never say what a help and comfort Edith has been to me," he told Corinne just before leaving Washington.

III

Despite Edith's help, getting out of Washington and into the war was no small feat. Once Roosevelt convinced McKinley and Long that he was really serious about fighting, they offered their assistance. Yet so well had the war party done its work that by the time the president asked for a war declaration, tens of thousands of young men who knew no more of armed conflict than the half-remembered and wholly glorified stories their daddies and granddaddies had told them about Manassas and Gettysburg were crying to throw their bodies into battle against the scurrilous Spaniard. Roosevelt's obvious avenue to Cuba—a commission in a New York regiment—was blocked by the crowd of would-be heroes.

However, when Congress authorized the raising of special units from the West—cavalry regiments of cowboys, hunters, wilderness scouts, and even Indians—Roosevelt saw his opening. He quickly reminded the top brass at the War Department that he had been a cowboy and a hunter; he certainly qualified for service in such a group. War Secretary Russell Alger agreed and in the tradition of American military politics offered Roosevelt the command of one such regiment.

Roosevelt rarely sold himself short and, despite his absence of experience at military command, was sorely tempted to accept Alger's offer. But even he recognized that he would require a few weeks to figure out just what a cavalry colonel was supposed to do: where to requisition supplies, how to arrange transport, what kinds of training the recruits required. From the number of people clamoring to go to Cuba, it was clear that the hardest fighting might occur on the gangplanks at the ports of embarkation. While he was learning on the job, others might beat him aboard, leaving him to guard some godforsaken blockhouse on the Gulf Coast. That would be worse than staying in Washington. Consequently, he declined Alger's offer of command in favor of a lieutenant-colonelcy under Leonard Wood, who as a career soldier knew all the things Roosevelt would have had to learn for himself.

The First Volunteer Cavalry immediately attracted the attention of the national press. A better story could hardly have been invented, for the cowboy cavalry combined two central strands of the American myth. It was the latest manifestation of the ideal of the citizen-soldier: the unsung patriot who set aside his plow and picked up his gun in the defense of liberty and justice. Yet in this case it wasn't the plow that got set aside but the lariat, for these were the Cincinnati of the western frontier, the knights-errant of the plains. They shot straight, lived straight (according to the myth), and rode like the wind; they had bravery in the blood and hardiness beyond measure. They broke broncos before breakfast, roped and branded longhorns until dinner, and shot wild Indians after supper. (The Indians of the First Volunteers were reservation Indians.) The Spaniards stood nary a chance against them.

Although the declaration of war came in April, it soon became apparent that logistical inertia would prevent any serious fighting before June. In the meantime the war correspondents had to earn their pay and file their stories. The "Rough Riders," as one anonymous alliterist christened the First Volunteer Cavalry, provided the best copy around. They were rounded up principally from the western territories; musters were held in Arizona, New Mexico, Oklahoma, and the Indian Territory. The call for volunteers produced an ensemble that impressed Roosevelt as much as it didn't surprise him. "They were a splendid set of men, these southwesterners—tall and sinewy, with resolute, weather-beaten faces, and eyes that looked a man straight in the face without flinching."

The original ceiling for the regiment was 780; when the War Department found funds to fill 1,000 saddles, the western volunteers were joined by a couple of hundred Ivy Leaguers and others from the polo and fox-hunting grounds of the eastern half of the country. (Total applications eventually reached 23,000.) Possibly feeling that the inclusion of the latecomers with the obviously qualified men of the plains and mountains had to be justified, Roosevelt, in his account of the regiment's exploits, took care to list their athletic credentials. One young man was "perhaps the best quarter-back who ever played on a Harvard eleven"; another was a close runner-up to this first as a football player and was the national tennis champion to boot (having, "in two different years, saved this championship from going to an Englishman"). Still other eastern volunteers were some Princeton footballers, a Yale high jumper, and the former captain of the Columbia crew. What such experiences had to do with soldiering, Roosevelt left unsaid; presumably he felt the connection was sufficiently obvious to make explanation unnecessary.

The regiment trained in Texas, outside the dusty old mission town of San Antonio. Roosevelt arrived late, after spending his last few days in Washington "stirring up everything as well as I knew how"—he explained to Leonard Wood—to ensure that their outfit wasn't overlooked in the bureaucratic scramble. He quickly made up for his tardiness. He wrote on May 19 to Lodge:

> We are working like beavers and we are getting the regiment into shape. It has all the faults incident to an organization whose members have elected their own officers—some good and more very bad—and who have been recruited largely from among classes who, putting it mildly, do not look at life in the spirit of decorum and conventionality that obtains in the East. Nevertheless many of our officers have in them the making of first rate men, and the troopers, I believe, are on the average finer than are to be found in any other regiment in the whole country. It would do your heart good to see some of the riding.

Not unnaturally, Roosevelt had harbored misgivings regarding the fit between the westerners and the easterners; he was pleased to report that the two groups appeared to be getting along fine. "You would be amused to see three Knickerbocker club men cooking and washing dishes for one of the New Mexico companies." The Indians who had volunteered for the regiment were, predictably, "excellent riders"; somewhat less automatically they seemed to be "pretty good fellows." Roosevelt had spent the day on the drill field, amid heat, dust, and sweat; in the evening the heat abated but the mosquitoes came out. "I am heartily enjoying it nevertheless."

The one thing Roosevelt really worried about was that the war would end before he got into it. To the surprise of most Americans who were not privy to the secret cables Roosevelt had sent to George Dewey, the conflict had commenced half a planet away from Cuba, its putative cause. As instructed, Dewey sailed for the Philippines at the outbreak of hostilities; catching the Spanish fleet there unprepared, he made a morning's work of destroying it and placing Manila Bay at his mercy. The victory transformed Dewey into an instant hero and rendered a confident American people overconfident. Already convinced that Spain would be no match for the United States in an open fight, many Americans began to doubt that the Spanish would put up a fight at all. On the evidence of Dewey's experience they seemed just as likely to run up the white flag and scurry back to Iberia.

"Do not make peace until we get Porto Rico," Roosevelt implored Lodge from Texas, "while Cuba is made independent and the Philippines at any rate taken from the Spaniards." The expansionist in Roosevelt was speaking here; for although the self-denying Teller amendment (not to mention America's sense of shame) stood in the way of taking Cuba explicitly for the United States, no such impediments blocked seizure of other Spanish possessions.

Yet the worried warrior was also speaking, for it seemed entirely possible that Spain would grant Cuba independence without even a landing of American troops. Roosevelt grew almost panicky at the thought that the war would end before he got his chance. He wished to be among the first troops to splash ashore in Cuba, but he was willing to go wherever he could get shot at. "We most earnestly hope we can be sent to Cuba," he said, "and if for any reason Cuba should fail, then to the Philippines—anywhere so that we can see active service." If he and his unit did not see active service, his departure from Washington would turn out to have been a bad, even stupid, move.

"But if we do, I shall feel amply repaid for the loss of what I liked to make myself believe was a career in the Navy Department."

While he fretted over the delays in getting off to the front, Roosevelt allowed himself to become more impressed than ever by his comrades in arms. "I really doubt if there has ever been a regiment quite like this," he told Lodge. His friend was used to Roosevelt's exaggerations, as Roosevelt realized, but this time he meant every word. "I know you will believe that more than ever I fail to get the relations of this regiment and the universe straight, but I cannot help being a little enthusiastic about it." As a militant nationalist he couldn't help being struck by the essential "Americanism" of the group, which corroborated nearly everything he had been saying about Americans in his historical works.

> It is as typical an American regiment as ever marched or fought. I suppose about 95 per cent of the men are of native birth, but we have a few from everywhere, including a score of Indians [whether he was including these among the native-born was unclear] and about as many men of Mexican origin from New Mexico; then there are some fifty Easterners—almost all graduates of Harvard, Yale, Princeton, etc.— and almost as many Southerners; the rest are men of the plains and the Rocky Mountains. Three fourths of our men have at one time or another been cowboys or else are small stockmen; certainly two thirds have fathers who fought on one side or the other in the civil war.

Almost none of the men had military training themselves, and their initial efforts showed the lack. "A regiment cannot be made in a week," he noted not long after the week had passed. But the men's hearts were in the right place, and also their heads. "These men are in it because they want to be in it. They are intelligent as well as game." Considering the unbroken nature of many of them, they were conducting themselves quite well. "Now and then a small squad goes to town and proceeds to paint things red, and then we get hold of them and put them into the guardhouse, but the great bulk of the men are as quiet and straight as possible. I am very confident there has been much less disturbance than there would have been with the ordinary National Guard or the ordinary regular regiment."

The officers, with certain exceptions, were as sound as the men. Wood was a trump. Roosevelt called him "one of the best fellows, as well as one of the best officers, that I know." His energy and executive capacity were "wonderful"; his combination of character and experience made him "the ideal man for Colonel." Others were in the same class, if in a slightly different mold. "The First Major is a dandy— Major Brodie, of Arizona—a grizzled old frontier soldier, who was in the regular army." One of the second lieutenants was a former captain of the Harvard crew; of his qualifications Roosevelt needed to say no more. Another officer, however, was "a pitiful failure"; a few besides this man were "very poor."

As to his own performance, Roosevelt was happy to report that he was fully measuring up. "I have been both astonished and pleased at my own ability in the line of tactics. I thoroughly enjoy handling these men, and I get them on the jump so that they execute their movements at a gallop."

In some other aspects of command, Roosevelt wasn't quite so proud of himself. He kept confusing his roles as the second officer in the regiment and therefore the superior of everyone besides Wood, and as the fellow cowboy and plainsman, and consequently just one of the boys. As throughout his life, Roosevelt wanted to be liked by these rough and ready types. Early in the training period at San Antonio he concluded a drill session by ordering his men to dismount; he then shouted, "The men can go in and drink all the beer they want, which I will pay for!" This elicited hurrahs from the men for the good old lieutenant colonel, and all retired to the nearest saloon for their brew. Roosevelt spent the next few hours reveling in the applause.

That evening, however, Wood called him in and pointed out that drinking with the enlisted men hardly conduced to good discipline. Roosevelt, embarrassed, accepted the reprimand and left the colonel's tent. His embarrassment mounted for several minutes afterward, until he couldn't restrain himself any longer. Returning to Wood's tent, he saluted sharply and announced, "Sir, I consider myself the damnedest ass within ten miles of this camp! Good night, sir!"

Roosevelt didn't share this particular experience with Lodge. Part of the reason was the obvious personal one of not wanting to look foolish in his friend's eyes. But as with nearly everything Roosevelt did, there was an element of calculation as well. Roosevelt realized that Lodge might be his ticket to the front. Lodge's stature in Washington had gained greatly upon the declaration of the war he had been promoting for many months; his string-pulling powers had increased commensurately. Consciously or unconsciously, Roosevelt wished to impress upon Lodge the fighting ability of the First Volunteer Cavalry; if the opportunity arose, Lodge might put in the crucial good word with the War Department or even the president. On this point Roosevelt was entirely frank. "If they begin to send troops to Cuba," he said, "I shall wire you to see that we go." He added for emphasis, "We are all ready now to move, and will render a good account of ourselves." Lest somehow Lodge miss the message, Roosevelt appended a special request: "Give my respects to the members of the Senate Committee on Foreign Relations and tell them I pin my faith to them."

Lodge's influence may have had some effect, for shortly thereafter the Rough Riders received the order to move. The people of San Antonio had mixed feelings on the unit's departure. The novelty and charm of a cowboy contingent was largely lost on the Texans; on the other hand, the attention of the national press had some head-turning effect. Yet even those who had bolted their doors and locked up their daughters at the arrival of this motley crew could join in a toast to their departure. The town threw a party, highlighted by a band concert. Professor Carl Beck, a prominent member of the large German-American community in Texas, conducted several stirring airs, including a rousing march that culminated in an explosion of sound. Concerned about the strength of his percussion section, Professor Beck augmented the drums with a cannon firing blanks.

But no one had told the Rough Riders that powder was on the program, and when the cannon went off, several of the soldiers concluded that they had come under fire, perhaps from some Spanish-sympathizing Mexicans. "Help him out, boys!" shouted one worthy, pulling out his pistols and racing to Beck's side. Other Rough Riders likewise leaped up and began firing into the night. Members of the audience, after a moment of absolute stupefaction, dove for cover under the chairs. In the melee the lights went out, multiplying the confusion.

Eventually things calmed down, and the Rough Riders spent the rest of their last night in San Antonio invading and occupying bars near the Alamo. A few brave concertgoers joined them, but most were happy to escape home with their lives. A shaken Professor Beck commented the next day, "I was in the Franco-Prussian War and saw some hot times, but I was about as uneasy last night as I ever was in battle."

IV

The next day the journey to Cuba began. The first leg was by train to Florida. Roosevelt oversaw the loading of the horses into one set of cars and the men into another. The train headed slowly east, trading the dry heat of central Texas for the marginally milder temperatures but more taxing humidity of the Gulf coastal plain. The nights brought some relief from the heat but exacted their own price. As Roosevelt explained in a letter to his children, written on arrival in Tampa, "We were all, horses and men, four days and four nights on the cars coming here from San Antonio, and were very tired and dirty when we arrived. I was up almost all of each night, for it happened always to be at night when we took the horses out of the cars to feed and water them."

A special surprise, beyond the anticipated shower and bed, awaited Roosevelt in Tampa. Clued by Lodge as to her husband's movements, Edith caught a train south from Washington and intercepted her husband. The visit did both of them good. Conjugal comforts aside, Roosevelt took reassurance that she was recuperating steadily. When he had left her, she was barely off her deathbed; now she was well enough for a long railroad journey. For her part, seeing him stilled, at least somewhat, the vague fears she always felt during his absence—fears now understandably magnified by the reason for this particular absence. Wood permitted Roosevelt to spend evenings and nights, from before dinner until after breakfast, with Edith at a hotel. They had "4 lovely days," he told his diary; to Corinne he called it "a regular spree."

(Roosevelt elided, to the point of misrepresentation, this part of the Tampa sojourn in his heroic account, *The Rough Riders*. "Over in Tampa town," he wrote, "the huge winter hotel was gay with general officers and their staffs, with women in pretty dresses, with newspaper correspondents by the score, with military *attachés* of foreign powers, and with onlookers of all sorts; but we spent very little time there.")

Roosevelt's unacknowledged spree ended when the thirty thousand soldiers gathered at Tampa commenced boarding transport ships for Cuba. The gathering of forces had been disorganized and helter-skelter to date, but much of the disorganization had been disguised by the dispersed locations of the training camps. Now the chaos was concentrated. "No words could describe to you the confusion and lack of system and the general mismanagement of affairs here," Roosevelt wrote Lodge. The mismanagement extended from the lack of such necessities as food and medicine to the duplication and contradiction of orders regarding who was to go where.

In the latter category Roosevelt discovered that the transport assigned to his regiment had also been assigned to two others; by no stretch of imagination or hull could the vessel accommodate all three units. Roosevelt's reasonably accurate portrayal of his reaction recorded his first triumph of the war: "I ran at full speed to our train; and leaving a strong guard with the baggage, I double-quicked the rest of the regiment up to the boat, just in time to board her as she came into the quay, and then to hold her against the Second Regulars and the Seventy-first, who had arrived a little too late, being a shade less ready than we were in the matter of individual initiative."

At first Roosevelt's men congratulated themselves on the pluck and dash of their leader, but before long some began wondering whether the laggards had got the better of the bargain. Unbeknownst to Roosevelt and nearly all the others at Tampa, reports had reached Washington of Spanish warships lurking in the Florida Strait. Although the Navy Department was skeptical, neither it nor the War Department wished to risk having the first transports sunk, with many hundreds or more lost to the depths and the sharks. Beyond the personal tragedies, the blow to American morale—and the prestige and credibility of the departments involved—would be devastating. Accordingly, the transports were ordered to wait in Tampa Bay.

For more than a week Roosevelt and the Rough Riders, along with thousands of other soldiers, stewed. Sewage from the town poured untreated into the harbor, suffocating the men with its rankness. "If the authorities in their wisdom keep us much longer in this ship," fumed Roosevelt, as uninformed of the reason for the delay as everyone else, "we shall certainly have some epidemic of disease." Jumping the chain of command, he wrote confidentially to Lodge ("I cannot speak publicly in any way; I should be courtmartialed if I did") to rail at the "inextricable confusion," "dilatory inefficiency," and "utter incompetence" of those responsible for the delay, and to urge his friend to do something to straighten out the mess. The one positive aspect of the experience was that the Rough Riders' horses didn't suffer: Shortage of space had forced the regiment to leave all but the officers' mounts behind.

Finally the phantom Spanish squadron—for phantom it proved to be—sailed over the horizon of Washington's nervousness, and the transports were released. Roosevelt's spirits rebounded at once. "We are steaming southward through a sapphire sea, wind-rippled, under an almost cloudless sky," he recorded. "There are some forty-eight craft in all, in three columns, the black hulls of the transports setting off the gray hulls of the men-of-war. Last evening we stood up on the bridge and watched the red sun sink and the lights blaze up on the ships, for miles ahead and astern, while the band played piece after piece, from the 'Star Spangled Banner' at which we all rose and stood uncovered, to 'The Girl I Left Behind Me.'"

The experience aroused in Roosevelt the welcome—and familiar—sense of playing a role in a grand saga. "It is a great historical expedition, and I thrill to feel that I am part of it. If we fail, of course we share the fate of all who do fail, but if we are allowed to succeed (for certainly we shall succeed, if allowed) we have scored the first great triumph in what will be a world movement."

V

As Roosevelt well knew and would have admitted, the most sweeping world movements often take shape through the most prosaic stages. And few aspects of even the most heroic military operations are more prosaic than a landing on an open beach. The American landing at Daiquirí was prosaic in the extreme. Next to none of the officers or men involved had any personal experience of getting troops ashore through surf, and the inexperience showed. Leonard Wood wrote his wife, "You can hardly imagine the awful confusion and lack of system which meets us on every hand in this business." Although the beach was undefended—the Spanish having withdrawn following a brief bombardment by American warships—the landing was slow and fraught with difficulty. The men staggered through the waves carrying packs and rifles, dodging each other and the wild-eyed mules and horses that had been driven off the transports in hopes they could find their way to the beach. Many didn't. "It is pitiful to see the poor brutes swim from one boat to another," declared one regular cavalryman. "Sometimes they get nearly to the shore, then turn around and swim to sea. Of course a great many of them are drowned, and the beach is covered with dead horses and mules." Miraculously, only two troopers—African-American horse soldiers of the Tenth Cavalry—died in the watery disorder; these deaths occurred despite the valiant efforts of one of Roosevelt's favorite and most colorful subordinates, Bucky O'Neill, a four-square former sheriff from the otherwise lawless mining camp of Prescott, Arizona, who dove into the surf to try to rescue the drowning men.

Roosevelt lost a horse in the landing, but having started with two, he had one to spare. By example and exhortation he encouraged the men to get themselves, their weapons, ammunition, provisions, and other impedimenta up the beach and onto dry ground. The site was unpromising, affording little shelter from either the elements or the enemy. The latter, fortunately, were nowhere to be seen, which was a lucky thing. "Five hundred resolute men could have prevented the disembarkation at very little cost to themselves," he estimated. As for the elements, they, too, cooperated, at least for the first night, which brought no rain. The next morning Roosevelt directed the construction of palm-frond lean-tos to keep the sun off.

The objective of this initial phase of the campaign was the town of Santiago de Cuba, some fifteen miles northwest of Daiquirí. Hoping to strike before the combined forces of tropical summer and tropical disease caught up with them, the commanding American general, William Shafter, ordered an immediate advance on the town. This order set in motion additional scrambling among the three divisions that made up the bulk of the Fifth Army Corps, as various unit commanders sought to push their way to the front of the column advancing inland.

General Joseph Wheeler commanded the mostly unmounted cavalry division that included the Rough Riders. Roosevelt and every other student of American military history knew Wheeler as a dashing leader of Confederate cavalry during the Civil War; a bit long in the tooth by now, he had been dragooned into service by President McKinley as living proof that the old wounds were healed—and also as evidence that McKinley, who had been beaten badly by Bryan in the South in 1896, had not written off the states below the Mason-Dixon line. (McKinley also reached out to Bryan but not so far. He commissioned Bryan as a colonel in the Third Nebraska Volunteers, commonly called the Silver Battalion after the sympathies of its leader and rank and file. Bryan and his men made it as far as Florida but not to Cuba. McKinley's advisers doubtless decreed that the Democratic leader was too valuable to his country to hazard making him a hero.)

Wheeler had lost none of the spirit that had earned him the name Fightin' Joe, although advancing years, the whiskey that he drank to ward off disease, and the overall confusion of the Cuba campaign occasionally muddled him. During one moment of excitement he was heard to shout, "We've got the damn Yankees on the run!"

Wheeler's zest for action caused him to interpret orders in a manner that allowed him to get a head start up the road toward Santiago; taking their cue from their commander, Wood and Roosevelt similarly elbowed their way to the van. "We marched fast," Roosevelt said, "for Wood was bound to get us ahead of the other regiments, so as to be sure of our place in the body that struck the enemy next morning. If it had not been for his energy in pushing forward, we should certainly have missed the fight. As it was, we did not halt until we were at the extreme front."

By then the men were more than ready to halt. A fish out of water is hardly more awkward than a cowboy off his horse; some of the Rough Riders probably hadn't walked a quarter mile at a stretch in years before they enlisted the previous month. With their horses back in Florida, the proud cavalrymen were ignominiously (as they saw it) and exhaustingly (as was obvious to any observer) transformed into lowly grunts. They were game enough but simply not in physical condition for an extended advance on foot. "I shall never forget the terrible march to Siboney," one of the Rough Riders later recalled of that afternoon's trek. Another survivor employed a metaphor: "Our march was like a pipe organ, having many stops." At each stop the men sank to the ground to catch their breath, only to have to rise again, pick up their gear, and resume their pace when the column momentarily commenced to move. "We were in full marching order; that means each man carries a carbine, a hundred rounds of ammunition, canteen, poncho, half a shelter tent, the army blanket, rations and other necessary articles we were obliged to have." With the passing miles, the men started to shed those items they considered less than absolutely essential. "As the sun beat down on us, the packs and bundles slid about as though they were alive and gained in weight from pounds to tons. In the woods the packs caught on overhanging underbrush and sent us stumbling and falling. In the open places, the sun was like a furnace and the packs were like lead. At last we could stand it no longer and we began to throw away our blankets; after the blankets went cans of meat, then our coats and underclothes, until some only had their guns and ammunition left." It didn't take long for those who had lightened their packs to feel the consequences; that night a downpour drenched the camp, soaking those without ponchos or blankets.

The effort of the march paid off the next day, however, when the Rough Riders got their first taste of action. At Las Guásimas on the Santiago road the advance units of the American column encountered a small Spanish force. The Spaniards were greatly outnumbered and evidently intended merely to slow the Americans' progress. The main body of the American force had nothing to do with the skirmish, but because of Wood's determination to be at the very front—at one point even Roosevelt began to grumble privately about the pace Wood was setting—the Rough Riders got in on the exchange.

Roosevelt was exhilarated by the scrape. "Yesterday we struck the Spaniards and had a brisk fight for 2½ hours before we drove them out of their position," he told Corinne and Douglas. "We lost a dozen men killed or mortally wounded, and sixty severely or slightly wounded [out of about five hundred]. One man was killed as he stood beside a tree with me. Another bullet went through a tree behind which I stood and filled my eyes with bark. The last charge I led on the left using a rifle I took from a wounded man. . . . The fire was very hot at one or two points where the men around me went down like ninepins." But the fire wasn't so hot that he didn't have time to collect souvenirs: three empty cartridges taken from a dead Spaniard "for the children."

The two hours of excitement made up for the many more hours of weariness and discomfort. On account of Wood's haste to be in on the fighting, the regiment's baggage remained behind; the men, including Roosevelt, slept on the ground and lived, wet with rain or sweat, in the same clothes day after day. Discomfort aside, the realities of war were sobering. Roosevelt described the vultures that circled overhead by the hundreds and descended on the deceased. "They plucked out the eyes and tore the faces and the wounds of the dead Spaniards before we got to them, and even of one of our men who lay in the open." Other scavengers scrambled through the brush. "The woods are full of land crabs, some of which are almost as big as rabbits; when things grew quiet they slowly gathered in gruesome rings around the fallen." Administrative confusion continued. "The mismanagement has been maddening. We have had very little to eat." But these were minor matters. "We care nothing for that, as long as we got into the fight."

VI

The skirmish at Las Guásimas proved merely a warm-up for the decisive engagement a week later. Although General Shafter still intended to push quickly to Santiago, he decided that he needed a few days to consolidate his forces, which had gotten dispersed along the road. He recognized that while the soldiers might manage to march a few days on cold rations, wet boots, and excitement, before long the lack of support would begin to tell. Some were already getting sick. General Wheeler was beginning to look and act like the old man he was; General Samuel Young, the Rough Riders' brigade commander, had been prostrated to the point where he had to be relieved by Wood—a shift that left Roosevelt in field command of the Rough Riders. Shafter himself was nearly immobilized. Obese, gout-ridden, and now laid low by the heat, he could scarcely straddle a horse and still less travel to the front to observe conditions personally.

Not everyone appreciated the respite. One sergeant figured that he had come to Cuba to do a duty, and he wanted to do it before being eaten alive by mosquitoes or land crabs or other vermin. Details of tactics and strategy left him cold. "Damn Strategy!" he swore. "I've never read about it, but I am getting blooming tired of the demonstration of it. There's Santiago, and the dagoes, and here we are, and the shortest distance between two points is a straight line; which is something everybody knows, and don't have to have strategy to find out. I am in favor of going up there and beating the faces off them dagoes, and then let the war correspondents make up the strategy, as they seem to be the only ones who are worrying about it."

The testiness of the men was exacerbated by the shortage of provisions, including the most basic rations. At one point Roosevelt had to pull rank on a commissary sergeant who said that a half-ton load of beans Roosevelt wanted for his men was reserved for the officers. Roosevelt responded with a straight face that his requisition *was* for the regiment's officers. "Why, Colonel, your officers can't eat eleven hundred pounds of beans," the sergeant objected. "You don't know what appetites my officers have," Roosevelt rejoined. The keeper of the beans grumblingly acquiesced in Roosevelt's demand but warned that they'd probably come out of his salary. (Apparently they didn't.)

For some soldiers other items were more essential than beans. Richard Harding Davis, the noted correspondent who became fast friends with Roosevelt, remarked that the shortage of tobacco during the week after the Las Guásimas skirmish worked hardships fully as trying as the lack of food and dry clothes. "With a pipe the soldier can kill hunger, he can forget that he is wet and exhausted and sick with the heat, he can steady his nerves against the roof of bullets when they pass continually overhead." Davis went on to record that desperate soldiers were reduced to smoking dried grass, ground roots, and pulverized horse manure in their frenzy for a nicotine fix; nothing worked. "For several nights the nerves of some of them were so unstrung for the need of the stimulant that they could not sleep."

Roosevelt doubtless congratulated himself on having avoided this now-debilitating habit, but he, too, was impatient to be moving forward again. He wasn't quite as anxious as he had been; his first taste of battle had taken the edge off his appetite. After the fight at Las Guásimas he told Lodge, "Well, whatever comes I shall feel contented with having left the Navy Department to go into the army for the war; for our regiment has been in the first fight on land, and has done well." Yet as the following days passed with no further action, he grew antsy once again.

On June 30 the order came to move out. The long column required considerable time to lurch into motion; though Roosevelt had his men ready shortly after noon, it wasn't until hours later that they were actually able to fall into line and begin the march. The road to Santiago varied drastically from mile to mile; in some places it was wide and smooth, in others no more than a cart path that doubled as a gutter in rainy weather. The road ran through the densest jungle that almost any of the Rough Riders—these men of the open plains and polo fields—had ever seen. The brush and small trees rose up like cliffs of green on either side of the road. The scorching sun entered the canyon from overhead, but not the slightest breeze penetrated the walls of vegetation. Between the heat of the sun and the humidity exuded by the jungle—not to mention the lack of conditioning for foot-soldiering—many of Roosevelt's men came perilously close to heat exhaustion. For some the frequent halts of the column served as breath catchers; others found that the starting and stopping simply made matters worse.

What with the late beginning and the slow pace, the column was still marching when dusk fell. Roosevelt's unit continued through the darkness to El Pozo hill, which they climbed with stumbling difficulty. Amid the ruins of a ranch and an abandoned sugar mill, they bivouacked for the night, sleeping on their arms and hoping for no rain.

Roosevelt got less sleep than most, what with the responsibility of checking on the sentries and the general excitement of the impending battle. He was up before dawn. Breakfast was beans, bacon, hardtack, and coffee—this last brewed from coffee beans ground on the spot with the handle of a knife or bayonet, since preground coffee spoiled too quickly in the sweathouse atmosphere. The sun rose on a setting that stuck in Roosevelt's memory. "It was a very lovely morning," he wrote afterward, "the sky of cloudless blue, while the level, shimmering rays from the just-risen sun brought into fine relief the splendid palms which here and there towered above the lower growth. The lofty and beautiful mountains hemmed in the Santiago plain, making it an amphitheatre for the battle."

The scene appeared less beautiful once American guns opened fire on the Spanish positions across the valley. The white smoke rings from the muzzles hung in the still air, making bull's-eyes for Spanish gunners to aim at. This particularly worried Wood and Roosevelt, who were sitting together when the firing began, in that the Rough Riders were situated in a direct line between the Spanish and American guns. Wood remarked that he wished the brigade could be moved; the words were scarcely out of his mouth when Spanish shells began bursting over their heads. A piece of shrapnel hit Roosevelt in the arm, causing a slight injury. Four of his fellows were less lucky, sustaining deeper wounds. A regular army soldier nearby lost a leg to a shard of flying metal. Not far away, several Cuban rebels, now allies of the Americans, were killed by a second shell. Disregarding the danger, Roosevelt leaped onto his horse and galloped this way and that among the men, hustling them to the other side of the hill to cover.

They remained there scarcely long enough to finish chewing their breakfast. With the battle now joined, they soon received orders to link up with another unit some distance to the right. Roosevelt had no exact knowledge of where this unit was, but impatient to enter the fray, he led his men in the direction indicated. After a brief and hurried march, they reached the San Juan River, a small stream they proceeded to ford. Spanish fire rained heavily around them, attracted by the approach of an American observation balloon hauled on a tether by another American unit heading for the ford at the same time as the Rough Riders. Cursing the criminal idiocy of those responsible for this foolish and costly attempt at aerial reconnaissance, Roosevelt exhorted his men to get across the river before the balloon entirely gave away the location of the ford to the Spanish gunners.

On the far side of the stream, the road ran along a defile between two elevated pieces of ground. To the left was San Juan Hill—actually the end of a ridge collectively called the San Juan Heights. To the right was a smaller rise the soldiers called Kettle Hill, after a large sugar-refining kettle they found at the top. Spanish forces were entrenched on both, and they directed a deadly fire down on the Americans. The Spanish riflemen were armed with German Mausers, which were far more effective than the antiquated Springfields the Americans carried. "The Mauser bullets drove in sheets through the trees and the tall jungle grass," Roosevelt wrote, "making a peculiar whirring or rustling sound; some of the bullets seemed to pop in the air, so that we thought they were explosive; and, indeed, many of those which were coated with brass did explode, in the sense that the brass coat was ripped off, making a thin plate of hard metal with a jagged edge, which inflicted a ghastly wound." The Spanish fire cut down several of Roosevelt's men, including Bucky O'Neill, who had just finished boasting that the

Spanish bullet hadn't yet been manufactured that could kill him. (It doubtless was cold comfort to his relatives that he died technically correct: The bullet was German.) Another trooper, whom Roosevelt had summoned to carry a message, was felled while saluting to go on his way; he slumped forward into Roosevelt's arms, spurting blood.

Roosevelt quickly shouted for another messenger, anxious to receive permission to get his men away from their exposed position. This man got off safely but couldn't locate Wood or anyone else with the appropriate authority. Neither could a third messenger, nor a fourth. Roosevelt was about to give the order on his own authority when the command finally came through. The Rough Riders were to move forward and support the regular troops in the assault on the hills.

Roosevelt again mounted his horse and began riding up and down the line of his men, urging them ahead. Some responded with alacrity; others required convincing. To one trooper who was slow to rise and join the assault, Roosevelt shouted indignantly, "Are you afraid to stand up when I am on horseback?" Stung, the man just had time to get to his feet before a bullet bored him from front to back and he fell down dead.

Roosevelt led his men forward, pushing through other units in his eagerness to reach the front. When he came up to the forwardmost regiment, he was dismayed to discover them lying down in the grass at the base of Kettle Hill. Judging that the hill could be taken only by storming, he looked around for the colonel in command of the regiment. The officer was nowhere to be seen. Seizing his opportunity, Roosevelt proclaimed himself the ranking officer present and gave the order to charge. The captain of the regulars appeared disinclined to enter upon such a dangerous assault on the orders of a mere volunteer officer. His reluctance infuriated Roosevelt, who demanded, "If you don't wish to go forward, let my men pass." (According to Richard Harding Davis, Roosevelt added a "please" here; one wonders.) The Rough Riders charged ahead, shaming the regulars into joining them.

The troops ran up the slope, cheering and yelling between shots. Roosevelt galloped about, trying to coordinate the efforts of the men, who were now joined by others attacking from different directions. Then he turned his horse and headed up the hill. At a stone's throw from the crest he ran into a wire fence and had to dismount. Turning his horse loose, he resumed the charge on foot. He was among the first to reach the top. Scores of others arrived just moments later. The Spanish soldiers, outnumbered and overwhelmed, fled as the Americans made the crest.

The thrill of triumph was intoxicating, and the men celebrated with backslaps and mutual congratulations. But the celebration was cut short by rifle and cannon fire from Spanish positions on the hill opposite. The Rough Riders took what shelter they could find; some huddled behind the giant sugar kettle. For several minutes they returned the Spanish fire but suffered substantial losses.

Roosevelt could see other American units charging San Juan Hill, and he determined to join them. Shouting at his men to follow, he scrambled over the wire fence and began running across the open ground toward the Spanish entrenchments. With bullets singing through the grass on either side of him and shells exploding to front and rear, it took a hundred yards for him to realize that almost no one was following him. Amid the noise of the battle his men hadn't heard his order. Incongruously embarrassed, considering the circumstances, he turned around, raced back to the lines, and tried again.

This time the assault took. The Spanish bravely kept up their fire for some minutes, but as they recognized the odds against them—they were outnumbered fifteen to one—those that could run did, making for Santiago, a mile away. By the time Roosevelt and his men reached the hilltop, the Spanish were nearly all gone. Roosevelt fired at one of the laggards at close range with a revolver salvaged from the *Maine;* in the confusion it was hard to tell whether his bullet or someone else's felled the enemy soldier.

The original American plan for the day had been to proceed immediately from San Juan Heights to Santiago. Roosevelt, emotionally supercharged by the battle, would have been happy to do so, but the fierceness of the day's fighting and the lateness of the hour caused his superiors to call a halt. The Americans dug themselves into the positions recently held by the Spanish. Darkness gradually silenced a sporadic and ineffective fire from Spanish guns near Santiago, while the American soldiers helped themselves to the dinner the Spanish had cooked but been forced to abandon.

Roosevelt and his comrades took their ease, the thrill of their triumph melting into weary satisfaction at a dangerous job well done.

Their losses had been heavy: more than two hundred killed at Kettle and San Juan Hills and in the surrounding area, and five times that many wounded. But the officers and men had proven their courage and capacity, and won a glorious victory.

Roosevelt had especially distinguished himself. Eyewitness Davis declared him, along with one other man, a general of the regulars, "the most conspicuous figure in the charge." The general was past his physical prime; his actions had inclined Davis to pray for his safety. "On the other hand, Roosevelt, mounted high on horseback, and charging the rifle-pits at a gallop and quite alone, made you feel that you would like to cheer. He wore on his sombrero a blue polka-dot handkerchief, à la Havelock, which, as he advanced, floated out straight behind his head, like a guidon. Afterward, the men of his regiment who followed this flag, adopted a polka-dot handkerchief as the badge of the Rough Riders."

Roosevelt himself was pleased with his conduct under fire—and it showed. A comrade who was also a friend of Edith's wrote to her describing her husband as "just reveling in victory and gore." Not long after the battle, General Wheeler mentioned that he intended to put Roosevelt's name forward for the Medal of Honor; at the least, Roosevelt could expect a promotion to colonel. In a letter to Lodge, Roosevelt declared with no false modesty, "I think I earned my Colonelcy and medal of honor, and I hope I get them." Several days later he added, "I do not want to be vain, but I do not think that anyone else could have handled this regiment quite as I have handled it during the last three weeks." He went on to say, "During these weeks it has done as well as any of the regular regiments and infinitely better than any of the volunteer regiments, and indeed, frankly, I think it has done better than the regulars with the exception of one or two of the best regular regiments."

Roosevelt turned melodramatic as he described the privations his men were still suffering in the way of short rations, inadequate clothing, and the like. "I hope you will not think I grumble too much or am too much worried; it is not in the least for myself; I am more than satisfied even though I die of yellow fever tomorrow, for at least I feel that I have done something which enables me to leave a name to the children of which they can rightly be proud and which will serve in some sense as a substitute for not leaving them more money."

A leader had to look after his men. And such men! (and, by implication, such a leader!):

> I am deeply touched by the way the men of the regiment trust and follow me. I think they know I would do anything for them, and when we got into the darkest days I fared precisely as they did. Certainly in battle or in the march or in the trenches I never went anywhere but I found them eager to follow me. I was not reckless; but with a regiment like this, and indeed I think with most regiments, the man in command must take all the risks which he asks his men to take if he is going to get the best work out of them. On the day of the big fight I had to ask my men to do a deed that European military writers consider utterly impossible of performance, that is, to attack over open ground unshaken infantry armed with the best modern repeating rifles behind a formidable system of entrenchments. The only way to get them to do it in the way it had to be done was to lead them myself.

The more Roosevelt reflected on the battle, the more impressed he grew with himself. Telling Lodge that it really didn't matter if he got his promotion and his medal, he said, "It doesn't make much difference, for nothing can take away the fact that for the ten great days of its life I commanded the regiment; and led it victoriously in a hard fought battle."

Roosevelt was half-candid in this disclaimer. Never one to shy from any honor that might be coming his way, he realized how important recognition of his valor could be to his future career. But in a deeper and more personal sense he was speaking the truth. It really did not matter whether the War Department or anyone else rewarded him for his actions. He had joined the army to test himself, to see if he measured up to the heroic ideal he had constructed in his imagination. The test, the supreme test of fire, had come, and he had indeed measured up. The inner glow of satisfaction that his achievement produced would never dim. Two decades later, only months before he died and after many intervening accomplishments of far greater worth to the world at large, he could look back and declare, "San Juan was the great day of my life."

CHAPTER FOURTEEN

Gunpowder Governor
1898–99

The battle of San Juan Hill didn't end the Spanish-American War for the United States Army or Roosevelt, but it might as well have for all the army or Roosevelt had to do with the matter. The Americans' capture of the San Juan Heights and of nearby El Caney disposed the commander of the Spanish naval squadron in Santiago Bay to evacuate his vessels lest they come under bombardment from American artillery. Evacuation would be dangerous, as a powerful armada of American battleships and cruisers lay in wait outside the bay; but like any blue-water man, Admiral Pascual Cervera preferred his chances at sea to those in the harbor, cooped up by land. He decided to make a run for it. The result was a disaster: All six Spanish warships were sunk or run aground, with more than three hundred men killed and seventeen hundred taken prisoner. Only one American sailor died, one other was wounded; damage to the American vessels was very light.

The destruction of Cervera's squadron essentially accomplished what the Fifth Army Corps had been sent to Santiago to do, leaving General Shafter and his superiors in something of a quandary as to what to do next. Without its ships, Santiago was simply a sleepy, inconsequential village, hardly worth losing lives over. Yet political considerations demanded that the town be taken: After the casualties at San Juan Hill, the United States Army couldn't very well turn around and walk away. Shafter sought to split the difference by nego-tiating a surrender.

Roosevelt wasn't privy to the thinking of either Shafter or his higher-ups in Washington—despite Lodge's intermittent efforts to keep him informed—but ignorance had never prevented him from making up his mind, and it didn't now. "Not since the campaign of Crassus against the Parthians has there been so criminally incompetent a General as Shafter," Roosevelt wailed from his jungle camp outside Santiago. "And not since the expedition against Walcheren has there been grosser mismanagement than in this." Roosevelt assumed that the delay in assaulting Santiago owed to Shafter's timidity. "It is criminal to keep Shafter in command," he repeated. "He is utterly inefficient; and now he is panic struck."

Shafter was indeed inefficient, but he wasn't panic struck, and after a desultory siege of two weeks he succeeded in persuading the Spanish commander to capitulate. The successful outcome mellowed Roosevelt only slightly. "Well, the fight is over now and we have won a big triumph, so there is no use in washing dirty linen," he conceded to Lodge, before adding the qualifier: "except that surely we ought to profit by our bitter experiences in the next expeditions." He then enumerated once again Shafter's deficiencies, going into great detail regarding the trials he and his men had suffered and still did.

Having unburdened himself on that score, Roosevelt switched to a lighter note. "Enough of grumbling. Did I tell you that I killed a Spaniard with my own hand when I led the storm of the first redoubt?" At least he thought he had; it was hard to be sure in the confusion. "Probably I did."

The destruction of the Spanish Caribbean fleet at Santiago, coming after Dewey's smashing of the fleet in the Philippines, broke the back of Madrid's war-making capability; an invasion of Puerto Rico by American forces and the investment of Manila by American (and Filipino insurgent) troops delivered the coup de grâce. On August 12, Spanish representatives in Washington accepted a preliminary peace accord, with the definitive treaty to follow further talks.

Roosevelt, with the rest of the Fifth Army Corps, spent the final weeks of the war as an observer—and an increasingly restive one. After the surrender of Santiago, the War Department determined to evacuate the troops in Cuba back to the United States, but with the other demands on American sea-lift capability, effecting the evacuation was a slow business. Meanwhile, yellow fever spread through the troops on the ground—literally—in Cuba. "The misery has been fearful," Roosevelt wrote to Corinne. "Today, out of my 400 odd men in camp 123 are under the doctor's care; the rest of the 600 with whom I landed are dead or in the rear hospitals." Now that the intoxication of live fire had worn off, Roosevelt reflected to Alice that war was "a grim and fearful thing." The sick and wounded suffered in the relentless heat; the women and children—"some like Archie and Quentin"—thrown onto the roads by the fighting caused a tear to well up in the eye of the bravest. "War is often, as this one is, necessary and righteous," Roosevelt told his elder daughter. "But it is terrible."

His remarks to Lodge were more pointed. "If the army is not brought away from here with all possible expedition," he declared on the last day of July, "and if an epidemic does really break out, the President and the Secretary of War will have incurred a debt as heavy as Walpole incurred when he wasted the lives of Admiral Hozier's 3,000 men in these same West Indian waters against this same Spanish foe. Perhaps you think I write too bitterly. I can only say, old man, that what I have seen during the last five weeks has been enough to make one bitter." Roosevelt again averred that he wouldn't begrudge dying now that he had done his part, and he repeated an earlier request. "Should the worse come to the worst I am quite content to go now and to leave my children at least an honorable name (and, old man, if I do go, I do wish you would get that medal of honor for me anyhow, as I should awfully like the children to have it, and I think I earned it)."

Roosevelt also wrote to his military superiors. He advised General Shafter to get the troops out of Cuba as soon as logistics permitted. "To keep us here, in the opinion of every officer commanding a division or a brigade, will simply involve the destruction of thousands. There is no possible reason for not shipping practically the entire command North at once." This letter was accompanied by a "round robin" letter making the same argument and signed by the divisional and brigade commanders of the Fifth Army Corps, including Roosevelt himself. Shafter allowed the letter to be published, which increased the pressure on the McKinley administration to get the troops out of Cuba before they wasted away from disease.

Administration officials in Washington didn't appreciate the pressure. The War Department already distrusted Roosevelt, who had written to Secretary Alger ten days earlier advising that the Rough Riders be withdrawn from Cuba and sent to join the invasion of Puerto Rico. As justification for such a move, Roosevelt asserted that the Rough Riders were "as good as any regulars and three times as good as any State troops." Alger wasn't in the habit of receiving advice from mere colonels (of volunteers, at that); he replied that while Roosevelt and his men had done well, they shouldn't overestimate themselves. "I suggest that, unless you want to spoil the effects and glory of your victory, you make no invidious comparisons. The Rough Riders are no better than other volunteers. They had an advantage in their arms, for which they ought to be very grateful." Upon reading the round-robin letter from Cuba, Alger released Roosevelt's earlier letter, apparently in the hope of making him out to be a gloryhound.

II

Alger doubtless believed that Roosevelt was letting his brief military success go to his head—a plausible enough assumption at the time. Richard Harding Davis and other correspondents were portraying Roosevelt as the great hero of the battle for San Juan Hill; their reports were relayed back to Roosevelt by Lodge and others. "You are one of the popular persons of the war and deserve to be," Lodge wrote shortly after the San Juan battle. Two days later Lodge wrote again: "You have won yourself a high place already as one of the popular heroes of the war." Another several days later, Lodge again effused, "You can't win more distinction than you have already won so far as mere personal heroism is concerned!"

Lodge had just come from a conference with influential friends at which they had discussed the war's effects on Roosevelt's political future. "What we want for you is the Senate but it looks as if the drift was very strong to make you Governor and that may lead to the Senate next winter." Lodge added, "You must not think that I am dreaming about these things because you can have no idea of your popularity here." Lodge told Roosevelt not to mess things up by doing anything else rash. "We know that you will take every possible opportunity to get killed if you can, but now that you are Colonel of the Regiment"—having spoken to McKinley, Lodge had inside word that Roosevelt's promotion was coming through—"we venture to suggest that your first business is to look after it and not run ahead of it in every charge that is made."

Soon others besides Lodge began inquiring about Roosevelt's availability for a race for governor. Roosevelt responded with manly modesty. To the author of one such feeler he replied that, intending no disrespect to the office of governor of New York, he had other business to attend to first. "Do not think that I underestimate the honor; on the contrary, I place it very high, but I would not feel it right to leave the regiment while the war is on."

With Lodge he was more candid. Whether he should remain in the army depended on whether there would be further opportunities for fighting and glory. "Of course, if I can possibly get out of it I do not intend to stay in the army merely for police work; I only want to be in while there is actual fighting on a fairly big scale." He appreciated the swell of support that was emerging in his home state. "The good people in New York at present seem to be crazy over me." But he wondered how lasting or effective such enthusiasm would prove. "It is not very long since on the whole they felt I compared unfavorably with Caligula. By the time election day comes round they may have reverted to their former feeling." More problematic still was the attitude of the New York Republican bosses. "I don't know how to get on with the New York politicians." If he had possessed the money to go into national politics, that would have been another matter. "The average New York boss is quite willing to allow you to do what you wish in such trivial matters as war and the acquisition of Porto Rico and Hawaii, provided you don't interfere with the really vital questions, such as giving out contracts for cartage in the Custom House and interfering with the appointment of street sweepers."

The end of hostilities two weeks later solved Roosevelt's problem of whether to stay in the army or get out. By this time the War Department had succumbed to the pressure to remove the troops from Cuba, and news of the peace agreement reached Roosevelt and the Rough Riders en route from Santiago to Montauk, Long Island—chosen because it was a more healthful spot than Tampa but sufficiently isolated to allow enforcement of a quarantine. After establishing their noncontagious condition, they would be mustered out.

III

"How are you, Colonel Roosevelt?" reporters shouted as his troopship pulled in.

"I am feeling disgracefully well . . ." he replied. "I feel positively ashamed of my appearance when I see how badly off some of my brave fellows are— Oh, but we have had a bully fight!"

And what about the governor's race? the reporters demanded.

Roosevelt deflected the question. It was his men's hour, he said; politics could wait.

What politics—and Roosevelt—had to wait for was Tom Platt. As Platt recollected later (doubtless giving himself some benefit of doubt), he had had his eye on Roosevelt for months. The then Republican governor, Frank Black, had run into trouble regarding irregularities in the financing of improvements to the Erie Canal. To make a long story short, the sum of one million dollars, entrusted to Black appointee George Aldridge, was missing and unaccounted for. A Boss Tweed might have laughed off a mere million as a slip of the pen, but the Tweed days were gone, and Black looked unreelectable. Platt wasn't one to let loyalty stand in the way of business; he cast about for a replacement.

About this time the Spanish-American War began, raising the possibility that some Republican would return from battle covered with sufficient glory to rout the Democrats as he had routed the Spaniards. When the Caribbean cable brought the news of the victory at San Juan Hill, it was clear that the man of the hour was Theodore Roosevelt. Platt would have preferred someone else—Frederick Grant, for instance—but he was a realist ready to work with the materials at hand. He called in Chauncey Depew, a longtime Republican politico, and asked him how he saw the situation as between Black and Roosevelt.

"Mr. Platt, I always look at a public question from the view of the platform," Depew replied. He explained that he had been giving stump speeches for years; he now tried to envision how a crowd would react to pitches for the two men. "If you nominate Governor Black and I am addressing a large audience—and I certainly will—the heckler in the audience will arise and interrupt me, saying: 'Chauncey, we agree with what you say about the Grand Old Party and all that, but how about the Canal steal?' I have to explain that the amount stolen was only a million, and that would be fatal." A Roosevelt candidacy would be a decidedly different affair.

> If Colonel Roosevelt is nominated, I can say to the heckler with indignation and enthusiasm: "I am mighty glad you asked that question. We have nominated for governor a man who has demonstrated in public office and on the battlefield that he is a fighter for the right, and always victorious. If he is selected, you know and we all know from his demonstrated characteristics, courage and ability, that every thief will be caught and punished, and every dollar that can be found restored to the public treasury." Then I will follow the colonel leading his Rough Riders up San Juan Hill and ask the band to play the "Star-Spangled Banner."

Platt still had misgivings. He recognized the likelihood that Roosevelt, once elected, would be hard to control, and in light of Roosevelt's reformist record, he feared that a Governor Roosevelt would try to undo much of the good work that Platt and other party bosses had done over the years.

But his advisers argued that he had no choice. Principal protégé Benjamin Odell, speaking of the need for a fresh face with polling power, later recalled, "There was in reality only one such figure on the horizon to pull us out of the awful mess the Aldridge scandal had got us into." That figure was Theodore Roosevelt.

Platt sent one of his lieutenants, Lemuel Quigg, to interview the colonel in camp at Montauk. When this initial contact went well, Platt invited Roosevelt to visit him at his hotel on Fifth Avenue. The boss wanted reassurances, as he had at the time of Roosevelt's appointment to the Navy Department, that Roosevelt would not use his new power to make war on the regular party; in exchange he was prepared to hand Roosevelt the Republican nomination.

Roosevelt had long since suppressed his reservations about working with Platt; the last time he had let such principles impede him, he had passed up the New York mayoral nomination, to his subsequent sharp regret. He would not make the same mistake now. He gave the boss the assurances he required.

"Apparently I am going to be nominated," Roosevelt told Lodge after the meeting with Platt. The conversation had been "entirely satisfactory." As usual, Roosevelt felt obliged to disclaim selfish interest in the matter. "Of course, I shall have great trouble in the governorship, but there is no use shirking responsibilities."

IV

Roosevelt's trouble began even before he officially received the Republican nomination at the party convention in late September. As they had repeatedly in the past, New York's mugwumpish types attempted to lure him away from regular Republicanism into clean-conscience candidacy as an independent. Perhaps from a desire to make the most of his new-won popularity, perhaps from simple inadvertence, he led the mugwumps to believe that he might accept an independent nomination. When he instead accepted the Republican nomination, with Platt's endorsement, the mugwumps felt betrayed again. Roosevelt, realizing that the race might be a close one, tried to assuage their wounded feelings; he crossed his heart and swore that he valued the support of independents and if elected would serve the interests of all the people of the state, not merely those of the Republican Party.

Another problem promised to cause more mischief than the disaffection of the mugwumps. During the previous several years Roosevelt had maneuvered to minimize his tax liabilities by claiming residence in low-tax Washington rather than high-tax New York. He had gone so far as to sign an affidavit declaring Washington residency. On the eve of the 1898 Republican state convention, some supporters of Governor Black, evidently with friends in the New York tax office, produced the affidavit. Since New York residency was—not illogically—a requirement for the governorship, Roosevelt's nomination appeared ruined.

But Tom Platt hadn't been a boss for all those years without learning that there were rules and there were rules. Convinced that voters wouldn't reject a son of Manhattan simply for serving his country in Washington—and, let it not be forgotten, in Cuba—the boss determined simply to ignore the residency requirement. He and the other party leaders commissioned Elihu Root to deal with the eligibility issue. In a masterpiece of obfuscatory rhetoric, Root explained to the convention the multiple meanings of the word "residence" and how those that seemed to disqualify Colonel Roosevelt did not, in reality, apply. He warned against niggling, which would serve only the enemies of the party; he exuded confidence that the delegates would perceive that the interests of the party and the state rested with a Roosevelt candidacy.

The delegates, additionally encouraged by the kinds of material arguments bosses such as Platt always made on behalf of their chosen, did indeed perceive the merits of a Roosevelt candidacy, and the Colonel, as he was now universally called, at least by his supporters, carried the convention.

V

Roosevelt proceeded to attack the general election with the same verve he had displayed in assaulting San Juan Hill. In fact, fully recognizing the basis of his nomination, he did his best to convert the general election into a referendum on the war. "There comes a time in the life of a nation, as in the life of an individual, when it must face great responsibilities," he pronounced in the kickoff speech of his campaign. "We have now reached that time. We cannot avoid facing the fact that we occupy a new place among the people of the world, and have entered upon a new career." As Roosevelt went on to explain how the United States must accept its destiny by carrying civilization and the American flag across the globe, by building an even stronger navy than that which had just smashed Spain, and by putting the other European powers on notice that America was not to be trifled with, voters might have been forgiven for forgetting just which office it was that Roosevelt was running for.

It made perfect sense for Roosevelt to run on the Republicans' national record, for there was nothing in their recent local history to recommend them but much, like the Erie Canal grafting, to recommend their opponents. National issues—the "large policy," the currency— were a safe and attractive alternative. The war was even more attractive. Roosevelt took every opportunity to remind voters where he had been the past few months. He brought a bugler and several Rough Riders along on his campaign train. "You have heard the trumpet that sounded to bring you here," he explained to those who came out to see him. "I have heard it tear the tropic dawn, when it summoned us to fight at Santiago." He introduced a wounded hero from his regiment, informing his audience that "a spent bullet from the same shell that wounded him struck me on the wrist." He invited his erstwhile comrades in arms to testify on his behalf. They did so, sometimes with more enthusiasm than forethought. "My friends and fellow citizens," one veteran declared, "my colonel was a great soldier. He will make a great governor. He always put us boys in battle where we would be killed if there was a chance, and that is what he will do with you." (Platt's machinists groaned at this buckskin touch. Benjamin Odell called the Rough Rider campaign followers "a failure and a hindrance from the start." He added, "I soon got rid of them.")

Roosevelt drew large crowds around the state, although in many cases curiosity vied with solid support as the main motivator of those who turned out. To the candidate's frustration the voters exhibited little enthusiasm for the big issues that were everything to him. "Taking it as a whole," he lamented to Lodge, "New York cares very little for the war now that it is over, except that it would like to punish somebody because the Republican administration did not handle the War Department well. It is not interested in free silver for it never looks more than six months ahead or behind and it thinks free silver dead." As a result, Roosevelt remarked, he was "not having an entirely pleasant campaign."

While Roosevelt believed he had a better chance campaigning on national issues than on local ones, in certain instances it was the national issues that cost him support. Carl Schurz came out against him, contending that a vote for Roosevelt was a vote for American imperialism. The charge was accurate enough—and would be even more accurate as soon as Roosevelt got himself in a position to really have his way—but Roosevelt did his best to duck it. Not wanting to lose the reform vote, he wrote Schurz to say, "The war is now over and I am as anxious for peace and quiet as you possibly can be." This statement was patently false: Roosevelt was not anxious for peace and quiet, let alone as anxious as Schurz was. Schurz saw through Roosevelt's protestation and refused to reconsider his opposition.

"I am in a hot campaign," Roosevelt told Bill Sewall in early October. "Just as hot as Santiago was." It got only hotter as election day approached, with both parties resorting to the various forms of regular and irregular political combat that made Gilded Age politics entertaining, if not edifying.

To Roosevelt's surprise, a local issue ended up deciding the election—in his favor. His Democratic opponent, Augustus Van Wyck, had been chosen by Tammany boss Richard Croker as carefully as Platt had picked Roosevelt; consequently, just as the Democrats kept returning to the question of the missing canal money, Roosevelt and the Republicans harped on the sins of Tammany. For a time it looked as though the former weighed more heavily with voters, Tammany not having been indictably corrupt lately. But shortly before the election Croker committed an uncharacteristic error. He refused renomination to a Democratic justice of the state supreme court on grounds that the jurist in question had been insufficiently attentive to Tammany's needs.

"This gave me my chance," Roosevelt explained afterward. Van Wyck was hard to get excited about, one way or the other, but Croker was another story. "The Trojan distrust of the Greeks," Roosevelt declared, "cannot begin to equal my distrust of Croker!" Certain that others felt the same way, Roosevelt hit hard again and again on the Tammany connections of Van Wyck; in the process he redefined the governor's race as a contest between himself, the war hero, and Croker, the unscrupulous boss who, needless to say, had been nowhere near the fighting front.

The strategy succeeded—barely. In one of the tightest contests in New York history, Roosevelt slipped into the governor's house by less than eighteen thousand votes out of 1.3 million cast.

VI

Roosevelt's election capped six months that utterly transformed his career. In April he had been a busybodied bureaucrat, beavering away at the Navy Department, making bellicose noises to all who would listen but uncomfortably aware that few outside his circle of friends were in fact listening. The political power brokers of the era distrusted him, with reason, as did independent-minded reformers, with equal reason. He was appointable but only to middling sorts of positions; the big helpings went to those who brought more to the table in terms of money or following. Because the bosses distrusted him and the public didn't know him, he was essentially unelectable. Almost two decades—half his life—after starting out in politics, his future was decidedly unpromising.

But then the war came and made him famous. Some people, even among his friends, had deemed his decision to forsake Washington for the front a gamble, a calculated risk that might make him a hero, or get him killed. It was a risk, all right, but it wasn't exactly calculated. Everything in his background compelled him to take up arms; he had little conscious choice in the matter. But whether conscious or not, the gamble paid off magnificently. A day's work in front of Santiago made him the darling of the nation. Now the bosses came to him rather than the reverse. Before he knew it, he was the governor of his home state, the largest in the country.

Roosevelt was fully aware of the role of fortune in his turnaround, although he thought it was about time fortune smiled his way. "I have played it in bull luck this summer," he told Cecil Spring Rice. "First, to get into the war; then to get out of it; then to get elected. I have worked hard all my life, and have never been particularly lucky, but this summer I *was* lucky, and I am enjoying it to the full." Lest he tempt luck, he disavowed expectations or desires of anything more. "I know perfectly well that the luck will not continue, and it is not necessary that it should. I am more than contented to be Governor of New York, and shall not care if I never hold another office."

VII

The future aside, Roosevelt's immediate problem was to demonstrate that he was, in fact, governor of New York. At the time of his nomination he had agreed to consult with Platt regarding appointments and other matters that bore on the interests of the boss. But "consult" admitted of different constructions. Platt believed that Roosevelt owed him, as leader of the party—not to mention a United States senator and the man most responsible for Roosevelt's election—substantial say in who received government jobs, contracts, and the like. Roosevelt had no difficulty with the idea of informing the boss of impending decisions, but he aimed to make absolutely clear that the people of New York had elected Theodore Roosevelt, not Thomas Platt, to be their chief executive. Besides, he understood that Platt and the regulars needed him—or had needed him, at least—just as much as he needed them. Benjamin Odell conceded the point, albeit not to Roosevelt. "If Theodore Roosevelt never did anything else politically," Odell recollected many years later, "I think there is no possible question that he saved us from a Democratic governor, that time."

Roosevelt had an opportunity to demonstrate his independence even before being officially sworn in. At a meeting with Platt, the boss congratulated the governor-elect on the fact that a particularly stellar individual had just agreed to be his superintendent of public works. Because of the scandal that had surrounded the Erie Canal, this was an especially sensitive post. Platt shared with Roosevelt the telegram the gentleman had sent accepting the appointment.

Roosevelt had been expecting some such show of force but not necessarily so soon. This was the first he had had heard of the appointment, and while he respected the individual's character and qualifications, he saw a potential conflict of interest arising from the fact that the man's home town lay along the canal. More to the point, he felt it necessary to establish the principle that the governor, not the boss, decided appointments.

Roosevelt politely informed Platt that he could not approve the planned nomination. "This produced an explosion," Roosevelt recalled afterward. Platt reminded Roosevelt, angrily and bluntly, who had chosen him as the Republican nominee and who had gotten out the vote for him. Roosevelt remained calm but unmoved. He did not mind accepting advice from the senator or from anyone else, but he insisted that he would accept dictation from no man.

Platt fulminated some more, doubtless questioning his own wisdom in backing this ungrateful wretch. Yet, pragmatic as ever, he eventually bowed to the inevitable and determined to make the best of the situation.

At the same time Roosevelt, having established his point, took pains not to insult or antagonize the boss. Indeed, he went out of his way to stay on good terms with him. The breakfast meetings between the governor and the senator, usually on Saturday mornings and often at Platt's New York hotel, became a regular feature of New York politics. To Roosevelt's reformist critics and to other observers as well, the fact of the meetings, and even more their location, appeared prima facie proof that Roosevelt was Platt's officeholder as much as he had been Platt's candidate. Roosevelt defended his consultations with the boss as being entirely within the tradition of political give and take. Platt could make Roosevelt's job as governor difficult, or he could make it easy. Roosevelt simply sought to make it easy for Platt to make it easy. As for the location of the meetings, that reflected not subserviency but geography. Platt spent his weeks in Washington, while Roosevelt was in Albany; New York City—to which Roosevelt often had occasion to travel anyway—was obvious middle ground. Besides, Platt was old and increasingly infirm; Roosevelt got around far more readily.

Yet Roosevelt wasn't immune to the criticism, which he tried to soften by maneuvering Platt, whenever possible, into meeting him at Bamie's house on Madison Avenue, where he stayed on his city visits. This had an advantage besides the obvious one of keeping him out of Platt's notorious "Amen Corner" at the Fifth Avenue Hotel, where every reporter in town could see the governor and the boss together. It allowed him to bring Bamie into their conversations. "She takes such an interest in what I am doing," Roosevelt would explain when Platt protested her presence. This was true enough, of course, but it wasn't the real reason. Bamie's job was to keep Platt off balance, which was simple enough since the boss wasn't accustomed to practicing his blunt brand of politics in the presence of women. Bamie also served as a witness—one friendly to the governor—in case questions arose regarding just what the boss had promised to do. Doubtless brother and sister had many a good chuckle at Platt's expense after the senator, exasperated, left.

VIII

War heroes in America tend to have short shelf lives, especially once they doff their khakis and put on the uniform of the politician. What makes the hero a hero is the romantic notion that he stands above the tawdry give and take of everyday politics, occupying an ethereal realm where partisanship gives way to patriotism, and division to unity, and where the nation regains its lost innocence and the people their shared sense of purpose. Some war heroes maintain this elevated station by recasting themselves in stone—or bronze or whatever is used for the statues that literally raise them up against the sky.

Roosevelt wouldn't have minded a statue or two, but still being alive, he didn't propose to sit around waiting for his sculptor to immortalize him. Instead he took the task into his own hands. He sought to have his heroism ratified by act of Congress—to wit, by receiving the Medal of Honor. Such slight diffidence as he had shown during the summer regarding his nation's highest decoration vanished completely during the governor's race. He fully appreciated what a coup it would be for him to receive the medal during the campaign; even if it arrived too late for that—and, in fact, the election came and went with no medal from Washington—it would still provide a confirmation of character that any opponent would be hard-pressed to match.

Besides, as he had concluded earlier, he thought he deserved the medal. "If I didn't earn it," he declared to Lodge, "then no commissioned officer ever can earn it." As he was wont to do, Roosevelt interpreted disagreement—in this case on the part of the War Department—as evidence of malicious motives. He believed that War Secretary Alger was still angry at his criticism of the department's handling of the troops in Cuba and had determined to prevent his receiving the medal. Roosevelt was at least equally determined that he should have the award. "I don't ask this as a favor—I ask it as a right," he told Lodge. He judged that he had already been insulted in not having received full recognition for his command of the brigade in Cuba and on the way home. "For this I don't care, but I am entitled to the Medal of Honor, and I want it."

Roosevelt may or may not have been right about deserving the medal, yet there was something unseemly about the effort he put into trying to get the McKinley administration to agree with him. He solicited letters from Lodge, from now-general Wood, from other officers who had been in Cuba, and from everyone else he thought might change the minds of the medal givers. The longer they held out, the angrier he became and the pushier he got. The contest did credit to none of the parties, least of all him.

Meanwhile, though, Roosevelt sought to immortalize himself by means more persuasive and permanent than ribbons and metal, namely ink. Various periodicals had approached him when he was preparing to ship out for Cuba regarding the possibility of preparing dispatches from the front. The market for articles by professional writers was already flooded, what with the presence on the ground of such tested sellers as Richard Harding Davis and Stephen Crane (who, having written *The Red Badge of Courage* without benefit of personal witness of war, thought he ought to have a look). But Roosevelt, being a soldier, as well as a seasoned author of heroic prose, offered a fresh angle. He initially put aside the offers; having waited thirty years to make war, he wasn't going to interrupt it simply to satisfy some publisher at home.

Yet he could never resist an audience, and he finally succumbed to the argument of the editors of *Scribner's* magazine that the public had a right to read the story from the hand of a man of action (and that this particular man of action ought to receive an advance of one thousand dollars). Shortly after his busy hour had passed, he began organizing his impressions into a narrative. The product of his labors was a series of articles that appeared in *Scribner's* between January and June 1899. "This will stand as the authoritative history of his regiment as a fighting machine," the *Scribner's* editors bragged, "as well as being a vivid narrative, with numerous anecdotes, showing the individual bravery of his men." Not long after the series ran, the articles were collected into a book, *The Rough Riders,* appropriately bound in khaki cloth.

As promised and as any reader of Roosevelt's earlier works could have guessed, his Cuban story was a tale of heart-swelling heroism. It began with an epigraph borrowed from Bret Harte—"Hark! I hear the tramp of thousands"—and ended with a letter from the schoolteacher of a few of the younger Rough Riders, relating how one of them had just died of meningitis but not before he and his fellows expressed their admiration for a Colonel who had looked after them so well and always listened to them as attentively as to any major-general; this followed by Roosevelt's own reaction: "Is it any wonder that I loved my regiment?" Obviously, the reader was supposed to love such men, too, and probably most did. More enthusiastically nationalist than anything Roosevelt had previously written, the articles and book portrayed America's motives in going to war as noble and selfless, and its actions in prosecuting the war as gallant and brave.

The most gallant and brave of all was the author. Roosevelt managed the delicate literary task of centering the story—and hence the victory—on himself without coming across as egregiously boastful. He made no effort to hide the fact that he was simply telling the tale of the Rough Riders, one regiment in a whole army. Yet such was the authoritative tone he adopted that it was easy to forget the rest of the cast of tens of thousands. How much influence his ongoing battle with the War Department over the Medal of Honor had on the writing of his story is hard to tell; Roosevelt never needed much encouragement to congratulate himself. Whatever may have been running through his mind at the time of the writing, what came out of his pen was a persuasive brief for himself.

This point was the one that most impressed the critics; of these, the one who skewered the author most tellingly was humorist Finley Peter Dunne. Dunne's Irish philosopher Mr. Dooley and his sidekick Hennessy were discussing the war and the "lithrachoor" it produced when Dooley recommended a new book he identified as "Th' Biography iv a Hero be Wan who Knows." Dooley paraphrased the book to his friend, explaining how "Tiddy Rosenfelt" had recounted the raising of the regiment from among his western companions. "'Together we had faced th' turrors iv th' large but vilent West,' he says, 'an' these brave men had seen me with me trusty rifle shootin' th' buffalo, th' elk, th' moose, th' moose, th' grizzly bear, th' mountain goat,' he says, 'th' silver man, an' other ferocious beasts iv thim parts.'" Dooley explained how within a few days Roosevelt had whipped his wild western companions into civilized soldiers so that on the voyage to Cuba they could admire the stars with him "'an' quote th' bible fr'm Walt Whitman.'"

Dooley especially enjoyed Roosevelt's account of the battle of San Juan Hill.

"We had no sooner landed in Cubia than it become nicessry f'r me to take command iv th' ar-rmy which I did at wanst. A number of days was spint be me in reconnoitring, attinded on'y be me brave an' fluent body guard, Richard Harding Davis. I discovered that th' inimy was heavily inthrenched on th' top iv San Joon hill immejiately in front iv me. At this time it become apparent that I was handicapped be th' prisence iv th' ar-rmy," he says. "Wan day whin I was about to charge a block house sturdily definded be an ar-rmy corps undher Gen'ral Tamale, th' brave Castile that I afterwards killed with a small ink-eraser that I always carry, I r-ran into th' entire military force iv th' United States lying on its stomach. 'If ye won't fight,' says I, 'let me go through,' I says. 'Who ar-re ye?' says they. 'Colonel Rosenfelt,' says I. 'Oh, excuse me,' says the gin'ral in command (if me mimry serves me thrue it was Miles) r-risin' to his knees an' salutin'. This showed me 'twud be impossible f'r to carry th' war to a successful con-clusion unless I was free, so I sint th' ar-rmy home an' attackted San Joon hill. Ar-rmed on'y with a small thirty-two which I used in th' West to shoot th' fleet prairie dog, I climbed that precipitous ascent in th' face iv th' most gallin' fire I iver knew or heerd iv. But I had a few r-rounds iv gall mesilf an' what cared I? I dashed madly on cheerin' as I wint. Th' Spanish throops was dhrawn up in a long line in th' formation known among military men as a long line. I fired at th' man nearest to me an' I knew be th' expression iv his face that th' trusty bullet wint home. It passed through his frame, he fell, an' wan little home in far-off Catalonia was made happy be th' thought that their riprisintative had been kilt be th' future governor iv New York. Th' bullet sped on its mad flight an' passed through th' intire line fin'lly imbeddin' itself in th' abdomen iv th' Ar-rchbishop iv Santiago eight miles away. This ended th' war."

Hennessy expressed his approval of Roosevelt's account. "I think Tiddy Rosenfelt is all r-right," he opined, "an' if he wants to blow his hor-rn lave him do it."

Dooley concurred, adding that if Roosevelt's valiant deeds didn't get in his own book, they'd be a long time appearing in Shafter's history of the war. Besides: "No man that bears a gredge again' himsilf 'll iver be governor iv a state. An' if Tiddy done it all he ought to say so an' relieve th' suspinse." But Dooley had one suggestion for the author. "If I was him I'd call the book 'Alone in Cubia.'"

When Dunne's send-up appeared, Roosevelt's acquaintances couldn't help chuckling. Even the victim himself had to laugh, and he sent Dunne a note: "I regret to state that my family and intimate friends are delighted with your review of my book." Roosevelt went on to say that he had long desired to meet the author, and he invited him to stop at the governor's mansion whenever he was in the area.

Dunne, recognizing the partial purpose of Roosevelt's good-natured note, replied that such friendliness disappointed him. "The number of persons who are worth while firing at is so small that as a matter of business I must regret the loss of one of them." Yet he calculated that if in losing a target he had gained a friend, he was ahead of the game after all.

In fact, Dunne did not accept Roosevelt's invitation, nor did he visit Albany after a second, more specific invitation. Apparently he decided that he needed targets more than friends. But the Rough Rider and the humorist did meet briefly later, during Roosevelt's vice-presidential campaign. Edith was there, and she nudged Roosevelt to tell a story on himself.

"Well, I oughtn't to," he replied. "But I will. At a reception I was introduced to a very pretty young lady. She said, 'Oh, Governor, I've read everything you ever wrote.'"

Roosevelt was impressed. "Really!" he said. "What book did you like best?"

"Why that one, you know, 'Alone in Cuba.'"

IX

Roosevelt had gone to war to prove his manhood; he had no such obvious objective in becoming governor. He had accepted the nomination principally because it was offered and it seemed like a good way to get back into politics. But he had no pressing agenda, no major reforms he hoped to accomplish. Even after election he had only the vaguest notion of how to employ his new authority. "I do not think that there is much in the way of constructive legislation to be done," he wrote to James Bryce in England. "At least, I do not see much that is needed. Just at present, all that seems to be necessary is honest administration, save that some change will have to be made ultimately in the State civil service laws; and the factory legislation must be enforced."

Roosevelt gradually realized that there was more to being governor than honest administration, although, given his ticklish relationship with Platt, administering the government honestly was no mean feat. Appointments were a constant headache during his first few months in office. Platt had strong opinions regarding the worthiness of particular individuals for particular posts; Platt's mugwumpish opponents had equally strong and generally opposite opinions. Roosevelt talked a fearless game. "I want a man of backbone, who realizes that the knife must be mercilessly used," he declared in describing the qualifications for one position charged with cleaning out corruption. But in practice he avoided carving into Platt's domain and sided with the senator whenever possible. "So far as politics can legitimately be considered in making appointments," he conceded to a friend, "I consider them from the standpoint of the organization." Perhaps he thought this gave the wrong impression, for he quickly added, "What I do not do for the organization, I do for the State and not for myself or for any faction."

At times Roosevelt seemed pleased enough with this modus vivendi. Applying what was for him the acid test, he told his uncle, "I can conscientiously say that I have done nothing of which I do not think father would approve if he were alive."

Yet at other times he wasn't so certain. He had long believed it a straightforward matter to distinguish good from evil; a man of character and moral courage should have no difficulty following the path of righteousness. But now the path often seemed dim and poorly marked. "You are right about the courage needed in a position like this being quite as much if not more than that needed at Santiago," Roosevelt mused to Bill Sewall. "The trouble is that right and wrong so often do not come up sharply divided. If I am sure a thing is either right or wrong, why then I know how to act, but lots of times there is a little of both on each side, and then it becomes mighty puzzling to know the exact course to follow."

Roosevelt didn't easily abide ambiguity; it made him nervous and uncomfortable. And when he was uncomfortable, he tended to lash out. In this case—as often—his target was the mugwumps, who were currently criticizing him for his cozy relationship with Platt. Roosevelt excoriated Carl Schurz as "the champion of dishonour in national relations and of dishonesty in civic matters." With but the flimsiest foundation in logic, Roosevelt charged Schurz with having backed the Tammany ticket in the recent governor's race—"for of course to support the ridiculous Goo-Goo ticket had no importance whatever, save as it gave comfort and aid to Mr. Croker." Roosevelt went on to declare Schurz the ideal negative role model. "We could do no greater harm to the youth of America at the present time than to hold up to them as a man to imitate one who like Mr. Schurz feels so bitterly opposed to those who believe that the nation should face its responsibility abroad, as to be willing, in order to defeat them, to work for the success of the most infamously corrupt government of modern times."

For all the acerbity and unfairness of his attacks on Schurz and the mugwumps, it gratified Roosevelt to be able to take the reformist side on occasional issues. The most important such issue during the 1899 session of the state legislature involved a proposal to levy taxes against franchises awarded by the state to private corporations. For decades the awarding of exclusive franchises to railroads and street-car lines had been a lucrative source of income for both the favored corporations and the political machines of both parties: the former from the monopoly control the franchises afforded, the latter from the open and covert compensation the corporations paid for their exclusive rights. The public lost coming and going: It lost to the corporations, who charged riders and other customers monopoly rates, and it lost to the bosses, who used the kickbacks and contributions to fasten themselves more firmly onto the body politic.

It had occurred to more than one reformer that the least the corporations could do in exchange for their franchises was pay a modest tax on their monopolies. Legislation to this effect had been introduced in the New York assembly, but had been ambushed by the bosses and left for dead. Roosevelt decided to attempt a rescue. He announced that he would support the franchise tax measure, which struck him as entirely reasonable.

From the reaction of the corporate community and the bosses, one would have thought Roosevelt had advocated outright socialism. To tax franchises, they contended, would upset the delicate balance of the free market, frightening investors and prompting who knew what kinds of calamities on Wall Street. A panic like that of 1893 couldn't be ruled out. Did the governor want that kind of debacle on his head?

Tom Platt wrote Roosevelt a long letter expressing his disappointment in the man he had done so much for. Describing his sentiments at the time Roosevelt's name was being bruited for the Republican nomination, Platt elaborated on the worry he had expressed then:

> I had heard from a good many sources that you were a little loose on the relations of capital and labor, on trusts and combinations, and, indeed, on those numerous questions which have recently arisen in politics affecting the security of earnings and the right of a man to run his own business in his own way, with due respect of course to the Ten Commandments, and the Penal Code. Or, to get at it even more clearly, I understood from a number of business men, and among them many of your own personal friends, that you entertained many altruistic ideas, all very well in their way, but which before they could safely be put into law needed very profound consideration.

Platt went on to say that Roosevelt's position on the franchise tax had "caused the business community of New York to wonder how far the notions of Populism as laid down in Kansas and Nebraska have taken hold upon the Republican party of the State of New York."

Roosevelt's reply reflected both his wariness of Platt and his determination to stick to his guns. He expressed regret that his actions should have caused the senator distress, and he assured him that he was no Bryanite. Indeed, he argued, a measure such as he was supporting was the most effective proof *against* Bryanism—and the most effective means of promoting both the public welfare and the interests of the Republican Party. It would steal the thunder of the rabble-rousers. Other states and countries taxed franchises, with no untoward consequences; by contrast, in those locales where the corporations had stonewalled such measures, popular outrage frequently built to bursting, resulting in public ownership of street railways and the like. The senator must certainly agree that such a reaction would benefit no one. "And as regards the effect on the party, I believe that the killing of this bill would come a great deal nearer than its passage to making New York Democratic a year from next fall." The corporate interests had no place to go besides the Republican Party. But the people did. And by passing the franchise tax, the party would demonstrate that it had the people's interests at heart.

In other words, with all due respect to the senator—who had "infinitely more experience" in such cases and whose judgment thereon was usually "far better than mine"—here was an instance where the enlightened self-interest of the party and of the public coincided. As governor he must stand by his decision.

Platt realized there was nothing he could do to change Roosevelt's mind, and the franchise tax bill became law. Its opponents retreated briefly before counterattacking through the courts. Not until Roosevelt was long gone from Albany was the constitutionality of the franchise tax definitively confirmed; not until he was gone from Washington—for the last time—did the New York legislature approve modifications that conferred on the franchise tax anything like the inevitability taxes are popularly reputed to have.

Tom Platt would be dead by then; for now he remained very much alive. The Easy Boss didn't forget Roosevelt's independent-mindedness, and neither did he forgive it.

X

Tom Platt was lucky he didn't have to deal with Alice Roosevelt, who was even more independent-minded than her father. Fifteen years old the month after Roosevelt's inauguration, Alice enjoyed the attention that came with being a war hero's child; she had particularly appreciated the admiring glances of the younger soldiers in her father's regiment when she visited him at Montauk. Being the first child of the First Family of the state had its points as well. The parties and receptions could be fun, and they furnished good excuses for buying new clothes.

But Albany, after a childhood spent in the environs of New York, Boston, and Washington, was on the whole rather boring. "She cares neither for athletics nor good works, the two resources of youth in this town," Edith remarked.

Nor did she care much for her parents at this stage. As Alice grew into adolescence she understood family dynamics in a way she had only intuited before. She recollected many years later:

My stepmother was terribly conscientious about me. She had insisted on keeping me with them when they married. My father obviously didn't want the symbol of his infidelity around. His two infidelities, in fact: infidelity to my stepmother by marrying my mother first, and to my mother by going back to my stepmother after she died. It was all so dreadfully Victorian and mixed up. My stepmother added a typically caustic twist by telling my brother Ted, who naturally repeated it to me, that it was just as well that my mother had died when she did because my father would have been bored to death staying married to her.

(The mature Alice came to agree with Edith. "The impression I gleaned from others"—certainly not from her father, who remained as silent as the first Alice's tomb on the subject—"about her was that she was charming and frivolous and rather hideously Dickensian. Little Dora the child bride in fact. . . . I don't think I would have liked my mother very much.") Regarding Edith, Alice continued: "I think she always resented being the second choice and she never really forgave him his first marriage." And she took out her resentment on those around her. "In many ways she was a very hard woman. She was Jonathan Edwards stock and she had almost a gift for making her own people uncomfortable."

Alice's relationship with her siblings was hardly easier. Ted—almost certainly responding to provocation—taunted her whenever he got the chance. At one point he pieced together—nearly—that after Alice's mother died, she must have had a wet nurse. "So this horrid little cross-eyed boy of about five would go around to all and sundry exclaiming, 'Sissy had a sweat nurse! Sissy had a sweat nurse!'"

As for her father, he seemed incorrigibly insensitive. Certain parts of the houses the family lived in were off-limits to the children. When they approached these forbidden sanctums—his attic gun room at Sagamore Hill, for example—he would literally frighten them away. "All my father had to do was to growl and moan and we would rush away in terror. It was a horrid, savage noise that quite petrified us." Even in fun he could be overwhelming. "Oh, those perfectly awful endurance contests masquerading as games!" she remembered. Alice had a particular fear of the water, which her father aimed to overcome by sheer willpower—his, not hers. "Although I like swimming, I couldn't dive. I can see my father at Sagamore shouting to me from the water, 'Dive, Alicy, dive.' And there I was trembling on the bank saying through tears, 'Yes, Father,' to this sea monster who was flailing away in the water, peering near-sightedly at me without glasses and with his mustache glistening wet in the sunlight. It was pathetic." Alice's cousin Eleanor, who was her same age and often her companion, simultaneously endured Uncle Theodore's demands. "She hated it as much as I did but was much more unprotesting. I was not. I cried. I snarled. I hated."

Previously Theodore and Edith had sent Alice back to Bamie's when things grew especially tense; Bamie's marriage to Will Cowles had essentially eliminated this option. Now they thought of packing her off to boarding school in New York. But the sort of places they had in mind didn't appeal to her, and she vowed to make a scene if they tried to force her to go. They let the subject drop. When she refused religious confirmation, they likewise abandoned that project.

The other children were considerably more agreeable. Ted had followed his father's military exploits with the closest curiosity. He had caught wind of the criticism occasioned by Roosevelt's decision to abandon the Navy Department for the fighting front, but he appreciated his father's thinking on the subject. "He said this morning that he knew you felt it was right for you to go to war," Edith reported, "because you had talked about it so much." The boy prayed as best he could for providential protection for his father. "He said, 'I want to pray to have Father brought home safe from the war, but when I try I get all mixed up with the 'ye's—but perhaps thinking it is just as good.'"

The younger ones lived more in their own worlds. Kermit was the same as ever, Roosevelt told his aunt: "a solemn, cunning mite, with queer little friends, whom he usually has to protect (he is now quite able to hold his own personally), and a really deep little nature under it all." Ethel was a "small, motherly home-body"; Archie a "merry, pretty mischief"; Quentin ("Quenty-quee") grew "more cunning every day."

Edith was in better health and spirits than in many a month. During the fighting she had experienced the bittersweet emotions of longing for a loved one far away. "Last night I slept better because I held your dear letters to my heart instead of just having them under my pillow," she wrote shortly before the San Juan fight. "I felt I was touching you when I pressed against me what your hand had touched." (Here a tear blotted the page.) After he survived his test of fire, she watched with amazement—modulated only by the belief that the recognition was deserved—while her husband was feted by press and public. She met him at Montauk, renting a room at a nearby boardinghouse, to which—in violation of quarantine—he repaired for their lovers' reunion. She proudly observed his campaign for governor, and upon his inauguration she assumed, somewhat tentatively in the beginning, the role of First Lady of New York.

Despite her reticent nature, she learned to like the job. The easiest part to like was the money. The governor's salary of ten thousand dollars was better than Theodore had ever made before (despite being only modestly larger than the inheritance income he had had in college, before he had sunk so much into Dakota); added to the salary was housing: the governor's mansion.

The mansion, if rather pretentious, was ideal for a family with six children. "We have a great big house which is very comfortable," Roosevelt wrote Spring Rice, "although in appearance and furnishing, painfully suggestive of that kind of elegance which one sees in a swell Chicago hotel or in the board room of the directors of some big railway." (Alice remembered the house less fondly as "a hideous building with dreary dark furniture and a funereal air.")

Besides paying for heating and lighting the house, the state provided a fund for renovations and the payroll for a staff to do the cooking, cleaning, and serving. These servants would naturally help with the entertaining, but other related expenses would come from the governor's salary—which meant that Edith would still have to watch the wine list and count the guests, if not so closely as before. She also still had to deal with people she didn't like but ought to be nice to. Yet on the whole she discovered that being a First Lady wasn't a bad thing at all. "Edith is thoroughly enjoying the position of governor's wife," Roosevelt remarked to her sister.

XI

Roosevelt himself was thoroughly enjoying the position of governor, as he conceded in the same letter. He loved being in the thick of things. "I am working under high pressure," he declared in a subsequent letter; although he himself didn't draw the analogy, he was like a steam engine in that he always worked best under high pressure.

Yet at times he continued to appear confused as to whether he was a state officeholder or a national one. To some degree the confusion was contrived: Recognizing that he and Platt got along better on matters of national politics than on state affairs, Roosevelt emphasized these topics of shared sentiments. To some degree it simply reflected Roosevelt's innate tendency to gravitate toward the largest stage available.

The biggest issue on the national stage during Roosevelt's first year as governor was imperialism. The question of the hour was whether the United States Senate should ratify or reject the lately negotiated treaty with Spain, which called for American annexation of the Philippines and Puerto Rico. The idea of attaching Puerto Rico to the United States occasioned a certain amount of soul-searching among committed self-determinationists, who wondered why Cuba should be independent but Puerto Rico not; but it was the Philippines that provoked by far the greatest debate.

Anti-annexationists included the usual (from Roosevelt's point of view) suspects. Carl Schurz feared that in the flush of victory Americans would throw away what their forebears had worked and fought to create. "The character and future of the Republic and the welfare of its people now living and yet to be born are in unprecedented jeopardy," Schurz warned. A republic could not be an empire. One war had ended, but another was about to begin, for the Filipinos would not submit meekly to annexation by the United States. "The Filipinos fought against Spain for their freedom and independence, and unless they abandon their recently proclaimed purpose for their freedom and independence, they will fight against us."

E. L. Godkin of the *Evening Post* and *Nation* argued that Americans had yet to demonstrate they could govern themselves—witness Kansas and other Populist strongholds—and, a fortiori, there was no reason to believe they could govern other people. Americans were "drunk with glory and flattery" from the Spanish war; their inebriation was about to cause them to commit a "gross fraud" in their pious professions of goodwill toward the Filipinos. With Schurz, Godkin feared for America's future. "I can not help thinking this triumph over Spain seals the fate of the American republic."

The anti-annexationist chorus included some less likely voices. Steelmaker Andrew Carnegie denounced annexation as the path toward war—not simply with the Filipinos but a real war with the European imperialists. The imperialists were at bayonet's point variously around the world, but in no region were they closer to hostilities than in the Far East. "It is in that region the thunderbolt is expected. It is there the storm is to burst." Carnegie ridiculed the argument that Americans might somehow uplift the Filipinos. "Has the influence of the superior race upon the inferior ever proved beneficial to either? I know of no case in which it has been or is." Even the mere occupation of the Philippines would corrupt the occupiers. "Soldiers in foreign camps, so far from being missionaries for good, require missionaries themselves more than the natives."

Other opponents of annexation harped on different issues. Jeremiah Simpson ("Sockless Jerry"), the Kansas Populist, accused McKinley of wanting to make himself an emperor. Spokesmen for American sugar, tobacco, and hemp interests decried the cheap imports that would put their constituents out of work. Race-baiters charged miscegenation, often in the most preposterously lurid language. A Virginia lawmaker called the Philippines a "witch's caldron" of races and declared straightfacedly, "The travelers who have been there tell us and have written in the books that they are not only of all hues and colors, but there are spotted people there and, what I have never heard of in any other country, there are striped people with zebra signs upon them." Such were the souls—if souls was the right word—that the annexationists wished Americans to clasp to their bosom. Annexation was fully that profound: "It is a marriage of nations. This twain will become one flesh. They become bone of our bone and flesh of our flesh. Henceforth and forever, according to the terminology of this treaty, the Filipinos and Americans are one."

Roosevelt rarely acknowledged intelligence or honesty in his opponents, and he certainly wasn't about to concede either to the ranters of such ravings as this. Governors have no constitutional responsibility for treaties, of course, but perhaps on the reasoning that war heroes have special obligations, he sallied into the fray. He contrived an occasion to present a sword to a distinguished naval veteran of the war; after a few words regarding the honored individual, he turned to the larger question. "You and your comrades at Manila and Santiago did their part well, and more than well . . ." he declared. "It now rests with our statesmen to see that the triumph is not made void." Roosevelt intimated that rejecting the Philippines would be tantamount to trampling on the graves of those who had died in the war; moreover, it would deny what destiny had placed in America's path. "To refuse to ratify the treaty would be a crime not only against America but against civilization."

At a time of tension with Tom Platt, the treaty afforded Roosevelt an issue on which he could in clear conscience join forces with the Republican boss. Platt perceived expansionism more as a party issue than as an existential mandate; all the same, he stepped up in the Senate and gave the treaty's opponents a sound whack. Roosevelt, in turn, stepped up before a gathering of prominent Republicans in New York City and gave Platt a rousing and congratulatory clap on the back. Platt's address in support of the treaty, Roosevelt declared, was "a speech admirable in temper and in tone, in which all of us as Republicans may take pride; a speech, also, which set forth in the broadest spirit the reasons why all patriotic Americans should desire the ratification of the treaty."

Roosevelt appended a few of his own thoughts to Platt's. As Schurz and other anti-imperialists had predicted, the prospect of annexation by the United States provoked the Filipinos to armed resistance. Ignoring the accuracy of the prediction, Roosevelt asserted that now more than ever were brave hearts and stern wills required. The civilizing work of the United States in the Philippines was precisely the same sort of thing other colonizers had been attempting elsewhere— to their lasting credit. "It is infinitely better for the whole world that Russia should have taken Turkestan, that France should have taken Algiers, and that England should have taken India," he declared. Should a revolt by Algerians or Indians against their colonial masters succeed, the result would be "a hideous calamity to all mankind," and whatever persons abetted such revolts should be branded "traitors to civilization." The situation in the Philippines was no different. "We must treat them with absolute justice, but we must treat them also with firmness and courage. They must be made to realize that justice does not proceed from a sense of weakness on our part, that we are the masters. . . . The insurrection in the Philippines must be stamped out as mercifully as possible; but it must be stamped out."

What the Spaniard had been taught, the Malay must learn: "that the American flag is to float unchallenged where it floats now."

Any other interpretation of recent events revealed folly or fear or both. Those who called for peace misunderstood whence peace emanated. Articulating what would become a constant theme, Roosevelt proclaimed, "You do not get peace by peace; you get peace as the result of effort. If you strive to get it by peace you will lose it, that is all." Peace in the present was the payoff for efforts past; to shrink from efforts now would condemn the future to anarchy and war. As for the tiresome assertion that the Filipinos should be left to look after themselves, this "idlest of chatter" simply grew more fatuous with each repetition. It hardly required rebuttal, except that it usually masked a baser motive. "It means that people are afraid to undertake a great task, and cover up their fear by using some term which will give it the guise of philanthropy." However disguised, such arguments couldn't change the truth. "If we refrain from doing our part of the world's work, it will not alter the fact that the work has got to be done, only it will have to be done by some stronger race, because we will have shown ourselves weaklings."

CHAPTER FIFTEEN

On Their Heads
1899–1901

As this speech suggested, Roosevelt was identifying with the nation to a greater degree than ever. His whole life, since his father's challenge at the age of eleven at any rate, had been a continuing effort to demonstrate that he wasn't a weakling. The war with Spain had given him the opportunity to put to rest whatever doubts he still harbored on the subject—or at least as fully to rest as he was ever likely to do. The war simultaneously afforded America as a country the opportunity to demonstrate that it wasn't a weakling among nations. Roosevelt had passed his personal test; America had passed the test of nations—so far as combat itself was concerned. Now Americans must demonstrate that they could win the peace as convincingly as they had won the war. Roosevelt was determined that they should do so, for their own self-respect and his.

Even as governor, Roosevelt could never identify with the state of New York the way he identified with the nation. States had no historic destiny—certainly not since the Civil War—and took no distinctive part in the struggle among nations. For Roosevelt the struggle was the thing; without the struggle, life wasn't worth living, for the individual or for the nation.

By contrast, old-line party bosses like Tom Platt *did* identify with their states. (City bosses like Richard Croker were more geographically particular still.) Platt had national connections and a national presence, but on the repeatedly proven premise that politics is overwhelmingly local, he paid primary heed to the concerns and affairs of New York and the Republican Party there.

And Platt could perceive that Roosevelt was bad news for the New York Republican Party. The boss had come to a working truce with the governor—one that, beyond the needed efficacy, included a certain measure of respect. "He is honest and he will do what he agrees to," Platt told Isaac Hunt. "I can't do what I want with him, he is willful as Hell, but if he agrees to do a thing he will do it." Roosevelt saw things similarly. Speaking of Platt and his associates, Roosevelt declared, "I always tell them just exactly what I will do, and then do it." He added a crucial point: "One of my great advantages is that Senator Platt knows I am not trying to build up any machine of my own."

Roosevelt may not have been building up a machine of his own, but some of his actions were certainly gumming up the gears of Platt's. For all that the Rough Rider had rescued the Republicans from Croker and the Democrats in the last election, his independence of mind rendered the victory a rather hollow one. At times Platt must have felt that the Democrats might just as well have won.

Consequently, the boss determined to rid himself of Roosevelt. Yet he realized he'd have to do so judiciously. He probably had the power to deny Roosevelt renomination for governor in 1900 (the two-year election cycle, originally devised to enhance popular accountability of governors, in fact increased the influence of the bosses by hindering governors from establishing independent bases of power). But if he cast Roosevelt aside in a callous, ham-fisted way, the voters would probably punish the party.

On the other hand, if he could engineer a graceful exit for Roosevelt, one seemingly inspired by respect for the war hero and devotion to the national welfare, the New York party might be twice rewarded. Roosevelt would become someone else's problem or at least a problem Platt would share with others; at the same time, Roosevelt's great popularity would reflect well on Republican candidates at all levels.

Roosevelt's popularity grew more apparent by the month. In June 1899 he headed west to New Mexico for the first reunion of the Rough Riders, at Las Vegas. All along the route large crowds turned out to meet his train. "It would really be difficult to express my surprise at the way I was greeted," he told Lodge. "At every station at which the train stopped in Indiana, Illinois, Wisconsin, Iowa,

Missouri, Kansas, Colorado and New Mexico, I was received by dense throngs exactly as if I had been a presidential candidate." Roosevelt's head had been turned by the war and the adulation that followed, but it hadn't been turned quite that much—yet. "My reception caused some talk, so I thought it better to come out in an interview stating that of course I was for President McKinley's nomination, and that everyone should be for it."

For the first time visions of being president began dancing in Roosevelt's head, but he was realistic enough to recognize that 1900 couldn't be his year. Determined incumbents almost never get evicted from the White House by members of their own party (a lesson Roosevelt would relearn in 1912); when the incumbent has presided over an economic recovery and a glorious war, as McKinley had, the odds become overwhelming. Roosevelt understood the situation and recognized that his first opening would be 1904. How to get from 1899 to 1904 was the question.

One route ran straight ahead through Albany. He could try for reelection; if he won, he would remain in the public eye and simultaneously demonstrate that his appeal went beyond his wartime exploits. The governorship had the added attraction of encompassing work he liked—"very absorbing . . . most interesting" work, as he explained to Uncle Jimmie Bulloch. Roosevelt always wanted to be at the center of things; his was an executive temperament—in contrast, for example, to a legislative one. As governor he was the state's chief executive. The drawback of the Albany strategy was that he might fail in an attempt at reelection; or, winning, he might so antagonize the regulars as to render his elevation to the presidency impossible.

The other route to 1904 was the vice presidency. Rumors were already circulating that McKinley might jettison his current backup, Garret Hobart, in order to strengthen his ticket on the stump against William Jennings Bryan, the likely Democratic nominee. Although the economic recovery and the war worked to the Republicans' favor, Bryan and his followers continued to pummel McKinley as the pawn of the plutocrats. McKinley considered it beneath his dignity as president, as well as against his easygoing temperament, to challenge Bryan in a duel of lung power; the staid Hobart was barely better equipped. But a tested campaigner like Roosevelt might be just the ticket's ticket.

On the other hand, in those days the vice presidency was hardly a reliable route to the White House. Not since Van Buren succeeded Jackson—which was to say, well before the consolidation of the current party system—had a vice president directly succeeded a still living president. Over that time the vice presidency had become a museum of anonymity, comprising such paragons of facelessness as Richard Johnson and William King—the latter who had died six weeks after being sworn in and hadn't been missed until months later, and then just barely.

Beyond this obvious drawback, the vice president didn't do anything. He presided over the Senate when he chose to, breaking the rare tie vote. But listening to other people argue and waiting for the moment when the partisan scales swung exactly into balance hardly appealed to an activist like Roosevelt. Conceivably, he could write books from the chair, but that might appear rude. Another, not immaterial disadvantage of the vice presidency was that the pay matched the job's responsibilities. And the government didn't even pick up the vice president's expenses.

II

During the last months of 1899 and the first half of 1900, Roosevelt received all manner of advice on the subject of his political future—advice that acquired urgency upon the untimely death of Vice President Hobart in November 1899. Cabot Lodge, the counselor Roosevelt listened to most carefully, argued in favor of the vice presidency, deeming it less fraught with political peril than the New York governorship. "I can put it most tersely by saying that if I were a candidate for the Presidency I would take the Vice-Presidency in a minute at this juncture." Yet Lodge conceded that on a matter as important as this, a man had to follow his own judgment. "Your own inclination is against it, and very likely it is correct, for I have great faith in your instincts about yourself."

Roosevelt's inclination indeed was very much against the vice presidency. "I really do not see that there is anything in the Vice-Presidency for me," he confided at the end of December 1899. "In the Vice-Presidency I could do very little; whereas as Governor I can accomplish a great deal." Moreover, if reelected governor he could reasonably accept an offer of a federal position, as secretary of war, perhaps, or governor-general of the Philippines. But if he were vice president, he wouldn't be offered such a job, nor could he accept it.

For a while the post of secretary of war seemed a real possibility. McKinley gradually came around to Roosevelt's opinion on Secretary Alger, and during the spring of 1900 the president began seeking a replacement. Yet having witnessed what a ruckus Roosevelt could cause as mere assistant secretary of the navy, McKinley had grave doubts about turning the entire army over to the Rough Rider, whose opinion of his own judgment on matters military certainly hadn't been diminished by all the laurels thrown his way since San Juan Hill.

With the War Department apparently out of bounds (McKinley eventually settled on the lawyerly Elihu Root), Roosevelt briefly fastened on the idea of being governor-general of the Philippines. He had long admired the great proconsuls of the British Empire—Curzon in India, Cromer in Egypt—and believed he would have made a good one himself. He probably would have, too, with his executive mindset and his racial and cultural self-confidence. "That is a job I think I could do," he said, "and it would be worth doing, although it would be a good deal like going on another campaign in the tropics." Not the least of the job's attractions was its relative freedom from interference by anyone else. The governor-general answered to the president, and the president was ten thousand miles away.

By contrast, the governor of New York—at least a Republican governor—had to answer to Tom Platt. And Tom Platt was always near at hand, either in person or in the form of one of his lieutenants. The fight over the franchise tax had pretty well cured Platt of the conceit that Roosevelt might be domesticated and brought into the fold; had any trace of the affliction lingered, repeated reminders from his corporate collaborators that they would never contribute to another Roosevelt gubernatorial campaign would have eliminated it.

During the spring of 1900, Platt played a canny game. To all outward appearances the old boss got on well enough with the young fellow. "I have learned to love that man," Platt told Isaac Hunt, who doubtless passed the word along. Roosevelt got a similar message from a source still closer to the original. "Personally both Platt and Odell like me," Roosevelt remarked to Joseph Bishop, an editor who was becoming a confidant. "Frank Platt explained the other day that his father liked me for the excellent reason that I never deceived him and he always knew I would do exactly as I said I would, and that he had never been thrown with a man in my position, who possessed my strength, and yet who treated him as I have treated him." Where someone like Odell didn't allow personal feelings to interfere with political business, Roosevelt said, Platt sometimes did. "He will often court defeat to get even with an enemy, and sometimes to stand by a friend." Roosevelt hoped Platt would stand by him.

Roosevelt knew, however, that Platt might take some persuading. "I need not speak of the confidence I have in the judgment of you and Lodge," he told Platt as part of an effort in that direction, "yet I can't help feeling more and more that the Vice-Presidency is not an office in which I could do anything and not an office in which a man who is still vigorous and not past middle life has much chance of doing anything." Roosevelt didn't have to tell Platt that his was an active personality or that he felt well suited to the governorship. "I have thoroughly enjoyed being Governor. I have kept every promise, expressed or implied, I made on the stump and I feel that the Republican party is stronger before the State because of my incumbency." Appealing to Platt's personal side, Roosevelt added, "As you know, I am a man of moderate means. . . . I should have to live very simply in Washington and could not entertain in any way as Mr. Hobart and Mr. Morton [Hobart's predecessor as vice president] entertained. My children are all growing up and I find the burden of their education constantly heavier." Roosevelt did not expect to leave his children much money, but he did desire to leave them something in the way of honorable achievements. "Now, as Governor, I can achieve something, but as Vice-President I should achieve nothing." Besides, being vice president wouldn't be any fun. "I would simply be a presiding officer, and that I should find a bore."

Roosevelt could have quashed speculation about his availability for a vice presidential draft; all he had to do was issue a straightforward statement that he didn't want the nomination and if nominated would not serve. He made a start on such a statement. In February he declared publicly that he was a candidate for governor, not for vice president. Meanwhile, he privately told Platt he wouldn't accept the vice presidency even if nominated unanimously.

But this didn't quite do it—as Roosevelt must have known it wouldn't. He definitely didn't want to be vice president if the governorship or some other more attractive post was available, but at the same time he was not going to rule anything out. The vice presidency would be better than nothing, and if nothing were the alternative, he would take the job.

III

The next few months were filled with maneuvering by Roosevelt to gain renomination for governor, and by Platt to get Roosevelt nominated for vice president. In April, Roosevelt wrote to Mark Hanna, McKinley's manager, explaining how much more valuable he would be to the party running for governor than for vice president. "I am convinced that I can do most good to the national ticket by running as Governor in this State. There will be in New York a very curious feeling of resentment both against myself and against the party leaders if I ran as Vice-President, and this will affect our vote I believe; whereas if I ran as Governor I can strengthen the national ticket in this State more than in any other way." He added, "I do not think we can afford to take liberties in this State."

While Roosevelt was trying to convince Hanna to keep him off the national ticket, Platt was trying to force Hanna to put him on. Platt may have liked Roosevelt, as Roosevelt thought and Platt himself said, or he may not have. But he certainly didn't like him enough to want to keep him around Albany. Whatever Roosevelt might hope, the boss placed business before pleasure. And Roosevelt continued to be bad for the business of the party. Roosevelt orchestrated the ouster of the state superintendent of insurance, Louis Payn, a man with unsurprisingly close connections to the insurance industry—too close, in Roosevelt's view, which was why he insisted on Payn's removal. (It didn't help Payn with Roosevelt that the insurance director, a crony of then-governor Black, had been instrumental in unearthing the story of Roosevelt's residency problems.) Platt had favored keeping Payn in office, for Payn was a convenient conduit from the corporate boardrooms to the party's coffers. Upon his ejection by Roosevelt, Payn came crying to Platt: "I warned you that this fellow would soon have you dangling at his chariot wheel. You would not believe me. He has begun by scalping members of your 'Old Guard.' He'll get you, too, soon." Whether or not Platt credited Payn's warning, the boss grew more convinced than ever that Roosevelt was trouble.

But Mark Hanna didn't want Roosevelt any more than Platt did. In electing McKinley in 1896, the Ohio boss had fashioned a finely balanced, carefully tuned machine that converted the money of Republican bankers and manufacturers into votes. Hanna's reward had been the satisfaction of seeing the man he admired installed in the White House and the country restored to prosperity. And, of course, there was the small matter of his own appointment to the Senate (to replace John Hay, named secretary of state). Despite some slight perturbations consequent to the Spanish war, which Hanna had resisted, the machine continued to operate smoothly. Hanna had no desire to see it thrown out of balance, and he had little doubt that a careless character like Theodore Roosevelt would do just that.

Nor did he have any love for Roosevelt as an individual. During the months before the war, Roosevelt had excoriated Hanna as one of those small-minded money-grubbers who placed prosperity ahead of what Roosevelt took for national honor. Roosevelt was reported to have confronted Hanna at one big-money dinner, shaking his fist at the boss and declaring, "We will have this war for the freedom of Cuba, Senator Hanna, in spite of the timidity of the commercial interests." Hanna might have overlooked this challenge to himself, but he couldn't abide Roosevelt's insults to his beloved McKinley. Roosevelt was widely reported to have slighted McKinley's character, comparing his backbone alternatively to a jellyfish and a chocolate eclair. Hanna already considered Roosevelt a fool for his exaggerated views of national honor (to a Roosevelt comment that Britain ought to be ejected from North America, Hanna replied, "You're crazy, Roosevelt! What's wrong with Canada?"), and now he deemed him an impudent boor as well.

As the Republican national convention approached, the jockeying to see who would get stuck with Roosevelt increased. Platt plotted with Matthew Quay, the principal boss of Pennsylvania Republicans, to orchestrate a groundswell in favor of Roosevelt. Quay didn't like Hanna, whom he was happy to try to embarrass. Meanwhile, western elements of the party, still stinging from their shellacking by the Bryanites in 1896, looked on Roosevelt as their best bet against another beating. The fact that Hanna didn't want Roosevelt simply made the westerners want him more: Few figures were more despised west of the Mississippi than Dollar Mark.

Amid all the maneuvering, Roosevelt grew increasingly coy. "The last position I wish is that of the vice presidency," he said again— which of course wasn't the same thing as saying he didn't wish it at all. What he *did* wish was to be reelected governor. But he recognized that the odds of his returning to Albany were getting slimmer all the time. "It is quite on the cards that I shall be beaten for Governor this fall," he remarked on one of his gloomier days. On another day, when he was feeling more chipper, he predicted that the big corporations would join forces with the gold Democrats in New York in an effort to oust him. "I do not think that they will succeed, but they will give me the fight of my life."

Although Lodge still wanted Roosevelt to take the vice presidency, the Massachusetts senator said that if his friend were really determined not to be nominated, then he ought to stay away from the Republican national convention. His presence at Philadelphia would provide a rallying point for his supporters—and for those enemies who wanted to employ his supporters to force him onto the ticket.

Roosevelt got the same advice from an even better source, Platt lieutenant Odell. "If you will remain away from Philadelphia," Odell said, "I will guarantee you will not be nominated for the Vice Presidency."

Roosevelt rejected this advice on the dubious grounds that failure to attend would make him appear weak. "I believe that I would be looked upon as rather a coward if I didn't go," he told Lodge. ("Then you will be nominated," Odell warned.)

Maybe he would have appeared weak—which to Roosevelt was unacceptable. More to the point, he would have jeopardized the career that was finally beginning to blossom. To defy Platt raised the very real possibility of being left without any job at all. Once out of the public eye, his popularity would wane. He had learned his lesson about letting opportunity pass; he wasn't going to take the chance of seeing it slip through his hands this time.

IV

Roosevelt not only did not stay away from the convention, he made quite a show of attending. He wore the same distinctive hat he had worn on the campaign trail in 1898, a Rough Rider knockoff that lent itself far more readily to a triumphal charge than to a determined retreat. The outcome of the main event—the nomination of the presidential candidate—being a foregone conclusion, attention focused on the fight for the vice presidency. Roosevelt's attendance and his style suggested a victory patterned after San Juan Hill. One observer, remarking Roosevelt's topper, quipped, "Gentlemen, that's an acceptance hat."

Roosevelt traveled to Philadelphia on the same train with Platt; by the time they reached the convention site, their purposes coincided. For form's sake the governor continued to protest that he was not a candidate for vice president, but both he and the boss knew that the steamroller Platt had set in motion would be nearly impossible to stop.

Mark Hanna, for one, saw that he was about to be run over. His exasperation got the better of him as he shouted at a visitor who came calling for guidance: "Do whatever you damn please! I'm through! I won't have anything more to do with the convention! I won't take charge of the campaign! I won't be chairman of the national committee again!" When the visitor responded to this outburst by asking what was the matter, Hanna exploded again: "Matter! Matter! Why, everybody's gone crazy! What is the matter with all of you? Here is this convention going headlong for Roosevelt for Vice President. Don't any of you realize that there's only one life between that madman and the Presidency?"

The madman in question handled himself sanely and adroitly. Everyone knew that Platt was working for Roosevelt's nomination; by holding out bravely, Roosevelt reinforced his image as one who wouldn't truckle to the New York boss. Such independence merited reward. At the same time, the fact that Hanna so violently opposed

Roosevelt allowed Roosevelt's supporters to slap the Ohio boss with the same vote.

Hanna could only watch in fury and disgust as one delegation after another declared for the Rough Rider. Even before the roll was called, the outcome was determined. Platt, Quay, and the others offered Hanna the chance to save face by a graceful surrender to the inevitable. Hanna, his habitual pragmatism once more getting the better of his anger, accepted; he announced that the nomination for vice president, like the nomination for president, should be unanimous.

V

"It was simply impossible to resist so spontaneous a feeling," Roosevelt explained to friend and ally Seth Low two days later. Someone was being kidded here, either Roosevelt or Low, for the stampede to Roosevelt, while sincere, was far from spontaneous. It had taken a great deal of hard work by Platt and Quay and others.

Yet Roosevelt preferred not to consider himself in the debt of the bosses for anything, even a nomination he hadn't wanted. Remarkably, he went on to boast that he had "stood the state machine on its head" in the business of his nomination. He liked this formulation so much that he repeated it in letters to Bamie, Corinne, John Hay, and others over the course of the summer. In the narrowest, hair-splitting sense, Roosevelt was right, for he was referring specifically to the fact that he had talked Platt into having the New York delegation initially announce for someone else. This ruse—for such it was— reconfirmed Roosevelt's apparent independence of Platt; as Platt, who didn't require much convincing, accurately guessed, it simply rendered Roosevelt more attractive to the many delegates who wanted to register a protest against the bosses. "The only effect was to make the rest of the country absolutely unanimous, and neither Hanna nor anyone else could stop it," Roosevelt crowed.

But if anyone did any headstanding in the affair, it was Roosevelt. Platt whistled all the way home from Philadelphia, congratulating himself on getting rid of Roosevelt and besting Hanna in the bargain. (Subsequently asked if he was planning to attend the inauguration in

March 1901, Platt chortled, "Yes, I am going to Washington to see Theodore Roosevelt take the veil!") Roosevelt had wanted to hold on to the governorship but had been forced out; the vice presidential nomination was a consolation prize.

As was his habit, however, Roosevelt soon started fashioning his sow's ear into a silk purse. "I believe it all for the best as regards my own personal interests," he told Lodge. "And it is a great load of personal anxiety off me." His misgivings about the vice presidency had disappeared amid the enthusiasm shown for him at Philadelphia. "I should be a conceited fool if I was discontented with the nomination when it came in such a fashion." Besides, there was nothing like a convention to stir one's blood. "It was horridly painful for three days, but the fourth was good fun."

Roosevelt took the opportunity of his nomination to wonder at how far he, and Lodge, had come. "It certainly is odd to look back sixteen years when you and I sat in the Blaine convention on the beaten side while the mugwumps foretold our utter ruin, and then in this convention, over which you presided [as permanent chairman], to think how you recognized me to second McKinley's nomination and afterwards declared me myself nominated in the second place on the ticket." Together they had proved the mugwumps wrong; together they had won the respect of the party. For his part he was "deeply sensible" of the honor the party had bestowed upon him. "I shall do my best to deserve it and not to disappoint those who trusted me and think well of me."

VI

Those who trusted and thought well of him might have had larger hopes, but his immediate job was to get McKinley elected. The president had held aloof from the skirmishing over the vice presidential nomination, leaving it to the party bosses to decide. But as with most things politically important, McKinley ended up getting what he wanted—in this case a popular number two who could shout just as loud as Bryan, thereby permitting the president to stay home and look presidential.

Roosevelt knew what was expected of him and aimed to deliver. A week after the convention he wrote to Hanna seeking instructions: "I wish in this campaign to do whatever you think wise and advisable— whatever is likely to produce the best results for the republican ticket. I am as strong as a bull moose and you can use me up to my limit." Roosevelt did raise one caveat, though, saying that in the governor's race two years before, his voice had just about given out after three hundred speeches in the space of four weeks. But at that time he had had to carry the whole campaign on his own shoulders, which wasn't the case now. "Exactly how much speaking should I do?" he asked. And where should he do it? He was prepared to travel west, into the heart of Bryan country. Yet he worried that a whistle-stop campaign on the order of Bryan's 1896 barnstorming tour would appear undig- nified. And if he spent too much time away from New York, he might risk losing that state for the ticket. "I am writing simply to try to place before you the situation as I see it, so that you can make use of me to the best advantage."

Predictably, Roosevelt (and other Republicans) pointed with pride to the accomplishments of the incumbent. McKinley had promised to restore prosperity, and prosperity had returned. He had vowed to uphold the national honor, and the nation had won a great victory in war. Not surprisingly, Roosevelt laid special stress on this latter issue. "Four years ago the nation was uneasy because at our very doors an American island was writhing in hideous agony under a worse than medieval despotism. We had our Armenia at our threshold. The situa- tion in Cuba had become such that we could no longer stand quiet and retain one shred of self-respect." The president had tried by peaceful methods to resolve the conflict in Cuba—naturally, Roosevelt didn't mention his own impatience at McKinley's temporizing—but finally had been forced to take up arms. "We drew the sword and waged the most righteous and brilliantly successful foreign war that this generation has seen."

At Hanna's insistence, Roosevelt concentrated his campaign efforts in the West. From Albany he traveled to Chicago, then across the plains to the Rocky Mountains and back. En route he rendezvoused with Rough Rider buddies—gatherings that replayed the war hero theme and made good copy for reporters who found the vice presi- dential candidate far more interesting than the president. In Colorado he escaped his train long enough for several outings on horseback, which generated still more favorable press. From his saddle as from the rear of his train and scores of platforms, he hammered home the dual message that McKinley meant good times at home and America's good name abroad.

To no one's surprise the Democrats had renominated Bryan. So had the tattered remnants of the Populist Party. Roosevelt seized every opportunity to remind his listeners of this lunatic fringe that rode the Democrats' coattails—without fail he referred to Bryan as the candidate of "the Populist Democracy." As a member now of the national ticket, Roosevelt restrained himself somewhat in his characterizations of Bryan, compared to his bloody rhetoric of the 1896 campaign. He dropped most of his analogies of Bryan to the leaders of the French reign of terror. But he did manage a few swipes at the loyalty and patriotism of the Democrats, likening them to the Copperheads of 1864.

Bryan was attacking the Republicans for the fighting that had broken out in the Philippines between Filipinos and the American occupation forces. To date, the conflict had conferred no honor on the American army (nor would it). The army's failure thus far to quell the insurrection, combined with persistent reports of atrocities by American troops and their Filipino collaborators, had soured many Americans on the imperialist project. The Democrats made the most of this dissatisfaction, calling imperialism the paramount issue in the campaign and decrying the trend toward militarism in American foreign policy.

Roosevelt roundly rejected any wrongdoing by America regarding the Philippines, and he snorted at the rest of the list of Democratic charges. "The simple truth is that there is nothing even remotely resembling 'imperialism' or 'militarism' involved in the present development of that policy of expansion which has been part of the history of America from the day she became a nation." The subordinate clause in this statement was not subordinate at all in Roosevelt's thinking: It was precisely the point. American expansion across the Caribbean and the Pacific was on a par with that pursued by Americans—including Democratic icons Jefferson and Jackson—for five generations. "This policy is only imperialistic in the sense that Jefferson's policy in Louisiana was imperialistic; only military in the sense that Jackson's policy toward the Seminoles or Custer's toward the Sioux embodied militarism."

The Democrats said they opposed expansion. Here they had matters wrong-end-to. "The question is now not whether we shall expand—for we have already expanded—but whether we shall contract." The Philippines were American territory; Americans had the obligation to provide order and stability and good government there. But good government was not the same as self-government. "To grant self-government to Luzon under Aguinaldo would be like granting self-government to an Apache reservation under some local chief." For America to relinquish control would not give the masses of the Filipinos even self-government. "They would simply be put at the mercy of a syndicate of Chinese half-breeds, under whom corruption would flourish far more than ever it flourished under Tweed, while tyrannical oppression would obtain to a degree only possible under such an oligarchy."

The Democrats spoke of oligarchies, too, although they were referring to the trusts that dominated American industry, intimidated labor, and increasingly strangled individual opportunity. Other Republican speakers—including Hanna, who took to the hustings this season with unaccustomed ardor—had difficulty replying, being so closely connected to the big business interests. Roosevelt conveyed greater credibility on account of his record of resistance to the corporations. "Let me point out to you," he told an audience in Michigan, "that within the last two years we have in New York established a franchise tax under which the corporations which owe most to the State, but who had hitherto largely escaped taxation, have been required to pay their just share of taxation." Unlike other Republicans, Roosevelt offered no defense of the trusts. "Beyond a question the great industrial combinations which we group in popular parlance under the name of trusts have produced great and serious evils." And there was every reason for the American people to attempt to abate those evils and make men of wealth carry their part of the burden of public affairs. But the wild and irresponsible representations by the Democrats and the actions those representations portended—in the unlikely event of a Democratic victory—would do more harm than good. "Hasty legislation of a violent type is either wholly ineffective against the evil, or else crushes the evil at the expense of crushing even more of good." What was required was "moderation combined with resolution."

Roosevelt did more speaking than he had intended, but the people wanted to see him, and he couldn't turn them down. "It seemed exceedingly hard to hurt their feelings when they were acting partly at least in a spirit of loyalty to me," he remarked after one outing. Although the effort drained him, the crowds energized him. They hailed the hero of Santiago and listened intently to his speeches, delivered staccato in that oddly high-pitched voice, accompanied by the characteristic gesture of his right hand, a quick, stabbing motion that from a distance recalled a sharp jab to an opponent's jaw.

Roosevelt could easily envisage himself punching Bryan or some other Democrat. As usual, he demonized his foes, if more privately than at certain times past. It was said of Bryan that in order to hate him, one had to avoid getting to know him; his sweet and open disposition won over nearly all he met. Roosevelt's path had occasionally crossed Bryan's, but he made a point of never getting to know the man. Consequently, he managed to maintain a full quotient of scorn. "What a thorough-paced hypocrite and demagogue he is," Roosevelt sputtered to Lodge. "And what a small man!" To Uncle Jimmie Bulloch, Roosevelt asserted that behind Bryan stood "every force of ignorance, evil and cowardice." This phalanx of corruption included not merely the usual grafters of Tammany and its machine-mates across the country, but also those anti-imperialists who opposed the glorious destiny toward which the Republicans were leading America. "I cannot express the anger and contemptuous indignation with which I regard the cultivated men from Schurz and Godkin down to the smaller vermin like Jack Chapman and Erving Winslow who at this great crisis show themselves to be traitors to the country."

Occasionally, Roosevelt's scorn got vented in public. At one rally a heckler asked him about the "embalmed beef" scandal of the Spanish war, in which (presumably Republican) suppliers foisted tainted meat off on the soldiers. "I ate it!" shouted Roosevelt in reply, slashing the air with his hand. "I ate it and you never did; and what's more, you'll never get within five miles of a hostile bullet, so long as you can run!"

Roosevelt continued to battle the cowards, the traitors, the vermin, the evil, and the ignorant until November when the election brought

McKinley a victory more sweeping than his first. The G.O.P. increased its margin in the House and added two seats in the Senate.

"I am delighted to have been on the national ticket in this great historic contest," Roosevelt told Lodge shortly after the returns came in. And he was quite ready to claim his share of the credit. "After McKinley and Hanna, I feel that I did as much as anyone in bringing about the result—though after all it was Bryan himself who did most."

VII

During the frenzy of the campaign Roosevelt forgot most of his reservations about the vice presidency. Any contest brought out the competitor in him, and at least while the contest lasted, he thought only of winning.

Edith wasn't so easily distracted. From the start she had opposed his candidacy, much preferring that he seek reelection to the governorship. She doubted the importance of the job, she dreaded the thought of another move—the fourth in six years—and she fretted about trying to provide for her growing family on an income effectively half of what Theodore was making as governor. Roosevelt's initial pleas against the nomination included concern for her opinion. "Even to live simply as a Vice-President would have to live," he told Lodge, "would be a serious drain upon me, and would cause me, and especially would cause Edith, continual anxiety about money." A few days later, speaking again to Lodge of a possible vice presidential nomination, he said that he had been going over it with Edith; as a result he intended, against Lodge's advice, to announce that he didn't want to be vice president. "Edith bids me to say that she hopes you will forgive me!"

Edith didn't change her mind during the following months, although she may have made a tactical error in March by leaving the country with her sister for a visit to Cuba—where, she said, she wanted to see how big a hill San Juan really was. By the time she returned, the Platt steamroller had gained critical momentum. Either because he didn't tell her of Lodge's and Odell's advice to stay away from the conven-

tion or because she ignored it, she made plans to attend the
Republican convention that summer, thinking attendance would be
fitting for the wife of the New York governor and exciting besides.
Revealing her plans to a dinner guest—Alton Parker, who turned out
to be Roosevelt's opponent in the 1904 election—he replied, perhaps
as a deliberate provocation, that it would indeed be exciting: She
would see her husband nominated for the vice presidency. "You disagreeable thing," she retorted. "I don't want to see him nominated for
the Vice-Presidency!"

But Edith's wishes hadn't prevailed against Platt any more than
Theodore's had, and now she found herself, none too happily, the wife
of the vice president–elect.

VIII

She also found herself alone—or at least husbandless. True to his
form, Roosevelt disappeared on a hunting trip while Edith completed
the evacuation from Albany and located a house to lease in
Washington. For five weeks, in the dead of the first winter of the new
century, he hunted big—and some medium—game on Colorado's
western slope. "We started soon after sunrise," he wrote to Ted, now
a student at Groton, following one typical day in the field, "and made
our way, hunting as we went, across the high, exceedingly rugged
hills, until sunset. We were hunting cougar and lynx or, as they are
called out here, 'lion' and 'cat.' The first cat we put up gave the dogs a
two hours' chase, and got away among some high cliffs. In the afternoon we put up another, and had a very good hour's run, the dogs
baying until the glens rang again to the echoes, as they worked hither
and thither through the ravines." The dogs set a faster pace than the
hunters' horses could manage across the wooded slopes and scree; at
times Roosevelt and his guide, John Goff, almost lost the pack.
Finally, the hounds treed the lynx, and the hunters caught up. Goff
then gave a command to three dogs that had lagged behind the others, apparently they were onlookers. What happened next astonished Roosevelt. "The dogs proceeded literally to *climb the tree,*

which was a many-forked piñon; one of the half-breeds, named Tony, got up certainly sixteen feet, until the lynx, which looked like a huge and exceedingly malevolent pussy-cat, made vicious dabs at him." After recovering from his amazement, Roosevelt finished off the quarry. "I shot the lynx low, so as not to hurt his skin."

Another outing was more exciting still. The hunters encountered the cold trail of a cougar; the dogs puzzled for a couple of hours, wandering this way and that, not knowing where to go. Then by chance they struck a fresh trail where the mountain lion had killed a deer the night before. The dogs took off in a frenzy. For half an hour they tore across the hillsides through the pines, with Roosevelt and Goff hard behind. "Soon we saw the lion in a treetop, with two of the dogs so high up among the branches that he was striking at them. He was more afraid of us than of the dogs, and as soon as he saw us he took a great flying leap and was off, the pack close behind." The chase continued until the dogs treed the cougar again. When the hunters arrived, the great feline again flew out of the tree. This time the dogs caught the cougar on the ground, and a terrific fight ensued. The dogs charged; the cougar swiped them with his vicious claws, sending them reeling and bloodied. They charged again; he slashed again. The dogs eventually would have worn the beast down, but likely not before being badly wounded themselves by the cougar. Roosevelt decided to take matters into his own hands—literally. "I ran in and stabbed him behind the shoulder," he told Ted, "thrusting the knife you loaned me right into his heart." It was a most satisfying day's work. "I have always wished to kill a cougar as I did this one, with dogs and the knife."

IX

Satisfaction of blood lust apart, one purpose of Roosevelt's hunting trip was to keep him out of sight and out of trouble until inauguration. During the campaign he had drawn more attention than McKinley, a matter that caused some ill feelings. "There is a strong disposition to make him jealous of me," Roosevelt had remarked at the time. Now, with inauguration just weeks away, he didn't want to do anything that might be interpreted as upstaging his boss.

His efforts to this end fell short. Although he kept away from reporters, he couldn't quiet the speculation that filled the papers regarding his exploits among the bears and wolves ("neither of which animals did I so much as see," he complained to a friend).

For the first time he started to feel personally the constraints that hedged in the life of an understudy to the president. He adjusted with some difficulty and not always with grace. When the taxidermist who was preparing the twelve cougar and five lynx skins he had bagged in Colorado invited the press to come and see the collection, Roosevelt rebuked him sharply. "Show them to no one from this time on, unless he has my written authority." For similar reasons he declined an invitation to attend a reunion of the Rough Riders. "My experience on the hunt increased my already existing respect for the infinite capacity of the newspaper press to manufacture sensations, and now the administration feels compromised whenever anybody says something of me which is not true!"

Inauguration day duly arrived in March, and Roosevelt was sworn in. As per custom in those days, the Senate met for a week before adjourning until year's end; Roosevelt gaveled the session open and closed. Then he and Edith and the children retired to Oyster Bay, with the intention of returning to Washington at the beginning of October.

For a time, Roosevelt recaptured the spirit of his youth at the old colony. "I am rather ashamed to say that I am enjoying the perfect ease of my life at present," he wrote William Howard Taft, the governor-general of the Philippines. "I am just living out in the country, doing nothing but ride and row with Mrs. Roosevelt, and walk and play with the children; chop trees in the afternoon and read books by a wood fire in the evening." The proximity of his offspring and their cousins brought out the child in him, which in any event was never far below the surface. On one occasion he allowed four of the young ones to go wading with their clothes on; wading deepened to swimming, and the quartet became soaked from head to toe. "I wish you could have seen the more than Roman-matron-like austerity with which Edith and Laura [the cousins' mother] received me when I headed the bedraggled procession back to them," he told Bamie. "The children were all given hot ginger and sent to bed on their return home, and on the part of both mothers there was evident a most sincere regret that it was not possible to give me hot ginger and send me to bed!"

But what had satisfied Roosevelt at seventeen didn't at forty-two. As vice president he had little to do. "I have very ugly feelings now and then that I am leading a life of unwarrantable idleness," he recorded. What was worse, as vice president there was little he *could* do. He couldn't speak without risking embroiling the administration in controversy; nor could he write more than the blandest prefaces to other people's books. He had already seen what trouble even hunting could get him into. He was at such a loss that he inquired into resuming his legal education—partly for something to do, partly as a hedge against the possibility that what he liked to call the "kaleidoscope" of politics should take a twist and turn him out of office.

One thing that was safe was writing letters. He exchanged views with Taft on the governance of the Philippines, on Republican politics, and on sundry other matters. He encouraged Leonard Wood, now military governor of Cuba, to carry on in the face of discouragements arising there and back home. He swapped naval strategy with Mahan. He debated the finer points of the Boer war with Speck von Sternberg. He bucked up Cecil Spring Rice when the British diplomat fell down in the mouth regarding the future of the English-speaking peoples (not least because of Britain's dismal showing against the Boers).

And of course he kept close contact with Cabot Lodge. Since the Republican convention the previous summer, Lodge, looking to 1904, had taken upon himself the role of Roosevelt's presidential campaign manager. At the convention's adjournment he had counseled his friend to be careful how he presented himself—forthright but not arrogant, decisive but not pushy, the energetic but ever-loyal lieutenant to McKinley. "My purpose in this is to secure by every righteous means the confidence and support for you of the President and of all his large following," Lodge explained. "This is going to be of immense importance to us four years hence, and that is why I desire that you should appear, not only during the campaign but after the election, as the President's next friend." Lodge went on, "There is today no one who could stand against you for a moment for the nomination for the Presidency, but no one can tell what will happen in four years. I believe myself that by judicious conduct we can have it just as surely within our grasp four years hence as it would be today, but we should make no mistakes."

Lodge applauded Roosevelt's conduct in the campaign, believing it brought 1904 that much nearer. He groaned when he read the reports of Roosevelt's heroics in the Rockies; he took reassurance when Roosevelt denied having done anything reckless or extravagant. He cheered louder than anyone else—except Ted and Kermit—at Roosevelt's inauguration. He helped arrange a joint appearance by Roosevelt and himself at the opening of the Pan-American Exposition in June; he exulted afterward, "Our speeches at Buffalo seem to have made quite a sensation."

Lodge was the readier of the two to discuss Roosevelt's political future; Roosevelt, not wanting to tempt fate, preferred for the moment to focus on the issues—although he allowed himself the occasional hypothetical. Efforts by the administration to amend or abrogate the 1850 Clayton-Bulwer Treaty with Britain, so that the United States might unilaterally build a canal across Central America, occasioned considerable discussion between Roosevelt and Lodge. "My own view, if I had the power," Roosevelt said, "would be that we should tell Great Britain that we wanted to be friendly and would like a treaty that would keep their self-respect as well as ours." But if this proved impossible, the United States should abrogate. In doing so, however, the American government must be prepared to deal with the consequences, including an unlikely but not unthinkable coalition of Britain and Germany. "In short, I wish to see us act upon the old frontier principles, 'Don't bluster, don't flourish your revolver and never draw unless you intend to shoot.'"

X

But the more he analyzed national affairs with Lodge and Mahan and Wood and Taft and others, and the more he hypothesized about what he would do if he had the power, the more painfully aware he became of the fact that he didn't and the more acutely conscious of what he called "the absolute innocuousness of the Vice Presidency."

McKinley was no help—indeed, just the opposite. "He is perfectly cordial and friendly to me . . ." Roosevelt said, "but he does not intend that I shall have any influence of any kind, sort or description in the administration from the top to the bottom." McKinley, Roosevelt belatedly realized, had been behind his nomination to the vice presidency, perhaps passively but no less effectively for that. "The President made up his mind that I was needed on the ticket with him last year and wanted me nominated, while Hanna did not." McKinley had gotten what he wanted and then been reelected. Now Roosevelt, having served McKinley's purpose, was no longer needed. "This he has made evident again and again, although always in an entirely pleasant and courteous way." McKinley apparently had never quite conquered his misgivings regarding Roosevelt. "The President in a cold-blooded way has always rather liked me, or at least has admired certain qualities in me. There are certain bits of work he would be delighted to have me do. But at bottom neither he nor Hanna (although I really like both) sympathize with my feelings or feel comfortable about me, because they cannot understand what it is that makes me act in certain ways at certain times, and therefore think me indiscreet and overimpulsive."

In his brighter moments Roosevelt accepted his fate philosophically. He said he couldn't sympathize with men like Tom Reed who, having received a great deal at the hands of their countrymen, became embittered when they didn't gain the highest distinction of all, the presidency. (Roosevelt's lack of sympathy for his old friend also had much to do with Reed's opposition to expansionism, a project he deemed driven by fatuity allied with cynicism. Regarding one proponent of the war with Spain who happened to own a marble quarry in Vermont, Reed remarked caustically, "Proctor's position might have been expected. A war will make a large market for gravestones.") As for himself, Roosevelt said, "I have been amply rewarded. I have led a very full and happy life, and have achieved certain things for the public which represent a substantial sum of good work, on which my children will have legitimate cause to look back with pleasure. If I never hold another public office I shall nevertheless always feel that I am away ahead of the deal!"

But the brighter moments were rare, and on most days he found it hard to be so accepting. "The Vice Presidency is an utterly anomalous office (one which I think ought to be abolished)," he complained to Leonard Wood. "The man who occupies it may at any moment be everything; but meanwhile he is practically nothing." McKinley continued to ignore him, in his usual jolly way; all the same, he had to watch his step, for the administration's sake as well as his own. The opposition press loved to lampoon him; yet where he had formerly felt free to defend himself, now the straitjacket of his office required him to suffer most slights in silence.

The one thing that kept him going, politically, was the prospect that he might be next to enter the White House. "Of course, I should like to be President," he told Taft, "and feel I could do the work well." Even while characterizing his spring and early summer of 1901 as a "time of slack water," he could still hear the roar of the cataract of the campaign—a roar that re-echoed when he went west to help Colorado celebrate its quarter-centennial in August. "I have been greatly astonished at the feeling displayed for me, not only in Colorado and Kansas, but in Missouri and even in Illinois. All the Colorado people, and all their leaders are a unit, and are perfectly straight out in their declarations. In Kansas and Missouri there have been genuine popular movements started on my behalf."

Yet such enthusiasm was like a prairie storm: Gathering quickly, it could dissipate just as fast. Besides, for all the excitement out west, Roosevelt couldn't even count on the support of the New York Republican machine, and for a candidate to gain the nomination without the backing of his own state was essentially unheard of. In any event, 1904 was a long way off, and much could happen before then.

XI

It did, starting two weeks later. On September 6 a self-proclaimed anarchist, Leon Czolgosz, shot McKinley at the Pan-American Exposition at Buffalo. The wound was grave; the stomach was perforated front to back. Whether the injury would prove mortal couldn't yet be known.

Roosevelt received the news on a speaking tour of Vermont. "Stunned amazement" was his initial response. The report seemed "literally incredible," he told Lodge. "You and I have lived too long, and have seen human nature from too many different sides, to be astounded at ordinary folly or ordinary wickedness, but it did not seem possible that just at this time in just this country, and in the case of this particular president, any human being could be so infamous a scoundrel, so crazy a fool as to attempt to assassinate him." Roosevelt noted that McKinley was not a wealthy man and could hardly be mistaken for a member of the plutocracy. On the contrary, he was a man of that class of people—merchants, mechanics, clerks, farmers—who were the backbone of the republic. Consequently, the attack on the president represented a blow at America's essence. "It was in the most naked way an assault not on power, not on wealth, but simply and solely upon free government, government by the common people."

Such was the reaction of Roosevelt the citizen—a reaction he assumed he shared with all Americans of sense and goodwill. But he, of course, was not just any citizen, and the attempted assassination placed him, as heir to the throne, in what he called a "most delicate" position. Not to go to Buffalo at once might appear callous and indifferent; to fly there too fast could give the impression of unseemly ambition.

In the event, he hesitated only momentarily before doing what he judged the "natural thing." He commandeered a train and raced to the president's bedside. By the time he got there, the physicians had stabilized McKinley's condition. Surgeons had opted against the use of recently invented X-ray equipment, although such was on display at the nearby exposition. They cleaned the wound and sutured the tears in the stomach and abdominal walls. This ended the immediate danger. During the next seventy-two hours the situation appeared to improve steadily. The president's fever fell, and he began to seem his usual sociable self. "It's mighty lonesome in here," he said in response to efforts to get him to be quiet and rest.

By all evidence the patient was on the mend. "Things are now progressing so favorably," Roosevelt wrote a friend on September 9, "that I believe the President will be out of danger before you receive this letter." The next day Roosevelt was even more sanguine: "Thank Heaven, the President is now out of danger."

Yet so mixed were Roosevelt's emotions that even this good news had an unhappy aspect (aside from whatever disappointment he may have felt—but certainly would never acknowledge—at learning that he wasn't to be president so soon). Roosevelt observed angrily that the capable work of the surgeons had simultaneously saved the life of the president's assailant, who now could be charged only with attempted murder, and even if convicted would be out on parole in seven years.

As he often did when conflicting emotions pulled him in opposite directions, Roosevelt lashed out. In this case the fact that Czolgosz was an anarchist—a member of that tribe that would assassinate moral order itself—added energy to his outburst. In a rambling letter to Lodge, Roosevelt contended that the blame for the attack rested not merely with Czolgosz but with all those who afforded the slightest encouragement to anarchists. They should be fought, one and all. "We should war with relentless efficiency not only against anarchists, but against all active and passive sympathizers with anarchists. Moreover, every scoundrel like Hearst and his satellites who for whatever purposes appeals to and inflames evil human passion, has made himself accessory before the fact to every crime of this nature, and every soft fool who extends a maudlin sympathy to criminals has done likewise. Hearst and Altgeld, and to an only less degree, Tolstoi and the feeble apostles of Tolstoi, like Ernest Howard Crosby and William Dean Howells, who unite in petitions for the pardon of anarchists, have a heavy share in the burden of responsibility for crimes of this kind."

XII

Not many people would have thought to indict Tolstoy for the attempt on McKinley's life, but the slightest hint of anarchy always set Roosevelt off, and in any event these were trying circumstances. As the president's condition continued to improve, Roosevelt's emotions stabilized, and on September 10 he left Buffalo "with a light heart." He stopped briefly in Oyster Bay before heading north to join Edith and the children on vacation in the Adirondacks.

The autumn rains had come early to the mountains; the slate clouds barred the view of anything much higher than the treetops above the two-story lodge at Tahawus, an old mining camp since converted to a rustic resort. But bad weather had never prevented Roosevelt from enjoying himself out of doors, and, especially after the turmoil of the past week, it wasn't going to keep him inside now.

His recent idle summer had produced one benefit: He was in better physical condition than in years. He would be heading to Washington in a few weeks; here was his opportunity to stretch his legs and test his wind. He determined on an ascent of Mount Marcy—no Matterhorn at a mere fifty-three hundred feet but still the highest in the neighborhood, and a stiff walk if not exactly a climb. Had he been by himself he almost certainly would have gone up and down in a day; Edith, however, wasn't going to let him disappear into the wilderness the way he so often did, and she announced that she would join him. Kermit and Ethel said they must go, too, and by the time the party set out at midday on September 12, there were nearly a dozen in the group.

They spent that night in cabins beside a small lake below the peak. The fire blazed, then died down; as Roosevelt stared into the embers he doubtless thought back on his close brush with the presidency and wondered if he would get that close again.

The next morning brought more rain, which again didn't discourage Roosevelt but this time caused Edith and the children to forgo the last leg of the ascent. They turned back toward Tahawus with one of the two guides who had brought them this far, while Theodore and the others headed up into the clouds.

They reached the summit and the top of the clouds at about the same time, just before noon. Roosevelt had never had the patience simply to enjoy a view for long, and, besides, despite the sunshine the wind was cold against clothes wet from both rain and sweat. They decided to start down and find some shelter before breaking out lunch.

It was while they were eating, relaxing on a shelf of land next to a small lake in a bowl a few hundred feet beneath the summit, that Roosevelt spied a man coming out of the woods on the trail from below. It was immediately obvious that he was no casual hiker; he was looking for them—in particular, for the vice president. "I felt at once that he had bad news," Roosevelt recalled later.

He did. "The President's condition has changed for the worse" read the telegram; it was signed by George Cortelyou, McKinley's personal secretary.

Roosevelt and the others stuffed the remains of their meal back into their rucksacks and immediately set out for Tahawus. Though downhill, the route was muddy and slippery from all the rain, and it was nearly six o'clock before they reached the lodge. Roosevelt asked if there was any further news; on learning that there was not, he changed into dry clothes and sat down to dinner.

By nine o'clock nothing further had been heard. He wondered what to do. Assuming that if the president's condition were really grave, there would have been a follow-up message, he prepared for bed. "I'm not going to go unless I'm really needed," he told Edith. "I've been there once and that shows how I feel. But I will not go to stand beside those people who are suffering and anxious."

Within two hours, however, a fresh report arrived that broke his sleep and changed his mind. The president was slipping fast; the end might come at any time.

Roosevelt threw on his clothes and called for a wagon to make the trip to the nearest railroad station. In the pitch night, the vice president set off through the forest with a single companion, the driver. Roosevelt must have reflected that it was a fortunate thing the driver had better vision than he did, and still more fortunate that the horses knew the steep, winding road. The travelers wore out one team, traded it for another, then repeated the process. By the time they reached North Creek, exhausted from lack of sleep and the nervous tension of the journey, the eastern sky was just starting to brighten above the mountains.

By that time, too, McKinley was dead. Roosevelt got the word from William Loeb, his secretary as vice president, who had arrived with a special train. Roosevelt clambered down from the wagon and climbed aboard the steaming train, which raced south to the main trunk line to Buffalo. Other traffic was shunted aside as Roosevelt's train hurtled west through the morning.

After receiving such details as Loeb had to convey—about how, unknown to the physicians until too late, infection had spread from the bullet wound throughout McKinley's abdominal cavity—Roosevelt spent most of the four-hundred-mile journey with his own thoughts. This time there was no question about propriety, none about appearances. The president was dead; the vice president had to pay the respects of the nation and demonstrate that whatever might befall any man, the government would continue to function.

He still had mixed feelings. To be president was a great honor—the highest to which any politician in America could aspire. But to achieve it this way materially diminished the luster. Far better to have won it in an open contest than by such default. He almost certainly reflected as well that sudden deaths seemed to have a habit of changing his life. What would his father have said on learning that his son was about to become president? What would Alice have thought?

The train reached Buffalo at 1:30 that afternoon. From the station he was driven to the house where McKinley's body lay. He stood silent beside the deceased for a moment; he offered condolences to the distraught widow.

Then he joined those members of McKinley's cabinet who had arrived in Buffalo. In their presence and that of some representatives of the press and a few others, he took the oath of office from a local judge and became the twenty-sixth president of the United States.

CHAPTER SIXTEEN

Suddenly in the Saddle
1901

If Roosevelt hadn't been hearing for three years that he ought to be president, he might have been overwhelmed or at least humbled by the responsibilities that befell him on September 14, 1901. But the hurrahs that had greeted him on his return from Cuba in 1898, at the Republican convention in 1900, on his campaign swings later that year, and on his journeys out west had prompted no little mental rehearsing of how he would bear the burdens of the nation's highest office. Moreover, since the time of his appointment as assistant navy secretary, he had been measuring McKinley, and on each visit to the White House he compared his own shadow to that cast by his boss. Roosevelt would have given McKinley the nod for political shrewdness—not least for the way he had turned the enthusiasm for Roosevelt to his own benefit and then turned Roosevelt out to pasture. But Roosevelt at this stage of his career respected shrewdness in a politician about the way a policeman (himself five years earlier, for instance) admires cleverness in a thief, and he certainly didn't feel himself deficient for coming up short in that category. An upstanding character mattered far more, and he judged himself a veritable obelisk next to McKinley's eclair.

Nor did it hurt Roosevelt's self-confidence as chief-executive-by-chance that at the outset of the twentieth century the office of the president was but a suggestion of what it would become during the next several decades. Congressional control had slipped somewhat since the legislature had placed Andrew Johnson under White House arrest, but the center of American political gravity was still well toward the eastern end of Pennsylvania Avenue. Although the emer-

gence of the United States as a world power carried the possibility of
greater executive control, McKinley had scarcely begun to exploit that
possibility. It remained for an incumbent of greater energy and imagination to make the presidency what it would become.

Roosevelt didn't judge McKinley a hard act to follow. "About the
President, I think I had better not put down on paper what I should
gladly tell you if we were talking together," Roosevelt had confided—
or not confided—to Bill Sewall in the spring of 1900. And though his
opinion of McKinley's cleverness had risen since then, Roosevelt's
overall estimate of the late president's character and capacity had not.

Of course, McKinley would have been even easier to follow in 1904
after a Roosevelt victory at the polls; but as he usually did, Roosevelt
accepted what fate threw in his path and prepared to make the most
of it. "It is a dreadful thing to come into the Presidency this way," he
told Lodge. "But it would be a far worse thing to be morbid about it.
Here is the task, and I have got to do it to the best of my ability; and
that is all there is about it."

Actually, the more he thought about it, the more Roosevelt realized
that his hadn't been such an unpromising path to the White House
after all. To be sure, he felt obliged to promise continuity; the people
had elected McKinley, not him, and the people deserved to have their
wishes respected. Accordingly, in almost the same breath as his oath
of office he had declared his intention "to continue absolutely unbroken the policy of President McKinley." On the other hand, he entered
the White House with fewer outstanding promissory notes than most
occupants. Any successful race for president entails the coordination
of the efforts of many people, and these people expect to be compensated in one form or another. Roosevelt assumed the presidency without having had to run for it and consequently without having had to
give explicit or implicit promises.

Moreover, Roosevelt at this time judged that the principal public
interest consisted in sound, honest, efficient leadership rather than any
specific policies. Although he wouldn't have put it quite so, he
believed in government of men rather than government of laws. If the
men were good, then good laws would follow; but if the men were
bad, the best laws on earth couldn't make them good. So even while
pledging continuity with McKinley's policies, Roosevelt reserved the
right to interpret and modify those policies in accord with his own

personal judgment of the demands of national honor and well-being.

Roosevelt didn't worry excessively about whether he was the perfect person for the presidency, any more than he had worried analogously at other critical moments in his life. As he told Lodge, the fact of the matter was that he now *was* president, and the only thing to do was get on with it.

Yet if he had been inclined to dwell on such subjects, he might reasonably have concluded that his preparation for the presidency was no worse than that of any but a few of his predecessors (the Adamses, for example) and better than that of most (including Lincoln). He had read more than any save possibly Jefferson and was broadly traveled both in the United States and overseas. He was as familiar with the West as with the East. A native northerner, he was by birth half a southerner. He understood local and state politics, from Manhattan's Mulberry Street to the governor's house in Albany. He knew the bosses and—more important—they knew him. He knew national politics, both from holding office in Washington under Republicans and Democrats and from frequent campaign tours across the land. He knew international affairs about as well as anyone other than a practicing diplomat (and even here got the benefit of friends such as Spring Rice and Speck von Sternberg, not to mention John Hay, who *were* diplomats); solid study and deep thought underpinned the "large policy" he had championed for a decade and that the nation had lately embraced.

All this suited Roosevelt for the responsibilities that tumbled down upon him in September 1901; yet there was something else that was still more important. While no man had ever made it to the White House without a taste for power, few ever relished that dish more than Roosevelt. Henry Adams considered Roosevelt a force of nature— "pure act." Adams, being pure thought, may not have been best qualified to speak on this subject, but his remark did capture how Roosevelt often appeared to Washington old-timers (the "cave dwellers," Alice called them). The capital was acclimated to political weather that changed as slowly and predictably as the prevailing patterns of the mid-Atlantic coast; Roosevelt blew in like a tornado off the Great Plains.

Cautious people weigh both sides of every issue, frequently finding as many reasons for leaving the status quo alone as for altering it;

Roosevelt cut through such intellectual inanition. His temperament cried out for bold thrusts and daring dashes, and his mind accommodated his temperament. When he spied a wrong, he sprang into action, rarely pausing to think that in this imperfect world, precipitate measures might merely replace the old evil with a new one.

Roosevelt held the romantic view that wrongs exist to be righted. He was sophisticated enough to recognize that, in a modern society at least, evil was not simply the deliberate work of bad men but of banal and pernicious institutional arrangements as well. Yet even so, he was naive enough to believe that for each of society's ills there was a solution. Intelligence could find that solution, and courage could effect it.

Courage combined with intelligence: For Roosevelt this was the formula for leadership. And the presidency afforded opportunities to exercise leadership in a way not given to other officeholders. The president possessed powers unrivaled elsewhere in American politics—or at least he did if the officeholder seized the opportunities the office held out to him. Roosevelt seized them more decisively than any president since Lincoln and any peacetime president since Jackson. Indeed, he developed what he called the "Lincoln-Jackson" philosophy of presidential power (and which he opposed to the "Buchanan-Taft" philosophy, so named subsequent to his falling out with Taft). Roosevelt refused to be deterred from some desirable action by the failure of the framers of the Constitution to sanction such action. "I declined to adopt the view that what was imperatively necessary for the nation could not be done by the President unless he could find some specific authorization to do it." Rather, the burden was on the framers or their heirs to stop him. "My belief was that it was not only his right but his duty to do anything that the needs of the nation demanded unless such action was forbidden by the Constitution or by the laws." This had the effect of inverting the Constitution, but Roosevelt never had any trouble reading upside down. "Under this interpretation of executive power," he admitted, with the satisfied warmth that came from plowing new political ground, "I did and caused to be done many things not previously done by the President and the heads of the departments. I did not usurp power, but I did greatly broaden the use of executive power. In other words, I acted for the public welfare, I acted for the common well-being of all our people, whenever and in whatever manner was necessary, unless prevented by direct constitutional or legislative prohibition."

In still other words, he had the time of his life. McKinley was hardly cold under the sod of Canton before Roosevelt was reveling in his new responsibilities. "I get real enjoyment out of the work," he said, "for I like work, and this is of course one of the three or four offices in the world best worth while filling."

II

Yet even Roosevelt knew enough not to start revising the Constitution right away. The current economic recovery was a McKinley recovery, and the stock market shuddered at McKinley's demise. The new president did what he could to reassure investors; as he told journalist friend Hermann Kohlsaat, "I don't care a damn about stocks and bonds, but I don't want to see them go down the first day I am President!" (Or so Kohlsaat recollected. While none of Roosevelt's intimates would have disputed the sentiment ascribed to him, many would have sworn he never uttered the word "damn." "I don't care a rap" was the way he usually indicated energetic indifference.) It was to soothe the speculators as much as anyone else that Roosevelt vowed to follow McKinley's policies. He announced that McKinley's cabinet would stay on. In nearly all cases he carried through appointments put in motion by McKinley but not yet consummated. On other appointments he took visible pains to consult with Mark Hanna, Tom Platt, Matt Quay, and other party headmen. He had dinner with railroader James J. Hill and lunch with the secretary of the New York merchants' association.

He also had dinner with Booker T. Washington—an engagement that quickly drove home to Roosevelt the difference between the presidency and every other office in the land. The famous African-American educator had been a national figure since the 1895 Cotton States Exhibition in Atlanta, at which he had proposed an implicit compromise on the issue of race relations in America. Blacks, Washington declared, would drop their insistence on immediate political equality if whites would support black educational and economic advancement. Although the "Atlanta compromise" eventually evoked opposition from members of what sociologist and outspoken Washington critic W. E. B. Du Bois called the "talented tenth" of the African-American community, it had enormous appeal for many whites. At a time when Jim Crow laws were sweeping the South and undoing the work of Reconstruction, Washington's message assuaged the consciences of those whites troubled at the country's retreat from the Fourteenth and Fifteenth amendments—not to mention the Declaration of Independence. The national press lionized Washington; he was held up as the archetype of the modern, sensible black man.

Washington was sensible, all right; he was also a master political operator. Recognizing that his message would appeal particularly to Roosevelt, a self-improver after his own heart, Washington invited the then vice president to visit his showcase Tuskegee Institute on a swing through the South in the autumn of 1901. Washington could spot an up-and-comer when he saw one, and he recognized that Roosevelt would fall in love with Tuskegee, where self-help was preached as gospel and where students and faculty combined strenuous outdoor labor with their intellectual endeavors. Roosevelt was finalizing plans for his visit when the McKinley assassination canceled them. But rather than miss seeing Washington altogether, Roosevelt invited him to call at the White House whenever he was in town.

Washington didn't have to be asked twice. Within weeks he was in the capital, and he duly received a request to join the president for dinner at the White House. On October 16, Roosevelt, Washington, and a few others sat down together. The discussion involved politics as well as education; Roosevelt sought Washington's advice regarding certain federal appointments that would have to be made in the South. Roosevelt aimed to weaken the Democratic stranglehold on the South. This, however, was a long-term project; more immediately and realistically he hoped to wean the southern wing of the Republican Party from its close attachment to Mark Hanna and the Ohio boss's allies. Booker Washington might be useful in this endeavor.

The evening confirmed Roosevelt's favorable opinion of Washington, but it also provoked a riot of protest across Dixie. "White men of the South," screamed the New Orleans *Times-Democrat,* "how do you like it? . . . White women of the South, how do YOU like it?" The Richmond *Times* read the darkest motives into Roosevelt's dinner invitation. "It means that the President is willing that negroes shall mingle freely with whites in the social circle—that white women may receive attentions from negro men; it means that there is no racial reason in his opinion why whites and blacks may not marry and intermarry, why the Anglo-Saxon may not mix negro blood with his blood." The Raleigh *Post* was moved to verse:

> Booker Washington holds the boards—
> The President dines a nigger.
> Precedents are cast aside—
> Put aside with vigor;
> Black and white sit side by side,
> As Roosevelt dines a nigger.

The Memphis *Scimitar* declared the president's action simply "the most damnable outrage ever perpetrated by any citizen of the United States."

Roosevelt was flabbergasted at the response. "No one could possibly be as astonished as I was," he told a British friend. Southern leaders were the very ones who had promoted Booker Washington as a spokesman for his race; now they were excoriating the president for acknowledging the wisdom of their judgment. With typical indignation Roosevelt lashed out—albeit privately—at his critics and vowed not to be intimidated. "The idiot or vicious Bourbon element of the South," he said, "is crazy because I have had Booker T. Washington to dine. I shall have him to dine just as often as I please."

In fact, however, Roosevelt did *not* have Washington to dine again. On the contrary, he attempted to minimize the importance of the visit, claiming that it was merely a spontaneous gesture of hospitality with no prior motives, and on at least one later occasion he said that the meal in question was lunch rather than dinner. In his disclaimers Roosevelt intended no disrespect to Washington—to whom he expressed his "melancholy" regarding the uproar the dinner had raised. A thinner-skinned man than Washington might have taken offense at Roosevelt's squirming, but Washington would never have reached the heights he attained if he had had a thin skin or if he hadn't understood the president's political purpose in inviting him to the White House. The southern editorialists also understood Roosevelt's partisan goal; while their response was couched in the language of race, it had an equally political objective: to prevent the president from tampering with the way things—political things in particular— were in the South. To this end, experience had shown that it was far more effective to cry "Nigger!" than "Republican."

Roosevelt was the person who hadn't understood the situation. "I never thought one way or the other about it, so far as outside effect was concerned," he said privately. Now, seeing that a public embrace of Washington would be counterproductive as an instrument for winning the South to his side, he quietly dropped the Tuskegee head from the White House dinner list and determined to avoid similar mistakes.

III

Roosevelt was much more careful in cultivating good relations with the Republican Capitol Hill contingent. Throughout the autumn of 1901 he held court in the White House for Republican members of Congress, especially such stalwarts of the Senate as Orville Platt of Connecticut, Nelson Aldrich of Rhode Island, John Spooner of Wisconsin, and William Allison of Iowa. With the Republicans in the majority in the upper house, this foursome largely controlled the operation of that body. Roosevelt hardly agreed with everything they stood for, nor did they always agree among themselves, but as he had with Tom Platt, he exercised great care to maintain cordial relations. "I suppose it is hardly necessary," he told Spooner in a typical note, "for me to say that during the coming three years I hope to keep in closest touch with you and to profit by your advice in the future as I have profited by it in the past." After consulting with Aldrich regarding the tariff, Roosevelt wrote, "Hearty thanks for your letter. I will follow exactly the course outlined therein and in my conversation with you." To Orville Platt, with whom he had discussed legislation to open corporations to public scrutiny, he said, "I shall get you together with the Attorney General as soon as you come on here to see if we can devise such a law."

The centerpiece of Roosevelt's consultation with Republican leaders during his first two months in office was the annual message he

delivered to Congress at the beginning of December. Other presidents—
less driven than Roosevelt, less self-confident, or simply less literary—
typically farmed out their annual messages to cabinet secretaries and
other interested persons; the results were predictably patchwork.
Roosevelt insisted on writing his own message. Yet he appreciated the
need to bring others in on the job. He recognized that there were
aspects of the federal government he hadn't mastered, and he didn't
wish to embarrass himself the first time he delivered a major message
as president.

Equally to the point, he understood that whatever he might say
would be simply so much wind without the backing of influential legislators. Consequently, he solicited the opinions of Spooner, Aldrich,
Allison, Oliver Platt, and others, and he encouraged them to critique
early drafts of sections touching issues close to their hearts. He wanted
them to feel responsible for the message and therefore for the success
of the program it outlined. To enhance their feeling of responsibility
he treated them almost as co-conspirators, keeping the consultations
as closely guarded as possible. He asked George Hoar for reactions
but apologized that he couldn't send the senator the draft speech to
examine in advance of their meeting. Copies of the speech might fall
into the wrong hands, Roosevelt intimated. "I have been careful not
to trust them out of my possession."

Roosevelt also consulted, of course, with key cabinet members such
as John Hay and Elihu Root. Secretary of State Hay was nearing completion of four decades in public life; McKinley's assassination
brought a painful reminder of the murder of Lincoln, the first president he had served. Hay also remembered the friendship of the first
Theodore Roosevelt, the new president's father, during the dark days
of the Civil War. Hay had one of the sharper tongues in Washington,
but his sardonic sense of humor now yielded to the sentimentality his
friends always knew lay beneath it. "If the Presidency had come to
you in any other way," he wrote Roosevelt the day after McKinley's
death, "no one would have congratulated you with better heart than I.
My sincere affection and esteem for you, my old-time love for your
father—Would he could have lived to see you where you are!—would
have been deeply gratified." Hay went on to say that even from his
sorrow and dismay he could still congratulate the new president.
"With your youth, your ability, your health and strength, the courage

God has given you to do right, there are no bounds to the good you can accomplish for your country and the name you will leave in its annals." Estimating that his official life was near an end, with his natural life not likely to last much longer, he concluded, "And so, in the dawn of what I am sure will be a great and splendid future, I venture to give you the heartfelt benediction of the past."

Root was a rather different sort than Hay. The secretary of war had a sense of humor even more wicked than Hay's, and even more than Hay he was happy to share his humor with the president, not least on those occasions when the joke was on Roosevelt. Edith thought Root was good for her husband, for among all Roosevelt's advisers Root was the one readiest to fight him when he was wrong. As for Roosevelt himself, he counted Root his most capable adviser, with the occasional exception of Will Taft.

Closer than either Hay or Root was Lodge. At the time of McKinley's assassination, Lodge was in France; upon his October return he went immediately to the White House, where he shared Roosevelt's new home, just as Roosevelt had often shared Lodge's home. Lodge offered constructive criticism of Roosevelt's proposed message to Congress, but for the most part he provided support and encouragement. "After careful reflection on all that has happened in these momentous weeks," he said a month after Roosevelt's accession, "I cannot see that you have made a single mistake. You have done admirably, splendidly." Following the flap over Booker Washington, Lodge stuck loyally by his friend. Writing from Massachusetts he reported, "Needless to say everyone here, literally everyone, is with you heart and soul on the Booker Washington matter. Needless for me to say how utterly right I think you are."

IV

Roosevelt didn't really need the encouragement. Once he got something in his head as the right thing to do, he rarely questioned it. But it didn't hurt to have Lodge cheering him on while he applied the final corrections to his annual message, for it was the most ambitious political statement he had ever made and one of the most ambitious by any American president. That its author occupied the White House by accident rather than election and that he had been there less than three months rendered the message all the more audacious.

It was a long statement, some twenty thousand words. (Mercifully, in those days presidents didn't deliver them orally.) Roosevelt commenced with the expected eulogy of McKinley, which led into an excoriation of anarchism and a call for stronger measures against this most dangerous form of political heresy. "Anarchy is a crime against the whole human race," Roosevelt asserted, "and all mankind should band against the anarchist." Those who thought to subvert democracy had better be warned, for the citizens of the United States would never stand for such nihilistic nonsense. "The American people are slow to wrath, but when their wrath is once kindled it burns like a consuming flame."

Doubtless by design, Roosevelt segued from this sentence to a long passage dealing with the need for greater government control of corporations. Since he had first challenged Jay Gould, Roosevelt had been skeptical, to say the least, that the interests of the corporate class were always those of the community as a whole. The reluctance of business leaders to embrace intervention in Cuba had convinced him that the moguls of finance and manufacturing would place profits before patriotism. The intimate ties between the trusts and the party bosses doubled his suspicions of both; these suspicions were borne out by the fight over the New York franchise tax and by the trusts' determination to have him placed on the shelf of the vice presidency.

Roosevelt had no desire to derange the stock market or trigger a run on the banks, so he couched his anticorporate message in reassuringly conservative language. "The captains of industry who have driven the railway systems across this continent, who have built up our commerce, who have developed our manufactures, have on the whole done great good to our people." Without them America never would have achieved the material prosperity of which it was justly proud. Moreover, these men could best do their wealth-making work unhampered by onerous regulation. "The mechanism of modern business is so delicate that extreme care must be taken not to interfere with it in a spirit of rashness or ignorance."

All the same, corporations must recognize their responsibility not merely to their shareholders but to the community at large. When they failed to do so on their own—as they often did fail—they must be made to mend their ways. "Corporations engaged in interstate commerce should be regulated if they are found to exercise a license working to the public injury. It should be as much the aim of those who seek for social betterment to rid the business world of crimes of cunning as to rid the entire body politic of crimes of violence." After all, it was the public, acting through laws regarding incorporation, that allowed the big businesses the opportunity to conduct their activities. "Great corporations exist only because they are created and safeguarded by our institutions; and it is therefore our right and our duty to see that they work in harmony with these institutions."

Having given the capitalists cause for alarm by promising regulation, Roosevelt gave them more by embracing organized labor. "With the sole exception of the farming interest," he said, "no one matter is of such vital moment to our whole people as the welfare of the wage-workers." Wage-workers must be protected: from overweening corporations by government regulation, from cheap imports by protective tariffs, from unfair competition by curbs on immigration. Women and children of the working class must be further safeguarded by special legislation forbidding excessive hours or unhealthy conditions. While the workers' betterment depended primarily on their own efforts as individuals, in the modern era it also required collective action. "Very great good has been and will be accomplished by associations or unions of wage-workers, when managed with forethought, and when they combine insistence upon their own rights with law-abiding respect for the rights of others." Government should encourage such responsible union activities.

Roosevelt didn't leave the business classes totally bereft. He endorsed the gold standard and the protective tariff—although he allowed that carefully crafted reciprocity treaties might lower the tariff with particular countries. He called for economy in government spending, to be accompanied by cuts in taxes.

But then he delivered more bad news—bad, that is, to advocates of a laissez-faire status quo. Railroads must be regulated. "The railway is a public servant. Its rates should be just to and open to all shippers alike." The banking system ought to be more carefully scrutinized.

The natural resources of the nation must be managed wisely and with care for future generations. Forest reserves ought to be expanded and placed under scientific management. The government should undertake flood control and irrigation projects. "Great storage works are necessary to equalize the flow of streams and to save the flood waters. Their construction has been conclusively shown to be an undertaking too vast for private effort."

Roosevelt's business-oriented auditors must have been relieved when he finally got to the part of his message treating foreign affairs, where he could do them less damage. He reiterated the essential righteousness of acquiring the Philippines, Puerto Rico, and Hawaii. Acknowledging the present difficulties with the Filipinos, he promised to stay the course. "Our earnest effort is to help these people upward along the stony and difficult path that leads to self-government." But self-government would not come overnight, nor would it be achieved by simply turning the Filipinos loose. "To leave the islands at this time would mean that they would fall into a welter of murderous anarchy. Such desertion of duty on our part would be a crime against humanity."

A similar sense of responsibility must guide American foreign policy in other areas. The United States must defend and strengthen the Monroe Doctrine, making certain and unchallengeable the American position in the Western Hemisphere against European interlopers. To this end, among others, the United States must continue to build up its navy. The current complement of nine battleships should be enlarged to seventeen by the timely completion of work under way and projected. The United States must arrange to construct a canal across Central America. "It is one of those great works which only a great nation can undertake with prospects of success, and which when done are not only permanent assets in the nation's material interests, but standing monuments to its constructive ability."

V

"I have never seen an annual Message followed with so much interest and attention in the Senate," Lodge reported, "and I am told it was even more marked in the House." Lodge could be expected to cheer his friend's maiden effort; but, indeed, the whole country was attentive, wanting to hear what this untested chief executive had to say.

The reaction was remarkably restrained. Evidently many conservatives had expected the "madman" of Mark Hanna's nightmares to storm the presidency frothing and foaming, and were surprised that he didn't. The Chicago *Journal* drew "a deep breath of satisfaction" on behalf of its readers, while the New York *Evening Post* observed, with obvious relief, that "the 'Rough Rider' and 'the Jingo,' the impetuous youth of a year ago, has disappeared." Finley Peter Dunne read ambivalence into Roosevelt's remarks; his Mr. Dooley paraphrased the president on the trusts: "On wan hand I wud stamp thim undher fut; on th' other hand not so fast." Yet the more skeptical remained leery: The Hartford *Courant* warned that federal control of the sort the president promised "is a few steps ahead of government ownership, and is in the same path."

Whatever readers made of the portents of Roosevelt's message, there was no mistaking its tone. This wasn't McKinley speaking; this was someone new, someone self-confidently assertive, someone with a far grander sense of the public purpose than anyone who had ever held the presidency. In this opening address Roosevelt set forth the themes that would inform his seven and a half years in office; the theme that was most obvious was his willingness—enthusiasm, rather—to grasp the power at his disposal and put it to use on behalf of the people.

VI

Of course, Roosevelt would have attracted attention even without firing a shot across the bow of the capitalist status quo. Not since Grant had the White House been occupied by a real war hero, and never by a man so young and vigorous—and prolific. Theodore and Edith allowed Mrs. McKinley all the time she needed to gather her spirits and her belongings and vacate the mansion, and then they and the children swept in and filled the place with characteristic Rooseveltian energy. The younger children found their new home particularly fascinating. It had all kinds of nooks and crannies that cried out for exploring. From the attic to the basement and all about the grounds they crawled and jumped and ran and swung and skated and bicycled. Their mother had grown used to ignoring everything but their most egregious boisterousness; only when they threatened dire harm to themselves or the premises did she intervene—and then as much to reprimand her husband, frequently the abettor of such escapades, as to chasten the young ones. "I play with the children almost every night," Roosevelt recorded, "and some child is invariably fearfully damaged in the play; but this does not seem to affect the ardor of their enjoyment."

The house would have been more crowded still had Ted not spent most of his time away at school. For his father, adjusting to the presidency came easily compared to coping with his son's adolescence. Like innumerable other fathers—and more than many of them—Roosevelt was torn between protectiveness toward his son and encouragement of manly activities and traits. He was pleased when Ted tried out for the football team at Groton but pained at the logical outcome of that adventure. "Blessed Ted," he wrote, "I was very sorry to learn that you had broken your collarbone; but I am glad you played right through the game, and that you seem to have minded it so little."

Yet the more he thought about it, the larger his misgivings loomed. "Pray do not think me grown timid in my old age until you read this note through," he wrote to the Groton headmaster, Endicott Peabody. "Ted would have a fit if he knew I were writing it." Roosevelt expressed concern that his boy was getting beaten up trying to play football. "In addition to Ted's collarbone, the dentist tells me that he has killed one front tooth in football, and that tooth will get black. Now I don't care a rap for either accident in itself; but Ted is only fourteen and I am afraid that if he goes on like this he will get battered out before he can play college." Roosevelt said he had it on the authority of both a Harvard player and Yale's quarterback that Ted was in over his weight. The latter expert deemed this especially unfortunate. "He thought it was a pity a young boy should get so battered up, if it came from playing larger ones, as it might interfere with other playing later." Roosevelt requested the headmaster to look into the matter.

Needless to say, Edith was just as concerned over Ted's health as

Theodore was; almost certainly she was partly responsible for her husband's inquiry into the nature of the football program at Groton. In other respects, however, her situation grew much more satisfactory during the autumn of 1901. She found the role of First Lady much preferable than that of Second Lady. Finances, so often the bane of her existence, were suddenly no problem. Theodore made fifty thousand dollars a year as president, far more than he had ever made before (and the equivalent of perhaps half a million dollars in the 1990s). Though expenses and entertainment had to come out of this amount, Edith had long since learned to manage money wisely. She presided over teas and receptions—modest at first, out of respect for the late president, but more elegant with the passing months.

The government *did* pay to renovate the Executive Mansion, which Roosevelt decreed should henceforth officially (as on stationery, press releases, and the like) be called by its traditional unofficial name, the White House. The latter he considered less stuffy and more in keeping with the democratic image he intended to convey of the presidency and of himself as president. While Roosevelt ordered the name change, Edith ordered the curtains, the carpets, and all the other items and alterations that made the gloomy old place lighter and more livable. In her own and more literal way, she contributed to her husband's project of adapting the White House to the twentieth century.

Not surprisingly in view of the circumstances of Roosevelt's elevation, Edith feared for her husband's safety. She had never quite gotten used to the dangers he deliberately courted—from grizzly bears to Spanish bullets—but the threat of assassination was something new and especially dreadful. If one malcontent had thought to bend history by murdering the inoffensive McKinley, wouldn't her more controversial husband be an even likelier target? "The horror of it hangs over me," she confessed to her sister, "and I am never without fear for Theodore." But the Secret Service, badly embarrassed by the McKinley shooting, was taking the most stringent precautions, and agents shadowed the president everywhere. Without being fatalistic, Edith placed her husband's ultimate safety in God's hands. "I try and comfort myself with the line of the old hymn, *Brought safely by His hand thus far, why should we now give place to fear?*" (It is unclear how much additional comfort Edith derived from her husband's practice of carrying a pistol. "If a man is willing to give his life for mine,"

Roosevelt remarked, "there is no way that he can be prevented from making the attempt. But such a man must be quicker than I am in the use of his gun.")

Her assassination worries apart, life in the White House suited Edith well. Friends and visitors remarked the dignity and dispatch with which she ran the place. She accomplished one of her husband's promised efficiencies when she eliminated the post of housekeeper; she assumed the task herself. If occasional grumbles that she ran too tight a ship were heard from friends and even family members who were politely but firmly made to know that appointments would be most appreciated, none could deny that the pages of the social calendar of the White House had never turned so smoothly.

Roosevelt valued his wife's virtues more all the time. "Edith is too sweet and pretty and dignified as mistress of the White House, and very happy with it," he told a mutual friend. She had never looked better, as he explained to John Hay. "She is forty, and I do not think I deceive myself when I say that she neither looks nor acts nor feels as if she was thirty." To their eldest son he similarly boasted of Edith; describing her on the afternoon horse rides they regularly took together, Roosevelt declared that she looked "so young and pretty." He added, "I heard the other day that someone had said 'she must be his daughter, for she is only a girl.'"

All his life Roosevelt had managed to find satisfaction and pleasure in even unpropitious circumstances. Now fortune was truly smiling, and he couldn't help smiling back. "It is no easy job to be President," he confided to Ted after a month in office. "But I am thoroughly enjoying it and I think so far I have done pretty well."

CHAPTER SEVENTEEN

Hand to Hand with the Coal Kings
1902

If the big story of American politics in 1901 had been the ascent of Theodore Roosevelt to the presidency, the big story of American business was the creation of the United States Steel Corporation. The steel trust—the first American corporation capitalized at over one billion dollars—represented a marriage of the greatest names in American industry and finance: Andrew Carnegie, the strongman of steel, and John D. Rockefeller, the oil magnate whose holdings had long since spilled across the natural resources line into iron. J. P. Morgan, the banking Croesus, officiated; his blessing made the match possible.

The steel trust was the largest and most visible of the corporate combinations that increasingly controlled American economic life. Rockefeller's Standard Oil overspread a sophisticated system that brought petroleum out of the ground and refined it into kerosene for the lamps of that large majority not yet connected to the growing electrical grids, as well as into gasoline for the automobiles of that as yet very much smaller group that had traded horse power for horsepower. The American Sugar Refining Company had the country by the sweet tooth, while the hand of the National Biscuit Company was in cracker barrels from coast to coast. The leather trust shod America; the life insurance trust consoled survivors with cash; the concrete trust put the country on a firmer foundation than ever before.

In 1890 Congress had passed an antitrust act. But the Sherman Act, especially as it soon found its way into practice, struck many as less an honest attempt to corral corporations than a prophylactic against real regulation by the populist types who already were alarming the boardrooms of America. The Supreme Court reinforced this view by its decision in the 1895 E. C. Knight case, in which the court ruled that efforts by the Justice Department to break up the American Sugar Refining Company's monopoly were constitutionally unwarranted. Congress, the eight justices of the majority said, had the right to regulate commerce but not manufacturing. The sugar trust engaged in commerce only incidentally; therefore, it was beyond the reach of federal law.

From the perspective of the corporate consolidators, the Knight decision opened the door to a new wave of mergers leading up to the U.S. Steel combine in 1901. From the perspective of the Bryanites and others less convinced of the beneficence of big business, the Knight decision and its denouement confirmed their suspicion that the captains of industry had captured the courts and suborned them to the plutocrats' profit-mongering purposes. The populist defenders of democracy counted scores of trusts fastened on the backs of the honest working folk of America; though this was many more than actually existed, the spectral ones were perhaps no less significant than the real in rallying the radicals and energizing their efforts against the corporate-kindly status quo.

While Theodore Roosevelt despised and abhorred the Bryanites as anarchists, he had scarcely more respect for the trustmakers. His disrespect evinced at once scorn for their narrow money-grubbing, recently at the expense of the expansionist national interest abroad, and disgust at the stupidity that failed to see that each megamerger simply strengthened the forces of radicalism. The fact that the corporate types reciprocated Roosevelt's distrust and had worked against his political advancement simply added a personal element to the president's determination to bring them to account.

His annual message of December 1901 constituted his fair warning; in February 1902 he assumed the battle in earnest. In the third week of that month he had his attorney general, Philander Knox, announce that the government was initiating a suit to force the breakup of the Northern Securities Company, a recently created holding company that comprised the leading railroads of the northwestern quarter of the country. Northern Securities wasn't the largest of the trusts (it weighed in at about $400 million soaking wet, substantially less when the water was wrung out of the stock). Nor did it enjoy the same kind of national market share as several other trusts, including the sugar, steel, and oil combines. But it had some other factors working against it. It was new and consequently lacked the precedent-forming attributes of age that kept the Justice Department at arm's length from some of the other trusts; moreover, having been formed on Roosevelt's watch, it was his responsibility to deal with, in a way its predecessors were not. It engaged indisputably in interstate commerce and therefore fell undeniably under the purview of the Constitution's commerce clause. Last and perhaps least—but perhaps not—it exercised its monopoly powers against the common farmers and ranchers of that part of the country that had been Roosevelt's adopted home. Roosevelt knew firsthand the tribulations of small cattlemen in their unequal contest with the railroads; in attacking James Hill, J. P. Morgan, and the other principals of Northern Securities, Roosevelt possessed a peculiar credibility he would have lacked in a fight against Carnegie or Rockefeller. (He also possessed political allies: Governors of the affected states were already seeking legal redress against the railroad combination.)

Roosevelt prepared his assault in strictest secrecy. An obvious adviser would have been Root, a former corporate lawyer and possessor of probably the sharpest mind and certainly the strongest spirit of the cabinet secretaries. But it was precisely because of this that Roosevelt bypassed Root. Certain that the war secretary would oppose the Northern Securities suit, the president preferred not to have to deal with his dissent. Roosevelt knew Root well enough to realize that once the decision to prosecute was announced, he would support it or at least keep his mouth shut.

Roosevelt also wanted to minimize the possibility of news leaks. As he recalled from the days of his battle with Jay Gould, the railroad business was unusually susceptible to speculative bubbles and raids; if word got out that the Justice Department was planning to attack Northern Securities, the raiders might spring into action, with disruptive effects that could ripple across the entire financial and commercial system.

Consequently, the administration kept quiet through the close of trading on February 19, 1902. Then, while the brokers were balancing their books for the day and getting ready to go home, Attorney General Knox dropped his bombshell. The news sent the market skidding the next day, with the bears driven from their dens by the explosion quickly taking control of the exchange.

J. P. Morgan, the underwriter of the railroad combine, interpreted the president's action as a direct affront. Ever since his bailout of the Cleveland administration during a run on the U.S. treasury's gold supply in 1894, Morgan had considered finance a fourth branch of government, with himself as its head. He thought it discourteous, indeed impertinent, for the president—and an accidental, stripling president at that—to treat him and his interests so cavalierly.

Morgan shortly came calling at the White House. The great financier didn't complain so much about the president's judgment that the railroad holding company contravened the principles of antitrust, although he certainly thought Roosevelt wrong in such a judgment. But Morgan did object to what he conceived as the ungentlemanly manner in which the president had gone about delivering his judgment. "If we have done something wrong," he said to Roosevelt (as Roosevelt recollected later), "send your man to my man and they can fix it up."

"That can't be done," Roosevelt replied. To which Knox, a railroad lawyer by background and one who had a few misgivings of his own about the president's hammer-and-tongs approach, loyally appended, "We don't want to fix it up; we want to stop it."

"Are you going to attack my other interests?" demanded Morgan. "The steel trust and the others?"

"Certainly not," said Roosevelt, "unless we find out that in any case they have done something that we regard as wrong."

Upon Morgan's departure, Roosevelt turned to Knox and declared, "That is a most illuminating illustration of the Wall Street point of view. Mr. Morgan could not help regarding me as a big rival operator who either intended to ruin all his interests or else could be induced to come to an agreement to ruin none."

In fact, Roosevelt's comment was probably more revealing of Roosevelt than of Morgan. Morgan may or may not have interpreted the battle over the trusts in personal terms, but Roosevelt certainly did. Roosevelt didn't object to trusts in principle. As he acknowledged in his first annual message and on numerous occasions afterward, the big corporations made possible the spectacular economic growth that underlay both prosperity at home and respect abroad. Even if he hadn't disliked Thomas Jefferson for political reasons, Roosevelt would have had scant sympathy for the Jeffersonian vision of a nation of farmers inoffensively minding their crops. Roosevelt liked farmers well enough, but his romanticism was of a different sort—not pastoral but martial, old-fashioned in virtue but modern in technique.

In Roosevelt's view, certain trusts were bad not because they were trusts but because they were run by bad men with evil motives. Such combinations deserved and should expect to be chastened by government, and Roosevelt made it his goal to see that they were. He explained his philosophy afterward: "If a corporation were found seeking profit through injury or oppression of the community, by restricting production through trick or device, by plot or conspiracy against competitors, or by oppression of wage-workers, and then extorting high prices for the commodity it had made artificially scarce, it would be prevented from organizing if its nefarious purpose could be discovered in time, or pursued and suppressed by all the power of government whenever found in actual operation." On the other hand, corporations run by good men with commendable objectives would be encouraged. "Where a company is found seeking its profits through serving the community by stimulating production, lowering prices, or improving service, while scrupulously respecting the rights of others (including its rivals, its employees, its customers, and the general public), and strictly obeying the law, then no matter how large its capital, or how great the volume of its business, it would be encouraged to still more abundant production, or better service, by the fullest protection that the government could afford it."

Such was Roosevelt's long-range goal. At the beginning of 1902 he had yet to demonstrate that corporations were subject to any meaningful federal control at all. Roosevelt likened his job to that of the monarchs of the Middle Ages who spent their reigns subduing unruly nobles. Referring to "the reactionaries of the business world and their allies and instruments among politicians and newspaper editors," he later declared: "These men demanded for themselves an immunity from governmental control which, if granted, would have been as wicked and as foolish as immunity to the barons of the twelfth century." Many of these men were evil by intention. Others were evil inadvertently: well-meaning, perhaps, but blind. "They were as utterly unable as any mediaeval castle-owner to understand what the public interest really was." Well-attuned to history, Roosevelt readily granted that aristocracy had once played an important role. "But we had come to the stage where for our people what was needed was real democracy." He added, "Of all forms of tyranny the least attractive and the most vulgar is the tyranny of mere wealth, the tyranny of a plutocracy."

Toppling this tyranny was Roosevelt's purpose in prosecuting the Northern Securities case. Northern Securities wasn't the worst trust in America—although if given time it might have become a contender for that title; but Roosevelt realized he had to start somewhere, and the railroad giant appeared as good a place as any. If Roosevelt had simply been interested in reforming the railroad, he might reasonably have cut a deal with Morgan. But Morgan and the railroad represented a whole category of corporate wrongdoing, and Roosevelt was determined to make an example of them. To have granted quarter would have eviscerated his entire enterprise.

II

Roosevelt wasn't a lawyer, and he had nothing to do with the legal proceedings of the case that became *Northern Securities Co. v. United States* (when the railroad holding company answered the Justice Department's suit with one of its own). Filed in federal court in Minneapolis, the case wended its way toward the Supreme Court where, as all parties understood from the first, it would be finally decided.

Nor did Roosevelt make much of the case politically. Some critics were already charging him with disrespect toward the judiciary, claiming that the Knight decision of 1895 had settled the issue and that the president was insolent in reopening it. Roosevelt let the critics rail; in public he held to the elevated ground of presidential impartiality.

Behind the scenes he was more active. A seat on the Supreme Court came open with the announced retirement of Associate Justice Horace Gray; Roosevelt carefully considered how best to fill the vacancy. The most widely touted candidate was Oliver Wendell Holmes, Jr., chief justice of the Massachusetts supreme court (as Gray had been before him) and author of *The Common Law,* a pioneering work of modern jurisprudence. Roosevelt had no doubt of Holmes's general qualifications for the post. "He possesses the high character and the high reputation both of which should if possible attach to any man who is to go upon the highest court of the entire civilized world," the president told Lodge. Moreover, some of Holmes's decisions on the Massachusetts court had gone against the big railroad and other corporate interests; this stood in his favor with Roosevelt.

All the same, Roosevelt harbored doubts as to Holmes's political reliability. Roosevelt mused,

> In the ordinary and low sense which we attach to the words "partisan" and "politician," a judge of the Supreme Court should be neither. But in the higher sense, in the proper sense, he is not in my judgment fitted for the position unless he is a party man, a constructive statesman, constantly keeping in mind his adherence to the principles and policies under which this nation has been built up and in accordance with which it must go on; and keeping in mind also his relations with his fellow statesmen who in other branches of the government are striving in cooperation with him to advance the ends of government.

Roosevelt pointed to John Marshall as an example of the kind of jurist he had in mind. Marshall was one of Roosevelt's heroes. "He is distinctly among the greatest of the great," the president averred, "and no man, save Washington and Lincoln, alone, deserves heartier homage from us." The greatness of the Federalist chief justice, like that of Washington and Lincoln, consisted in his acceptance of the duties of "a statesman of the national type." The counterpoint to Marshall and the exception that proved the rule of the judicial statesman's responsibilities was Marshall's successor, Roger Taney. "Taney was a curse to our national life because he belonged to the wrong party and faithfully carried out the criminal and foolish views of the party which stood for such a construction of the Constitution as would have rendered it impossible even to preserve the national life."

Roosevelt neglected to mention that Marshall spent most of his judicial career in opposition to the governing party and philosophy; in seeking a Supreme Court nominee, Roosevelt wasn't looking for

Marshall's independence of mind but rather his loyalty to the politics of the party that chose him. Roosevelt deemed such loyalty critical at this precise moment of American history. The court was narrowly balanced between those justices who, in upholding forward-looking policies, had rendered "a great service to mankind and to this nation" and a reactionary clique that aimed to hamper "well-nigh hopelessly" the American people in their efforts to do "efficient and honorable work for the national welfare." Roosevelt didn't doubt the upright character of the reactionary justices. "But this no more excuses them than the same conditions excused the various upright and honorable men who took part in the wicked folly of secession in 1860 and 1861."

Roosevelt would frequently liken himself to Lincoln; in the presidential self-image he was creating, he aimed high. Lincoln hadn't allowed constitutional scruples to prevent the vigorous exercise of executive authority; neither would Roosevelt. Lincoln had packed the court with cooperative justices; Roosevelt would, too, if he had his way.

This was precisely the issue as Roosevelt weighed Holmes's nomination. The Massachusetts justice had given a speech in which he expressed what appeared to Roosevelt to be insufficient appreciation for Marshall's virtues. "It may seem to be," Roosevelt told Lodge, "but it is not really, a small matter that his speech on Marshall should be unworthy of the subject, and above all should show a total incapacity to grasp what Marshall did." This lapse on Holmes's part was causing Roosevelt some qualms about his reliability. "I should like to know that Judge Holmes was in entire sympathy with our views." Justice Gray had been a strong voice for progressive government action. "I should hold myself as guilty of an irreparable wrong to the nation if I should put in his place any man who was not absolutely sane and sound on the great national policies for which we stand in public life."

Roosevelt made inquiries about Holmes during the next few weeks. What he turned up revealed that even if Holmes was a bit mushy on Marshall, he was a better bet than anyone else in Massachusetts—and for political reasons Roosevelt wanted Gray's seat on the court to stay with a Bay Stater. In addition, Roosevelt found Holmes personally charming. He was witty and well-read, and as able a conversationalist as his father, whom Roosevelt had long admired.

The president decided to go ahead with the nomination. When it was received with broad public acclaim, he wrote Holmes a congratulatory letter. "Pettigrew said that South Carolina was too small for an independent republic and too large for a lunatic asylum. The Senate is not too large for a lunatic asylum, and if there is any opposition whatever to your confirmation, I shall certainly feel that it fulfills all the conditions of one."

III

The favorable response to the Holmes nomination erased most of Roosevelt's misgivings about the judge; it also counterbalanced the beating he was taking in conservative circles for his attack on Northern Securities. Roosevelt found a fellow sufferer of regular Republican opprobrium in Philander Knox, who was even more reviled in the boardrooms than the president, being an apostate rather than a mere heretic. The president chuckled at their common unpopularity; in May he sent the attorney general a note introducing a friend who happened to write for the London *Times*. "I want him to have a talk with you because in New York he lives at the Metropolitan Club and meets largely gentlemen who since the merger suit cross themselves at the mention of our names." Even as it elicited his humor, the criticism confirmed Roosevelt in his estimate of his own righteousness. "I am sorry that the financial men should be tempted to criticise me but I have never been more certain of anything than that I was right in taking the actions which they criticised." These critics were too blinkered to recognize that he was actually doing them a favor by demonstrating that democracy could deal with the excesses of capitalism. "It is above all to the interests of the men of great wealth that the people at large should understand that they also have to obey the law."

Controversy had never been a stranger to Roosevelt, and it certainly wasn't now. The anti-antitrust outrage was his own doing; other brouhahas were bequests from his predecessors. The fallout from the Spanish war continued to rain down on the political landscape, soaking the just and unjust alike. In the latter category, in Roosevelt's opinion, was the great crybaby of the conflict, General

Nelson Miles ("merely a brave peacock," he had called Miles at the time). For reasons best known to himself, Miles had felt obliged to publicly challenge the judgment of a naval board of inquiry in an essentially silly dispute over who had done what during the battle of Santiago Bay in July 1898. War Secretary Root, with Roosevelt's approval, had reprimanded the general for his breach of the code of military etiquette.

The reprimand injured the general's sensitive feelings, and he marched straight to the White House to let his former subordinate, the colonel of volunteers, know how he felt. Roosevelt was occupied when Miles arrived; he asked the general to wait in the cabinet room. But Miles wouldn't be put off. He grew loud and, Roosevelt thought, rude. The president thereupon told the general what he thought of his impulsive and unacceptable behavior. This incensed Miles further, and he left in a huff. Shortly thereafter his version of the encounter, asserting that the president had treated him with discourtesy both unworthy of the commander in chief and disrespectful of the highest ranking officer in the army, appeared in the papers.

Roosevelt ground his teeth but publicly bit his tongue; he bruised his molars the more when Miles requested permission to go to the Philippines to take command of the military situation there. This struck Roosevelt as the dumbest idea Miles had had since suggesting, prior to the 1900 election, that they join forces to unseat McKinley— a double-khaki candidacy, with Miles for president and Roosevelt for vice president. At the time Roosevelt had thought Miles merely an idiot; now he deemed him "a perfect curse." To a journalist friend he dropped a leaden hint meant for Miles: "Of course General Miles' usefulness is at an end and he must go."

But Miles was beyond taking hints, and Roosevelt wasn't ready for an open row just yet. The general had a following in Congress, which was considering an important army reorganization bill that Root was trying to push through. Miles opposed the reorganization, and Roosevelt had no desire to make a martyr out of him. Instead he just ignored him.

Roosevelt eventually got his army bill, and Miles eventually had to retire on account of age. Yet in going he created another controversy, for Roosevelt declined to write him a special letter commending him for long and distinguished service, and Miles's fans raised a hue and

cry at this shocking display of executive ingratitude. Roosevelt refused
to be moved. "Miles has for the two years of my presidency, and of
course for some years before that, shown himself the most dangerous
foe and slanderer of the army which he was supposed to command,"
the president told Lodge. "Nothing will hire me to praise him." To a
pro-administration editor in Philadelphia he likened Miles to General
James Wilkinson, the co-conspirator of Aaron Burr and a man infamous for subordinating national interest to private ambition. "I am
not sure that I did right in letting him serve out his term, but most certainly I should have been wrong and I should have inflicted harm on
the army if I had thanked him for his treachery and misconduct."

IV

The backbiting after the Spanish war might at first glance have
seemed odd. Winners usually leave such squabbling to the losers. But
though the United States had handily defeated the Spanish, it wasn't
doing so well against the Filipinos who picked up where the Spanish
left off, and the festering that often punishes lack of success at arms
soon infected American politics. The anti-imperialists predictably
pointed fingers at their erstwhile antagonists in the debate over the
Paris treaty. Somewhat less predictably, so did many other people
who, while not opposing imperialism in principle, objected to the way
it was being practiced in the Philippines.

That way included a dirty war against Filipino guerrillas, an unsavory struggle that recalled some of the tactics used by the Spanish
against Cuban guerrillas—tactics that Roosevelt and other interven-
tionists had denounced as barbaric and intolerable. American forces
in the Philippines adopted a variant of the *reconcentrado* policy made
notorious by the Spanish in Cuba; more shocking still was the "water
cure." This interrogative technique, designed to elicit information
from reluctant prisoners regarding the whereabouts of guerrilla leaders and other matters of military significance, entailed holding the
prisoner on the ground, forcing a gallon or so of water down his
throat, and then kicking and beating his swollen belly until he talked
or it burst—the latter with grave, frequently fatal, effect.

The war in the Philippines even produced an American counterpart to the Spaniard "Butcher" Weyler of Cuban notoriety. General Jacob Smith ("Hell-Roaring Jake") had been given the job of suppressing resistance in the guerrilla stronghold of Samar. A veteran of the Indian wars in the American West, as well as of the Civil War, Smith set to his work with a vengeance. "I want no prisoners," he told his principal subordinate. "I wish you to kill and burn; the more you kill and burn the better you will please me. I want all persons killed who are capable of bearing arms in actual hostilities against the United States." The subordinate, a hard-bitten major with few qualms himself, asked the general to specify a lower age limit. "Ten years," Smith said. The major wanted to make sure he heard this right. "Persons of ten years and older are those designated as being capable of bearing arms?" "Yes," Smith replied. In another order Smith declared that Samar "must be made a howling wilderness."

Roosevelt initially tried to ignore the complaints about Smith, just as he had ignored Miles. He judged the criticism of American actions in the Philippines overblown and he reasoned that in any case even good wars have their nasty sides. But when reporters obtained and published a copy of Smith's "howling wilderness" order, the president had no choice but to respond. He ordered Root to convene a committee to investigate the charges of brutality and other kinds of misconduct.

Privately Roosevelt couldn't contain his annoyance at Smith's arrant stupidity. Besides embarrassing the president, the general's violent and brutal directives had a distinctly demoralizing effect on the men serving under him. Roosevelt hardly sympathized with those who would place all stern responses to guerrilla operations beyond the pale; he explained to Speck von Sternberg that in ordering the inquiry into Smith's behavior he had not given the slightest impression of softness. "I have taken care that the army should understand that I thoroughly believe in severe measures when necessary, and am not in the least sensitive about killing any number of men if there is adequate reason." But Smith had gone too far. "I do not like torture or needless brutality of any kind, and I do not believe in the officers of high rank continually using language which is certain to make the less intelligent or more brutal of their subordinates commit occasional outrages."

The president's public statements were more circumspect. On

Memorial Day 1902 he gave a speech at Arlington Cemetery promising to rectify any wrongs. "Determined and unswerving effort must be made, and has been and is being made, to find out every instance of barbarity on the part of our troops, to punish those guilty of it, and to take, if possible, even stronger measures than have already been taken to minimize or prevent the occurrence of all such acts in the future."

Yet Roosevelt refused to retreat from the goals the United States had established for itself in the Philippines. "The Republic has put up its flag in those Islands, and the flag will stay there," he vowed. "Where wrong has been done by any one the wrong-doer shall be punished, but we shall not halt in our great work because some man has happened to do wrong."

Typically, Roosevelt responded to the attacks on his administration with a counterattack. In a daring non sequitur he defended American actions in the Philippines on grounds that Americans had done worse elsewhere. Specifically, he asserted that lynchings in the United States constituted "cruelty infinitely worse than any that has ever been committed by our troops in the Philippines." Roosevelt didn't have to mention the South by name; his listeners knew what he meant. Nor, when he castigated "the men who fail to condemn these lynchings, and yet clamor about what has been done in the Philippines," did he have to single out the Democrats.

It was a nice maneuver. It allowed him to register respect for, if not agreement with, Republican anti-imperialists like George Hoar, who did lash lynching, while slamming the Democrats, who generally didn't. It also served to change the subject. And it provided the additional bonus of furthering Roosevelt's southern strategy of speaking out for suffering (and Republican) blacks against racist (and Democratic) whites.

V

While Roosevelt's baiting of southern Democrats was deliberate, his antagonizing of another group—American Catholics—was accidental. Events in the Philippines triggered this controversy as well. In pursuit of McKinley's astonishing pledge to "Christianize" the Filipinos, American administrators in the islands discovered what anyone with any historical perspective already knew: that the job had been done long before by Spanish missionaries. In bringing (Catholic) Christianity to the Philippines, the Spanish friars had simultaneously acquired title to large tracts of Philippine real estate. The current American governor-general, William Howard Taft, recalled that popular antipathy to the friars had helped precipitate the anti-Spanish rebellion that preceded the American occupation, and in any event he desired to remove this vestige of European feudalism. Taft and his associates sought to break up the religious orders' estates by purchasing them and redistributing the land to the peasants who worked it. This would simultaneously serve the second purpose of encouraging the Spanish friars to go back to Spain; American priests would take their place.

Unfortunately for Taft, and for Roosevelt, the friars resisted this encroachment of the temporal sphere into what they interpreted as the realm of religion. They appealed to the pope in Rome for support, and their appeal echoed among American Catholics—a largely Democratic constituency and one always difficult for Roosevelt. As usual Roosevelt had trouble finding any merit in his opponents' case. He told Archbishop John Ireland that he was "very indignant" at the Catholic criticism, not least since his administration's policy toward the friars followed suggestions by Ireland himself. To another Catholic acquaintance he declared, "I am pained and concerned to find that a large number of Catholics seem to feel that the movement to get rid of the friars is in some way a movement against the Catholic Church by the government at Washington." Nothing could be further from the truth. It was the fact that the friars were Spanish, not that they were friars, that was the source of the problem, for the Filipinos had an historical hatred of the Spanish priests and still harbored "the most bitter indignation" against them. "If only these Spanish friars could be taken away, then their places can be at once taken by friars of other nationalities or by other orders of priests to whom the people will listen." As always his administration had nothing in mind but the best interests of the Filipinos—the great majority of whom were, of course, Catholic. "We have been endeavoring in all these matters to meet the wishes of the catholic population of the Philippine Islands."

Roosevelt grew more irritated the more he thought about the Spanish friars—"a lecherous lot of scoundrels," he called them in a less diplomatic moment—but upon due reflection he determined to approach the problem calmly, and in the spirit of J. P. Morgan, of all people. He sent his man, Taft, to see the friars' man, Pope Leo XIII. Taft found the pontiff surprisingly agreeable. "The old boy is quite bubbling with humor," he noted afterward. "He was as lively as a cricket." Leo's liveliness didn't prevent him from driving a hard bargain, and for the time being the negotiations stuck on price.

Roosevelt probably would have pushed the pope more vigorously but for the beating the American bishops and their flocks were giving him. "There has been the most extraordinary agitation among the Catholics here in the United States," Roosevelt wrote Taft, "caused by your negotiations at Rome. I was prepared to be attacked by the extreme anti-Catholic people for your going there, but I was completely taken aback by the violent attack made upon us by the Catholics." Roosevelt told Taft that he wasn't wavering regarding the prudence or propriety of what they were trying to accomplish. He declared, "Our action has been just and wise and entered upon on the highest grounds." But there were other angles to consider. "I am afraid we may be hurt thereby this fall in the congressional elections."

VI

Roosevelt always anticipated elections with eagerness; what he called "the hurly burly of a political campaign" provided the closest intersection between politics and personal combat. The elections of 1902 possessed additional significance as the first, albeit indirect, referendum on his performance as president.

The dignity of his office required him to modulate the tone of his stump speeches; it wouldn't do for the head of state to sling around charges of anarchy and treason the way Roosevelt had in previous elections. But he certainly couldn't sit at home, not so long as there were blows to be struck for righteousness and votes to be won for his wing of the party.

Accordingly, he left Oyster Bay in late August for a tour through New England. The region had never been as strong for him as certain other parts of the country; perhaps the Puritan reserve found his unbuttoned enthusiasms a bit much. But he hoped to do better this year. The beginning of September saw him in Massachusetts, warming to his themes and gaining momentum for the fall.

A mishap on September 3, however, cut short his campaigning and almost his life. In Pittsfield an out-of-control trolley car hurtled into the president's carriage, killing one of his bodyguards on the spot and sending the other passengers—Roosevelt, Massachusetts governor W. Murray Crane, and Roosevelt's private secretary George Cortelyou—flying across the pavement. Crane and Cortelyou walked away with minor injuries, but Roosevelt had his face smashed into the ground and a leg badly bruised.

Roosevelt minimized the extent of his injuries, and after a brief return to Oyster Bay, resumed his speaking schedule. He swung west through Tennessee and into Indiana. All the while his face got better, with the swelling diminishing and the lacerations healing over. But his leg stubbornly refused to mend. Indeed, it turned strange colors and grew disconcertingly painful. By the time he got to Indianapolis, the doctors who examined it were becoming alarmed. Infection obviously had set in, and blood poisoning threatened. The nation had lost one president to infection just a year earlier, and no one—with the possible exception of the hardest core of Roosevelt's opponents—wanted to lose another.

Apprised of the gravity of his condition, Roosevelt submitted to surgery. The wound was laid open all the way to the bone, and the putrified tissue cut away. The operation wasn't difficult, but the recovery would be painful, and especially in those days before antibiotics, there was real risk of additional infection.

Yet this time the wound began to heal—not least because on doctors' orders, and Edith's, Roosevelt curtailed his activities. He returned again to Oyster Bay, where he was confined to bed briefly. For some weeks thereafter he was not allowed to put weight on his leg, and he learned to get around in a wheelchair.

He still made light of his injury. He told an acquaintance that his enforced idleness was due to "one of the bruises I got in the trolley accident having developed in a mildly unpleasant way."

All the same, he realized that he had been close to something far more serious. The doctors got to his leg "just in time," he informed journalist friend Joseph Bishop with a strict injunction to secrecy; any further delay, he explained, and he would have been flat on his back for months, or worse.

As it was, Roosevelt found his relatively brief period of inactivity frustrating. He couldn't exercise; he couldn't even engage in a heated discussion, which for him had always involved full-motion body language. Yet with characteristic industriousness he resolved to make the most of his confinement. He contacted the librarian of Congress, who happened to be a fellow Harvard man, and asked for some reading material. "As I lead, to put it mildly, a sedentary life for the moment I would greatly like some books that would appeal to my queer taste." He asked about histories of the peoples of the Mediterranean; also works on Mesopotamia and Poland. He had read an interesting book by an author named Oman on the art of war; was a second volume out yet?

VII

Roosevelt had reason to brush up on the art of war, for at precisely this time he was caught in the middle of what was shaping up as another round of the industrial warfare that had been plaguing America since the Molly Maguire troubles of the 1870s. Conditions in the coalfields hadn't improved much since then, for although demand for coal had increased with the ongoing industrialization of the American economy, the continuing flood of immigration had effectively capped wages in mining and other unskilled occupations. The distinctly unfriendly attitude of the executive branch and the courts—evidenced by the Cleveland administration's injection of federal troops into the Pullman strike and by the courts' granting of injunctions against organized labor and their interpretation of antitrust laws in an antilabor fashion—had thrown additional hurdles in the path of union organizers.

Nonetheless, union leaders such as John Mitchell persisted. The economic upturn of the late 1890s promised gains, for with orders pouring in from steelmakers, railroads, steamship lines, and other industrial consumers of coal, the managers of the coal companies wouldn't want to risk missing out on profits. Moreover, in a strong market the managers could expect to pass wage increases along to their customers.

These propitious circumstances moved Mitchell and the other officers of the United Mine Workers to call a strike in the summer of 1900. Their timing couldn't have been cannier: With Bryan raving about the trusts and the oppression of the working man, the Republicans were primed to prove their concern for the lunch-bucket brigade. Mark Hanna warned the mine operators that the 10 percent raise the miners were demanding was cheap insurance against the havoc they would face if Bryan won. The operators took Hanna at his word and conceded victory to the miners.

Two years later Mitchell and the miners tried the same tactic. Even with their recent raise they were still paid miserably; moreover, their hours were backbreakingly long and appallingly dangerous. The companies controlled nearly every aspect of the workers' existence, owning the houses where they lived, the stores where they bought food, the churches where they prayed, the graveyards where they were buried, often prematurely. The companies also controlled the conditions under which they worked, including the weighing of the coal they dug. Whether from deliberate cheating or from generous (to the companies) interpretation of what constituted a ton, the workers often found themselves bringing three thousand pounds or more to the surface and getting paid for only a ton. In the spring of 1902, Mitchell again led his men out of the mines, demanding another raise, a shorter day, and no fiddling with the scales. Within a week some 140,000 men had put down their picks and shovels, and mines throughout the anthracite region were idle.

Roosevelt instantly appreciated the potential of a long coal strike for causing economic and political distress. When nearly everything ran on coal, nearly everything would stop without it. The president quietly encouraged Hanna to approach the mine operators and try to reproduce his success of two years earlier. But the operators would have nothing to do with Hanna this time. They felt they had been played for fools before—what had their concessions got them but another strike?—and they vowed not to be fooled again.

Roosevelt thought they were fools for their intransigence. He monitored the situation carefully, ordering an investigation into the causes and unfolding of the strike. In late June he asked Knox to give him an opinion as to his legal options in the matter. Knox responded that in the absence of a breakdown of order in the coalfields, the situation was constitutionally out of his hands.

As president, Roosevelt rarely conceded that anything was really out of his hands, but for the time being he chose not to act. The Northern Securities suit had already convinced much of the business class, which was supposed to be reliably Republican, that the White House was enemy territory. As things stood, Republican dunners would have a hard time keeping the corporate chieftains from sitting on their wallets this campaign season; Roosevelt wasn't eager to make the task of shaking down the boardrooms any harder.

The summer brought conflicting reports of violence in the coalfields. By some accounts the region had reached the edge of anarchy, with the miners solely to blame; by other accounts the situation wasn't so bad, with such outbreaks as had occurred being the work of provocateurs or trigger-happy sheriffs.

The one thing that couldn't be argued was the dwindling stockpiles of coal. While the warm weather lasted, the principal consequence of the production shortfall was higher prices, which pinched the profits of industrial consumers of coal. This was a problem for a Republican administration but not a dire one. The dire problem was the one that loomed ahead in the autumn when fuel shortages would provoke widespread layoffs and, more ominously still, when a coal famine would starve the furnaces and fireplaces that kept people warm across the northern parts of the country. If the strike persisted into November and December and beyond, it was entirely conceivable that hundreds of people or more would freeze in unheated tenements and ill-insulated shacks. What such a calamity would produce in the way of social and political convulsions was impossible to know but thoroughly unpleasant to imagine. Under such circumstances even a far less forceful president than Roosevelt would feel compelled to act.

Some chief executives take a Fabian approach to decisions, waiting patiently until all the pieces necessary to a policy's success are in place before moving. McKinley was this sort, as his handling of the Cuban war attested. Roosevelt was just the opposite. Constitutionally—in both senses of the word—impatient, he refused to let events run ahead of him. He strove whenever possible to avert crises through timely preparation and bold preemptive action. "My rule," he once remarked, "is a simple one: Do the best you can, with what you have, and do it now."

Roosevelt applied his rule to the coal strike. By the end of September the price of coal had quadrupled from five dollars a ton to twenty dollars; in parts of the country mobs were seizing coal cars of trains passing through their communities. Life-threatening hardship had yet to hit large numbers of people, but the discomfort level was growing rapidly. And with the congressional elections approaching, this was bad news for the party in power—that is, the Republicans. "Of course, we have nothing whatever to do with this coal strike and no earthly responsibility for it," Roosevelt remarked to Hanna, who was as frustrated as he was. "But the public at large will tend to visit upon our heads responsibility for the shortage in coal precisely as Kansas and Nebraska visited upon our heads their failure to raise good crops in the arid belt, eight, ten or a dozen years ago."

Roosevelt found himself at a loss. "I do not see what I can do, and I know the coal operators are especially distrustful of anything which they regard as in the nature of political interference. But I do most earnestly feel that from every consideration of public policy and of good morals they should make some slight concession."

With each passing week Republican officeholders and candidates sent increasingly urgent warnings to Washington of the debacle that lay ahead. Mayor Seth Low implored the president, "in the name of the City of New York," to take action to stave off the approaching peril; the continuance of the current situation would guarantee "great suffering and heavy loss to the inhabitants of this city, in common with many others." Cabot Lodge warned of "political disaster" in New England. Massachusetts governor Crane traveled to Washington with a personal message of approaching doom.

Though still not sure what he could do, Roosevelt calculated that doing almost anything was better than doing nothing. He discerned a "vital need" to get the mines back into operation before the cold weather set in. "You were no alarmist," Roosevelt told Crane shortly afterward, "and when you saw the coal famine impending, with untold misery as the result, with the certainty of riots which might develop into social war to follow, I did not feel like longer delaying." Roosevelt acknowledged that at this point he had neither constitutional duty nor constitutional right in the matter. "But I felt that the crisis was not one in which I could act on the Buchanan principle of striving to find some constitutional reason for inaction."

VIII

His first move was the relatively modest one of inviting representatives of the two sides in the strike to meet with him and each other. (Yet even this step provoked cries of protest from the friends of the corporate community. The New York *Sun* called it "extraordinary" and "dangerous"; the New York *Journal of Commerce* accounted it additional evidence of "Mr. Roosevelt's seemingly uncontrollable penchant for impulsive self-intrusion.") Edith was redoing the White House at this time; consequently, the meeting was held in the president's temporary office on Lafayette Place. The key operators of the coal companies came: George Baer, W. H. Truesdale, E. B. Thomas, Thomas Fowler, R. M. Olyphant, Alexander Cassatt, and John Markle. Representing the miners was John Mitchell.

Roosevelt was hardly up to form. His injured leg kept him in his wheelchair, substantially curtailing the gesticulations he customarily employed to emphasize his arguments. Yet at the same time his confinement suited the restraint he intended to project. Knowing the suspicion with which he was viewed by big capital, he wished to offer some reassurance. He opened the conference by welcoming his guests and then attempted to set the operators' minds at ease by explicitly disclaiming any constitutional or legal right or duty to intervene in the strike.

On the other hand, though, the situation at hand was very serious, and he couldn't simply stand—or sit—idly by. "The urgency and terrible nature of the catastrophe impending," he continued, "requires me to use whatever influence I personally can." Circumstances were rapidly growing intolerable; the country faced a calamity. The two sides must come together in the name of the public welfare. "I appeal to your patriotism, to the spirit that sinks personal consideration and makes individual sacrifices for the general good."

The miners' Mitchell seized the floor as soon as the president finished speaking, and accepted the challenge. Mitchell looked more like a Presbyterian minister than a labor leader: His neatly trimmed brown hair and clean-shaven face rose above a trademark reversed collar and dark suit, vest, and tie; his sober demeanor and careful phrasing completed a picture that was utterly at odds with the stereotype of the radical union organizer.

"I am much pleased, Mr. President, with what you say," Mitchell declared. He proposed a tribunal, to be selected by the president, to arbitrate the matters at dispute. "If the gentlemen representing the operators will accept the award or decision of such a tribunal, the miners will willingly accept it, even if it be against our claims."

Roosevelt nodded approvingly, his previous favorable opinion of Mitchell strengthened. But the operators were outraged. Baer, the spokesman of the group, was the antithesis of Mitchell. One of his favorite portraits of himself showed him sitting in a chair that could easily have passed for a throne; his silver mustache and goatee, with his long Roman nose and heavy eyelids, gave the impression of bored royalty. On this occasion Baer left no doubt that he considered Mitchell an intolerable instigator of lèse-majesté and Roosevelt an illegitimate upstart. Speaking to the president, he condemned the "crimes inaugurated by the United Mine Workers, over whom John Mitchell, whom you invited to meet you, is chief." The president shouldn't waste the operators' time negotiating with "the fomenters of this anarchy"; he ought to enforce the laws that guaranteed property rights and dissolve the miners' union as a conspiracy in restraint of trade.

The other operators joined in the attack on the president. "Are you asking us to deal with a set of outlaws?" demanded John Markle. He, for one, would never stand for it. In chorus the operators asserted that Roosevelt should long since have sent in the army to break the strike, and in an agreed statement they declared that the administration would be "a contemptible failure" if it could secure the lives and property and comfort of the people "only by compromising with the violators of law and the instigators of violence and crime."

Roosevelt seethed at this display of arrogance. "If it wasn't for the high office I held I would have taken him by the seat of the breeches and nape of the neck and chucked him out of that window," he said of one of the operators. To former president Cleveland, hardly a labor sympathizer, Roosevelt described the operators' words and actions as "very exasperating." He reported to Hanna: "The operators assumed a fairly hopeless attitude. None of them appeared to such advantage as Mitchell whom most of them denounced with such violence and rancor that I felt he did very well to keep his temper. Between times they insulted me for not preserving order (and they evidently ignored such a trifling detail as the United States Constitution) and attacked Knox for not having brought suit against the miners' union as violating the Sherman Antitrust Law."

Roosevelt's hopes of achieving a settlement crashed upon the operators' obduracy. "I have tried and failed," he told Hanna. If anything, the meeting was counterproductive, for Mitchell could only come away from the conference confirmed in his belief that the operators were troglodytes who would never, unless forced, give working men a fair shake. Nor could Roosevelt gainsay the union leader's judgment. He told journalist Albert Shaw: "The operators do not seem to understand that the present system of ownership, or at least of management of the anthracite fields, is on trial."

Roosevelt struggled to find the silver lining in this soot-colored cloud. "I am glad I tried anyhow. I should have hated to feel that I had failed to make any effort." He wasn't quite sure what his next move would be, but the meeting had convinced him that he couldn't expect any compromise or even rational assessment of self-interest from the operators. And now that he knew where he stood, he was better able to gauge which direction he ought to go. "I feel most strongly that the attitude of the operators is one which accentuates the need of the Government having some power of supervision and regulation over such corporations. I would like to make a fairly radical experiment on the anthracite coal business to start with!"

IX

Having met the miners and the operators, and taken the measure of each, Roosevelt was able to conceive the problem between the two sides in personal terms. He had already been inclined to believe that the miners deserved better treatment than they were getting; Mitchell's dignified demeanor, combined with the arrogance of the operators, pushed the president even further into the miners' camp. The operators didn't do themselves any favors by certain statements they made in the course of the dispute. The most provocative pronouncement emanated from the office of George Baer. Responding to an appeal from an inhabitant of Wilkes-Barre, Pennsylvania, to settle the strike, Baer intoned, "The rights and interests of the laboring man will be protected and cared for—not by the labor agitators, but by the Christian men to whom God in His infinite wisdom has given the control of the property interests of the country, and upon the successful Management of which so much depends. Do not be discouraged. Pray earnestly that right may triumph, always remembering that the Lord God Omnipotent still reigns, and that His reign is one of law and order, and not of violence and crime."

Baer's letter soon found its way into print, causing some observers to suggest that he had been set up, and it provoked a squall of outrage. The New York *Evening Post* called the letter "extraordinary"; the New York *Times* said it seemed to "verge very close upon unconscious blasphemy." The religious press was more incensed still. The Chicago *Standard*, a Baptist paper, castigated "the selfish, ignorant cant that this captain of industry mistakes for religion." An Episcopal paper from New York called Baer's statement "a ghastly blasphemy," while another Baptist journal, from Boston, declared, "The doctrine of the divine right of kings was bad enough, but not so intolerable as the doctrine of the divine right of plutocrats to administer things in general with the presumption that what it pleases them to do is the will of God."

Baer's attitude dispelled some of what Roosevelt called the "painful fogginess" of the American popular mind regarding the coal strike, and not to the benefit of the companies. And the shift in public thinking encouraged Roosevelt to blame the operators even more. "I have been so indignant with the mine-owners that it has been difficult for me to control myself in reference to them," Roosevelt wrote to Jacob Riis. The operators were simply oblivious to the import of their actions. "One great trouble," the president told Bamie after the worst of the crisis had passed, "was that the little world in which the operators moved was absolutely out of touch with the big world that included practically all the rest of the country."

Roosevelt determined to put the operators back in touch with the country by one means or another. Lately he had been rereading the life of Lincoln by John Hay and John Nicolay. "In this present crisis it is curious to see exactly the same tendencies of the human heart coming to the front," he told Robert Bacon. "Just as Lincoln got contradictory advice from the extremists of both sides at every phase of the struggle for unity and freedom, so I now have carefully to guard myself against the extremists of both sides. The men who wish me to proceed under the Sherman antitrust law against the miners' union are if possible one shade more foolish than the others who wish me to proceed under the same law against the coal operators."

Roosevelt was writing to Bacon as one old friend and Harvard grad to another; he was also writing as president to a partner of J. P. Morgan. Bacon and Morgan were urging Roosevelt to act in the coal case before the turbulence and violence in the minefields swept across the American economy and American society; Roosevelt replied significantly, "My dear Bob, as you write frankly, let me with equal frankness in return say that the turbulence and violence you dread is just as apt to come from an attitude of arrogance on the part of the owners of property and of unwillingness to recognize their duty to the public as from any improper encouragement of labor unions."

Roosevelt didn't intend to be seen as improperly encouraging labor unions. He contacted Mitchell and again proposed to have the miners return to work while a presidential commission examined the issues in dispute; he said he would then try to get the operators to accept a settlement on the basis of the commission's report. Roosevelt didn't really expect the union boss to agree to this one-sided proposal, which committed the miners but not the operators. "I suppose Mitchell will refuse my suggestion," he wrote. When Mitchell did refuse, Roosevelt declined to take it amiss. Mitchell held that the miners had come more than halfway; it was the operators' turn to make concessions. Roosevelt couldn't disagree.

The president began laying plans to pressure the operators into just such concessions. Quietly, but not so quietly that they wouldn't hear the sabers rattling, he prepared to have the army seize control of the mines. He summoned General J. M. Schofield and asked if he would be able to occupy and operate the mines. Saying that the situation in the coalfields was more dangerous than anything since the Civil War,

Roosevelt explained that the action he had in mind would be practically a war measure. The general must act in a purely military capacity, "paying no heed to any authority, judicial or otherwise, except mine." Schofield declared that he was ready and willing to do what was desired. The president need only give the order.

The constitutional basis for Roosevelt's plan was dubious to say the least. The president mentioned a common-law tradition under which a peasant might take wood that wasn't his if the wood was necessary to his survival. The common law being the fuzzy thing it was, there existed some question whether such a tradition existed; there was even greater question whether, assuming it did exist, it applied to the president of the United States. But Roosevelt had decided that he couldn't let constitutional scruples stand in his way any more than such scruples had stood in the way of Lincoln and other Union leaders during the Civil War. "I do not know whether I would have had any precedents, save perhaps those of General Butler at New Orleans," he admitted afterward, "but in my judgment it would have been imperative to act, precedent or no precedent—and I was in readiness."

To underline the seriousness of his intent, Roosevelt sent his secretary of war, Root, to talk with Morgan, who was in constant communication with the coal operators. Precisely how far Root tipped Roosevelt's hand remains unclear, but within a short time the operators signaled a willingness to bend a little. They reiterated the thorough fairness and justice of their treatment of the miners and reemphasized the entire responsibility of the miners for the shocking violence to life, limb, and property in the anthracite region; but they agreed to binding arbitration by a panel of experts if the miners would return to work. The catch was the narrow restrictions they placed on the membership of the expert board. It must consist of an officer of the engineer corps of the U.S. army or navy, a civilian mining engineer, a federal judge from eastern Pennsylvania, and a mining operator or other active participant in the business of mining and selling coal. As a slight concession, the operators allowed that the board might also include "a man of prominence, eminent as a sociologist."

Roosevelt was encouraged, since this was more than the operators had agreed to thus far. But he doubted that the miners would accept a panel stacked so heavily in the operators' favor. And, indeed, Mitchell rejected the offer as it stood. Instead, in a meeting with the president on the morning of October 15, the union leader made a counteroffer: The union would accept arbitration and go back to work if the operators would agree to expand the arbitration board to seven members—the five they had specified plus two to be named by the president. "This seemed reasonable," Roosevelt remarked afterward, "and I told him I would try."

Roosevelt did try, but at first he didn't get anywhere. As the two additional members, the president had intimated to Mitchell that he would appoint E. E. Clark, the head of the railway conductors' union, and Bishop John Spalding, a Roman Catholic prelate respected by the largely Catholic miners. Subsequently, Roosevelt proposed the name of former president Cleveland to replace the military engineer; he didn't want the army or navy getting mixed up in a labor dispute except under his own direct control.

The operators rejected this plan. It was either their proposal or nothing. That evening Bob Bacon and George Perkins came down from the Morgan office in New York. Bacon and Perkins let Roosevelt know that they had been authorized to negotiate for the operators, but under no circumstances would the operators agree to expand the specified panel.

Of course, this left them precious little room to negotiate, and as the meeting wore on and Roosevelt refused to accept the operators' take-it-or-leave-it proposition, the two Morgan men grew tense and nervous. "Bacon and Perkins were literally almost crazy," Roosevelt told Lodge shortly after the fact. The three went round and round about the composition of the commission. "Argue as I could, nothing would make them change, although they grew more and more hysterical, and not merely admitted, but insisted, that the failure to agree meant probable violence and possible social war."

Hysterics were not Roosevelt's style. While he was more frustrated than ever, he was also mystified that the operators would risk so much on what appeared to be a point of pride. Were they really that stupid?

The break came when Bacon let slip that the operators would probably grant the president leeway in naming individuals to the commission as long as the appointments were made under the headings the operators had specified. Once Roosevelt received this piece of intelligence, the situation "cleared tremendously," as he explained shortly thereafter. "I at last grasped the fact that the mighty brains of these captains of industry had formulated the theory that they would rather have anarchy than tweedledum, but that if I would use the word tweedledee they would hail it as meaning peace."

Switching tweedledum for tweedledee entailed, in this case, calling Clark, the conductors' union head, the sociologist the operators allowed. "I instantly told them that I had not the slightest objection whatever to doing an absurd thing when it was necessary to meet the objection of an absurd mind on some vital point, and that I would cheerfully appoint my labor man as the 'eminent sociologist.'" This answered his earlier question regarding the operators: They really *were* that stupid. "It was almost impossible for me to appreciate the instant and tremendous relief this gave them. They saw nothing offensive in my language and nothing ridiculous in the proposition, and Pierpont Morgan and Baer, when called up by telephone, eagerly ratified the absurdity! And accordingly, at this utterly unimportant price, we bid fair to come out of as dangerous a situation as I ever dealt with."

As usual Roosevelt exaggerated both his own exploits and the iniquity, or in this case folly, of his foes. The coal crisis was worrisome, to be sure, but it hadn't really reached the danger stage. And the operators were rather shrewder than he made them out to be. They bluffed as long as they thought they could; when they recognized the need to retreat, they forced the president into saving their face, and their future, for them. There would be other negotiations and other standoffs; to cave in to the union would simply encourage future strikes. On the other hand, to yield to the president on a minor point here or there could be defended as the mark of magnanimity and patriotism.

And, indeed, the operators did yield on a couple of small points once the big dam broke. They accepted the addition of Bishop Spalding to the commission and allowed Roosevelt to name Carroll Wright, the federal commissioner of labor, as recorder. Roosevelt, in turn, withdrew his objection to an army officer serving on the commission—which let former president Cleveland off the hook. (The operators' concessions had "totally changed" the situation, Roosevelt explained in informing Cleveland that the nation wouldn't be requiring his services.)

The commission convened at the end of October and spent the next four months gathering information and hearing testimony. Meanwhile, the miners went back underground, coal prices fell, and furnaces were fired up. In the end the commission awarded the miners a 10 percent pay hike but refused to recognize the United Mine Workers as the bargaining agent for all the miners. Each side got enough to claim victory.

The corporate heads, and not just those in the mining industry, continued to complain about Roosevelt and wish him ill, but on the whole his handling of the coal strike evoked applause. One Republican paper called it "a great personal triumph"; another sympathetic writer declared that the president's actions during the previous few months had "given the color of romance and knight errantry" to his office.

Roosevelt took the positive feedback with a grain of salt. "Now I am being very much overpraised by everybody," he told Joseph Bishop, who was one of the chief culprits. "And although I suppose I like it, it makes me feel uncomfortable too. Mind you I speak the literal truth when I say I know perfectly well I do not deserve what you have just said of me in that editorial. It really seems to me that any man of average courage and common sense who felt as deeply as I did the terrible calamity impending over our people would have done just what I did."

To another friendly editor Roosevelt predicted that he had let himself in for no end of troubles. "Every strike will mean that some people will accuse me of being the cause of it by having settled this coal strike, and others will insist that I interfere to stop it, heedless of the fact that such interference or intervention of mine, as in the case of the coal strike, must occur only in extreme cases." Yet the principle involved in the anthracite strike warranted risking this potential for future complications. "It was essential that organized capital and organized labor should thoroughly understand that the third party, the great public, had vital interests and overshadowing rights in such a crisis as that through which we have just passed."

CHAPTER EIGHTEEN

The Kaiser and the Canal
1902–3

Roosevelt's rescue of the Damsel Public in the coal strike made dramatic headlines just before the 1902 elections, which returned solid Republican majorities to both houses of Congress. Taking this as ratification of his bold use of executive power, the president declared himself "well contented" with the results of the polling.

Although things had turned out right in the end, Roosevelt recognized that the constitutional bridge he had galloped over to save the fair lady was relatively flimsy and might not bear many more such crossings; for this reason he intended to leave most future forays to less exalted officials expressly armed with congressional warrants. Yet his blood was up (and his leg was healing), and he must continue to seek dragons to slay.

During the several months after the coal strike he found his dragons overseas. This was just as well (and not entirely coincidental), since presidents have always been granted greater autonomy in foreign affairs than in domestic. Roosevelt took what he was granted—and more. To an even greater degree than in domestic matters, he believed that his arm wielded the sword of righteousness in international affairs. That he swung the sword in earnest much less often than he merely brandished it didn't indicate any lack of confidence in his moral authority; it rather reflected a recognition that weapons have multiple uses.

II

The dragon that most worried Roosevelt during his whole presidency (and for a decade thereafter) was Germany. Since the late

1890s, Germany had been shadowing the United States: in the Pacific, as earlier, and increasingly in the Caribbean. During the Spanish-American War, Roosevelt (and Lodge and Mahan and their co-conspirators) had feared that Spain would appeal to Germany for help. Spain did, but the Germans judged Madrid's chances too slim to justify provoking the Americans. All the same, the German navy made rude gestures at Dewey in the vicinity of Manila (affording annexationists such as Roosevelt an additional argument for holding the Philippines after the war). Since the war, moreover, German banks and businesses had been enlarging their commercial claims in several countries of South America, lending money to governments and private concerns and assisting Berlin in an energetic diplomacy of the mark.

Roosevelt and his fellow Republicans couldn't credibly object to German economic efforts in the hemisphere—the Republicans (under McKinley) having pioneered the "open door" theory of equal access to foreign markets and investment opportunities—but the president considered drawing the line when Germany supplemented mark-manship with marksmanship. For some time German investors had grown impatient with the Venezuelan government's laxity in meeting schedules of debt repayment. Had Cipriano Castro, the current ruler of the country, pleaded simple inability to repay, the Berlin bondsmen might have rescheduled the debts, as they had done on more than one occasion previously. But Castro used the debt dispute as a rallying point for Venezuelan nationalism—one of the few issues on which he could count on support for his unpopular regime—and all but dared the Germans to compel Venezuela to cough up the cash. Berlin took the dare. In conjunction with Britain, which had similar financial problems with Castro, and Italy, which tagged along as the much junior partner, Germany announced that it would use force to collect its debts. In December 1902, German and British warships imposed a blockade of the Venezuelan coast. Venezuela resisted long enough to have several of its ships seized and two of its coastal fortifications bombarded.

Roosevelt viewed the Venezuela affair with profound ambivalence. On one hand he deemed Venezuela deserving of just about whatever chastisement the Europeans dished out. The country's government scarcely deserved the name. "Castro is an unspeakably villainous little monkey," he told John Hay a couple of aggravations later. During a period when the United States was enforcing civilized behavior on the Filipinos—and the Puerto Ricans and only slightly less directly on the Cubans—Roosevelt had difficulty working up resentment at Germany and Britain for doing the same to the Venezuelans. Just the previous year he had told his German diplomat friend Speck von Sternberg, "If any South American State misbehaves towards any European country, let the European country spank it." At that time Roosevelt was still vice president, but either then or after his accession to the presidency his sentiments surely found their way to the upper echelons of the German foreign ministry.

On the other hand, the European use of force against an American republic—even a republic as compromised as Venezuela—grated on Roosevelt's Monroe Doctrinal sensibilities. Berlin and London disavowed any territorial aims; after they made their point and got their money, they said, they would lift the blockade and return the customhouses and harbors to Venezuelan control. Roosevelt was willing to accept London's assurances in this regard; Britain's good behavior during the past few years had allowed his sense of Anglo-Saxon solidarity to gain the advantage over his perfidious–Albionist suspicions.

But Roosevelt distrusted Germany. Kaiser Wilhelm II was a hard man to fathom. He had flashes of brilliance. "The more I have heard of the Kaiser the more my respect for him has grown," Roosevelt told Spring Rice during the summer of 1901. Wilhelm was ambitious for his country and determined to implement his ambitions; on days of particular frustration with Democrats, mugwumps, and other timid types, Roosevelt must have felt a certain envy for the kaiser's comparative unaccountability. At the same time, however, this very unaccountability left the emperor ballastless, so to speak, with the result that Germany's foreign policies veered to starboard one week, to port the next. Wilhelm's wayward style diminished Roosevelt's respect for him even as it complicated the president's task of dealing with Germany.

To Roosevelt's thinking, Germany posed the sole serious threat to American overseas interests. "It seems to me," he mused in April 1901, "that Germany's attitude toward us makes her the only power with which there is any reasonable likelihood or possibility of our clashing." As recently as a few years earlier he had feared that the United States might have to teach Britain a lesson; but the British had done a competent job of educating themselves. "There is no danger to us from England now in any way. I think there never will be." Germany was another story. "Germany is the great growing power, and both her faults and her virtues, at least of the superficial kind, are so different from ours, and her ambitions in extra-European matters are so great, that she may clash with us."

Roosevelt realized that Germany wasn't the only country with an unpredictable foreign policy; America's had been marked by fits and reversals as well. The president fretted that the combination would prove combustible—that American inconstancy would encourage Germany to adventurism, which the United States would then be compelled to counteract by military force. After Congress failed to fund what Roosevelt considered a necessary addition to the American fleet, he wrote forebodingly to Lodge:

> Some friends of mine who have been at the German field maneuvers last year were greatly impressed with the evident intention of the German military classes to take a fall out of us when the opportunity offers. I find that the Germans regard our failure to go forward in building up the navy this year as a sign that our spasm of preparation, as they think it, has come to an end; that we shall sink back, so that in a few years they will be in a position to take some step in the West Indies or South America which will make us either put up or shut up on the Monroe doctrine; they counting upon their ability to trounce us if we try the former horn of the dilemma.

Roosevelt's wrestling match with the coal bosses during the autumn of 1902 distracted him from a full consideration of the potential consequences of the German-British blockade of Venezuela, which was signaled to Washington well in advance of the fact. Through John Hay, the president declined to dispute the legitimacy of the joint action. But once he had beaten the bosses—and been invigorated by the victory—he changed his mind and decided to challenge the kaiser. He doubtless would have done so even if America's newspaper nationalists hadn't raised the hue and cry about this latest instance of European interloping in the Americas, which they did. But the editorial agitation enhanced his resolve. Roosevelt was accustomed to being accused of being too bellicose; he privately enjoyed it. He *wasn't* used to being called too soft; he didn't like that at all.

Precisely what he did next became the subject of considerable controversy during subsequent decades. According to a letter he wrote
some fourteen years later, Roosevelt grew convinced that Germany
had far grander designs than it was admitting—"that Germany
intended to seize some Venezuelan harbor and turn it into a strongly
fortified place of arms, on the model of Kiaochow [the Chinese penin-
sula Germany had recently grabbed], with a view of exercising some
measure of control over the future of the Isthmian Canal, and over
South American affairs generally." Roosevelt had recommended that
the Germans arbitrate their differences with the Venezuelans; they had
refused. Berlin's envoy simply repeated his government's pledge that
the occupation of Venezuela would be temporary—"which might
mean anything," Roosevelt remarked. "I finally decided that no useful
purpose would be served by further delay, and I took action accordingly. I assembled our battle fleet, under Admiral Dewey, near Porto
Rico, for 'maneuvres,' with instructions that the fleet should be kept
in hand and in fighting trim, and should be ready to sail at an hour's
notice."

Then he called in the German ambassador, Theodor von Holleben.
He informed the ambassador that Berlin's refusal to settle its differ-
ences with Venezuela peacefully was unacceptable to the United
States. Holleben again repeated the formula that the occupation of
Venezuelan territory was temporary. Roosevelt replied that Germany
had called its occupation of Kiaochow temporary as well. He would
not stand for a Kiaochow on the Caribbean coast of South America.
Holleben reiterated that his government could not arbitrate its dispute
with Venezuela. "I then asked him to inform his Government,"
Rosevelt explained, "that if no notification for arbitration came during the next ten days I would be obliged to order Dewey to take his
fleet to the Venezuelan coast and see that the German forces did not
take possession of any territory."

This got the ambassador's attention. He asked gravely whether the
president realized the serious consequences that might follow such a
course. Roosevelt assured Holleben he did. "I answered that I had
thoroughly counted the cost before I decided on the step, and asked
him to look at the map, as a glance would show him that there was no
spot in the world where Germany in the event of conflict with the

United States would be at a greater disadvantage than in the Caribbean sea."

Suitably chastened, the ambassador returned to the embassy and presumably passed the message along. But nothing happened. A week later he had another interview with Roosevelt at which the two chatted amiably for several minutes on inconsequential topics. To Roosevelt's surprise Holleben then got up to go. Roosevelt stopped him. "I asked him if he had any answer to make from his Government to my request." He said he did not.

At this point Roosevelt delivered his ultimatum. "I informed him that in such event it was useless to wait as long as I had intended, and that Dewey would be ordered to sail twenty-four hours in advance of the time I had set."

This statement finally produced a result. "Less than twenty- four hours before the time I had appointed for calling the order to Dewey, the Ambassador notified me that His Imperial Majesty the German Emperor had directed him to request me to undertake arbitration myself."

Roosevelt's recollection of the events surrounding the German agreement to arbitrate elicited skepticism. The timing alone was doubt-provoking. Roosevelt's letter was written in August 1916 to William Thayer, who, quite evidently with Roosevelt's permission, published it as an appendix to a new printing of Thayer's life of John Hay. It seemed striking that the former president should tell his story publicly for the first time precisely when he was berating the man who had defeated him in 1912, Woodrow Wilson, for failing to stand up to the same German kaiser and his gang of aggressors.

Roosevelt's letter ran light on details that might have corroborated his story, and in fact supporting evidence was scarce. Subsequent studies of German archives unearthed nothing that looked like an ultimatum. Neither did anything in contemporary official American documents, in the files of either the State Department or the Navy Department. Roosevelt's correspondence at the time is likewise silent. One would have thought he would inform Cabot Lodge, whose devotion to the Monroe Doctrine had helped inspire his own, of the sturdy defense he had made of that cherished principle; if he did, he did so in person, for not a word on the subject passed in their written exchanges.

Theodore, Corinne, Edith, Elliott.
Theodore Roosevelt Collection, Harvard

T.R.'s room at Harvard. *Harvard*

Alice Lee, at about the
time of her marriage
to T.R. *Harvard*

MADE HARMLESS AT LAST!

The reformer (with Grover Cleveland) in *Puck*, 1884. *Harvard*

Home on the range (Chimney Butte ranch house). *Library of Congress*

Dakota, 1885. *Harvard*

Baby Alice and Bamie,
c. 1886. *Harvard*

Thomas Nast on
the Civil Service
commissioner:
"Stick to your
saddle and don't
be bounced."
Harvard

Police
commissioner.
Harvard

Assistant secretary
of the Navy.
Harvard

With his men, 1898. *Library of Congress*

THE ROUGH RIDERS.

As hero, 1898. *Harvard*

T.R. (*center*) and Thomas Platt (*with beard*) at Republican
convention, 1900. *Harvard*

South Carolina, 1902. *Library of Congress*

At Yellowstone with John Burroughs, 1903. *Library of Congress*

The First Family: Quentin, T.R., Ted, Archie, Alice, Kermit,
Edith, Ethel. *Library of Congress*

Panama, 1906.
Library of Congress

With Gifford
Pinchot, 1907.
Library of Congress

Sagamore Hill. *Library of Congress*

Taking a fence.
Library of Congress

Recreating, while president.
Library of Congress

Edith, 1908.
Library of Congress

On safari, 1909 or 1910.
Library of Congress

With Ethel on the Nile,
1910. *Harvard*

Europe, 1910. *Library of Congress*

Heading aloft, 1910. *Library of Congress*

On the road to Armageddon, 1912. *Harvard*

Returning from South America, 1914. *Library of Congress*

Editorialist at work, 1916. *Library of Congress*

Campaigning for preparedness, 1916. *Library of Congress*

Circa 1917. *Library of Congress*

With Grace and Archie, Jr., 1918. *Harvard*

A few years after the Venezuela affair Roosevelt referred vaguely to a lesson in resolve he had given Germany. "When I first came into the Presidency I was inclined to think that the Germans had serious designs upon South America," he wrote Spring Rice in November 1905. "But I think I succeeded in impressing on the Kaiser, quietly and unofficially, and with equal courtesy and emphasis, that the violation of the Monroe Doctrine by territorial aggrandizement on his part around the Caribbean meant war, not ultimately, but immediately, and without any delay." Scattered other references occurred in his correspondence in subsequent years.

Yet despite the dearth of supporting evidence, it is entirely possible that things happened more or less as Roosevelt recalled them. Roosevelt wasn't one to launch into histrionics to make a point. For one thing it violated the code of conduct he had learned on the western frontier, where a man did what he had to do without carrying on about it. For another, he recognized that he would have to deal with the kaiser again, and it would only make future relations more difficult if the German leader were embarrassed by an obvious show of American force. The fewer people who knew about any ultimatum, the better. As for Dewey and the Caribbean fleet, the absence of any record of special orders from the White House means only that the maneuvers remained merely maneuvers; the president's ultimatum, if any, worked.

It may have been that Holleben—and perhaps even Roosevelt at the time—did not perceive his warning as an ultimatum per se. In a 1906 letter to Henry White in which he described the incident, Roosevelt said he had had "to make a display of force and to convince him [the kaiser] definitely that I would use the force if necessary." Yet Roosevelt went on to tell White that he had couched his message in terms of American public opinion, which, he contended to Holleben, was so adverse to Germany's actions in Venezuela that any president might feel obliged to act. "This was not in any way intended as a threat," Roosevelt said of his warning; it was simply a statement of the political facts of life. Shortly thereafter Wilhelm had agreed to arbitrate. Roosevelt added, in the letter to White, "I do not know if it was a case of post hoc or propter hoc." The president proceeded to characterize his treatment of the German leader: "Where I have forced him to give way I have been sedulously anxious to build a bridge of gold for him, and to give him the satisfaction of feeling that his dignity and reputation in the face of the world were safe. In other words, where I have had to take part of the kernel from him, I have been anxious that he should have all the shell possible, and have that shell painted any way he wished."

Indeed, it would have been ideal for Roosevelt's purposes if the ultimatum had produced its effect without the kaiser's realizing he had been directly threatened. Wilhelm had other reasons for abandoning whatever designs he had on Venezuela. The German government had taken care to coordinate with Britain regarding Venezuela, but an outburst of unfavorable feeling in Britain regarding both Germany and the Venezuela venture caused London to back off almost before its troops landed. Berlin faced the prospect of being the lone villain in the piece. The kaiser might well have decided on his own, before or in the absence of any explicit warning from Roosevelt, to agree to arbitration.

On balance, Roosevelt's story seems likely even if his memory was a bit hazy regarding details. What is still more likely—indeed, nearly unquestionable—is that by the time he told the story to Thayer, he *believed* it had happened as he said it did. Some of Roosevelt's critics, then and after, accused him of concocting the story from whole cloth. He didn't. Roosevelt's stories always contained a substantial element of fact. He sometimes embellished them or allowed the heroic version the benefit of the doubt—as in the case of his growing certainty that he had killed a Spaniard with his own hand in the battle for San Juan Hill, and in the many instances of his demonizing his opponents—to make himself feel more principled. But he wasn't a liar.

Whether or not the climax of the Venezuela crisis transpired just as Roosevelt related, only the most querulous observers disputed his description of the denouement as "very satisfactory." Roosevelt declined the kaiser's invitation to act as arbitrator, despite perceiving "some real advantages" in such a course; instead he recommended turning the matter over to the international tribunal at The Hague. When Wilhelm accepted the principle of Hague arbitration, the danger seemed to have passed. "Of course complications may at any time arise in connection with the settlement of the terms of arbitration," the president remarked on the day after Christmas 1902; but complications over terms were what the diplomats got paid to iron out—as in this case they did.

On the whole, Roosevelt was quite pleased. "We have sustained the Hague court, have done good service to the cause of arbitration, have taken a step onward in preparing a code of international ethics, and have also taken a step onward in securing European acknowledgement of the Monroe Doctrine." Even for a person of Roosevelt's energy and ambition, this was a good couple of weeks' work.

III

In the spring of 1903, Roosevelt ventured west from Washington to complete the trip he had been required to cut short the previous fall when his injured leg festered. As president he traveled considerably more conspicuously than he had just two years earlier as vice president. He hoped for a reprise of his cougar hunt with John Goff but was forced to settle for a guided tour of Yellowstone Park and a ceremonial cornerstone-laying at the entrance. At Yosemite in California he roughed it with John Muir; afterward he wrote his appreciation to the famous naturalist: "I shall never forget our three camps; the first in the solemn temple of the giant sequoias; the next in the snowstorm among the silver firs near the brink of the cliff; and the third on the floor of the Yosemite, in the open valley, fronting the stupendous rocky mass of El Capitan, with the falls thundering in the distance on either hand."

Along the way he picked up the expected honorary degrees and made the required patriotic gestures. The University of Chicago dubbed him a doctor of laws; he replied by defending the Monroe Doctrine and asking for a bigger navy. The University of California also granted him the law degree he never got at Columbia; he crossed the San Francisco Bay to break ground for a statue of McKinley in Golden Gate Park.

It was not the college crowds, however, that rendered the trip worthwhile in Roosevelt's view but the throngs of common folk who rode and walked from near and far to see the first president they really felt to be their own. Roosevelt afterward told John Hay,

Wherever I stopped at a small city or country town, I was greeted by the usual shy, self-conscious, awkward body of local committeemen, and spoke to the usual audience of thoroughly good American citizens—a term I can use in a private letter to you without being thought demagogic! That is, the audience consisted partly of the townspeople, but even more largely of rough-coated, hard-headed, gaunt, sinewy farmers and hired hands from all their neighborhood, who had driven in with their wives and daughters and often with their children, from ten or twenty or even thirty miles round about. For all the superficial differences between us, down at bottom these men and I think a good deal alike, or at least have the same ideals, and I am always sure of reaching them in speeches which many of my Harvard friends would think not only homely, but commonplace.

Roosevelt conceded that curiosity inspired much of the turnout to see him. "Most of these people habitually led rather gray lives, and they came in to see the President much as they would have come in to see a circus. It was something to talk over and remember and tell their children about." But even so he felt a personal bond. "I think that besides the mere curiosity there was a good feeling behind it all, a feeling that the President was their man and symbolized their government, and that they had a proprietary interest in him and wished to see him, and that they hoped he embodied their aspirations and their best thought."

Whether or not the people possessed the feelings he ascribed to them—many did, certainly, but many of these same people had flocked to see William Jennings Bryan, with whom Roosevelt shared nothing except a common touch—Roosevelt *believed* they did. As always he felt revitalized by a journey to the West. He declared,

> As soon as I got west of the Missouri I came into my own former stamping ground. At every station there was somebody who remembered my riding in there when the Little Missouri roundup went down to the Indian reservation and then worked north across the Cannon Ball and up Knife and Green Rivers; or who had been an interested and possibly malevolent spectator when I had ridden east with other representatives of the cow men to hold a solemn council with the leading gangsters on the vexed subject of mavericks; or who had been hired as a train hand when I had been taking a load of cattle to Chicago, and who remembered well how he and I at the stoppages had run frantically down the line of cars and with our poles jabbed the unfortunate cattle who had lain down until they again stood up and thereby gave themselves a chance for their lives; and who remembered how when the

train started we had to clamber hurriedly aboard and make our way
back to the caboose along the tops of the cattle cars.

Like all such stories, these doubtless improved with the telling, bur-
nishing the romantic patina that already colored Roosevelt's memories of his western days.

In the guise of the returning hero, Roosevelt visited Medora and the
region of the Little Missouri. (In corresponding with friends from the
area he had taken to signing himself "The Medora President.") He
saw Sylvane and Joe Ferris; also the man named Paddock who had
lent him the rifle hammer he had used on his first hunting trip to the
area, the sheriff to whom he had delivered the three boat thieves, and
scores of others.

> The older men and women I knew well; the younger ones had been
> wild towheaded children when I lived and worked along the Little
> Missouri. I had spent nights in their ranches. I still remembered meals
> which the women had given me when I had come from some hard expe-
> dition, half famished and sharpset as a wolf. I had killed buffalo and
> elk, deer and antelope with some of the men. With others I had worked
> on the trail, on the calf roundup, on the beef roundup. We had been
> together on occasions which we still remembered when some bold rider
> met his death in trying to stop a stampede, in riding a mean horse, or in
> the quicksands of some swollen river which he sought to swim.

The passage of time, not to mention the celebrity that surrounded
the president, had conspired to smooth the rough edges of memory.
"They all felt I was their man, their old friend; and even if they had
been hostile to me in the old days when we were divided by the sinister bickering and jealousies and hatreds of all frontier communities,
they now firmly believed they had always been my staunch friends and
admirers." It hardly became a fellow frontiersman, let alone a politician, to disabuse them of such beliefs.

Roosevelt's typical letter was two pages or less; this one to Hay,
recounting his adventures in the West, ran ten times as long. He
described a meeting in Arizona with one of his Rough Riders, a man
named Ritchie who was a career bartender but doubled as a justice of
the peace. Ritchie one evening had found himself in a poker game
when a particularly unfortunate player grew surly. Sensing trouble,
Ritchie walked over to the bar to get his gun. The angry cardplayer

stood up and attempted to shoot Ritchie; instead he was the one killed. "Had he drawn his gun, Ritchie?" queried Roosevelt. "He didn't have time, Colonel," said Ritchie coolly. To Hay, Roosevelt added that Ritchie had been cleared of any wrongdoing in the scrape.

Roosevelt also ran into Seth Bullock, another Rough Rider friend, who recounted the misadventures of a man named Llwellyn, a captain in the Rough Riders. "The excellent captain is a large, jovial, frontier Micawber kind of personage, with a varied past which includes considerable man-killing," Roosevelt explained to Hay. As a veteran of the Badlands, Roosevelt didn't necessarily hold man-killing against a person; some miscreants deserved sudden death. Bullock had killed many men but was at bottom a tenderhearted soul. Llwellyn was a harder case. Bullock told how Llwellyn had been brought to trial on a murder charge, and only with great difficulty had he—Bullock—been able to persuade the jury to acquit him. "Under the circumstances, Colonel," Bullock related to Roosevelt, "I wouldn't have killed that man, and you wouldn't either, Colonel." "Which I thought was very likely true," Roosevelt remarked wryly to Hay.

In Montana, Bullock arranged a special bodyguard for the president. Roosevelt had recently incurred the wrath of the violently radical Western Federation of Miners (by comparison with whom the United Mine Workers of John Mitchell were milquetoasts) for sending federal troops to restore order in an Arizona strike. The president's arrival in Butte had brought out the radicals along with hundreds of others. "The ordinary procession in barouches was rather more exhilarating than usual and reduced the faithful secret service men very nearly to the condition of Bedlamites. The crowd was filled with whooping enthusiasm and every kind of whiskey, and in their desire to be sociable broke the lines and jammed right up to the carriage. There were a lot of the so-called 'rednecks' or dynamiters, then men who had taken part in the murderous Coeur d'Alene strike, who had been indulging in threats as to what they would do to me, and of course the city is a hotbed of violent anarchy."

Accordingly Bullock had arranged for extra protection. He selected some associates on whom he could rely, tough characters all and uniformly quick with a pistol. "By occupation they were, as he casually mentioned, for the most part gamblers and 'sure thing' men," Roosevelt told Hay. For this very reason they were just the sort for the job. "They had no sympathy whatever with anarchy in any form. They thoroughly believed in men of wealth, for they wished to prey on them." This special guard allayed whatever concerns Roosevelt had for his own safety, although he couldn't rule out the possibility of an innocent—admittedly a relative term in a place as wild as Butte—but overly exuberant observer getting shot by mistake.

The parade down Butte's main street claimed no casualties, but for a time it looked as though dinner might. Politics and related matters had divided Butte into warring camps, which called a truce long enough to host a banquet. The two factions were equally represented, by fifty men apiece. "In Butte every prominent man is a millionaire, a professional gambler, or a labor leader; and generally he has been all three," Roosevelt explained. "Of the hundred men who were my hosts I suppose at least half had killed their man in private war, or had striven to compass the assassination of an enemy. They had fought one another with reckless ferocity." The setting recalled scenes of feasting that Roosevelt had read about in his romances. "As they drank great goblets of wine the sweat glistened on their hard, strong, crafty faces. . . . They were accustomed to taking their pleasure when they could get it, and they took it fast and hard with the meats and wines." Roosevelt couldn't say he admired these men, but one had to respect them. "They had made money in mines; they had spent it on the races, in other mines, or in gambling and every form of vicious luxury. But they were strong men for all that. They had worked and striven and pushed and trampled, and had always been ready, and were ready now, to fight to the death in many different kinds of conflict. They had built up their part of the West." They were, in their own way, much like the sturdy, reckless frontiersmen Roosevelt had eulogized in his *Winning of the West*.

After the dinner the stories began and the drinking continued. "To my horror," Roosevelt recorded, "I found that Seth Bullock had drunk too much." Roosevelt urged his friend and ostensible protector to go back to the train and sleep it off. But Bullock demurred on grounds that an early retirement would be insulting to their hosts and ignominious to himself. He did agree, however, to relinquish his sidearm, a long forty-five. He survived the evening without it, as did the other guests.

The balance of Roosevelt's trip was less riotous. The president touched every state of the Far West and nearly all of the principal cities. He inspected the navy yard at Bremerton, south of Seattle. He reviewed cavalry troops at Cheyenne. On behalf of his children he accepted a gift of a badger from a girl in Kansas. He visited the tomb of his hero and model—Lincoln—at Springfield.

On June 5 he arrived back at Washington. Edith had dressed the children in their finest clothes, and she and they were waiting in the window of the East Room when he pulled up the drive from the station. Edith had been sick, but, wearing one of Roosevelt's favorite dresses, she was a splendid sight for a homesick heart. "It is not good taste to speak about one's wife," Roosevelt confided to Lodge. "But in writing to my closest friend perhaps I can be allowed to say that though Edith looked frail she looked so pretty that upon my word she seemed to me just as attractive as seventeen years ago when I crossed to England to meet her."

IV

Roosevelt stayed in Washington only a few weeks; at the end of June he and the family departed for Oyster Bay. In those days of modest federal government and no air-conditioning, Washington regularly emptied out during the summer. Roosevelt would contribute to remedying the first deficiency by expanding the scope of federal activities; he wouldn't have introduced air-conditioning even if he could have, since he valued the excuse to remove himself to Oyster Bay for a few months with Edith and the children. (He also occasionally used the heat to political effect. During one dog-day session of Congress when the legislature wasn't giving him all he wanted, a delegation from Capitol Hill reported the great suffering being experienced there. "Let them sweat," Roosevelt retorted with a wicked smile. "I hope it will get hotter. Perhaps after a while they will see their duty and be able to do it.")

The summer of 1903 was, by Roosevelt's accounting, "as lovely a summer as we have ever passed." Such a statement has to be discounted for the fact that he was constantly uttering such superlatives. But he was indeed in high spirits that season. He was fresh from his triumphs over the kings of coal and Prussia, and his western tour indicated that he was as popular as ever among the people whose opinion he valued most. And it was too early to be worrying about the election of 1904.

Most of all the three months away from the White House gave Roosevelt a chance to resume the outdoor and family activities he loved. Writing to Corinne about himself and Edith, he explained, "We have ridden horseback much together, and have frequently gone off for a day at a time in a rowboat, not to speak of the picnics upon which everybody went. In the intervals I have chopped industriously." The children and their cousins were gloriously underfoot. Alice managed to escape to Newport and other more fashionable watering holes, which was probably just as well for everyone concerned. "But all the rest of the children—ours, Laura's, and Christine's and Emlen's—have been here, and we have had the happiest, healthiest, most old-fashioned kind of a summer together." The cousins matched up well by age and interest; Quentin, in addition, made particular friends with the Secret Service men who followed his father night and day.

As president, Roosevelt had the luxury of holding court wherever he went, including Oyster Bay. Eminent and interesting men of all professions and persuasions went out of their way—literally—for the chance of an audience with the most powerful and arguably the most charismatic man in the country. "Grant La Farge and Dan Wister came out on Wednesday night," Roosevelt informed Lodge in late September, "and Friday morning I took them on a three hours' ride." Wister explained how he was adapting his best-selling novel *The Virginian* for the stage. Lyman Abbott joined them for lunch; also naturalist George Grinnell, "with whom I wanted to talk Indian reservations, and incidentally some points on big-game zoology."

The lunch table discussion was followed by postprandial tennis and other physical recreation, which resumed the next morning. "Saturday I took Edith off in a rowboat, and we were out all day, rowing down to the great marsh at the end of Lloyd's Neck, where we took our lunch and watched the white sails of the coasters passing up and down the Sound. I had a stiff row home against wind and tide."

V

Roosevelt returned to Washington shortly after this outing. A deskful of issues, some more vexing than others, awaited him. The tariff lobby was attacking the Cuban reciprocity treaty, which would lower the impost on goods from Cuba in exchange for a reduction on duties on goods exported to Cuba from the United States. While the lobbyists condemned the agreement on economic grounds, Roosevelt defended it as crucial to American and hemispheric security. "This is not like an ordinary reciprocity treaty," he explained. "It stands by itself; it is demanded by our military needs in Cuba." Under reciprocity, Cuba would thrive—and, equally important, become indissolubly linked to the United States. After all the trouble he had had with the kaiser over Venezuela's debts, Roosevelt didn't want Cuba to tempt the Germans or other foreigners by running up similar deficits. If the Cubans owed anyone money, let them owe Americans. Besides, the Platt amendment gave the United States extraordinary rights of intervention in Cuban affairs; for the United States to deny Cubans access to American markets would put "a most unpleasant aspect" on the Platt clause.

Roosevelt dismissed many of the opponents of Cuban reciprocity as "foolish extremists." But one opponent couldn't be disregarded so easily—despite his being dead. The protectionists were circulating statements by Thomas Reed, who had passed away the previous December; these statements criticized the treaty and Roosevelt for supporting it. Roosevelt had never forgiven Reed for failing to back the Spanish war and the annexation of the Philippines (Reed derided the Paris treaty, which specified an American payment of $20 million to Madrid for the transfer of title to the islands, as the "purchase of Malays at $2 per head"). Reed's subsequent opposition to the Northern Securities suit had additionally riled the president. It was difficult to tell whether Roosevelt was more upset at Reed for disagreeing with him or at himself for previously having admired the Maine legislator so extravagantly. In either case, the latter's death didn't deter Roosevelt from lashing out at him. "The figures of his estate show that he had made immense amounts of money in New York through the Morgan people and certain others," Roosevelt told Lodge. "I have no doubt that he kept technically honest; and I have also no doubt that he got the money as the equivalent or consideration for using his name and influence against me personally, and against all others who were striving to make good the promises given before election. If the man were alive now he would be the rallying point for all the disaffected elements."

Roosevelt's displeasure at Reed aside, what made Cuba a particularly sensitive subject for the president was its proximity to the Central American isthmus. By the autumn of 1903 negotiations over an American right to construct a canal across the isthmus had reached an impasse. During his first months in office Roosevelt had overseen the conclusion of talks with Britain that led to London's release of the United States from the Clayton-Bulwer Treaty of 1850, which prevented either country from building a canal without the consent of the other. In 1850 this pact had served the United States by tying the hands of Britain, the country more likely to have been in a canal-building frame of mind. By 1900 the positions were reversed; this reversal was what had provoked Roosevelt's remarks during that period about unilateral abrogation if the British didn't bow out gracefully. But the British did, in keeping with their continuing hands-across-the-Atlantic campaign.

This left Roosevelt to conclude a deal with the locals—either the government of Nicaragua, which controlled one proposed route, or the government of Colombia, which at that time controlled Panama, the location of the other route. Few negotiations ever involved American officials in such intrigue and with such dubious characters. Representatives of the two governments vied for American favor; middlemen and speculators joined the dog and pony show. The star of the production, by his own reckoning and most others', was Philippe Bunau-Varilla, a Frenchman of questionable birth but undeniable ambition and energy. Bunau-Varilla had become enamored of the idea of a Panama canal when, as an engineering student in Paris in the 1880s, he had heard the great Ferdinand de Lesseps, the conqueror of Suez, describe his dream of another grand canal, this one linking the Atlantic and Pacific. Jungle, mountains, and tropical disease defeated de Lesseps, but they only intensified the desire of Bunau-Varilla to succeed where his countryman had failed.

At the time Roosevelt entered the White House, expert opinion remained divided on the technical merits of the competing routes. The Nicaragua route was longer but being at sea level needed no locks. The Panama route was more direct but involved moving mountains and building large and elaborate combinations of dams and locks. Roosevelt took no strong position in the dispute, although he was leaning toward Nicaragua. He wanted a canal; he wasn't finicky about where it was located.

In December 1901, however, he received an engineering report that convinced him that Panama was the better route. Improvements in excavation and construction technology made lowering the highlands and raising the rivers of Panama more feasible than before, while the growing size of oceangoing ships rendered critical Nicaraguan waterways increasingly cramped.

This report persuaded the president to look to Panama; it also involved him with Bunau-Varilla and entangled him in the coils of Colombian and Panamanian politics. Since Colombia's independence from Spain in 1821 (as New Granada), the district of Panama had been but loosely and uncomfortably joined to the rest of the country. Part of the problem was geographical: The vertiginous mountains and ax-breaking hardwood forests that separated Panama from the populated regions of Colombia made overland travel and communication essentially impossible. For all that contiguity counted, Panama might as well have been a foreign country.

Such was precisely the opinion of influential Panamanians, a group that included some characters well attuned to the scheming of the likes of Bunau-Varilla. From the days of Balboa, Panama had attracted more than its quota of drifters, adventurers, and ne'er-do-wells; on the whole these weren't people upon whom authority rested easily, especially when that authority was exercised intermittently and from a distance, as by Colombia. Over the decades one faction or another of Panamanians was almost constantly in revolt against Colombia; by some counts the number of rebellions topped fifty before the beginning of the twentieth century.

Until Roosevelt's time, the revolts had all failed—more than a few on account of American opposition. In 1846 the Polk administration had negotiated a treaty with Colombia guaranteeing America's right of transit—currently by rail, prospectively by canal—across the isthmus. The benefit to the United States was obvious; the benefit to Colombia was the stake the agreement gave Washington in preventing a breakaway by the Panamanians, perhaps encouraged by a foreign power. In accord with this treaty, the American government acted to frustrate several secessionist efforts by the Panamanians. In the 1880s, Grover Cleveland dispatched warships and a contingent of marines to Panama to suppress a rebellion. Roosevelt himself edged into the game in the autumn of 1902 when he approved the use of an

American battleship as the forum for negotiations that led to the end of the Thousand Days' War between Colombia and Panama's latest crop of nationalist hopefuls.

But during the first several months of 1903, Roosevelt reconsidered his and America's position in the matter of independence for Panama. Congress lately had weighed in on the canal question, voting in favor of a Nicaraguan route. This prompted Bunau-Varilla to bend all his wit, charm, and capacity for misrepresentation to reversing the vote. He buttonholed influential senators and representatives, delineating the technical advantages of the Panama route. He explained how the experience acquired by de Lesseps would speed the construction. He dropped dark hints of the instability that would endanger a canal through Nicaragua as contrasted with Panama, across which Americans had been traveling safely for decades.

But it was another form of instability that clinched his case. In the spring of 1903 a volcano erupted on Martinique, killing tens of thousands. Martinique was nowhere near Nicaragua (Florida was closer to the volcano), but America's legislators had always been weak on geography, and the idea of volcanoes in the Caribbean jolted Congress into asking whether any such uproarious things existed near the proposed canal. The Nicaraguan government announced that there was nothing to worry about; yes, there were volcanoes in Nicaragua, but they were all slumbering peacefully.

Not so! cried Bunau-Varilla. Mount Momotombo, one of the signature sights of Nicaragua, had in fact belched messily just months before. So pleased had the Nicaraguan government been, in fact, at the monumental picturesqueness of its powerful peak that it had immortalized it on a postage stamp. The gleeful Bunau-Varilla scoured the stamp shops and snatched up every copy he could find. He then sent greeting cards to leading American legislators—cards bearing this official witness to both the unreliability of the Nicaraguan government and the instability of the Nicaraguan landscape. Shortly thereafter Congress cast new ballots on the canal issue, mandating that the passageway be located in Panama.

This change of heart pleased the government of Colombia, which found itself in the apparently happy position of monopolist regarding an American-built canal. Roosevelt was also pleased; he directed John Hay to draw up the papers. The secretary of state proceeded to negotiate a treaty granting the United States control for ninety-nine years of a strip of territory six miles wide across Panama, in exchange for an annual payment of $250,000 and a signing bonus of $10 million.

Roosevelt was delighted with Hay's work and looked forward to the commencement of construction. Ratification by the Senate could never be taken for granted, especially when refusal required a mere one-third plus one. But a canal was so manifestly in the American national interest that even the Democrats and anti-imperialist Republicans would have to go along.

VI

To Roosevelt's great surprise, and that of most other Americans, the Colombian senate decided that *it* didn't have to go along. In August the Colombian body rejected the treaty by a unanimous vote. The charitable interpretation, from Washington, was that the Colombians were so attached to their native soil that they couldn't stand to relinquish control of even a small portion of it; the cynical interpretation was that they hoped to squeeze more money out of the *norteamericanos*.

Roosevelt wasn't inclined to be charitable. He likened the Colombian rejection to extortion, which he angrily determined to defeat. "I do not think that the Bogota lot of jack rabbits should be allowed permanently to bar one of the future highways of civilization," he told Hay. The president briefly toyed with the idea of telling the Colombians to dig their canal themselves, if they could; the United States would build an American canal in Nicaragua. But the longer he thought about it, the more incensed he grew at the Colombians, and he refused to accept a second-best route simply because some greedy low-lifes in the Colombian legislature wanted more money. "What we do now will be of consequence, not merely decades, but centuries hence, and we must be sure that we are taking the right step before we act."

Roosevelt pondered his options. One was simply to go ahead and start digging in Panama. Under an ingenious interpretation of the 1846 treaty with Colombia, the United States had the right to dig a canal in Panama even against the wishes of the Colombian government. Roosevelt was tempted. "If under the treaty of 1846 we have a color of right to start in and build the canal," he told Hay, "my off-hand judgment would favor such proceeding."

Yet he didn't want to rush into anything. As he said, his administration was building for the ages; a month this way or that would hardly justify hastiness. From Oyster Bay in mid-September he wrote to the also-vacationing secretary of state: "I shall be back in Washington by the 28th instant, and you a week or two afterwards. Then we shall go over the matter very carefully and decide what to do. At present I feel that there are two alternatives. (1) To take up Nicaragua; (2) in some shape or way to interfere when it becomes necessary so as to secure the Panama route without further dealing with the foolish and homicidal corruptionists in Bogota. I am not inclined to have any further dealings whatever with those Bogota people."

During the next six weeks Roosevelt set aside for good the Nicaraguan option. His engineers continued to advise that Panama was better; some went as far as to say that having no canal would be preferable to having a canal through Nicaragua. Roosevelt was more convinced than ever that Panama was the place. But acting on this conviction, against a recalcitrant Colombian government and a potentially skeptical Congress (Roosevelt guessed that the legislature would balk at anything requiring boldness), was the rub. The ethics of the matter concerned the president not in the slightest. He told Mark Hanna, "I feel we are certainly justified in morals, and therefore I believe justified in law, under the treaty of 1846, in interfering summarily and saying that the canal is to be built and that they shall not stop it."

Roosevelt's reservations had to do, rather, with appearances—which was to say, politics. "As yet the people of the United States are not willing to take the ground of building the canal by force," he told Albert Shaw of the *Review of Reviews* in the first week of October. But the Colombian government had done its best to ensure that force was the sole option—"literally the only way" treaty rights could be obtained on reasonable terms. All the same, Roosevelt told Shaw that "to obtain such terms now by bribery or violence would be wrong." Writing to an influential editor like Shaw (as opposed to an insider like Hanna), Roosevelt may have wished to convey the notion that he thought bribery and violence were morally wrong. In fact, although he always looked down on bribery as uncouth, he never had any problem with violence in a good cause, which he certainly considered this to be. The wrongness of overt violence against Colombia would lie in the damage it might do to America's good name, not in any sort of sinfulness against abiding standards of good and evil.

In this same letter Roosevelt knowingly gave Shaw a hint of what the future might hold. He suggested that there could be other paths to a Panama canal besides direct American seizure. "Whether in the future there will be misconduct among the people of the Isthmus, or among those controlling the Isthmus, such as to bring about a condition of things that will warrant the action we desire being taken openly, honestly, and in good faith, I do not know."

He could guess. The Colombian senate's rejection of the canal treaty had flummoxed Bunau-Varilla even more than it had Roosevelt, for while the American president had only immortality to win by building a canal, the French engineer-entrepreneur had millions of dollars to gain. Yet where Roosevelt could afford to bide his time, Bunau-Varilla couldn't, for the concession he had taken over would expire in 1904. During the two months after the Colombian rejection of the American offer, the Frenchman haunted the halls of the American State Department, the corridors of the Capitol, and the private parlors of influential individuals like Hay and John Bassett Moore, a former diplomat and a lawyer whose legal opinion and political advice Roosevelt valued. In the second week of October he met with Roosevelt personally.

"I was received with the characteristic open-heartedness which has won this remarkable man so many friends," Bunau-Varilla recollected later. The Frenchman described the unsettled situation in Panama, declaring the isthmus the victim of detestable political passions that were frustrating the Panamanians' legitimate desire for independence.

Roosevelt inquired of his visitor what the outcome of the current situation might be.

"It was then or never," Bunau-Varilla recalled. "I could by my answer know exactly what the President had in mind. I remained silent for a moment, and I pronounced the following four words in a slow, decided manner: 'Mr. President, a Revolution.'"

According to Bunau-Varilla's story, Roosevelt reacted with "profound surprise." This response may have suited the Frenchman's tale, but it seems unlikely if only because Roosevelt wasn't a good enough actor to convincingly feign ignorance of what he knew perfectly well to be the revolutionary predilections of the Panamanians.

But whatever his response, it didn't include any kind of commitment as to what he would do in the event Bunau-Varilla was right. "He had no assurances in any way, either from Hay or myself, or from anyone authorized to speak for us," the president said some weeks later, certainly in perfect truth. At the same time Roosevelt conceded that explicit assurances had hardly been necessary. "He is a very able fellow, and it was his business to find out what he thought our Government would do. I have no doubt that he was able to make a very accurate guess, and to advise his people accordingly. In fact, he would have been a very dull man had he been unable to make such guess."

What Bunau-Varilla guessed was that Roosevelt would guarantee the success of a Panamanian revolution in exchange for the canal he coveted. And this was exactly what happened. The French middleman let Panama's eager founding fathers know that the American president favored their project, and accordingly in early November they proclaimed yet another independent Panamanian republic. Within twenty-four hours an American cruiser conveniently in the area landed marines, effectively neutralizing those Colombian officers and men who hadn't been bought off by the revolutionaries and by the private interests connected to the canal concession. Within another forty-eight hours Roosevelt recognized the new government of Panama, essentially ensuring its survival against what efforts Bogota might have planned for suppressing the rebellion.

Negotiating a new treaty required a bit longer. Bunau-Varilla proposed to speak for the Panamanian government; with the millions he stood to gain from the deal now so tantalizingly close, he couldn't bear the thought that delay might cause it to unravel at this eleventh hour. To facilitate acceptance by the American Senate, Bunau-Varilla sweetened the deal substantially from what Roosevelt had negotiated with the Colombians. When the real Panamanian representatives arrived in Washington, they were astonished at what the unaccredited Frenchman had done. Yet they could hardly do more than mop their brows and consider their reception back in Panama if they refused to

go along. Their country's fragile existence depended on the goodwill
of the United States; their personal safety (against Colombian wrath,
for instance) likely did, too. They swallowed their misgivings and
took the treaty back to Panama where the legislature similarly swallowed the pact.

VII

The Panamanian affair gave Roosevelt the canal he wanted—or
rather the chance to build the canal—but it also gave him heartburn.
He spent the next several weeks explaining how his actions in the matter had been entirely honorable and aboveboard. "I did not foment
the revolution on the Isthmus," he told Albert Shaw. If fault existed in
the matter, it lay not with American officials but with the Colombians.
"The latter signed their death warrant when they acted in such infamous bad faith about the signing of the treaty." The United States had
done a good turn for the Panamanians, if not for the Colombians,
who didn't deserve it. "Unless Congress overrides me, which I do not
think probable, Colombia's grip on Panama is gone forever."

To Spring Rice, Roosevelt protested his innocence with greater
vehemence. "The Colombia people proved absolutely impossible to
deal with," Roosevelt said. "They are not merely corrupt. They are
governmentally utterly incompetent. They wanted to blackmail us and
blackmail the French company; but the main trouble was that they
would not or could not act on any terms. The treaty we offered them
went further in their interests than we by rights ought to have gone,
and it would have given them a stability and power such as no other
Spanish-American republic possessed between Mexico and Chile. But
in spite of the plainest warnings they persisted in slitting their own
throats from ear to ear."

To other correspondents Roosevelt offered additional justification
for his actions and further proof of his innocence. He told Lyman
Abbott, who had just left Washington, that he wished he had shown
him the draft of the annual message he had been working on. "It was
written at the very end of October—that is, less than a week before
the outbreak occurred—and by it you would have seen that at that

time neither Hay nor I was preparing for the outbreak, and that the message was drawn up on the supposition that there would be no outbreak." To a lawyer friend from Chicago he dismissed suggested analogies between Panama's secession from Colombia and the South's secession from the Union. The South was part of a great democracy, he explained; its secession would not have expanded the sphere of freedom but rather, through southern insistence on slavery, narrowed it. By contrast, the Panamanians were striking a blow for liberty against the corrupt and incompetent Colombian government. "By every law, human and divine, Panama was right in her position." Which meant, of course, that he had been right to support Panama.

Not everyone agreed, of course, which was why Roosevelt was protesting so strenuously. Chronically anti-Roosevelt papers, as well as some that weren't, lambasted the president for hypocritical high-handedness. William Randolph Hearst's Chicago *American* assailed Roosevelt for "a rough-riding assault upon another republic over the shattered wreckage of international law and diplomatic usage." The New York *Evening Post* was slightly more generous: "The same result could have been achieved with some regard for appearances. The booty could have been bagged just the same, yet the burglar could have looked, to the casual eye, more like a church member." Senate Democrats delighted in the opportunity to make the president squirm, knowing that he knew that they had the numbers to consign the canal to continued limbo.

As ever, Roosevelt ascribed the basest motives to his foes. The suggestion that the United States should have surrendered—or should still surrender—the Panamanian people to the demonstrated incapacity of Colombia was infamously wrong. "Nothing could be more wicked," he declared. Those who advocated such a course were "a small body of shrill eunuchs who consistently oppose the action of this government whenever that action is to its own interests, even though at the same time it may be immensely to the interest of the world, and in accord with the fundamental laws of righteousness."

Roosevelt always liked to believe that the American people endorsed his actions; yet when evidence cast such belief into some question, as it did now, he was quite capable of appealing to a higher court. "Whether the people of the United States as a whole do or do not approve of what I have done to the extent of making them wish to continue me in my present place, I cannot say," he told British friend Arthur Lee. "But I am very confident that from the standpoint of the country's interest and honor, my actions have been both wise and right, and if the people do not take this view, why I shall be sorry, but it will not in the least alter my convictions." To his son Ted he once more likened himself to Lincoln. "I get an idea of what he had to stand after Bull Run and again after McClellan's failures in '62 and the party defeat in the elections of that year, and again after Fredericksburg and Chancellorsville."

Roosevelt's critics commonly charged him with having an oversized ego, but even most of them probably didn't imagine that he was comparing the flurry over Panama with the ordeal of the Union during the Civil War. For indeed it was nothing more than a flurry, as Roosevelt in his less melodramatic moments recognized. "While I have had a good deal of worry and trouble over Colombia and the Isthmus of Panama," he explained to Kermit, "so far things have come out exactly as I wished them." A more apt parallel than Lincoln would have been Thomas Jefferson at the time of the Louisiana Purchase. Of course, Roosevelt, detesting Jefferson, would never have drawn the parallel, but apt it was. Jefferson's Federalist critics had threatened to make trouble over the treaty with France, but in the end they couldn't bring themselves to reject such an obvious bargain. Similar considerations prompted Roosevelt's Democratic foes to fall into line after the requisite hand-wringing and public soul-searching.

Thus America got its canal—a decade of construction later—and Roosevelt got his place in the history of world geography. He also got two of the more enduring comments in the history of the American presidency, both at his expense. At a cabinet meeting Roosevelt asked Attorney General Knox to explain the legal justification for the administration's actions in the affair; Knox responded: "No, Mr. President, if I were you I would not have any taint of legality about it." When Roosevelt demanded, "Have I answered the charges? Have I defended myself?", War Secretary Root replied: "You certainly have, Mr. President. You have shown that you were accused of seduction and you have conclusively proved that you were guilty of rape."

CHAPTER NINETEEN

The Life of the Party
1904

Roosevelt would consider the acquisition of rights to the Panama Canal the signal achievement of his tenure as president. He thought the American people would, too, and he was surprised when Republican spokesmen in the campaign of 1904 didn't make more of the great work he had done on behalf of America and the world. "Can you not tell our speakers to dwell more on the Panama Canal?" he asked Senator Nathan Scott, chairman of the Republican speakers' bureau. "It does not seem to me that nearly enough stress is laid on this." The more the Republicans pushed the issue of the canal, the better off they would be. "We have not a stronger card."

The fact that Roosevelt needed to make this suggestion indicated that not all the Republicans agreed that Panama was their trump against the Democrats. Their assessment reflected a belief that imperialism—a term Roosevelt resisted but one that fairly captured his strong-armed assertion of American influence in the Western Hemisphere and beyond—wasn't as popular among the American people at large as it was in the circles Roosevelt frequented. This belief was well founded, especially in the aftermath of the Philippine war. Roosevelt could talk all he wanted about America's responsibility to the benighted Filipinos (as to the almost equally underprivileged Puerto Ricans and Cubans), but the idea never caught on outside a rather small group of mostly Republicans. Short, glorious foreign wars like that with Spain were acceptable; dirty wars that dragged on for years, like that in the Philippines, were demoralizing and distasteful. Fortunately for Roosevelt, the war in the Philippines ended by the summer of 1902, essentially removing it as a campaign issue; if he had had to campaign on that, he would have been in trouble.

Imperialism aside, the hesitancy of all the Republicans to embrace Panama also reflected substantial lingering hesitation about Roosevelt himself. As of the end of 1903, Roosevelt could hardly claim a mandate among the movers of the G.O.P. The draft that had carried him to the vice presidency in 1900 had been genuine enough, but the whole point was to make him *vice* president, not president. Since inheriting McKinley's mantle, Roosevelt had hardly endeared himself to the big-money men who dominated the party. Quite the contrary: His pro-labor position in the anthracite strike branded him a dangerous radical in the minds of the more reactionary corporate bosses, and the ongoing prosecution of the Northern Securities suit struck even relative moderates like J. P. Morgan as provocatively progressive. A widely quoted speech delivered at Spokane, Washington, attacking the "criminal rich" made the president less popular still in the boardrooms; his use of the adjective in the restrictive rather than the inclusive sense was lost on many listeners, among both those who thought the two words always went together and those who thought they rarely or never did.

Roosevelt recognized the cloud he walked under, and whereas he never let real rain hamper his appreciation of the outdoors, he had no desire to have this cloud dump a downpour on his parade to a victory he could call his own. Roosevelt liked to boast that he refused to let fear or favor mold the positions he took on issues. His positions, he claimed, were entirely shaped by his perception of the public good. Such claims were true as far as they went, but in election season they didn't go very far. Like most great men, and like many who fancy themselves great, Roosevelt convinced himself that his own advancement was crucial to the public welfare. Ever impatient—not least from bad conscience—with the mugwump types who placed principle above political efficacy, Roosevelt believed that his first job was to attain, or in this case keep, office. Safely past the election he would wade to his waist in the work that needed doing. Until then he would stick closer to shore.

II

Roosevelt essentially commenced his 1904 campaign with his annual message to Congress in December 1903. "The country is to be congratulated," he declared with not a trace of false modesty, "on the amount of substantial achievement which has marked the past year both as regards our foreign and as regards our domestic policy." He praised himself on the settlement of a vexatious but essentially minor wrangle with Britain over the boundary between Alaska and British Columbia; he expressed satisfaction that the dispute between Venezuela and its creditor-assailants was proceeding smoothly through arbitration at The Hague; he lauded the continued buildup of the United States Navy.

He defended his handling of the Panama affair. Providing an overview of the turbulent history of the region, to the point of listing fifty-three riots, insurrections, rebellions, and attempted revolutions since 1850, he concluded that "the experience of over half a century has shown Colombia to be utterly incapable of keeping order on the Isthmus." The chronic disorder had blocked work on a project that would benefit all mankind.

> Under such circumstances the government of the United States would have been guilty of folly and weakness, amounting in their sum to a crime against the nation, had it acted otherwise than it did when the revolution of November 3 last took place in Panama. This great enterprise of building the interoceanic canal cannot be held up to gratify the whims, or out of respect to the governmental impotence, or to the even more sinister and evil peculiarities, of people who, though they dwell afar off, yet, against the wish of the actual dwellers on the Isthmus, assert an unreal supremacy over the territory.

Such self-congratulation was hardly unexpected from a sitting president, and still less, by now, from Roosevelt; but what the corporate captains really wanted to hear was what the president proposed to do for, or to, them. Here his tone was distinctly more temperate than of late—as befitted a candidate who would soon be asking the big guys for their political and especially financial support. Roosevelt patted himself on the back for the creation of the Department of Commerce and Labor, of which the money men weren't overly fond, and for the establishment within that department of the Bureau of Corporations, which they liked even less; but then he allayed their alarm by emphasizing the strictly informational aspects of the bureau's work. The president stressed the "sane and conservative" character of recent measures affecting business. "Nothing revolutionary was attempted. . . . The legislation was moderate. It was characterized throughout by the idea that we were not attacking corporations, but endeavoring to provide for doing away with any evil in them; that we drew the line against misconduct, not against wealth; gladly recognizing the great good done by the capitalist who alone, or in conjunction with his fellows, does his work along proper and legitimate lines." So important did Roosevelt consider the message of his moderation that he essentially repeated himself a few paragraphs later. "The progress has been done by evolution, not by revolution. Nothing radical has been done; the action has been both moderate and resolute."

The business barons were not so foolish as to take Roosevelt's avowed moderation at face value; there was no telling what he might do once reinstalled in the White House. But at least his choice of words was a decided improvement over the "criminal rich" language of the recent past, and if it didn't bind him beyond the election, at least it suggested that business wouldn't become his football during the campaign. A fractious president might be dealt with; a Congress swept into office on a wave of anticorporate indignation would pose a considerably larger problem.

III

Besides, the businessmen could still hope that their friends on high might exercise restraint over the president. Some placed their trust in Mark Hanna. The relation of Hanna to Roosevelt was a curious one. McKinley's death had devastated Hanna personally; it also reversed the balance of power between Hanna and Roosevelt. Roosevelt nonetheless recognized the importance of cultivating Hanna and consequently took an early opportunity to reach out to the boss. Hanna indicated he could be reached but only on two conditions. The first was that Roosevelt implement McKinley's policies—as Roosevelt himself had pledged he would. Hanna's second condition was that Roosevelt cease his annoying habit of calling him "old man." "If you don't," Hanna warned, "I'll call you 'Teddy.'" Roosevelt, who privately detested the nickname as undignified (Alice Lee was one of the few who had called him Teddy, which doubtless was another reason he disliked hearing it from others), accepted the conditions.

This pact facilitated the changing of the Republican guard but didn't complete it. (That Roosevelt couldn't quite keep his promise about addressing Hanna—"Good luck to you, old man!" he wrote Hanna not many months later—may have had something to do with its falling shy.) Roosevelt remained the accidental president, and Hanna remained the party's kingmaker—and potential king-unmaker. Still kicking himself over the defeat at the 1900 convention that had allowed Roosevelt's ascendancy, Hanna considered himself as worthy an heir to McKinley as Roosevelt was. He may have entertained hopes of winning the Republican nomination for himself in 1904; perhaps he simply wanted to determine who *did* win the nomination. But in either case he desired to keep the issue open as long as possible.

Roosevelt, for obvious reasons, wanted to nail the nomination down; for less obvious reasons, certain other members of the party wanted to help in the hammering. Senator Joseph Foraker, also of Ohio, had tired of operating in Hanna's shadow, and in the summer of 1903 he devised a scheme for weakening his Senate colleague. Foraker proposed that the Ohio Republican Party endorse Roosevelt's nomination a year early. Such a maneuver was hardly unheard of; several state conventions had already endorsed Roosevelt, and Hanna himself had used the ploy for McKinley in 1895. In this instance Foraker hoped his motion in favor of Roosevelt would flush Hanna out of the bushes and onto open ground where he would be more vulnerable. For Hanna to support the motion would fairly rule out his own candidacy; for Hanna to oppose it would mark him publicly as a foe of the president. By his own admission Roosevelt was never especially accurate with a gun, but even he wouldn't have any trouble hitting Hanna with that much time to aim and shoot.

Roosevelt, then on his barnstorming tour through the West, could almost hear Hanna muttering in Ohio as the senator paced back and forth, trying to find a way out of his fix. The best Hanna could come up with was an assertion that the Ohio Republican convention of 1903 had no right to bind the convention of the following year in the matter of a presidential nomination or presumably anything else. As he rationalized to Roosevelt, "The issue which has been forced upon me in the matter of our state convention this year endorsing you for the Republican nomination next year has come in a way which makes it necessary for me to oppose such a resolution; when you know all the facts I am sure you will approve my course."

Roosevelt didn't wait for all the facts. "I thought the matter over a full 24 hours . . ." Roosevelt told Lodge, "and decided that the time had come to stop shilly-shallying, and let Hanna know definitely that I did not intend to assume the position, at least passively, of a suppliant to whom he might give the nomination as a boon." He composed a reply to Hanna that skewered the senator even more deftly than Foraker's maneuver had done. "Your telegram received," the president said. "I have not asked any man for his support." (This statement caused one longtime Roosevelt watcher to jibe, "Hurrah for George Washington!") Roosevelt continued, "I have had nothing whatever to do with raising this issue. Inasmuch as it has been raised of course those who favor my administration and my nomination will favor endorsing both and those who do not will oppose."

When Roosevelt released this reply—while shrewdly refraining from mentioning Hanna's telegram—the Ohio senator had no recourse. He wired back his surrender: "In view of the sentiment expressed I shall not oppose the endorsement of your administration and candidacy by our state convention."

Roosevelt accepted the surrender with satisfaction. "I am pleased at the outcome . . ." he told Lodge. "It simplified things all around, for in my judgment Hanna was my only formidable opponent so far as the nomination is concerned." Roosevelt had just given his "criminal rich" speech at Spokane. "I made it particularly with reference to having a knockdown and dragout fight with Hanna and the whole Wall Street crowd, and I wanted them to understand that if they so desire they shall have all the fighting they wish." With or without Hanna, the money men would put up a struggle. "The big New York and Chicago capitalists—and both the criminal rich and the fool rich—will do all they can to beat me." Yet the idea of a fight had its appeal, especially after several enjoyable but rather unchallenging weeks on the road. "This whole incident has served one temporarily useful purpose, for it has entirely revived me."

Roosevelt applied the finishing touch to his immobilizing of Hanna by writing him a soothing letter two days later. He explained that the apparent rift that had developed between the senator and the administration had given heart to their common foes and threatened to prevent the achievement of their common goals. "I had to take a stand," he explained, adding that he did so with the greatest reluctance. "I hated to do it because you have shown such broad generosity and straightforwardness in all your dealings with me that it was peculiarly painful to me to be put, even temporarily, in a position of seeming antagonism to you." Yet he was sure a man of Hanna's courage and magnanimity would understand. "No one but a really big man—a man above all petty considerations—could have treated me as you have done during the year and a half since President McKinley's death. I have consulted you and relied on your judgment more than I have done with any other man."

IV

Putting Hanna on the shelf effectively guaranteed Roosevelt's renomination; but the president proposed to leave nothing to chance, and he set out to gain a grip on that portion of the party that Hanna had controlled. The Republican Party, as a party, had next to no influence on the affairs of the South, which remained as staunchly Democratic as since the end of Reconstruction; but the converse was not true. Southern Republicans, while nonentities in the politics of their own states, still possessed pull with the national party—for example, at nominating conventions. The South had resisted Roosevelt's charms in 1900 until the last moment, remaining loyal to Hanna. Roosevelt's desire to establish his own base in the South had led to his much denounced dinner with Booker Washington; it also led, or perhaps pushed, him to take a stronger stand on racial issues generally than he might have taken otherwise.

No racial issue was more explosive than lynching. To blacks in the South, lynching was an especially terrifying instrument of the broader oppression by which whites kept blacks poor and powerless despite the paper guarantees of the Thirteenth, Fourteenth, and Fifteenth amendments. To southern whites, lynching was an understandable, if (to some) regrettable, expression of white outrage at blacks' propensity for criminal violence. As with everything else about the race question, lynching was a subject on which southern whites were exceedingly sensitive to criticism from outsiders.

Roosevelt, like many whites of his day, had mixed feelings about lynching. At times he could interpret it as a rough form of popular justice, an inevitable corrective to the failings of the formal criminal justice system. Referring to a recent rash of lynchings, Roosevelt remarked to Attorney General Knox, "Among the causes that have produced this outbreak of lynching—I say only 'among them,' for I do not know how prominent it should be put among them—is, in my judgment, unquestionably the delays of the law, and the way in which clever criminal lawyers are able ofttimes to secure the acquittal, and almost always to secure long delay in the conviction, of men accused of offenses for which the penalty should be absolutely certain and the punishment as quick as possible." Roosevelt had been asked to pardon a murderer said (by friends and sympathizers) to be insane at the time of killing his wife; he refused, not believing the convicted man insane enough to warrant escaping punishment but also not wanting to give the lynchers any more cause for exacting extrajudicial justice. "Every pardon of a murderer who should have been executed is to my mind just so much encouragement to lynching, just so much putting of a premium upon lawlessness."

On the other hand, it was this lawlessness that constituted the principal argument against lynching—this and what Roosevelt called the "inhuman aspect of putting to death by torture—usually by burning alive," as was often the case when blacks were lynched. In the summer of 1903, Roosevelt wrote a letter of congratulation to Governor Winfield Durbin of Indiana, who had acted boldly and bravely to halt a race riot in Evansville (and whose need to do so served as a reminder that the South didn't have a monopoly on racial troubles). Roosevelt expected his letter to be published (it was); consequently, the message was drafted as a public statement on the subject of lynching, which had done much to precipitate the riot.

As in his letter to Knox, Roosevelt acknowledged the sentiments that often lay behind lynching. "In a certain proportion of these cases the man lynched has been guilty of a crime horrible beyond description; a crime so horrible that as far as he himself is concerned he has forfeited the right to any kind of sympathy whatsoever." All the same, Roosevelt continued, honest and upright citizens could look upon the rise of lynchings only with trepidation. "All thoughtful men must feel the gravest alarm over the growth of lynching in this country, and especially over the peculiarly hideous forms so often taken by mob violence when colored men are the victims—on which occasions the mob seems to lay most weight, not on the crime but on the color of the criminal."

A glaring problem with many lynchings was that they wreaked their violence on the wrong persons. "It is of course inevitable that where vengeance is taken by a mob it should frequently light on innocent people, and the wrong done in such a case to the individual is one for which there is no remedy." But the evils of lynching ran deeper than this, to the heart of what it meant to be a civilized society.

> Even where the real criminal is reached, the wrong done by the mob to the community itself is well-nigh as great. Especially is this true where the lynching is accompanied with torture. There are certain hideous sights which when once seen can never be wholly erased from the mental retina. The mere fact of having seen them implies degradation. This is a thousandfold stronger when instead of merely seeing the deed the man has participated in it. Whoever in any part of our country has ever taken part in lawlessly putting to death a criminal by the dreadful torture of fire must forever after have the awful spectacle of his own handiwork seared into his brain and soul. He can never again be the same man.

Such horrendous punishment was sometimes defended as necessary to avenge and deter what Roosevelt called "the inhuman and hideous crime of rape." The president disagreed that it was necessary even in such cases, and besides, it rarely stopped there. "Every violent man in the community is encouraged by every case of lynching in which the lynchers go unpunished to himself take the law into his own hands whenever it suits his own convenience. In the same way the use of torture by the mob in certain cases is sure to spread until it is applied more or less indiscriminately in other cases. The spirit of lawlessness grows with what it feeds on, and when mobs with impunity lynch criminals for one cause, they are certain to begin to lynch real or alleged criminals for other causes." Citing recent statistics, Roosevelt asserted that three-fourths of lynchings were not for rape at all; in many cases they were for very ordinary crimes.

The president was speaking out because he felt he could not keep silent. Nor, he contended, could other honorable citizens.

> Surely no patriot can fail to see the fearful brutalization and debasement which the indulgence of such a spirit and such practices inevitably portends. Surely all public men, all writers for the daily press, all clergymen, all teachers, all who in any way have a right to address the public, should with every energy unite to denounce such crimes and to support those engaged in putting them down. As a people we claim the right to speak with peculiar emphasis for freedom and for fair treatment of all men without regard to differences of race, fortune, creed or color. We forfeit the right so to speak when we commit or condone such crimes as these of which I speak.

The obvious emotion conveyed in this letter demonstrated quite clearly that it came from Roosevelt's heart. Lynching was a great evil, partly because it violated the rights of (mostly black) citizens but equally because it challenged the rule of law, which was the only thing that stood between society and anarchy. Roosevelt was a reformer, but a cautious one; he was about as far from a revolutionary as a person could be. Indeed, it was precisely his fear of uncontrolled change that led him to espouse measured change. Roosevelt thought himself an enlightened conservative, and he never grew more exasperated than when confronted with Neanderthals like coal master George Baer whose resistance to any change whatever threatened to make it impossible to conserve what really needed conserving. To Roosevelt, anarchy was the wolf perpetually at the door, and lynching loosened the lock. As he told Governor Durbin, "Mob violence is simply one form of anarchy."

Yet if Roosevelt's antilynching letter came from the heart, it also came from the head. The letter could be expected to provoke a virulent reaction among white southerners, which it did, with editors lambasting the president's misbegotten meddling in matters of which he had no understanding. But it also could be expected to hearten southern blacks, who looked to the president for support against the lynch law regime. The president in turn looked to them for support against the conservative whites who formed the basis of Hanna's support in the southern wing of the Republican Party.

Roosevelt never spoke of his southern strategy in such calculating terms; given his facility for blurring the distinction between conscience and convenience, he likely never even thought of it in such terms. As usual, he felt that he was serving justice, and he would scarcely be surprised if justice served him. But it was a tricky business. His strategy depended on continued political participation by southern blacks; if recent trends toward exclusion persisted and they were shut out of politics, he would only have accomplished the alienation of whites.

As things were, he was surprised at the vehemence of the white response. "I have been greatly puzzled to account for the yell of bitter anger caused by my action," he confided to Carl Schurz, who was again on Roosevelt's list of people to be cultivated, in this case by sharing confidences. Indeed, Roosevelt confessed to being "greatly puzzled" regarding the race question generally. "Do not misunderstand me. I do not mean that I was puzzled as to whether what I did was right, for I have never been clearer about anything." But how to frame his actions most effectively was a real poser. "I have found it difficult to know how far I ought to go at certain points, and exactly what I ought to say. . . . I have on the one hand been very desirous not to shock southern sentiment, subject, however, on the other hand, to my not flinching from what by right should be done."

Schurz had evinced concern over the obviously orchestrated campaign to deprive southern blacks of their constitutional rights. Roosevelt concurred, yet added that out of deference to white southern opinion, and to the limits of efficacy, he had not made an issue of the matter. "I feel just as you do about the nullification of the 14th, 15th and even 13th Amendments in the South; but as it has not as yet seemed absolutely necessary that I should notice this, I have refrained from doing so." At the same time, Roosevelt said, he would not collaborate in the exclusion. Many southern whites wanted him to appoint only whites to federal positions in the South. He had refused. "I have felt that it would be a base and cowardly act not to appoint occasional colored men. I did not want needlessly to excite alarm and resentment. On the other hand, in the interest of both the white and the black in the Southern States, I could not afford to connive at, and thereby strengthen, a movement of retrogression which in its essence was aimed at depriving all colored men, good and bad, intelligent and degraded, alike, of the elementary rights of citizenship."

Roosevelt really *was* torn as to where wisdom resided on the race question. No other issue found him resorting so often—and not just rhetorically—to the "on the one hand . . . on the other" construction. For Roosevelt it was truly the rare and vexing case where a single hand—if not a single index finger—failed to suffice.

Nor could he say that the results of his actions had borne particular testimony to the wisdom of his actions. In South Carolina his appointments had been overwhelmingly white; most were Democrats, and some were even ex-Confederates. But the odd black appointment had produced "a literally frantic denunciation of me." The reaction in Mississippi had been still more astonishing. There an even greater majority of appointees were white Democrats, and not simply conservative gold Democrats but even some populistic silver Democrats. Yet again the rare black appointment, combined with the fact that he had consulted with Booker Washington before making the appointments, had precipitated a hail of abuse. "There has been no species of foul assault which the victorious faction of the democratic party in Mississippi, headed by Governor Vardaman, has not made upon me."

At this point Roosevelt was prepared to concede that his southern strategy had failed miserably. "I have of course, in both Mississippi and South Carolina, as in most of the other Southern States, completely lost control of the republican machine by what I did, so that if a fight is made against my nomination, I have no question that most of the southern delegates will be against me." The president added that this outcome ought to give the lie to those who claimed that expedience had motivated his actions. "One would think that anyone would see that my course was not dictated by my political self-interest." Yet he wouldn't have changed a thing. "I am very confident that I have acted as a president must act if he intends to use whatever influence he may have on the side of decency and civilization in the South."

V

As things turned out, Roosevelt's weakness in the South didn't matter much. Hanna's hold on the party continued to slip during the early weeks of 1904 until the senator fell ill in February. By the time typhoid fever was diagnosed, Hanna was in mortal danger. Roosevelt called on him at his hotel—"as a matter of course," the president told

Elihu Root. This gesture evidently affected Hanna greatly, for shortly afterward he penciled a note to the White House: "My dear Mr. President: You touched a tender spot, old man, when you called personally to inquire after me this A.M. I may be worse before I can be better, but all the same such 'drops' of kindness are good for a fellow."

The end came a short while later. "Poor Hanna has died," Roosevelt wrote. "I am very, very sorry." The president characterized the death as "a veritable tragedy"—although he appreciated that, from his own perspective, the timing of the senator's illness and death could have been more tragic still. "Thank Heaven, before he became sick the whole opposition to me had collapsed."

Collapsed, yes, but not disappeared, and now Roosevelt couldn't help realizing that Hanna's death had deprived the conservatives within the party of their focal point, their most experienced manager, their directing intelligence. Once more Roosevelt had benefited by another man's death—not so strikingly as when McKinley died but measurably nonetheless. Death had sometimes been hard on Roosevelt personally, but it did wonders for his career.

Perhaps this was what he was thinking, or perhaps he felt he hadn't treated Hanna as well as he should have; in either event, he fairly gushed in a confidential eulogy: "He was a big man in every way and as forceful a personality as we have seen in public life in our generation. I think that not merely I myself, but the whole party and the whole country have reason to be very grateful to him for the way in which, after I came into office, under circumstances which were very hard for him, he resolutely declined to be drawn into the position which a smaller man of meaner cast would inevitably have taken; that is, the position of antagonizing public policies if I was identified with them." Hanna could have wreaked havoc on the administration and the country if he had attacked the policies on Panama, the Philippines, and other crucial questions. "But he stood by them just as loyally as if I had been McKinley."

VI

This was vintage Roosevelt: judging the character of a man in terms of whether that man sided with him or not. Root, the recipient of this letter and the most quizzical of Roosevelt's intimates, must have rolled his eyes at these words. At the same time, though, Root appreciated the president's gifts and on the whole thought the country could hardly do better in a chief executive.

This, at any rate, was what he told a gathering of skeptical influentials at the Union League Club of New York. Root stoutly defended Roosevelt as "the greatest conservative force for the protection of property and our institutions in the city of Washington." Corporate leaders might not agree with everything the president proposed, but he was far preferable to the likely alternatives—namely, the Democratic candidates—and indeed was the most potent proof against the radicalism many Democrats were espousing. Evidently Root got his point across: One of those in the audience wrote Roosevelt the next day that he ought to send Root "a gold watch, or a diamond necklace, or a house and lot or any little thing that occurs to you," so laudatory and effective had Root's speech been.

Roosevelt appreciated Root's support. He doubtless recalled how Root had almost single-handedly saved his candidacy in the 1898 governor's race after the irregularities in his residency and tax paying became an issue. Just as it had then, so now Root's credibility with conservatives served Roosevelt well.

Root was one of Roosevelt's envoys to the conservatives; another was the man the president chose to replace Hanna as chairman of the Republican National Committee. At first Roosevelt offered the chairmanship to Cornelius Bliss of New York, former secretary of the interior, close Hanna associate, current treasurer of the party, and a man whom Roosevelt hoped would allow the oft-bickering Platt and Odell wings of the state party to join hands in support of his nomination. Moreover, Bliss was a well-known businessman; his appointment could be expected to appeal to Wall Street.

Roosevelt made a strong pitch: "You were in McKinley's Cabinet; you were Hanna's right-hand man; you are known all over the country as a public servant of marked ability and the highest probity; you are known to the business world; you have the confidence of the people as no one else whom we could choose for the place could have it." On the chance that flattery failed, Roosevelt promised power. "You would become of right one of the trusted and intimate advisers in all matters before the administration for the next four years, if we were successful."

But Bliss's head would not be turned, as it had not been turned by McKinley's efforts to have him accept the vice presidential nomination Roosevelt wound up with in 1900. He said he wanted to stay on as treasurer.

Having paid his respects to the Hanna wing, Roosevelt then turned to one of his own. He had long had high regard for the abilities of George Cortelyou, a former court reporter who had become personal secretary to President Cleveland and then McKinley. By 1901 he was something of a fixture in the White House, and Roosevelt inherited him along with numerous other appurtenances of the office. Partly because of his partiality toward ordinary folks who had made good, partly because of Cortelyou's obvious enchantment with him, and mostly because of the man's quick mind and astute organizational gifts, Roosevelt elevated him to a cabinet executive post, as the first secretary of the new Department of Commerce and Labor. He was sufficiently pleased with Cortelyou's performance in that capacity to offer him the job of Republican national chairman when Bliss declined.

Roosevelt knew the nomination might cause trouble. Neither Platt nor Odell liked the idea of honoring a man who was not a practical politician or, by background, even a reliable Republican. Many members of the Republican National Committee had similar reservations. But an incumbent president of good health and great vigor is hard for his party to resist. "If I am to run for President," Roosevelt announced, "then Cortelyou is to be Chairman of the National Committee. I will not have it any other way." Somewhat more ominously Roosevelt requested information on those who were balking. "Please give me names of people opposed to him . . ." Roosevelt asked George Meyer, a Boston friend of his and Lodge's and a prominent Republican. "The choice of Cortelyou is irrevocable and I will not consider any other man for the position, and shall treat opposition to him as simply disguised opposition to the republican party." For emphasis he repeated himself: "I regard opposition or disloyalty to Mr. Cortelyou as being simply an expression of disloyalty to the republican party."

In personal affairs Roosevelt had long treated opposition as the mark of moral failing on the part of his opponents, but not until now had he felt strong enough to apply this egocentric standard to the national Republican Party as a whole. His power play paid off. Few committeemen wanted to risk the wrath of a president almost certain to be reelected; with Roosevelt writing down names, the resistance to Cortelyou rapidly melted away.

Nor was Roosevelt content to dominate the party. He fully believed that the nation, for its own good, needed to return him to the White House. "I am sure that the policies for which I stand," he told a supporter, "are those in accordance with which this country must be governed, and up to which we must all of us live in public or private life, under penalty of grave disaster to the nation."

VII

By now Roosevelt had guaranteed success in the first step toward averting this national disaster. He had locked up the nomination, fully as tightly as McKinley had locked up renomination in 1900. No one stepped forward to oppose the president; when the Republicans gathered in convention in Chicago in June, they embraced him by acclamation.

The vice presidential nomination, on the other hand, was just as unpredictable as it had been in 1900. Roosevelt wanted the position to go to Robert Hitt, a longtime congressman from Illinois and a friendly hand at the helm of the House Foreign Affairs Committee. "I very earnestly hope that Mr. Hitt will be nominated for Vice-President with me," Roosevelt told Ted. "He would be an excellent candidate, and if I should be elected he would be of all men the pleasantest to work with." What Roosevelt meant, of course, was that Hitt would help deliver the large electoral vote of Illinois and wouldn't argue with him.

But Roosevelt wasn't to have his way. Although the challenge to Cortelyou as party chairman had evaporated, the resentment his appointment had engendered transmuted into opposition to Hitt. Exercising the small scope for independence left to it, the convention tapped Charles Fairbanks, a senator from Indiana who before McKinley's death had evinced presidential aspirations for 1904.

Roosevelt, having personal experience of the unimportance of the vice presidency and entirely intending to live for another four years, accepted this minor setback graciously.

The party platform was perfectly predictable. It pointed with pride to the prosperity that even now was elevating American living standards, to the national glory and international improvement that followed the party's wise and courageous decision for war with Spain in 1898, and to the numerous other boons the American people had enjoyed during the previous eight years. It viewed with alarm the actions and promises of the Democrats during that same period and warned of dire consequences should that deeply flawed party unaccountably prevail in the autumn.

The one bit of excitement at the convention was a stirring message from Roosevelt—not to the convention, but to the American consul in Morocco, of all people and places. Two months earlier an American named Ion Perdicaris and a relative traveling with him had been kidnapped by a bandit called the Raisuli, who demanded a ransom for their release. Bandits had been engaged in this sort of behavior in that part of the world for centuries; what disturbed Roosevelt was the apparent apathy of the Moroccan government in the affair. To encourage action he ordered an increase in the American naval presence off Tangier; there was even a hint of an American landing. These measures helped concentrate the mind of the Moroccan sultan, who preferred to keep his problems within the country, and he arranged the captives' release. But before this good news got back to the United States, Roosevelt took the opportunity to resuscitate the somnolent Republican convention. At a moment of maximum drowsiness he arranged with the chairman of the convention, House Speaker Joseph Cannon, to have the clerk read an ultimatum that was going out to Morocco: "We want either Perdicaris alive or Raisuli dead."

This brought the delegates to their feet, cheering the dash and energy of their president. When the hostages turned up alive shortly afterward, the president's boldness drew another round of applause, this time from the nation at large. John Hay, who drafted the cable to Tangier—the more prosaic parts of which weren't read to the convention—could only marvel at Roosevelt's flair for the dramatic. "My telegram to Gummeré had an uncalled-for success," Hay noted in his diary. "It is curious how a concise impropriety hits the public."

VIII

After the maneuvering and manipulation that won him command of the party, Roosevelt found the campaign itself confining. The heavy lifting he had to leave to others: Sitting presidents, even unelected ones, were still expected to stay off the stump. His formal contribution consisted chiefly of his letter officially accepting the nomination. He lambasted the Democrats for irresolution and misrepresentation; he waved the bloody shirt over the issue of veterans' pensions; he shamelessly defended the rights of business against Democratic encroachments, saying that "fundamentally ours is a business people"; he extolled the tariff as "part of the very fibre of the country"; he averred, without exception, that there was not a policy of the present administration "which it would not be disastrous to reverse or abandon."

As Roosevelt's reference to business and the tariff demonstrated, he was continuing his efforts to cultivate the capitalists. The Democrats made a halfhearted gesture toward the boardrooms by nominating Alton Parker, a New York jurist, a pillar of the eastern establishment, and a man about as far removed from William Jennings Bryan as he could be and remain a living, breathing Democrat. Parker had almost no issues to run on. The party abandoned silver at the same time that it abandoned Bryan; Roosevelt had spiked the Democrats' antitrust guns with his Northern Securities suit and drained their supply of labor indignation by his Baer-baiting in the anthracite strike. Democratic anti-imperialism didn't cut much ice, either, with the war in the Philippines over.

Although tradition kept Roosevelt off the campaign trail—for the first time in a presidential contest in twenty years—he involved himself intimately in the efforts on his behalf. He wrote instructions to George Cortelyou nearly every day, ordering rebuttals to Democratic attacks, directing strategy for appealing to important interest groups, worrying about opposition inroads in one state or another.

He realized he might be holding the levers too tightly. "I wonder whether President McKinley bothered Hanna as I am bothering you!" he remarked to Cortelyou early on. But wondering didn't make him stop. "Did you notice in the *Tribune* today the exposure about Parker having interpolated in his speech a strong affirmation about the gold standard with the perfectly transparent purpose of having the official copy go all through the West, and the copy with the interpolation reserved for circulation in Eastern financial centers? I think this should be brought out in the strongest possible way by your publication bureau."

IX

While nudging Cortelyou, Roosevelt applied his persuasive skills to reporters and editors. Presidents could speak more freely to journalists in those days than later; convention decreed that a chief executive could never be quoted or even directly attributed unless speaking in public or unless he granted specific authority to do so. Roosevelt improved on this policy by semiformalizing sanctions against those who violated the convention. He created the "Ananias Club" for reporters who heard something at the White House and repeated it outside; members were denied further access to confidential information. The Ananiases accepted their punishment with greater or less grace; what was harder to bear was Roosevelt's bald denial of statements they knew perfectly well—and *he* knew perfectly well—he had made.

Roosevelt justified his denials on grounds that otherwise he would never be able to speak freely with his numerous paid and unpaid advisers. "I see hundreds of men each day," he explained, exaggerating greatly, "and they say many things to me, and I make many references." These exchanges were informal and should be kept so, unburdened by the weight of official policy. "What I have to say to the public will be in public speeches, messages to Congress, or proclamations. No man can become my mouthpiece." More succinctly: "I reserve the right to deny any statement attributed to me in these personal conversations."

Reporters and others might have accepted this reasoning as it applied to conversations with cabinet members, legislators, and others invested with public office, but many thought Roosevelt went too far when he included journalists in the ban. Roosevelt defended his policy adamantly, if somewhat sophistically. Following a White House denial of a statement attributed to Roosevelt by a French reporter, Roosevelt asked Hermann Kohlsaat if he had seen the denial. "Yes," Kohlsaat replied, "and I believe you said what the Frenchman sent to his paper, because you have said the same thing to me." Unrepentant, Roosevelt rejoined, "Of course I said it, but I said it as Theodore Roosevelt and not as the President of the United States!"

Yet however much the journalists disliked not being able to say what they knew, they liked even less the idea of not knowing it in the first place, and the great majority accepted Roosevelt's ground rules. Consequently, he felt free to think out loud to editors and their subordinates, explaining his side of things without worrying that what he said might be used against him. He gained important information in return regarding the state of public opinion; of equal value, he created what often amounted to an influential cabal of co-conspirators.

During the 1904 campaign Roosevelt worked his news network almost around the clock. With few other demands on his time— Congress being in recess and the world comparatively quiet for the moment—he had ample opportunity to write letters to journalists near and far. Dictating from his desk, dictating while pacing about the office, while being shaved or having his hair cut, while playing with Quentin and his friends, he conducted what amounted to a back-channel campaign.

To well-known investigative journalist Ray Stannard Baker, for example, he sent a long defense of his position as between labor and management. Baker had suggested in an article that people were confused by the president's reception at the White House of a delegation of miners from Montana; how did he reconcile this with his treatment of the Miller case (in which Roosevelt had rejected the idea of union membership as a condition of employment in the government printing office and, by extension, in other executive agencies)?

Roosevelt registered exasperation that people couldn't understand his insistence on steering a middle course in labor-management disputes. "When we get hold of a fool who thinks that my refusing to sanction the tyranny of capital over labor is contradicted by, instead of complemented by, my refusal to allow labor in its turn to tyrannize, why, I don't see that any explanation will make the matter clear to him." The facts were simple. As they involved business: "I believe in corporations. If a corporation is doing square work I will help it so far as I can. If it oppresses anybody; if it is acting dishonestly towards its stockholders or the public, or towards its laborers, or towards small competitors—why, when I have power I shall try to cinch it." Likewise toward labor: "I believe in labor unions. If I were a wage-worker I should certainly join one; and I am now an honorary member of one and am very proud of it. But if the members of labor unions indulge in rioting and violence, or behave wrongfully either to a capitalist or to another laborer or to the general public, I shall antagonize them just as fearlessly as under similar circumstances I should antagonize the biggest capitalist in the land."

Roosevelt urged Baker to keep these two principles in balance in writing about the administration. "My action on labor should always be considered in connection with my action as regards capital, and both are reducible to my favorite formula—a square deal for every man." Roosevelt liked the formula so much that he was willing to lend it to Baker for an article. "I wish you could put that as the title." (Baker declined the offer, but Roosevelt adopted the phrase as the label for his domestic policies generally.)

X

As always Roosevelt grew hot with indignation at what he conceived to be the duplicity of his rivals. "What an insincere canvass our opponents are waging this year!" he exclaimed to a friend. "They are trying to carry New York by putting Cleveland on the stump and keeping out Bryan; and Indiana by putting Bryan on the stump and keeping out Cleveland; and are explaining in the East that if Parker is elected Bryanism is dead; and in the West that if Parker is elected it means that Bryan, as a sharer in the triumph, will gain an immense amount of political influence." New York Democrats were playing particularly foul, damning the president for the alleged sins of Governor Odell. "They are scandalously and iniquitously unjust and mendacious." Nor could Parker hide behind the actions of his handlers and supporters. "I used to think Parker only a fool, but I guess he is as much of a knave as his associates. He lies like a trooper all the time."

What Roosevelt particularly resented were charges by Parker and other Democrats that Cortelyou and others on the Republican National Committee were buying the support of the trusts with promises to go easy on antitrust prosecution after November. For most of the autumn campaign the Democratic press, lacking much else to hit the incumbent with, seized on the stick of "Cortelyouism"; Parker himself joined the chorus as defeat drew nearer.

Roosevelt roundly rejected the very idea that he would entertain for even a moment the suggestion that corporate contributions to his campaign should have the slightest influence on the actions of his administration. To the extent that businessmen chose to support his election, they were doing so simply from an understanding that his policies were most likely to create a constructive climate for business activity. "The big business corporations have a tremendous stake in the welfare of this country," he declared. "They know that this welfare can only be secured through the continuance in power of the Republican party; and if they subscribe for the purpose of securing such national welfare, and with no thought of personal favors to them, why they are acting as is entirely proper."

All the same, the president conceded that appearances mattered. Certain people, misled by the malicious, might mistake a coincidence of views for collusion. Consequently, even while giving the order to "attack Parker" and demanding "an aggressive fight against the insincerity and double dealing of the Parker campaign," Roosevelt directed a minor tactical retreat. He didn't tell Cortelyou to stop asking for corporate money; in fact, he said almost nothing to the party chairman regarding fund-raising. But after a journalist uncovered a report that Rockefeller's Standard Oil trust had sent Cortelyou a check for one hundred thousand dollars, Roosevelt decided that political propriety required him to step in. He told Cortelyou to return the check at once.

Having elevated himself above even Caesar's wife, Roosevelt grew righteously wrathful when, just days before the election, Parker amplified the charges of a Republican shakedown of the bosses of Wall Street. Desperate, the normally judicious jurist let the word "blackmail" slip past his lips.

Roosevelt pounced upon the statement. He broke his official silence to castigate the Democratic calumny as "monstrous." Speaking as if to a grand jury, he declared, "The assertion that there has been any blackmail, direct or indirect, by Mr. Cortelyou or by me is a falsehood. The assertion that there has been made any pledge or promise or that there has been any understanding as to future immunities or benefits, in recognition of any contribution from any source is a wicked falsehood." Voters must surely take note of the infamy of these charges. "Heavy must be the condemnation of the man making them."

Roosevelt always felt better when he was on the attack, and he always attacked better when he was convinced that he was in the right and his opponents in the wrong, as he almost always did. In this case there was some of both right and wrong on each side. Roosevelt definitely did not give any hints of easy treatment to potential donors; for the most part he didn't even know who had made Cortelyou's short list of deep pockets. That was the whole point of having a national chairman and a national committee: *They* were the ones who had the lists, who hit up the people on the list, who remembered afterward who had contributed and who hadn't. The candidate remained innocently in the dark—at least until after the balloting. This tradition was not unique to the Republican Party, but since the days of Grant it had especially marked the party of business. "Mr. Cortelyou has really run the election," Roosevelt confessed to Kermit, referring particularly to the financial side of the race. "And I have had little to do with it."

As a matter of fact, Parker was far closer to the truth than Roosevelt knew or cared to know. Cortelyou and party treasurer Bliss, the latter having learned the art of massaging for money from Mark Hanna, conducted a thorough sweep of the head offices of the major businesses. In estimating how much each corporation could afford to give, they may or may not have used information improperly gathered, perhaps from the Bureau of Corporations. If they intimated anything in the way of reciprocation, they certainly didn't have Roosevelt's authorization to do so. And given Roosevelt's record of high-profile skepticism of business motives, the corporate executives would have been foolish indeed to think they were buying any reliable goodwill. On the other hand, they definitely didn't desire to incur any more of the president's wrath than they already had, as a group or individually. For a company like Standard Oil, $100,000 (or $125,000, as subsequent evidence indicated) was a comparatively cheap insurance premium.

And a nonrefundable premium at that. Despite Roosevelt's direct order to Cortelyou, the oil company didn't get its money back. Bliss made plain why he hadn't wanted to give up the treasurer's post for the chairmanship: As treasurer he opened the books to no one, not even the president. Knowing that all would be forgiven in the event of victory, and nothing forgiven in the event of defeat, he deposited the money and kept his mouth shut. Standard Oil was hardly in a position to complain, and Roosevelt didn't have to know. (The facts came out only years later.)

XI

Despite his apparent advantage over Parker, Roosevelt grew increasingly nervous as the day of decision approached. His composure had already been shaken by the surprise appearance in his camp of some longtime antagonists. On learning that the New York *Sun* had endorsed him, he said he was "very much concerned and alarmed." But he took reassurance from the fact that the *Sun*'s endorsement was hardly unqualified. "Theodore! with all thy faults—" ran the editorial head. The president was painfully aware of the deficiencies of his knowledge regarding the state of mind of the electorate. "A candidate can never tell much about his own prospects," he observed—in a remark as revealing of his appreciation of the perception-skewing effects of his own hopes as of the rudimentary condition of public-pulse-taking. He added, "I shall be confident of the result only after the votes are counted."

Sometimes Roosevelt affected unconcern. Writing to Kermit he laid out the odds for and against his victory in November, then asserted: "In the meanwhile we must possess our souls in patience. If things go wrong remember that we are very, very fortunate to have had three years in the White House, and that I have had a chance to accomplish work such as comes to very, very few men in any generation; and that I have no business to feel downcast or querulous merely because when so much has been given me I have not had even more."

At other times his agitation showed through. To a friend who told him he had nothing to worry about, he replied, "Good Heavens, I wish the election were over as you say it is! I am lying still under shell fire, and I mortally hate the experience."

Until the final hour he considered the outcome too close to call. "I haven't an idea what effect Parker has produced by the infamous campaign of personal slander which he has recently inaugurated," the president said on November 3. "I should think it would make every decent man disgusted with him. But it may be that he may deceive some decent men into believing the falsehoods that he is spreading." To Kermit he wrote: "Parker is as I learned from first-hand sources entirely confident of his election. My friends are equally confident in my election. I have not the vaguest idea which is right."

The latter were, by miles. Roosevelt won a tremendous victory over his Democratic rival, receiving 7.6 million votes to Parker's 5.1 million. As usual the margin was magnified in the electoral college, with the incumbent besting the challenger by a tally of 336 to 140. Roosevelt swept every state outside the almost automatically Democratic old Confederacy; he even carried Missouri, whose voters (at least the reading ones) may have recalled his esteem for Thomas Benton. His strength was especially impressive in the West: California endorsed him by better than 2 to 1, Oregon and Washington by almost 4 to 1. He owned the Dakotas, Nebraska, and the upper Midwest; his majority in Michigan was nearly 230,000 out of 500,000 votes cast. He had worried that squabbles between the Odell and Platt wings of the New York party would jeopardize his chances there; his cushion in the Empire State turned out to be 175,000.

"Have swept the country by majorities which astound me," Roosevelt cabled Lodge as the results rolled in. Catching his breath, he declared, "I had no idea there would be such a sweep."

CHAPTER TWENTY

The Logic of Power
1904–5

Roosevelt's breathtaking victory stunned his opponents and gratified his supporters; an announcement he made on the evening of his triumph stunned his supporters and gratified his opponents. Declaring himself deeply honored by the great vote of confidence that even then was pouring in, the president said he would consider the three-and-a-half years between September 1901 and March 1905 as equivalent to a full first term, in the sense that George Washington had understood such things. "The wise custom which limits the President to two terms regards the substance and not the form," he continued. "Under no circumstances will I be a candidate for or accept another nomination."

Roosevelt's statement shocked even those closest to him. Quite evidently he had been thinking the matter over; several days later he wrote to W. Murray Crane: "You saw that I acted upon the conclusion we had reached, and made public what I had to say about the third term at the earliest possible moment." Lodge was also aware of Roosevelt's third-term thinking. "I know of course how you felt in regard to another term," Lodge wrote from Massachusetts. But he hadn't realized his friend was going to reveal that thinking so soon. "It had not occurred to me that you would say it at that precise moment."

Apparently it hadn't occurred to Edith, either. Roosevelt may have raised with her the general subject of serving only two terms, but he seems to have kept her in the dark that he was going to abjure a third term even before his second term began. Doubtless he did so for the same reason he declined to tell Lodge: that he feared she would try to change his mind—as indeed she would have tried, as she later admitted to Owen Wister. Personally, Edith was getting used to being First Lady; it wasn't a bad position at all, despite her continued worries about the possibility of Theodore's assassination. More to the point, though, she understood the difficulties that a lame-duck president would labor under, especially when that lame duck couldn't count on the support of his own party. The American people might love Roosevelt—Edith had no trouble believing that—but it remained obvious that Republican conservatives, not to mention most Democrats, didn't.

Even more to the point, Edith must have sensed—even though she seems not to have put it into words—that her husband would have difficulty adjusting to life after the presidency. He was forty-six years old now; he would be fifty when he left the White House. What would he do then? She had seen him pace his study at Sagamore during the spring and summer of 1901; in five months he had nearly worn through the floorboards. Being an ex-president appeared hardly more engaging than being a vice president had been. To be sure, he had his pastimes: riding, rowing, hunting, chopping, birding, writing. He could keep busy. But he had always felt the need for achievement, and after the presidency, whatever he could achieve in other areas would almost certainly seem second-rate.

And there was something else. She couldn't help feeling hurt that he hadn't confided his thinking to her. Did he still hold his missed chance for the New York mayorship against her? That hardly seemed likely in one who now held an office far more important than that of any mayor. Had she complained too loudly about not wanting him to be nominated for vice president? Well, he had objected, too. She could accept that he had to make his own political decisions for himself, but those decisions were life decisions for her and the children. Didn't she deserve a hearing?

II

At subsequent moments of frustration, Roosevelt would agree with Edith and Lodge that he may have spoken too soon. "I would cut my hand off right there," he reportedly told Hermann Kohlsaat, laying his finger on his wrist, "if I could recall that written statement." (Like Roosevelt, Kohlsaat knew how to tell a story; but the phrasing, as well as the sentiment, sounds like the Roosevelt revealed by other evidence.)

Yet however impolitic Roosevelt's election night statement, it was entirely in character. Indeed, its political imprudence—which Roosevelt fully appreciated—was its very purpose, and his decision to make it anyway was, in certain fundamental respects, the defining moment of his presidency. For someone who spent almost his entire adult life in the public arena, Roosevelt was exceedingly sensitive to criticism. The criticism that stung the most came from his perennial antagonists, the mugwumps. No one who dismissed the independent reformers as completely as Roosevelt said he did would have expended such emotional energy on them. Even in his moment of stunning triumph, he lashed out at "Carl Schurz and the *Evening Post* crowd" (a group that overlapped with "the lying scoundrels who write for *The Nation*"—an earlier slam). These men were "hypocritical and insincere," Roosevelt insisted. "They have loudly professed to demand just exactly the kind of government I have given, and yet they have done their futile best to defeat me." In this letter to Owen Wister the president went to considerable length to defend himself against the criticism of Schurz and the others—and this *after* the election, when their criticism was largely moot.

Almost certainly Roosevelt reacted so strongly to the mugwump attacks, which centered on a concern that in his quest for reelection Roosevelt had compromised with the corporate underwriters of the Republican Party, because of a nagging sense that there was something to the charges. He had indeed trimmed his sails during the last year, after the fearless actions of his first year in office; and his campaign did indeed depend on the generosity of the capitalists, to a degree Roosevelt could easily guess even if he couldn't specify. While the pragmatist in him justified the modulation of his tone toward business as the price principle paid to practicality, as nothing more than a temporary and tactical retreat, the romantic in him wanted to storm the fortress at once, to win all or go down trying.

It was the romantic in Roosevelt that announced on November 8 that he would not be a candidate again. This statement was

Roosevelt's riposte to those who alleged that a love for power had warped his sense of right and wrong. In the very moment of victory, when delusions of grandeur should have held him in their grasp, if they ever would, he renounced power. A nobler or more dramatic gesture was hard to imagine of a politician; in making it, Roosevelt believed he would confirm once and for all his claim to serve not his own self-interest but only the public good.

Not until late in life would Roosevelt acquire significant capacity for self-reflection. Until then he continued to conflate the reality of his life with the role he imagined himself playing. Professional politicians and career observers of the political scene, their faculties honed by tawdry experience to a keen edge of skepticism, had great difficulty accepting Roosevelt at face value. Hypocrisy seemed the only explanation for his ability to say one thing and do something else. In most cases the criticism was wrong, for it assumed a self-knowledge that Roosevelt simply didn't have.

Roosevelt's romanticism may have been lost on the pols, but the polis loved it. The 1904 election revealed as much. Never had a presidential candidate amassed such a margin of the popular vote. Roosevelt boasted to Kermit, "The only States that went against me were those in which no free discussion is allowed and in which fraud and violence have rendered the voting a farce"—which was to say, the South. "I have the greatest popular majority and the greatest electoral majority ever given to a candidate for President." (In his excitement Roosevelt might have been forgiven for exaggerating slightly. He did indeed roll up a larger total and a larger percentage of the popular vote than any candidate since popular tallies began to be kept, in the 1820s; but Grant in 1872 beat Roosevelt's percentage of the electoral vote, although, due to the smaller number of states and electors, not his total.)

If the people responded to Roosevelt, he responded to them. "It is a peculiar gratification to me," he told Wister, "to have owed my election not to the politicians primarily, although of course I have done my best to get on with them; not to the financiers, although I have staunchly upheld the rights of property; but above all to Abraham Lincoln's 'plain people'; to the folk who work hard on farm, in shop, or on the railroads, or who own little stores, little businesses which they manage themselves." These plain people had placed their trust in him; this trust was a sacred responsibility. "I would literally, not figuratively, rather cut off my right hand than forfeit by any improper act of mine the trust and regard of these people. I may have to do something of which they will disapprove, because I deem it absolutely right and necessary; but most assuredly I shall endeavor not to merit their disapproval by any act inconsistent with the ideal they have formed of me."

III

Of course, the ideal the public had formed of Roosevelt was largely a reflection of the ideal he had created for himself. Better than any president since Lincoln, Roosevelt embodied a romanticized view of American life. His was no rags-to-riches story, to be sure, but then the rags of that hoary tale had never been as popular as the riches, as long as the rich man didn't put on airs, which Roosevelt conspicuously didn't. Many politicians affected the common touch; some affected it quite persuasively. But for Roosevelt it was no affectation. He really *did* feel a bond with the "plain people" of America. Not for years had he shared their life, the way he did in Dakota, but his political trips across the country, especially through the West, periodically reconnected him to his adopted roots.

Roosevelt cultivated his connections with the ordinary people of the country however he could. In an age of large families, he appreciated the popular appeal of his own large family, and where it didn't intrude excessively on the children's privacy, he allowed the public, through the press, to have a look. The children attended the obvious public events, such as his inauguration in March 1905, and while they weren't paraded before the cameras, neither were they hidden from view.

Of course, coverage of the children—like coverage of himself—inevitably produced inaccuracies. If the errors weren't too grievous, Roosevelt generally suffered them in silence, believing that calling attention to such errors would simply multiply their ill effect. But now and then he reacted strongly to what he considered outlandishly flagrant misreporting. A correspondent for the Boston *Herald* wrote that at the White House Thanksgiving celebration of November 1904, the smaller children had delighted in chasing a frightened turkey about the grounds while their father laughed at their antics. The story, which alleged cruelty in the affair, aroused Roosevelt's ire; he promptly ordered an embargo on news from all federal departments in Washington to the offending paper—which, perhaps not coincidentally, had registered reservations regarding administration policies unrelated to animal rights. Roosevelt also fired off an angry letter to the *Herald*'s editor. The president charged "deliberate falsification" in the paper's editorial columns heretofore; but against these, he reminded, he had refrained from objecting. He could not stay silent, however, in the face of this slander against his children. "Dispatches such as this dispatch about alleged cruelty to the turkey are not only false but are wilfully false; they are malicious inventions." On behalf of his children, the president demanded a retraction and an apology.

Although other papers screamed foul at this high-handed use of executive power, intimating when they didn't state outright that if the president could wring the neck of the *Herald* over a turkey, he could probably throttle other critics on other issues, the *Herald*'s editor yielded. The requisite retraction appeared, and the embargo was lifted.

Controlling coverage of the older children, who spent much of their time away from home, was more problematic. An uneasy truce, interrupted by occasional outbursts, held between Alice, on one hand, and her father and stepmother, on the other. At times Alice thrived on being the center of attention as First Daughter. Her debut ball in early 1902 was the first event of its kind in the White House and one of the highlights of that social season. The occasion brought the most stylish and eligible young men and ladies of Washington society to the executive mansion; among the guests were the daughters of the British ambassador, the Misses Pauncefote; the daughter of the Russian ambassador, Countess Marguerite Cassini; and Alice's dashing distant cousin, Franklin Delano Roosevelt.

Though Alice was the empress of the evening, the fete failed to live up to her expectations, which ran much more toward the extravagance of the Newport set than the simplicity (if often elegant simplicity) of the Oyster Bay crowd. She complained when her parents declined to offer the guests the lavish favors—gold watches, silver cigarette cases—that were de rigueur among the fashionable Four

Hundred. Alice demanded that these be supplied out of the allowance she got from her Lee grandparents; when Edith and Theodore still refused, explaining that since they were giving the party, they would decide what was appropriate, she threw a snit.

Protocol occasionally required Alice to perform official functions. During the late winter of 1902 the brother of the German kaiser came to America. Prince Heinrich was to accept delivery of a yacht being built for the German royal family at a New Jersey shipyard; he also intended to wave the flag and promote German-American amity. Royalty was right in Alice's line, and she volunteered to show the prince around. She christened the vessel, escorted Heinrich to dinner, accepted a diamond bracelet sent by the kaiser, and generally had a glorious time. The anti-Roosevelt press made much of Alice's airs, calling her Princess Alice and suggesting that a taste for royalism in the daughter betrayed similar tendencies in her father. Roosevelt might have been more annoyed had he not found the prince to be a regular fellow: a delightful dinner guest and a game companion on a two-hour ride through the rain.

Relations between the father and daughter remained rocky. She was convinced he didn't love her. "Father doesn't care for me," Alice asserted in her diary; "that is to say one eighth as much as he does for the other children." It was scarcely surprising that she felt this way. She still resented her father's having abandoned her during her first three years of life, and she always felt that she didn't fit into the family he had created with Edith. Ethel had Edith to turn to; Alice, the stepdaughter, didn't, at least not in the same way. Edith tried to understand Alice and to sympathize, but at least as often she felt obliged to instruct her stepdaughter in the ways of civilized society. "I meant to warn you about talking continuously of yourself," Edith wrote in one letter. "It is quite the natural subject for a girl of your age, but except with family, is neither well bred nor nice." On another occasion she reminded Alice, whose allowance from the Lees gave her more independence than any of the other children enjoyed, that such independence entailed responsibilities—foremost, to settle up with her creditors. "If you have debts they must be paid." (In this case Edith spoke too soon. Upon learning that Alice had already paid the merchants in question, she apologized: "I feel quite repentant for your letter came this morning so I need not have scolded you last night.")

Theodore was little help. He wasn't good with girls: They couldn't box or wrestle or play football or do most of the things that bonded him to his boys. Besides, his was simply an overpowering personality. All the children felt it. Ted attempted to live up to his father's example and expectations by doing the things Roosevelt liked—boxing, football, hunting—and the strain had nearly broken his spirit and his health, although he seemed to be finding himself lately. Alice adopted the opposite expedient of not even trying to please her father; she rebelled instead. She stayed out late and consorted with individuals he judged a bad influence. Realizing that there was only so much he could do with her, he resigned himself to hoping that she would not find *too* much trouble. He told Ted: "Sister continues to lead the life of social excitement, which is all right for a girl to lead for a year or two, but which upon my word I do not regard as healthy from the standpoint of permanence." Wistfully, he continued, "I wish she had some pronounced serious taste. Perhaps she will develop one later."

(At times Roosevelt doubtless wished Alice took after her more responsible cousin Eleanor, who chose the late winter of 1905 to marry that other, more distant cousin, Franklin. Alice was a bridesmaid in the wedding, which Theodore and Edith attended in New York on Saint Patrick's Day. The president congratulated the groom: "Well, Franklin, there's nothing like keeping the name in the family.")

For the most part, Roosevelt tried to ignore Alice's willful behavior. When a friend asked why he didn't look more closely after his daughter, Roosevelt reportedly replied, "I can be president of the United States, or I can attend to Alice. I can't do both."

IV

He didn't always have to do both, because he had help. Bamie was watching out for Alice, as she always had, and when things got difficult between Alice and Edith, as they so often did, Bamie lent a more sympathetic ear than her stepmother supplied. "Alice came in with her amber-colored hair," Bamie recalled of her niece's lament at the imposed frugality of her debut, "and shed an amber-colored tear."

Bamie also watched out for Theodore. She had moved to Washington at the end of 1899 when Will Cowles was posted to the Bureau of Navigation of the Navy Department. Though this terminated her breakfast sessions with her brother and Tom Platt, she soon established in the nation's capital a niche that arguably was more influential. Her house at 1733 N Street, just a few blocks from Cabot and Nannie Lodge's and Du Pont Circle, became a regular stop for the diplomatic and social elites; every Tuesday, almost without fail, the carriages and the odd automobile lined up outside her door to deposit their distinguished owners. "Here come the 'dips,'" her English maid would say.

When Roosevelt suddenly became president in 1901, Bamie was well positioned to greet him—in fact, he and Edith stayed with Bamie while Mrs. McKinley was pulling herself together after her husband's death. It was at this time that 1733 N Street became known as the "Little White House," and the name stuck, with reason. Theodore dropped by frequently to meet friends, family, and influential individuals who for personal or political reasons he preferred not to invite to the real White House.

Theodore's visits also afforded the president an opportunity to try out ideas on Bamie. According to Eleanor—who by the time she spoke these words knew a good deal about how presidents seek advice, and who had lived with her aunt for two years before marrying Franklin— "Uncle Theodore made no major decision in foreign or domestic policy without first discussing it with Auntie Bye." Precisely what counsel Bamie offered on any specific topic is impossible to tell. She was the soul of discretion—"Bamie has never given anyone away," a longtime intimate explained—and in any event such advice was usually spoken rather than written. Quite likely she served principally as a sounding board: a critical intelligence to whom her brother could think aloud more freely than with nearly anyone else. A president has few disinterested advisers among his political associates, and Edith's opinions, valuable though they might have been, came clouded with personal considerations that didn't affect Bamie. Theodore was nearly as discreet as Bamie regarding their sessions together, but he revealed something of the nature of his relationship with his sister in a letter to Alice. "Auntie Bye is as dear as ever," he wrote, "and oversees the entire nation."

V

It was a good thing Bamie was watching the nation, because her brother had decided to supervise the hemisphere. In December 1904, Roosevelt announced a policy that went beyond anything any of his predecessors in the White House had conceived of: He declared that the United States—meaning, in effect, himself—would henceforth act as sheriff of North and South America.

The Roosevelt Corollary, as this policy was soon called, followed from the Monroe Doctrine, as the name and circumstances suggested. It also followed from Roosevelt's trying experience with the German emperor regarding Venezuela. Although the president was pleased to count as a quiet triumph the German acceptance of arbitration, he recognized that the temptation for Germany and other European countries to meddle in Latin American affairs persisted. Several Latin American governments had followed the Venezuelan example—or set precedents of their own—in running up big debts to European bond-holders. When those governments, or sometimes successors ushered into office by the dissatisfaction the debts evoked, failed to make timely payment on their obligations, Berlin, London, Paris, and Rome came under pressure to act as collectors, as had happened in Venezuela.

As before, Roosevelt was of two minds about such matters. He had no respect for the politics of most of the countries of Latin America, and though in principle a partisan of self-determination, he had no doubt that incompetent and unruly regimes like those of Venezuela and Colombia required chastisement now and then by better-governed out-side powers. On the other hand, he was loath to allow any European powers to administer the chastisement, fearing, again as in the case of Germany and Venezuela, that troops landed to spank bad rulers and collect bad debts might readily discover reasons to extend their stay. This would violate the Monroe Doctrine; in other words, it would dent the sphere of American interest in the Western Hemisphere that President Monroe had claimed and that the United States, under the spur of leaders like Roosevelt and Lodge, had been actively reinforc-ing during the last decade.

At the time of its enunciation in 1823 the Monroe Doctrine had applied to the whole Western Hemisphere; as Roosevelt had alluded to in his earlier letter to Cecil Spring Rice, Monroe and John Quincy Adams worried as much about Russian encroachment in the far Northwest as about Spanish or French aggrandizement to the south. In theory the hemispheric construction still applied, but in practice Roosevelt and his generation concentrated their attention on the Caribbean basin. Canada was Britain's problem; countries like Argentina and Chile were too distant and generally too civilized to attract much American concern. But Central America and the islands of the Caribbean were close, often chaotic, and, now that the canal in Panama was abuilding, perilously proximate to what would become one of America's vital arteries. Having gone to such trouble to get the digging started, Roosevelt wasn't about to let some deadbeat dictator throw a wrench into the steam shovel.

Disturbingly, something like this seemed about to happen in Santo Domingo, as the Dominican Republic was often called at that time. A revolution, the latest in a long line of insurrectionary violence, broke out at the end of 1903, just weeks after the conclusion of the negotiations that produced the Panama Canal treaty. Roosevelt grew anxious and annoyed as the fighting spread, for trouble in the Caribbean might complicate approval of the Panama pact by the Senate (whose "idiotic jealousy of the Executive," in Roosevelt's view, made that body only too eager to place hurdles in the path of a responsible foreign policy). As had happened in Cuba in 1898, certain elements in Santo Domingo decided that insulting the United States might work to their advantage, and in February 1904, not long after an American sailor was killed on the docks in the town of Santo Domingo, insurgents fired on an American warship in the harbor.

Roosevelt responded with an order to the American commander in the area to employ immediate measures to safeguard American lives and property. As interpreted by the commander, these measures included shelling insurgent positions and landing marines to patrol the neighborhood of the waterfront.

The bombardment and landing stabilized the situation briefly but left the underlying sources of strife unresolved. "Santo Domingo is drifting into chaos," Roosevelt told Ted, "for after a hundred years of freedom it shows itself utterly incompetent for governmental work. Most reluctantly I have been obliged to take the initial step of interference there. I hope it will be a good while before I have to go further." Yet he wasn't overly sanguine. "Sooner or later it seems inevitable that the United States should assume an attitude of protection and regulation in regard to all these little states in the neighborhood of the Caribbean. I hope it will be deferred as long as possible, but I fear it is inevitable."

The military action in Santo Domingo, following Roosevelt's role in the Panama affair, prompted speculation in the American press that Roosevelt might try to negotiate a protectorate over Santo Domingo or perhaps annex the country outright. This speculation borrowed credence from efforts by the beleaguered Dominican government to win American help against its enemies. At an earlier time—before he became president, for example—Roosevelt might have entertained the idea of annexation. But with the all-important Panama treaty still awaiting action by the Senate, he had no wish to give his critics any additional opportunity for obstruction. He told journalist Joseph Bishop, often his channel for messages he couldn't state directly, "I have been hoping and praying for three months that the Santo Domingans would behave so that I would not have to act in any way. I want to do nothing but what a policeman has to do in Santo Domingo. As for annexing the island, I have about the same desire to annex it as a gorged boa constrictor might have to swallow a porcupine wrong-end-to. Is that strong enough?"

On the very day that Roosevelt issued this disclaimer, however, the international tribunal that was adjudicating the earlier controversy between Venezuela and its creditors issued a ruling that compelled Roosevelt to reconsider his distaste for porcupine. The Hague court found in favor of the Germans and British, thereby conferring prima facie approval on the kind of gunboat diplomacy that had brought the case to court in the first place. Force worked and consequently could be expected to be repeated.

Roosevelt understood the portents of The Hague court's ruling, but with the 1904 election approaching, he declined to do anything drastic. To be sure, he firmly believed that the most beneficial thing for the Santo Domingans would be an American protectorate of some sort. "If I acted purely in accordance with the spirit of altruistic humanitarian duty," he said confidentially, "I would grant the prayers of the best people of the island and take partial possession of it tomorrow." But circumstances prevented bestowing such a boon. "I do not do this, chiefly because if I did many honest people would misunderstand my purposes and motives." These honest but potentially misunderstanding people included many American voters—hence the desirability of putting off action until necessity absolutely forced his hand, or the election intervened.

While politics precluded a public démarche, in private Roosevelt prepared the ground for an important shift in policy. To a Philadelphia editor the president explained his view of the uproar in Santo Domingo and adjacent locales, and of the appropriate American response. He repeated that he had no acquisitive sentiments toward Santo Domingo or its neighbors, or any pressing desire to get involved in their internal affairs. But American national interests might still compel such involvement. "It is our duty," he said, "when it becomes absolutely inevitable, to police these countries in the interest of order and civilization."

Roosevelt was a bit more forthcoming in a letter to Elihu Root: "All that we desire is to see all neighboring countries stable, orderly and prosperous. Any country whose people conduct themselves well can count upon our hearty friendliness. If a nation shows that it knows how to act with decency in industrial and political matters, if it keeps order and pays its obligations, then it need fear no interference from the United States." On the other hand, nations that did not conduct themselves well were asking for interference. "Brutal wrongdoing, or an impotence which results in a general loosening of the ties of civilized society, may finally require intervention by some civilized nation; and in the Western Hemisphere the United States cannot ignore this duty."

As Roosevelt intended, Root read this letter to a gathering celebrating the second anniversary of the establishment of the republic of Cuba. The reaction of the immediate group was favorable enough, but critics in the wider world of opinion taxed the president for hubris and related sins, and he decided to keep quiet for the duration of the election campaign. As always, of course, he castigated his critics for ignorance and maliciousness. "What I wrote is the simplest common sense," he told Root, "and only the fool or the coward can treat it as aught else. If we are willing to let Germany or England act as the policeman of the Caribbean, then we can afford not to interfere when gross wrongdoing occurs. But if we intend to say 'Hands off' to the powers of Europe, then sooner or later we must keep order ourselves. What a queer set of evil-minded creatures, mixed with honest people of preposterous shortness of vision, our opponents are!"

An unanticipated resurgence of the Venezuelan troubles that had started all the thinking about an American police power in the Caribbean pushed Roosevelt still closer to a decisive statement. President Castro reacted to The Hague award to the Europeans by refusing to pay and by seizing foreign holdings, including some American. He also arrested and briefly held an American national connected to one of the confiscated properties.

"It looks to me as if Castro was riding for a fall," Roosevelt told John Hay, "and my present impression is that if he has to have a fall, we had better give it to him." Roosevelt went on to say, "Of course we do not want to act in the closing weeks of the campaign, but I think we should make up our minds to take the initiative and give Castro a sharp lesson." The president proposed sending in the marines to seize control of Venezuelan customs houses. To demonstrate that it wasn't bent on conquest, the United States might subsequently turn the customs over to a representative of The Hague court. "This would put into deeds the policy announced in my letter read by Root at the Cuban dinner. I think it will have a very healthy effect, in the first place because it will do away with the foreign nations having any pretext for interference on this side of the water, and in the next place it will show those Dagos that they will have to behave decently."

After all his hints of a more rigorous attitude toward misbehavior, it came as no great surprise when Roosevelt, safely elected, unveiled his corollary to the Monroe Doctrine. Like Monroe eighty-one years before, Roosevelt incorporated his new policy into his annual message to Congress. The essence of his initiative appeared in a single, albeit substantial, sentence: "Chronic wrongdoing, or an impotence which results in a general loosening of the ties of civilized society, may in America, as elsewhere, ultimately require intervention by some civilized nation, and in the western hemisphere the adherence of the United States to the Monroe Doctrine may force the United States, however reluctantly, in flagrant cases of such wrongdoing or impotence, to the exercise of an international police power."

But Roosevelt was never one to let a few words suffice where more would serve. He went on to say that the United States had no desire to interfere in the affairs of its neighbors. "We would interfere with them only in the last resort, and then only if it became evident that their inability or unwillingness to do justice at home and abroad had violated the rights of the United States or had invited foreign aggression to the detriment of the entire body of American nations." Good citizenship applied to nations as to individuals. "It is a mere truism to say that every nation, whether in America or anywhere else, which desires to maintain its freedom, its independence, must ultimately realize that the right of such independence cannot be separated from the responsibility of making good use of it."

It went without saying that Roosevelt reserved to himself the right to determine when a nation—at least one whose shores were lapped by the Caribbean—was making good use of its independence and when it wasn't. Roosevelt had always considered himself, and other Americans who held similar opinions, peculiarly suited to passing judgment on the legitimacy of the actions of foreign countries. Not until now, however, returned by an unexampled margin to the most powerful office in the New World, had Roosevelt enjoyed such scope for enforcing his judgment. It was enough to go to a man's head.

VI

It sometimes did. And perhaps because it did, Roosevelt soon showed that he wasn't satisfied being the most powerful man in the New World; he aimed for decisive influence in the Old World as well. Since the beginning of 1904, Japan and Russia had been locked in a deadly contest for supremacy in northeastern Asia. The war began with a stunningly successful Japanese sneak attack on the Russian fleet at Port Arthur; although this hardly comported with Marquess of Queensbury rules, Roosevelt couldn't help admiring Japan's daring and initiative. He followed the fighting closely. "How absorbing the far eastern business has been!" he declared to journalist Whitelaw Reid in mid-February. "I cannot understand Russia having been caught so unprepared and supine." Laxity aside, the president thought the Russians had brought their current troubles on themselves. "For several years," he told Ted, "Russia has behaved very badly in the far East, her attitude toward all nations, including us, but especially toward Japan, being grossly overbearing." Roosevelt had expected a clash between Japan and Russia; his principal fear had been that Russia might beat Japan and become more obnoxious than ever. "I was apprehensive lest if she at the very outset whipped Japan on the sea she might assume a position well-nigh intolerable toward us." Just the opposite had occurred, to the president's private satisfaction. "Between ourselves—for you must not breathe it to anybody," he told his son, "I was thoroughly well pleased with the Japanese victory, for Japan is playing our game." As an additional caution to confidentiality, Roosevelt appended a warning: "Be sure not to let this letter stay around where it could be seen by anyone, for it might cause trouble."

As long as Japan continued to play America's game, Roosevelt kept his distance from the fray. He had next to nothing good to say about the current condition of Russia. "I believe in the future of the Slavs if they can only take the right turn," he told Spring Rice. "But I do not believe in the future of any race *while it is under a crushing despotism.* The Japanese are non-Aryan and non-Christian, but they are under the weight of no such despotism as the Russians; and so, although the Russians are fundamentally nearer to us, or rather would be if a chance were given them, they are not in actual fact nearer to us at present. People who feel as we do would be happier today living in Japan than living in Russia."

Yet while Roosevelt didn't complain that Japan had knocked the smugly boorish smile off Russia's official face, neither did he welcome the thought of a decisive Japanese victory in the war. "If the Japanese win out, not only the Slav, but all of us will have to reckon with a great new force in eastern Asia." For the other contenders for influence in the area, including the United States, the lands bordering the Japanese and Chinese seas represented one interest among many; for Japan, they were everything. Until now a rough balance of power among the several contenders had kept any one from grabbing the great prize of eastern Asia: China. A decisive victory over Russia might well tip the balance in Japan's favor and tempt Tokyo to seize that prize.

And it might produce such a civilization-shattering transformation as occurred only once or twice each epoch. If Japan set about to reorganize China, all the world would have to take notice. "There will result a real shifting of the center of equilibrium as far as the white races are concerned. Personally, I believe that Japan will develop herself, and seek to develop China, along paths which will make the first and possibly the second great civilized powers; but the civilization must of course be of a different type from our civilizations." Race would play a part but not the determining part. "I do not mean that the mere race taken by itself would cause such a tremendous difference. I have met Japanese, and even Chinese, educated in our ways, who in all their emotions and ways of thought were well-nigh identical with us. But the weight of their own ancestral civilization will press upon them, and will prevent their ever coming into exactly our mold."

All this said, Roosevelt conceded that at the present stage of the war, when the outcome remained in the balance, such thoughts were simply speculation. "No one as yet can fully understand what the Japanese strategy is," he told Ted, "or what the reserve power of the Russians will amount to." To Spring Rice he observed, "It may well be that the two powers will fight until both are fairly well exhausted, and that then peace will come on terms which will not mean the creation of either a yellow peril or a Slav peril."

As the spring and summer progressed, a yellow peril appeared rather more likely than a Slav. Japanese forces invested Port Arthur and threatened to drive the Russians out of Manchuria. In June the president had lunch with the Japanese ambassador, Kotoro Takahira, and an influential civilian, Kentaro Kaneko, who happened to share Harvard with Roosevelt as alma mater. Roosevelt expressed admiration for the success of Japanese arms but remarked frankly that he feared that Japan might become intoxicated with victory and embark on a career of insolence and aggression. Needless to say, this would be unpleasant for Japan's neighbors; perhaps more needful of expression, it could be still more unpleasant for Japan. Having voiced this concern, Roosevelt assured his guests that he didn't deem such an outcome at all predestined. He said he hoped Japan would assume its place among the great civilized nations, with something to teach them as well as something to learn. He wouldn't object to Japan's being paramount in the region around the Yellow Sea, just as the United States was paramount in the Caribbean. Yet he hoped that Japan would show no more desire to conquer weak nations than the United States had shown with respect to Cuba and no more truculence toward the strong than America had shown toward Britain and France in the West Indies.

Guests at the White House table customarily commented on the president's tendency to dominate a conversation, even with several guests at once, shifting from subject to subject to suit the different diners but frequently allowing them little more than monosyllables in reply. In this meeting with Takahira and Kaneko, Roosevelt wasn't reticent; he still directed the conversation and made certain to get his point across. But he also wanted information from them, and when they spoke, he listened more closely than usual.

They assured him that Japan would not allow a victory over Russia to go to its head. Japan had limited aims in northeastern Asia; once it received the satisfaction it deserved, it would call a halt. Americans who engaged in loose talk about a yellow peril should remember that Japan had experience of the same thing—a yellow peril of its own, in the form of the Mongol invasions of the thirteenth century. Many Americans seemed to think Japan endangered the American position in the Philippines; this was entirely false. Japan would respect America's preeminence in those islands.

Roosevelt replied that he wasn't worried. He said the United States would give Japan no cause for aggression. Yet he added significantly that if aggression came, the United States would be quite competent to defend itself.

"The Japs interest me and I like them," Roosevelt wrote to Spring Rice by way of recapitulating the meeting. "I am perfectly well aware that if they win out it may possibly mean a struggle between them and us in the future; but I hope not and believe not." Roosevelt dismissed the notion that the racial difference would place Japan permanently at odds with the West. The Russians were closer in race to Americans than the Japanese were, but Japan had made far more progress toward a civilized society than the Russians had. Something similar could be said of other ethnic groups. "The Turks are ethnically closer to us than the Japanese, but they are impossible members of our international society, while I think the Japs may be desirable additions." Not all Japanese were paragons of virtue, but that was hardly unusual. "That there are large classes of the Japanese who will sometimes go wrong, that Japan as a whole will sometimes go wrong, I do not doubt. The same is true of my beloved country." At the moment Roosevelt saw no reason to believe that Tokyo would prove itself superior in morality to Berlin or Vienna or Paris, let alone London or Washington; but neither did he expect it to act egregiously worse. "I see nothing ruinous to civilization in the advent of the Japanese to power among the great nations."

During the succeeding months Roosevelt resolved to help usher Japan into the company of the great nations. As in much else, the American election postponed any dramatic initiatives; so also did Japan's continuing success in the field and at sea. With matters falling their way, the Japanese weren't in any hurry to trade bayonets for briefcases.

Roosevelt's respect for the Japanese grew with each report of their prowess; likewise his wariness. He told George Meyer in late December,

> The situation in the far East is one which needs careful watching. I am not inclined to think that Tokyo will show itself a particle more altruistic than St. Petersburg, or for the matter of that, Berlin. I believe that the Japanese rulers recognize Russia as their most dangerous permanent enemy, but I am not at all sure that the Japanese people draw any distinctions between the Russians and other foreigners, including ourselves. I have no doubt that they include all white men as being people who, as a whole, they dislike, and whose past arrogance they resent; and doubtless they believe their own yellow civilization to be better.

Again Roosevelt remarked that Russia had brought most of its troubles on itself by, among other things, its "literally fathomless mendacity." But Japan might not be much better on this score. "Japan is an oriental nation, and the individual standard of truthfulness is low." What this might mean for the United States, none could say. Vigilance and resolve were even more necessary than usual. "The summing up of the whole matter," Roosevelt told Spring Rice, "is that we must trust in the Lord and keep our powder dry and our eyes open."

The first months of 1905 brought additional Japanese victories. In February, Port Arthur fell and Japanese troops drove deep into Manchuria. Still the Russians refused to seek an end to the struggle, placing their hopes in the Baltic battle fleet that was racing across the Indian Ocean on its way to crush the Japanese armada. The Russian ships arrived in late May; to the astonishment of the world, they were utterly annihilated in the battle of Tsushima Strait.

Roosevelt was as shocked as the rest. He had thought the Japanese might hold their own, but he certainly didn't expect them to smash the Russians so thoroughly. "No one anticipated that it would be a rout and a slaughter rather than a fight," he told Lodge, "that the Russian fleet would be absolutely destroyed while the Japanese fleet was left practically uninjured."

This climactic battle convinced all parties that the fighting had gone just about far enough. The Russians finally realized that they weren't going to win back what they had lost; the Japanese believed they had proved their point and didn't want to overreach; the European powers hoped for a quick settlement that would preserve at least some semblance of a balance in northeastern Asia. In addition, the German emperor feared that the disaster in the Far East would unleash the demons of revolution in Russia, whence they might burst forth against regimes in other countries, including his own.

Roosevelt took much the same view as the Europeans, although he wouldn't have minded a little revolution in Russia. He responded favorably to a highly confidential approach by Takahira asking him, while trying not to ask him, to persuade the Russians to deal. The Japanese, in short, wanted the war to end but didn't want to be seen as wanting it to end. The president proceeded to sound out the Russian ambassador, who initially replied with what Roosevelt called "his usual rigmarole, to the effect that Russia was fighting the battles of the white race." Roosevelt answered this with a query as to why, then, Russia treated other white people so badly. Exasperated with St. Petersburg's envoy, Roosevelt contacted the czar through the American ambassador in the Russian capital. This time the response was not unfavorable but still diffident; the Russians didn't wish to be seen suing for peace any more than the Japanese did.

The two sides shuffled and coughed, each angling for the most favorable conditions under which to negotiate. "I am having a good deal of difficulty in getting Russia and Japan together," Roosevelt told Kermit in the second week of June. Part of the problem was the president himself—or rather his initial unwillingness to have the warring parties bring their troubles to the United States. "Curiously enough both of them want to meet at Washington. I think it would be far better for them to meet at The Hague. I feel that if they meet here each side will expect me to do the impossible, whereas, if they meet at The Hague, I may at some critical moment render unexpected and therefore very valuable assistance." Each side seemed to harbor exaggerated notions of what it might win through negotiations. Basing his forecast on Tokyo's recent actions, Roosevelt predicted, "Doubtless Japan will desire even more than her interest requires." The Russians were worse. "The chief trouble is with Russia, which keeps being shifty and which will try to escape without paying any penalty whatever that is adequate for the defeat into which her own policy led her."

Roosevelt did his best to bring the expectations of both sides into consonance with reality. To this end he reluctantly accepted Washington as the venue for discussions, and he acted as go-between in setting the ground rules. The Japanese intended to vest their negotiators with full decision-making power; at the same time that the president urged the Russians to do likewise—"so as to convince even the most doubting" that Russia was negotiating in earnest—he told Tokyo that the issue of the precise powers of the negotiators was "not in the least a vital question," certainly not something to hold the talks hostage to.

Roosevelt never would have made a good full-time diplomat; he was too impatient. And now he ached to cut through the niceties of form and start pickaxing at the obdurate substance underneath. "It is for the real interest of Japan to make peace," he told Lodge, "if she can get favorable terms, rather than fight on for a year at great cost of men and money and then find herself in possession of eastern Siberia (which is of no value to her) and much strained by the struggle. Russia had far better make peace now, if she possibly can and find her boundaries in east Asia left without material shrinkage from what they were ten years ago, than to submit to being driven out of east Asia." American interests, too, indicated a settlement about now. "For the rest of us, while Russia's triumph would have been a blow to civilization, her destruction as an eastern Asiatic power would also in my opinion be unfortunate. It is best that she should be left face to face with Japan so that each may have a moderative action on the other."

This mutually moderative action was Roosevelt's goal. He continued to jawbone the Russian and Japanese governments to cease their posturing and cancel their preconditions and get down to the business of ending the war. Those two governments continued to take one step forward, then one step back, then two steps sideways, trying to gain an edge in the peace conference that everyone agreed was impending if not exactly imminent. Meanwhile, of course, soldiers on both sides continued to die. Finally Roosevelt's persistence paid off, and St. Petersburg and Tokyo agreed to send their foreign ministers to America for peace talks.

VII

Had Roosevelt not taken personal command of the mediation between Russia and Japan—had he left it to the State Department—an untoward development of July might have tossed the negotiations off track. John Hay died at the beginning of the month. The secretary of state's passing marked another turning point in Roosevelt's life. "John was my father's friend; I dearly loved him," the president wrote by way of consolement to Hay's widow. "There is no one who with any of us can quite fill the place he had." In a certain sense Hay had represented to Roosevelt the generation of his father; that generation was now truly gone, leaving the world to the care of Roosevelt's own and to the president personally.

Not surprisingly, Hay's death caused Roosevelt to reflect on human mortality. The way the secretary died—still at his job, still honored and respected—seemed all that a man could ask. "John Hay's death was a severe personal loss to me entirely aside from his position as a public man," Roosevelt told Spring Rice. "But after all, Springy, it is a good thing to die in the harness at the zenith of one's fame, with the consciousness of having lived a long, honorable and useful life. After we are dead it will make not the slightest difference whether men speak well or ill of us. But in the days and hours before dying it must be pleasant to feel that you have done your part as a man and have not yet been thrown aside as useless, and that your children and children's children, in short all those that are dearest to you, have just cause for pride in your actions."

The political consequences of Hay's passing were hardly less important than the personal. McKinley's assassination had made Roosevelt president on sufferance; the election of 1904 had made him president in his own right; now Hay's death made him truly master of his office. By nudge and attrition, Roosevelt had replaced most of the top men he had inherited from his predecessor; Hay was the last important cabinet holdover from the McKinley administration. In either personal or political conscience, Roosevelt couldn't have removed Hay, but for some time the secretary of state had been a bit of a bar to the kind of diplomacy Roosevelt wanted to pursue. "Of course, what I am about to say I can only say to a close friend, for it seems almost ungenerous," he confided to Lodge. "But for two years his health has been such that he could do very little work of importance. His name, his reputation, his staunch loyalty, all made him a real asset of the administration. But in actual work I had to do all the big things myself, and the other things I always feared would be badly done or not done at all." Hay's shortcomings had particularly hampered relations with Germany; the secretary so despised the kaiser that the president had to redo most of what Hay did regarding Berlin. "But all this is only for you and me to talk over together," Roosevelt concluded, "for it is not of the slightest consequence now, and what is of consequence is that America should be the richer by John Hay's high and fine reputation."

To replace Hay, Roosevelt approached Elihu Root. The war secretary had returned to private life in 1904 with such evident relief and satisfaction that Roosevelt half-expected him to decline this offer of the State Department. But he didn't, deciding that for all the remunerative advantages of law practice, it lacked the zest of real power. Roosevelt was pleased. "In Elihu Root I think I have the very best man in this country for Secretary of State," he told Spring Rice.

Except himself, that is. Having grown accustomed to playing the piano of foreign policy, the president didn't intend to give up the keyboard even to one as talented and capable as Root. Roosevelt liked being his own secretary of state, and he was in a position to do what he liked.

VIII

Despite his earlier acceptance of Washington as the site of the Russo-Japanese conference, Roosevelt succeeded in deflecting the negotiations several hundred miles. Summers in the capital were trying even for the natives, the president pointed out; for diplomats from the cooler climes of Russia and Japan, August would be downright debilitating. New England would be far more comfortable. Besides, he wasn't going to be in Washington anyway but would have relocated to the summer White House at Oyster Bay. What went without saying was that an off-the-beaten-track location such as Portsmouth, New Hampshire, would help keep the conference from dissolving under the glare of public scrutiny, and would limit, although certainly not prevent, a perception of presidential liability in ensuring a favorable outcome. Between the Washington heat and an accurate guess that Roosevelt would loom large in negotiations held anywhere in America, the Russian and Japanese governments accepted the Portsmouth venue with no serious complaint.

En route to Portsmouth, the foreign envoys visited the president on Long Island. The chief Japanese negotiator, Jutaro Komura, arrived first and enhanced Roosevelt's largely positive opinion of the Japanese. "I have seen Baron Komura and am favorably impressed with him," Roosevelt told Will Taft, Root's replacement as secretary of war. Komura's counterpart, the Russian Sergei Witte, struck Roosevelt less well. Witte, Roosevelt complained to Spring Rice, had "talked like a fool" to the press regarding Japan. "The only possible justification of his interviews is to be found in his hope that he may bluff the Japanese; in which he will certainly fail."

The central sticking point of the talks was whether Russia would pay an indemnity to Japan. The Japanese government had led its people to expect a handsome indemnity, which would help compensate loved ones for lives sacrificed in fighting that meant little intrinsically to most Japanese. The Russians, having lost so much already, naturally resisted having to give up more.

While maintaining physical distance from the negotiations, Roosevelt kept thoroughly apprised of the progress and lack of progress at Portsmouth. The Russian ambassador, Roman Rosen, frequently came to see him at Sagamore Hill; likewise Kaneko for Japan.

As before, the Japanese appeared to Roosevelt far more reasonable than the Russians, who still seemed unable or unwilling to accept the depth of their disaster in the war. The Japanese quietly set aside a number of their initial demands, and were willing to entertain a smaller payment from St. Petersburg than they had initially proposed.

Moreover, they offered to drop the terminology of indemnity and let the Russians call it a payment for transfer of control of the southern half of Sakhalin Island to Japan; the northern half of the island would be restored to Russia by Japan.

This struck Roosevelt as fair of Tokyo, and he told the Russians as much. He wrote Czar Nicholas urging him to accept. "It seems to me that if peace can be obtained substantially on these terms," the president said, "it will be both just and honorable, and that it would be a dreadful calamity to have the war continued when peace can be thus obtained." At the same time he wired his old friend Speck von Sternberg, now German ambassador to the United States, relating what he was telling the czar and suggesting that Kaiser Wilhelm apply his own persuasive skills to the task.

While awaiting a response from Nicholas to his efforts to push St. Petersburg closer to Tokyo, Roosevelt attempted to tug Tokyo closer to St. Petersburg. He urged the Japanese to moderate their indemnity demand further. However reasonable in principle a payment might be, it would prove unreasonable if it caused the negotiations to fail. "You know how strongly I have advised the Russians to make peace," he told Kaneko. "I equally strongly advise Japan not to continue the fight for a money indemnity. If she does, then I believe that there will be a considerable shifting of public opinion against her." Public opinion aside, if Japan continued the war, it would quickly squander on the fighting whatever it might hope to squeeze from the Russians as an indemnity and would come out no better than at present.

Roosevelt made this same argument to the British ambassador. Since 1902, Britain had been Japan's ally, and although the alliance didn't pertain to the war with Russia, Roosevelt hoped it would afford London leverage in bringing Japan to see reason. Until now the British had declined to get involved; Roosevelt thought they ought to, at once. "If Japan shows to the world that she is fighting simply to get money," he told the British ambassador, "I think the effect will be bad upon her in every way, and that, moreover, there is a fair chance that in the end she will find she has lost more, instead of getting any. I wish your people could get my views."

When the Russians remained reluctant, Roosevelt pounded again on the point that Russian self-interest, if nothing else, required accepting something close to Japan's terms. "To decline to try to make peace on these terms it seems to me is to invite terrible disaster to Russia," he warned Witte. Placing himself in the Russian foreign minister's boots, he said, "I should hate to be responsible for the possibility of such disaster when the alternative is an absolutely just and honorable peace."

As another nudge to Japan, Roosevelt reiterated what that country had won from the war—and, by implication, what it stood to lose if it didn't make peace soon. "She has won the control of Korea and Manchuria; she has doubled her own fleet in destroying that of Russia; she has Port Arthur, Dalny, the Manchurian railroad, she has Sakhalin." The president appealed to Japan's self-interest to stop the conflict; he also cited Japan's ethical responsibilities. "Ethically it seems to me that Japan owes a duty to the world at this crisis," he told Kaneko. "The civilized world looks to her to make peace; the nations believe in her; let her show her leadership in matters ethical no less than in matters military. The appeal is made to her in the name of all that is lofty and noble; and to this appeal I hope she will not be deaf."

Still the talks stuck. As a final attempt to knock a deal loose, Roosevelt proposed that, in lieu of a specified indemnity, the two sides accept arbitration of the amount of a transfer payment for Sakhalin. The Japanese agreed, albeit reluctantly. The Russians still balked.

Roosevelt now wrote directly to the German kaiser to get him to work on Nicholas. Japan's terms, the president declared, were "extremely moderate." But the czar seemed distrustful of anything that came from Washington. Perhaps Wilhelm could allay Nicholas's fears. "I feel that you have more influence with him than either I or anyone else can have. As the situation is exceedingly strained and the relations between the plenipotentiaries critical to a degree, immediate action is necessary. Can you not take the initiative by presenting these terms at once to him? Your success in the matter will make the entire civilized world your debtor." The czar respected the kaiser and would surely listen to him. "I am unable to see how Russia can refuse your request if in your wisdom you see fit to make it."

But Russia did refuse, throwing the conference into what seemed almost certain to be terminal deadlock. Roosevelt could hardly contain his anger and frustration at the czar's uncomprehending perversity. "The Japanese ask too much, but the Russians are ten times worse than the Japs because they are so stupid and won't tell the truth," he wrote to Kermit. To American diplomat William Rockhill, who had raised some unrelated examples of Chinese refractoriness, Roosevelt fumed, "Bad as the Chinese are, no human beings, black, yellow or white, could be quite as untruthful, as insincere, as arrogant—in short as untrustworthy in every way—as the Russians under their present system. I was pro-Japanese before, but after my experience with the peace commissioners I am far stronger pro-Japanese than ever."

For forty-eight hours the conference verged on collapse. Nicholas, fearing incipient revolution in his own country more than a resumption of fighting in the Far East, and fearing that weakness against the Japanese would encourage the revolutionaries, persisted in his *nyet*.

At the last possible moment, however, Roosevelt's arguments took hold—not with the Russians but with the Japanese. Tokyo finally came around to the president's view that an indemnity wouldn't cover the costs of continuing the war, and it dropped the demand.

"Tell Baron Komura that I am overjoyed at the news," Roosevelt wired Portsmouth. To the Japanese emperor he conveyed his "earnest congratulations upon the wisdom and magnanimity" Japan had displayed. Roosevelt's message to Russia's Nicholas was more restrained. "I congratulate you upon the outcome," he told the czar, "and I share the feelings of all other sincere well-wishers to peace in my gratitude for what has been accomplished." To Germany's Wilhelm, Roosevelt expressed his "profound appreciation" for the kaiser's cooperation.

Privately, Roosevelt credited Tokyo for the settlement. "I think the Japanese government has acted most wisely," he said. Regarding the Russians, he was still angry. "There were moments during the peace conference at Portsmouth," he confided to Arthur Lee, "when I earnestly wished I could get the entire Russian government to the top of Cooper's Bluff and run them violently down a steep place into the sea!"

Yet now that it was over, the president was satisfied with the solution. "It all came out right in the end," he told Lee. The deal was a sound one, and not only for the belligerents. "I think the peace is just to Russia and Japan, and also good for England"—this letter was to Spring Rice—"and the United States."

CHAPTER TWENTY-ONE

Square Dealing
1905–6

As trying as Roosevelt's dealings with the Japanese and especially the Russians were, they seemed delightfully simple and straightforward compared to his struggles with Congress. "Congress does from a third to a half of what I think is the minimum it ought to do, and I am profoundly grateful that I get as much," he grumbled to Leonard Wood. In a letter to Spring Rice he was more emphatic: "There are several eminent statesmen at the other end of Pennsylvania Avenue whom I would gladly lend to the Russian Government, if they cared to expend them as bodyguards for grand dukes whenever there was a likelihood of dynamite being exploded!"

But there was no avoiding grappling with those eminent statesmen. As much as Roosevelt relished the freedom of foreign affairs, where the scope of his power was comparatively unconstrained by constitutional checks and balances, he understood that a president earned his keep—or didn't—at home. "Our internal problems are of course much more important than our relations with foreign powers," he wrote British historian George Trevelyan in the midst of his Russo-Japanese diplomacy. Summarizing what he saw those problems to be, he explained, "Somehow or other we shall have to work out methods of controlling the big corporations without paralyzing the energies of the business community and of preventing any tyranny on the part of the labor unions while cordially assisting in every proper effort made by the wageworkers to better themselves by combinations."

This letter was revealing of the philosophy that underlay Roosevelt's "square deal" and that later emerged as his "new nationalism." He accepted large size in corporations as an ineluctable element of the modernizing process. The problem wasn't the corporations' size, which afforded them and their customers the advantages of economies of scale; the problem was the lack of public control over the corporations' behavior. Roosevelt had launched the progressive campaign of trust-busting with his suit against the Northern Securities combination—which by now had succeeded but only over the dissent of Justice Holmes, who as a result fell out of Roosevelt's favor. "It broke up our incipient friendship . . ." Holmes remarked some years later, "as he looked on my dissent to the *Northern Securities* case as a political departure (or, I suspect, more truly, couldn't forgive anyone who stood in his way.)" Holmes went on to say: "He was very likeable, a big figure, a rather ordinary intellect, with extraordinary gifts, a shrewd and I think pretty unscrupulous politician. He played all his cards—if not more." Perhaps most revealing of the difference between the two men was a line Holmes quoted from a contemporary, a remark the Supreme Court justice considered a grave criticism but one Roosevelt would have deemed an at least backhanded compliment: "What the boys like about Roosevelt is that he doesn't give a damn for the law."

Despite his success in the Northern Securities suit, Roosevelt refused to adopt trust-busting as a philosophical cause. Partly because he had never been a farmer or a small businessman, partly because he reveled in power, he never embraced the Arcadian ideal of a nation of yeomen and mechanics. The modern age was the age of steel—needed not least for his beloved navy—and steel wasn't made on the hearth at home. A powerful nation had to employ the most advanced industrial techniques.

At the same time, the inevitably large influence of these corporate combines should be offset by judicious combinations of workingmen. Just as Roosevelt aimed for a balance of power between Russia and Japan, so he sought a balance of power between management and labor. Roosevelt had never had close personal relations with industrial workers, but he assumed that they were generally of the same honest stock as the lumberjacks he had known in Maine and the cowboys in Dakota. (He made significant—negative—exception for workers of socialist and anarchist persuasion as well as those immigrants who refused to adopt appropriately American attitudes.) Roosevelt believed that workers had a right to organize as a means to better their condition and that of their families. In the process, healthy and active unions would restrain the ambitions of the corporations.

Under present and foreseeable circumstances, however, unions lacked the heft to stay long in the ring with the biggest corporate combinations. Moreover, union leaders were subject to the same temptations as the corporate captains, and a war between organized labor and organized capital would serve the interests of no one—certainly not the public at large. To enforce rules of responsible behavior upon both sides was the task of government.

In particular, it was the task of the federal government. Roosevelt had earlier alluded to federal refereeing of capital-labor relations, but in the run-up to the 1904 election he had muted his horn, especially as it sounded tones that might upset the corporations that Cortelyou was dunning for donations. Yet now elected, he took the mute off and blew what Wall Street could only interpret as a charge. "In the vast and complicated mechanism of our modern civilized life," he declared in his postelection annual message to Congress, "the dominant note is the note of industrialism; and the relations of capital and labor, and especially of organized capital and organized labor, to each other and to the public at large come second in importance only to the intimate questions of family life." Delicacy wouldn't deter Roosevelt from addressing the intimate questions of family life, but on this day he stuck to topic two. He said that state governments had their part in addressing the industrial issue, but, divided as they were, the states were poorly positioned to deal with industries that spanned the entire nation. "It has proved exceedingly difficult, and in many cases impossible, to get unanimity of wise action among the various States on these subjects. From the very nature of the case this is especially true of the laws affecting the employment of capital in huge masses." Consequently, if the people hoped to guarantee good behavior by big capital, they would have to act through the federal government. "The National Government alone can deal adequately with these great corporations."

Roosevelt targeted railroads as peculiarly in need of federal oversight. By their nature they often exercised monopoly power over the lives and fortunes of the people in the districts through which they ran. (For this reason, although Roosevelt didn't mention it, the railroads were perennially unpopular and as a result represented an easy political target.) The Elkins Act, which he had happily signed into law in 1903, had forbidden rebates, the often-secret price reductions that afforded large shippers an edge over their smaller rivals. But the law proved too loosely drafted to actually stamp out rebates or to eradicate many of the other practices decried by progressives, who soon began agitating for tougher reforms.

Roosevelt snatched the reformers' banner and raised it high. "The government must in increasing degree supervise and regulate the workings of the railways engaged in interstate commerce," he declared. Ever eschewing radicalism, even when embarked on a course many considered radical, Roosevelt explained the essential conservatism of what he intended: "Such increased supervision is the only alternative to an increase of the present evils on the one hand or a still more radical policy on the other."

The most obvious sort of supervision was authority over rates. Without such authority, it was very difficult for the Interstate Commerce Commission, the pertinent body, to enforce fairness between big shippers and small and to iron out anomalies like those that often caused customers sending goods a short distance to be charged for a much longer haul. Some advocates of regulation asserted that the I.C.C. ought simply to set rates, telling the roads how much they must charge for traffic on any given route. Others wanted only to fix maximum charges, leaving the roads free to offer lower prices where they chose.

Roosevelt vacillated between these two positions. Temperamentally he leaned toward straightforward rate fixing, which seemed the more transparent and the more likely to prevent shenanigans between the railroads and their largest customers. Yet while he himself had no qualms about the great power this would hand over to a small board of unelected bureaucrats, he recognized that other people did. (One reason for his lack of qualms was that the president got to choose the members of the I.C.C.) Among those other people were several justices of the Supreme Court, which as a body remained leery of such sweeping assertions of government control over private industry.

Roosevelt explained his views in a letter to reporter Ray Stannard Baker in November 1905. "I am inclined to think that it would be better if the Commission had the power to fix a definite instead of a maximum rate," he said. But on the advice of Attorney General William Moody (who had replaced Knox), he estimated that while a maximum rate would almost certainly pass constitutional muster with the courts, a mandated rate might not. "The Supreme Court's attitude is more than doubtful on it." Roosevelt hoped to avoid constitutional problems. "The one thing I do not want is to have a law passed and then declared unconstitutional." Such an outcome would result in the stock and bond markets being upset twice: once when the law was passed and again when it was voided. Roosevelt was willing to upset the markets but only in a good and lasting cause.

Anti-railroad zealots, however, wanted mandatory rates, and when they continued to push for them, Roosevelt found himself in the unlikely—but not entirely uncongenial for a Republican president—position of having to defend the roads against excessive interference. "I have had a great deal to do with railroads in the West," he subsequently told Baker, who hadn't been convinced by Roosevelt's earlier arguments, "and a great deal to do with eastern legislatures which were dealing with railroads. I have often been impressed by the swinish indifference to right by certain railroad men in dealing both with the people and with railroads; but I am bound in honor to say that I have seen ten such exhibitions of indifference to the rights of railroads among legislatures and even among communities for one that I have seen among the railroad people themselves."

Plain justice required treating the railroads fairly; so did plain prudence. "Any movement conducted not on the ground of insisting on justice *to* the railroads as well as *from* the railroads—any movement which limits itself simply to an attack upon railroads or upon the big corporations—is necessarily carried on in a spirit which invites disaster." Casting himself in the mold of the two great heroes of American history, Roosevelt reiterated his belief that success required hewing to the via media. "In social and economic, as in political, reforms, the violent revolutionary extremist is the worst friend of liberty, just as the arrogant and intense reactionary is the worst friend of order. It was Lincoln, not Wendell Phillips and the fanatical abolitionists, who was the effective champion of union and freedom; it was Washington, and not the leaders of the 'liberty mobs' who did the real work in securing us national independence and then the national unity and order without which that independence would have been a curse and not a blessing."

II

Yet for all the objections of Baker and other progressives, the Republican conservatives were the ones Roosevelt really provoked in his quest for railroad regulation. The most formidable of these defenders of the status quo formed a bloc in the Senate, headed by Aldrich of Rhode Island, Foraker of Ohio, Depew of New York, and Stephen Elkins of West Virginia. The anti-regulators also included Philander Knox, now senator from Pennsylvania, and Roosevelt's old friend and usually reliable ally Cabot Lodge of Massachusetts.

If the rate fight brought out the political differences between Roosevelt and the conservatives, it simultaneously revealed the personal shift that was taking place in Roosevelt's relations with Lodge. The two men remained friends, as did Edith and Lodge's wife, Nannie. But Roosevelt's elevation to the presidency, and especially his independent victory in 1904, subtly but unmistakably altered the dynamics between the two. Prior to 1901, Lodge had always been the more influential and accomplished of the two; Roosevelt had frequently found himself a protégé and a project of Lodge. But since that time Roosevelt had raced ahead of Lodge, gaining power, prestige, and popularity that Lodge could only dream of. Lodge lacked the personal magnetism that made Roosevelt irresistible to so many people; the Senate was as high as Lodge could go in electoral politics, and he knew it.

Roosevelt knew it, too, and although he refrained from making a show of the advantage his office gave him over Lodge, neither did he deny it. "I try to look at Lodge disinterestedly, and try not to let my personal friendship mislead me," Roosevelt told Lyman Abbott. "In this very railway fight he is against me. But he is a man of the most sensitive honor, and while I think he is entirely mistaken in being against us and hope we will get him around, I am certain he is absolutely conscientious in his attitude."

Roosevelt was conscientious enough in return, but he wasn't above some minor misdirection in trying to bring his friend aboard. As the rate fight—embodied in a bill bearing the name of sponsor William Hepburn of Iowa—moved toward a showdown, the president approached Nannie Lodge about an opportunity to change her husband's mind. "Dear Nannie," he began, "I write to you because I feel more confidence in my ability to exert a favorable response from you than from Cabot. Can you have me to dinner either Wednesday or Friday? Would you be willing to have Bay and Bessie [Lodge] also? Then we could discuss the Hittite empire, the Pithecanthropus, and Magyar love songs, and the exact relations of the Atli of the *Volsunga Saga* to the Etzel of the *Nibelungenlied,* and of both to Attila—with interludes by Cabot about the rate bill, [Senator] Beveridge, and other matters of more vivid contemporary interest."

Roosevelt had little luck moving Lodge or the other hard-liners. Progress, when it came at all, arrived in grudging increments. "The rate bill fight is dragging slowly along," Roosevelt told Kermit in March. "I think we shall win out on it, but as yet it is doubtful." And most of the doubt was the work of the old guard. "The Republican leaders have tried to betray me." Accordingly, the president considered crossing party lines himself and soliciting the support of the Democrats. Speaking of the Hepburn bill he said, "I am now trying to see if I cannot get it through in the form I want by the aid of some fifteen or twenty Republicans added to most of the Democrats."

The spring of 1906 saw Roosevelt engaged in nearly constant negotiations with allies, especially Republican William Allison of Iowa, with waverers, and with opponents. The battle shifted ground as opponents offered amendments that would have gutted the bill, supporters parried with amendments that, while mitigating its force somewhat, would leave the essentials intact, and waverers trolled for favors in the murky waters behind each version. Roosevelt eventually determined that his Democratic strategy wouldn't work; the party of Bryan insisted on more than he was willing to offer. From Roosevelt's perspective this turned out to be just as well, for even a tactical coalition with such as Ben Tillman—"one of the foulest and rottenest demagogs in the whole country," he privately labeled the South Carolina legislator on another occasion—had troubled Roosevelt's usually sound sleep.

The process wasn't pretty, as legislating often isn't, but it finally proved effective. Roosevelt accepted an amendment proposed by Allison that increased the power of the courts to intervene in rate-setting matters; this right turn was the crucial maneuver that left Tillman and the Democrats stranded. At the same time it allowed

Roosevelt to regain the Republican center, where he was more comfortable anyway. Tillman and friends cried double-cross, as expected;
Roosevelt denied any such thing, as equally expected. The president
shrugged off the old populist's allegations of betrayal: "As for the
Tillman incident, it is one of those likely to happen at any time. I am continually obliged to see a great many men, and it is impossible to be sure
that some scoundrel will not lie about me—which, as I am President,
he can do with impunity."

The tactical amending opened the way to victory. "If the Hepburn
bill goes through substantially in its present form, but with that
amendment," Roosevelt told Allison early in May, "I regard the outcome as excellent." It did, and he did. On May 18 the Senate
approved the bill; in the end only a smattering of holdouts decided
that they should stand clearly with the railroads and against the president and the people. "The rate bill went through in fine shape,"
Roosevelt recorded with satisfaction. Six weeks later, after the measure returned from House-Senate reconciliation, he still thought it
fine, and he made it law with his signature.

III

By bromide, the only process as unsavory as lawmaking is
sausage-making, which would suggest that the process most off-
putting of all would be lawmaking about sausage-making. Even
while fighting the railroads over rates, Roosevelt took on the big
meatpackers. Not as a matter of course especially fastidious in
things culinary, Roosevelt had had his attention riveted on the packing industry at the same time half the country had, by the work of
probing reformer Upton Sinclair. If a tentative alliance with the populist Tillman had seemed a stretch for Roosevelt, common cause
with the socialist Sinclair required even greater elasticity. Sinclair's
celebrated *The Jungle* was only inadvertently a call to clean up the
packing industry, which in Sinclair's novel was a metaphor for capitalism collectively. The author wanted workers to can capitalism,
not canned beef. He later lamented, "I realized with bitterness that I
had been made a 'celebrity,' not because the public cared about any-

thing about the workers, but simply because the public did not want to eat tubercular beef."

Roosevelt didn't eat much canned beef, since he could afford better, but he immediately spotted a winner in a campaign against abuses in the packing industry. He had hardly put Sinclair's book down before he directed Agriculture Secretary James Wilson to conduct an investigation into the conditions Sinclair described. Referring to his attorney general, who had done some digging of his own, the president told Wilson, "The experiences that Moody has had in dealing with these beef trust people convinces me that there is very little that they will stop at. You know the wholesale newspaper bribery which they have undoubtedly indulged in."

Roosevelt also wrote to Sinclair. Needless to say, the president had scant sympathy for Sinclair's politics. "I wish he had left out the ridiculous socialistic rant at the end, which merely tends to make people think his judgment is unsound and to make them question his facts," Roosevelt said of Sinclair. He told Sinclair himself essentially the same thing. Sinclair had written the president earlier, enclosing an endorsement of his work by an enthusiast who likened him to Tolstoy, Zola, and Gorki; Roosevelt replied that, however intended, this was hardly praise. Gorki was noteworthy only for "the kind of leadership which can never lead anybody anywhere save into a Serbonian bog"; Zola appealed to "the lascivious, the beast side" of human nature; Tolstoy had written some good novels but was, in the final reckoning, "a man of diseased moral nature, a man in whose person the devotee and debauchee alternately obtain sway, as they sometimes do in successive generations of decadent families or in whole communities of unhealthy social conditions." Sinclair would do well to avoid such company. "But all this," Roosevelt concluded in a handwritten postscript, "has nothing to do with the fact that the specific evils you point out shall, if their existence be proved, and if I have power, be eradicated."

The investigation into the meat industry revealed that Sinclair spoke substantial truth in his stomach-churning passages about everything that went into what came out as potted chicken and kindred concoctions. In May, Senator Beveridge introduced a measure—an amendment to that year's agriculture appropriations bill—requiring that the packing industry submit to inspection by federal officials and accept other reforms, such as the stamping of the date of production on canned goods.

Roosevelt had reservations about Beveridge. "I was not very much impressed by his argument," he confided after one session with the Indiana lawmaker. And he judged Beveridge occasionally too quick to present himself as a spokesman for the administration. But Beveridge was the instrument at hand on the meat inspection issue, and for the most part the president backed him heartily. "The information given me seems to show conclusively that as now carried on the business is both a menace to health and an outrage on decency," he wrote James Wadsworth, Republican chairman of the House agriculture committee and author of a substitute amendment more acceptable to the packers and their political allies. "No legislation that is not drastic and thoroughgoing will be of avail." Until this point Roosevelt had withheld the particulars of the investigative committee's report on industry abuses, but now, confronted by foot-dragging by the packers' partners on Capitol Hill, he ordered the report released. "Under such circumstances I feel that the facts upon which I base my judgment must now be laid before Congress."

Typically, Roosevelt considered himself the steward not merely of the interests of those endangered by the abysmal practices in the packing industry but also of the interests of the industry itself—including that dependent branch dear to his heart, the cattle business. "The misdeeds of those who are responsible for the abuses we design to cure will bring discredit and damage not only upon them but upon the innocent stock growers, the ranchmen and farmers of the country. The only way permanently to protect and benefit these innocent stock growers, these farmers and ranchmen, is to secure by law the thorough and adequate inspection for which I have asked."

Roosevelt initially deemed the Wadsworth amendment insufficiently rigorous to accomplish his goal, which he characterized as "a thorough and rigid, and not a sham, inspection." Yet as on the Hepburn bill, the president refused to tie himself to any masts that might have to be cut away to prevent the bark of reform from swamping. He told Wadsworth his amendment fell short of the Beveridge amendment on important particulars; at the same time, he added, "I care not a whit for the language of the amendment. What I am concerned with is to have it accomplish the object I have in view."

Roosevelt's flexibility proved critical. "We may have long and ugly fighting," the president predicted regarding the inspection bill, and events made him a prophet. Wadsworth's substitute won the support of influential farm state and industry-friendly legislators, who believably insisted that they would stifle anything stronger. Roosevelt ultimately had to concede that this version, cosmetically modified, was the best he could get. After Congress passed the measure, he declared victory and signed it. Sending the pen to Beveridge, he accorded the Indianan and himself congratulations that neither entirely deserved: "You were the legislator who drafted the bill which in its substance now appears in the amendment, and which will enable us to put a complete stop to the wrongdoing complained of."

IV

Regulation of railroads and the packing industry were causes Roosevelt could readily warm to; both included clear villains (the monied monopolists of the roads, in the first instance, and the conscienceless adulterators of the nation's food, in the second) and readily identifiable victims (the small farmers and shippers, and the men, women, and children who unknowingly or unavoidably ate that horrible stuff).

Another issue evoked an uncharacteristic ambivalence from the man who saw most matters in a light clearer than truth. The tariff, to Roosevelt, was a muddle. It wasn't an issue of conscience for him, for although he recognized the irregularities and dubious causes that hid under the skirts of protection, he was too much of a nationalist and too much of a Republican to endorse free trade. At the same time, however, no issue provoked such regular calls for revision, especially among those distrusters of Wall Street who were looking to this progressive president for inspiration and leadership.

Had the tariff question been entirely up to him, he would have taken his customarily strong stand and done something about it. "If I were the legislative as well as the executive," he remarked during the summer of 1906, "I would revise the tariff right away, although I am not at all sure that at least half of those who are loudest to demand revision would be satisfied with the revision I would give." But as things stood, he had troubles enough with his own party, and he chose to husband his energies for other fights. "I doubt whether it would be possible to get the tariff revised prior to the next Presidential election," he said by way of explaining why he was ducking the issue. "If this were my first term I should certainly count upon taking up a revision of the tariff as one of the things that I would have to do in my second term." But he had pledged not to run in 1908, and he could hardly presume to commit his successor, whoever that might be.

Lack of time was a lame excuse for a president whose tenure would fall just six months shy of the historical maximum, but it was the best he could come up with. To an ally who remarked the strength of western demands for tariff revision and who suggested sending Congress a reform measure, the president replied, "No, God Almighty could not pass a tariff bill and win at the election following its passage. The only time to pass a tariff bill is the first year of a new administration, and trust to have the effects counteracted before another Presidential election."

Roosevelt wasn't proud of his record on the tariff; when he boasted of his accomplishments in the White House, he conspicuously—and with cause—omitted any reference to the tariff. But the issue's complexity and its absence of drama numbed his attention, as it generally did the public at large. With nothing to gain from an attack on that portion of the status quo, and much to lose, he chose to leave ill enough alone.

V

At times it seemed that the tariff was about the only thing he did leave alone. During the couple of years after his 1904 election, Roosevelt appeared to have his hand in everything else. His critics contended that, eschewing alcohol, the president was drunk on power. "That fellow at the other end of the Avenue," said House Speaker Cannon in a moment of especial exasperation, "wants everything, from the birth of Christ to the death of the devil." Even his friends occasionally wondered whether there wasn't any custom or practice too minor for him to try to regulate, update, or otherwise improve.

The state of sport in America was a natural for the most visibly sporting president in the nation's history. Perhaps partly on account of Ted's batterings on the football field, his father called a White House conference of the leading football figures of the country to devise rule changes that would diminish the danger to participants. Roosevelt didn't intend to eliminate the occasional broken nose or fractured arm; without a certain element of physical risk the game would lose its zest and character-building qualities. But the head and neck injuries that were literally killing dozens of players every year were hardly improving the physical or moral health of the nation. Roosevelt judged, not entirely accurately, that the injuries resulted chiefly from unworthy tactics—what he called "mucker play"—by ignoble types who didn't understand the uplifting possibilities of the game. In issuing his invitation to the White House conference, he declared, "I want to take up the football situation and try to get the game played on a thoroughly clean basis."

In the matter of football, as in most others, Roosevelt considered himself the enlightened conservative. Strong voices were calling for banishing the game altogether; among these was Charles Eliot, still president of Harvard. Eliot, not the sporting type himself, saw few redeeming qualities in football and many damning ones, and thought Harvard could do quite well without the game. Roosevelt realized that even he couldn't overrule Eliot, but he could try to shame him if necessary. "I am perfectly willing to say I think Harvard will be doing the baby act if she takes any such foolish course as President Eliot advises!" he told a friend and fellow football enthusiast. Roosevelt's advocacy of a cleanup of the sport was his contribution to the effort to save the game from radical abolitionists like Eliot.

His football offensive succeeded. The White House session produced a resolution affirming the participants' "honorable obligation" to eliminate foul play, and it set in motion changes in the nature and enforcement of football rules. "Believe me I appreciate your action," Roosevelt cabled to Walter Camp, the Yale coach who was working on becoming a legend in the sport. "I can not tell you how pleased I am at the way you have taken hold." Roosevelt may have been most pleased at frustrating Eliot of Harvard: With the president's (President Roosevelt's, that is) high-profile support, the Harvard board of overseers decided not to yield the gridiron to Yale and other lesser schools.

VI

Roosevelt had greater direct authority in another area also related to the moral and physical development of the nation's young men. In February 1906 he granted a pardon to a midshipman at the Naval Academy at Annapolis who had been convicted by a court-martial on the charge of hazing. Regulations required that any midshipman found guilty of hazing be dismissed from the academy. Roosevelt judged this unfair. He didn't approve of hazing, but he thought offenses of this nature needed to be kept in perspective. "In many cases, these amount to nothing more than exhibitions of boyish mischief attended with no consequence of any moment to those hazed, and indicating on the part of the hazers only some exuberance of animal spirits." He recommended rewriting the law governing such matters; Congress, taking much the same tolerant view as the president, agreed.

Roosevelt didn't stop at setting overall policy for the Naval Academy; he went right down into the classroom—or, in this case, gymnasium. Upon hearing that the academy was dropping some of the martial arts from the curriculum, he quickly contacted the secretary of the navy to register his concern. "I am not satisfied about the giving up of the judo or jujitsu at the Naval Academy," he declared. "It is not physical exercise so much as it is an extraordinarily successful means of self-defense and training in dexterity and decision." Naturally the old fogies who knew nothing about it opposed it. "But I know enough of boxing, wrestling, rough-and-tumble fighting, and of the very art in question to be absolutely certain that it is of real and on occasions may be of great use to any man whose duties are such as a naval officer's may at any time become." The president concluded, "I should like to have it continued next year at the Naval Academy." And so it was.

Roosevelt stuck his presidential finger in sundry other pies as well.

Disliking the look of the coins coming out of the national mint, he ordered new dies made to enhance the relief on the coins, especially the twenty-dollar gold piece, "which is the one I have most at heart." He intervened on behalf of a Chicago sausage grinder who contended that truth in labeling went too far when it forbade him from calling his foremost product "Bologna sausage" since it wasn't actually made in that Italian city. "I think on this he is right," the president told agriculture secretary Wilson. "Bologna sausages are not commonly understood to be made in Bologna any more than Castile soap is understood to be made in Spain." Roosevelt added, "Not one in a thousand persons knows where Bologna is—and I personally am not that one."

When the navy developed a prototype of a new war vessel that traveled under the water, he couldn't content himself with merely christening it; he had to go for a ride. He shrugged off expressed worries about his safety. To the German Speck von Sternberg, who likely read about this undersea boat with great interest, Roosevelt explained, "I went down in it chiefly because I did not like to have the officers and enlisted men think I wanted them to try things I was reluctant to try myself." He added, doubtless to Sternberg's further interest, or at least that of his friends in the German admiralty: "I believe a good deal can be done with these submarines."

VII

Of all Roosevelt's pet projects, none produced a greater reaction than his attempt to reform the spelling of the American language. Roosevelt had long tripped over spelling, lately relying on copy editors and secretaries to repair the injuries he did to the language of Samuel Johnson and Noah Webster—if not the more imaginative idiom of presidential predecessors George Washington and, most notoriously, Andrew Jackson. The emergence during the late nineteenth century of a movement to reform the spelling of archaic survivals like "through" and "comptroller" had caught Roosevelt's attention, and after the movement gained the legitimacy of the support of such academic notables as David Starr Jordan of Stanford and Nicholas Murray Butler of Columbia—and, more important, after he gained the power to hope to put his preferences into effect—he noisily joined the camp of reform. In August 1906 he directed the government printing office to adopt revised spellings for a core list of three hundred words compiled by the most prominent group of spelling reformers, an outfit calling itself the Simplified Spelling Board.

The simplifiers made much of the savings to be accomplished by straightening out American orthography. They pointed to the inordinate time spent on spelling in American schools, as compared to schools in countries like Italy and Spain where spelling followed pronunciation so closely that spelling as a separate subject of study did not exist. They noted that a cleaner orthography would shorten sentences by up to a sixth in printed books and magazines, affording commensurate savings of ink and paper. Perhaps with a mind to Roosevelt's years with the Civil Service Commission, they pointed to the large number of qualified applicants turned aside for mere misspellings.

In justifying his spelling order, Roosevelt did not promise important savings, perhaps recognizing that the startup costs of a program of spelling change would swallow any savings for some time to come. Rather, he intended to strike a blow for common sense. "There is not the slightest intention to do anything revolutionary or initiate any far-reaching policy. The purpose is simply for the Government, instead of lagging behind popular sentiment, to advance abreast of it and at the same time abreast of the views of the ablest and most practical educators of our time as well as the most profound scholars." Roosevelt remarked how the spelling of English had been changing for centuries. Who now wrote "fysshe," as the Elizabethans had, or "publick," like the American founding fathers? The reform he was ordering fell comfortably into that category of evolutionary, progressive change. "It is not an attempt to anything far-reaching or sudden or violent; or indeed anything very great at all. It is merely an attempt to cast what slight weight can properly be cast on the side of the popular forces which are endeavoring to make our spelling a little less foolish and fantastic." To lend additional weight of authority and precedent to his decision, Roosevelt ordered his annual message of December 1906 printed and distributed according to the simplified stylebook.

During his five years in office, Roosevelt had annoyed most members of Congress on one issue or another, in style or substance; more than a few, on the extreme left and the far right, he had alienated entirely. Yet sufficiently shrewd had he become as a political tactician that his opponents were usually unable to organize the assorted provocations into anything amounting to unified opposition, as his success in winning approval of his railroad and meat inspection bills demonstrated.

The cause of language reform, however, provided a lightning rod for the discharge of all the congressional frustrations. Following the lead of the Supreme Court, which summarily threw out Roosevelt's spelling order as it applied to the court's own publications, Congress roundly rejected the spelling initiative. One after another, lawmakers rose to the defense of the traditional values of language. They roasted Roosevelt as a czar who would dictate to the American people on a matter so personal as how they communicated—a hornbook tyrant who was attempting to usurp authority that by no stretch of constitution or imagination lay within legitimate presidential purview. In highest dudgeon, the House overwhelmingly endorsed a resolution calling on the printing office to "observe and adhere to the standard of orthography prescribed in generally accepted dictionaries of the English language."

The congressional opposition joined a river of ridicule that poured into the White House from every direction. The New York *Times* haughtily promised to treat each of the president's "heterographical freaks" as a misprint and to correct it accordingly. The *Evening Post*, quoting humorist Artemus Ward, who had made his reputation misspelling things, declared, "This is 2 mutch." The Baltimore *Sun* wanted to know how the name Roosevelt would appear in the new spelling. "Will he make it 'Rusevelt' or will he get down to the fact and spell it 'Butt-in-sky'?" The editor of the Louisville *Courier-Journal* suggested the spelling "Rucevelt," with "the first silabel riming with goose." This writer went on to summarize much sentiment regarding Roosevelt's latest bright idea:

> Nuthing escapes Mr. Rucevelt. No subject is tu hi fr him to takl, nor tu lo for him tu notis. . . . He now assales the English langgwidg, constitutes himself a sort of French Academy, and will reform the spelling in a way tu soot himself.

The ridicule did Roosevelt in. He had habitually made jokes on himself; friends and visitors found it one of his most engaging qualities. But he didn't like others to be the ones making the jokes on him, and he had grown increasingly sensitive on the subject since entering the White House. To some extent his heightened sensitivity was merely a matter of power tending to intoxicate, as his critics alleged; to some extent it resulted from his concern for the honor and prestige of the presidency. In any event, by the time the House passed its resolution to keep the old spelling books, Roosevelt realized his error. He rescinded his order to the printing office, although he determined to continue using the new style in his own correspondence. To Brander Matthews, an ally in the struggle, he explained, "I could not by fighting have kept the new spelling in, and it was evidently worse than useless to go into an undignified contest when I was beaten." Typically, he denied having any regrets. "I am mighty glad I did the thing."

VIII

A much happier subject than spelling reform was Alice's wedding. During his daughter's often-difficult twenty-two years, Roosevelt doubtless dreamed of the day when she would become someone else's problem. He likely didn't envision Nicholas Longworth, although, knowing Alice, he shouldn't have been surprised. (Roosevelt's feelings about a prospective son-in-law surfaced in an incident at Sagamore Hill in which a young man with a strange gleam in his eye drove a carriage up to the gate and insisted that he had to get in; he was to marry Alice. The Secret Service guard tried to turn him away, but he was adamant. A scuffle ensued, revealing a pearl-handled pistol in the young man's possession; needless to say, this provoked rather firmer gestures from Roosevelt's bodyguards. The noise attracted the president, who came outside to see what was going on. Apprised of the intruder's announced mission, he immediately recognized that he was dealing not with an assassin but a lunatic. "Of course he's insane," he commented. "He wants to marry Alice.")

Nick Longworth wasn't insane, but he was fifteen years older than Alice, which caused some parental concern. And in those extra years of life he had acquired something of a reputation as a man of the world, which elicited additional concern. But his background was respectable enough: his family were pillars of Cincinnati society. And he had embarked on what Roosevelt could only endorse as an honorable career: politics. A second-term congressman, he was already making a name among younger Republicans.

Recognizing, in any event, that Alice would have her way, her father and stepmother welcomed Longworth into the family. For Edith the crucial issue was Alice's feelings toward Nick. "Alice is really in love, and it is delightful to see how softened she is," Edith remarked, although she couldn't help adding: "I still tremble when I think of her face to face with the practical details of life."

Theodore concentrated on his future son-in-law's strengths. "Longworth is a good fellow," he informed an English friend. "He is a Harvard man, like myself, was on the varsity crew, was a member of my club, the Porcellian, and was and is much the best violinist who ever left Harvard." (Roosevelt had to take this last on faith: His lack of musicality was a family joke.) He added, "He has worked his way along in politics and has shown that he has good stuff in him. I hope he can continue, and I believe that my daughter will be of some assistance to him for she gets along well with politicians."

If Alice had occasionally chafed under the restraints of her parents' comparative frugality, all was forgotten amid the blizzard of gifts that descended on the White House during the first weeks of 1906, preparatory to the February wedding. Foreign governments vied to honor the daughter of the president; influential Americans and those who aspired to influence felt that while lavish gifts to the master of the mansion might be misconstrued, no one could object to generosity to the master's daughter.

Alice dispensed with bridesmaids, not wishing to share what she realized would be her last moment at the center of the nation's attention. She rode her father's arm down the aisle of the East Room to a makeshift altar where Longworth awaited her. When the presiding bishop asked who gave this woman to this man, her father's emotions evidently overcame him, and he was unable to speak, merely placing Alice's hand in Nick's. Following the exchange of vows, she surprised her stepmother and gratified her father by walking purposefully over to Edith and kissing and embracing her warmly.

If the wedding was Alice's moment, the reception was more to Roosevelt's democratic taste. Protocol went by the board as invited guests, reporters, servants, and assorted passersby helped themselves to the food and drink. "If the Secretary of State ranked the chambermaid no one worried about it this day," remarked Ike Hoover, longtime White House usher. Hoover, who sometimes questioned Edith's thriftiness, admitted that this time she and her husband did themselves proud. "It can truthfully be said that this was once, and only once, in this house when everybody was amply supplied with all the inner man might desire."

IX

Alice obviously thrived under the spotlight, much like her father; Ted, on the other hand, didn't. Roosevelt's oldest son had followed his father's footsteps to Harvard but was achieving something less than the success they both had hoped for. Part of the problem was the public scrutiny that never left the lad alone. During the previous autumn reporters had followed him about Harvard Yard, snapping his picture at awkward moments and broadly making nuisances of themselves and a nervous wreck of him. At one point his concerned father felt obliged to write President Eliot to inquire whether something might be done to shield the boy. "I am inclined to tell him, if he sees any man taking a photograph of him, to run up and smash the camera, but I do not like to do this if you would disapprove." On second thought Roosevelt realized that this would probably cause more harm than good. Yet even while refraining from asking any special favors, he wasn't above dropping a hint. "I do not suppose you could interfere; I don't even suppose it would be possible to tell one or two of the influential college men to put an instant stop to the cameras, and to the newspapermen running around after Ted."

Ted survived the attentions of the press without resort to violence, but he had a more trying time in the classroom. Just the week after Alice's wedding, Roosevelt received a letter from the dean of the college informing him that his son had been placed on academic probation. Roosevelt was at something of a loss as to how to respond. He knew he had to admonish Ted to do better, yet he recalled Ted's history of reacting adversely to paternal pressure.

The letter Roosevelt wrote to his son reflected an effort to strike a balance:

> There is not leeway for the smallest shortcoming on your part. Under no circumstances and for no reason short of sickness which makes you unable to leave your room, should you cut a lesson or a theme or fail to study hard right along. If you cannot study at Claverly (and I bitterly regret that I ever engaged you a room there) hire a quiet room outside of college and I will pay for it. I need not say to you to pay no heed whatever to athletics, to social life, or to anything else that will in the slightest degree interfere with your studies. It is of no use being popular in the class if you are going to be dropped out of the class.

Besides, it was crucial to impress his instructors with his seriousness.

This said, there was no call to be discouraged. "I know you have thought of all this and I have unlimited confidence in your ability to pull yourself together, not to get depressed, not to be misled by the fools who will tell you that probation is nothing, and to peg away as hard as you know how at your work, being careful only not to work up to the point where you break down." In a handwritten addendum he offered further encouragement: "Good luck, old boy! You'll come out all right. I know you have the stuff in you, and I trust you entirely. Any one might come a cropper like this; now get up and retrieve it."

While Ted wasn't meeting the mark academically, his youngest brother Quentin's failings were of a rather different sort. Quentin was a bright lad but disposed to follow his own inclinations and not overly respectful of authority. In other words, as Roosevelt interpreted the situation, he was an eight-year-old boy. And he should be treated as such.

Consequently, Roosevelt was mildly annoyed when Quentin's teacher sent a note home complaining that her charge was misbehaving and creating "general disorder." What annoyed him was neither the misbehavior nor the note but the ineffectual attitude the note conveyed. Evidently the young teacher was intimidated by the presidential presence that surrounded the boy and hesitated to reprimand him.

Roosevelt told her to quit worrying and whale away. "Mrs. Roosevelt and I have no scruples whatever against corporal punishment. We will stand behind you entirely in doing whatever you decide is necessary." Assessing his son (somewhat contradictorily), he explained, "He is a docile child, although one that needs a firmness bordering on severity. . . . If you find him defying your authority or committing any serious misdeed, then let me know and I will whip him." The president postscripted: "If he brings play toys to school, confiscate them and keep them."

X

Personal problems of another sort spilled over into the public arena. In March 1906, Roosevelt felt obliged to request the resignation of Bellamy Storer as ambassador to Austria-Hungary. Roosevelt and Edith had come to know Bellamy and Maria Storer during the early 1890s when Roosevelt had been civil service commissioner and Storer an Ohio congressman. The two couples had hit it off well, and the Roosevelts were pleased to see Storer's career advance through diplomatic appointments to Belgium and then Spain. If Maria Storer seemed the more ambitious of the two, that was hardly remarkable in an age that offered few avenues for independent accomplishment by women. Following his accession to the presidency, Roosevelt was happy enough to elevate Storer to the ambassadorship in Vienna.

He gradually grew concerned, however, when Maria Storer turned her ambition from the acceptable goal of pushing her husband forward to one more dubious: of promoting Archbishop John Ireland of Minnesota to be a cardinal. Maria was a convert to the Catholic Church, and after converting her husband she evidently hoped to convert much of the rest of America. She recognized, though, that in order for this to happen, the church needed to become a vibrant force in American life, with leaders of singular energy and vision. The comparatively (for a Catholic) progressive Archbishop Ireland appeared just such a leader.

Roosevelt agreed. "It would please me greatly to see him made Cardinal," Roosevelt wrote Bellamy Storer in late 1903. But Roosevelt realized that it would never do for an American president to endorse a candidate for the college of cardinals. Rome would rightly resent such meddling; Protestant America—which was to say, the overwhelming majority of people in the United States—would resent it even more. He made his point quite plainly to Storer: "I could not as President in any way try to help any clergyman of any denomination to high rank in that denomination."

Maria didn't get the message. She continued to lobby on behalf of Ireland, intimating to friends in the Vatican that the American president actually supported the nomination even if political sensitivities in America precluded an open avowal of such support. Roosevelt repeatedly told her to cease and desist, but friendship kept him from speaking quite as bluntly as he might have. Only after her representations persisted long past any reasonable excuse of confusion did he take the necessary step of firing Bellamy.

Storer's sudden recall vexed him and enraged Maria. In the autumn of 1906 they told their side of the story to sympathizers on Capitol Hill, whence it found its way—complete with Roosevelt's confidential letters—to curious journalists. Papers all over the country carried the "Dear Maria" scandal on page one. For a week or so editors and other commentators kibitzed on what the president had or had not done in the way of interfering in Catholic politics and whether he or the Storers had been the more indiscreet. Roosevelt defended his actions as resolutely as he always did, declaring that if he had erred in the matter, it was as the result of a "certain chivalric feeling" toward a friend and his wife.

The flap did no lasting damage to Roosevelt. While it suggested—accurately—that the president sometimes misjudged friends and tolerated their faults longer than was prudent, most Americans were willing to forgive this venial sin. Many probably agreed with the Philadelphia editor who contended that the real lesson to be learned from the affair was that the Catholic Church was wise in not letting its officials marry. "Considerate married men of long experience will surely find reason for regarding Bellamy with mournful commiseration."

XI

Compounding Roosevelt's personal troubles were the aches and pains of passing years. He still tried to squeeze regular exercise into his schedule, with greater or less success depending on the demands of official business. He delighted in taking visitors for "scrambles," as he called his hikes-cum-climbs-cum-swims along Rock Creek, northwest of the White House. The worse the weather and the more treacherous the footing, and the greater the discomfort of his guests, the more he liked it; he judged the jaunts a test of his visitors' mettle. He held those who passed the test in the highest regard.

None did better than French ambassador Jean Jules Jusserand, who felt that not simply his own personal standing but the honor of France rested on his ability to keep up. One day in response to a presidential invitation to take a walk, Jusserand arrived at the White House in afternoon coat and silk hat, having in mind something like a stroll in the Tuileries or along the Champs-Elysées. To his surprise Roosevelt appeared in knickerbockers, heavy boots, and a well-worn felt hat. A few others joined them, and off they went, heading out of the city. They tramped pell-mell through woods and across fields, splattering mud, stumbling in the water, and thoroughly ruining Jusserand's stylish outfit. He managed to stay with the group but quite obviously only by keeping the glory of *la belle France* firmly before his eyes. Finally, they came to a stream that was too wide to jump and too deep to ford. Jusserand's relief that now they must turn back was palpable. But to the ambassador's horror Roosevelt began to strip off his clothes in order to swim the creek. Jusserand gamely followed suit, yet insisted on leaving on his lavender kid gloves. When Roosevelt cocked an eyebrow at this, the ambassador replied that in case they met ladies, he didn't want to be underdressed. Roosevelt laughed heartily, appreciating not only the ambassador's determination but also his good humor under trying circumstances. His reward was the president's confidence—which served France well.

Hiking, however, even in Roosevelt's take-no-prisoners mode, lacked the zing of more bellicose pursuits. When the opportunity arose, he liked to stick-fight with Leonard Wood. At first the two former comrades-in-arms used relatively light sticks; when these kept splintering, they switched to stouter ones. Thereafter it was calcium that shattered instead of cellulose; one especially sharp blow broke Roosevelt's right arm. "I have had to temporarily stop singlestick with General Wood," the president recorded sheepishly.

A different man might have inferred from this that hand-to-hand combat was best left to his juniors; not Roosevelt. He took up the singlesticks again once his bone mended, and on off days he boxed with young military officers. Following one boxing bout in late 1904, he reported further injuries. "I am sorry to say I have wrenched my thigh again and succeeded in breaking a blood vessel in one eye." Although the thigh slowly mended, the eye never did. Indeed, the injury precipitated a gradual deterioration of the left eye that ended in Roosevelt's losing sight on that side. Meanwhile the president continued to box, and to receive additional bruises.

Roosevelt was hardly the first or last to deny the obvious—that he, like everyone else, was getting older. But for him the inexorable loss of strength, flexibility, and recuperative powers came particularly hard. From the age of eleven his self-esteem had been intimately entwined in his conception of his physical prowess. Of course, what he had accomplished in the literary and especially the political fields vastly outstripped anything he had done as an athlete or outdoorsman. And sometimes this afforded solace. "Gracious me!" he declared a few weeks after the 1904 election. "I am so glad I am elected President, so that it does not make any difference really whether I am or am not as physically fit as formerly." On other occasions, though, the corporal toll came harder. "I eat too much and have very little exercise, and work all the time in sedentary fashion," he complained to Kermit, "and so naturally I get out of condition." To a longtime friend he lamented that he had become "both old and fat."

As he lost the battle of the calendar and the belt, Roosevelt discovered that peace and quiet, rather than the boisterous activity he had customarily employed, were what he required to revive himself. "I have been having a real rest this summer," he wrote Cabot Lodge in August 1906, "and incidentally have grown to realize that I have reached that time of life when too violent physical exercise does not rest a man when he has had an exhausting mental career."

But Roosevelt wasn't ready for the rocking chair. He continued to play an energetic, if unaccomplished, game of tennis. Indeed, the tennis court at the White House became famous as the meeting ground for his "tennis cabinet," the shifting group of athletic intimates who also talked politics with the president, although not so often or with such effect as the conspiracy-minded of his critics imagined.

And he continued to hurt himself. "Last Monday I strained my ankle playing tennis," he told Kermit after one excessively strenuous afternoon on the court, "but did not think it amounted to anything and played a couple of sets more, with the result that I have had to abandon even riding, and am now engaged busily in doing nothing when I am not at my Presidential work!"

CHAPTER TWENTY-TWO

Neither War nor Quite Peace
1906–7

A Providence editor, writing at the time of Roosevelt's fight over simplified spelling, commented, "President Roosevelt is a lucky man; this Cuban business gives him a fine opportunity to let go the tail of the simplified spelling bear."

The Cuban business at issue was a continuation of the fight Roosevelt had been waging for reciprocal tariff reduction; this fight in turn was an outgrowth of the political settlement that had concluded the Spanish war. The American victory in the war against Spain delivered control of Cuba to the United States, although the self-denying Teller amendment prevented outright American annexation. From 1898 until 1902, American troops occupied the island; during most of that period they were commanded by Roosevelt's fighting and hiking friend Leonard Wood. Negotiations for an American withdrawal commenced before Roosevelt assumed the presidency; another Roosevelt intimate, Elihu Root, handled the bargaining on the American side. Fearing that internal disorder would both endanger American property in Cuba and invite intervention by foreign powers, Root arranged for a right of American intervention to be written into American law, into a U.S.-Cuban treaty, and into the Cuban constitution. The Platt amendment, as this provision was known in the United States (after the Connecticut Platt, not the New York one) took effect during the summer of 1901.

Most Cubans were less than enthusiastic about the Platt provision, which seriously compromised the independence Cuba was about to gain. Yet with German ships cruising the Caribbean and with the country still deeply torn by the late rebellion against Spain, an American commitment to preserve partial independence (that is, against Europeans and other non-American outsiders) and to guarantee internal order didn't seem a uniformly bad idea. Moreover, the Cuban merchant class hoped for favorable tariff treatment by the United States, which would go far toward ensuring economic viability for the merchants and the country as a whole; raising a ruckus about the Platt amendment would probably harden the already hard hearts of the protectionists in the American Congress. Finally, the Americans made clear that if Cuba wanted to get rid of the U.S. troops, Platt was the price.

During the initial part of his presidency, Roosevelt waged his lonely struggle for tariff reciprocity. The president understood the antipathy of his party toward tariff reductions. But this case was special. "A moral question is involved," he told Nicholas Murray Butler. Unfortunately, so were political questions, and Roosevelt recognized that getting the reductions Cuba really needed—on agricultural products—would take some doing. "I wish that Cuba grew steel and glass," he lamented.

What Cuba grew, of course, was sugar, and American beet sugar growers lobbied energetically and for the most part successfully to keep Cuba's cane on the list of imports paying full freight. For two years the beet men blocked Roosevelt's reciprocity treaty. The break came only in the autumn of 1903 when a major merger of sugar producers folded some of the biggest beet growers into a trust comprising Cuban cane interests as well. The trust called off the protectionist police, and Cuban reciprocity rolled through.

Whatever it did for the sugar trust's profits, reciprocity didn't cure Cuba's ills. Cubans accustomed to centuries of foreign domination had difficulty adapting to the demands of self-government. President Tomas Estrada Palma, a naturalized American citizen and former upstate New York schoolteacher who had returned to join the anti-Spanish rebellion, complained, "In Cuba we have a republic, but no citizens." Palma and his fellow Moderates did little to encourage a civic sense, packing government posts with cronies, stuffing ballot boxes, and generally using every device at hand to shut out the opposition Liberals. Cuban politics grew nastier than ever; the Moderates took to calling the Liberals "tartars," and the Liberals responded by calling the Moderates "cossacks." Before long the two sides were hurling more than epithets at each other: The summer of 1906 saw outbursts of regular fighting. As the anti-Palma insurgency gained strength, the Cuban leader turned to the United States, invoking the Platt amendment and calling on Roosevelt to send troops.

In 1898, Roosevelt had been only too eager to intervene in Cuba; now he evinced the greatest reluctance. He had been younger then, with spurs still to be won; now, having proved his manhood, he could afford to take a more measured approach. Then he had enjoyed the luxury of irresponsibility; now the burden of responsibility rested squarely on his shoulders. Then he had had no other concerns against which to weigh the consequences of intervention; now he had to deal with an increasingly fractious Congress, which included rivals in both parties who would exploit a slip on Cuba to attack him on a dozen other fronts. Perhaps most important, intervention in 1898 had been a blow against Spain and, by extension, Europe; now Spain was long gone, and the hegemony of the United States in the Caribbean was essentially unquestioned.

For all these reasons Roosevelt resisted intervention mightily. "If I am forced to intervene it will not be until it is evident that no other course is left me," he told Whitelaw Reid. Indeed, he resented even the thought of intervention. "Just at the moment I am so angry with that infernal little Cuban republic that I would like to wipe its people off the face of the earth," he declared in September 1906. "All we have wanted from them is that they would behave themselves and be prosperous and happy so that we would not have to interfere. And now, lo and behold, they have started an utterly unjustifiable and pointless revolution and may get things into such a snarl that we have no alternative save to intervene—which will at once convince the suspicious idiots in South America that we do wish to interfere after all, and perhaps have some land-hunger!"

Roosevelt's antipathy to intervention caused him to try to prevent Palma from even making a request. "I have just been notified by the Cuban Government that they intend to ask us forcibly to intervene in the course of this week," he told George Trevelyan on September 9, "and I have sent them a most emphatic protest against their doing so." To reenter Cuba would risk saddling the United States with a heavy and thankless burden, the likes of which it had enough already.

"I loathe the thought of assuming any control over the island such as we have over Porto Rico and the Philippines. We emphatically do not want it."

Certainly Americans at large did not want it; popular enthusiasm for colonial adventures had never recovered from the Philippine war. Roosevelt understood this, and it reinforced his own reluctance. He wasn't about to walk away from obligations already incurred, such as those in the Philippines and Puerto Rico, but neither did he have any desire to add to them.

Unfortunately, the existing obligations to Cuba pulled him inexorably toward intervention. The Platt amendment linked the United States politically to Cuba; equally important to Roosevelt, the intervention against Spain and the subsequent occupation had tied the United States by conscience to the island. As president, he could not simply stand aside while Cuba dissolved into chaos. "I dread the creation of a revolutionary habit," he told Trevelyan, "and the creation of a class of people who take to disturbance and destruction as an exciting and pleasant business." If action were required to forestall such a development, he would have to order it. "We cannot permanently see Cuba a prey to misrule and anarchy."

Even so, Roosevelt wasn't going to do anything hasty. Dubious of some of the reports he was receiving from Cuba, he ordered William Taft, now secretary of war, and Bob Bacon, lately transferred from Morgan's employ to the State Department, to go to Cuba to assess the situation personally. (He would have sent Root, but the secretary of state was on a tour of South America.) He granted Taft authority to order American troops ashore if an emergency arose in which there was no time to contact Washington, but he cautioned the war secretary to avoid using the term "intervention" or analogously loaded labels. "Simply say that they are landed to save life and property in Havana," Roosevelt explained.

Taft's initial impressions offered hope that a compromise between the opposing parties would render American intervention—however labeled—unnecessary. He proceeded to develop such a compromise. Meanwhile, Roosevelt wrote Palma urging him to support Taft's mediative efforts. "It is evident that under existing circumstances your government cannot stand," Roosevelt said, "and that to attempt to maintain it or to dictate your own terms about the new government

merely means disaster and perhaps ruin for Cuba." Roosevelt congratulated Palma on the birth of Cuban independence during his four
years in office; the American president implored his Cuban counterpart not to spoil his reputation at this late hour. "I adjure you for the
sake of your own fair fame not so to conduct yourself that the responsibility if such there be for the death of the republic can be put at your
door."

But Palma spurned Roosevelt's advice, causing the president to consider throwing American support to the insurgents, who expressed
willingness to go along with Taft. "I am inclined to think that unless
you have reason to the contrary of which I am ignorant," Roosevelt
told Taft, "it would be better to proceed with the insurrectos along the
exact lines that you have proposed, simply notifying them that as
Palma will not act we will appoint some man to act in his place until
the plan you have sketched out and to which they have agreed can be
put thru." Roosevelt hoped by this means to avoid the necessity of an
American occupation, which he feared would end badly. "I do not
believe we should, simply because Palma has turned sulky and will not
act like a patriot, put ourselves in the place of his unpopular government and face all the likelihood of a long drawn out and very destructive guerrilla warfare."

Taft talked Roosevelt out of backing the insurgents and into sending the marines. The secretary of war judged the rebels incapable of
providing the leadership Cuba needed; the mere thought of handing
the government over to them made him "shiver at the consequences,"
he said. Taft contended that a Cuban solution to Cuba's problems was
beyond reach; both parties seemed determined to have the Americans
intervene.

Roosevelt was developing substantial faith in Taft's judgment.
"With Taft in Havana I feel quite easy, and cheerfully turn over all my
volcanic responsibilities in that island to him," the president
remarked. Accordingly, he acceded to the force of Taft's argument,
and to the weight of circumstances in Cuba. The president acknowledged the drawbacks of sending troops and probably becoming burdened with responsibility for fashioning a new government in
Havana. Among these drawbacks was the signal it would send to
Cubans that insurrectionary force might successfully be employed to
change an unsatisfactory government. "It is undoubtedly a very evil

thing that the revolutionists should be encouraged and the dreadful example afforded the island of success in remedying wrongs by violence and treason to the government," he observed to Taft. But with the likes of Palma in charge, the United States had little choice.

In authorizing intervention, however, Roosevelt repeated his admonition to Taft to shun that term. "Avoid the use of the word intervention in any proclamation or paper of yours and if possible place the landing of our sailors and marines on grounds of conservation of American interests emphasizing the temporary character of the landing."

Roosevelt consistently prided himself on his immunity to semantical considerations; he was always saying that he cared "not a rap" what something was called as long as it accomplished what needed to be accomplished. His pride in this regard was often excessive; particularly after becoming president he paid close attention to what things were called, for the good reason that labels *did* matter. They shaped the thinking of people positioned to do the president harm or help. Ignoring this fact would be foolish and counterproductive.

Having already been ensnared by congressional opposition to the Santo Domingo treaty, Roosevelt wanted to do everything possible to minimize further upset on Capitol Hill. In warning Taft against letting "intervention" pass his lips, the president explained, "This as I say is important not merely for the sake of the Cubans but for the sake of meeting our opponents at home."

Those opponents assaulted the president for militaristic egomania, for collusion with the sucrose capitalists, and for failings less credible and more tangential to the situation in Cuba. The most telling, and potentially most damaging, criticism, however, was that Roosevelt was poaching on Capitol Hill. There was little precedent for his sending marines to occupy a country with which the United States was not at war, and there was considerable question whether he had the authority to do so without consulting Congress.

Roosevelt himself wasn't sure he did, which was why he wished to avoid calling his action in Cuba intervention. Paradoxically, or so it might have appeared to one not familiar with Roosevelt's thinking, this was also one of the few factors pushing him *toward* intervention. As evidenced in the anthracite strike, in the Panama affair, and in numerous other incidents, Roosevelt believed that power was meant to be used. "While I am a Jeffersonian in my genuine faith in democracy and popular government," he once explained, "I am a Hamiltonian in my governmental views, especially with reference to the need of the exercise of broad powers by the National Government." And more especially still was this true with reference to the powers of the president in foreign affairs. "You know as well as I do," he told Taft, "that it is for the enormous interest of this Government to strengthen and give independence to the Executive in dealing with foreign powers." By contrast to the executive branch, the legislative branch was poorly suited to handling foreign affairs, particularly in moments of crisis. "A legislative body, because of its very good qualities in domestic matters, is not well fitted for shaping foreign policy on occasions when instant action is demanded."

It was partly to demonstrate—or create, depending on one's view of the situation—his authority to send troops into action that Roosevelt approved the landing in Cuba. While the operation remained several days in the future, the president wrote Taft, "If it becomes necessary to intervene I intend to establish a precedent for good by refusing to wait for a long wrangle with Congress." Legislative leaders would complain, some out of principle, more out of partisan pettiness. But the point was worth the political cost. "The important thing to do is for a President who is willing to accept responsibility to establish precedents which successors may follow even if they are unwilling to take the initiative themselves."

II

Roosevelt wrought better than he dreamed in establishing the interventionist precedent. His immediate successors would intervene repeatedly in the Caribbean basin, and throughout the twentieth century presidents would ignore Congress far more frequently than they would consult it in sending soldiers overseas. Eventually, American forces would fight full-scale wars without the congressional declaration even Hamilton had considered necessary.

Yet those critics who tagged Roosevelt with militarism missed the point. In his callow youth he had praised war as moral calisthenics;

now that he was president he took a rather different view. War was the crucible in which one's character was tested; he had passed his test brilliantly. The hero didn't need to prove his bravery every day; having won his laurels, he could afford to let prudence temper boldness. And prudence was most becoming in a president.

There may have been another element that contributed to his thinking, although it probably didn't rise to the level of consciousness. As president he was one of the few able-bodied men in the country who would be guaranteed *not* to have a chance to ride into battle; instead he would have to watch while war made *other* men heroes. It certainly said something about Roosevelt that no sooner would he leave the White House than he would be volunteering for military service again, and that at the first serious post-presidential opportunity he would resurrect his war-as-vital-for-national-health arguments.

In any event, Roosevelt in office placed a higher premium on order than on conflict. In Venezuela, in northeastern Asia, and most recently in Cuba, he had sought to maintain or restore order. For several months during 1905–6, order was threatened again, this time in Europe, and once more Roosevelt stepped into the breach. And once more he found himself face-to-face with Germany's Wilhelm. The president's respect for the kaiser continued to be tempered by puzzlement. Wilhelm was often his own worst enemy: Convinced that the world was ganging up on him, he acted in a fashion that begot ganging. In an age when pushiness was expected in international relations, the Germans were pushier than most; but when faced with opposition, they—or at least their leader—took offense and started shouting for satisfaction.

It was just such shouting that involved Roosevelt in the Algeciras conference. During the course of 1905 the kaiser became convinced that the other European powers were trying to elbow Germany out of Morocco, one of the few countries of the African continent not claimed by the colonialists (if it had been so claimed, Roosevelt wouldn't have had the opportunity to send his "Perdicaris alive or Raisuli dead" ultimatum). Morocco itself was hardly a great prize; it hadn't been left out of the imperial scramble for nothing. But Morocco meant more to Germany than fezzes and dates and perhaps a railroad or two; it signified respect, or the absence thereof. Wilhelm described to Roosevelt a plot whereby Spain and especially France, the latter with England's assistance, were colluding to keep Morocco's markets and resources to themselves. Germany could not allow this to happen. German firms had every right to do business in Morocco. Speaking through Speck von Sternberg, the kaiser added that Germany had deeper concerns in the matter: "She is bound to think of her national dignity." For thirty-five years France had been testing Germany. "As soon as France discovers that Germany meekly submits to her bullying, we feel sure that she will become more aggressive in other quarters."

Hoping to use the Americans as a counterbalance to France and Britain, Wilhelm asked the president to sponsor an international conference to determine the fate of Morocco. Such a conference would apply the principles of the open door, championed by the United States in China, to Morocco, thereby guaranteeing the equal rights of all nations in that country. "A word from you to England will mean a great deal," Sternberg declared, at Wilhelm's direction, "and I'm sure the Emperor will be most grateful to you for intimating that you would like to see England and Germany in harmony in their dealings with Morocco." Wilhelm himself was characteristically more forceful. The kaiser warned that if Germany did not receive satisfaction, he would be compelled to act alone. In a typically third-person memorandum to Roosevelt, Wilhelm went as far as to utter the word that seasoned diplomats reserve for the direst emergencies. "He would have to choose between the possibility of a war with France and the examining of those conditions which France may have to propose, so as to avoid a war."

Roosevelt was no stranger to extravagant language, but he took care to shun the stuff when speaking as president and chief American diplomat, when issues of war and peace hung on his wording. Being conscientious in this regard himself, he hardly knew whether to take the mercurial Wilhelm seriously. Roosevelt's uncertainty, joined to his assessment that Morocco meant nothing to the United States, initially inclined him to put the German emperor off. "The Kaiser's pipe dream this week takes the form of Morocco," Roosevelt remarked to Taft. The United States should stay out. "We have other fish to fry and we have no real interest in Morocco. I do not care to take sides between France and Germany in the matter."

But the emperor persisted in his expostulations about the iniquity of France and Britain. Once again he wrote Roosevelt threatening war if Germany failed to receive due respect. Both Sternberg and French ambassador Jusserand grew increasingly agitated and worried. "It really did look as if there might be a war," Roosevelt explained later.

The president came to conclude that while Morocco didn't matter to the United States, Europe did, and a war between the two largest continental powers wouldn't benefit Americans or anyone else— whatever the kaiser might think. Ticking off the reasons for changing his mind and acceding to Wilhelm's request for mediation, he wrote, "I felt in honor bound to try to prevent the war if I could, in the first place, because I should have felt such a war to be a real calamity to civilization; and in the next place, as I was already trying to bring about peace between Russia and Japan, I felt that a new conflict might result in what would literally be a world conflagration; and finally for the sake of France."

On this last point Roosevelt feared that the French didn't realize what they were up against. He tried to explain the danger to Jusserand, and through Jusserand to the government in Paris. He noted that even if France had Britain's backing, that backing wouldn't mean much in a war with Germany. Britain's strength lay in its navy, which could hardly prevent German troops from crossing the Rhine. He urged Paris to agree to a conference. Whether or not the kaiser's complaints about Morocco had any merit, Wilhelm had worked himself into such a huff that he might well go to war out of wounded pride. Under the circumstances, magnanimity in giving Wilhelm a way back down from this particular limb would benefit everyone.

When the French agreed in principle to the president's proposal, Roosevelt took pains to prevent Wilhelm from spoiling the victory either by gloating or by holding out for additional concessions France might be unwilling to give. In a letter to Sternberg for the kaiser's attention, Roosevelt offered flattery and a warning. He declared of Wilhelm that "he stands as the leader among the sovereigns of today who have their faces set toward the future." Roosevelt added: "He has won a great triumph; he has obtained what his opponents in England and France said he never would obtain, and what I myself did not believe he could obtain. The result is a striking tribute to him personally no less than to his nation, and I earnestly hope that he can see his way clear to accept it as the triumph it is."

Things didn't happen quite so easily as this. Paris and Berlin haggled over the terms of the conference and its agenda. Once more Jusserand and Sternberg fretted that war impended. Just before the negotiations broke down, however, Roosevelt sliced through the bickering with several bold strokes of a pencil. He scribbled, "The two Governments consent to go to the conference with no program, and to discuss there all questions in regard to Morocco, save of course where either is in honor bound by a previous agreement with another power." He gave this note to Sternberg and a copy to Jusserand; the statement—and the fact that it came from Roosevelt, respected by both sides as an honest broker—provided just the impetus to break the deadlock.

The conference itself commenced at Algeciras in Spain during the third week of January 1906. Roosevelt attended only in spirit but continued to mediate between France and Germany through the agency of Jusserand and Sternberg, both of whom he held in the highest regard. (By contrast, he considered the British ambassador, Mortimer Durand, hopeless. "He seems to have a brain of about eight-guinea-pig-power. Why, under Heaven the English keep him here I do not know! If they do not care for an Ambassador, then abolish the embassy; but it is useless to have a worthy creature of mutton-suet consistency like the good Sir Mortimer." Further on, Roosevelt lamented, "Oh Lord, what a difference it would make if Spring Rice were here as Ambassador!")

In acting as go-between, the president generally spoke with Jusserand directly, while Sternberg and the kaiser preferred getting their messages in writing. Wilhelm was as suspicious and skittish as ever—as well he might have been, given that most of the major powers took France's side against Germany. Roosevelt spent the better part of two months reassuring the kaiser that a settlement at Algeciras made more sense than a breakdown of negotiations and a likely war. On February 19 the president offered a four-point plan; Wilhelm accepted three points but rejected the fourth. Additional sessions with Sternberg and Jusserand ensued, and the bills for transatlantic cablegrams climbed.

When finally, in mid-March, Wilhelm seemed to have dug himself into a position from which diplomatic niceties didn't appear likely to dislodge him, Roosevelt tried something more forceful. He threatened to publish the entire correspondence between himself and Wilhelm, which, he intimated to Sternberg, would cast Germany's honor and good faith in a bad light. On the other hand, if the emperor could find it possible to come to terms, he—Roosevelt—would keep the correspondence confidential and go out of his way to give Wilhelm credit for wisdom and graciousness.

This provided the kaiser the encouragement he needed to acquiesce in what by most measures was a bad bargain for Germany. The conference nominally confirmed Morocco's independence and the principle of equality for all comers commercially; but France got control of Morocco's state bank, and France and Spain authority over Morocco's police.

The Algeciras conference enhanced Roosevelt's reputation considerably less than the Portsmouth conference had. Part of the reason was that the president's role in the latter was obvious and acknowledged, while his actions regarding Algeciras were mostly hidden from view. More important was that while Portsmouth produced the measurable result of ending a war, Algeciras yielded nothing so neat or definitive. The Spanish conclave may have averted a war, assuming the kaiser meant what he said about pushing Paris on Morocco. Yet none of those attending the conference, and certainly not Roosevelt, thought they had bought more than time. "I think the outcome of the Morocco business was satisfactory, don't you?" the president wrote King Edward of Britain, who did, too. But no more than satisfactory: While the great powers avoided war in 1906, Algeciras demonstrated Germany's isolation and left Wilhelm feeling more put upon than ever.

III

The Japanese were feeling put upon as well. To some extent the bad feelings were their own fault. Prior to Portsmouth, government officials in Tokyo had made grand promises about an indemnity; when they came home empty-handed, the Japanese people were predictably disappointed. No more than politicians anywhere did Japan's leaders like to confess their folly in raising expectations unreachably high;

seeking a scapegoat, they blamed Roosevelt. Anti-American riots erupted in Tokyo and other Japanese cities; even as the Nobel committee in Norway was choosing him for its peace prize for bringing reconciliation to the Far East, committees of public protest in Japan were targeting him for abuse for bringing shame to their country. Hotheads went as far as to talk of war with the United States.

Yet if some of the Japanese outrage against America was undeserved, no small part was fully earned. The anti-Asianism that had motivated the Chinese Exclusion Act of 1882 (which had been extended in 1892 and rendered permanent in 1902) had lately focused on Japanese immigrants. As before, the animus against the immigrants from across the Pacific was informed by influences economic, cultural, and racial. West Coast workers objected to the low-wage competition of Asian "coolies," and they and their neighbors feared and despised the immigrants' exotic beliefs and lifestyle. The immigration issue, thought to have been settled by the laws barring Chinese, the earliest and most numerous of the Asian immigrants, had recently flared up again following the annexation of Hawaii in 1898. Scores of thousands of Japanese had migrated to Hawaii before annexation; thousands continued to do so. Under the terms of the treaty of annexation, they could move on freely to the American mainland.

The Japanese immigration issue came to a head during Roosevelt's second term. In October 1906 the San Francisco school board mandated the segregation of Asian schoolchildren into an institution called the Oriental Public School. The order embraced Korean and Chinese children as well as Japanese, but both Korea and China had troubles aplenty without worrying about what school their emigrant children were attending in far-off California. For Japan, however, lately accustomed to thinking itself the equal of the Western countries—a belief underscored by the thrashing just administered to Russia—the San Francisco action came as an egregious insult. First the Americans had deprived Japan of its hard-won indemnity; now they were classing Japanese children as no better than Chinese and Koreans.

Roosevelt, for all his embrace of the democratic ideal and his confidence in the common people, had never held state or local governments in particularly high esteem. The pests of the democratic process, he believed, fed most freely on the grass roots. He knew this to be true in the New York City of Tammany Hall and the Albany of the black-horse cavalry; he suspected it was true of California as well. Since the Portsmouth conference he had grown concerned over the deteriorating condition of U.S.-Japanese relations; the edict of the San Francisco school board promised to deal those relations a sharp—and utterly unnecessary—blow. He told Kermit he was "horribly bothered about the Japanese business"; he added: "The infernal fools in California, and especially in San Francisco, insult the Japanese recklessly." Considering the sensitivity of the Japanese people and the idiocy of the Californians, Roosevelt didn't deem war entirely out of the question. "However," he said, "I hope to keep things straight. I am perfectly willing that this Nation should fight any nation if it has got to, but I would loathe to see it forced into a war in which it was wrong."

Roosevelt immediately set to dampening the combustibles. He wrote to Baron Kaneko expressing his "gravest concern" at this affront to Japan and assuring him that the San Francisco action no more represented American opinion than recent misdeeds against Americans by some Japanese seal poachers represented Japanese opinion. He said his Justice Department was taking measures through the courts to invalidate the school board's directive. At the same time, though, he had to acknowledge the constraints under which even a president operated. "Our form of government, which has many advantages, has some disadvantages, and one of them is in dealing with movements like this."

Roosevelt laid plans to use federal troops to protect Japanese immigrants from mob violence, if things came to that; meanwhile, he sought to strike the problem of anti-Japanese feeling at its source. "In the Japanese matter the crux is the bringing in of the Japanese laboring men," he explained to Lyman Abbott. "Whether we like it or not, I think we have to face the fact that the people of the Pacific slope, with the warm approval of the labor men thruout our whole country, will become steadily more and more hostile to the Japanese if their laborers come here, and I am doing my best to bring about an agreement with Japan by which the laborers of each country shall be kept out of the other country. I want to make things so pleasant for Japan, if I possibly can, that with entire self-respect they can propose or assent to such a proposition."

Roosevelt's posture in this regard was partly rhetorical. The situation between the two countries was nowhere near as symmetrical as he suggested. American laborers were not lining up to enter Japan; the flow was all in the other direction. Yet by pointing to barriers to American entry into Japan, he could construct a case for keeping Japanese workers out of the United States.

Though not a zealous immigration reformer like Lodge or any number of other contemporaries, Roosevelt conceded the legitimacy of part of the restrictionists' argument. Speaking of businessmen who wrapped themselves—cynically, as he saw it—in the mythology of immigration as a vital part of the American dream, Roosevelt asserted, "I have not the slightest sympathy for big men who want to bring in cheap labor, whether Japanese, Chinese or any other." Neither did he have any moral qualms about limiting the number of Asian workers allowed to enter the United States: America was not the world's dumping ground for the overflow of other countries.

Yet he insisted that his country do justice to any it did allow in. Rumblings in the West indicated a desire to prevent Asians from exercising voting rights and other aspects of citizenship. This would be unfair and unwise. "It does no possible good to deprive those who are here of the franchise. On the contrary, I think that we should studiously give the franchise and school facilities to, and in other ways treat as well as possible, all the Japanese that come." What Roosevelt feared was not immigrants per se but immigrants kept beyond the pale of full participation in American life. "We cannot afford to regard any immigrant as a laborer; we must regard him as a citizen."

It was no accident that the Japanese issue boiled over on the eve of the 1906 congressional elections; nor did it surprise the president to find his opponents posturing on the issue even after the election. Samuel McCall, a Republican congressman from Massachusetts, and Richard Olney, the former attorney general and secretary of state, and still an important figure among Democratic conservatives, spearheaded the opposition to a measure that would have granted the president leeway in deciding whom to let in and whom to keep out. Roosevelt predictably impugned the motives of the two men. "McCall and Olney," he said, "in a spirit of folly so gratuitous that it looks like deliberate mischief-making, are now adding to the difficulties of the Nation in coming to a peaceful solution of the Japanese imbroglio."

But it was the Californians who angered Roosevelt the most. Out of either parochial ignorance or fatuous selfishness, he judged, they were putting the narrow—and misguided—interests of one city and state ahead of the interests of the nation as a whole. To drive home the likely consequences of their actions, Roosevelt invited—all but ordered, in fact—members of the San Francisco school board and the city's mayor to Washington. He called in California's congressional delegation. He wrote long letters to the newly elected, and conveniently Republican, governor of California.

To this last individual, James Gillett, Roosevelt explained that the "violent extremists" who were stirring up the Japanese issue were making it nearly impossible for him to accomplish the very goal they professed to pursue. Roosevelt shared the objective of keeping out Japanese laborers, but he argued that gratuitously insulting the government of Japan was hardly the way to accomplish it. Congress had not seen fit to bar entry to workers from the advanced (and even those not-so-advanced) countries of Europe; to single out Japan for special and unfavorable treatment would needlessly aggravate tensions that already existed between the United States and the most advanced and powerful country of Pacific Asia.

The president went on to say that he had been engaged in quiet negotiations with the Japanese government, which had pledged to prevent the emigration of laborers to the United States as long as Japanese already in America suffered no official discrimination. Moreover, in his continuing conversations with members of the San Francisco board he had elicited an agreement that promised to save the face of both sides: All foreign children, whether Japanese or other nationality, would be placed in separate schools or classes when either their advanced age or their lack of fluency in English prevented their participating in regular classes. A solution satisfactory to almost everyone was near. "The National Government has met with only one difficulty in securing this object," Roosevelt explained to Governor Gillett, "and that is the difficulty caused by these foolish or designing agitators who most loudly repeat the cry of Japanese exclusion at the very moment that they are doing all they can to prevent its becoming a fact." Roosevelt wasn't so blunt as to tell Gillett to crack these crazies into line; the president didn't know who else would be reading the letter, and, besides, Gillett could no more dictate to Californians than Roosevelt could. But he expected the governor to derail some additionally insulting bills that were working their way through the California legislature at that very moment.

Roosevelt's stiffening letter paid off. The governor shared the president's sentiments with leaders of the California senate, which duly turned back the measures in question.

Yet Roosevelt soon learned of another anti-Japanese initiative afoot in Sacramento, and he felt obliged to address another, longer, and even more forceful letter to the governor. The agreement with Japan was essentially complete, he explained. "It therefore appears that we now have absolute power to exclude all Japanese laborers from this country, and that the only obstacle to thus securing their exclusion lies in the action of those unwise and sinister agitators who seek to delude the good people of California, and especially of San Francisco, into a course of action which will defeat the very object they profess to have in view."

With this additional encouragement, Gillett throttled the latest provocative measure, allowing the so-called Gentlemen's Agreement with Japan to slide sedately into effect. The bargain was as Roosevelt had explained it earlier: no formal American barriers to Japanese immigration and no legal discrimination against Japanese in the United States, but informal measures by Tokyo to prevent additional emigration to America by Japanese workers.

Gentleman that he was, Roosevelt refused to crow publicly over what amounted to a significant victory for his method of quiet but firm diplomacy. Yet he did allow himself one private boast. He told Andrew Carnegie, "In this Japanese matter I can say with all sincerity that I doubt if any President could have done more to secure peace than I have done." He added with an indeterminable degree of exaggeration, "The situation was at times a very dangerous one."

IV

The flap over Japanese immigration might have been settled a bit sooner except that in the middle of it Roosevelt rendered himself incommunicado. For some time he and Edith had been looking for a place where they could drop out of sight; Sagamore Hill, which was seasonally besieged by the press, hardly qualified. Besides, like all parents, they wanted a spot where they could get away from their children as well as from outsiders. Accordingly, when Roosevelt heard about a piece of property in the woods near Charlottesville, Virginia, they decided to give it a look. They liked what they saw, made an offer, and became landowners of the Old Dominion.

At the beginning of November 1906, Roosevelt and Edith traveled to Pine Knot, as they called their hideaway. For three days they enjoyed simple pleasures that had become all but impossible in Washington or even Oyster Bay. Edith puttered around, unbothered by servants or company of any kind, save her husband's. Theodore took to the woods. "I hunted faithfully thru all three days," he told Kermit, "leaving the house at three o'clock one day, at four the next, and at five the next, so that I began my hunts in absolute night; but fortunately we had a brilliant moon on each occasion." The game was scarce the first two days, and for most of the third, but on the afternoon of the last day his luck changed. For a moment the troubles with Japan, with the kaiser, and with the other fools of the world faded before the important business at hand. "The turkey came out and started to fly across the valley, offering me a beautiful side shot at about thirty-five yards—just the distance for my ten-bore. I killed it dead, and felt mighty happy as it came tumbling down thru the air."

Roosevelt and Edith returned to civilization long enough for him to vote at Oyster Bay, as per his custom; then they set out on another journey, this one no less diverting but considerably more newsworthy. From George Washington through William McKinley, no president had ever left American soil (or territorial waters) while in office. Roosevelt abided by this hoary tradition for more than five years— long enough to get elected on his own hook and to preserve the Republican majority in Congress in the 1906 races. But never a stickler for tradition when it stood in the way of something he thought he ought to do—or simply wanted to do—he judged that modern techniques of communication made him just as available aboard ship in the Caribbean as anywhere else (and more available than at Pine Knot), and he determined to visit Panama. On November 8 he and

Edith clambered up the gangway of the U.S.S. *Louisiana* and headed south to see how his pet project was progressing.

Accommodations for a president and first lady were rather cushier than for a volunteer lieutenant colonel and a band of scruffy cowboys, but the Caribbean voyage brought back memories nonetheless. The Windward Passage stirred the romantic strain in his imagination just as it had in 1898. He recounted to Kermit:

> All the forenoon we had Cuba on our right and most of the forenoon and part of the afternoon Haiti on our left; and in each case green, jungly shores and bold mountains—two great, beautiful, venomous tropic islands. These are historic seas and Mother and I have kept thinking of all that has happened in them since Columbus landed at San Salvador (which we also saw), the Spanish explorers, the buccaneers, the English and Dutch seadogs and adventurers, the great English and French fleets, the desperate fighting, the triumphs, the pestilences, all the turbulence, the splendor and the wickedness, and hot, evil, riotous life of the old planters and slave-owners, Spanish, French, English and Dutch; their extermination of the Indians and bringing in of negro slaves, the decay of most of the islands, the turning of Haiti into an island of savage negroes, who have reverted to voodooism and cannibalism; the effort we are now making to bring Cuba and Porto Rico forward.

The weather was good and his mal de mere in abeyance; the trip southward was a "perfection." Under the circumstances, Roosevelt would have enjoyed the voyage even had his vessel simply sailed around in circles. His rivals couldn't reach him, he had time to stroll the deck with Edith, and he had brought a short stack of reading, including Tacitus, Milton, and a modern German novel. He also got to play captain, courtesy of the real captain. The whole experience did his patriotic heart good. "It gives me great pride in America to be aboard this great battleship and to see not only the material perfection of the ship herself in engines, guns and all arrangements, but the fine quality of the officers and crew."

The pleasures of the voyage were gratifying indeed, but destination made it doubly worthwhile. Panama was "a great sight," a land "strange and beautiful with its mass of luxuriant tropical jungle, with the treacherous tropic rivers trailing here and there through it." Roosevelt delighted in the brilliantly colored birds, the enormous butterflies, the breathtaking orchids, the sinister snakes and exotic lizards. He tramped the old Spanish towns with their crumbling walls and the native villages with their thatched huts.

But what really brought Panama to life for Roosevelt was what the five thousand Americans there were accomplishing. An isthmian canal had been a hobbyhorse for him, then an obsession, then the cause of the most controversial act of his presidency, until he had become almost a hostage to its successful completion. The construction was not going as well as hoped. Technical troubles vexed the project; no one had ever moved so much dirt, under such difficult conditions, in all of history. Administrative headaches, aggravated by political wrangling among congressional oversight committees, bogged the engineers down almost as badly as the sticky red Panama clay did. Roosevelt couldn't expect to do much about the technical problems, but he did hope to push the project along politically by his presence.

Politics aside, Roosevelt thrilled to feel he had made possible something the whole procession of conquistadors and pirates who had trod this crossroads of the world had failed to accomplish.

> I kept thinking of the four centuries of wild and bloody romance, mixed with abject squalor and suffering, which made up the history of the Isthmus until three years ago. I could see Balboa crossing at Darien, and the wars between the Spaniards and the Indians, and the settlement and the building up of the quaint walled Spanish towns; and the trade, across the seas by galleon, and over land by pack train and river canoe, in gold and silver, in precious stones; and then the advent of the buccaneers, and of the English seamen, of Drake and Frobisher and Morgan, and many, many others, and the wild destruction they wrought.

The president traced the rebellions and civil wars that had wracked the region, and the failed attempts of the French and others to carve a canal across this spine of land.

"Now we have taken hold of the job." Problems persisted; a task as enormous as this could never be easy. "But I believe"—considering his personal and political stake in the canal, he certainly *wanted* to believe—"that the work is being done with a very high degree both of efficiency and honesty; and I am immensely struck by the character of American employees who are engaged not merely in superintending the work, but in doing all the jobs that need skill and intelligence." Simply seeing the crews took Roosevelt back to his days in the Maine lumber camps and on the Dakota range. "From top to bottom these men are so hardy, so efficient, so energetic, that it is a real pleasure to look at them." John Stevens, the chief engineer of the project, was an imposing figure, "a man of daring and good sense, and burly power." Taken together they were more than a match for any who had gone before. "All of these men are quite as formidable, and would if it were necessary do quite as much in battle as the crews of Drake and Morgan."

Yet they were doing far more important work than Drake or Morgan and their crews. "Nothing remains to show what Drake and Morgan did. They produced no real effect down here. But Stevens and his men are changing the face of the continent, are doing the greatest engineering feat of the ages, and the effect of their work will be felt while our civilization lasts."

Roosevelt had been striking poses since he was a young man; it was only natural that he should do so in the midst of this heroic undertaking. The most famous picture to survive the trip shows him at the controls of one of the great steam shovels that were conquering the mountains that had defied all comers until then. Having seized the canal zone for the United States, Roosevelt was now digging the canal. The photograph neatly fit the popular image of the president, and the president's image of himself.

V

After a brief stopover in Puerto Rico, Roosevelt returned home to deal with the escalating inanities over the Japanese in California, and also to confront another brouhaha that had blown up since he had left. In August 1906 some black soldiers in Brownsville, Texas, had gotten into a violent scrape with some white townsfolk; several of the latter had been shot, one fatally. Initial evidence pointed to about a dozen soldiers, but the investigation stalled when they and their fellows refused to testify against one another.

Roosevelt was outraged at this apparent insubordination, which seemed to him to strike at the heart of military discipline—and which touched that eternally raw nerve of his, the one attuned to anarchy.

He declared that if the innocent men—or, rather, those who were innocent before entering into this conspiracy of silence—were so determined to stand by the guilty, then they could stand by them right out of the army. On November 5, shortly before leaving for Panama, he ordered the three companies involved dishonorably discharged and barred forever from reenlistment.

While the president cruised the Caribbean and acted as inspector general and engineer in chief in Panama, the nation's press refought the Civil War over the Brownsville incident. This time Roosevelt found himself aligned uncomfortably with the South. Editors from the old Confederacy by and large applauded the president's firm response; many northern papers and nearly all black papers took a critical view—the black papers vehemently so. Among those drummed out of the army in Roosevelt's summary judgment were several winners of the Medal of Honor; this circumstance underscored what many believed was an unfair and thoroughly un-American imputation of guilt by association. More than a few skeptics on the subject of Roosevelt remarked the fact that the president's decision was handed down on the eve of election day—early enough to deflect charges that he had deliberately withheld the verdict in order to keep black voters in the Republican camp but late enough to accomplish precisely that.

Roosevelt, needless to say, hotly denied that political or any other considerations save justice had influenced him one iota. "When the discipline and honor of the American Army are at stake I shall never under any circumstances consider the political bearing of upholding that discipline and that honor." He went on to declare that "no graver misfortune could happen to the American Army than failure to punish in the most signal way such conduct as that which I have punished."

As the furor continued to mount, the president defended his actions more vigorously than ever. "I have been amazed and indignant at the attitude of the negroes and of shortsighted white sentimentalists as to my action," he stated. "It has been shown conclusively that some of these troops made a midnight murderous and entirely unprovoked assault upon the citizens of Brownsville." In fact, the evidence against the black soldiers was proving to be less conclusive than initially thought, and in any event Roosevelt knew that the troops had been provoked mightily. Yet he refused to accept that the slurs and insults to which the soldiers had been subjected really constituted provocation. "The fact that some of their number had been slighted by some of the citizens of Brownsville . . ." he explained, "is not to be considered for a moment as provocation for such a murderous assault." Roosevelt remained utterly unrepentant of having discharged the whole companies. He judged that by taking the side of the miscreants against the duly constituted authorities, the others had brought the ignominy of the crime—and the weight of its punishment—willfully upon their own heads.

The criticism didn't cause Roosevelt to reconsider his discharge order; rather, it had the paradoxical effect of making him rethink something else—his earlier condemnation of lynching. Heretofore the president had dismissed as racist rationalization the argument that whites had to step outside the law to exact justice because blacks banded together to shelter the criminals among themselves from prosecution. Now the black troops from Brownsville were apparently confirming what the lynchers had said. Roosevelt believed that blacks made a critical moral and political error in assuming they ought to protect wrongdoers. "I condemn such attitude strongly," he said, "for I feel that it is fraught with the gravest danger to both races." If for no other reason than to deter such illegitimate race feeling, Roosevelt would hold his ground. "I should be recreant to my duty if I failed by deeds as well as by words to emphasize with the utmost severity my disapproval of it."

This point in particular stuck in Roosevelt's mind. He wrote Ray Stannard Baker several weeks later:

> I have been really deprest over this Brownsville (Texas) business, not so much by the attitude of the colored troops themselves, altho that was sufficiently ominous, but by the attitude taken by the enormous majority of the colored population in regard to the matter. I had never really believed there was much justification for the claim of the Southern whites that the decent Negroes would actively or passively shield their own wrongdoers; or at least I had never realized the extent to which this statement was true; but this Brownsville business has given me the most serious concern on this very point.

If the troops were white, Roosevelt ventured, the situation would not have arisen, or at least not in the same way.

The president's most prominent antagonist on the Brownsville matter was Senator Joseph Foraker. Roosevelt characteristically refused to believe that the Ohio lawmaker could honestly disagree with him. "It is simply not supposable that he seriously questions the guilt of the Negro troops, both of those among them who are actively concerned in the shooting and the attendant murder, and of the others who were accessory before or after the fact." The only conclusion Roosevelt could draw was that Foraker was angling for the black vote or was simply retaliating against the administration for championing corporate reform. Either way, Foraker was taking gullible blacks for a ride in the wrong direction. "The overwhelming majority of the colored people have stood by him heartily and have been inclined to lose sight of every real movement for the betterment of their race, of every real wrong done their race by peonage or lynching, and to fix their eyes only upon this movement to prevent the punishment of atrociously guilty men of their race."

VI

Roosevelt's animus toward Foraker, and vice versa, burst spectacularly into the open in late January 1907 at the annual Gridiron Club dinner of Washington pressmen and political worthies. One version of the evening's activities dubbed the impromptu debate that transpired between Roosevelt and Foraker a "battle royal"; Foraker himself deemed it a final parting of the ways. "The relations of President Roosevelt and myself were strained before the Gridiron Club encounter," he wrote. "They were practically broken off by that incident."

Roosevelt should have known he was in for a bad time; the entire purpose of the Gridiron dinners was to tweak the high and mighty, and after five and a half years in the White House, Roosevelt was feeling about as high and mighty as he ever would. Besides, he was never so touchy as when charged with dealing unfairly with honest men (and soldiers to boot), as he was in this case. The tone of the evening was set in the souvenir booklet distributed to the diners; a cartoon showed the hyperkinetic Roosevelt at his desk, drafting something literary with his right hand, shooting a bear with his left hand, and kicking a black man with his foot. The accompanying jingle described the president's routine:

> "I'm busy with things night and day,"
> A Rough Rider was once heard to say,
> "Writing views, singing tunes,
> Killing bears, firing coons,
> Or composing an old Irish lay."

Roosevelt wasn't the only one lampooned. Foraker was pictured being hailed by two gratefully smiling black soldiers; the caption ran:

> "All coons look alike to me,"
> J. B. Foraker, says he, says he,
> "Even if they is black as kin be,
> An' is dressed in blue or yaller khaki.
> All coons look alike to me,
> Since 'mancipation set 'em free,
> Nigger vote hold de balance,
> All coons look alike to me."

The fireworks commenced in earnest when Roosevelt remarked to the guests that the Senate investigation Foraker was directing was "academic" in that the Senate had no jurisdiction over the Brownsville matter. Needless to say, Roosevelt, who was rarely given to short speeches, made other comments on other topics, but it was this that got the attention of the audience. As one indirect press account (the rules of the evening precluded straightforward reportage) had it, "Mr. Roosevelt was forceful—more than strenuous—and cuttingly incisive. It is said to have been a speech of biting sarcasm, interlarded with a vigorous vocabulary. . . . It was taken by all who heard it as a direct challenge to Senator Foraker. More, indeed. It was taken as a lecture to him as an individual and the Senate as a whole, reprobating both for stirring up the Brownsville mess. It was delivered in a high, strident pitch, and sandwiched with gestures more than emphatic."

Ordinarily, presidential protocol dictated that the head of state got the last word at any gathering. Roosevelt may well have thought that his remarks would go unanswered. But the Gridiron was famous for irreverence, and so no one, except perhaps Roosevelt, was shocked when the master of ceremonies, explaining that it was time "to bridge the bloody chasm," called on Foraker to respond.

The Ohio senator gave as good as he got. The same news story reported: "When Foraker arose to reply he was ashen white. He felt he had been singled out in a promiscuous company to be insulted. From the opening sentence he was more than virile. He did not mince words. He hurled back the gratuitous flings at himself and the Senate over his head. He denied even to a President the right to instruct him in his duties as a Senator."

Roosevelt grew more and more restive during Foraker's defense of the Senate's honor and his own. When Foraker finally finished, the president leaped up to rebut. But such a stir had the two men already created that some time was required for the hubbub to die down. "Those who were pleased with Foraker's utterances forgot the courtesy due the President of the United States, and continued cheering for a minute after Mr. Roosevelt rose to his feet. . . . For a few seconds it looked as if a deliberate effort was being made to howl him down, just as if the affair were a political convention instead of a dinner attended by gentlemen."

Roosevelt eventually managed to get in a few more words, additionally defending his handling of the Brownsville case and reiterating that the matter was closed. Then, in the interest of party unity—and perhaps realizing that he was looking rather foolish at what was supposed to be a lighthearted event—he avowed his respect and appreciation for the support Senator Foraker had given to the administration in the past, their current differences notwithstanding.

No one believed him. But by now everyone was eager to adjourn and gossip about this most exciting Washington dinner in years. The toastmaster led the guests in "Auld Lang Syne" to signal a formal end to the evening. A large group gathered around Foraker, while the bulk of the crowd headed outside to escape the cigar smoke and to compare notes. Roosevelt returned to the White House bruised, slightly embarrassed, but exhilarated by the battle nonetheless.

CHAPTER TWENTY-THREE

Heir Apparenting
1907

Theodore Roosevelt was not a good judge of character. He had guessed wrong about Tom Reed, thinking that they shared far more in the way of politics than they did. He underestimated McKinley, not realizing how that apparently unassertive individual generally got what he wanted, including Roosevelt for vice president. He allowed his friendship for the Storers to blind him to the damage Maria's maneuverings were doing to his administration and the interests of the country.

But he never made such a mistake as with Will Taft—a fatal error of judgment that would blight both of their lives and alter the course of American politics. Taft was an easy man to misjudge. He was smart, but like many fat men—he weighed well over three hundred pounds, at six foot two—he often gave the impression of laziness. His father had constantly chided him to get moving, recalling that one of his teachers "hit your case when he said that you had the best head of any of my boys and if you was not too lazy you would have great success." Taft's amiable disposition fit the fat-man stereotype, allowing him to laugh off jokes made at his expense. (As governor-general of the Philippines, he wrote Elihu Root that he had just taken a long horseback ride about his domain and felt fine afterward. "How is the horse?" came Root's reply.) His face was positively cherubic in childhood; even as an adult, when a walrus mustache hid half of it, his smile was like "a huge pan of sweet milk poured over one."

Taft hadn't intended to go into politics. Law was his field. From Yale Law School he returned to his home state of Ohio, where in due course he advanced from bar to bench. Before long he was the presiding judge of the sixth federal circuit, which comprised Ohio, Tennessee, Kentucky, and Michigan. His judicial gifts and judicious temperament prompted McKinley to select him to head the Philippine Commission in 1900; Taft hesitated, but accepted when the president made clear that the post wouldn't sidetrack his legal career. A Supreme Court appointment, when a seat came open, was mentioned. After the Philippine Commission completed its task—with no vacancy yet on the high court—McKinley persuaded Taft to stay on as governor-general.

Roosevelt naturally watched this man who got the proconsular job he had wanted, and what he saw impressed him. Taft quite obviously took his colonizing mission seriously—so seriously that when Roosevelt, now president, offered him the promised Supreme Court seat, he respectfully declined, saying he had work yet to do among the Filipinos. Roosevelt grew all the more impressed. "Old man," he told Taft while the latter was weighing the court offer, "whatever you decide to do I shall be absolutely satisfied, and shall believe not only that you have done what you thought right but actually was right." Roosevelt rarely granted such moral carte blanche to anyone.

Only after Root resigned from the War Department did Roosevelt succeed in persuading Taft to come to Washington, and then by pointing out that as secretary of war he would have oversight of the Bureau of Insular Affairs, which administered the Philippines. In other words, he could continue his civilizing work on a higher level. This convinced Taft, who in any event was finding the tropical climate and its attendant itches, sweats, and eternal internal rumblings tiresome.

In Washington, Taft became Roosevelt's right-hand man and cabinet confidant, improving on Root—who had never gotten over his habit of talking back to the president. "Taft is a splendid fellow and will be an aid and comfort in every way," the president told Ted. Roosevelt saw much of himself in Taft—and wasn't alone in doing so. Edith observed that on precisely this account Taft wouldn't measure up to his predecessor. "As mother says," Roosevelt continued to his son, "he is too much like me to be able to give me as good advice as Mr. Root was able to because of the differences of character between us."

Yet Roosevelt didn't want Taft as a devil's advocate. Exactly what he did want is harder to say. From shortly after Taft's arrival in

Washington in 1904, it seemed to insiders that the president was grooming him as an heir. This was true enough, as became evident. But more was involved. The personal relationship that developed between Roosevelt and Taft transcended politics. In a curious way Taft became for Roosevelt something of a younger brother (although Taft was actually the older of the two by a year). It was almost as though Roosevelt, having lost Elliott a decade before and never having discovered a replacement, now turned to Taft.

Roosevelt's real friendships had always been few. He possessed innumerable acquaintances, people with whom he shared interests—not least because his interests were so catholic. He had allies: men who could further his political career and whose careers he in turn could advance. And of course he had Edith, who knew him better than anyone and who shared his family life, even if he still kept her at arm's length regarding politics.

But of close friends, individuals outside his family to whom he could entrust his feelings, there was only Cabot Lodge. "You see I never make friends atall easily," he had written to Nannie Lodge in 1886. "Outside of my own family you two are really the only people for whom I genuinely care." Roosevelt's circumstances had changed in the intervening twenty years, but not his underlying personality; if anything, real friendships came harder now that he was famous. And of late even Lodge was drifting away, partly from the changed relative status of the two men and partly because Lodge's politics were too conservative for Roosevelt's current tastes. It probably wasn't coincidence that the further Roosevelt felt himself slipping from Lodge—his surrogate older brother—the closer he drew to Taft—his stand-in for Elliott.

Sibling rivalry with Theodore had often made Elliott's life miserable; something comparable would destroy Taft's political career. But for now, everything was gentleness and light between Roosevelt and his protégé. "You cannot know how absolutely you have the trust and confidence of all our people whose trust and confidence are best worth having," the president declared when still trying to woo Taft to the capital. Anxious that Taft might have gotten the wrong idea from one of his arguments as to why it was time to quit the Philippines and come to Washington, he explained: "The feeling of admiration and respect for you, and of appreciation of your work, is so great among all those for whose opinion I give a rap, that it simply never occurred to me that you could dream I wanted to change you, except for the reason that I wanted to put you in what I regarded as an even bigger post, near me." A few weeks later Roosevelt gushed some more: "I wonder if you realize how much I respect and admire you!"

Roosevelt's affection only intensified as time passed. "You beloved individual," Roosevelt greeted Taft during the summer of 1906, saying that he had thoroughly enjoyed a long letter Taft had written. In this letter Taft had explained that he was coming under criticism for a particular recent action. Roosevelt continued,

> One element in my enjoyment was, as it always is with you, my unchristian delight in finding that you, whom I admire as much not only as any public man of the present but as any public man of the past, bar Lincoln and Washington—indeed, whom I suppose I admire more than any other public man, bar these two—get into just the same kind of hot water from time to time that I get into myself. The water is not as hot, and you never deserve to have gotten into it, as I am sorry to say I abundantly do; but it is a comfort to feel that the man I love and admire and respect encounters the difficulties that I encounter.

II

The reason Taft was in hot water was that Roosevelt's intentions for him were becoming apparent, and not everyone in the party liked the idea of a Roosevelt clone in the White House after 1908. Some preferred Charles Evans Hughes, the governor of New York; others pushed Philander Knox, still senator from Pennsylvania. Elihu Root was generally conceded to be as capable as anyone in the party, if perhaps too clever to suit some voters. Charles Fairbanks, approaching the end of four years of enforced idleness, daydreamed of being the second vice president in a row to succeed to the top job.

But Roosevelt wanted Taft. And he was willing to fight for him. Indeed, his tussle with Foraker at the Gridiron dinner was as much about Taft as about the dismissal of the Brownsville troops. Foraker did *not* want Taft—even entertaining some faint hopes of the presidency for himself—and by investigating this military matter hoped to embarrass both the president and the secretary of war.

Having taken his own swing at Foraker, Roosevelt urged Taft to do the same. The president depicted the difference between the two men in the starkest moral shades: "I know no man in public life who would be prompter than you to follow his own conscience without regard to the fact whether it hurt his future or not, while I am certain that Foraker would never for a moment follow what he is pleased to call his conscience unless he thought it would be to his own advantage." Taft was too willing to let Foraker hide behind his hypocrisy. While Taft's was a "fine and manly" approach, it wasn't what was called for at present. The problem was that Foraker not only didn't have a conscience but acted "so as to outrage the consciences of all the best men" and was, besides, "the tool of unscrupulous corporate wealth."

Taft never warmed to hand-to-hand combat the way Roosevelt did, but that failure didn't diminish the president's respect for him, nor did it lessen Roosevelt's efforts on Taft's behalf. From time to time since the night of his 1904 triumph, Roosevelt had reiterated his intention to leave the White House in March 1909, but for various reasons various groups refused to take him at his word. In the West, longtime Roosevelt partisans genuinely wanted him to serve a third term. Recalling how they had rushed him into the vice presidential nomination in 1900, they thought they might be able to do the same with the presidential nomination in 1908. In other regions, presidential hopefuls whose success hadn't yet met their dreams wanted him to remain at least a nominal presence in the race until their chances improved.

Tactical considerations of his own caused Roosevelt to refrain from a Shermanesque door-closing. As long as he allowed people to speculate on his future, he enjoyed the best of both worlds: of being on the record as having high-mindedly denied himself another term, while simultaneously keeping his enemies off balance regarding the future. Besides, all the guessing focused attention on him, which was where he always thought it belonged.

Meanwhile, it enabled him to immobilize opposition to Taft. "Taft's friends in New York believe that if I repeated that statement too often," Roosevelt told William Allen White, referring to his 1904 pledge, "the result would be that we should have a New York delegation solidly anti-Taft—probably for Hughes, possibly for Knox. In the Southern States many of the Taft people have told me that they wanted me to keep clear for the moment because any further repetition of what I had said might result in the delegations being captured definitely away from Taft." In this letter Roosevelt went on to applaud, for the benefit of any whom the Kansas editor's words might reach, the "courage, sagacity, inflexible uprightness and disinterestedness, and wide acquaintance with governmental problems" of the secretary of war.

Roosevelt would have gone public with such applause if not for the tradition that barred a president from anointing his successor. While he might have ignored this tradition as tradition, he feared that his and Taft's enemies would use an early endorsement against Taft. To his son Kermit, Roosevelt freely declared, "I most earnestly hope and I am inclined to believe that we shall be able to nominate Taft for President"; but he added, "Of course this is to be kept strictly quiet, as I cannot, as President, take any part in getting him the nomination."

Through the summer and autumn of 1907, Roosevelt lay low. His enthusiasm for Taft, however, continued to increase. After a Taft speech on the rights and obligations of labor, given at Seattle, a hotbed of labor radicalism, Roosevelt congratulated his protégé: "No ordinary candidate would venture to say what you do, but you are not an ordinary candidate; and I believe that your courage, your entire willingness to sacrifice your own interests for a principle, and the instinctive feeling that everyone must have as to your utter disinterestedness, are the qualities which (taken together with the fact that your ability and experience put you head and shoulders to the front of all other possible candidates) will force your nomination." Looking toward that nomination, the president revealed how much it meant to him: "I really believe I am quite as nervous about your campaign as I should be if it were my own."

Gradually, a Taft nomination came to appear irresistible. Roosevelt's rivals resented the president's assumption of an almost royal prerogative in selecting his successor; this scarcely seemed democratic, they complained. But the democratic bona fides of those doing the complaining—the old bosses, chiefly, and the corporate fat cats—weren't exactly unimpeachable. More to the point, the president had put himself in an impregnable position. By all (admittedly impressionistic) indications his popularity in the nation at large remained nearly as great as in November 1904. This alone was enough to give pause to any who would defy him, from within the Republican party or without. Equally important—and more immediately so—after six years in office he was firmly, if not unchallengeably, in control of the party machinery. Rebels such as Foraker might confront him rhetorically, but how many people owed anything to Foraker? For six years Roosevelt had been appointing people to federal jobs in Washington and throughout the country; lots of people owed the president a great deal. If he wanted Taft for a successor, he could have Taft—as long as Taft was electable, which was the bottom line for those whose principal interest was keeping their jobs. Republican candidates for Congress and state offices had similar concerns: A winner at the top of the Republican ticket would give them a leg up on their Democratic rivals. Roosevelt himself would have been ideal, but since he wasn't going to run, his man Taft looked like the next best thing.

III

At another time Roosevelt's corporate critics might have mounted a sterner challenge to what appeared likely to be (and what Roosevelt certainly hoped would be) a continuation of his policies under Taft. But the autumn of 1907 was a period of panic on Wall Street. The corporocrats had started jittering early in the year when the stock market suddenly turned south and business went bad in several sectors of the economy at once. Naturally, they blamed Roosevelt's innovations as the cause of the unsettlement; just as naturally, and even more vehemently, Roosevelt denied responsibility. On the contrary, he rejoined, if blame was to be assigned, it deserved to go to "certain malefactors of great wealth" who were deliberately trying "to bring about as much financial distress as possible, in order to discredit the policy of the government and thereby secure a reversal of that policy, so that they may enjoy unmolested the fruits of their own evil-doing." The president vowed to stand like Gibraltar against these cynical manipulators. "I regard this contest as one to determine who shall rule this free country—the people through their governmental agents, or a few ruthless and domineering men whose wealth makes them peculiarly formidable because they hide behind the breastworks of corporate organization."

If investors had been looking for a soothing sign, this wasn't it, and during the next several weeks the economic jitters worsened. In October it became a full-blown breakdown when a run developed on the Knickerbocker Trust Company of New York. For a day and a half agitated depositors filled the lobby of the venerable old firm and spilled out into the street, where policemen had to be called in to maintain order. At noon on the second day—October 22—the bank exhausted its reserves and was forced to close its doors. The swooning of the Knickerbocker, in the heart of the New York financial district, sent the stock market spinning out of control and led to runs on other financial houses.

Roosevelt was finishing a bear hunt in the cane breaks of Louisiana when he heard that another species of bear was terrorizing Manhattan. He hurried back east to corral the critter and restore calm to the currency and stock markets. He immediately huddled with Root, Bob Bacon, and George Meyer, his most important advisers still on speaking—rather than his own shouting—terms with the corporate community. He arrived too late to consult Treasury Secretary Cortelyou, who had already left for New York and an emergency meeting with J. P. Morgan.

Roosevelt himself never met with Morgan during the critical weeks at the end of October and the beginning of November. The two men—the nation's political leader and its financial leader, each at the apex of his power—circled each other warily, even as the country drew closer to the brink of a depression that might ruin them both and much of the rest of the nation besides. Morgan distrusted Roosevelt as a demagogue who knew nothing of the way the world really worked; Roosevelt resented Morgan as a man whose power derived from mere money rather than character or popular confidence.

For one of the few times in his public life, Roosevelt felt himself the victim of circumstances beyond his control. Not that he was alone: "In the panic here," he wrote to Whitelaw Reid in London, "as was inevitable, most people lost their heads—this is, of course, what panic means." As he generally did during moments of trial, Roosevelt looked to Lincoln for guidance. He remembered how the sixteenth president was forever being confronted by some impossible aspect of the slavery question and hounded by shortsighted partisans who demanded that he take this action or that to overcome the impossibility. They insisted that if he didn't act as they advised, the war effort would fail, and he would be responsible. "He answered," Roosevelt remarked, "that whether he was or was not responsible for the failure, he knew that he would be held responsible. Of course the same thing is true now. Whether I am or am not in any degree responsible for the panic, I shall certainly be held responsible." Already the president was hearing "the usual paroxysm of screams and yells about me"; yet until now the screaming was largely confined to people who bitterly opposed him already. This could be expected to change. "The feeling will spread to those who have been my friends, because when the average man loses his money he is simply like a wounded snake and strikes right and left at anything, innocent or the reverse, that presents itself as conspicuous in his mind."

Financial matters had always puzzled Roosevelt, and they did so now. "Whether I can do anything to allay the panic I do not know." He certainly wasn't lacking for advice, especially of a narrowly interested kind. "All the reactionaries wish to take advantage of the moment by having me announce that I will abandon my policies, at least in effect. . . . The big financial men, moreover, seize the occasion to try to escape from all governmental control, and believe they can now thus escape." But they were wrong. His policies were sound and just, and he would hold fast to them. Even so, he had to do something to stem the panic; the question was—what? "The situation is unpleasant and perplexing."

Roosevelt resolved the puzzle as best he could, giving the money men something but less than they wanted. When Cortelyou arrived at the Morgan offices at the corner of Broad and Wall streets, Morgan explained how he and his banker friends were arranging an infusion of liquidity into the nation's beleaguered banking system. Some hundred million dollars in gold would flow in from overseas, principally from Britain; lesser amounts would come from the coffers of John D. Rockefeller and other Americans who would demonstrate their patriotism by pledging their millions to defend the dollar (and who, as

Roosevelt realized, in the process would help prevent those millions from melting into mere hundreds of thousands or less). The government's contribution to this confidence-building scheme should be the deposit of 150 million of the federal treasury's dollars into major banks around the country.

Roosevelt approved this part of the plan. He felt awkward finding himself in cahoots with the men he had made a career of lambasting. Yet he had swallowed Blaine and Platt; and if necessary he could choke down Morgan. In the interest of the national economic health, he went as far as to offer public congratulations to "those conservative and substantial businessmen who in this crisis have acted with such wisdom and public spirit," and to declare that "by their action they did invaluable service in checking the panic which, beginning as a matter of speculation, was threatening to destroy the confidence and credit necessary to the conduct of legitimate business." As a final fillip to investor confidence, the president asserted, "No one who considers calmly can question that the underlying conditions which make up our financial and industrial well-being are essentially sound and honest. Dishonest dealing and speculative enterprise are merely the occasional incidents of our real prosperity."

IV

Roosevelt's action and statement beat the bears back momentarily, but they remained hungry and aggressive. Each time one bank or broker was rescued, they attacked another. At the beginning of November they had singled out the brokerage firm of Moore & Schley, whose financial fate hung on the price of a large number of shares of the Tennessee Coal and Iron Company, held as collateral for loans. Cash was scarce to prop up that price, but some of Morgan's men had the bright idea of a stock swap with U.S. Steel, the shares of which were, if not quite as good as gold, just about as good as cash. The big steel trust would take over the Tennessee, paying the shareholders with its own stock. The crucial side effect of the transfer would be the salvation of Moore & Schley—and, it was hoped, the final defeat of the bears.

Elbert Gary and Henry Frick, directors of the steel trust, accepted the idea with one important condition. President Roosevelt must grant his approval. The Tennessee was a competitor with U.S. Steel in certain markets, and Gary and Frick wanted to make sure that the president wouldn't use the merger as grounds for an antitrust suit.

Time being of the essence, the two men arranged for a special train to carry them overnight from Manhattan to Washington, where Roosevelt interrupted his breakfast to meet with them. Gary explained that he and his associates at U.S. Steel had only the highest motives in contemplating the purchase of the Tennessee; as a strictly business proposition, it made little sense, at least at the price to be offered. But for the good of the nation, the company was willing to sacrifice. The two men added that even counting the Tennessee's assets, U.S. Steel would control less than 60 percent of the country's steel properties.

Roosevelt was out of his depth in this matter. Fearing what he labeled "a general industrial smashup," he had to take the word of Gary and Frick that such a calamity could be averted only by his approval of their scheme. They didn't mention Moore & Schley by name, and he didn't ask—obviously not wishing to convey the impression that he was acting on behalf of any particular firm. He also had to take the word of the two men that an immediate decision was required and that he didn't have time to check out their story.

But Roosevelt was nothing if not decisive, even when his decisions were based on patchy knowledge. In less time than Gary and Frick required to present their case, he told them he wouldn't stand in their way. As he explained in a memo written just after the meeting, "I answered that while of course I could not advise them to take the action proposed, I felt it no public duty of mine to interpose any objection."

During this meeting the White House operator had kept a telephone line open to Morgan's offices in New York; as soon as the interview ended, the glad tidings were relayed north, where they had the desired effect. The bears, recognizing that they were now up against the combined resources of Morgan and Roosevelt, snarled but gave ground. Their snarls continued for several weeks more, during which time neither Roosevelt nor Morgan—nor anyone else—could confidently rule out another attack. But gradually, one by one, they returned to their dens.

In time, when memories of the panic faded, Roosevelt would find himself excoriated for falling for the old capitalists' trick of threatening to commit suicide. The excoriations gained plausibility when rising prices for mineral resources, of which the Tennessee Coal and Iron Company had plenty, made that company's takeover by U.S. Steel seem a bargain. The excoriations grew still sharper after Roosevelt parted ways with Taft, who in 1911 launched an antitrust action against the steel combine. Taft's partisans found it irresistibly tempting to brand Roosevelt a dupe of—or a panic-stricken colluder with—the evil steelmen.

Roosevelt didn't have to wait until 1911 for the smaller carp to start quibbling. Gary and Frick had hardly left the White House before congressional Democrats were alleging that in a financial crisis all Republicans acted alike. Tom Watson, the old Populist whom Roosevelt had scorned on the stump but since made up with, wrote wanting to know if the allegations were true. "My dear sir," Roosevelt responded, "I trust I need hardly assure you that I shall not 'surrender' to the bankers, or to anyone else, and there will be no 'secret midnight conferences' with any big financier, or anyone else." The country could count on the integrity of the president. Roosevelt did confess, however—at a time when the markets remained touchy—to continuing perplexity. "As to the financial situation, I am not yet by any means clear what I ought to do."

Roosevelt didn't like not knowing what to do. While he felt obliged to back the bankers in public, he privately damned them for having gotten him and the country into this fix. To his brother-in-law Douglas Robinson, Roosevelt reiterated his helplessness in the face of recent events: "I am doing everything I have power to do; but the fundamental fact is that the public is suffering from a spasm of lack of confidence. Most of this lack of confidence is absolutely unreasonable, and therefore we can do nothing with it." But a substantial part of the failure of faith had a perfectly reasonable basis. "There has been so much trickery and dishonesty in high places; the exposures about Harriman, Rockefeller, Heinze, Barney, Morse, Ryan, the insurance men, and others, have caused such a genuine shock to people that they have begun to be afraid that every bank really has something rotten in it." Roosevelt held that a panic of one sort or another had become inevitable. "The growth of the speculative spirit and the scandalous dishonesty among some high financiers combined, made it absolutely certain that we would come a cropper." The president granted that one or more investigations set in motion by his administration may have precipitated the panic, but it would have happened eventually, and would have been "far more severe" if delayed.

Roosevelt remained heroically unrepentant. A panic worse than that already experienced might yet be in the offing. "If it comes we may as well make up our minds to the fact that for the time being at any rate, and perhaps permanently, I will be blamed and that the administration will be held to have gone out under a cloud." Even so, he would not be swayed by "what really amounts to hydrophobia about me." He would hold his ground. "There is nothing that I have done that I would not do over again, and I am absolutely positive that the principles which I have sought to enforce are those that must obtain if this government is to endure." Roosevelt was willing to guess that if the country survived the present panic, it would benefit, albeit painfully, from the experience. "If we check it, I think it will mean ultimate good; tho it will also mean depression for a year."

V

While Roosevelt's great trial of the last part of 1907 was the financial panic, his great triumph was the launching of the round-the-world voyage of the American battleship fleet. The Gentlemen's Agreement of the previous February had failed to eliminate tensions between the United States and Japan, for the simple reason that a sizable number of those responsible for the tensions were not gentlemen. In May, anti-Japanese riots convulsed San Francisco, as Californians discontented with Roosevelt's executive accord sought to vent their anger on the Japanese population of California's first city. Meanwhile, the counterparts in Japan to the Californians refused to accept any curbs—imposed by the Japanese government or anyone else—on the right of Japanese to migrate to America. Although statistics were hard to come by, the complaints of this group seemed to have caused the Tokyo government to be less stringent in upholding its end of the bargain than it might have been.

Roosevelt was annoyed by Tokyo's failings, but he was incensed at the Californians and their supporters elsewhere in the country. "Our people act infamously when they wrong in any way the Japanese who are here," the president asserted. And those individuals who inflamed the situation for their own benefit acted most infamously of all. Upon hearing scurrilous rumors being retailed as fact by certain journalists, Roosevelt responded that he "would like to trepan the various editors who are striving to cause trouble with Japan."

But in his cooler moments he recognized that not even his generous construction of executive powers allowed drilling skulls. Consequently, he resorted to the tested technique of jawboning, applied first to his Japanese acquaintances. He wrote to Kaneko ("My Dear Baron"), reassuring his friend that the more responsible and enlightened elements in American society respected the Japanese and cherished their goodwill. "Among the friends whom I especially value," he volunteered, "I include a number of Japanese gentlemen." But relations between the United States and Japan were too new for this respect to have filtered down to the masses. "We must not press too fast in bringing the laboring classes of Japan and America together." The president pointed out that American workers weren't unique in their fear of foreigners. "If scores of thousands of American miners went to Sakhalin, or of American merchants to Japan or Formosa, trouble would almost certainly ensue." He told Kaneko that he was doing what he could to facilitate good relations between the two countries, and he hoped Kaneko would do the same.

Through the course of the summer Roosevelt continued to try to pour oil on the troubled waters of the northern Pacific. "I have the Japanese Ambassador and a Cabinet Minister out here the day after tomorrow," he informed Lodge from Oyster Bay in July. "I shall continue to do everything I can by politeness and consideration to the Japs to offset the worse than criminal stupidity of the San Francisco mob, the San Francisco press, and such papers as the New York *Herald*." Hotheads on both sides of the ocean were talking loosely about war. Roosevelt didn't pay inordinate attention to such stupidities, although he couldn't help noting them. "I do not believe we shall have war; but it is no fault of the yellow press if we do not have it. The Japanese seem to have about the same proportion of prize jingo fools that we have."

The cabinet minister Roosevelt spoke of to Lodge was actually a former cabinet minister, but this minor inaccuracy was more than off-set by the fact that the individual in question was Admiral Isoroku Yamamoto, ex-navy secretary (and later prime minister) and a man who was roughly Japan's equivalent of A. T. Mahan and Roosevelt rolled into one, in terms of strengthening and modernizing his nation's fleet. Yamamoto arrived in a bad mood and remained huffy through-out the meeting. He demanded indignantly (the indignation only partly filtered out by his interpreter) that Japanese laborers must be allowed to enter the United States on exactly the same terms as European workers. Anything less was an insult to Japan's honor.

Roosevelt was polite, but he wasn't going to take this, even from a (former) cabinet minister. Japanese arrivals in the United States were up from the previous year, despite the Gentlemen's Agreement ("Many of them who come as petty traders are really laborers," Roosevelt explained to Root). To Yamamoto, Roosevelt didn't quite accuse the Japanese government of cheating, but he stoutly and repeatedly rejected the admiral's demand. "I kept explaining to him that what we had to do was to face facts; that if American laboring men came in and cut down the wages of Japanese laboring men they would be shut out of Japan in one moment." Roosevelt asserted that economics, not racial thinking, lay behind his administration's insistence on curtailing Japanese immigration. And his administration would indeed insist. "I told him emphatically that it was not possible to admit Japanese laborers into the United States."

Yamamoto may or may not have been impressed by Roosevelt's defense of American prerogatives in establishing American immigra-tion policy; but the admiral could not have helped listening carefully when Roosevelt let drop that the United States battleship fleet was preparing for massed exercises in the Pacific. From the time of the Russo-Japanese War, Roosevelt and American naval officials had spo-radically entertained the idea of sending America's biggest warships from the Atlantic, where they were regularly stationed, to the Pacific. The voyage would be a shakedown cruise, revealing where logistics needed to be improved; it would also serve as a reminder to the Japanese, who not surprisingly felt rather proud of themselves, that the United States was a Pacific power to be reckoned with.

Yet precisely this latter purpose seemed to some an argument against the voyage. Amid the rapid deterioration of U.S.-Japanese relations, the Japanese government might interpret a redeployment of the American fleet as a provocation. If Tokyo were contemplating war, it might not wait for the big ships to arrive in the Pacific but would instead strike first, thereby triggering the conflict Washington wanted to avoid. A second argument against the voyage, more or less important in various quarters, was that it would cost millions of dollars that didn't really need to be spent.

Roosevelt paid no mind to the argument that an audacious American move might provoke a war. He had built a career on provocation of one sort or another; more to the point in the present case, he felt that weakness was far more provocative than strength. Consequently, the worse relations with Japan grew, the more necessary he deemed the voyage. As for the expense, a war would be far more costly than any practice cruise.

While the president refused to skimp on the costs of preparation for war, in his conversation with Yamamoto he economized somewhat on the truth. He described the anticipated journey of the fleet through the Pacific, then declared (as he recounted the meeting to Root) that "it would return home very shortly after it had been sent out there; at least in all probability." In fact, Roosevelt had something far more ambitious in mind. As he had told Lodge a few days earlier: "This winter we shall have reached the period when it is advisable to send the whole fleet on a practice cruise around the world."

A Pacific run doubtless would have taught the navy nearly everything it needed to know about equipping and servicing the fleet for action far from home; moreover, not even Roosevelt could conceive a mission for the U.S. Navy in the Indian Ocean or off the Cape of Good Hope. But Roosevelt intuitively grasped the public relations possibilities of a circumnavigation of the globe. A later president would stir America's soul by pledging to put a man on the moon; Roosevelt's decision to send the fleet around the world was technologically less challenging but in the same grandly ambitious mold. Nothing like this had ever been attempted. For the United States to be the first to accomplish it would be a cause for national pride—not to mention a distraction from the trembling of the financial markets.

Roosevelt's political opponents were slightly slower to grasp the meaning of the great voyage, but once they caught on, they were no less determined to prevent him from achieving his coup than he was to achieve it. As was so often the case, the president's principal opponent in the matter was a member of his own party, in this case Eugene Hale, chairman of the Senate Naval Affairs Committee. "I have almost as much trouble with our own people, like Senator Hale, who are always giving the impression to Japan that we are afraid of them, as with the other people, who insult the Japanese," Roosevelt muttered.

Again as usual, Roosevelt ascribed objective evil to the attempt to prevent him from doing what he wanted to do. He judged Hale "blind to every consideration of broad national honor and interest" and said the senator suffered from "downright cowardice." He went on to assert, "If he were actuated by a sinister desire to bring on trouble with Japan and to impair the efficiency of the United States Navy, he would be following exactly the course he is now following." Roosevelt lampooned his opponent in a letter to Lodge: "Hale would like to introduce into our naval and military affairs a system of supervision based upon the proceedings of the Aulic Council of Vienna and flavored with the spirit of Moorfield Storey's Anti-Imperialist League, plus the heroism of the average New York financier." The president concluded his diatribe by calling Hale a "conscienceless voluptuary" and—partially repeating himself to deliver the most damning judgment he could think of—a "physical coward."

VI

Roosevelt's critics once more detected autocratic tendencies in the president—in particular, the belief that he was above answering to others, most notably Congress. The critics had cause for their complaints. "I shall tolerate no control by an individual Senator or Congressman of the movements of the fleet," Roosevelt boasted to Root. To Speck von Sternberg he went on: "I decline for one moment to consider any protest against sending our entire battle fleet to any part of our own dominions which it seems advisable"—advisable to Roosevelt, needless to say—"the fleet should visit." Besides: "I think a cruise from one ocean to the other, or around the world, is mighty good practice for a fleet."

Roosevelt later admitted that the voyage of the fleet was chiefly an exercise in domestic politics. "My prime purpose was to impress the American people," he stated—adding, with characteristic modesty, "This purpose was fully achieved." The disarray in the economy reminded Roosevelt of an earlier theme in his writing and speeches: how Americans were succumbing to the softness of luxury. "We of the United States suffer in aggregated form from all the evils attendant upon our luxurious, pleasure-loving, industrial, modern civilization," he complained to Sternberg. Roosevelt granted that good qualities still existed among the American people, qualities like those that had animated the nation during the Civil War. "There are nevertheless certain ominous signs of frivolity, of a lack of sense of proportion in ideals, and of inordinate love of ease and of pleasure, and an overemphasis upon merely material well-being."

Roosevelt aimed to reawaken America's ardor for the manly virtues, including military preparedness. "This cruise around the world will be a striking thing," he predicted. "The people I hope will be interested in it." To ensure that they were, the president took pains to arrange favorable publicity. "In no way can their interest be better stimulated, with better result to the Navy, than by properly writing it up," he enjoined Acting Navy Secretary Truman Newberry. Not just any journalism would do. "It is absolutely essential to have men whom we can entirely trust on such a trip, and of course every article they send must be submitted to the Admiral." The president granted the necessity of consulting the major press organizations, but he reserved the right to veto the names put forward. "We will take no one of whom we do not entirely approve."

For all his attention to the public relations of the voyage, Roosevelt couldn't ignore the foreign relations. The diplomatic pouch from Europe transmitted a sense there that the Japanese were spoiling for a war with the United States, and might well get it. Sternberg relayed a report from a German official in Mexico that Japan had infiltrated several thousand former soldiers, under the guise of immigrants, into the regions of that country bordering the United States. Sternberg explained, "Our representative says: 'This news sounds rather adventurous, but it does not seem entirely out of question that Japan is contemplating the idea to use her men of the reserve in Mexico for the formation of a strong body of troops, in case of a war with the United States.'"

Roosevelt recognized the possibility of war, not least because he knew he couldn't read the Japanese mind—nor the Japanese read the minds of Americans. "This whole Japanese business is very puzzling," he told Sternberg, "I suppose because there are such deep racial differences that it is very hard for any of us of European descent to understand them or be understood by them." For his own part Roosevelt had a clear conscience regarding Japan. To be sure, the troubles in California weren't pleasant to watch; indeed, they were an outrage to any sense of fair play or American honor. But they were isolated, sporadic, and, in the end, insignificant. "Nothing that has been done affords the slightest justification or excuse for the Japanese thinking of war." On the other hand, the Japanese lately had developed an exaggerated notion of their prowess and importance. "Their heads seem to be swollen to a marvelous degree."

All the same, he considered war unlikely. "I do not think they will attack us," he told Root. He added, however, "But there is enough uncertainty to make it evident that we should be very much on our guard and should be ready for anything that comes."

This was precisely what motivated him to send the fleet on its way. "My own judgment is that the only thing that will prevent war is the Japanese feeling that we shall not be beaten, and this feeling we can only excite by keeping and making our navy efficient in the highest degree." The cruise would enable the Navy Department to maximize efficiency: to discover and remedy deficiencies in coaling, repairs, and communication, and to provide officers and men opportunities to practice and perfect their skills under stressful, near-warlike conditions.

Equally to the point, the fleet—of sixteen battleships, numerous escort craft, and some eighteen thousand uniformed personnel—would be an awesome sight. Never had so much naval power been gathered in one place, let alone sent on a grand tour around the globe. The Japanese, who could be counted on to be watching, couldn't help being impressed, even intimidated. To observe such an armada plowing the Pacific would give pause to even the most reckless fire-eaters in the Japanese admiralty.

Preparations for the voyage filled the autumn of 1907; while they did, tensions with Japan remained high. The latter circumstance convinced Roosevelt all the more that he was making the right decision in sending the fleet west. In mid-November he noted with satisfaction, "The fleet is in good condition; Evans [the fleet commander] is a good man; it starts for the Pacific inside of a month. The wisdom—indeed, I may say the absolute need—of its going there has been amply demonstrated." Roosevelt still couldn't rule out a Japanese attack, but it seemed increasingly improbable. "I should hardly suppose that the Japanese would hit us while the fleet was there." And if they did, the big ships would be precisely where they were needed.

Roosevelt didn't quite get his differences with Senator Hale and the rest of Congress ironed out by the December starting date. The legislature continued to balk at spending the money that the voyage would cost. Roosevelt cut through this obstruction by the simple expedient of announcing that he was sending the fleet to the Pacific with funds already appropriated. If Congress chose to withhold additional funds, the fleet could simply stay in the Pacific. Roosevelt knew his audience, which consisted of Hale of Maine and various other influential lawmakers with roots on the Atlantic coast. Easterners had been among the harshest critics of the voyage, contending that their states would be left defenseless in the event of war. Roosevelt reckoned that an Atlantic war was nearly out of the question. "Our relations with all European powers are so good that it seems in the highest degree unlikely that trouble will occur," he said privately. But he wasn't above letting the East Coasters worry just enough to authorize the funds to bring the battleships back. His strategy paid off; as he remarked afterward, with more than a trace of smugness, "There was no further difficulty about the money."

Roosevelt knew how to manage Congress, but his mastery of certain other elements was less sure. After all the political, diplomatic, fiscal, and logistical preparations, bad weather nearly kept the fleet from leaving on time. A late autumn storm pounded Hampton Roads in the days just before Roosevelt was to review the fleet and bid officers and men a presidential bon voyage. But in the end even wind and rain succumbed to his desires. The sixteen battleships turned out in full dress under sparkling skies, their rails manned, bands playing, pennants flying. With carefully orchestrated precision, the vessels thundered a simultaneous twenty-one-gun salute as the presidential yacht came into view.

Roosevelt hadn't been so thrilled in years. He strode excitedly up and down the deck of the *Mayflower*, exclaiming to all within earshot, "Did you ever see such a fleet? Isn't it magnificent? Oughtn't we all feel proud?"

CHAPTER TWENTY-FOUR

The Breathless End of a Rousing Run
1908–9

The voyage of the Great White Fleet (named for the shade of the ships, not of those who sailed them) provided constant favorable publicity during Roosevelt's last full year in the White House. Under the censorship he imposed, the reports that came home hid such deficiencies in logistics and operations as surfaced, and played up the bold and heroic aspect of what was, by any measure, an ambitious and impressive undertaking.

The voyage also afforded Roosevelt additional leverage in international affairs. In the spring of 1908, when the kaiser was acting petulant regarding a change of ambassadors in Berlin, Roosevelt sent him a soothing missive with a pointed tail. "I trust you notice," he told Wilhelm, "that the American battleship fleet has completed its tour of South America on schedule time, and is now having its target practice off the Mexican coast." The president traced the itinerary—Australia, Japan, China, the Philippines, Suez—leaving unsaid that the German navy had never done anything like this. And he couldn't resist a final note: "Their target practice has been excellent."

The addition of Japan to the list of stops came at the special request of the Japanese government. Roosevelt recognized that it was not out of friendliness that the invitation arose. The president remained convinced, with statistical reason, that Japan was fudging on visa numbers. And he had no doubt that Tokyo would take advantage of a visit by the fleet to gain every ounce of naval intelligence possible. But he deemed the psychological impact of this formidable display of military power to be worth whatever risks were involved.

At the same time he insisted that those risks be no greater than absolutely necessary. He ordered the fleet commander to "exercise the most careful watch thruout the time that you are in Oriental waters." The admiral must be on the lookout for "fanatics" but equally for misconduct by his own men. "If you give the enlisted men leave while at Tokyo or anywhere else in Japan, be careful to choose only those upon whom you can absolutely depend. There must be no suspicion of insolence or rudeness on our part." In what was an uncharacteristic display of caution, he concluded, "Aside from the loss of a ship I had far rather that we were insulted than that we insult anybody under these peculiar conditions."

This unusual attitude reflected an underlying concern, indeed discouragement, on the president's part. The voyage of the fleet was a grand show, but for all that, it was still a show. It might momentarily hide but couldn't materially change the fact that the position of the United States in the western Pacific was fundamentally weak. A decade earlier Roosevelt had agitated for the annexation of the Philippines, assuming in his enthusiasm that the islands would make a glorious addition to American power and decrying as defeatist and unpatriotic anyone who thought otherwise. The Philippine war had demonstrated that annexation wasn't going to be as easy as he had guessed, and subsequent American apathy—occasionally outright antagonism—to developing the military facilities of the archipelago had rendered them vulnerable to the growing power and ambitions of an obviously expansionist Japan.

"The Philippines form our heel of Achilles," the president told Taft. "They are all that makes the present situation with Japan dangerous." Roosevelt couldn't help recognizing that he had misjudged the American people. "I wish our people were prepared permanently, in a duty-loving spirit, and looking forward to a couple of generations of continuous manifestation of this spirit, to assume control of the Philippine Islands for the good of the Filipinos. But as a matter of fact I gravely question whether this is the case." The American people had difficulty understanding the requirements of their country's security even in such obvious areas as the Caribbean, as demonstrated by their tepid reaction to the recent events in Cuba and Santo Domingo. Their failure was the more apparent regarding the Philippines, and it forced the president to consider a reversal of policy.

"To keep the islands without treating them generously and at the same time adequately fortifying them and without building up a navy second only to that of Great Britain, would be disastrous in the extreme," he wrote. The Philippines had benefited from their American connection more than the United States had—"save, of course, as we benefit and as all people benefit by doing well a piece of duty that ought to be done." Unfortunately, a majority of Americans didn't appreciate the benefits of duty well done. "I do not believe our people will permanently accept the Philippines simply as an unremunerative and indeed expensive duty." This being so, the United States ought to consider granting early independence to the Philippines— "much sooner than I would think advisable from their own standpoint, or than I would think advisable if this country were prepared to look ahead fifty years and to build the navy and erect the fortifications which in my judgment it should." However, any withdrawal from the Philippines, perhaps accompanied by some international guarantee for the preservation of order, must come of America's own volition and not in response to pressure from Japan. "I would rather see this nation fight all her life than to see her give them up to Japan or any other nation under duress."

II

If the president was ambivalent about the Philippines, he was absolutely lost on the fiscal crisis that continued to wrack the country. The stopgap measures of the autumn of 1907 had calmed the situation momentarily, but the bondholders had been badly spooked, and during the next several months they remained skittish and consequently dangerous to the nation's economic health.

The essential problem was a lack of control by the government—or anyone else—of the money supply of the nation. The American corporate economy was already well into the twentieth century, but the money system remained stuck in the 1830s when Andrew Jackson had waged successful war against the second (and last) Bank of the United States. Since then the money supply had been a hodgepodge of gold, silver, and notes and bonds issued by a motley collection of states, banks, corporations, and sundry other entities of diverse and often dubious reliability. The confusion had contributed to the panics that occurred with roughly the regularity of sunspots; it also gave rise to the recurrent manias for greenbacks and, most recently, free silver.

The 1907 panic spawned a new crop of nostrums. Nearly everyone agreed that a more flexible system of ensuring liquidity during crises was necessary. Republicans, typically trying to address economic problems from the perspective of the boardroom, proposed to put greater control of the money supply into the hands of the bankers and the corporate sector generally. Democrats and other distrusters of Wall Street wanted the government to keep control and to issue new notes directly to the people.

Roosevelt didn't know what to do. He recognized his inadequacy on money questions. "I have more difficulty about dealing with the currency than with anything else," he confessed to Tom Watson, "for I feel less sure of my ground in the matter." Watson had urged the president to issue $50 million in greenbacks—notes unsecured by gold or by anything else except the government's promise to pay. Roosevelt was tempted but skeptical.

> It seems to me that the trouble about issuing greenbacks as you suggest is that it is like a man temporarily relieving himself by issuing notes of indebtedness. He can do it with safety if he exercises severe self-control; but a government will not permanently exercise such self-control. I have no doubt that $50,000,000 of greenbacks, if it was absolutely certain that no more would be issued, would achieve something of the purpose that you have in mind; but I also believe that most people would think that it foretold an indefinite issuance of greenbacks and that in consequence it would have a frightening effect.

Roosevelt refused to go the greenback route, instead throwing reluctant support to an alternative proposed by Senator Aldrich. The Aldrich bill was much more in keeping with Republican convention and corporate concerns; this was the source of Roosevelt's reluctance, and of considerable frustration that he had no better answer himself. His frustration spurred him to a fresh series of diatribes against those he—mistakenly—considered responsible for the continuing derangement of the nation's economy.

In January 1908, Roosevelt wrote Charles Bonaparte to congratulate the attorney general on a hard-hitting speech vowing to enforce the law against the rich just as rigorously as against the poor. It was a speech along thoroughly Rooseveltian lines, and in applauding Bonaparte the president applauded himself.

> It was time to say something, for the representatives of predatory wealth, of wealth accumulated on a giant scale by iniquity, by wrong-doing in many forms, by plain swindling, by oppressing wageworkers, by manipulating securities, by unfair and unwholesome competition, and by stockjobbing, in short by conduct abhorrent to every man of ordinarily decent conscience, have during the last few months made it evident that they are banded together to work for a reaction, to endeavor to overthrow and discredit all who honestly administer the law, and to secure a return to the days when every unscrupulous wrongdoer could do what he wisht unchecked, provided he had enough money.

Speaking of himself as much as of Bonaparte, Roosevelt asserted, "They attack you because they know your honesty and fearlessness, and dread them." Roosevelt delineated how these corporate corruptionists perverted legislators with campaign contributions, bought newspaper editors with advertising and college presidents with donations, and—especially disheartening to observe—occasionally soiled even the ermine of the bench. Of late their hydra-headed assault had targeted the present administration. "The amount of money the representatives of the great monied interests are willing to spend can be gauged by their recent publication broadcast thruout the papers of the country from the Atlantic to the Pacific of huge advertisements, attacking with envenomed bitterness the Administration's policy of warring against successful dishonesty." These advertisements, Roosevelt alleged, as well as a pamphlet titled "The Roosevelt Panic," had been authored by agents of the Rockefeller and Harriman interests. Yet the very furor of the attack gave cause for satisfaction, for it revealed "the anger and terror which our actions have caused the corrupt men of vast wealth to feel in the very marrow of their being."

By no means did Roosevelt confine such fevered opinions to his private correspondence. At the end of January 1908 he sent a special message to Congress outlining what he perceived to be the great danger to American democracy. The president again characterized criticism of the administration as being the work of "writers and speakers who, consciously or unconsciously, act as the representatives of predatory wealth—of the wealth accumulated on a giant scale by all forms of iniquity, ranging from the oppression of wageworkers to unfair and unwholesome methods of crushing out competition, and to defrauding the public by stock jobbing and the manipulation of securities." The monied malefactors were corrupting the nation's youth, committing "the hideous wrong of teaching our young men that phenomenal business success must ordinarily be based on dishonesty." They had banded together in a conspiracy "to overthrow and discredit all who honestly administer the law, to prevent additional legislation which would check and restrain them, and to secure if possible a freedom from all restraint which will permit every unscrupulous wrongdoer to do what he wishes unchecked provided he has enough money."

In this message Roosevelt recommended a variety of measures to level the playing field between the rich and the rest, but his rambling statement—well over ten thousand words—was most noteworthy for its tone of moral combat. A citation of Abraham Lincoln, the wielder of the sword of wrath during the Civil War, hardly reassured those who wondered what he was driving at. Their concerns were only amplified by his explicitly combative closing: "There is grave need of those stern qualities shown alike by the men of the North and the men of the South in the dark days when each valiantly battled for the light as it was given to see the light. Their spirit should be our spirit, as we strive to bring nearer the day when greed and trickery and cunning shall be trampled under feet by those who fight for the righteousness that exalteth a nation."

III

Roosevelt's ranting brought responses of a sort that should have given him pause. William Jennings Bryan sent a note of warm congratulations, which Roosevelt acknowledged warmly. By contrast, his old friend and ally Nicholas Murray Butler reported "sorrow and regret" among Roosevelt's supporters at the intemperance of his language, and predicted that the political effect of the message was "to bring Mr. Bryan measurably nearer the White House than he has ever been before." (This may have accounted for the warmth of Bryan's letter.)

Roosevelt rejected all criticism of his actions and words. He branded as nonsense the idea that by going after the speculating class he was interfering with the nation's prosperity. "I have interfered with prosperity just about as much as a raid on Canfield's [a notorious gambling house] would interfere with New York City's business well-being," he told one correspondent. And indeed, after the initial shock of the panic, he was starting to appreciate the opportunity it afforded. "I was feeling rather badly about the depression and hard times," he told Corinne. "And of course I still feel very badly about the poor people; but the New York contingent have succeeded in awakening in my mind a good healthy desire to take the tuck out of them!"

Roosevelt was even more emphatic in his rejoinder to Butler. "You regret what I have done," he wrote. "To me your regret is incomprehensible." He scoffed at the notion that his strong stance would drive away supporters. Quite the contrary; it would simply show who his true supporters were.

> I have the right to the fullest and heartiest support of every good man whose eyes are not blinded by unhappy surroundings, and who has in him a single trace of fervor for righteousness and decency without which goodness tends to be an empty sham. If your soul does not rise up against corruption in politics and corruption in business, against the unspeakable degradation and baseness of a community which will accept Rockefeller and Harriman, Foraker and Black, and Chancellor Day, as its leaders in the business world and in political thought, and which will tolerate the vileness of the New York *Sun* and kindred newspapers in its family— why, then naturally you are out of sympathy with me.

On the other hand, if Butler would open his eyes to the "unspeakable degradation" toward which these men colluded, a fate which if not opposed and checked "would work a ruin such as was worked in the last days of the Roman Republic by similar forces," then he would throw his backing to the president.

Rarely had even Roosevelt so clearly classed his enemies as agents of evil, and rarely had he so scorched the earth with overheated language as to render any middle ground—between himself and his foes—uninhabitable. One might have thought that the criticism of reasonable men like Butler and, even more so, the applause of Bryan would have caused Roosevelt to reconsider at least his language if not his policies. But the only thing it made him reconsider, and then only fleetingly, was his decision not to seek a third term. "The events of the last three months," he said privately in February 1908, "have made me for the first time sincerely regret that this is not my first term, and that I cannot have a showdown with my foes both without and within the party." He was certain he could win. "There would not even be a fight west of the Alleghenies; and if I were a betting man I should like to bet heavily on the fight in New York."

But Roosevelt placed too much store in his reputation as a forthright truth teller to go back on his promise to retire from the presidency come March 1909. Despite considerable pressure to recant and considerable evidence that he could indeed have swept to the nomination and to a third term, he stuck with his earlier decision.

IV

As it does every four years, the political process reduced to essentials during the spring and summer of 1908. Lawmaking and other irrelevancies were suspended as both parties prepared for the quadrennial clutching for the big brass ring on the front door of the White House.

Roosevelt, having removed himself from the contest for the substance of political power, contented himself with the symbolism. In May he hosted a conference on conservation of natural resources. The conference was almost wholly symbolic, committing no one to anything in particular or inconvenient; but for all that, it was not insignificant.

Roosevelt's interest in natural resources, of course, dated back decades, at least to that day when he encountered the dead seal on Broadway that kindled his curiosity regarding the natural world. Conservation hadn't been a major concern during those several years when he couldn't spot a winged or pawed creature without reflexively reaching for his gun, although as he grew older and learned to tame or at least cage the killer instinct in himself, he appreciated more fully the value of wildlife *in vivo*. His hunting trips to the West brought home the significance of preserving habitat if only to ensure the existence of game for future hunters to kill. Other activities soon distracted him from the work of the Boone and Crockett Club, but he never lost touch with those who made the preservation of wild natural habitat a priority. His ranching venture—and especially the debacle it became in the winter of 1886–87—made painfully clear the importance of balance within biological niches.

Yet Roosevelt was hardly a preservationist. His romanticism was not of the Thoreauvian variety, which valued wilderness for wilderness' sake. Roosevelt's romanticism ran closer to that of Daniel Boone and Davy Crockett (not for nothing was the name of his club chosen), who opened up the frontier to human habitation. With other progressives Roosevelt believed that natural resources existed to be used. They had to be used wisely, of course; like a family trust (of which Roosevelt knew something), they provided a regular surplus that might—and should—be employed to human benefit, but to take more than this surplus was as shortsighted and foolish as to spend down one's capital (of which he knew something as well).

Roosevelt was a conservationist rather than a preservationist. Even when he supported setting aside certain spectacular areas—Yosemite, Yellowstone—he did so primarily out of a judgment that the highest use of such spots was as scenery. More commonly he advocated allowing forests to be cut for lumber, rangeland to be opened to grazing, rivers to be dammed for irrigation and electrical power. He had no desire to close woodlands wholesale to loggers like those bluff fellows he had met while hunting with Bill Sewall, nor did he desire to run his cattlemen friends off the ranges of the West. Such people, he remained convinced, were the bedrock of the republic; their activities ought to be encouraged and their livelihoods protected.

Unsurprisingly, Roosevelt believed that the appropriate agent of conservation was the federal government. In certain fields there was simply no alternative. Roosevelt supported and gladly signed the Reclamation Act of 1902, which authorized the construction of flood-control and irrigation projects across the arid and predominantly federally owned West. In this case he could see—and few disputed—that in the absence of federal action, the rivers in question would continue to flood and to dump their waters unexploited (by humans) into the sea. In the presence of federal action, by contrast, the desert would bloom, cities would thrive, and the population would grow. A later generation of environmentalists would consider these to be dubious goals, but to Roosevelt they represented the essence of national life and the purpose of government.

Characteristically, Roosevelt deemed himself the chief steward of America's resources. He delighted to be able, with the stroke of a pen, to designate certain federal tracts as game reserves. Informed that the bird population of Florida's Pelican Island was mortally endangered by hunters greedy for the elaborate plumes of the showy waterfowl there, he inquired cursorily whether there was anything to prevent his banning hunting on the island; told there wasn't, he imposed the ban at once.

The nation's forests became a special project. In 1891, Congress had passed a law allowing the president to place certain federally owned properties into "forest reserves," the equivalent of what later would be called national forests. By 1901 presidents Harrison, Cleveland, and McKinley had transferred some 50 million acres of timberland into the reserve system. Roosevelt continued the practice and expanded it. For chief of the Bureau of Forestry he tapped Gifford Pinchot, a well-educated, well-heeled, well-connected advocate of scientific forest management and a man who, in Roosevelt's judgment, combined "entire disinterestedness and sanity" with "great energy and knowledge." On Pinchot's advice and encouragement, Roosevelt placed another 150 million acres into the reserved category.

The purpose of the protection was to prevent the continued strip-mining of forests by cut-and-run companies that grabbed the salable logs and left denuded, eroding moonscapes behind. Predictably, those companies and their political allies objected to Roosevelt's intervention in what they judged the beneficent operation of the free market. By 1907 they had garnered enough support in Congress to force a revision of the 1891 law; the new measure sharply curtailed the president's authority to create additional reserves.

Roosevelt would have vetoed the measure, but it was attached to an agriculture bill that couldn't be rejected without risking political suicide. Instead he evaded the clear meaning of the law and the intent of its framers by huddling with Pinchot and selecting the best of the parcels remaining outside the reserve system; with the time running out on his power as lord of the forests, Roosevelt issued a decree expanding the reserve system by 16 million midnight acres.

Roosevelt defended his move as reflecting "the utmost care and deliberation," but he fooled no one. It was patent that, Congress having outmaneuvered him, he was fighting a spirited rearguard action, using his power before it vanished. He went as far as to dare his opponents to roll back his reserve extensions. "If Congress differs from me . . ." he declared, "it will have full opportunity in the future to take such position as it may desire." (Many in Congress did differ, but not so many as to overturn his coup.)

The case of the forests exemplified the crux of the conservation struggle. More than any president before him—and than most after—Roosevelt recognized that natural resources were a wasting asset if not husbanded carefully. "We are prone to speak of the resources of this country as inexhaustible; this is not so," he declared in his annual message at the end of 1907. Indeed, the nation's resources were being exhausted at an alarming rate. Roosevelt congratulated himself for having saved as many forest acres as he had. "But it is only a beginning." The danger to the forests, and to those generations that ought to be able to count on the products and opportunities the forests supplied, persisted. "There are persons who find it to their immense pecuniary benefit to destroy the forests by lumbering. . . . A big lumbering company, impatient for immediate returns and not caring to look far enough ahead, will often deliberately destroy all the good timber in a region, hoping afterward to move on to some new country."

Similar judgments applied to the nation's other resources. Coal and oil were fast being lost to the public. "In the Eastern United States the mineral fuels have already passed into the hands of large private owners, and those of the West are rapidly following." Public lands generally had been subject to "great fraud" by individuals and corporations with no objective save the largest profit in the shortest time. Roosevelt typically spoke in superlatives and always sincerely; but he was never more sincere than when he declared the conservation of natural resources to be "the fundamental problem which underlies almost every other problem of our national life."

It was to address this problem that in the spring of 1908 he summoned to Washington the nation's governors and assorted other notables interested in conservation—or who, in his opinion, ought to be interested. He gave them the use of the East Room of the White House for three days in May. He greeted the guests, applauded their concern for an issue close to his heart, and by his presence ensured front-page coverage for their deliberations.

Though the grand generality of the gathering guaranteed that no one could object too strenuously to the various motions and resolutions, the affair was not without its moments of petty intrigue and personal pique. Gifford Pinchot had done most of the legwork in organizing the conference and had footed many of the bills; on the reasoning that he who writes the agenda and the checks ought to write the speeches as well—especially when he also holds the post of director of the national forest service—he did just that for several conferees whose desire to be associated with a worthy cause outpaced their mastery of the matters involved. John Muir, who had crossed staffs with Pinchot before, accused him of ramrodding his multiple-use views down the throats of the conferees and not letting preservationists like himself speak. Afterward, the sage of Yosemite was heard to mutter that Pinchot "never hesitates to sacrifice anything or anybody in his way."

Roosevelt ignored the grumbling and accounted the conference a splendid success, as did most observers. When the commission established under the auspices of the conference delivered its predictably progressive report the following January, Roosevelt praised it as "one of the most fundamentally important documents ever laid before the American people." A month later he convened a hemispheric conference on conservation, again at the White House. Once more he was delighted at the response—so delighted, in fact, that at the time he left the White House in March 1909, he was working on the guest list to a global conservation conference.

V

This last conference never took place; Will Taft found conservation less engrossing than Roosevelt did. But in 1908, Roosevelt didn't realize how much their views diverged (and not only on conservation), and he spent the summer and autumn of that year getting Taft nominated and elected. The principal obstacle to Taft's nomination was Roosevelt—precisely, the lingering hope on the part of Roosevelt's partisans that he could be stampeded into accepting a draft. Roosevelt wasn't exaggerating much when he told Lyman Abbott in May, "There has never been a moment when I could not have had the Republican nomination with practical unanimity by simply raising one finger." But still he declined to make a definitively forthright declaration of his intentions. His critics, ever detecting hypocrisy where there was really only sincere solipsism, concluded that he was conniving. Naturally, Roosevelt accused his critics of the basest behavior. Speaking of the possibility of his renomination, he declared, "Any man who supposes that I have been scheming for it, is not merely a fool, but shows himself to be a man of low morality."

Roosevelt also bridled at accusations that he was employing his powers as president to favor Taft—despite the fact that he indisputably was. As early as January he had penned a note: "Dear Will: Do you want any action about those Federal officials? I will break their necks with the utmost cheerfulness if you say the word!" Yet just weeks later he branded as "false and malicious" the charge that he was using the offices at his disposal to favor Taft. "It is the usual imaginative invention which flows from a desire to say something injurious."

With the opposition to Taft intimidated or otherwise neutralized, all went according to presidential plan. One by one the state Republican delegations swung into line; well before the delegates convened at Chicago in June, Taft's rivals had fallen by the wayside.

The convention also followed the script—albeit a raucous and demonstrative one. Cabot Lodge, the permanent chairman, primed the crowd with a litany of the administration's accomplishments; as he began to praise the president by name, the delegates and the galleries burst into cheers and shouting; they waved American flags madly and stamped their feet until the house sounded as though it would come crashing down. The uproar went on for five minutes, then ten, then twenty. The chairman, not dissatisfied at what he had unleashed, nonetheless affected unconcern. By one press account: "Up on the platform, Senator Lodge strolled about like the father of triplets, resigned and half bored at the prolongation of the tumult. Various national committeemen sitting near the speakers' platform proffered kind advice as to how they would calm the galleries if they had the gavel. The Senator shrugged his shoulders, looked at them pityingly and took another stroll up and down." The band struck up

"The Star-Spangled Banner," which did nothing to stem the torrent of noise. Someone brought forward a large stuffed toy bear (a "teddy bear," so called after Roosevelt's much embroidered sparing of a bear on a 1902 Mississippi hunt). This was carried to the stage and then offered to the crowd. Eager hands grabbed it and thrust it high, then tossed it about. At this point the demonstration began to look like a riot.

When the galleries took up the chant, "Four, four, four years more!" a shudder of alarm went through the Taft people. But Lodge quickly squelched any intimations of a stampede for Roosevelt. "His refusal of a renomination, dictated by the loftiest motives and by a noble loyalty to American traditions, is final and irrevocable," the chairman intoned, his voice steadily rising above the sea of sound. "Any one who attempts to use his name as a candidate for the Presidency impugns both his sincerity and his good faith, two of the President's greatest and most conspicuous qualities, upon which no shadow has ever been cast." Lodge's phrasing was just the cold water needed to dowse the last hopes of those who thrilled to the thought of Roosevelt but nodded off at the mention of Taft.

From the distance of Oyster Bay, Roosevelt judged that it had been a close call. Just before Lodge's address he had not seen "any danger of a stampede"; but immediately afterward he asserted that preventing the rush had required "some lively work." Lodge had done "splendidly" in corraling the convention before it got out of hand.

Lodge didn't refuse the congratulations, but observers at Chicago doubted that a stampede was ever really likely. "The demonstration, prolonged and enthusiastic as it was, gave no sign of any movement in the convention to nominate Roosevelt," opined the correspondent for the New York *Tribune*. "It was the tribute of the throng to the President's popularity and the emphatic answer to the vicious campaign waged against him by selfish interests."

Roosevelt wasn't about to split hairs; he was simply glad not to have to have dealt with a draft. "It would have been well-nigh impossible for me to refuse the nomination, and perhaps ruin the party thereby, if the nomination had actually been made; and yet if I had accepted, my power for useful service would have forever been lessened, because nothing could have prevented the suspicion that I had not really meant what I had said, that my actions did not really square with the highest and finest code of ethics."

Roosevelt's escutcheon survived this scrape intact, and the convention otherwise proceeded according to design. Taft was duly acclaimed as the heir apparent. The platform provoked little excitement; the only noteworthy development occurred when the Taft wagon, failing to entice Charles Evans Hughes aboard as number two nominee, hauled up James Sherman of New York. Taft's handlers hoped that "Sunny Jim" would brighten a ticket that couldn't help looking gray after Roosevelt.

Roosevelt registered thorough satisfaction with the outcome. Breaking his official silence, he congratulated the country and the party on a stellar nominee, a man, he suggested, who would make as good a president as almost any who had served. Roosevelt's private assessment was no less enthusiastic. "Always excepting Washington and Lincoln," he told George Trevelyan, "I believe that Taft as President will rank with any other man who has ever been in the White House."

In this same letter Roosevelt reflected once more on his now accomplished decision to relinquish power. He said that having made the original statement in 1904, he never seriously considered going back on it. Yet so intense had grown the battle with the entrenched forces of evil during his second term that he sometimes wondered whether he was doing the right thing. "When I felt obliged to insist on retiring and abandoning the leadership, now and then I felt ugly qualms as to whether I was not refusing to do what I ought to do, and abandoning great work on a mere fantastic point of honor." He didn't wish to be one of those who, like Dante's Pope, were "guilty of 'il gran refuito.'" (He added parenthetically, "I am a trifle uncertain as to the correctness of the Italian." He was close: it was *il gran refiuto*.) When there was a fight to be fought, he wanted to be in the thick of it.

On balance, however, he judged he had acted correctly. Power was a fine thing for a man of action to wield, and he had wielded it to the full. "While President I have been President, emphatically; I have used every ounce of power there was in the office and have not cared a rap for the criticisms of those who spoke of my 'usurpation of power'; for I knew that the talk was all nonsense and that there was no usurpation." Yet if power served a president well for a time, the nation was not well served when one man was president too long. "I believe in a strong executive; I believe in power; but I believe that responsibility should go with power, and that it is not well that the strong executive should be a perpetual executive." The plain people of the country, Roosevelt told Trevelyan, considered him peculiarly their president, and he didn't wish to do anything that might cause them to change their minds. "The chief service I can render these plain people who believe in me is not to destroy their ideal of me."

Roosevelt related a recent, relevant incident that had touched him deeply. Three common, backcountry farmers had arrived in Washington. "They were rugged old fellows, as hairy as Boers and a good deal of the Boer type. They hadn't a black coat among them, and two of them wore no cravats; that is, they just had on their working clothes, but all cleaned and brushed. When they finally got to see me they explained that they hadn't anything whatever to ask, but that they believed in me, believed that I stood for what they regarded as the American ideal, and as one rugged fellow put it, 'We want to shake that honest hand.'" The encounter confirmed Roosevelt's insistence on sticking with his original plan to retire. Having said he would leave, he could do no other.

VI

Roosevelt could retire, but he couldn't be retiring. As he told Trevelyan, he was much reassured to know that in Taft he had a candidate after his own heart, "a man whose theory of public and private duty is my own, and whose practice of this theory is what I hope mine is." Roosevelt went on to say that "if we can elect him President we achieve all that could be achieved by continuing me in the office."

Roosevelt spent the next four months working hard to guarantee this secondhand second lease on political life. His sense of political decorum continued to prevent his mounting the stump as openly for Taft as he would have wished, but he made his feelings quite obvious in letters to numerous individuals and groups, intended for publication—and duly published. To a Montana Republican leader, for example, who happened to be an old friend from his ranching days, Roosevelt declared that "the honest wageworker, the honest laboring man, the honest farmer, the honest mechanic or small trader, or man of small means, can feel that in a peculiar sense Mr. Taft will be his representative." By the same token, Taft could be expected "to exact justice from the railroads"—those bugbears of westerners.

While praising his Republican protégé, Roosevelt blasted his old Democratic bête noire, third-time nominee Bryan. Notwithstanding Bryan's praise of the attacks by the White House on corporate corruption, Roosevelt lashed the Democratic candidate privately as "the cheapest faker we have ever had proposed for President" and roughed him up publicly in an exchange of printed letters. "Bryan gave me a bully chance to hit him and I think I have hit him to some purpose," Roosevelt bragged to Taft. The president urged the candidate to do the same. "Hit at Bryan & the Bryanites," he said.

Roosevelt had plenty of other advice to offer as well. He recommended Frank Kellogg for campaign manager (Taft chose Frank Hitchcock instead). He told Taft not to play golf (the candidate's favorite pastime): It was having a bad effect in the West. He alternately urged Taft to speak up and to keep quiet. In the latter vein he said, "I believe you will be elected *if we can keep things as they are;* so be *very* careful to say nothing, not one sentence, that can be misconstrued, and that can give a handle for effective attacks." Writing as one who knew, he explained, "I have always had to exercise lynxeyed care over my own utterances!" Weeks later, however, Roosevelt was hot for verbal blows. "Hit them hard, old man!" he pleaded. Yet he didn't want to turn Taft into a pit bull. "Good for you!" he congratulated him in September. "I am glad to see you hitting Bryan. You have done it just the right way—good naturedly and gentlemanly, but as a fighter." On another occasion he exhorted: "Let the audience see you smile *always,* because I feel that your nature shines out so transparently when you do smile—you big, generous, high-minded fellow." Obviously trying to convince himself as much as Taft, Roosevelt went on, "Let them realize the truth, which is that for all your gentleness and kindliness and generous good nature, there never existed a man who was a better fighter when the need arose."

The problem was that Taft *wasn't* a fighter, at least not in the exuberant Rooseveltian sense. The harder it became to deny this, the more impatient Roosevelt grew. "I am not very much pleased with the way Taft's campaign is being handled," he told Nick Longworth. "I do wish Taft would put more energy and fight into the matter. He ought to throw Foraker with a bump." Regarding Foraker, who had lately been embarrassed by the revelation of some dubious payments from the Standard Oil Company and who consequently was embarrassing the party and the ticket, Roosevelt complained to Lyman Abbott that Taft was simply being too nice. "Taft is quite right in saying that he does not wish to hit a man when he is down; but this is not a case of that kind. This is a case of a fight to the finish, and in such a fight (if you will pardon the simile by an old-time boxer) if a man wishes to win it is absolutely necessary that he shall knock out his opponent when he has the latter groggy."

While urging Taft to pound his opponents, Roosevelt himself remained as sensitive to criticism as ever. The opposition press regularly sent him into a rage. "I don't think the worst politicians or the worst businessmen reach the level of infamy attained by so many newspapermen," he said. After listing his least favorites, he declared, "I happen to have seen recently editorials from all of these papers which for malignant mendacity, whether purchased or unpurchased, come well up to anything I have known. I do not think that there is any form of lying slander at which these men would stop." Roosevelt pondered answering the attacks openly but wondered whether the height of the election campaign was just the time. "Skinning skunks is not a pleasant occupation, and tho I am glad to get rid of the skunks, it is at least an open question whether the game is worth the candle."

The skunks were suffered to survive the campaign despite a recurrence of Roosevelt's quadrennial nervousness. "What curious changes we see among the people!" he mused in mid-September. Just a few months earlier the feeling in the West for Taft had been "overwhelming"—largely, the president continued, "because he was accepted as the exponent of the policies and principles for which I stood." Lately, though, the nominee appeared to be losing ground. "The advices I have received from the West are anything but reassuring," he told Frank Hitchcock, admonishing the Republican chairman to tighten up the campaign organization at Chicago.

Gradually, the reality of the situation sank in even on the fidgety father of the bride. "Most certainly I do not wish to be overoptimistic, and I need not say that there must be no let-up of any kind," Roosevelt wrote Taft in early October, "but I believe not only that we are going thru all right, but that we shall have substantially the elec-

toral vote of four years ago." The balloting bore out Roosevelt's prediction, substantially: Taft won by a large majority, although a smaller
one than Roosevelt's in 1904.

"The result is a great victory and a mighty good thing for the whole
country," the president declared on the morning after the election.
"Naturally I am greatly pleased." As well he might have, Roosevelt
interpreted the vote for Taft as a triumph for his own policies; with
somewhat slighter justification he deemed Taft's victory a guarantee
that those policies would continue. "Taft will carry on the work substantially as I have carried it on," he forecast to George Trevelyan.
"His policies, principles, purposes and ideals are the same as mine. . . .
I have the profound satisfaction of knowing that he will do all in his
power to further every one of the great causes for which I have fought
and that he will persevere in every one of the great governmental policies in which I most firmly believe." Roosevelt judged that the election's outcome absolved him of any possible lingering blame for *il
gran refiuto* (he got it right this time). "Renunciation is so often the
act of a weak nature or the term by which a weak nature seeks to
cover up its lack of strength." Roosevelt had never really thought himself guilty of such weakness, but the objective damage might have
been the same had Taft lost. "Naturally the relief is very great to have
the event justify me."

VII

Taft's election left Roosevelt with little presidential to do until
March 1909, when he would officially hand over power. Although the
(now really) lame-duck president would have to deal with a lame-
duck Congress, neither could be expected to do much except hiss and
nip at the other, as waterfowl do.

Yet the nipping could get nasty. The 1908 session of Congress produced an amendment restricting the activities of the Secret Service,
which certain legislators with paranoid tendencies or simply bad consciences suspected Roosevelt of turning into what one likened to "the
hated Black Cabinet of St. Petersburg." Roosevelt didn't have any
deep designs for espionage against his opponents, but he did think

some of them, and especially some of their allies, certainly deserved investigating. Moreover, as he always did, he resisted restraints on his authority. With the end of his administration in sight, he eschewed the measured language of politics; instead he lashed the backers of the amendment, impugning their motives all. "The chief argument in favor of the provision," he proclaimed, "was that the Congressmen did not themselves wish to be investigated by Secret Service men." For good measure he added: "This amendment has been of benefit only, and could be of benefit only, to the criminal class."

Not surprisingly, such a blanket indictment inflamed the situation. Senator Aldrich demanded an investigation into the president's own behavior. Members of the House rose in high dudgeon to defend the dignity of their chamber. Roosevelt retreated slightly, disavowing any desire to use the Secret Service to probe the activities of members of Congress, but he stood by his contention that circumscription of the activities of the service would benefit the criminal class. The House, by a margin of 212 to 35, voted to chastise the president for disrespect of a coequal branch of the government.

Roosevelt's irritation with his opponents spilled over into his relations with the press and provoked him to one of the least judicious actions of his presidency. Ever since 1903 his handling of the Panama affair had come in for criticism, but when Joseph Pulitzer's New York *World* in December 1908 accused him of "deliberate misstatements of fact" in rebutting a recent renewal of the criticism (which this time besmirched his brother-in-law Douglas Robinson and Taft's brother Charles in addition to himself), he decided he could stand it no longer. He demanded that the Justice Department bring charges. "I do not know anything about the law of criminal libel," he conceded to Henry Stimson, federal district attorney for New York, "but I should dearly like to have it invoked about Pulitzer." The president went on: "Pulitzer is one of these creatures of the gutter of such unspeakable degradation that to him even eminence on a dunghill seems enviable."

Charles Bonaparte reminded the president that libel was difficult to prove, criminal libel more so, and that in any event it was almost always considered a state offense, if an offense at all. The attorney general succeeded as far as making Roosevelt acknowledge that "unfortunately, the Nation has a very indirect jurisdiction in the matter," but Roosevelt didn't want to debate the law. He was morally convinced that Pulitzer had done wrong and must be punished, law or no law. At the president's insistence the case went ahead. The government's lawyers managed, by determination and ingenuity, to win indictments. But the prosecution stalled when the defendants challenged the jurisdiction of the federal courts and the courts concurred. The affair ended in clear defeat for by-then-former President Roosevelt's expansive interpretation of the law of libel.

VIII

Other matters were more enjoyable. Shortly after the election, Roosevelt amused himself by taking the entire general staff of the army and the faculty of the National War College—some fifty officers altogether—on one of his famous scrambles up Rock Creek. "We did not go fast because of course with such a number we had to wait for the tail-enders, and there were about a dozen who could not have gotten thru at all if we had kept at any gait," he told Ethel. "But they all climbed gallantly up the cliffs, waded the stream (up to their chins), and wriggled along the hillsides."

In the same realm of military self-improvement, the president shamed those officers complaining at a directive of his that they all demonstrate the capacity to ride ninety miles in three days, by himself covering ninety miles in a single day. He left before dawn and, employing a relay of four horses, rode nearly fifty miles to the community of Warrenton, Virginia, where he shook hands with the prominent locals and addressed the schoolchildren. Then he remounted and returned home. He hadn't had such fun in years. "The last fifteen miles were done in pitch darkness and with a blizzard of sleet blowing in our faces," he told Kermit proudly. Amid the storm, military aide Archie Butt suggested that the icy streets of the capital might be too slick for safety and that perhaps they should take a carriage for the final mile or so. Roosevelt rejoined: "By George, we will make the White House with our horses if we have to lead them." And so they did. "We were all covered with ice," Butt noted afterward, "but the President in his black riding jacket, with fur collar and pockets, and broad-brim black hat, looked for all the world like the pictures of

Santa Claus." Edith was waiting at the door for them. "It was a perfect picture," Butt remarked. "She had on some light, fluffy evening gown and I don't believe that Dolly Madison, even in her loveliest moments, ever looked more attractive than did Mrs. Roosevelt at that moment, standing there, framed in the big doorway with the strong light on her and the wind blowing her clothes in every direction." The First Lady extended the hospitality of the White House to the entire party. "Mrs. Roosevelt made us come in and gave us each a julep," Butt gratefully recorded.

While single-handedly whipping the military into shape, Roosevelt stuck the fingers on his other hand into the customary assortment of pies large and small. He read even more than usual and engaged in his customary robust criticism; he attacked Jack London as a purveyor of "nonsense" masquerading as realism—only a "nature faker" could have a lynx killing a wolf, as London did in *White Fang*. He delivered an esthetic verdict on a bronze cherub adorning the Mammoth Hot Springs at Yellowstone Park: "A more ridiculous and incongruous thing cannot be imagined." He ordered the offending angel removed forthwith. He engaged in a detailed and at times heated correspondence over whether a particular American runner had committed a foul in a race at the recent Olympic games. Even while asserting that government officials shouldn't bother themselves with such trivial matters, he did just that. Of course he had no direct knowledge of the incident in question, but he nonetheless ventured a judgment. "Carpenter is a Cornell man," he explained, adding that he had it from a young cousin who had competed against Carpenter in the Ivy League that he was "a good, straight fellow and that there has never been a suspicion of crookedness about him." Roosevelt averred that the charges against Carpenter arose from "a bitterness of hostile feeling" against Americans on the part of certain Britons, "a bitterness so discreditable to them that it deprives them of all right to criticize others."

A last run-in with California failed to spoil his final weeks. After the California legislature discovered some novel ways to insult the Japanese, Roosevelt again urged Governor Gillett to block the offensive measures; meanwhile, he gnashed his teeth at the antics of half the California senatorial delegation. "One of the Senators, Flint, has stood by me like a trump," he related to Ted. "I would like to break the neck of the feebly malicious angleworm who occupies the other seat as California's Senator; he is a milk-faced grub named Perkins." But eventually the worm turned and in doing so helped frustrate the Japan-baiters in Sacramento. What might have been another major confrontation with Japan blew by.

The president didn't waste his time thanking Perkins for doing what he thought the California lawmaker should have done from the start; if credit was due to anyone for making the Pacific live up to its name, he was happy to claim it himself. In a letter to Arthur Lee he asserted that this latest flap confirmed the wisdom of his way of handling Japan, which consisted of polite but definite insistence that the Japanese government keep its workers at home, and a simultaneous buildup of the United States Navy.

IX

The navy gave Roosevelt a going-away present (which was the least it could do after all he had done for it) by getting the battleship fleet home just days before he left the White House. Roosevelt wouldn't have missed the return for the world. Not even a family crisis could keep him away: On the eve of the great moment he learned that his nephew, Corinne and Douglas's son Stewart, had died tragically in an accident at Harvard. "I am heartbroken at the dreadful news," he wired the grieving parents, but he begged off from going to them in their time of sorrow. As he explained to Archie, it would have been "impossible" for him not to greet the fleet. "No President can let any private matter interfere with a great public duty."

Roosevelt joined the scores of thousands who flocked to Hampton Roads on George Washington's birthday to witness the return of the warships from their fourteen-month voyage. Civilian vessels of all sizes and states of seaworthiness braved squally skies and rough water to watch the white ships (already slated to be scraped and repainted a less gaudy gray) materialize out of the mist on the eastern horizon.

Roosevelt welcomed the battleships as he had sent them out, from the rail of the *Mayflower*. He received another simultaneous salute from all the big guns, then twenty-one more from each ship as it steamed past the presidential yacht. The column of vessels stretched more than seven miles; the thunder of the guns—answered by return salutes from the armada of onlookers—filled the better part of an hour.

The president nearly burst with patriotic pride. "This is the first battle fleet that has ever circumnavigated the globe," he reminded the officers and men, speaking from the deck of the admiral's flagship. "Those who perform the feat again can but follow in your footsteps." With censorship lifted, scores of papers had sent correspondents; all agreed that the president had never been so triumphant. One journal aptly captioned the occasion "the apotheosis of Roosevelt," the "one supreme, magnificent moment" of his career.

Part Four

RESTLESS STILL

CHAPTER TWENTY-FIVE

Lions and Lesser Royalty
1909–10

"**I** want him to be the simplest American alive after he leaves the White House," Edith said just before they both did. "And the funniest thing to me is that he wants to be also and says he is going to be, but the trouble is he has really forgotten how to be. I try to think of his year in Africa and my year in my sister's little cottage on the Mediterranean as having the effect the forty years of wandering had for the Jews. At the end of that time we will enter the home at Oyster Bay as gladly and as meekly as ever the Children of Israel entered the Promised Land."

It was a wonderful notion. After ten years at the center of America's attention, the First Couple would escape the spotlight by the simple expedient of escaping the country. Theodore would head for Africa to go on a safari he had long dreamed of but never, until lately, thought he would be able to experience. Edith had no more interest in killing wild beasts than she ever had or in spending more than the odd night out under the stars; while he played great white hunter, she would recuperate from the cares and responsibilities of running the executive mansion in a snug retreat in the Ligurian hills outside Genoa. Travels about Italy and the neighboring countries would afford diversion when desired.

Yet for all its attractions, this arrangement wasn't what she really wanted. She would have much preferred being with Theodore. During the last ten years he had been close at hand, usually just down the hall in his office. But he had often been so busy that he might just as well have been miles away. She had longed for the day when they would be merely Mr. and Mrs. Roosevelt and would have a chance to get to know each other again.

But it wasn't to be. Theodore must have his safari—which meant, of course, that she would have the children, as always. He was taking Kermit, yet that only made matters worse: Of all the children he was the one with whom she could most easily share her feelings. Alice had her own life now, as did Ted for the most part. But she would still have Ethel and Archie and Quentin to care for. And in a foreign country, no less.

As if that weren't enough, her mind wouldn't even be able to rest regarding Theodore's safety. For seven and a half years—since the moment she learned McKinley had been shot—she hadn't lived a day without the fear that her husband would be murdered by another such lunatic. At times the only thing that had kept her sane was the knowledge that this potential death sentence would run out on March 4, 1909. No one would risk his life to kill an ex-president.

And what did Theodore do to celebrate his freedom—and hers? He insisted on throwing himself in front of charging lions and elephants. And taking Kermit along, no less.

As she had always done when Theodore got something in his head that he had to do, she hid her feelings and bade him go. She put on her best dress and her bravest face, kissed him and Kermit good-bye, and waved from the piazza at Sagamore as they drove down the hill to meet their ship.

But Kermit saw what his father didn't. The next day he encountered Archie Butt at the dock; the White House aide asked about her. "He told me that she was perfectly calm and self-possessed when they had left," Butt recorded, "but that he felt her heart was almost broken."

Edith herself conceded nearly as much. Almost before her husband and son's ship had cleared the Narrows, she wrote to Kermit: "If it were not for the children, I would not have the nervous strength to live through these endless months of separation from Father."

II

Roosevelt's departure for Africa in March 1909 culminated almost a year of planning. The wildlife of Africa had fascinated him since his boyhood days on the Nile; more recently the great beasts of the East African highlands had implicitly challenged his prowess as a hunter. He had killed the most fearsome animals America had to offer—the cougar and the grizzly bear—but what were these against the lion, the elephant, the rhinoceros? "I have never shot dangerous game," he wrote to Frederick Selous, a famous hunter and explorer with long experience in Africa, "unless you can call the very few grizzly bears I have shot dangerous." In fact, one certainly could call grizzlies dangerous, but Roosevelt realized that he was a mere tyro compared to a veteran of the veldt like Selous.

Consequently, he consulted Selous and other experts in laying plans for his safari. "I quite appreciate what you say as to the need of taking a certain number of delicacies on a trip of this kind and traveling in comfort, and anything that you think proper I will take," he told Selous during the summer of 1908. He inquired as to the best armaments, the optimal pursuit techniques, the appropriate season for the different game species. "People have told me that I can not start with a caravan in the rainy season," he wrote to an outfitter in Nairobi. "Other people have told me that it is entirely possible and, indeed, that that is a good season." Where lay truth in the matter?

Sensitive to the charge of bloodthirstiness, Roosevelt took pains to cast his safari as a scientific expedition. He pledged his prizes to the Smithsonian museum; the animals, stuffed, would depict the large-mammal life of East Africa to future generations of students and other museum-goers. He explained his strategy to a British official in Kenya: "Except for actual food—and these only to the extent that I am permitted under your general regulations—I shall merely desire to get one specimen, or perhaps one specimen of the male and one of the female of each of the different kinds of game, for the National Museum at Washington." Only he and his son Kermit would be shooting; the professional naturalists who would join them on the journey would not, as a rule.

The company of Kermit was one among the several attractions of the trip for his father. Far more than Ted, Kermit possessed the adventurous, romantic spirit Roosevelt had always admired—in himself and in others. Probably Kermit felt obliged to distinguish himself from conventional Ted; doubtless he saw what constant laboring in the shadow of their famous father had cost Ted in terms of peace of mind.

Perhaps some of his restless spirit came from his uncle Elliott, whom he resembled in another way: He later developed a severe alcohol addiction which led directly to his death (in Kermit's case by overt suicide). Whatever the reasons, Kermit would never require more than the slightest invitation to be off to the ends of the earth. Africa sounded splendid.

Yet as much as Roosevelt admired Kermit and as much as he looked forward to this time together in the field with him, he still fretted paternally over his safety and well-being, and occasionally wondered if he wasn't putting the boy (young man, actually: Kermit would turn twenty in Africa) at unnecessary risk. "I have been a little worried about him in connection with the fever," he wrote to one of his expert consultants, who had described a trip to the headwaters of the Nile. But in the next sentence he guessed that perhaps his worries were overblown. "In British East Africa, where most of our hunting is to be done, I should suppose that the fever was not so bad as in Uganda and the Upper Nile." In any event, Kermit was anticipating the expedition with such eagerness that his father couldn't tell him no. "It would absolutely break Kermit's heart if I now left him behind."

Kermit's anticipation scarcely exceeded his father's. "I fairly dream of the trip," Roosevelt told Selous as early as September 1908. "It seems too good to be true." He admitted that he lacked the toughness and endurance he had prided himself on as a young man. "I shall be absolutely soft and out of condition after ten years of close office work." But even so, he could hardly wait. "Hurrah for Africa!" he wrote two months before Taft's election.

Indeed, it was Taft's election that provided the final fillip to Roosevelt's desire to visit the dark continent. As vehemently as he denied having imposed Taft on the Republican Party, the outgoing president realized that the incoming president would labor under that popular (and accurate) impression. Taft would never become effective—either for himself or in terms of the goals Roosevelt hoped to achieve through him—until he could demonstrate that he was his own man. If Roosevelt remained in America or anywhere within earshot of a reporter, he would constantly be asked to comment on Taft's performance. Roosevelt may have known himself well enough to recognize that he would find it nearly impossible to decline comment indefinitely. Better to leave the country for someplace even the most intrepid correspondents would have trouble following him.

As if distance weren't enough, Roosevelt noisily warned off journalists who might have wanted to follow him. He declared that he would refuse to talk to any reporter who had the effrontery to try to track him down; pleading the privacy of the ordinary citizen, he demanded to be left alone to hunt in peace. His experience in the American West had demonstrated that reporters were invariably a nuisance on a hunt. When they weren't busy getting themselves nearly killed by bullet or beast, they were frightening away the game. "I feel absolutely ferocious at times when I am not allowed to have a moment to myself," Roosevelt grumbled to Archie Butt regarding the prospect of being chased across Africa. "I do not think any English newspaper men will attempt to follow me, for the English are rather decent in such matters, and if our own people pursue me as they did when I hunted in the West I may be able to get the authorities to intervene until I elude them in the wilds." He promised to give them the slip—or (half-jokingly) worse. "They will never catch up with me if I get ahead of them once, and if they do in the jungle you may see my expense report to the National Museum read something after this order: 'One hundred dollars for buying the means to rid myself of one *World* reporter; three hundred dollars expended in dispatching a reporter of the *American;* five hundred dollars for furnishing wine to cannibal chiefs with which to wash down a reporter of the New York *Evening Post.*'"

III

Roosevelt had a less disinterested motive in declaring a preemptive embargo on news about his safari: He didn't want to scoop himself. While gathering his guns and packing his trunks for the trip, he also lined up a lucrative contract with Scribner's, the magazine and book publisher, for a series of articles on his African adventure. He would get fifty thousand dollars for twelve articles, which would run monthly from whenever the first one arrived out of the bush. In addition he would receive royalties from the book the articles would constitute after serialization. *Collier's* and *McClure's* had offered him more money than Scribner's, but he liked the treatment Scribner's had given his earlier hunting stories and *The Rough Riders,* and he decided to stay with that house.

Whatever the coverage of the details of his expedition, the fact of the safari was no secret. Wall Street, not surprisingly, applauded his departure; J. P. Morgan was reported to have raised a glass and declared, "America expects that every lion will do his duty." (One of Roosevelt's hunting partners later suggested that the president himself had originated the idea of lions doing their duty. Carl Akeley, an old Africa hand, was having dinner at the White House with Roosevelt and telling about a particular cave in East Africa from which he had once seen sixteen lions emerge. The image appealed to Roosevelt, who was then exasperated even more than usual at the antics of his opponents in Congress. The president remarked that he wished he had those lions to set loose in the Capitol. One of the guests—a friendly but now somewhat nervous congressman—wondered whether the president didn't worry that the lions might make mistakes. The legislator was hardly reassured by Roosevelt's reply: "Not if they stayed long enough.")

For a decade America had never been without its Teddy, and his disappearance into deepest Africa created a dramatic void that gave his return, when he did return—initially by magazine article, later in person—all the greater impact. He played the role of explorer to the exotic for all it was worth. "I speak of Africa and golden joys," he quoted, writing for Scribner's from Khartoum: "the joy of wandering through lonely lands; the joy of hunting the mighty and terrible lords of the wilderness, the cunning, the wary, and the grim." Roosevelt painted the scene as Homer might have:

> In these greatest of the world's hunting-grounds there are mountain peaks whose snows are dazzling under the equatorial sun; swamps where the slime oozes and bubbles and festers in the steaming heat; lakes like seas; skies that burn above deserts where the iron desolation is shrouded from view by the wavering mockery of the mirage; vast grassy plains where palms and thorn-trees fringe the dwindling streams; mighty rivers running out of the heart of the continent through the sadness of endless marshes; forests of gorgeous beauty, where death broods in the dark and silent depths.

The denizens of this wondrously formidable land likewise embodied imminent death amid abundant life. "The land teems with beasts of the chase, infinite in number and incredible in variety. It holds the fiercest beasts of ravin, and the fleetest and most timid of those beings that live in undying fear of talon and fang." Death yielded no quarter to even that highest of the animals. "On the land and in the water there are dread brutes that feed on the flesh of man; and among the lower things that crawl and fly and sting and bite, he finds swarming foes far more evil and deadly than any beast or reptile; foes that kill his crops and his cattle, foes before which he himself perishes in his hundreds of thousands."

And yet there were men who willingly ventured into this deadly land. Roosevelt didn't dwell on his own bravery, but neither did he give it short shrift. Why did such men court such dangers? For an experience equaled nowhere else. "The hunter who wanders through these lands sees sights which ever afterward remain fixed in his mind. He sees the monstrous river-horse snorting and plunging beside the boat, the giraffe looking over the tree-tops at the nearing horseman, the ostrich fleeing at a speed that none may rival, the snarling leopard and coiled python with their lethal beauty, the zebras barking in the moonlight, as the laden caravan passes on its night march through a thirsty land." The hunter saw also the tawny boldness of the lion, the great gray bulk of the elephant, the uncomprehending truculence of the rhinoceros.

"These things can be told," Roosevelt wrote after doing just that.

> But there are no words that can tell the hidden spirit of the wilderness, that can reveal its mystery, its melancholy, and its charm. There is delight in the hardy life of the open, in long rides rifle in hand, in the thrill of the fight with dangerous game. Apart from this, yet mingled with it, is the strong attraction of the silent places, of the large tropic moons, and the splendor of the new stars; where the wanderer sees the awful glory of sunrise and sunset in the wide waste spaces of the earth, unworn of man, and changed only by the slow change of the ages through time everlasting.

IV

Not every aspect of the safari was so romantic. For one thing, the journey entailed much tedious slogging through country that, though often scenic, was rarely spectacular. Indeed, Roosevelt remarked that it reminded him of Dakota. He and his companions alternately roasted and shivered—the first during the equatorial day, the second in the highland night. Insect pests were a constant trial. Ticks were everywhere: in the grass, in the bushes, in the bedding, under one's trousers, stockings, shirt. Humans had to pick them off carefully and frequently or risk tick fever, which even the most stringent precautions frequently failed to avert. The horses had things worse; every evening the aboriginal attendants, called *saises,* spent hours plucking the ticks off the party's mounts. The ticks plagued the native hoofed beasts, with neither fingers of their own nor those of humans to tend to them, more sorely still. Roosevelt noted repeatedly how the animals the hunters killed were infested with ticks; the blood-sucking insects often formed solid mats around the animals' eyes and other vulnerable spots.

The local human inhabitants had come to terms with the ticks and the other aspects of their surroundings. "The natives of East Africa are numerous; many of them are agricultural or pastoral peoples after their own fashion . . ." Roosevelt related. "They are in most ways primitive savages, with an imperfect and feeble social, and therefore military, organization; they live in small communities under their local chiefs; they file their teeth, and though they wear blankets in the neighborhood of the whites, these blankets are often cast aside; even when the blanket is worn, it is often in such fashion as merely to accentuate the otherwise absolute nakedness of both sexes." (Whether or not Roosevelt made the connection consciously, these Victorian observations on the nakedness of the natives recall the entries in his travel diary for Alexandria, written at age fourteen.)

Speaking as a rancher and a conservationist, Roosevelt couldn't help commenting on what seemed to him the foolish practices of these local herders. "These savages are cattle-keepers and cattle-raisers, and the women do a good deal of simple agricultural work; unfortunately, they are wastefully destructive of the forests." At the same time they carried their concern for their cattle to ridiculous lengths. "Except for the milk, which they keep in their foul, smoky calabashes, the natives really make no use of their cattle; they do not know how to work them, and they never eat them even in time of starvation. When there is prolonged drought and consequent failure of crops, the foolish creatures die by the hundreds when they might readily be saved if they

were willing to eat the herds which they persist in treating as ornaments rather than as made for use."

Roosevelt had never pretended to be an anthropologist, but even he
ought to have asked himself where the Masai and their neighbors
would have found replacements for the cattle he recommended they
eat in times of drought; unlike wealthy American ranchers, they
couldn't fetch new herds by train from the next state. It was partly this
lack of imagination, and partly his predisposition to believe that imperialism was the same thing as progress, that caused Roosevelt to interpret the British presence in Africa as a signal step forward for the
human race. He lauded the courage and fortitude of the planters, mag-
istrates, army officers, and other Englishmen dedicated to uplifting
those "out-of-the-way regions where the English flag stands for all that
makes life worth living." He derided the notion that self-government
suited all people. Of one tribe he declared, "The Wakamba are as yet
not sufficiently advanced to warrant their sharing in the smallest
degree in the common government; the 'just consent of the governed'
in their case, if taken literally, would mean idleness, famine, and endless internecine warfare. They cannot govern themselves from within;
therefore they must be governed from without; and their need is met
in highest fashion by firm and just control, of the kind that on the
whole they are now getting."

Roosevelt reckoned that the upland region of East Africa was ripe
for civilized settlement. "It is a white man's country," he said—echoing
exactly the view of the British imperial government. Again noting sim-
ilarities to the American West, he advocated conservation and capital
improvement projects similar to those he had promoted at home.
"There should be storage reservoirs in the hills and along the rivers—
in my judgment built by the government, and paid for by the water-
users in the shape of water-rents—and irrigation ditches; with the
water stored and used there would be an excellent opening for small
farmers, for the settlers, the actual home-makers, who, above all others, should be encouraged to come."

Among the whites already in East Africa were members of a group
toward which Roosevelt felt a particular affinity. The Boers, descendants
of Dutch settlers who left Holland about the same time Roosevelt's
Dutch ancestors departed for America, had reached East Africa from
the south. In their new home they continued to display the singular

self-reliance that had made them such doughty foes to the British in the late South African war. Roosevelt was as thoroughly taken by the Boers he met as they, fully aware of his Dutch roots, were by him. He congratulated them on their large families and joined them in singing a Dutch lullaby he remembered from childhood.

Between the British and the Boers, Roosevelt judged, the white race was well represented in Africa. "There could be no better and manlier people than those, both English and Dutch, who are at this moment engaged in the great and difficult task of adding East Africa to the domain of civilization."

Roosevelt had no doubt that white settlements in Africa would have a beneficial effect on the black races there; for proof one had only to look at the condition of the black race in America. "To an American, who must necessarily think much of the race problem at home," he wrote, "it is pleasant to be made to realize in vivid fashion the progress the American negro has made, by comparing him with the negro who dwells in Africa untouched, or but lightly touched, by white influence." The relative advancement of American blacks was underlined by the presence in Kenya of a black man from the States who was working as a doctor; Roosevelt and his party quickly came to respect and admire this man for his courtesy and intelligence. They felt much the same way regarding a Jamaican black who managed one of the colonial government's farms and whose skills and temperament likewise bespoke the ameliorative influence of white culture. "No one could fail to be impressed with the immense advance these men represented as compared with the native negro."

V

But Roosevelt hadn't come all the way to Africa to discover the civilizing genius of the white race, of which he was completely convinced already. He had come for the hunting. Even so, just as he felt obliged to defend the institutions that made a great white hunt politically possible, so he felt compelled to defend the values that made it scientifically—as he saw it—necessary. During the course of his debates with the "nature fakers," one of the targets of Roosevelt's scorn had responded to the president's complaint that they didn't know the heart of wild things by declaring, "Every time Mr. Roosevelt gets near the heart of a wild thing he invariably puts a bullet through it." Perhaps this jibe still stung, or perhaps he simply recognized that the *Scribner's* audience wasn't quite that of *Field and Stream*. In any event, he mounted a sturdy defense of hunting. He recited "certain facts that ought to be self-evident to every one above the intellectual level of those well-meaning persons who apparently think that all shooting is wrong and that man could continue to exist if all wild animals were allowed to increase unchecked." Notable among these facts was that the argument-from-Eden for the sanctity of animal life was illogical and untenable. Roosevelt pointed out that humans and wildlife were engaged in a constant struggle for the resources of the planet; if humans didn't kill animals, the animals would end up killing humans, by eating them out of crops and home. He didn't advocate indiscriminate slaughter, to be sure. "Game-butchery is as objectionable as any other form of wanton cruelty or barbarity," he said. "But to protest against all hunting of game is a sign of softness of head, not of soundness of heart."

Roosevelt killed hundreds of animals on this trip; yet he insisted in each installment of his story that he did so only in the interests of science and sustenance (what wasn't stuffed to make dioramas for the museum was stewed to make dinner for the baggage-bearers). Despite his disclaimers, however, his thrill at the chase and the kill gleamed through his prose. For each of dozens of encounters, he described in exquisite detail the tracking, stalking, shooting, and expiring of the victim. After a while all the giant and common elands, harnessed and unharnessed bushbucks, Jackson's and Nilotic hartebeests, Vaughn's and white-eared kobs, common and Singsing waterbucks, and Grant's, Roberts's, Notata, and Thomson's gazelles started to run together. But a few of the encounters were undeniably gripping, and as recounted by the great man himself, they demonstrated that he hadn't lost the physical courage in which he took such pride and which made him so irresistible to so many of his compatriots.

Roosevelt bagged his first lion on the Kapiti plains between Nairobi and Mount Kilimanjaro. The expedition's beaters had been creating a commotion in the tall grass, driving suspected lions in the direction of Roosevelt and the other rifles. But they raised only two cubs, which were dispatched despite their innocence (thereby preemptively extinguishing the species "teddy lion").

Disappointed, Roosevelt and the other hunters mounted their horses and proceeded back toward camp. On the way they spotted fresh signs of lions and detoured toward a thicket to flush out any big cats hiding there.

> We rode up to it and shouted loudly. The response was immediate, in the shape of loud gruntings, and crashings through the thick brush. We were off our horses in an instant, I throwing the reins over the head of mine; and without delay the good old fellow began placidly grazing, quite unmoved by the ominous sounds immediately in front. I sprang to one side; and for a second or two we waited, uncertain whether we should see the lions charging out ten yards distant, or running away. Fortunately, they adopted the latter course. Right in front of me, thirty yards off, there appeared, from behind the bushes which had first screened him from my eyes, the tawny, galloping form of a big, maneless lion. Crack! the Winchester spoke; and as the soft-nosed bullet ploughed forward through his flank the lion swerved so that I missed him with the second shot; but my third bullet went through the spine and forward into his chest. Down he came, sixty yards off, his hind quarters dragging, his head up, his ears back, his jaws open and lips drawn up in a prodigious snarl, as he endeavored to turn to face us. His back was broken; but of this we could not at the moment be sure, and if it had been merely grazed, he might have recovered, and then, even though dying, his charge might have done mischief. So Kermit, Sir Alfred, and I fired, almost together, into his chest. His head sank, and he died.

Roosevelt killed eight other lions, eight elephants, thirteen rhinoceroses, seven hippopotamuses, twenty zebra, seven giraffes, six buffalo (the real thing, not the bison of North America), and scores of lesser mammals, as well as dozens of birds, from ostriches (two) and great bustards (four) down to the odd duck and songbird, and three pythons.

Like other hunters, he developed opinions regarding the character of his various foes. He judged the lion the most formidable, combining great strength with courage—although Roosevelt conceded wide variance among lions, as among certain other dangerous animals. One lion would charge when another would retreat. By contrast, rhinoceroses were uniformly stupid, and on precisely that account could be quite terrifying—not least because the only sure way to bring down a rampaging rhino was to put a bullet in its brain, a small target indeed.

The quirks of animal behavior caused Roosevelt to reflect on animal emotions, which in turn caused him to reflect on human emotions. Roosevelt knew that it was unscientific to impute emotions to animals, since there was no way of knowing what any given animal was thinking or if it was thinking anything at all. Yet the subject of animal emotions served as his literary gateway to the topic of human emotions; and in any event he was just as sure that animals thought and felt as he was of nearly everything else in his life. He mused,

> Watching the game, one was struck by the intensity and the evanescence of their emotions. Civilized man now usually passes his life under conditions which eliminate the intensity of terror felt by his ancestors when death by violence was their normal end, and threatened them every hour of the day and night. It is only in nightmares that the average dweller in civilized countries now undergoes the hideous horror which was the regular and frequent portion of his ages-vanished forefathers, and which is still an every-day incident in the lives of most wild creatures. But the dread is short-lived, and its horror vanishes with instantaneous rapidity.

This was all the more reason why the tenderhearted should not weep for those animals killed by hunters—or for those uncivilized people brought under the rule of law.

> Life is hard and cruel for all the lower creatures, and for man also in what the sentimentalists call a "state of nature." The savage of to-day shows us what the fancied age of gold of our ancestors was really like; it was an age when hunger, cold, violence, and iron cruelty were the ordinary accompaniments of life. If Matthew Arnold, when he expressed the wish to know the thoughts of Earth's "vigorous, primitive" tribes of the past, had really desired an answer to his question, he would have done well to visit the homes of the existing representatives of his "vigorous, primitive" ancestors, and to watch them feasting on blood and guts.

Roosevelt did just this, and, through his writing, so did his readers.

> Around the dead rhino the scene was lit up both by the moon and by the flicker of trees. The porters made their camp under a small tree a

dozen rods to one side of the carcass, building a low circular fence of branches on which they hung their bright-colored blankets, two or three big fires blazing to keep off possible lions. Half as far on the other side of the rhino a party of naked savages had established their camp, if camp it could be called, for really all they did was to squat down round a couple of fires with a few small bushes disposed round about. The rhino had been opened, and they had already taken out of the carcass what they regarded as the tidbits and what we certainly did not grudge them. Between the two camps lay the huge dead beast, his hide glistening in the moonlight. In each camp the men squatted around the fires chatting and laughing as they roasted strips of meat on long sticks, the fitful blaze playing over them, now leaving them in darkness, now bringing them out into a red relief.

Roosevelt entered far enough into the spirit of the country to eat the heart of the first elephant he killed, a great bull with monumental tusks, bagged on the slopes of Mount Kenya. But for the rest he remained distinctly an outlander, a keeper of civilization in the wildest region of the earth. Roosevelt may or may not have intended the stark—to the point of humorous—juxtaposition of one scene in which he had just put his knife through the brain of a deadly puff adder. "I slipped it into my saddle pocket," he wrote, "where its blood stained the pigskin cover of the little pocket 'Nibelungenlied' which that day I happened to carry." Roosevelt wrote of reading Poe on the upper Nile, of feeling a flush of patriotic pride on receiving a cable telling of Peary's winning the race to the North Pole, of listening with delight to the pupils of an American missionary sing the first two lines of "The Star-Spangled Banner"—phonetically: They had no idea what the words meant.

Seeing all the sights he described and killing all those animals took a long time: The grand safari lasted nearly a year. It ended at Khartoum in March 1910. "Kermit and I parted from our comrades of the trip with real regret; during the year we spent together there had not been a jar, and my respect and liking for them had grown steadily." Roosevelt also regretted taking leave of his "faithful black followers." He noted that he had been sick, with fever, only five days out of the whole; he ventured the opinion that this malady had nothing to do with Africa but rather was a recurrence of an illness contracted in Cuba on the Santiago campaign. Thus the great hunter closed his account with a reminder that he was also a war hero.

VI

Roosevelt's published version was how he wanted his public to perceive his expedition. He didn't dwell on certain other aspects of the journey—for example, the relatively soft life of the hunter who could afford to travel first class, as he did. "My tent is so comfortable (a warm bath and a cup of tea always ready for me when I come in after the day's hunt) and the food so good, that I feel rather as if I was having more luxury than was good for me," he wrote Bamie. And this comfortable tent was the rudest of his accommodations. During several stretches of the safari he stayed in the houses of the British settler aristocracy, including the Lord and Lady Delamere, master and mistress of a one-hundred-thousand-acre spread in Kenya, where they had established themselves as the foremost members of a modern, if comparatively enlightened, feudal nobility. Only slightly less elegant was the ranch of Sir Alfred Pease, an inveterate hunter who, having sampled the game of most of the African continent, had settled in the East African highlands for the moment. He also stayed with the William McMillans, a pair of American expatriates who felt honored to play host to their native country's former chief executive. "After returning from hunting today," he reported to Bamie from the McMillans', "I am sitting on the cool verandah of a very nice house with a beautiful garden around it."

Roosevelt and Kermit were treated to the best hospitality the white settlers of the region could provide, which, reflecting the pains they took to re-create the life of England in the bush, was quite good. From the evidence of the meals the two Roosevelts were served, they might as well have been in London. July 1909 found them in Nairobi for a transplanted version of race week at Ascot. Roosevelt was too old to take a mount in the running, but Kermit did, to his own amusement and his father's pride.

Indeed, Kermit's growing competence was one of the highlights of the trip for Roosevelt. From the time Seth Bullock had taken the boy hunting in the Badlands and told his father that it was "really astonishing how the little fellow can ride and shoot," Roosevelt had known he had the makings of a hunter on his hands. But even he was surprised at the prowess his second son now displayed. "Do you remember how timid he used to be?" Roosevelt asked Corinne. "Well, my trouble with him now is that he is altogether too bold, pushing daring into recklessness." Roosevelt related how Kermit had approached a rhinoceros just the day before. "He was as cool as if it had been a rabbit." Early in the trip Kermit experienced some trouble mastering aim with the big hunting rifles; this made his habit of exposing himself to charging rhinos, elephants, and lions the more disconcerting. But with practice he improved markedly. "Kermit has become a really notable hunter," Roosevelt said toward the end, "and has accomplished feats that would have been utterly beyond me even in my prime."

Shooting wild animals and worrying about Kermit occupied most of Roosevelt's hours in Africa, but not all of them. Writing his articles for *Scribner's* filled a regular portion of every day. Since becoming vice president he had essentially stopped writing for publication—with the obvious exception of his official presidential messages to Congress and the like. He realized that, whatever disclaimers he might make, there was no such thing as an unofficial published opinion by the president of the United States; consequently, he had to weigh every word for its effect on the stock market, on the state of U.S.-Japanese relations, on editorial opinion in the South, and on a hundred other situations, ninety of which no one could know in advance. It was easier simply not to.

Now he was a comparatively free lance. Of course his writings would certainly be scrutinized, but the scrutiny given the scribblings of an ex-president were of an entirely different order than that applied to an incumbent. And whatever unwarranted conclusions people might draw from their scrutiny were *their* problem, not his—and not that of the United States. For the *warranted* conclusions, Roosevelt was happy to assume responsibility.

Since becoming governor of New York he had always had a stenographer handy to take dictation; not so in the African bush. Each day after the hunt he pulled out a pencil and a thick pad of paper and wrote his articles in the hand he had always complained about being so slow and painful. As regular as clockwork he filed his dispatches, sending them by runner from camp or ranch to the nearest outpost of civilization, whence they would be forwarded to New York. He often sent a second copy by an alternate route, in case lion, hippo, or other mischance befell the first runner. Although *Scribner's* doubtless would have tolerated some slippage from an ex-president encountering unusual circumstances far from home, he never missed a deadline.

His promptness was mostly a matter of personal pride; having committed to deliver the goods at a particular time, he was determined to make good his pledge. But it also reflected his appreciation that now that his political career was over, writing was going to supply most of his income, and consequently it behooved him to heed the business end of the craft. He urged his editors at *Scribner's* to begin running his articles as soon as possible. "My coming here has attracted attention to the country and everybody is starting to forestall the market by writing a book about it." He had heard that no less than eight volumes on hunting in East Africa were in the works. "The object of course is to forestall our book. Therefore if our first chapter can come out in the October or November issue of the magazine, it will be from every standpoint advisable."

Money matters of another sort caused him concern as well. The expedition was proving quite expensive, more than Roosevelt or its sponsors had reckoned. The party eventually numbered more than two hundred, counting porters, saises, tent-boys, gun-bearers, and other helpers. Although the natives came cheap by American standards, they didn't come free. And the special requirements of a scientific expedition added to the costs. As Roosevelt pointed out in a letter to Andrew Carnegie, the principal underwriter of the trip, hauling four tons of salt—for preserving the hides—across the outback of East Africa ran through money pretty rapidly. By the beginning of June 1909 it appeared that the expedition would have to be cut short if more support couldn't be summoned fairly soon. Roosevelt calculated that thirty thousand dollars would be necessary to do the job right. "My dear Sir," the ex-president addressed the ex-steelman, "I know the multitude of demands made upon you, and it may very well be that it is out of the question for you to give such a sum." But if not, the money would be put to good use. "If you feel that you can give it I shall of course be greatly relieved and I believe that you will be rendering a great service to science."

Carnegie came up with the money, partly from love of science and learning but also, no doubt, from hope that it would cause Roosevelt to listen to what his benefactor had to say on subjects rather removed from natural history. As he had for some years, Carnegie was pushing arbitration as an alternative to war in solving international disputes. He knew that Roosevelt would be speaking to various heads of state and government in Europe after emerging from Africa; if Roosevelt, the apostle of armed strength, could be persuaded to pitch arbitration, Carnegie's thousands would be well spent.

In the event, Roosevelt did put in a word for Carnegie's cause, although not as loud a word as the philanthropic pacifist would have liked. Whether Carnegie thought he got his money's worth out of the African expedition is uncertain.

For himself, Roosevelt judged the trip worth the cost. He spent some twenty thousand dollars of his own money on the year's diversion for himself and Kermit. This was more than would have been required to amuse them at Oyster Bay, although not out of line on a per capita basis (per animal capita, that is) with what he had been known to spend bagging big game in the American West. He had the additional satisfaction of knowing that he was contributing to the advancement of science and that his children and many others down the decades would gaze in wonder at the depictions of African wildlife made possible by the exploits of Theodore Roosevelt, Hunter. Sagamore Hill would also benefit, as several of the finest trophies were heading back to the shores of Long Island Sound.

VII

By the end of the safari Roosevelt wished that he himself were heading back there, too. "I want to go home!" he wrote in February 1910. "I am homesick for my own land and my own people! Of course it is Mrs. Roosevelt I most want to see; but I want to see my two youngest boys; I want to see my own house, my own books and trees, the sunset over the sound from the window in the north room, the people with whom I have worked, who think my thoughts and speak my speech."

This particular letter has to be taken with a few grains of all that salt Andrew Carnegie was buying, for it was written to Carnegie by way of explaining why Roosevelt couldn't do everything Carnegie wanted for arbitration, disarmament, and peace. Yet Roosevelt's feelings were no less genuine for being convenient. He did indeed miss Edith. "Oh, sweetest of all sweet girls," he wrote her from camp in November 1909, "last night I dreamed that I was with you, and that our separation was but a dream; and when I waked up it was almost too hard to bear. Well, one must pay for everything; you have made the real happiness of my life; and so it is natural and right that I should constantly [be] more and more lonely without you."

A recent happening of no intrinsic consequence had brought to mind happy memories of their life together.

> The other day I sat down under a tree and found my clothes covered with "pitch-forks"; and laughed so as I thought of the Sweet Cicily at home. Do you remember all about the Sweet Cicily, you darling? Do you remember when you were such a pretty engaged girl, and said to your lover "no Theodore, that I cannot allow"? Darling, I love you so. In a very little over three months I shall see you, now. When you get this over three-fourths of the time will have gone. How very happy we have been for these twenty-three years! Five days hence, on the 17th, is the anniversary of our engagement.

He closed this letter, "Kiss Ethel and the two little boys for me— they really are hardly 'little boys' any longer. . . . YOUR OWN LOVER."

Roosevelt was delighted and gratified that Edith undertook the arduous and hardly hazard-free journey up the Nile to meet him and Kermit at Khartoum. Ethel accompanied her mother; Archie and Quentin had gone back to America to school.

Besides bringing herself and Ethel, Edith brought exciting news that Ted was engaged to be married. Amid the emotions of his reunion with Edith, this news afforded Roosevelt occasion to reflect again on what his own marriage had meant in his life; he related some of these reflections to his son and the bride-to-be, along with his hopes that they be so lucky. To Eleanor Alexander, Ted's betrothed, he wrote that he welcomed her into the family "with all my heart"; he added, "There is nothing in the world that equals the happiness that comes to lovers who remain lovers all through their wedded lives, and who are not only devoted to each other, but wise and forbearing and gentle, as well." To Ted he explained: "Cunning Mother, looking very pretty and triumphant and mischievous, told me that she had advised Eleanor, with me as an awful example—but would not tell me what she had said! She was so charming, and felt so much that she had both been wise and scored off me that I had to keep kissing her while she told me."

Roosevelt went on to offer some paternal advice, which he asked Ted to pass along to Eleanor as well. "Greatly tho I loved Mother I was at times thoughtless and selfish, and if Mother had been a mere unhealthy Patient Griselda, I might have grown set in selfish and inconsiderate ways. Mother, always tender, gentle and considerate, and always loving, yet when necessary pointed out where I was thoughtless and therefore inconsiderate and selfish, instead of submitting to it. Had she not done this it would in the end have made her life very much harder, and mine very much less happy."

VIII

Roosevelt's regard for Edith was one cause, among several, of his getting into what he described as "every kind of muss" on the return trip through Europe. From Khartoum, the four—Theodore, Edith, Kermit, and Ethel—traveled by steamer and train downriver to Cairo. Along the way they took in the sights, ancient and less so. Much was the same as on Roosevelt's visit forty years earlier, but much, including the British occupation, was different. In British East Africa, Roosevelt had remarked that he was "a pretty good Imperialist"; it had showed then, and it showed now. He thoroughly approved of the civilizing work the British were doing in Egypt—although skeptics might have asked, and did, what the British could teach the country that had invented civilization thousands of years before the inhabitants of what would be called Britain stopped running around in skins and face paint. Roosevelt waved the imperialist flag in an address at the National University at Cairo, praising the British and telling them to keep up the fine job.

From Alexandria the party sailed to Italy, where Roosevelt provoked what he called "an elegant row." He hoped to see the pope, and Pius X indicated he would be willing to grant an audience. But the pontiff imposed the condition that the former president refrain from visiting an American Methodist mission in the city. Roosevelt refused the condition, which caused the Methodists to gloat in unseemly triumph—whereupon Roosevelt canceled his visit to *them*. He settled for meeting King Victor Emmanuel—and for recharging his supply of righteous indignation. "As for the Vatican incident," he told a friend, "really I don't see how there is room for the slightest difference of opinion. I acted in the only possible way that anyone could act, and in my judgment no man is a good American who fails heartily to support me for it."

Shortly after leaving Rome, Roosevelt caused the stir involving Edith. Kaiser Wilhelm invited the former president to stay at the royal palace—the Schloss—in Berlin. But the invitation said nothing about Edith. Roosevelt replied that while he was honored at the invitation, he could not be separated from his wife; the couple would stay at the American embassy. American diplomats, recognizing the mercurial character of the kaiser, momentarily panicked: Lesser slights than this had caused the emperor to threaten war. Roosevelt stood firm; any place he went, Edith must go.

Fortunately, the kaiser proved a gentleman as well as a monarch. His spokesman sent word that the failure to include Edith had been an oversight; of course the former First Lady was invited to the palace.

Roosevelt had what he called "a most interesting time with the Kaiser," whom he had never met until now. The highlight of the visit was a mock battle the Prussian forces staged for Roosevelt's benefit. Photographers recorded the event; Wilhelm sent Roosevelt prints, with some "really amusing comments of his own pencilled on the backs," as Roosevelt informed Lodge.

With each passing week the agenda grew more crowded. Everyone wanted a piece of Roosevelt, by this time quite possibly the most famous man on earth. He and Edith spun across the continent in "a perfect whirl" of activity. They breakfasted, dined, and supped with majesties, ministers, and diverse other dignitaries in the capitals of Austria, Hungary, France, Belgium, Holland, Denmark, and Norway. In Norway, Roosevelt delivered a belated acceptance speech for his 1906 Nobel Peace Prize. The broad topic, appropriately, was international peace, but while the address lacked the robustness of many of his speeches, it was rather more forceful than Andrew Carnegie would have wished. "Peace is generally good in itself," Roosevelt allowed, "but it is never the highest good unless it comes as the handmaid of righteousness." And righteousness came only to the brave. "No man is worth calling a man who will not fight rather than submit to infamy or see those that are dear to him suffer wrong. No nation deserves to exist if it permits itself to lose the stern and virile virtues." This said, Roosevelt went on to endorse measures to facilitate arbitration treaties, to lend greater authority to The Hague courts, to encourage a carefully qualified disarmament, and to establish a "League of Peace," a consortium of like-minded great powers that would enforce good behavior on potential miscreants.

For six weeks the pace never slackened. Roosevelt had long since become adept at fending off invitations, but even he found it a "soul-harrowing business" trying to make and keep a schedule devised on the fly across several countries. "Literally every minute of my time in Europe seems to be disposed of," he complained. The worst offenders were royalty, who appeared to think he had nothing better to do than arrange, rearrange, and rearrange again his and Edith's itinerary to suit them. Of the royal offenders, the worst was Edward VII of England. "I am mad as a wet hen, and I know that you will pardon my democratic soul for wishing the royalties would be a trifle more considerate," he wrote Arthur Lee.

Edward's final act of inconsiderateness was to die suddenly, which threw Roosevelt's—and, it seemed, half of Europe's—schedule utterly awry. Roosevelt attended the funeral as President Taft's special emissary; in the process he upstaged the deceased. Everyone wanted to see the former president, including (the new) King George and Queen Mary, Kaiser Wilhelm (again) and the other royals (ditto for most of them) in town for the funeral, Rudyard Kipling, Arthur Conan Doyle, Edward Grey, George Trevelyan, the Lord Mayor of London, Andrew Carnegie (who came to critique the Nobel speech), and a host of others. One person Roosevelt avoided was Winston Churchill, whom he considered a shady self-promoter.

While in England, Roosevelt received honorary degrees from Oxford and Cambridge, and gave a number of speeches, including two full-dress lectures. The first, at London's Guildhall, was billed "A Plain Talk on Egypt"; in it Roosevelt returned the favor for all the hospitality he had received in East Africa and along the Nile. The second, the annual Oxford Romanes lecture, put a Rooseveltian spin on Social Darwinism, drawing analogies between the biological and historical spheres. The great nations were great, he said, because of their peculiar fitness for the conditions of the modern age. But they would remain great only as long as they served the interests not merely of themselves but of less advanced nations and peoples. Roosevelt called for imperialism with a conscience. "In the long run there can be no justification for one race managing or controlling another unless the management and control are exercised in the interest and for the benefit of that other race." Bearing this in mind, countries like the United States and Britain must forge ahead, doing what they did best, for their own benefit and that of those peoples who fell under their sway.

In the process they might make themselves more prosperous and powerful; but they might not. Historical evolution, like biological evolution, held no guarantees. Yet they would gain the satisfaction of having attempted great things. "Let us strive hardily for success, even if by doing so we risk failure, spurning the poor souls of small endeavor, who know neither failure nor success. Let us hope that our own blood shall continue in the land, that our children and our children's children to endless generations shall arise to take our places and play a mighty and dominant part in the world. But whether this be denied or granted by the years we shall not see, let at least the satisfaction be ours that we have carried onward the lighted torch in our own day and generation."

CHAPTER TWENTY-SIX

Retirement Ruined
1910–11

T he president of the United States may or may not have read Roosevelt's ode to struggle; Will Taft was a busy man in the spring of 1910, with much on his calendar and more on his mind. But if he did read it, he surely groaned, for he could have sensed that Roosevelt's incessant need to be fighting something would soon afflict his administration and his equanimity.

The rift that developed between Roosevelt and Taft was a political fiasco. It revealed, among other things, how little lasting imprint Roosevelt had left on his party and how tenuous were his triumphs as president. In taking on Taft, Roosevelt rode to the rescue—he hoped—of his own legacy.

Yet the split between these two friends was more than a political fiasco; it was a personal tragedy. Even as it fractured the Republican Party, it revealed the corrosive egotism intrinsic—if often latent—in Roosevelt's romantic conception of life. It broke Taft's heart; it would have broken Roosevelt's if he hadn't long ago placed his heart out of reach of such things.

II

The first slight was barely perceptible—except to Roosevelt. On election night in November 1908, even as the returns were tallying his victory, Taft wrote Roosevelt an effusive letter conveying his "deep gratitude" to the president and acknowledging that "you have always been the chief agent in working out the present status of affairs." This was music to Roosevelt's ears and doubtless reconfirmed his high opinion of his protégé. But in this same letter Taft also mentioned his older half-brother, whose money had financed much of the campaign. "You and my brother Charley made that possible which in all probability would not have occurred otherwise," the president-elect declared.

In the glow of their great mutual triumph, Roosevelt responded in the same warm language he had been employing with Taft for years: "You are the only man whom we could have nominated that could have been elected. . . . All those who love you, who admire you and believe in you, and are proud of your great and fine qualities, must feel a thrill of exultation."

Yet Taft's reference to Charley bothered him. Almost certainly Roosevelt never consciously thought of himself as Taft's older brother; even so, the obvious affection he lavished on Taft made clear that much more was involved than a political succession. In his own mind, Roosevelt refashioned Taft into a younger version of himself. He kept projecting his own fighting qualities onto Taft; he insisted that they had the same enemies and the same friends. And they had the same goals: Taft would carry on in his footsteps.

Before long, Roosevelt would discover that he was mistaken about Taft politically. But even before then, the reminder that Taft already *had* an older brother, who could help in him ways Roosevelt could not, irked him. He seems to have kept his annoyance on this point to himself for nearly two years; yet he didn't forget it. And after he found other reasons for questioning his judgment regarding Taft, he gave it voice. During the summer of 1910 he was privately recorded as saying that attributing Taft's victory to himself and Charley was like saying that "Abraham Lincoln and the bond seller Jay Cook saved the Union."

III

Other slights were more prosaic. Just after receiving the nomination in June 1908, Taft evidently made some statement to Roosevelt to the effect that he would be happy to retain those members of the president's cabinet who wished to stay on. Roosevelt, taking this as endorsement of his own judgment, apparently shared this welcome intelligence with the individuals involved. But during the next several months the candidate and then president-elect decided that in certain cases he might be better served by individuals who owed their appointments to him rather than to Roosevelt. The fact that he failed to consult with Roosevelt in the replacements didn't help matters.

The background of Taft's appointees caused Roosevelt further concern. Six of the nine cabinet secretaries were lawyers by training and profession; as Republicans in good standing they had been found far more often on the side of business than of labor, consumers, or the other groups Roosevelt loved to champion. Taft defended his choices on the ground that none knew better how to regulate corporations than corporate lawyers; to Roosevelt and even more to those Roosevelt partisans who had hated to see their hero relinquish the presidency and harbored hopes that he would reclaim it, Taft's cabinet looked as though it might have been selected by Pierpont Morgan himself.

Among the many who refused to transfer their loyalty to the new occupant of the White House was Cabot Lodge. A few other leading Republicans might reasonably have complained of being overlooked by the new administration; not Lodge, who was the person first offered the position of secretary of state. But Lodge liked his seat in the Senate and didn't want to give it up to serve with Taft, and he declined. Despite this recognition, Lodge soon started whispering in Roosevelt's ear (to be sure, via mail delivered across six thousand miles, the last leg often covered by barefoot runner) at the disappointment that was developing about Taft. Gubernatorial elections in the fall of 1909 saw significant Democratic gains; Lodge, looking to the future, was worried. "I feel anything but easy about next year," he said.

A noisy squabble during that winter led to the removal of Roosevelt's friend and fellow forest-lover Gifford Pinchot. As Lodge acknowledged, Pinchot brought his ouster upon himself by allowing disagreement with Interior Secretary Richard Ballinger to escalate into insubordination. But the political repercussions for the party might be drastic and dangerous. "The general feeling in the country is that Pinchot represents the people and your policy of Conservation, which is true, and that Ballinger and the administration represent opposition, which is not true. But that is what the country thinks and you cannot get it out of the public mind."

Lodge wasn't the only one providing Roosevelt political intelligence. Pinchot pleaded his own case in a sixteen-point indictment of Taft. A few of the points of this bill of particulars were substantive; most were of the guilt-by-association variety ("He has affiliated himself in Congress with the leaders of the opposition to the Roosevelt policies and the makers of personal attacks upon yourself"). Pinchot averred, unconvincingly, that he was giving Taft "the benefit of every doubt"; if so, he wouldn't have been so quick to declare, "We have fallen back down the hill you led us up." Like Lodge he argued from popular perception: "There is a general belief that the special interests are once more substantially in full control of both Congress and the administration." Unlike Lodge, he forthrightly added, "In that belief I share."

Precisely how general this belief was remained an item of no little controversy during the spring and summer of 1910. But the increasing influence of the reactionaries inclined many Republican progressives to recall their leader from his self-imposed exile. "There is a constantly growing thought of you and your return to the Presidency," Lodge reported.

IV

Roosevelt could have squelched such thoughts by simply stating that his no-third-term pledge still applied. But he didn't. For one of the few times in his life he was of two minds about a subject. Half of him wanted to give Taft the benefit of the doubt, at least for a while longer. "It is a very ungracious thing for an ex-President to criticize his successor," he wrote Pinchot. All administrations had troubles; Taft ought to be allowed the opportunity to work his administration's troubles out. On this same side there was the additional consideration that Taft's failure would, in a certain sense, be Roosevelt's own failure—failure of judgment, if nothing else. Roosevelt wasn't ready to admit that he had made a mistake in tapping Taft as his successor.

On the other hand, Roosevelt remained as ambitious as ever, and as committed to the national interest. And, as ever, he couldn't tell the difference between the two. He had loved the spotlight of the presidency, both for what it did for him and for what it enabled him to do for the country. After telling Pinchot how ungracious it would be to criticize Taft, in the next breath he declared, "And yet I cannot as an honest man cease to battle for the principles which you and I and Jim [Garfield] and [Herbert Knox] Smith and Moody and the rest of our close associates stood." Roosevelt had devoted decades to the struggle for these principles, and he couldn't allow excessive fastidiousness to hold him back from the fight now.

This ambivalence caused Roosevelt to keep his options open. Following Lodge's advice, he declined during his European tour to comment publicly on the situation in the United States. Against Lodge's advice, he met with Pinchot, who came over to Italy. Lest this seem a slap at Taft, Roosevelt also met with Elihu Root, now a New York senator but rightly still judged a Republican regular and a Taft supporter.

In maintaining silence on American politics, and on his own intentions, Roosevelt naturally believed he was acting out of devotion to the nation's best interests. "I am absolutely free to act as I deem wise for the country, in any way, and shall keep my freedom," he assured Lodge. When Lodge again raised the possibility of a return to the White House, Roosevelt responded that he desired nothing for himself. "I have had the crown, I have had everything possible, and there is nothing left for me to grasp at." He went on to assert that the question had to be considered "purely from the standpoint of the needs of the party and the country." He added, "I shall neither seek nor shirk responsibility."

V

From the distance of several thousand miles it was possible for Roosevelt to believe that the apparent enthusiasm for him might simply be a case of absence making the heart grow fonder. Safari life had left him time to ponder such matters, and he did. Writing from the slopes of Mount Kenya, he told Lodge that perhaps a life outside politics would afford him the greatest opportunity to do good. Indeed, he wasn't sure how much good he could do even as an outsider. "People easily grow tired of the advice of a man whose day is past," he said. Lest Lodge think this melodramatic, he continued, "The last statement sounds melancholy, but it really isn't; I know no other man who has had as good a time as I have had in life; no other President ever enjoyed the Presidency as I did; no other ex-President ever enjoyed himself as I am now enjoying myself, and as I think it likely I shall enjoy myself in the future. The American people have left me heavily in their debt; and I appreciate the fact."

But the closer he got to home, the more he realized that the enthusiasm for him was real, and that he would probably enjoy himself most of all back in the thick of the political fight. He had refused any elaborate farewell ceremony in March 1909, explaining that his safari might prove "a flat failure"; if this happened, it would be "most ridiculous and humiliating to look back on anything in the nature of a send-off." Now, of course, it was obvious that the trip had *not* been a failure but a great success—followed by a still greater success in the capitals of Europe. Even had he wanted to, which he didn't, he couldn't have prevented the riotous greeting that welcomed him back to New York.

The gods set the stage, bowing to what was widely interpreted as the "Roosevelt luck." Just hours before his arrival a tremendous storm raked across the city; more than a dozen people died in the rain, wind, and lightning. But the thunder fell silent, the clouds parted, and the sun broke through as the *Kaiserin Augusta Victoria* approached Staten Island on the morning of June 16, 1910. As the ship steamed majestically up the harbor, hundreds of small watercraft vied for the honor of being nearly rammed by it or being sucked into its wake or crashing into one of the six battleships or sundry smaller vessels of war that constituted the Navy Department's greeting to its most famous former assistant secretary. A twenty-one-gun salute from Fort Wadsworth rolled across the water but was almost lost amid the shrieks, blares, gongs, and booms of the whistles, horns, bells, and sirens of the unofficial armada. The hero himself answered the summons by going topside. "When he reached the bridge," an eyewitness recorded, "such a shout went up from the shore as to waken the stones."

The mayor of New York met the ship at the Battery, offering the city to its favorite son. Roosevelt descended the gangway to more cheers, then entered a carriage—one of fourteen—for a parade up Broadway. A regiment of mounted Rough Riders and a hundred-piece military band, along with assorted other Spanish war veterans and two Oklahoma boys, aged six and ten, who had ridden horseback all the way from their home for the great occasion, accompanied the former president's vehicle. For five slow miles north, the hero rode a wave of adulation through a sea of sound.

On this day all loved him; all were thrilled to have the hero back. Those who knew and loved him best were most thrilled, but they were also slightly puzzled. He seemed changed. Archie Butt noted:

> He was just the same in manner, in appearance, in expression, yet there was something different. We, all of us who had been closely associated with him in the past, felt it. I spoke of it. Senator Lodge spoke of it. Secretary Meyer, who is not keen to see much, he even spoke of it; and so did Nick [Longworth]. Loeb and I, for we rode together in the procession, talked almost entirely of him and each of us felt that there was a change in him. Mr. Meyer thought he had grown older, but it wasn't that. Loeb, Senator Lodge, and I figured it out to be simply an enlarged personality. To me he had ceased to be an American, but had become a world citizen. His horizon seemed to be greater, his mental scope more encompassing.

Butt conceded that he couldn't offer any single bit of irrefutable evidence to document the change. "But it is there. He is bigger, broader, capable of greater good or greater evil, I don't know which, than when he left."

VI

Good or evil: That was the question on everyone's mind during the summer of 1910—with the answer, needless to say, depending on one's relationship to Roosevelt. The question was certainly on the mind of Taft, who didn't know but definitely wondered what his relationship to Roosevelt was. To find out he invited his mentor to Washington.

Roosevelt refused the invitation, politely but decidedly. "I don't think it well for an ex-President to go to the White House, or indeed to go to Washington, except when he cannot help it," he told Taft without saying quite why.

Taft might have been forgiven for thinking that Roosevelt didn't want to share the glory he was basking in, or that he was plotting a return to power. The former reason for Roosevelt's standoffishness may have applied, but not the latter—yet. He simply didn't know where he stood or ought to stand on Taft. Should he listen to Lodge and the other whisperers or stick with the man he had installed as his successor?

Yet not even the most famous man on earth could wholly snub the president of the United States, and on a trip to Massachusetts to see Lodge—and weigh his political options further—Roosevelt detoured to Beverly, Taft's summer residence. Lodge came along for moral support and perhaps to act as a witness to what was said, if witnessing became necessary.

The meeting began warmly enough. Taft offered both his hands to his guest, saying, "Ah, Theodore, it is good to see you."

Roosevelt took the hands and replied, "How are you, Mr. President? This is simply bully."

"See here now, drop the 'Mr. President,'" Taft said, clapping Roosevelt on the shoulder.

"Not at all. You must be Mr. President and I am Theodore. It must be that way."

Perhaps it was the force of habit, as he claimed, or perhaps something in him decided that if Roosevelt was going to be formal, so was he; but from whatever cause, Taft spent the rest of the visit calling his guest "Mr. President." The atmosphere was strained, notwithstanding Taft's further efforts at ice-breaking, including the body language of taking Roosevelt by the arm and leading him to an easy chair on the veranda. Roosevelt obviously felt the strain; when the butler appeared and inquired what the gentlemen would like for refreshments, Roosevelt uncharacteristically responded that he needed a Scotch and soda.

The two men talked about New York politics; they agreed that the Republican Party looked hard up and likely would lose the governor's race in the fall. The tension of the gathering grew with the arrival of Mrs. Taft, who was known to be very suspicious of Roosevelt's intentions.

Taft tried to improve the mood by changing the subject. "Now, Mr. President, tell me about cabbages and kings," he said.

"Ah, I see you remember *Alice in Wonderland*," Roosevelt replied. Evidently as eager as Taft to get onto safer ground, Roosevelt proceeded to describe his adventures among the crowned heads of Europe. From this point the conversation went smoothly, indeed swimmingly, since neither Taft nor anyone else got a chance to inject more than an infrequent word into Roosevelt's soliloquy.

After an hour Roosevelt rose to take his leave. Lodge suggested that the president and the former president decide on a statement to release to the several score of reporters waiting outside the gate. Roosevelt proposed saying simply that he had paid a personal call on the president and that the two had had a delightful afternoon. "Which is true as far as I am concerned," he added.

"And more than true as far as I am concerned," Taft answered. "This has taken me back to some of those dear old afternoons when I was Will and you were Mr. President."

VII

Though Taft clearly desired to recapture the friendliness of those dear old days, they were gone forever. With each passing week, and each disgruntled progressive who dropped by Oyster Bay to mutter, Roosevelt grew ever more convinced that the president wasn't the man he had hoped he would be. "I very keenly share your disappointment in Taft," he confided to Pinchot, "and in a way perhaps feel it even more deeply than you do, because it was I who made him President."

All the same, Roosevelt, a loyal party man his entire career, at this stage saw no alternative to closing ranks behind the president. "It behooves us to realize that it is not only possible, but probable, that two years hence circumstances will be such as to make it necessary to renominate Taft, and eminently desirable to re-elect him over anyone whom there is the least likelihood of the Democrats naming."

A sizable and growing portion of the Republican Party couldn't have disagreed more strongly, certainly with the first part of

Roosevelt's statement. The progressive insurgents were disgusted with Taft and the congressional old guard led by Aldrich in the Senate and Cannon in the House. Particular issues—the Payne-Aldrich tariff of 1909, conservation, child-labor laws, the use of the injunction in strikes—divided the insurgents from the regulars, but beneath the dissatisfaction of the former was their conviction that the latter were delivering control of the party, and the government, back to the same big-money mossbacks from whom Roosevelt had rescued it nine years earlier.

The divide deepened as the campaign of 1910 heated up. Each camp sought to enlist Roosevelt's support. The ex-president found himself "in a position of inconceivable difficulty," as he told Arthur Lee. "The ultra-Taft people have been bent on making me come out for Taft in a way which would, in the first place, represent insincerity on my part, and in the next place, would simply cause me to lose all my hold on my own supporters." Roosevelt remarked the folly of such demands, noting that if he lost his supporters he wouldn't be able to do Taft any good. On the other hand, the insurgents were shouting for him to announce his opposition. "The extremists have been wild to have me break with Taft." Issues of party loyalty aside, the extremists tended hard toward impracticality, rendering much of their energy self-defeating. Roosevelt reiterated that Taft appeared the best of the available alternatives. "I am not satisfied with him, but you and I who have been in practical politics and have actually tried public life, know that it is not often that one is able to be thoroughly satisfied; and when we cannot do the best, then, as Abraham Lincoln said, we have to do the best possible." Referring to his own role in elevating Taft, Roosevelt concluded, "It is to my personal interest that Taft should succeed himself; and all that I can conscientiously do to effect this will be done."

Roosevelt would have been incensed to hear himself described as slippery, but, consciously or not, he almost always managed to leave himself enough wriggle room to go in either of opposite directions. (The exception that—temporarily—proved the rule was his no-third-term pledge of 1904, which he was now in the process of reinterpreting.) The operative word in his letter to Lee was "conscientiously": As soon as he decided that supporting Taft ran against his conscience, he would release himself from any obligation. Nor in this case was his choice of language any accident: He repeated his argument almost word for word in a letter to James Garfield.

Roosevelt's self-releasing began shortly. He had hoped that the prospect of defeat in the coming election would concentrate the minds of his fellow Republicans long enough for them to present a semblance of unity to the voters. He was briefly encouraged as Taft and certain of the less extreme progressives collaborated on some modestly reformist legislation. But various elements among both the insurgents and the old guard appeared to prefer purity to success, and the bickering resumed, more bitter than ever.

Publicly, Roosevelt adopted a position of neutrality between the two factions. "I am not taking sides for or against any man in any contest for the nomination for any position," he declared in July. Yet this was a temporary expedient—perhaps sustainable in a season of congressional elections but probably untenable when the race for the grand prize of the White House drew closer.

With the party dissolving beneath his feet, Roosevelt wondered what it meant to be a Republican. "I am a practical politician," he told Nick Longworth, "and a believer in practical politics, but at the same time I am a Republican primarily because the Republican Party is the best instrument through which to do good to the nation." He hoped the party would continue to be the best instrument, but he was no longer as sure as he had been. "Really I feel rather despairing," he said.

Part of Roosevelt's discouragement reflected his age. At fifty-two he was hardly decrepit, but he had lost some of the boundless energy he'd had at thirty. Train rides seemed longer, his voice gave out sooner, and he suffered fools—including those who needed to be suffered in exchange for their votes—less gladly than before.

More of his discouragement resulted from his inability to decide precisely what the role of an ex-president ought to be. (If he now recalled a prophecy of Nicholas Murray Butler, his alienated former friend, the memory didn't improve his mood. "I do not fear for you in the presidency, Theodore," Butler had said in 1901. "Your most difficult task will come when you finally leave the White House. . . . It will be a lot harder for you, Theodore, to be an ex-President than President.") In theory Roosevelt admired the example of John Quincy Adams, who had not considered the House of Representatives to be beneath a former chief executive; but in practice he found demotion rather unappealing. His unwillingness to endorse Taft essentially shut him out of national Republican politics; this left the New York state party, for the moment at least, as the obvious vehicle for such ambitions as he hoped to indulge. "It is not a pleasant thing to have to go back twenty years and struggle for control in the State organization as I did when I was a young man," he remarked to Arthur Lee.

Most of all, though, Roosevelt's lack of enthusiasm for politics reflected his uncertainty as to what was the right thing for him to do. A large part of his famous energy had always derived from his moral certitude—which, if not quite the same as moral certainty, was even more effective in impelling him to action. Now he just didn't know. He couldn't support the administration without disappointing the most ardent of his followers and without himself swallowing what he deemed an unhealthy dose of corporate-coddling reaction. Yet he couldn't break with the administration without becoming that most despised of political pariahs—despised by himself, at any rate, for a quarter century—a mugwump. It was a grim choice. Commenting on a western speaking tour he had previously committed to, he said the very thought filled him with "perfect dread."

VIII

Dread, however, was not an emotion Roosevelt habitually harbored for long. And in any event the fresh air and big sky of the western plains always revived his spirits. Of course, the cheers that greeted him at every town and whistle-stop didn't hurt, either. New York, with its high concentration of millionaires, financiers, lawyers, and corporate officers, had always been a tough sell for Roosevelt; Kansas, Nebraska, the Dakotas, and the rest of the trans-Mississippi region, where the earth was liberally salted with farmers, ranchers, and other common folks, were far more friendly.

Roosevelt responded to the cheers with a series of speeches that put the nation on notice that, if he wasn't yet willing to break openly with the administration, he certainly was thinking about it. His most striking statement came at Osawatomie, Kansas—ominously, to those who already spied the mark of the zealot on Roosevelt's forehead, a central battlefield of the "bleeding Kansas" era of the 1850s. Roosevelt reminded his Republican listeners that theirs had been the party of labor—free labor, as opposed to slave labor—before it was the party of capital. "Labor is prior to, and independent of, capital," Roosevelt quoted Lincoln. "Capital is only the fruit of labor, and could never have existed if labor had not first existed. Labor is the superior of capital, and deserves much the higher consideration." Now, even more than in Lincoln's day, the Republicans must be the party of labor. Roosevelt conceded that capital had rights, too, but he laid far more stress on capital's obligations. "The true friend of property, the true conservative, is he who insists that property shall be the servant and not the master of the commonwealth; who insists that the creature of man's making shall be the servant and not the master of the man who made it. The citizens of the United States must effectively control the mighty commercial forces which they have themselves called into being."

Roosevelt proceeded to specify how this control should be effected. Extending the principle behind the establishment of the Bureau of Corporations, he advocated "complete and effective publicity of corporate affairs." Declaring antitrust legislation a demonstrated waste of time, he called instead for closer government supervision of business. "The effort at prohibiting all combinations has substantially failed. The way out lies, not in attempting to prevent such combinations, but in completely controlling them in the interest of the public welfare." He called for an effective ban on the use of corporate funds for political purposes. (This plank particularly galled those corporate donors whom George Cortelyou and Cornelius Bliss had strong-armed on Roosevelt's behalf in 1904.) He insisted that the directors of corporations be held directly responsible for lawbreaking by the firms they headed. He called for tariff revision, not by the business-as-usual means of logrolling and palm-greasing but on the advice of a commission of impartial experts. He urged the passage of workmen's compensation acts, laws regulating labor by women and children, and the establishment of practical job training for students not bound for higher education. Getting personal, he advocated a progressive income tax on the wealthy, and a graduated and effective inheritance tax.

Roosevelt called his program the "New Nationalism," although, as he pointed out when conservatives immediately cried revolution, there wasn't much really new about it. Most of the items on his agenda had appeared in one or another of his annual messages as president. Yet he had never stated his objectives so comprehensively or packaged them so concisely as a single approach to the country's problems. And the fact that he made the speech as part of a ceremony memorializing militant John Brown added a chilling edge to his demands for change.

Although Roosevelt rejected the label of insurgent, this speech, and his continued refusal to endorse Taft, identified him in the minds of both the insurgents and the regulars as a potential standard-bearer of the former. The Taft camp tried to smoke him out, hoping that his loyalty to the party would cause him to reconsider and close ranks against the Democrats. In mid-August, Roosevelt received a visit from Lloyd Griscom, a leader of the New York Republican regulars, inquiring as to whether he would accept the temporary chairmanship of the Republican state convention. Roosevelt, still ambivalent about an official return to politics, especially state politics, but concerned that otherwise the convention would fall to the control of the most hidebound of the old guard, with the inevitable corollary of a Tammany victory in the November elections, answered that he would.

At the same time Griscom delivered a message that Roosevelt interpreted as coming from Taft. Griscom explained that the president was distancing himself from Senator Aldrich and Speaker Cannon and the other reactionaries in Congress; henceforth he would take his cue from more moderate types. According to Griscom, the president's new advisers could include Roosevelt, if Roosevelt would declare outright for the president and his administration.

Roosevelt refused to bite. "I answered that the time to choose me, and those like me, as his advisers had gone by," he reported to Lodge, "and that in any event what was needed in the present was leadership, and not willingness to give the lead to Aldrich, Cannon and Tawney as long as they seemed strong, and to throw them over when they got weak." Roosevelt declared that responsibility for the break between himself and the president rested entirely with the latter; by his actions during the eighteen months after his election Taft had "deliberately abandoned" the close relations that had previously existed between them.

Undeterred by Roosevelt's negative response, Griscom tried again a few weeks later to bring the president and the former president together. Taft was coming to New York; Griscom asked Roosevelt if he would be willing to meet with him. Roosevelt said he would, adding that he would have done so even if Griscom had not made the suggestion.

As it turned out, the meeting, which was arranged in secrecy to minimize press speculation, took place in New Haven rather than New York—and almost didn't take place at all. The plan was for Roosevelt to cross over from Oyster Bay and rendezvous with Griscom at Black Rock Harbor, near Bridgeport; they would then drive to New Haven. But a gale blew up in the hours before Roosevelt set out, and nearly swamped Roosevelt's boat. An observer from the New York Yacht Club watched through binoculars as the former president's launch, a twenty-seven-knot speedster, leaped from one wave to the next—with Roosevelt "swaying from side to side as it bucked the waves and talking most energetically with the engineer." To all appearances the former assistant navy secretary was telling the engineer how to do his business—as he doubtless was.

The tempest prevented the boat's reaching Black Rock Harbor; instead it put in at Stamford, where Roosevelt—soaking wet and cold, but exhilarated—hired a car and driver. They drove to Bridgeport, with Roosevelt intending to transfer to Griscom's car, but discovered that that vehicle had a flat tire. So Griscom's group crowded into Roosevelt's rental, and with a police escort leading the way, all raced toward New Haven. They were nearly there when part of the transmission fell out of the car onto the road. Everyone clambered out while the driver rolled underneath to make repairs. Eventually the gears were reconnected, and the party completed its journey. By now, however, the secrecy surrounding the meeting had been shredded.

The session was unproductive. "Taft and [his secretary Charles] Norton were more than cordial, and made a point of being as pleasant as possible," Roosevelt remarked to Lodge shortly afterward. But this positive effect was spoiled when Norton, uncorrected by Taft, let out to reporters that Roosevelt had requested the meeting, hoping to gain Taft's support for the fight that was developing over control of the New York party convention.

Roosevelt was angered by Norton's maneuver, but unsurprised and indeed somewhat relieved. "It was probably necessary that one such incident should occur," he told Lodge, "and this was about as good a time as any other. Scores, I am inclined to say hundreds, of good people have kept asking me why I did not call and see the president, why I did not talk with him; and if they ask me anything more about it, I shall simply tell them that this experiment has shown me that when I do call, those close to the President industriously seek to try to humiliate me and put me in a wrong position because I have called."

The New Haven meeting and its denouement killed any hope that the breach between Roosevelt and Taft would be repaired in the near term. Feeling himself wronged (whether he really was wronged was a matter of interpretation), Roosevelt began to gather once again the moral momentum that had always powered his political crusades.

IX

The New York Republican convention, held at Saratoga in late September, quickly revived that part of Roosevelt's combative spirit which his meeting with Taft hadn't. "By George, this is bully!" he declared. "It is great to be back in the thick of the fight again. It reminds me of the old days when I was a member of the state Assembly." He judged that the actions of the regulars had absolved him "from all responsibility" for the party's welfare; consequently, he could make his fight purely on principle. And he thought he could win. When his train stopped at Troy on the way to Saratoga, he announced, "We are going to beat them to a frazzle; do not forget the word, frazzle. I came back from Africa with some trophies and when we get back from Saratoga we shall have some trophies."

"Frazzle" overstated the actual outcome. To be sure, Roosevelt was the center of attention. Several of the old guard were sitting on the porch of their Saratoga hotel when a young girl came up and asked, "Is Teddy Roosevelt here?" He wasn't just then, but the regulars took the query as indicative of their plight. "Oh, hell! What's the use?" one moaned. "Even the babies cry for Roosevelt. He is the whole three rings, ringmaster and elephant. Maybe he will let us into the show if we carry water for the elephant."

And Roosevelt did win his fight for the convention chairmanship.

With help, he persuaded the group to endorse the comparatively progressive accomplishments of Governor Charles Evans Hughes. He
also assisted in the nomination of friend and ally Henry Stimson for
governor. On the other hand, convention conservatives went considerably further than Roosevelt deemed desirable in congratulating
Taft and the Republican Congress for their fine work. Roosevelt
made the required nod in the direction of party unity by acknowledging "the credit which is rightly due to the Congress and to our able,
upright, and distinguished President, William Howard Taft," but his
list of worthy achievements had a decidedly different emphasis than
that of the Taftites. Although Roosevelt came away from Saratoga
claiming an "overwhelming" victory, less interested observers estimated that the balance of power in the party remained with the pro-
Taft forces.

Not that this meant much when election day arrived. The 1910
congressional balloting was a disaster for the Republicans. The G.O.P.
lost fifty-eight seats in the House of Representatives, yielding control
of that chamber to the Democrats for the first time since the
Democratic debacle of 1894. The Republicans maintained control of
the Senate but only because (as always) a mere third of the upper
house was vulnerable to replacement. As things were, the Democrats
slashed the Republicans' margin in the Senate from 29 to 10.

Some of Roosevelt's progressive friends indulged in a species of
schadenfreude toward the conservatives, believing that this discredit-
ing of the Republican regulars would pave the way for a progressive
takeover of the party. Roosevelt wasn't so sure. "The Tower of Siloam
is very apt to fall upon the just as well as upon the unjust when there
is an earthquake such as that through which we have just been," he
warned William Allen White. Yet Roosevelt did concur that the defeat
presented an opportunity. "While the Republican Party may be beaten
even if it stands for progressive policies, it will surely be beaten, and
what is more, deserve to be beaten, if it does not."

The Republicans' thrashing completed Roosevelt's reconversion to
politics. A few days after the election he wrote to Herbert Parsons: "I
want to see you and talk over certain things with you when we once
get far enough away from the election so that our meeting will not
cause too much comment." He didn't want to specify these "certain
things" in a letter, but Parsons, a progressively minded Republican

congressman who had just been swept away by the Democratic tidal wave, could guess—and hope. To White, Roosevelt was equally vague but more emphatic: "Win or lose, I am in this fight to a finish."

X

Yet the problem remained: What form should the fight take? The presidential contest of 1912 was two years away. What to do until then? For the first time in three decades Roosevelt found himself somewhat at loose ends. Before leaving for Africa he had arranged to become a contributing editor to the *Outlook,* Lyman Abbott's journal. He would write perhaps a dozen articles a year and in exchange receive twelve thousand dollars. Other journals had offered him more money, but he liked Abbott's approach. "The *Outlook* is of all the publications the one that comes nearest to representing my convictions," he told Lodge, "and its editors, altho I do not always agree with them by any means, are sincere, patriotic, painstaking men, who always try to practise what they preach." But an article a month was decidedly part-time work for Roosevelt; in younger years he could have fulfilled this obligation before breakfast and had the whole day free for other occupations.

To be sure, these weren't younger days. He lacked the energy he had had then; more tellingly, he lacked the drive. Writing to Ted from Sagamore Hill, he described his comparatively aimless routine. "Mother and I had a three hours ride yesterday; in the evening we sat in the north room before the blazing log fire, while a snow storm outside gradually turned into a blizzard." For once in his life inactivity suited him. "Twenty years ago, or even ten years ago, I should not have been contented, simply because I would have felt I had not any business not to be doing work. But I have not that feeling at all now. I am fifty-two, I have worked very hard for thirty years, and while I am perfectly willing to do more work if it comes in the line of a duty, I don't in the least feel that I must at all hazards find it to do; and I am perfectly willing to acquiesce in the view that it may be much the wisest thing not to try to do it, but to let duty jump with inclination, and stay home."

In his own house and under Edith's influence, Roosevelt began to luxuriate in his role as paterfamilias. The role, never hard, grew easier when word arrived that he was to be a grandfather. Ted and Eleanor had been married in June, just days after his and Edith's return from Europe; now, seven months later, Eleanor was pregnant. "It is all too good for anything," Roosevelt wrote Ted. "Home, wife, children— they are what really count in life. I have heartily enjoyed many things; the Presidency, my success as a soldier, a writer, a big game hunter and explorer; but all of them put together are not for one moment to be weighed in the balance when compared with the joy I have known with your mother and all of you." He added, "As merely a secondary thing, this house and the life here yield me constant pleasure. Really, the prospect of grandchildren was all that was lacking to make perfect mother's happiness and mine."

XI

Under other circumstances Roosevelt might have been content to live out his life in quiet retirement among his books and trophies. Such wasn't likely, but it was possible. His diverse intellectual interests could have kept him as busy as he wanted to be. During the winter of 1910–11 he was elected vice president of the American Historical Association, preparatory to being elevated to president the next year. As one who on occasion had scorned academic historians as small-minded seekers after the obscure and insignificant, he wasn't initially overwhelmed by the honor. On the other hand, it was nice to have his historical vision ratified by the leading group of professionals. During this same period he undertook to raise funds for the Smithsonian Institution, to be used to promote the publication of works dealing with such worthy projects as his trip to Africa. His touch, however, turned out to be less persuasive than that of his father, and he soon left the fund-raising to others. Meanwhile, he engaged in a lively, at times acrimonious, published debate regarding the function and purpose of protective coloration in birds and other small vertebrates.

But even had Roosevelt been willing to content himself with science and history, his fans wouldn't let him; they maneuvered to draw him back into the political fray. Republican progressives interpreted the party's shellacking in the 1910 elections as evidence of the necessity of a wholesale reorganization of the party. In January 1911, Senator Robert La Follette of Wisconsin and such other insurgents as Pinchot, William White, and California governor Hiram Johnson linked arms in something called the National Progressive Republican League. Not surprisingly, the rebels sought Roosevelt's imprimatur on their charter. "Now, Colonel," wrote La Follette, employing the title he knew Roosevelt liked best, "can't you consistently give this movement the benefit of your great name and influence? Practically all thoroughgoing progressives, senators, congressmen and governors have already joined." The Wisconsin lawmaker made a further pitch before finishing: "I do not presume to urge you"—although he had done just that—"but do sincerely hope that you will conclude to wire me that I may sign for you."

Roosevelt was skeptical. For some time he had treated the term "progressive" with caution, saying that he did not use it "in any factional spirit." Now La Follette and the others were asking him to do so, and to act on the new usage. Roosevelt wasn't sure he was ready for the change.

For one thing, he had mixed feelings about La Follette. "I think well of La Follette," he told Ted. "He is an able, forceful enthusiast. With most of his policies I am in entire accord. He is, however, an extremist, and has the touch of fanaticism which makes a man at times heedless of means in attaining his ends."

Moreover, it was only *most* of La Follette's policies Roosevelt was in accord with. He accepted such archetypally progressive measures as corrupt-practices laws, preferential primaries, and the direct election of senators; but he had reservations about others, including the initiative, referendum, and recall. These, he felt, should be used sparingly if ever. Otherwise, in the progressives' zeal to strengthen democracy, they might simply short-circuit it.

But most fundamentally, he wondered whether the La Follette group wasn't missing the point. Their proposed reforms were purely political; they didn't address what Roosevelt believed was the more crucial question of political economy: to wit, how to regulate industry in the public interest. To Roosevelt, La Follette and his allies were focusing on forms; what was needed was attention to substance.

Finally, Roosevelt questioned whether what appeared destined to be a third party was the most potent vehicle for achieving progressive reforms. For all his upset at the direction Taft was going, Roosevelt wasn't ready to abandon the party of his youth. He had been a Republican through victory and defeat, and the party had been very good to him in return. The conservatives held the upper hand at present; how long they would continue to do so was anyone's guess.

Yet even in registering his skepticism, Roosevelt refused to close any doors. He declined to join La Follette's league, but he expressed general support for its progressive principles—which, he assured La Follette, he would continue to endorse in such venues as the *Outlook*.

XII

He was as good as his word. Indeed, he was better—by many thousand words. Between January and April 1911, Roosevelt wrote a series of articles for the *Outlook* defining and defending what he called "the great movement of our day, the Progressive Nationalist movement against special privilege and in favor of an honest and efficient political and industrial democracy." As he did with most things he was associated with, Roosevelt defined Progressive Nationalism almost as much in terms of its enemies as of its objectives. These enemies included, most notably, "the dishonest man of swollen riches whose wealth has been made in ways which he desires to conceal from the law, and the politician who does not really believe in the right of the people to rule and who prefers to trust to corruption and class favoritism rather than to honesty and fair dealing in politics." Added to these were men who, while sincere and honest by their own lights, were misguided: the rich man who hadn't broken any laws but who had made his money by relying on special privilege, and the man who put property rights above human rights and rejected the idea that government might regulate business in order to secure the larger public interest.

Roosevelt applauded a recent book by journalist Herbert Croly, *The Promise of American Life,* calling it "the most profound and illuminating study of our national conditions which has appeared for many years." Roosevelt's applause obviously had much to do with the fact that Croly agreed with him on the need for energetic government activities to restrain the overweening power of corporations.

As promised, Roosevelt spoke warmly of La Follette's work, and with his earlier reservations somewhat eased, he embraced the Progressive Republican platform. He suggested certain additions: regulations to limit work by women and children, a program of workmen's compensation, guarantees of the right of labor to organize and bargain collectively, government inquiries into the causes of labor disputes.

Occasionally, Roosevelt animated his political exposition a bit. "The democracy, if it is to come to its own in this country, must set its face like steel against privilege and all the beneficiaries of privilege," he wrote. "It must war to cut out special privilege from our frame of government, and in doing so it must count upon the envenomed hostility, not only of the great industrial corporations and individuals who are the beneficiaries of privilege, but of their servants and adherents in the press and in public life." But compared to the vividness of his historical prose, his political essays were pretty dull—reminding readers why the Populists, for all the wackiness of some of their ideas, had been far more entertaining than the Progressives were.

XIII

Yet it wasn't just the Progressives; it was Roosevelt, who still hadn't committed himself emotionally to the battle La Follette and the Progressives were waging. During March and early April 1911 he and Edith crossed the country to California. One reason for the journey was to see Ted, who had taken a job with a San Francisco company, and Eleanor and the new baby; a second reason was to fulfill speaking engagements Roosevelt had made before leaving the White House; a third was to visit his old haunts in the West and see if he was still as well loved as ever. For months beforehand he complained that only a sense of obligation was motivating him to make so many speeches; and, indeed, the speaking side of the trip proved something less than a joy. "Thank heaven!" he wrote to Taft from San Francisco. "I am coming to the end of the last speaking tour I shall ever make."

Doubtless Roosevelt protested more vigorously to Taft than he might have—or did—to certain other people; it was one way of forestalling any lingering ideas on Taft's part that he might be persuaded to stump for the party in 1912. Yet even so, lacking a standard to fight under, Roosevelt found that politics had lost its zest. Western crowds still responded to him, but the most enjoyable and rewarding part of the journey was the ten days he and Edith spent with Ted, Eleanor, and Grace. The baby quickly won her grandfather's heart. He confessed to Lodge that he would "a little have preferred" a grandson to a granddaughter, but that was neither here nor there. "I am so pleased about it anyhow that whether it is a boy or a girl is a matter of entirely minor importance.

The return trip took the couple through North Dakota. This stretch of the journey reminded Roosevelt how quickly time passed. "The old country that I knew so well has absolutely vanished," he told Owen Wister. The land had filled in so thoroughly as to be unrecognizable. One location, formerly a desolate patch where Roosevelt had once got lost in a snowstorm, was now a thriving town complete with an active chamber of commerce.

Other evidence of time's passing greeted him on the return to Oyster Bay. Grudgingly, the Roosevelt family had entered the age of automobiles, which Theodore characterized as "distinct additions to the discomfort of living." The horse-drawn carriages that used to be pulled up Sagamore Hill to the front door of the house had largely given way to horseless models. But the front drive was too steep for the wheel-driven vehicles, especially during the spring when their tires spun vainly in the muddy ruts. Consequently, guests took to coming up the back road, which deposited them at the rear of the house. The back door was fine for servants and delivery men, but both Theodore and Edith thought it rather casual, if not downright gauche, for guests. Since few people seemed willing to abandon their cars and return to their carriages, the only solution was to build a new road with a modern weatherproof surface. "This will mean much expense all told," Roosevelt explained to Bamie. Beyond this, the noisy cars drastically altered the ambiance of the old homestead, where until recently children had been the loudest entities.

Those children were mostly grown (Quentin, the baby, was now nearly fourteen), but memories of their childhood lingered. Roosevelt reminisced to Eleanor about Ted's infancy, how he used to wake early and sing what Edith called his "hymn to the light" and how, when he got a little older, he would climb out of bed and come into his parents' room. "If I was unwary enough to give the least sign of being awake," Roosevelt recalled, "he would swarm into bed with me and gleefully propose 'a story,' keeping a vigilant watch on me for any sign of sleepiness on my part while I told it."

Time's passing continued to tell on the body. The aches and pains of the strenuous life added up. Roosevelt wrote to Endicott Peabody, the Groton headmaster and a longtime sharer of outdoor escapades, apropos of a possible visit in the fall: "I am afraid I am aged a good deal, Cotty, and I won't be at all a companion, athletically, for you now. The African trip was my final burst, so to speak." Somewhat later he wrote in a similar vein to Arthur Lee: "I do wish I could be with you in your Scotch Lodge. Unfortunately my infernal body is bothered more or less with rheumatism, and I doubt if I shall ever be much good for long walks again."

XIV

At such times it was easy for Roosevelt to conclude that his life in public affairs was over. He had never known politics as anything but a full-contact sport, and when his shoulders throbbed on rainy mornings or his knees and breath gave way on a walk that wouldn't have winded him before, the north room at Sagamore Hill seemed far more congenial than a smoke-filled convention hall or a jerry-built stand on a sun-baked square in one of a score of towns on another speaking tour. "I have revelled in being home," he wrote Lady Delamere, his Kenya hostess, "and if fortune favors me I shall never again leave Mrs. Roosevelt and my own belongings."

But on occasions when his rheumatism didn't flare up, some of the old spark did. In 1910 a revolution erupted in Mexico; by the spring of 1911 the turbulence from the revolution was spreading toward the border of the United States. Alarmists sketched out scenarios in which a resentful Japan or an aggressive Germany would throw its support to Mexico for an effort to undo the war of 1846. To allay the alarm and to keep Mexico's troubles in Mexico, Taft sent twenty thousand troops to the border.

Roosevelt, in his own way, likewise rose to the challenge. "I don't suppose there is anything in this war talk," he wrote Taft, "and I most earnestly hope that we will not have to intervene even to do temporary police duty in Mexico." But just in case, he was volunteering in advance to serve. "Of course I would not wish to take any part in a mere war with Mexico—it would not be my business to do peculiarly irksome and disagreeable and profitless police duty of the kind any occupation of Mexico would entail. But if by any remote chance—and I know how remote it is—there should be a serious war, a war in which Mexico was backed by Japan or some other big power, then I would wish immediately to apply for permission to raise a division of cavalry, such as the regiment I commanded in Cuba."

Roosevelt obviously had given this idea some thought. He laid out to the president what his division would consist of, how it would be organized, and who the senior officers would be. He reminded Taft of the brilliant performance of the Rough Riders in the Spanish-American War, and he guaranteed, in effect, comparable performance by an entire division. "If given a free hand, I could render it, I am certain, as formidable a body of horse riflemen, that is, of soldiers such as those of Sheridan, Forrest and Stuart, as has ever been seen."

Roosevelt was right about one thing in this matter: the unlikelihood of the war he anticipated. The trouble passed, sparing Taft the difficulty of determining how to treat Roosevelt's awkward request. But the president certainly must have come away from the affair guessing that, whatever Roosevelt might be telling friends, he wasn't committed very seriously to retirement.

XV

In fact, what Roosevelt was telling friends was that he expected Taft to be renominated and that he expected to work for the president's reelection. "Taft is stronger than he was," Roosevelt explained to Arthur Lee in late June 1911, "because his opponents in his own party have largely gone to pieces, and his worst advisers have been eliminated from their positions of power." Roosevelt still couldn't bring himself to work for Taft's nomination; this in any case was probably unnecessary and certainly would produce dismay among Roosevelt's progressive followers. But the Democrats were as corrupt as ever and as needful of being beaten in the general election. For this reason honest Republicans ought to rally behind Taft against anyone the party of Jefferson put forward. "I shall do whatever I can for his re-election," Roosevelt wrote Spring Rice.

As for his own prospects, Roosevelt dismissed them. In May 1911 he told a friend and supporter: "I feel that my nomination in 1912 would be not only a misfortune to me, but undesirable from the standpoint of the Party and the people." He actively discouraged efforts on his behalf. "I expect every real friend and supporter of mine to do everything in his power to prevent any movement looking toward my nomination."

At times he felt the discouragement might be unnecessary. In June he dismissed a question as to whether he would accept a nomination by declaring the matter "academic." "I won't have to decide it," he predicted flatly. Later that month he told Arthur Lee, "I think all danger of my nomination has passed, partly because the big monied interests, with their enormous control of the press, are more determined than ever that I shall not be nominated, and partly because my own friends have definitely accepted my statement that I will not be a candidate." In August he told Spring Rice, "I do not think there is a chance that I shall ever again be back in political life."

But another groundswell rose during the autumn, and once more he felt obliged to deny interest. "Neither you nor any of my friends must permit any movement looking toward my nomination," he wrote an Oklahoma supporter in October. To William White he said the same thing more strongly: "I do most emphatically feel that I have a right to expect every friend of mine to do everything in his power to prevent any movement looking toward my nomination, no matter what the circumstances may be."

Roosevelt wasn't just feigning reluctance. He really did not want the nomination. Earlier he had declared that the question of leadership in the movement for reform was "not of the slightest consequence except in so far as the leader helps to win success." On the whole he still felt that way: that whether a particular person—himself, in the present case—should step up or step aside ought to be determined solely on the basis of what propelled the movement forward. In this light the fact that he didn't want to serve—that he would be happier staying home with Edith—shouldn't have counted.

But it did, if only in conjunction with larger issues. In a letter to Hiram Johnson, Roosevelt said that under other circumstances he would be willing to lead the reform movement into the fray even if the odds of immediate success were small. "I would not feel that I had a right to object to being sacrificed if it were necessary to sacrifice me, if we had to lead a forlorn hope and I was the best person to lead it."

Yet such wasn't the present situation, he contended. "I do feel very strongly that I ought not to be asked to have my throat cut when the throat-cutting would damage me and in addition, what is infinitely more important, would damage the progressive cause we have at heart." At one time he had had the confidence of the people, but now he wasn't so sure. "Certainly I have no cause to think that at the moment there is any real or very widely extended liking for or trust in me among the mass of the people."

CHAPTER TWENTY-SEVEN

To the Barricades Once More
1912

Neither Hiram Johnson nor the other progressives had to be geniuses to recognize that this was far short of the definitive denial that would have taken Roosevelt out of the race for good. Indeed, by premising his refusal on grounds of his presumed unpopularity, Roosevelt made obvious what was necessary to bring him into the race—namely, a draft.

Many skeptics on the subject of Roosevelt reckoned, especially in light of the events of the next several months, that this was exactly what he had in mind. But those skeptics didn't know Roosevelt. The former president was absolutely sincere in not wanting to be nominated. Campaigning was hard work, and where he once had embraced hard work as a necessary part of every man's responsibility, his thinking had changed. "Twenty or even ten years ago, I should have felt sorry to retire from the activities of the universe," he told a friend, "because I should have felt that I had not earned the right thus to retire." But no more. "Now I feel that I have worked hard for thirty years, I have done everything I could, and have accomplished a certain amount." The old compulsion had dissipated. "I no longer feel that I am recreant unless I have the harness on." There was a season for everything. "I am glad to rest and to turn my attention to other things, and I am enjoying myself to the full for I feel that I thus enjoy myself with a full heart and without any unpleasant suspicion that I am not doing my duty unless I am hard at work."

Roosevelt went on to reflect on his place in history. "I hope you won't think me priggish or affected or conceited, when I add that I concern myself comparatively little with what the general repute in which I am held is or will be. I am entirely sure that whatever may be said of me at the moment, in the long run decent people will think fairly well of me, so that my children and my children's children will not have cause to feel ashamed of me, and my living friends will not have cause to regret their friendship." Beyond this, not much mattered. "If at Santiago I had been shot, I should not when dying have wasted any thought as to how people would think of me in the future or whether they would ever remember me at all. I should have thought of my family and should have been glad that they and a few friends would know that I had done my duty fairly; and as for the rest, my code is that the duty must be done and that the doing of it must be the chief reward and often the only reward, and though I could not very clearly give my reasons why I do hold this code, yet I am perfectly sure it is the right code to hold."

Roosevelt had always considered it a prime part of duty to be fruitful and multiply. This he, and Edith, had accomplished, and now they could enjoy the pleasure of watching their offspring begin to make their own way in the world. Alice was well married—and "much improved" by the match, he thought—with her husband gaining increasing distinction in the House of Representatives. Ted was making a good start in business in San Francisco and lately had even commenced a political career of his own with a speech on "Our Civic Duties." "It immensely amused me," Roosevelt remarked to Spring Rice regarding Ted, "for he is just the age I was when I first went to the New York Legislature." Kermit had enrolled at Harvard, although, as always, the taste for the wild was still strong in him. At the moment he was in Mexico dodging revolutionaries and hunting sheep. "His mother is slightly uneasy about him. I take a more philosophical view, partly because I have great confidence in his hardihood, and partly because I feel that he has got to take risks, and that there is no use worrying about it." Ethel was twenty and "becoming quite a staid young lady"; Archie and Quentin divided their time between boarding school and home.

Counting ahead, Roosevelt wanted to see Kermit, Archie, and Quentin through college; this would require another eight years. "Then all the children will have been launched in life, and I shall be sixty years old, and I shall feel that I have a right to draw out of work entirely." Until then he would continue to write for the *Outlook*, which would provide the income necessary to pay the bills at Harvard and Groton for the three younger boys.

Income aside, the *Outlook* remained a congenial connection. "My fellow editors have the same high purpose and sanity that, for instance, the members of the Tennis Cabinet had," Roosevelt explained to Spring Rice. "I can work with them in complete sympathy, and as long as they continue to think me valuable I shall continue to work with them because I feel that, though there probably is not much effect from what I am doing, yet whatever effect there is is good and wholesome; and it is an honorable thing to cast even a little weight on the side of decency and fair and honest dealing."

II

Another circumstance influenced Roosevelt's thinking on his future. On the last day of September 1911 he and Edith were out riding, as was their daily habit. Archie was along, which probably spurred Roosevelt to ride a bit faster than usual, and Edith kept up at a gallop. Suddenly and for no reason that any of them could discern, and certainly none that Edith anticipated, her horse swerved to the side. Edith was hurled to the ground, hitting her head on the hard macadamized surface of the road. The blow knocked her senseless, and although her husband and son were relieved to see her breathing, their efforts to revive her were unavailing. Roosevelt flagged down a passing delivery automobile; together he and Archie lifted her into the vehicle, which transported her back to the house. Roosevelt summoned a doctor while she lay unconscious on her bed. For the balance of that day and through the night he kept watch; she remained unconscious and, but for her faint breathing, as still as death.

Finally, the next day, she began to come to. The doctor examined her and declared that nothing was broken and the brain hadn't been shaken quite as violently as he had feared; whatever danger had existed was now past. But she would have to stay in bed for a week or two. Edith, her head throbbing excruciatingly, didn't argue.

In the event, the week or two stretched much longer. Edith's headache persisted; she was in "frightful pain," Roosevelt recorded, and could "hardly talk or even be read to." She had also lost her sense of smell. As in many such cases, this not only took much of the savor out of life but posed a potential risk because it left her with almost no appetite. Her strength ebbed by the day. She was "very frail and wasted," her worried husband wrote to an old family friend in late October. To their eldest son he explained, "She has had a very serious time, and I cannot form any idea when she will really be herself again."

Fortunately, Edith's condition gradually turned for the better. By late November she was up and moving about, carefully. Although her improvement wasn't uninterrupted, her sense of smell slowly returned, and with it her appetite and a portion of her strength.

But the shock and fright of the experience lingered, for her husband probably more than for herself. Briefly, Roosevelt had thought he might lose her; for weeks after that he wondered if she would ever be as she was before. The experience would have elicited reflection in anyone, and it did in Roosevelt. He understood that she—and he—had had "an exceedingly narrow escape," and even more than previously he appreciated the human treasure that resided beneath his roof at Sagamore Hill.

At the same time, though, Edith's close brush, by fostering a renewed awareness of the evanescence of life, reminded Roosevelt of the swift passing of each man's opportunity to make his mark. Whether or not a direct and conscious connection existed in his mind between Edith's injury and his decision to return to the political arena is impossible to say. His letters and reported remarks reveal no such direct link, but then this was not the kind of thing he would ordinarily comment on. The fact remains, however, that even while Edith was recovering from her blow, he was getting ready to rejoin the battle he had been fighting for decades.

III

Yet for all the gravity of his feelings toward Edith, their relations were anything but grave. Archie Butt took a few days off from his duties at the Taft White House to visit Sagamore Hill at the end of January 1912. He arrived half-frozen, having driven to Oyster Bay from New York in an open car. As he thawed himself before the dancing fire in the north room, he filled Edith and Ethel in on the latest news of Washington personalities—"from Mrs. Townsend down to Alice, the black scullery maid at the White House." They shared several hearty laughs and in the process attracted Roosevelt's attention. Butt recorded:

> The Colonel heard us laughing once, and he rushed in and made us repeat what had just been said. He never could stand being left out of a good laugh. Then, turning to Ethel, he took her in his arms and said:
> "And how is my sweet little apostle? [Ethel had just returned from teaching Sunday school.] I'll wager none propounded the Scripture as convincingly as she did today, with her apple red cheeks."
> "It is a very good thing that you did not go to church, Father. They sang abominable hymns, and you would have disgraced us all by trying to sing them."

Butt inquired as to Roosevelt's favorite hymn.

> He put his finger on his forehead, as if giving an imitation of a man thinking deeply, and said jerkily:
> "Archie, I think my favorite hymn is 'Lord, Abide with Me,' that being the nearest mention to patience which I can now recall in the hymnal."
> "Why, Father," said Ethel, "you told someone the other day that your favorite hymn was 'Weary of Earth and Laden with My Sin'!"
> "Never," said the Colonel, "never! I don't feel laden with sin, and I have never felt laden with sin—have I, Edie? Or if I did say it, I must have been more tired than I knew. But always remember one thing, Ethel, you are blessed with a father who has many opinions on the same subject. Yes," he continued thoughtfully, "I am quite sure that my favorite hymn today is 'Abide with Me.' To-morrow it may be 'The Son of God Goes Forth to War,' but to-day it is 'Abide with Me.' I think I will let it stand at that," he said, laughing, and leaned over and kissed his wife and vigorously left the room."

Butt recognized that the laugh, and more especially the selection of hymns, were intended for his ears—and Taft's.

With Jusserand, the French ambassador, who also happened to be there, Butt stayed for lunch. The meal consisted of the same basic fare Roosevelt had always enjoyed. "Our menus are a legacy from my Georgian mother," he explained. "She taught us to have rice twice a day and hominy every morning for breakfast, and we group simple meats around it."

Near the end of the meal one of the men who worked on the grounds came in. The telephone had been out of order, and now the explanation surfaced.

> "Colonel, the telephone man has been here, sir, and he says you cut down all the trees this morning which had the wires on them, and he said, sir, that you didn't even pull the wires out after the trees fell."
>
> The Colonel looked guilty as Mrs. Roosevelt began to laugh, but he stopped her quickly by saying:
>
> "Now, Edie, don't you say a word. It was your own fault. You always mark the trees I am to cut down, and you did not do it. No, Edie, you did not do your duty as forester of this establishment, and you ought to be punished, but I will say nothing more about it and not hold you up to scorn before your children if you will let the subject drop once for all."

Jusserand—unnecessarily—came to Edith's defense, pointing out that she hadn't said a word. Roosevelt, with a very bright twinkle in his eye, refused to let the matter drop.

> "Ah! But you don't know my wife. She has a language all her own. That telephone will never ring now that my wife will not chuckle to herself, and if the cursed thing ever gets out of order, which it most frequently does, she will tell the servant to see if the wires are still up or the trees are down. No, my dear Mr. Ambassador, people think I have a good-natured wife, but she has a humor which is more tyrannical than half the tempestuous women of Shakespeare."

And he laughed out loud once more.

IV

Roosevelt's hard-core partisans had never stopped talking up the chance of another nomination for their hero. In November 1911 the talk grew louder and more insistent when a group of Ohio Republicans endorsed Roosevelt for the party's nomination. The endorsers included such recognizable (family) names as Jim Garfield and Dan Hanna; the real significance of the move, however, was that it emanated from Taft's home state.

"Of course that action made me uncomfortable," Roosevelt complained to Garfield. Yet his discomfort owed not so much to the action itself as to the possibility of its misinterpretation. From this point on, Roosevelt's lamentations about the undesirability of his returning to active politics diminished and then disappeared; to the extent that he continued to protest, his protests increasingly sounded like those of a man positioning himself to be drafted. "I do hope you will explain to the La Follette leaders," he told Garfield, "and to men like Gilson Gardner and Ray Stannard Baker, for instance, that no friend of mine, and nobody in any kind of touch with me, had anything to do with the sudden expression in my favor." But he didn't disavow the expression. Shortly thereafter Roosevelt received a letter from Garfield asserting that only "a flat-footed final statement from you that under no circumstances would you accept the nomination" would prevent the pro-Roosevelt tide from continuing to rise; Roosevelt conspicuously declined to make such a statement.

In keeping open the possibility of another run at the presidency, Roosevelt had to answer allegations that he was reneging on his no-third-term pledge of 1904. As usual, Roosevelt interpreted the statement to suit his present purposes, and he assailed all who differed with him as imbecilically or malevolently obtuse. To one correspondent, Herbert Parsons, who querulously raised the question, Roosevelt responded, "I have not the slightest sympathy with your third-term position. As I said in connection with accepting the nomination last time, what we need to do in the third-term matter is to pay attention to the substance and not the form. I cared nothing for the fact that I have not had two elective terms, for of course the only possible justification for the third-term theory is that it shall be a third consecutive term." The point was to prevent an incumbent from monopolizing power and maintaining himself illegitimately in office. As a non-incumbent, Roosevelt didn't fall under that proscription. "Oh! good Herbert, I cannot help grinning as I dictate these words at your solemnity over the possible danger to free institutions from the

Contributing Editor of *The Outlook* who has just come to Town hanging onto a strap in a crowded car." Lest he leave his critic with nothing, however, Roosevelt closed with his stock but decreasingly convincing disclaimer: "I am a good deal more anxious not to be nominated than you can possibly be not to have me nominated."

With practice, Roosevelt refined his response to the third-term questions. Skeptics asked why, if he had meant no third *consecutive* term, he hadn't said so before. Roosevelt drew a homely analogy. "Frequently when asked to take another cup of coffee at breakfast, I say 'No thank you, I won't take another cup.' This does not mean that I intend never to take another cup of coffee during my life; it means that I am not accepting the offer as applying to that breakfast, and that my remark is limited to that breakfast." As with coffee, so with the highest office in the land.

In moving closer to candidacy, Roosevelt also refined his views of his likely rivals, although, as with the third-term issue, it was impossible to know how much was cause and how much consequence of his desire to try for the White House again. At the moment, Roosevelt felt forgiving, if condescending, toward Taft. "I am really sorry for Taft," he wrote in December. "I am sure he means well, but he means well feebly, and he does not know how! He is utterly unfit for leadership, and this is a time when we need leadership. All kinds of people influence him on the unimportant things where he does know his own mind but generally makes up his mind wrong; and on the important things he does not know his own mind and changes it every which way."

As for La Follette, the man had a decent track record but dubious prospects. "La Follette has done admirable work in Wisconsin, but hitherto he has not succeeded in impressing himself favorably on the public mind east of the Mississippi. The Progressives in Michigan and Ohio, in New York and New Hampshire, who have been to see me tell me they are against Taft for almost any man, but for him against La Follette."

And regarding the Democratic contenders, they carried the burden of their party. Roosevelt never allowed evidence to shake his lifelong view that the national Democratic Party was essentially Tammany Hall writ large. Republicans might have their faults, but the deficiencies of the Democrats were always greater. Woodrow Wilson, the

Democratic front-runner, had shown early promise but never really blossomed. "Down at bottom Wilson is pretty thin material for a President," Roosevelt said. "He lacks the fundamental sincerity, conviction and rugged strength, and yet I think he is the strongest man the Democrats have."

While denigrating his opponents, Roosevelt idealized himself. The old romantic streak surfaced again; more than ever he identified with the heroes of American history, especially Lincoln. He contended that to the extent he was challenging the Republican establishment, he was simply trying to return the party to its Lincolnian roots. "My loyalty to the Republican party is naturally very great," he wrote to Governor Augustus Willson of Kentucky. "But remember, my dear Governor, that my aim is to make it and to keep it the Republican party that it was in the days of Lincoln." For the benefit of persons insisting that he say something to silence those critics who charged him with a deep and devious plan for seizing the nomination, he quoted Lincoln (who himself cited a rather higher authority): "Those who will not read or heed what I have already publicly said would not read or heed a repetition of it. If they heed not Moses and the Prophets, neither would they be persuaded though one rose from the dead." To demands for a direct answer as to whether he would accept a proffered nomination, he again referred to the first Republican president: "Why! don't you think I ought to be allowed to quote Abraham Lincoln's statement that no one ought to ask any man to cross that bridge before he comes to it?"

Most tellingly and most characteristically, Roosevelt cast himself as the agent of the people's will. During the winter of 1911–12 this agency was still merely potential. "I am not a candidate," he told one correspondent, among many. "I will never be a candidate." What he really meant was that he wouldn't be a candidate for the nomination in the sense of taking an active part in trying to win it. "But I have to tell the La Follette men and the Taft men that while I am absolutely sincere in saying that I am not a candidate and do not wish the nomination, yet that I do not feel it would be right or proper for me to say that under no circumstances would I accept it if it came; because while wildly improbable, it was yet possible that there might be a public demand which would present the matter to me in the light of a duty which I could not shirk." By early January 1912 he was willing to put his position more clearly, albeit negatively and confidentially. "If the people make a draft on me," he told Colorado reformer Benjamin Lindsey, "I shall not decline to serve."

V

It was supremely important to Roosevelt to believe that self-interest played no part in his decision. "As far as I know my own soul," he explained to Governor Herbert Hadley of Missouri, "I am telling you the exact truth when I say that I do not wish and will not take this nomination unless it comes to me as a public duty. I would not touch it if it were to come in such fashion as to look like the gratification of a desire on my part again to hold the Presidency. If I am to be nominated, it must be made clear that it is because the people think that at this time I am the man to do the job which in their interests they want done." To Elihu Root, Roosevelt insisted, "As far as I am able to judge of my motives, I am looking at this purely from the standpoint of the interests of the people as a whole, from the standpoint of those who believe in the causes which I champion."

Roosevelt's protests were largely lost on Root, who had always cast a quizzical eye on Roosevelt's motives even while he cherished the man. Less forgiving Roosevelt watchers angrily interpreted the former president's disclaimers as additional evidence of his infuriating hypocrisy.

In fact those disclaimers were part and parcel of the romantic identity he had long ago created for himself. As before, Roosevelt saw himself as the champion of the common people, the hero of those many endangered by the depredations of the few. It was an ennobling vision and a reassuring one—both for Roosevelt and for those others who held it of him. And it was what allowed him to square the circle of pursuing the presidency even as he honestly disclaimed any desire to do so. The people called, and he could not but answer.

Roosevelt's vision was reassuring and ennobling—and untenable, at least in the form he initially conceived it. As he knew full well, a political leader might express the people's will, but the people usually had to be alerted to that fact. The very existence of political parties testified to the need for institutions to direct and channel the wishes of the masses; for thirty years Roosevelt had accepted this need and played by the rules it implied. No group had earned a greater measure of his scorn than the mugwumps, who denied the necessity of parties to make the machinery of democracy work. As the election of 1912 approached, Roosevelt increasingly realized that he would either have to become what he had despised—a mugwump—or continue to accept party politics and the partisan imperatives such politics imposed on activists like himself.

As it turned out, he did both—first the latter, then the former. Discussions with progressive types from across the country made plain that, whatever the will of the people, if Roosevelt were to have a prayer of becoming the instrument of that will, he would have to announce his candidacy openly. Republican politicians—governors, congressmen, state legislators—would be putting their careers in jeopardy bucking Taft and the party leadership to follow Roosevelt; they could hardly be expected to take such a risk for a man who wasn't willing to take some chances himself. Certain influential individuals who would have preferred Roosevelt had already announced for La Follette; others reluctantly stuck with Taft. The longer Roosevelt kept silent, the fewer people would be left to join him.

Gradually, Roosevelt accepted this analysis. Yet he still wished to maintain the appearance that he was acting only in response to popular demand. In mid-January he contacted a handful of progressive-minded Republican governors and suggested that they write him a letter asking point-blank what his intentions were. "It seems to me that if such a group of four or five Governors wrote me a joint letter," he explained, "or wrote me individual letters which I could respond to at the same time and in the same way, that such procedure would open the best way out of an uncomfortable situation. I am now inclined to think, as I did not even think as late as a month ago, that the evil of my speaking out publicly is less than the evil of my refraining from speaking." Getting down to specifics, Roosevelt continued: "The letter to me might simply briefly state the writer's belief that the people of his State, or their States, desire to have me run for the Presidency, and to know whether in such a case I would refuse the nomination." Reiterating that he was not consulting his own interest but only that of the people, Roosevelt made plain that his answer would be in the affirmative. "If it is the sincere judgment of men having the right to know and express the wishes of the plain people that the people as a whole desire me, not for my sake, but for their sake, to undertake the job, I would feel in honor bound to do so."

VI

"Things are boiling in the political pot," Roosevelt told his brother-in-law Will Cowles a few days later, without mentioning the log he himself had just thrown on the fire. The boiling caused confusion among some progressives. Hiram Johnson of California, for example, having endorsed La Follette on the understanding that Roosevelt was not a candidate, now wanted to change his mind. He traveled east to talk to Roosevelt; after a meeting at Sagamore Hill at the beginning of February, he decided to jump the La Follette ship for the Roosevelt craft and to bring aboard as many of his fellow Californians as he could.

Johnson's defection was one among many. Already struggling, the La Follette candidacy slowly sank during the next several weeks. Many Republicans had backed La Follette as the only alternative to Taft, but for all his bellicose nickname, Battle Bob failed to ignite much fight in his followers. Roosevelt was by far the more charismatic figure, and with excuses that varied according to the conscience and circumstances of each, most of La Follette's pledged supporters found their way to Roosevelt's side.

Roosevelt was encouraged by the trend, but he insisted on keeping matters in cautious perspective. He dampened his supporters' hopes, and his own. "The situation changes so rapidly that any conclusion must be tentative," he explained.

In the second week of February the requested letter from the governors arrived. The seven authors told Roosevelt that "a large majority of the Republican voters of the country favor your nomination, and a large majority of the people favor your election as the next President of the United States." They went on to say that no other man represented so well the principles and policies necessary for the happiness and prosperity of the nation. They recited Roosevelt's specified formula that they were not considering his personal interest but only the interest of the people at large. "We feel that you would be unresponsive to a plain public duty if you should decline the nomination."

Even to this direct, carefully scripted appeal, Roosevelt didn't respond at once. He recognized that the nation—or, at any rate, the nation's newspapers—hung on his answer, and he appreciated the publicity value of a certain continuing dramatic tension. He let the tension build for several more days before heading off to the very den of the lion. He had consented to address a constitutional convention in Ohio; without doubt every paper in the country would give full coverage to the challenge he was expected to make in Taft's backyard. He added to the interest by tossing off a remark to a reporter: "My hat is in the ring." The phrase wasn't original with Roosevelt, but neither did it yet have the full import it would acquire shortly—after becoming connected to the decision he would soon announce unambiguously. In any event, no one, including the reporter who recorded the remark, paid it much heed at the time.

What everyone noticed instead was what Roosevelt told the Ohio constitutional convention. Wrapping himself closely in the cloak of the sainted Lincoln, he likened his foes to that reviled doughface, Buchanan. He openly called himself a "Progressive," and he endorsed such progressive reforms as the initiative, referendum, and recall (these with certain exceptions), the direct election of senators, the short ballot, and, significantly, preferential primaries for presidential nominations. The lead he provided the pressmen, however, was something more radical, namely, popular review of judicial decisions. He contended that when courts—state courts in particular—frustrated the will of the people, the people ought to be able to overrule the courts. "Again and again in the past," he declared, "justice has been scandalously obstructed by state courts." This was especially so when some state court invalidated a reform duly passed by the state legislature and supported by a large majority of the people. Under such circumstances the people ought to have the last word: a referendum on the court's decision. "If it is sustained, well and good. If not, then the popular verdict is to be accepted as final." True democracy could countenance no less.

As food for thought for a convention of delegates devising a new constitution for Ohio, this recommendation was arguably appropriate; but it nearly gagged those conservatives and others who had long deemed Roosevelt an enemy of property and order and good government. The courts were generally seen as the last refuge of property rights, and now Roosevelt was advocating that they be subject to overrule by the whims of the masses—doubtless inflamed by demagogues like himself. In fairness to Roosevelt, he applied his doctrine of popular review only to the states; the federal courts (for now) would be above such oversight. In fairness to his critics, what he was proposing was the overthrow of the traditional system of checks and balances.

Roosevelt's proposal provoked controversy, as he knew it would—and, indeed, as an earlier version essayed in the *Outlook* had. While the storm swirled, with him at the hurricane's eye, he conspicuously huddled with various advisers. He traveled to Boston for a meeting of the Harvard board of overseers; while there he sounded out New England progressives. The trip took on the air of a circus, with reporters tracking his every step, inquiring of all who had seen him as to what he said and to whom.

In Boston, Roosevelt stayed at the home of friend and ally Robert Grant, who, realizing the historic nature of what was happening within his walls, recorded his impressions of and conversations with the prospective candidate. "Everyone was on tiptoe to know what his answer was to be," Grant wrote, "though it was generally assumed that Barkis was willing." Grant was impressed by Roosevelt's bearing and demeanor. "I never saw him in better physical shape. He is fairly stout, but his color is good, and he appeared vigorous." Roosevelt's enemies were circulating scurrilous tales about him; the least unlikely, although still ludicrously unfounded, had him taking heavily to drink, while others posited creeping megalomania or other form of clinical lunacy. Grant felt obliged, for the record, to offer personal refutation. "I saw no signs of unusual excitement. He halts in his sentences occasionally; but from a layman's point of view there was nothing to suggest mental impairment, unless the combination of egotism, faith in his own doctrines, fondness for power and present hostility to Taft—of which I will speak presently—can be termed symptomatic." As to alcohol, he drank only the wine served with dinner.

Far from being a lush or a lunatic, Roosevelt struck Grant as a most delightful guest. "I have never spent a more absorbing twenty-four hours." And he certainly seemed ready and eager for battle. At mid-

night, at the end of a long and full day, Grant—himself feeling worn
and jaded—showed his guest where he would be sleeping. "I saw him
upstairs, and, as he stood at the threshold of his room, he stretched
out his arms and exclaimed 'I feel fine as silk.'"

At an appropriate moment Grant broached the subject of Taft, intimating that some people would consider Roosevelt disloyal for abandoning his successor. "'What do I owe Taft?'" came the reply, as quoted
by Grant. "'It was through me and my friends that he became
President. I had him in the hollow of my hand and he would have
dropped out.' He had his pocketknife in his palm and suited his action
to the word." Grant wasn't quite satisfied with this answer and
returned to the subject of Taft and loyalty later in Roosevelt's visit.
Roosevelt brushed off the implied criticism. As Grant noted, "It was
perfectly evident from his point of view that this did not disturb him."
Roosevelt did allow, though, that he would support Taft—"as one
who preferred 20 to 19"—if Taft received the nomination.

Grant was fully aware of the charges of hypocrisy that followed
Roosevelt. These were unfounded, he believed. "That Theodore is in
earnest and sincere, there is no room for doubt in my mind."
Roosevelt was convinced, and told Grant, that if he failed to heed the
governors' call he would be guilty of Dante's *il gran refiuto*. Grant
thought Roosevelt was wrong, that he had made "a great mistake—an
unnecessary and possibly fatal blunder." But he couldn't gainsay his
guest's sincerity.

VII

Roosevelt emerged from his Boston conclave to finally make a formal announcement of his intentions. "I will accept the nomination for
President if it is tendered to me," he declared. He added, "I will
adhere to this decision until the convention has expressed its preference." He said he had always stood for, and now, especially, still did
stand for, the genuine rule of the people. "Therefore I hope that so far
as possible the people may be given the chance, through direct primaries, to express their preference as to who shall be the nominee of
the Republican Presidential Convention."

Though not unexpected, Roosevelt's announcement still hit the Republican Party like a thunderclap. It caused no end of emotional and professional anguish among those career Republicans who had developed a personal or philosophical affinity for the Rough Rider but who weren't eager to help him split the party. Elihu Root told his and Roosevelt's mutual friend Bob Bacon, "Theodore has gone off upon a perfectly wild program, most of which he does not really believe in, although of course at this moment he thinks he does." Root expanded on this idea in a letter to another associate. "He is essentially a fighter and when he gets into a fight he is completely dominated by the desire to destroy his adversary. He instinctively lays hold of every weapon which can be used for that end. Accordingly he is saying a lot of things and taking a lot of positions which are inspired by the desire to win. I have no doubt he thinks he believes what he says, but he doesn't. He has merely picked up certain popular ideas which were at hand as one might pick up a poker or chair with which to strike." As for Root's own reaction to Roosevelt's latest enthusiasm, he told Bacon, "I wish to fall upon your neck and weep. I wish to walk up and down in your congenial and unrestraining presence and curse and swear and say things which I would not have repeated for the world."

The situation was still more wrenching for Cabot Lodge. "I have had my share of mishaps in politics," Lodge wrote his friend of thirty years, "but I never thought that any situation could arise which would have made me so miserably unhappy as I have been during the past week." He said he had known that he and Roosevelt differed on certain points, but he hadn't realized that the difference, as on popular review of judicial decisions, was so deep. Consequently, he couldn't in good faith support his candidacy. But neither could he go against him. "There is very little of the Roman in me toward those I love best, and I hope a good deal of loyalty in my affection." Standing aside when his friend was fighting was hard, but he had no choice. "I cannot tell you how much I have suffered from these harsh necessities, and so I shall say no more."

The situation was the most distressing for Taft. Root and Lodge foresaw a defeat for their party in the next election; Taft realized he was witnessing the ruin of his career. Win or lose the nomination, Roosevelt had made a Democratic victory almost inevitable. The only question for Taft was whether he should be repudiated by his own party or by the electorate at large.

Actually, there was another question, one that caused the sensitive Taft enormous pain. Why had Roosevelt turned on him so? Roosevelt complained that Taft had compromised with the bosses; but hadn't Roosevelt himself cultivated Tom Platt and Mark Hanna when necessity dictated? And hadn't Roosevelt endlessly excoriated the mugwumps for placing philosophical purity above practical efficacy? Roosevelt charged him with colluding with the corporate bigwigs; but who had forced the breakup of Rockefeller's Standard Oil trust, and who had brought more antitrust lawsuits in one term than Roosevelt had in two? Roosevelt alleged that Taft had sold out friends and allies at the insistence of the big money men; but who was it who even now was turning on one who had placed his faith in Roosevelt's friendship? After one long day defending himself against Roosevelt's allegations, Taft wearily retired to his train car. A reporter caught him, slumped in a lounge chair, head cradled in his hands. "Roosevelt was my closest friend," Taft lamented. And then, exhausted and despondent, he began to weep.

VIII

Roosevelt's reactions to the turmoil he was causing ranged from the empathetic to the characteristically self-righteous. To Lodge he wrote, "I don't know whether to be most touched by your letter or most inclined to laugh over it." While declaring that nothing could make him lose his affection for his old friend, he said he had sensed that he and Lodge were moving apart on political issues for some time. Of course Lodge should stand by his convictions, just as he must stand by his own. To Root he asserted that, whatever the arguments against his making a race, the arguments in favor were even stronger. The welfare of the American people demanded that he challenge the president in support of policies the nation needed—policies "which most reluctantly I have come to believe he either does not understand at all, or else is hostile to."

Roosevelt's treatment of Taft did the former president scant credit. Perhaps the two old friends could have avoided personal assaults if they hadn't received such goading from the galleries. Taft certainly hoped they could. A mutual friend, Henry White, reported a conversation with Taft in a letter to Roosevelt. White had raised the topic of Roosevelt's Columbus speech and his challenge to the judicial status quo; Taft evidently disagreed with Roosevelt's view but declined to object in this conversation. "He said however," White related, "that nothing would induce him to say, or to allow anyone whom he can control, to say anything against you personally; that he has never ceased to avail himself of every opportunity to express his gratitude for all that you have done for him; that you made him President (he said nothing about his brother Charles in this connection!) and that he never can forget the old & happy relations of intimacy between you & him." Taft described how various persons were endlessly urging him to attack Roosevelt but said he was determined to resist such pressure. To this White remarked frankly that certain things had been said and done that might cast doubt on such a statement. "He made no reply to this," White related to Roosevelt, "but said he could not help hoping that when all this turmoil of politics had passed, you and he would get together again and be as of old."

But as Taft had observed, the galleries refused to let their champions tilt in peace. Conservative commentators and longtime Roosevelt critics leaped all over the new candidate. Major New York papers, taking a special interest in Manhattan's native son, branded his plan for tampering with the courts a "charter of demagogy," an "invitation of anarchy," and a "proposal of revolution." They deemed his decision to enter the race "vulgar" and "boorish." Roosevelt was assailed as a liar, an ingrate, and an aspiring Caesar. A New York supreme court justice characterized Roosevelt as having the "daring of a madman" and the "instincts of a beast." His former friend Nicholas Murray Butler of Columbia University called him and his followers a band of "Cossacks," "political patent medicine men," and "sandlot orators."

With such encouragement, and receiving no sign of reconciliation from Roosevelt, Taft reluctantly picked up the gage his predecessor had thrown down. The president's judicial instincts and experience took particular umbrage at Roosevelt's assault on the courts. Taft asserted that making the courts subservient to the momentary passions of the people would hazard turning the United States into a replica of revolutionary France or the more chaotic of the South

American republics. Those who advocated such subservience were extremists. Taft didn't mention Roosevelt by name, but he didn't have to. Taft concluded: "Such extremists are not progressives—they are political emotionalists or neurotics."

Roosevelt had never accepted criticism kindly, but being called a "neurotic" incensed him, and it ruined any chance that the campaign might climb from the muck of personal name-calling to the higher ground of reasoned argument. He judged that the hysterical response of the reactionaries to his judicial review proposal indicated bad consciences and bad intentions. Their criticism was really a criticism of popular government, for if the people did not know what was best for them, who did? Singling out the president, he declared, "Mr. Taft's position is perfectly clear. It is that we have in this country a special class of persons wiser than the people, who are above the people, who cannot be reached by the people, but who govern them and ought to govern them; and who protect various classes of the people from the whole people." This was an ancient doctrine—and a dreadful one. And it was going to be repudiated, as well it should. Roosevelt averred that he was willing to work with moderate, rational conservatives, provided that they saw the light and strove toward it. "But when they halt and turn their backs to the light, and sit with the scorners on the seats of reaction, then I must part company with them. We the people cannot turn back."

Roosevelt had long infuriated his critics, and dismayed even some of his friends, by his blithe and proprietary identification with "the people." He continued to infuriate and dismay them now. But he had little choice, having entered the race on the belief that the people were demanding that he do so. At the same time, the strength of the pro-Taft response forced him to abandon any notions of waiting quietly at Oyster Bay for the people to come and hand him the nomination. In the days after his announcement he had toyed with the idea of a Sagamore Hill strategy. "I do not think it would be wise for me to give the impression of going about stumping through the country as if I were in an ordinary campaign." But reality soon set in, and he had to concede that though the people might want him to serve, they had to be shaken alive to that fact.

He wasn't complaining, however. Or when he did, he didn't really mean it. "I am having a horrid time," he told family friend Robert

Ferguson before explaining: "I did not feel that I could shirk leadership in this moment. A great many of my friends said they wished I would wait until 1916 and I told them that I wished I could too; but, as Mark Sullivan said, the time to set a setting hen was when the hen wanted to set." And there was a certain compensation for all the criticism he was receiving from the circles of the staid and proper: Alice now visited home more often. Following one such visit, Roosevelt remarked to Kermit, "I think she felt she just had to see me because of course all respectable society is now apoplectic with rage over me."

For the first time since 1898, Roosevelt felt free to fight a campaign with coat off and both sleeves rolled up. He hit the road hard, traveling from the East Coast far out to the West. In interviews and full-dress speeches he answered every charge and criticism leveled against him. The allegation of disloyalty he rebutted by saying that it was Taft and the bosses who had been disloyal to the principles of Lincoln. Accusations that he was preaching class hatred he rejoined by declaring that he was preaching only hatred of crookedness in business and in politics. Old assertions of irregularities in funding the 1904 campaign he dismissed as evidence of despair on the part of his foes. Claims that he had taken a high-handed approach to presidential power he did not deny directly but said that whatever power he wielded had emanated from the people and had redounded to the people's benefit. He told the story from the Santiago campaign as to how he had cut through army red tape to feed his hungry men, paying for half a ton of beans out of his own pocket. That was what power should be used for—the welfare of the many, not the enrichment of the few. He offered Panama as another example. If he had heeded the naysayers, the canal would be fifty years in the future. "Instead of doing that, I took the Isthmus and started the Canal, and I let Congress debate me instead of the Canal."

IX

Fulminating aside, the strategies of the two sides were obvious to all observers. Taft would work through the regular machinery of the party and employ the usual instruments of incumbency—patronage, pork, and pull on key committees. Roosevelt would take his case to the people, relying on primaries and popular challenges to rules that favored the party regulars who wrote them. "There is not one state out of ten in which Mr. Taft would have any chance if the vote were left to the people themselves," Roosevelt told an audience in Nebraska. He may have given himself some benefit of doubt, but the general idea was correct, and it guided his approach to the fight for the nomination.

Taft's strategy appeared most promising in the South, where Republicans, that endangered minority, had long looked to Washington and the national party leadership for protection and sustenance. William B. McKinley, Illinois congressman and currently Taft's campaign manager, had watched Mark Hanna work the levers for the party below the Mason-Dixon line, and now he did the same. Republican officeholders quickly learned that the slightest display of Rooseveltian sympathies would cost them their jobs; those in positions of responsibility were warned to deliver delegations for Taft to the state conventions or face the consequences.

Roosevelt's strategy, by contrast, was better suited to the North and West. Western Republicans had long had a soft spot for Roosevelt and a rebellious streak toward the national party, while several northern states had adopted or were in the process of adopting primaries, which allowed Roosevelt to reach out to voters over the heads of the bosses. The northern tier of midwestern states, moreover, had lately been a hotbed of progressivism.

Yet, unlike canny generals who retreat in the face of unfavorable odds, neither Taft nor Roosevelt would concede any state to the other; each side fought for every delegate to the national convention. In all states supporters of the two candidates came to verbal blows; in several states the verbs were backed by fists and other blunt weapons. One contested district in Missouri witnessed what went down in the history of that border state as the "ball bat convention," after the number of baseball bats brandished by delegates. In Michigan a riot broke out at a district gathering, cleaving the caucus down the middle; amid total confusion, the Taft and Roosevelt sides conducted competing business from the same stage, choosing contradictory sets of delegates. In Oklahoma, where the Rough Rider tradition remained strong, some two hundred Roosevelt supporters stormed the convention hall in defiance of a state central committee mandate that they be barred. The pro-Taft chairman received death threats, which were rendered entirely credible by the ominous presence, immediately behind the chair, of a Roosevelt partisan with loaded pistol at the ready.

Although order never returned to the campaign, certain patterns emerged. Taft, as expected, ran strongest in states closely controlled by the party organization, while Roosevelt gained ground where primaries afforded voters more direct access to the delegate selection process. The South went solidly for Taft; so did New York, Indiana, Michigan, and Kentucky. Massachusetts, where Lodge had quietly reinterpreted his pledge to sit out the campaign and was discreetly aiding the incumbent, gave the president a narrow victory. Roosevelt, meanwhile, won majorities in Illinois, Minnesota, Nebraska, South Dakota, and California. Maryland and Pennsylvania, for reasons peculiar to their local politics, also joined the Roosevelt camp.

In May the battle shifted to the crucial ground of Ohio. For Taft to lose his home state would be disastrous—more so than the loss of New York was to Roosevelt, who explained defeat there as additional evidence of the fear he inspired in the corporate and party bosses. The fight for Ohio brought out every speaker, precinct walker, and hand-shaker either side could summon; it also brought out the most concentrated nastiness of the campaign to date. "I am a man of peace," Taft avowed, "and I don't want to fight. But when I do fight I want to hit hard." He did. He branded Roosevelt a "demagogue," a "dangerous egotist," and a "flatterer of the people." He added, "I hate a flatterer. I like a man to tell the truth."

Roosevelt slashed back. Taft, he said, was an apostate to reform. He had turned his back on the people. He was a "fathead" and a "puzzlewit"; his intellect fell slightly shy of a guinea pig's. The Ohio papers gleefully reported the exchange of such additional elevating epithets as "Jacobin" (said of Roosevelt) and "honeyfugler" (of Taft). Perhaps afraid that he was missing something, the floundering La Follette (whom Roosevelt had lately accused of trying "to wreck the Progressive cause") arrived at the eleventh hour, just in time to join the smearing.

When the mud stopped flying and the primary votes were counted, Roosevelt claimed a stunning victory. He had bested home-state Taft by nearly fifty thousand votes out of three hundred thousand cast (La Follette garnered less than twenty thousand). The people of Ohio had spoken, and if they didn't shout with quite a single voice, substantially more said "Roosevelt" than "Taft."

X

Yet Roosevelt knew enough not to place too much importance on that one result or, for that matter, on all the primary results taken together. To give him the nomination, his delegates still needed to carry the national convention. This wouldn't be easy, and Roosevelt expected the worst from the regulars. "Evidently, Taft and his associates have prepared to steal the convention if they are able," he wrote a friend.

The president and his supporters obviously wouldn't have phrased it so. They intended to play by the existing party rules, which, as they pointed out, had been good enough for Roosevelt in 1904 and 1908 when he had been on the inside instead of the outside. Perhaps Roosevelt was right, some of them conceded, when he asserted that the majority of the Republican rank and file were behind him. Perhaps not: Primaries left much to be desired, as evidenced by the fact that most states did not employ them. But the matter was moot. The Constitution specified representative government, not mob rule; and the American people, in their collective wisdom, had evolved the present party structures as the most reliable means of implementing representative government.

As the national convention, slated for Chicago, approached, some 250 delegates were in dispute. If Roosevelt could win just 70 or so of these, he would gain the nomination. The sticking point—perhaps an insuperable one—was that the credentials of the delegates would be determined by a committee that had been carefully packed with Taft men.

This didn't prevent Roosevelt's partisans from having a show. The committee deliberated regarding the disputed delegates; delegate by delegate it awarded nearly all of them to Taft. Yet in the background, and frequently in the foreground, Roosevelt's supporters yelled, gesticulated, and otherwise demonstrated their outraged disapproval. Events never quite reached the degree of violence of some of the state conventions, but at times they came close. As the drift of the deliberations grew apparent, the Roosevelt camp denounced the proceedings as illegitimate and worse. The awarding of two California seats to Taft spurred Roosevelt's on-site management to remarkable feats of rhetoric:

> The saturnalia of fraud and larceny now in progress under the auspices of the National Committee took on new repulsiveness today with the announcement of the committee's action in the case of California. It was thought that the limit of folly and indecency had already been reached by this doomed and passion-drunk committee which in the last four days have issued the party's credentials to bogus delegates, reeling with fraud and straight from the cesspools of Southern corruption. Hitherto it was supposed that the National Committee was content with the political emoluments of pocket-picking and porch-climbing. Today, however, they essayed the role of the apache and the garroteer.

Roosevelt was hardly less creative in his denunciation of the committee and all its works. The decision on the delegates essentially determined the nomination, as everyone concerned recognized. Warned by his lieutenants in Chicago that he was about to be shut out, Roosevelt boarded a train from New York and raced to the convention city. There he addressed his followers in the Chicago Auditorium. The chief issue separating the two sides in this contest, he declared, was clearer than ever. "It is not a partisan issue; it is more than a political issue; it is a great moral issue." Taft and his followers were perpetrating a "great crime," which if let stand would jeopardize "not merely our Democratic form of government but our civilization itself." Roosevelt charged Taft with lying when he said he did not represent the bosses of the party; the president's very actions condemned him. These actions amounted to nothing less than "treason," both to the party and to the American people at large. The self-proclaimed party leaders called themselves regulars, as if this accorded them special status. It did not. "Theft and dishonesty cannot give and never shall give a title to regularity."

Roosevelt repudiated the decision of the national committee, and he urged his followers to join him in the repudiation. Evil often succeeded when good men resisted only feebly. "We who are in this fight are not feeble, and we intend to carry the fight to the end." Certain individuals had spoken of a compromise. "There can be no compromise in such a contest." Nor would there be any yielding or flinching. "We have the people behind us overwhelmingly. We have justice and honesty on our side. We are warring against bossism, against privilege social and industrial; we are warring for the elemental virtues of honesty and decency, of fair dealing as between man and man."

Roosevelt asserted that the corruptionists had targeted him in particular, as he had known all along they would. "When I undertook this contest I was well aware of the intense bitterness which my re-entry into politics would cause, I knew that the powers that prey would oppose me, with tenfold the bitterness they would show in opposing any other progressive candidate, simply because they do not fear any other progressive candidate, whereas they very greatly fear me." And well they should, for behind him were arrayed the masses of the people—"the men of faith and vision, the men in whom love of righteousness burns like a flaming fire, who spurn lives of soft and selfish ease, of slothful self-indulgence, who scorn to think only of pleasure for themselves, who feel for and believe in their fellows, whose high fealty is reserved for all that is good, that is just, that is honorable."

The bosses did not know with whom they had tangled. They would know soon. "The trumpets sound the advance, and their peal cannot be drowned by repeating the war-cries of bygone battles, the victory shouts of vanished hosts." It was fitting that the battle should be joined in the foremost city of the state of Lincoln. Were Lincoln alive, he would certainly link arms with the progressives in striving to restore his party to the honest toilers who had given it birth.

Just as Lincoln's struggle had morally transcended the frontiers of America, so did the current struggle. "Nowhere else in all the world is there such a chance for the triumph on a gigantic scale of the cause of Democratic and popular government." The consequences of failure would be equally great, for failure would dispirit all those who looked with fond hope to America for an example of beneficent self-government.

Roosevelt's audience had listened with rapt attention through his long speech, interrupting only to roar assent. The cheers fell silent, gathering force for a tremendous explosion as he drew to the end.

"What happens to me is not of the slightest consequence; I am to be used, as in a doubtful battle any man is used, to his hurt or not, so long as he is useful, and is then cast aside or left to die." But whatever happened to him, the fight must and would continue. The victory might not come at once. "But the victory shall be ours, and it shall be won as we have already won so many victories, by clean and honest fighting for the loftiest of causes. We fight in honorable fashion for the good of mankind; fearless of the future; unheeding of our individual fates; with unflinching hearts and undimmed eyes." Roosevelt's final phrase sent the spirits of his supporters soaring even as it brought down the house: "We stand at Armageddon, and we battle for the Lord!"

XI

Roosevelt judged this moment his finest hour; his foes deemed it his worst; many of his friends considered it his most embarrassing. Each group might well have asked—and some among them did, explicitly—what Roosevelt was doing bringing the Lord into politics at this late hour. Roosevelt's views on religion had always been quietly conventional. Once asked to summarize his thoughts on the subject, he cited the Book of Micah: "To do justly, to show mercy, and to walk humbly before the Lord thy God." That, he said, was the whole of religion. By the standard of his own code, the public Roosevelt had always been strongest on justice, weaker on mercy, and often conspicuously deficient in humility. But heretofore he had left the Lord pretty much out of his politics.

Now he was bringing the Lord smack into politics, and even many of his sympathizers winced. Of course, his talk about Armageddon was thoroughly in character: Leave it to Roosevelt to place himself at the center of the biggest battle in the history, or future, of heaven and earth.

Whether or not he was correct about the Lord's preferences in this particular contest, Roosevelt was right on the money with his statement that the regulars and the corporocrats feared him. Well they might have. To judge by his recent statements, no one else was so likely to stir ordinary people with the passions of class warfare. An outright socialist like Eugene Debs at least had the courtesy to be honest about preaching the overthrow of the capitalist system; Roosevelt, many conservatives believed, would accomplish the same result by deception. And as loopy as Debs was on the subject of the relations of labor and capital, he lacked Roosevelt's flair for demagoguery and his hunger for power. There seemed nothing Roosevelt wouldn't do in the name of the people.

But for Roosevelt the hijacking—as he interpreted it—of the delegates, while depriving him of the nomination, awarded him a greater prize: confirmation of the fundamental righteousness of his candidacy. From the beginning he had recognized the odds against him. He had taught Taft how to employ the machinery of party leadership, and his pupil had learned well. Yet in losing, Roosevelt judged that he had revealed the bosses for what they were and guaranteed that they wouldn't be able to win again, at least not without learning some new tricks. The people were aroused, and there was no telling what they could accomplish.

In the long term they would accomplish the regeneration of American democracy; in the short term they would organize a new party. Following his Armageddon speech, Roosevelt rejected tentative, and perhaps not entirely honest, feelers toward a compromise candidate—"I'll name the compromise candidate," he had said after his Ohio victory. "He'll be me. I'll name the compromise platform. It will be our platform"—and called on his supporters to boycott the further proceedings of the convention. It was the progressives, he said, not the regulars, who represented "eighty per cent of the rank and file of the Republican Party, and ninety-nine per cent of all the men who have the slightest claim to spiritual kinship with Lincoln, or who stand as the heirs of his principles and policies." When his supporters followed his directive, and Taft officially won the party's nomination, Roosevelt announced that he would accept nomination by a new party should his supporters see fit to organize such a party and tender him the offer. "I shall accept the progressive nomination on a progressive platform, and shall fight to the end, win or lose."

Roosevelt harbored no illusions as to the difficulty of running a third-party race. "My feeling is that the Democrats will probably win if they nominate a progressive," he privately predicted. In light of the lead enjoyed by Woodrow Wilson, the progressive governor of New Jersey, this was saying something significant. Yet Roosevelt was convinced that he had to make the fight. The alternative to the kind of reform he was advocating was "a general smashup of our civilization." He added, "Succeed or fail, I hold it to be the duty of every decent man to fight to avoid such a smash."

In early July, while Wilson remained merely a prospective opponent, Roosevelt revised somewhat his earlier judgment and conceded that the governor was an "excellent man." But once the Democrats nominated him, Roosevelt again spied shortcomings. By the beginning of August, Wilson had been downgraded to a "good man" and moreover "one who has in no way shown that he possesses any special fitness for the Presidency." As a professor and subsequently president of Princeton, Wilson had "advocated with skill, intelligence and good breeding the outworn doctrines which were responsible for four fifths of the political troubles of the United States." Originally a conservative who "was being groomed by a section of Wall Street as the special conservative champion against me and my ideas," he had "turned an absolute somersault" on about half of his basic doctrines after being elected New Jersey governor. "He still clings to the other half, and he has shown not the slightest understanding of the really great problems of our present industrial situation."

The platform Wilson was running on was even more dismal than the candidate. "The Democratic platform shows that the Democratic Party now is as stupid, bourbon and reactionary as ever before," Roosevelt declared. "It shows a combination of complete muddleheadedness, with great insincerity." One hardly knew whether to despair more at its domestic or its foreign planks. "It is, to my mind, one of the worst platforms that any party has put out for over forty years."

Roosevelt had already written off Taft and the regular Republicans; now he felt justified in dismissing the Democrats (again). Consequently, when the newly hatched Progressive Party convened at Chicago during the first week of August and made him its nominee, he was morally fortified for the final leg of the contest.

The Progressive convention had all the air of an Episcopal synod. The Progressives were a sober-minded lot, imbued with a sense of virtue and high purpose; even if they hadn't been, the presence in their ranks of a large number of earnest women, entering politics for the first time, would have dampened the holiday-making tendencies of the delegates. Their speeches sounded like sermons, and they sang hymns—especially "Onward, Christian Soldiers" and "The Battle Hymn of the Republic"—at the slightest provocation. One eyewitness from the suburbs remarked, "To see good old Oscar Straus [one of the most prominent Jews in the country] singing 'Onward, Christian Soldiers' with all his might was worth coming in from Lake Forest to see." Another sight that would have been worth coming much farther to see was advertised—whether in faith or fun wasn't clear—by an anonymously circulated flyer: "At Three o'Clock Thursday Afternoon, Theodore Roosevelt Will Walk on the Waters of Lake Michigan."

Roosevelt contributed to what he conceded was the "fairly religious fervor" of the gathering with a sermon of his own. He congratulated the delegates on their boldness and proclaimed the wisdom and necessity of their break with the old parties. "The time is ripe, and overripe, for a genuine Progressive movement, nation-wide and justice-loving, sprung from and responsible to the people themselves, and sundered by a great gulf from both of the old party organizations, while representing all that is best in the hopes, beliefs, and aspirations of the plain people who make up the immense majority of the rank and file of both the old parties." He ran through the list of reforms he had been espousing and which, not surprisingly, became the platform of the new party, and he perorated much as in his earlier Chicago speech. "Our cause is based on the eternal principles of righteousness; and even though we who now lead may for the time fail, in the end the cause itself shall triumph." Undaunted, as usual, by the criticism of his pretentious moralism, he plagiarized himself: "We stand at Armageddon, and we battle for the Lord."

XII

Roosevelt's strategy during the campaign for the general election was to portray Taft and Wilson as two of a kind, creatures of the bosses, and to distance himself from both. In his speeches he alternated the usages "Taft-Wilson" and "Wilson-Taft" in characterizing policies implemented or advocated by his two rivals. But while Taft played along, himself drawing away from his erstwhile party mate, Wilson complicated matters by cozying up to Roosevelt, or at least to the progressive principles Roosevelt stood for.

Yet although both Roosevelt and Wilson could fairly be labeled progressives, there was a substantial philosophical difference between their brands of the reform doctrine. As Roosevelt pointed out (exaggerating in the process), Wilson was uncomfortable with power. In attempting to restore the balance among business, labor, and consumers, Wilson preferred weakening the first, while Roosevelt advocated strengthening the second and third. Wilson wished to return to the competitiveness of an earlier, preindustrial, pretrust era; he would knock big businesses back down to size and then let the rules of laissez-faire do the rest. Roosevelt, by contrast, accepted great size as an inescapable consequence of modernization; he would control the corporations not by hobbling them but by bolstering the government agencies that would regulate their affairs.

Roosevelt carried his message across the continent on a barnstorming tour that began in New England in late August, traversed the northern tier of states to Washington, dropped down to California in mid-September, and wended back east via the Midwest and South. He arrived home at the beginning of October. He conferred briefly at Oyster Bay with the men who were raising money for his campaign; they informed him that there was enough in the kitty for another swing before election day. So he took off again.

Hoping to capitalize on the strength of progressivism in the upper Midwest, he returned to Michigan and Minnesota before reviewing a parade of Progressives through the streets of Chicago. He still thought Wilson had the edge over him in the three-way race (with Taft third), but fired as he always was by the excitement of campaigning, he could hope for an upset.

With just three weeks to go, his train pulled into Milwaukee on October 14. While making his way from the hotel to the auditorium where he would speak, Roosevelt was approached by an unfamiliar man, presumably one of his many supporters. Suddenly the man pulled a gun and shot the candidate at close range. During the previous weeks, Roosevelt's long-windedness had worn down his voice, which grew hoarser at each campaign stop; now it may have saved his life. The bullet plowed through the folded speech manuscript in the breast pocket of his coat before hitting his metal eyeglass case; together the bulky manuscript and the case slowed the slug sufficiently that it did no lasting harm.

Roosevelt understood the situation at once. "As I did not cough blood," he told Kermit a few days later, "I was pretty sure the wound was not a fatal one." All the same, the doctors who examined him didn't want to take any chances and ordered that he be driven to a hospital at once.

Roosevelt refused. Staggering painfully onto the podium—although the wound wasn't mortal, it felt as if he was being stabbed with each breath—he delivered his most dramatic performance ever. "Friends, I shall ask you to be as quiet as possible," he said. "I don't know whether you fully understand that I have just been shot; but it takes more than that to kill a Bull Moose. . . . The bullet is in me now, so that I cannot make a very long speech, but I will try my best." He unbuttoned his vest and showed the bloodstained shirt to the audience, which gasped in a combination of horror and admiration.

The peculiar circumstances gave special weight to Roosevelt's insistence that he hadn't taken on this candidacy for his own welfare but for that of the country. "I have altogether too important things to think of to feel any concern over my own death; and now I cannot speak to you insincerely within five minutes of being shot. I am telling you the literal truth when I say that my concern is for many other things. It is not in the least for my own life. I want you to understand that I am ahead of the game, anyway. No man has had a happier life than I have led; a happier life in every way. I have been able to do certain things that I greatly wished to do, and I am interested in doing other things. I can tell you with absolute truthfulness that I am very much uninterested in whether I am shot or not."

Roosevelt recalled his days as colonel of the Rough Riders, when he had thrown himself into battle, heedless of his personal safety. He tied the present attempt on his life to the infamous attacks his political enemies had been making on him. "It is a very natural thing that weak and vicious minds should be inflamed to acts of violence by the kind of awful mendacity and abuse that have been heaped upon me for the last three months." The Republicans, Democrats, and Socialists, and the newspapers that spouted their propaganda, shouldn't be surprised at the consequences of their unceasing untruthfulness, especially on unbalanced natures. "They cannot expect that such natures will be unaffected by it."

As he spoke, Roosevelt's advisers repeatedly beckoned him to finish. Journalist friend O. K. Davis, concerned that he had lost color and seemed to be struggling more than before, gently laid his hand on the candidate's arm. "He stopped and glared at me ferociously . . ." Davis recorded afterward. "He said, 'No Sir, I will not stop. You can't stop me nor anybody else.'" Turning to the audience, Roosevelt explained, "My friends are a little more nervous than I am. Don't you waste any sympathy on me. I have had an A–1 time in life and I am having it now."

He certainly was. Although accustomed to commanding the attention of the country, he realized that he had never had such a stage as this. He also guessed that this might be his last public appearance before the election. "I know these doctors, when they get hold of me, will never let me go back," he confided to the crowd. "And there are just a few things more that I want to say to you." He warned that Wilson, whatever he professed, was not a true progressive; he reminded that Taft had stolen the nomination, not so much from him but from the people. Disavowing yet again any personal interest in the outcome, he advocated a vote for the Progressive platform in November—"for only by voting for that platform can you be true to the cause of progress throughout this Union."

XIII

Needless to say, the attempt on Roosevelt's life and his heroic if melodramatic speech with a bullet lodged beside his heart captured the imagination of the country. Wilson and Taft immediately cabled their concern; Wilson pledged to suspend his own campaigning until Roosevelt recovered.

The recovery began almost with the speech itself. "The Colonel was feeling very good, in excellent spirits," O. K. Davis wrote, describing Roosevelt at the hospital awaiting X rays. "His color had returned and he looked better than he had at any time since leaving Chicago.

He dictated several telegrams to Mrs. Roosevelt and sat upon the operating table talking and joking with the doctors and nurses." The X rays and examinations revealed that the bullet was buried in the muscle of the chest wall, where it posed little danger and might easily be reached if it started to. The doctors decided to leave it there.

Notwithstanding the rapid rebound and positive prognosis, the physicians confined Roosevelt for several days to a hospital bed in Chicago, which had better facilities than Milwaukee. He felt considerable discomfort, but his spirits remained high. Edith, who naturally had been stunned by the news of the attempt on her husband's life— despite his telegram reassuring her that his wound was "trivial" and not "a particle more serious than one of the injuries any of the boys used continually to be having"—came quickly from New York to oversee his recovery. The iron law she imposed upon the sickroom, keeping nosy reporters and even most well-wishers at bay, caused a chuckle among observers who recalled her husband's diatribes against boss rule. Platt, Hanna, and the others were pushovers compared to Mrs. Roosevelt, reckoned one journalist.

> That sedate and determined woman, from the moment of her arrival in Chicago, took charge of affairs and reduced the Colonel to pitiable subjection. Up to her advent he was throwing bombshells into his doctors. . . . The moment she arrived a hush fell upon T.R. . . . He became as meek as Moses. Now and then the Colonel would send out secretly for somebody he knew and wanted to talk to, but every time the vigilant Mrs. Roosevelt would swoop down on the emissary. . . . No such tyrannical sway has ever been seen in the history of American politics.

Roosevelt thrived on the attention of his wife, as well of Alice, Ted, and Ethel, who joined their mother at his bedside. "I am in great shape," he told Bamie. "Really the time in the hospital, with Edith and the children here, has been a positive spree, and I have enjoyed it. Of course I would like to have been in the campaign, but it can't be helped and there is no use crying over what can't be helped!"

To the public he issued a more solemn message. "It matters little about me but it matters all about the cause we fight for. If one soldier who happens to carry the flag is stricken, another will take it from his hands and carry it on." He reiterated that he had not chosen to run but had been chosen, as Lincoln and his generation had been chosen.

"Only the call that came to the men of the sixties made me answer it, in our day, as they did more nobly in their day." It didn't matter whether he personally lived or died, for the cause would continue. Speaking through fellow Progressive Albert Beveridge, he said, "Tell the people not to worry about me, for if I go down another will take my place. For always, the army is true. Always the cause is there, and it is the cause for which the people care, for it is the people's cause."

Roosevelt left the hospital and returned to Oyster Bay two weeks before the election. He mustered sufficient strength for a brief speech at Madison Square Garden and another at his home during the last few days of the campaign. "The greatest of all issues is honesty—honesty in business and honesty in politics alike," he declared. The election of Wilson would mean the enthronement of Tammany in New York and its counterparts elsewhere; the election of Taft would reentrench the Republican bosses who had held sway during the last four years. The Progressives offered the only true alternative. "We, and we alone, stand for the real right of the people to rule their own government."

The people didn't agree. Or perhaps they had other reasons for electing Wilson, who garnered 6.3 million votes to 4.1 million for Roosevelt and 3.5 million for Taft.

CHAPTER TWENTY-EIGHT

The River of Doubt
1913–14

"Well, we have gone down in a smashing defeat," Roosevelt conceded the day after, adding, "Whether it is a Waterloo or a Bull Run, time only can tell." He had some ideas on the subject and on the general significance of what he and the Progressives had wrought. "I had expected defeat," he told Arthur Lee, "but I had expected that we would make a better showing." In New York and Massachusetts, for instance, he had thought he would run second to Wilson; as it happened, he had lost to Taft as well. "But I suppose that I ought not to expect that in three months we could form a new Party that would do as well as we have actually done. We had all the money, all the newspapers and all the political machinery against us and, above all, we had the habit of thought of the immense mass of dull unimaginative men who simply vote according to the party symbol." Looking ahead, Roosevelt couldn't say whether the Progressive Party per se would persist; too many unknowable influences were at work. "But the Progressive movement must and will go forward." The country required it. "The alternative is oscillation between the greedy arrogance of a party directed by conscienceless millionaires and the greedy envy of a party directed by reckless and unscrupulous demagogues."

Would Roosevelt go forward with the progressive movement? That was more problematic. For public consumption he was as eager as ever. He declared that he was "proud to have made the fight" and that "the next four years will make the 1916 fight much easier." He promised his continuing best efforts, telling one supporter, "You may be sure that I am in this fight to stay and that from now on all I can do will be done to help the Progressive Party to victory." But even this formulation left him some maneuvering room, for he might conclude that the best thing for the movement was for him to stand aside. He told another backer that it would be "a real misfortune" if the Progressive Party didn't develop another leader by 1916.

He was more forthcoming to Arthur Lee. "As things were this year," he explained, "there was no human being who could have made any fight or have saved the whole movement from collapse if I had not been willing to step in and take the hammering. But it doesn't seem to me as if I could ever make up my mind to repeat the experiment." Roosevelt admitted to his old friend that he personally shrank from putting himself through another such ordeal. Besides, there were sound political reasons that he shouldn't carry the banner again—reasons that, indeed, had applied to the late campaign. "While the fight could only have been made under my leadership, yet it is also true that an infinitely stronger attack was made upon me than would have been made upon any other Progressive leader."

The relation of the leader to the party, and of the party to the political system as a whole, occupied Roosevelt during the several months after the election. It occupied his fellow Progressives even more. Roosevelt had risked only reputation—and life, if one counted the assassination attempt—in his divorce from the Republicans; his colleagues had hazarded their careers. Roosevelt could retire to Sagamore Hill, comfortable financially and in the pride of what he had accomplished; they might retire from politics—might be forced to—but most would still have to find livelihoods.

A few, fainter-hearted and farther-seeing than the rest, were already resigning themselves to a return to the Republican Party. Recognizing the historical habit of American democracy to chew up third parties, swallow the kernel, and spit out the husk—the most recent morsel being the Populists—they perceived no future for the Progressives. Others, like Roosevelt fascinated with the Lincolnian roots of Republicanism, saw the crisis of modern industrialism as being no less fundamental than the sectional crisis of the 1850s, and perceived the Progressive Party as the latter-day equivalent of the Republican Party of Lincoln's era and the harbinger of a new alignment in American politics.

Despite the evidence of the election, the romantic in Roosevelt dearly hoped for the latter to be the case. "The Progressive Party has come to stay," he had prophesied to his nephew a week before the election, when it was already apparent he wasn't going to win. Shortly after the election he told a supporter from a district that had gone Progressive: "I only wish the rest of the country had followed your example. However, perhaps they will see the light a little later on."

Considering the blame he had heaped on the Republicans lately and the Democrats since his political baptism, Roosevelt could hardly do anything other than hope for a new alignment. Concern for the spirits of his followers also drove him in the direction of optimism—at least in public. A month after the polling, the Progressives met, again in Chicago, to lick their wounds and buck up one another's courage. "We have fought a great fight," Roosevelt told the assembly. "We have accomplished more in ninety days than ever any other party in our history accomplished in such a length of time."

Precisely what the Progressives had accomplished was somewhat harder for Roosevelt to say. He claimed that the Progressives had "overthrown the powerful and corrupt machine that betrayed and strangled the Republican party"—this despite the fact that the bosses were still in charge and, with the Progressives departed, no longer encumbered by them. He declared that the Progressives had forced all parties and candidates to pay "at least lip service to Progressive principles"—but he supplied no concrete evidence that the service went beyond the lips to the minds or hearts, especially of the Republican Party.

Achieving such results as they had achieved, however, had been personally exhausting, and even while forecasting a bright future for the Progressive movement, Roosevelt hinted that it might have to go forward without him. He asserted that "in the matter of leadership, both local and national, we may trust the events of the next year or two to develop our ablest and most resourceful man." He reminded his listeners that, in any case, the leader mattered less than the mission. "The Progressive party is the servant of the people. No man should come into this party with the idea that he can establish a claim on it; he must be content with the opportunity it offers for service and for sacrifice."

II

This last warning was aimed at those who *were* making claims on the party. The defeat at the ballot box predictably provoked finger-pointing and postmortem repositioning. Principal among those blamed for the loss was George Perkins, the Morgan partner, who perhaps from aching conscience and certainly from admiration for Roosevelt, had embraced progressivism, to the extent of underwriting a major part of the 1912 campaign. Roosevelt spent much of the following winter defending Perkins against the assaults of Gifford Pinchot, his brother Amos Pinchot, and others who couldn't believe that a Morgan man could be an honest—or at any rate an effective—Progressive. The squabbling brought out the best in none of those involved, except perhaps Roosevelt, who loyally stuck by his financial angel. "I don't think we could have carried on the fight at all without him," Roosevelt told Gifford Pinchot. To the other Pinchot, Roosevelt spoke more sharply regarding Perkins: "I feel that this whole assault on him has been not only thoroughly unjustifiable, but contains the greatest element of menace which we now face as to the future of the Progressive Party." Those who wanted to jettison Perkins to purify the party were those who would render the party forever ineffectual. "Do you not know that Lincoln's fight was half the time a fight to prevent foolish extremists from ruining the antislavery cause and ruining the union by insisting upon ostracizing the moderate men?"

The attempted purge of the moderates elicited third thoughts among many Progressives regarding the wisdom of their earlier apostasy; a new wave of recantations followed. The most noted of the recanters, not least because he provided his own news coverage, was magaziner Frank Munsey, whose journal and pocketbook had contributed about equally to the 1912 campaign. It was a measure of Roosevelt's own ambivalence regarding the new party that he, uncharacteristically, didn't question Munsey's motives in retreating to Republicanism. "He sympathizes with the Progressive Platform," Roosevelt told Hiram Johnson, "but he is not a crusader, and he is suspicious of some of the extremists in our ranks." Munsey apparently estimated that the Progressive Party wouldn't amount to anything without substantial defections from the Democrats, which, after the election of Wilson, didn't seem likely. "Therefore very naturally and from entirely proper motives, although as I think very unwisely, he is openly casting about for some scheme that will bring the [Progressive and Republican] parties together."

All the same, Roosevelt himself wasn't about to return to the Republican fold. Maybe Munsey didn't take politics personally, but he—Roosevelt—did. He still seethed over what he judged the theft of the nomination by the Taftites. "It is for the Taft Republicans to come to us, and not for us to go to them," he insisted. "The nomination of Mr. Taft was a stolen nomination, deeply discreditable to every beneficiary of it." Even after the inauguration of Wilson gave Roosevelt, Taft, and their various supporters something to complain about in common, Roosevelt refused to forgive or forget. His younger daughter Ethel was married in April 1913; Sagamore Hill hosted several hundred friends and acquaintances. But Roosevelt pointedly declined to invite such old friends as Taft and Elihu Root; they would have been "unwelcome guests," he explained.

During the first months of 1913, Roosevelt repeatedly urged his followers to keep the faith. In January he wrote a circular letter to several prominent Progressive committeemen, saying, "It is imperatively necessary for every true Progressive to make it clearly understood that this party has come to stay, and that under no circumstances will there be any amalgamation with either of the old parties." Shortly thereafter he vowed, "I shall fight as strongly as I know how for the perpetuation of this party exactly in its present shape and with no more attempt at fusion with one of the old machines than with the other." He wrote and spoke on behalf of Progressive candidates; in March he made a special trip to Michigan to campaign for Progressives there.

At the same time, he began to hedge his bets—emotionally and privately, if not politically and publicly. He wrote to Arthur Lee, "As for the Progressive Party, no human being can tell what will happen." If the Democrats split, the Progressives might provide a home to one wing. But if the Democrats held together, the future of the Progressives would be bleaker. "It may be that the Progressive Party will be eliminated." To his sister-in-law Emily Carow, Roosevelt said much the same thing—in a form he would have vehemently repudiated during the campaign: "If the Democrats do well, then the reason for a Progressive Party will be so small that the ground may be swept from under our feet."

III

During this same period, Roosevelt spent as much time looking backward as looking forward. Having largely suspended his editorial attachment to the *Outlook* during the campaign, he had since committed himself to providing serial installments of an autobiography. These ran in the journal during several months starting in February 1913; many newspapers ran them as well. At the end of the year they were published in book form.

Roosevelt's autobiography, even more than most such exercises by political figures, read like an extended campaign speech: part homily, part platform, part defense of past actions. Even more than elsewhere, Roosevelt identified himself with the nation. He took as his theme the proposition that, in the life of the nation as in the life of the individual, principled performance required the melding of often-opposite qualities: practical efficiency with lofty vision; zeal for righteousness with love of peace; personal responsibility with willingness to employ collective power; respect for the state with an embrace of the family; duty with joy for life. His own life became a case study of just how this melding should be accomplished.

In an age of immigration (which peaked just about the time of the book's publication), he honored his immigrant ancestors, emphasizing the modest circumstances of the first couple of generations rather than the affluence of Grandfather Cornelius. In an age that sought to tie up the wounds of the Civil War, he highlighted the southern roots of his mother that complemented the northern antecedents of his father. To an audience increasingly of city dwellers but who recalled the simpler life of the country, he told of growing up in Manhattan but blossoming outside the city. To a nation fast converting the frontier from real estate to myth, he described his life as a rancher. He spoke knowingly of the habits of wild Indians, western outlaws, grizzly bears, mountain lions, and political and corporate bosses. He extolled the "strenuous life" and refought battles that covered the landscape of his career from Albany and Dakota to Cuba and Washington. He brought peace to the Pennsylvania coalfields and northeastern Asia; he set dirt flying in Panama and sent the fleet around the world. When someone occasionally exhibited greater proficiency or sounder judgment than the author, that person invariably sprang from the ranks of ordinary people—the Bill Sewalls of America—from whom no public official should be embarrassed to take instruction. It was, in sum, a work that revealed next to nothing important about Roosevelt that wasn't already common knowledge.

The book differed from Roosevelt's stump speeches in being more circumspect about the numerous opponents he had encountered during his career. He wrote scathingly enough at times, but rarely about individuals identifiable by name—although astute readers didn't have much difficulty supplying the deficiency. His reticence was calculated; he aimed, he said privately, to strike "just the happy middle" between candor and discretion. "The hardest task I have is to keep my temper," he explained to Cabot Lodge, "and not speak of certain people, the editors of the *Evening Post,* for instance, anti-imperialists, universal peace and arbitration men and the like, as they richly deserve. The various admirable movements in which I have been engaged, have always developed among their members a large lunatic fringe; and I have had plenty of opportunity of seeing individuals who in their revolt against sordid baseness go into utterly wild folly."

IV

During the same period that saw him writing his memoirs, Roosevelt directed his literary energies in other directions as well. He had been duly promoted from vice president to president of the American Historical Association and consequently delivered the keynote address at the annual winter meeting. The audience at Boston included more than the usual crowd of academics taking advantage of the cheap hotel rates in the dead week between Christmas and New Year's. A former United States president and recent presidential candidate was an oddity among the professional historians; on this account and because Roosevelt still captured the imagination of millions of Americans, newspapers and magazines gave the speech far wider coverage than the head of the historians' guild had ever received before or would again.

Roosevelt ranged in his address from ancient Egypt to modern

America in arguing for the restoration of the romantic element in historical literature. In the early twentieth century, most academic historians had abandoned the idea of history as art in favor of history as science. Roosevelt knew more science than nearly all of even the most scientifically minded historians, and yet he contended that the scientific approach was sterile and ultimately self-defeating. The amassing of facts—the preoccupation of the scientific historians—was necessary to first-rate historical writing, but it was scarcely sufficient. In the same way that an inspired architectural imagination was required to fashion piles of stones into a soaring cathedral, so an inspired historical imagination was required to fashion piles of facts into a moving historical narrative. The point of historical writing, Roosevelt asserted, was to edify and ennoble. The great historian must also be a "great moralist," and the highest use of history was "to thrill the souls of men with stories of strength and craft and daring, and to lift them out of their common selves to heights of high endeavor." Roosevelt nodded in the direction of recounting the daily business of life, but his examples betrayed his strong preference for the grandly romantic and heroic.

> The true historian will bring the past before our eyes as if it were the present. He will make us see as living men the hard-faced archers of Agincourt, and the war-worn spearmen who followed Alexander down beyond the rim of the known world. We shall hear grate on the coast of Britain the keels of the Low-Dutch sea-thieves whose children's children were to inherit unknown continents. We shall thrill to the triumphs of Hannibal. . . . We shall see conquerors riding forward to victories that have changed the course of time. . . . Dead poets shall sing to us the deeds of men of might and the love and the beauty of women. . . . We shall sit at feast with the kings of Nineveh when they drink from ivory and gold. With Queen Meave in her sun-parlor we shall watch the nearing chariots of the champions. For us the war-horns of King Olaf shall wail across the flood.

After more along these lines, Roosevelt left his listeners with the forecast that future historians—future true historians—would see similar grand and heroic themes in American history. Although he modestly declined to cite his own work by name, his audience had no difficulty catching echoes of *The Winning of the West* in his lyrical description of the "hesitating early ventures into the Indian-haunted forest" and of the "endless march of the white-topped wagon-trains across plain and mountain to the coast of the greatest of the five great oceans." Future historians would have to account for the hard materialism of the modern age, but those who sought the wellsprings of American life would find them in a unique character and spirit. "A people whose heroes are Washington and Lincoln, a peaceful people who fought to a finish one of the bloodiest of wars, waged solely for the sake of a great principle and a noble idea, surely possess an emergency-standard far above mere money-getting."

Roosevelt projected his romantic view from the past into the future. "When the tale is finally told," he predicted, "I believe that it will show that the forces working for good in our national life outweigh the forces working for evil, and that, with many blunders and shortcomings, with much halting and turning aside from the path, we shall yet in the end prove our faith by our works, and show in our lives our belief that righteousness exalteth a nation."

V

Righteousness and exaltation were for the long term; meanwhile the blunders and haltings prevailed. Roosevelt spent much of the spring and summer of 1913 critiquing the performance of the first Democratic president since Grover Cleveland. Roosevelt's already sour impression of Wilson continued to acidify with each month the new chief executive occupied the office Roosevelt had wanted back.

Wilson, like nearly every other American president, had been elected chiefly for his presumed ability to handle the country's domestic problems. He had claimed no particular abilities pertinent to foreign affairs, and voters attributed none to him; but such was the apparently settled state of the world that none seemed required of him. So little concern did he have regarding international affairs that he used the secretaryship of state, the nation's top diplomatic job, as a device to soothe the ruffled feelings of the man he had displaced as leader of the Democratic Party, William Jennings Bryan. The Great Commoner had his gifts—even if Roosevelt often found them hard to discern—but no one claimed that they included mastery of the game of nations.

So it was ironic that Wilson spent most of his presidency caught in the coils of international affairs. The troubles began almost with his arrival at the White House. The Mexican revolution was boiling again; two weeks before Wilson's inauguration, Francisco Madero, the man who had pushed aside longtime strongman Porfirio Diaz, was himself deposed and shortly thereafter killed. (Roosevelt evidently shed few tears for Madero, although just months earlier he had accepted the then-Mexican–president's condolences on losing the 1912 election and offered "all good wishes" in return.) Wilson and Bryan found the method of succession-by-murder offensive, and the White House refused to recognize the new government of Victoriano Huerta.

Whatever nonrecognition may have done for the moral sensibilities of Wilson and Bryan, it accomplished little by way of restoring stability to Mexico. Roosevelt was no longer offering to lead a division of volunteer cavalry across the Rio Grande, but he did suggest indirectly that the president should seek the aid of some of the Latin American states in an effort to arrange a settlement. "What it has seemed to me might be done," he told an editor with connections to the White House, "is to ask powers such as Chile, Argentina, Brazil—big, stable South American powers—to join with us, or else join in helping us as to just what to do to get order in Mexico somewhat along the lines of what we have done in Santo Domingo and Cuba." Yet Roosevelt didn't desire at this very early stage to lecture the president in public on how to handle his job. His suggestion, he said, "must be entirely confidential, as I do not want to seem to be advising Mr. Wilson."

The Mexican situation, at the moment, was merely a bother; more menacing was renewed tension with Japan. Nativists in California were up to their old ugliness once more, this time barring Japanese and other Asians from owning land in the state. Roosevelt didn't deny the principle behind the restriction: He still opposed the immigration of large numbers of Japanese to the United States, and he believed that the people of the United States had every right to determine who should be admitted to citizenship and on what conditions. But he insisted that this was a matter for the national government, not any state, to decide, and he contended that it should be handled in a manner that didn't needlessly aggravate tensions with Japan.

Even in saying this, however, he held that the Japanese government must be made to know that America was prepared for any trouble

Tokyo might precipitate; and it was on this score that he thought the Wilson administration fell particularly short. Bryan was taking the position he had long espoused, namely that nearly every difference was negotiable, including, in this case, the issue of Japanese immigration and land ownership. Wilson backed his secretary of state. Roosevelt again refrained from criticizing Wilson in public, and in private correspondence with his Japanese friend Kaneko he supported the overall aims of the administration even while conceding that he would have handled things differently.

Under his breath, though, he was fuming. He derided what he—following others—called Bryan's "grape juice diplomacy." The label derived originally from prohibitionist Bryan's banning of alcohol from receptions and dinners hosted by the State Department, but to Roosevelt it seemed a perfect metaphor for the spineless talking Bryan and Wilson seemed to be substituting for real diplomacy. "Well!" Roosevelt snorted. "Grape juice diplomacy under Wilson does not bid fair to be much better than dollar diplomacy under Taft."

Roosevelt's opinion of Wilson and Bryan slid steadily during the following months. The situation in Mexico grew more confused and threatening, Japan swaggered as belligerently as ever, and one Balkan crisis in a series of several roiled the once again troubled surface of European politics. Yet the Democrats made no move to prepare to counter military challenges to American interests. In failing to do so, Roosevelt believed, they rendered such challenges the more likely. In a letter to Lodge in September 1913, Roosevelt declared Bryan "the most contemptible figure we have ever had as Secretary of State." But Bryan was no worse than Wilson, who had to bear responsibility for his subordinate. "I regard Wilson with contemptuous dislike. He has ability of a certain kind, and he has the nerve that his type so often shows in civil and domestic affairs where there is no danger of physical violence. He will jump up and down on cheap politicians, and bully and cajole men in public life who are anxious not to part company with their political chief. But he is a ridiculous creature in international matters. He is a narrow and bitter partisan, and he is intellectually thoroughly dishonest."

Events of the next few years would give Roosevelt a legitimate basis in fact for criticizing Wilson, but to this point the Democratic president's sins, such as they were, hardly merited the intemperance of

Roosevelt's language. Of course, Roosevelt had always been intemperate regarding his political opponents; his maligning of Wilson's motives and methods surely came as no surprise to Lodge (who himself developed a dislike for Wilson that had a more fateful impact on world affairs than Roosevelt's) or to others familiar with Roosevelt. Taft, for example, knew all about Roosevelt's tendencies in this regard. Indeed, Roosevelt's animus toward Wilson was probably of a piece with much of the ill will he bore toward Taft—in short, the resentment of one used to the limelight for whoever steals it. Roosevelt had conjured up reasons for despising Taft; now he did likewise for Wilson. But to a large extent these reasons were merely rationalizations for something simpler but less consciously acceptable: envy.

VI

By July 1913, Roosevelt had spent a longer period living continuously at Sagamore Hill than he had spent living in any one house since he was a child, and his feet began to itch. The itching intensified from the absence of Edith, who had been called to Europe to tend her ailing sister Emily; without Edith, the big house on the hill seemed empty.

Not that it actually *was* empty. If anything, the house was more crowded than it had been for years. Alice and Nick spent much of the summer of 1913 there; as with most things involving Alice, this was a mixed blessing. The previous twelve months had been hard on her and Nick. Roosevelt's candidacy placed Nick in the excruciating position of having to choose between his family and his future. To be sure, Roosevelt himself didn't ask his son-in-law to commit political suicide: "Of course you must be for Taft." And Nick *had* been for Taft. But the campaign made his life miserable. Alice couldn't flaunt her support for her father without making Nick look bad, while he couldn't work as hard for the Republican ticket as an up-and-comer ought to—as his father-in-law, for example, had at his age—without annoying Alice. Things just got worse when Nick lost his own bid for reelection. Not unreasonably, and not alone, he judged Roosevelt's rending of the party a strong contributing factor to his defeat. And if this weren't enough, his loss, by forcing a relocation from Washington to Cincinnati, sent Alice into a state of chronic ill humor.

Ted's situation wasn't any happier. Deciding that his prospects weren't bright enough in California, Theodore and Edith's eldest son had returned east to take work with a New York financial firm. He joined a fast social set in Manhattan, began drinking heavily, and started neglecting Eleanor and Grace. When he chose to spend Christmas Day of 1912 at the Ritz rather than at Sagamore, Edith was infuriated, declaring that his highest aspiration in life seemed to be to make himself "a tin pin in a pin cushion." Theodore was less visibly hurt, but he must have wondered whether his son wasn't entering that dark place that had devoured Elliott.

Fortunately, Kermit was faring better. A flurry of application had compensated for his safari-making and gotten him through Harvard on schedule; with the prosaic matter of academic education out of the way, he began looking for something more exciting. He found it in the form of a job with a company constructing railroads in Brazil. Part of his father probably wished he could go off on this adventure with his son, but at the time Kermit set sail in the summer of 1912, the older man was girding for Armageddon.

As a result, Kermit wasn't home during Edith's absence during the summer of 1913, but the other children were. Ethel, who resided with her husband Richard Derby in Manhattan, popped in and out. Alice fled Ohio for the more civilized haunts of the East Coast, including Oyster Bay; Nick came along for part of the visit. Ted brought Eleanor and Grace as well as Eleanor's mother out to Sagamore for vacation. Archie and Quentin were home from Harvard and Groton, respectively, for the summer.

To Edith in Italy, all the comings and goings sounded horribly stressful—"just when everything should be managed to shield Father." She complained to Kermit that his siblings had settled upon his father "like vampires, filling the house with people they want to know, using Father as a bait!"

But Father didn't mind. He had always liked to have people about—his children especially—and he recognized the comparative freedom they enjoyed with their mother gone. "Ted and Eleanor and Alice had a feeling as if in the absence of mother they could impose all their least desirable friends on pagan old father," he told Kermit.

"Accordingly they planned various delightfully wicked feasts of friends whom they thought mother would not like to have." But in the end, he explained with a chuckle, nothing transpired "except two very small and stodgily virtuous dinners!"

VII

Yet even the presence of the children could relieve his itching feet only so long; consequently, just after Independence Day he and Archie and Quentin boarded a train in New York, bound for the Southwest. The trip combined sightseeing (the Grand Canyon, the Painted Desert, Hopi villages) with hunting (most notably cougars in northern Arizona). The colonel of the Rough Riders touched base with old comrades-in-arms, and on the return trip met with some Progressive leaders at Chicago.

Although interesting in its own right—and valuable for the time Roosevelt got to spend with his younger sons—this southwestern trip was a mere warm-up for a much more ambitious journey. Since childhood Roosevelt had been fascinated by South America, especially the great Amazon rain forest, home to more plant and animal species than anyplace else on earth. Moreover, the Amazon was the last great uncharted wilderness; decades after Roosevelt's heroes Speke and Livingston traced the course of the Nile and mapped most of interior Africa, large swaths of the Amazon still defied and tantalized explorers and cartographers. Roosevelt had proved himself as a hunter and frontiersman and soldier, but he had never done any real exploring. He couldn't help wondering if he had the stuff.

He had first started thinking seriously about a South American expedition late in his second term as president. John Zahm, a Holy Cross priest connected to Notre Dame University and a philosopher-naturalist whose work Roosevelt admired, visited the president and regaled him with stories of his journeys across the southern continent, and suggested something similar for him. At that time Roosevelt was already laying plans for his African safari, and he set thoughts of Amazonia aside. But his triumphal 1910 tour of Europe inspired certain South American governments to issue invitations for analogous attention, and as he weighed the invitations he recalled Father Zahm's suggestion. Letters, telegrams, phone calls, and personal consultations eventually supplied the itinerary: He would travel by ship to Rio de Janeiro, then overland across southern Brazil to Uruguay, Argentina, and Chile. On this phase of the trip he would discharge his obligations as former president, Nobel laureate, and famous world figure. Edith would accompany him; Kermit, who was between jobs in Brazil and as eager for adventure as ever, would join them in Bahia.

The real fun would begin following a return to Buenos Aires, where he and Kermit would put Edith aboard a ship for home and would head north to Paraguay. Ascending the Paraguay River into Brazil, they would connect with a couple of American naturalists and a Brazilian expeditionary force headed by one Colonel Rondon, a famously intrepid veteran of numerous explorations into the wildest parts of the continent. The group would cross the divide separating the waters flowing south into Paraguay and Argentina from those flowing north into the Amazon. They would embark on a voyage down a large river that disappeared off the maps into the unknown vastness of the equatorial rain forest. Gravity dictated that the river's waters ultimately mingled with those of the main channel of the Amazon, whose course was well charted. But where the mingling took place and what route the river—aptly called the Rio da Dúvida, or River of Doubt—followed between its headwaters and its final destination, no one could say.

As before, Roosevelt arranged institutional backing, in this case from the American Museum of Natural History and the Brazilian government. He also arranged publicity, again in the form of a series of articles he would write and send to *Scribner's*.

The trip commenced slowly, from a literary if not a geographical point of view. To quicken the pace, and the reader's pulse, Roosevelt related the dangers to come. He dwelled especially on the deadly snakes that infested the forests. A visit to a herpetological research institute afforded what excuse he required to provide a detailed description of the serpents his party could be expected to meet. Nor could he resist recounting, in the most egregiously—but nonetheless engagingly—anthropomorphic terms, a (staged) fight to the death between two formidable snakes. The villain of the piece was the "vicious" jararaca, perhaps the most lethal creature to crawl the brush and branches of the jungle; the hero was the peace-loving (and non-venomous) mussurama. The hero triumphed through pluck and bravery (and biochemical immunity to jararaca venom), causing Roosevelt, who had handled the mussurama before the fight, to exult, "I never saw cooler or more utterly unconcerned conduct; and the ease and certainty with which the terrible poisonous snake was mastered gave me the heartiest respect and liking for the easy-going, good-natured, and exceedingly efficient serpent which I had been holding in my arms."

Roosevelt made much of the malevolent ferocity of nature in the rain forest. To the snakes were added myriad species of maddening and frequently death-dealing insects: termites that chewed through tents, boots, books (of which Roosevelt brought his usual ample supply), and anything else they could lay mandibles on; mosquitoes and ticks that carried malaria and other tropical fevers; carnivorous ants that found human legs a tasty break from monkey and peccary carcasses. The skies were the home of bloodsucking vampire bats, which siphoned the very life liquid out of mammals of the four- and two-legged varieties. A person seeking relief from the insects or the bats might take refuge in the nearest stream; if so, he wouldn't last long if that stream were home, as it likely was, to piranhas, the flesh-eating fish that could strip every ounce of soft tissue from the body of a horse or man within minutes, leaving only bare bones awash in bloody water.

Roosevelt invested his tale with almost gothic grotesqueness, the better to highlight the heroism of those explorers, not excluding himself, who braved such perils to extend the realm of scientific knowledge and modern civilization. As matters transpired—in a way the serially reporting Roosevelt couldn't foresee—the tale needed no enhancement, for the expedition turned out to be considerably more challenging than Roosevelt or any other member of the party had anticipated.

From the time they launched their canoes into the headwaters of the Dúvida, the group repeatedly encountered rapids and waterfalls that forced them back onto the banks. Each set of cataracts necessitated a painstaking portage of cargo along trails that had to be hacked out of the jungle by hand (usually the hands of the two dozen

Brazilian rivermen, but often supplemented by a Roosevelt arm or two). On the majority of the rapids the boatmen would then run the empty boats down the chutes; if the craft capsized, they could be righted with no loss of foodstuffs or other supplies. The most daunting of the rapids required a portage of the canoes as well, which was an even more exhausting operation.

The frequent portages slowed the pace of the expedition annoyingly at first, and then alarmingly, with the alarm arising from the fact that they carried a limited supply of food and medicine. In the dry season they might have lived off the land, but this was the rainy season, and the rising waters had driven most game animals far back from the river. Fish were equally scarce, having been liberated from their normal channels to swim across hundreds of square miles of flooded valleys and plains. The one semi-reliable source of sustenance was the palm tops that grew in the trees along the river; but although these filled the belly, they didn't provide much strength.

After the first few weeks, the alarm over dwindling supplies transmuted into grave fear that the party might run out of food before it ran out of river. To make matters worse, they lost a couple of the canoes to the rapids; these could be replaced only by the primitive application of ax to tree. Roosevelt marveled at the facility of the Brazilian woodsmen, who put even Bill Sewall to shame with their blades; but each day devoted to hewing canoes was a day lost to travel downstream.

The strains of the portaging and canoe-making, exacerbated by the increasingly necessary rationing of food, laid the explorers open to disease, which in that climate required scant opening. The expedition's doctor dosed everyone with quinine; this worked, but not perfectly. Roosevelt managed to avoid serious illness until one day when two of the canoes escaped the boatmen and were dashed down a cataract to a whirlpool at the bottom. There they were pinned by the current against some rocks. Roosevelt leaped into the water to rescue the boats, and with help and great difficulty accomplished his purpose. In the process, however, he badly bruised his leg—the same one that had been injured in the streetcar crash in 1902 and become infected afterward. The wound quickly gave rise to fever, which prostrated him for forty-eight hours and came close to carrying him off.

Kermit subsequently related the critical period:

There was one particularly black night. . . . We had been working through a series of rapids that seemed interminable. There would be a long carry, a mile or so clear going, and then more rapids.

The fever was high and father was out of his head. Doctor Cajazeira, who was one of the three Brazilians with us, divided with me the watch during the night. The scene is vivid before me. The black rushing river with the great trees towering high above along the bank; the sodden earth under foot; for a few moments the stars would be shining, and then the sky would cloud over and the rain would fall in torrents, shutting out the sky and trees and river.

Father first began with poetry; over and over again he repeated "In Xanadu did Kubla Khan a stately pleasure dome decree," then he started talking at random, but gradually he centred down to the question of supplies, which was, of course, occupying every one's mind. Part of the time he knew that I was there, and he would then ask me if I thought Cherrie had had enough to eat to keep going. Then he would forget my presence and keep saying to himself: "I can't work now, so I don't need much food, but he and Cherrie have worked all day with the canoes, they must have part of mine."

Although this initial crisis passed, the former president was a sick man for the rest of the journey. Against Kermit's urging, he did indeed shorten his own rations so that the boatmen could have more. This marginally strengthened them but substantially weakened him. Kermit had to watch his father lest he weaken himself beyond recovery. At one point Roosevelt—according to his later recounting—considered telling Kermit and the rest to leave him behind and save themselves. But he realized that Kermit would insist on transporting his body out of the jungle, and he reckoned that a dead man would be even more of a burden than a sick man.

By this time the entire group was in bad shape. One man had been drowned in the rapids; another was murdered by one of his fellows, who apparently went insane from the unrelenting heat, humidity, hunger, and fatigue. After shooting his companion, the murderer fled into the bush, where he most likely fell victim to the arrows of hostile indigenes; in any event, he was never heard from again. Kermit earlier had fallen ill with fever; now he came close to drowning—a fate that would have been rendered all the more tragic by the circumstance that he had recently become engaged to be married, with the wedding set for shortly after he and his father were expected to complete their journey.

The party had put into the Dúvida on February 27, 1914. They were still struggling downstream on April 15. Of late the fishing had improved: For Easter Sunday dinner they feasted on piranha, a species that had the saving grace of being almost as good eating was it was *at* eating. Roosevelt was still feeling the effects of his injury and the ensuing infection, despite a drainage tube that the expedition's doctor had inserted into the wound.

Then, finally, in the late morning of April 15 they came upon a small hut, evidently the recent lodging of a rubber tapper. An hour farther on they encountered some tappers themselves, who initially fled at the approach of the expeditionary party, mistaking them for tribal raiders—the only people they had ever seen coming *down* the river. At this point Roosevelt and the others knew that the expedition as a whole wouldn't fail. They wouldn't all starve in the jungle even though there might be more difficulties ahead.

There certainly were for Roosevelt, whose fever returned with a vengeance. As he explained to *Scribner's* readers: "It is not ideal for a sick man to spend the hottest hours of the day stretched on the boxes in the bottom of a small open dugout, under the well-nigh intolerable heat of the torrid sun of the mid-tropics, varied by blinding, drenching downpours of rain."

But Kermit and the doctor looked after him, and he and the rest of the party made it safely back to civilization. By the time they happily forsook their canoes for a local milk-run steamboat, they had covered nearly five hundred river miles in sixty days and mapped a river larger than all but a handful of streams in the United States. The Brazilian government commemorated the expedition by renaming the Rio Dúvida the Rio Roosevelt.

VIII

As impressed as the Brazilians were with his waterborne exploits, Roosevelt raised scarcely a ripple in the pool of American politics on his return to New York in May 1914—in starkest contrast to his riotous homecoming from Africa and Europe in 1910. Part of the difference owed to the remoteness of the Amazon as compared to East

Africa and particularly the courts of the Continent; when he disappeared down the Rio Teodoro, as his river came to be called by locals whose tongues couldn't quite get around "Roosevelt," he was really gone from sight. But most of it was the result of the continued turning of the wheel of politics. By the spring of 1914, Woodrow Wilson was clearly the darling of American progressives. His legislative agenda, which differed in political practice rather less from Roosevelt's than it had in campaign rhetoric, was sailing through Congress, powered by the billowy phrases that the Democratic president crafted with such facility. The press found Wilson as fascinating in his own way as it had Roosevelt during the previous decade.

There was something else that drew attention away from Roosevelt during the middle months of 1914. The ominous ticking that had disturbed the sleep of European diplomats—and internationally minded Americans like Roosevelt—since the late nineteenth century grew noticeably louder in June when a Serbian nationalist murdered the Austrian archduke. The ticking grew louder still as the neighbors of Serbia and Austria stuck their noses in the Serb-Austrian argument.

The ticking was loud enough for Roosevelt to hear even in the middle of the Atlantic. After recuperating at Oyster Bay for a month, he had traveled to Washington to address the National Geographic Society and pay a very formal courtesy call on President Wilson; then he was off to Spain for the wedding of Kermit to Belle Willard, the daughter of the American ambassador at Madrid. Edith, oddly, stayed home, contending that family and household matters required her attention; she may also have been less than pleased at Kermit's decision to marry a girl who didn't appear good enough for her favorite son. From Spain, Roosevelt hopped over to England. There he renewed acquaintance with Arthur Lee, James Bryce, Edward Grey, and others, and got in a most satisfying tussle at the Royal Geographic Society regarding the significance of his Amazonian exploration. It was on his return voyage that he heard of the assassination at Sarajevo.

After his presidential efforts to keep the European powers from one another's throats, Roosevelt naturally paid close attention to the exchanges of threats and ultimatums, and he feared what a European war might entail for the United States. But he wasn't president anymore, and for the time being there was little he could do.

So he spent July discussing the future of the Progressive Party. Congressional and state elections were approaching rapidly, and most of those who had followed him out of the Republican Party in 1914 wanted to know whether he would lead them again.

He didn't say yes, but he couldn't say no. "This jungle fever hangs on," he explained by way of excusing himself from the kind of barnstorming he had done in 1912. To Leonard Wood he declared, "I am now an old man." At the same time, he acknowledged that the cause required sacrifice. "The call of duty is supreme whatever the cost may be." And if he couldn't speak in a hundred cities, he might yet speak in a dozen. "Even as it is I am pretty good in a pinch!"

Though Progressive campaign managers could still appeal to Roosevelt's progressive ideals and his combative spirit, his attachment to the Progressive Party continued to loosen. He accepted that there were races in some states and districts where progressive policies might best be pursued by running candidates on joint Progressive and Republican tickets. Most of the Progressives were, like Roosevelt, old enough to recall what had happened to the Populist Party when it adopted a similar fusionist strategy with the Democrats: It had disappeared. Many thousands of Republicans had burned their bridges to the old party in 1912; now Roosevelt was hinting that they must take their lives in their hands and crawl back across the charred beams.

With an imprecision that reflected tactical ambiguity, honest uncertainty, and an unwillingness to concede what was growing more apparent—that any course might be doomed to failure—Roosevelt sent out mixed signals. He insisted that he hadn't moved an inch from where he had planted the progressive flag in 1912 and that any collaboration with the major parties must be on strictly progressive terms. Yet what his followers needed to know was whether progressive terms meant Progressive terms, and here Roosevelt waffled. "I would welcome into alliance with us the rank and file of both the old parties and make it easier for them to fight under our banner and for our principles," he declared to an Arizona Progressive. "But I would stand like flint against any amalgamation with either of the old machines." A month later he advocated collaboration with both Republicans and Democrats in New York. "If necessary, I should be entirely willing to run the same candidates on three different tickets: Progressive, Republican, and Progressive-Democrat. Or, if the

Republicans and Democrats did not like the name Progressive, I should have it called Anti-Boss, or Anti-Machine, or Good Government Republican and Democratic ticket." Another week later he stated, "Where either Republicans and Democrats come out and endorse our platform I think we should make every effort to co-operate with them so as to make it easy for them to come over to us entirely." He closed, this time with more bravado than confidence: "I cannot imagine any other course being right from the standpoint of common sense."

CHAPTER TWENTY-NINE

The Irregular's Return
1914–16

"The cataclysm was just about what I expected it would be," Roosevelt told his son Archie shortly after the 1914 elections. Ticket-leading Progressive candidates in every state but California (where Roosevelt's recent running mate, Hiram Johnson, proved the single exception) went down to defeat. The future looked bleaker than ever: "I should suppose that the Progressive party now would probably disband." From one perspective this was a shame. The Progressives were good men with high ideals. They were simply too far ahead of the rest of the country. From another perspective, though, Roosevelt shed no tears. "It will be, from the selfish standpoint, a great relief to me personally when and if they do disband." The 1912 presidential campaign had been exhausting and fruitless, and he didn't want to be pressured to repeat it.

The evident demise of the Progressives set Roosevelt once more to thinking about leaving politics for good. "The people are tired of all reformers, and especially of myself," he told a California Progressive. To William White he declared, "As far as making political speeches or taking part in any more party activities is concerned, my duty for the time being is to obey the directions of the New Bedford whaling captain when he told his mate that all he wanted from him was 'silence; and damn little of that!'" Looking back, Roosevelt said that on the night of the 1912 election he had judged the odds against the Progressives gaining a permanent foothold to be immense. They hadn't gotten any better. "When we failed to establish ourselves at the very outset as the second party, it became overwhelmingly probable that politics would soon sink back into the conditions that had been normal for the previous half century, that is, into a two-party system, the Republicans and the Democrats alternating in the first and second place. Under such circumstances it was likely that we would keep only the men of high principle and good reasoning power and the cranks. The men in between left us."

Unsurprising as this was, it did test one's faith in democracy. "The average American in his party affiliations is largely influenced by a feeling quite as unreasoning as that which makes the average fan depressed or exultant over the victory of a professional baseball team." The opportunity for fundamental change had passed. Roosevelt descried a "general revulsion against reform." Once again times were uncertain economically, making people hesitant to take the leap that real reform required. "Under such circumstances the stomach vote numerically far outweighs the conscience vote." Moreover, preaching—which was what progressives did best—inevitably produced a backlash among voters. "They were tired of us all."

But no more tired than Roosevelt was. He spent the period just after the election lying low, enjoying the company of Edith and various children and grandchildren. At the end of November he wrote to Ethel, "We've had the most delightful three weeks imaginable. I never wish to leave Sagamore again."

II

He had said as much before and subsequently snapped out of it. He did so again, this time under the spur of the greatest global calamity of his lifetime.

The world war began when the threats of June and the ultimatums of July gave way to the guns of August. The first victim of the war was Belgium, overrun by the forces of Wilhelm and Germany. Briefly, Roosevelt hesitated to condemn the kaiser. "I simply do not know the facts," he pleaded on August 8. But very soon he decided that Germany was thoroughly in the wrong, at least in its attack on the neutral and inoffensive Belgians. "There is not even room for an argument," he told Arthur Lee. "The Germans, to suit their own purposes, trampled on their solemn obligations to Belgium and on Belgium's rights."

Within a week of the war's outbreak, Roosevelt received a message from the kaiser himself. Speaking through an informal envoy, Wilhelm said he would always remember with pleasure the time when he had entertained the former president at Berlin and Potsdam; he felt sure that he could count on Roosevelt's sympathy and understanding in Germany's present position. Relating the interview to his daughter-in-law, Roosevelt described his response to the kaiser's messenger: "I bowed, looked him straight in the eyes, and answered, in substance, and nearly in words: 'Pray thank His Imperial Majesty from me for his very courteous message; and assure him that I was deeply conscious of the honors done me in Germany, and that I shall never forget the way in which His Majesty the Emperor received me in Berlin, *nor the way in which His Majesty King Albert of Belgium received me in Brussels.*'"

For all of Roosevelt's disapproval of the German assault on Belgium, he was by no means convinced that right, justice, and wisdom lay entirely on the side of the Allies. He credited Britain and, to a lesser extent, France with most of the virtues of civilization, but he had deep reservations about Russia and Japan. "I do not agree with you when you speak of this as being the last war for civilization," he told Lee. "I see no reason for believing that Russia is more advanced than Germany as regards international ethics, and Japan with all her politeness and her veneer of western civilization is at heart delighted to attack any and every western nation whenever the chance comes." With an incomplete prescience that echoed his earlier themes and vaulted him decades into the future, he warned, "If Germany is smashed it is perfectly possible that later she will have to be supported as a bulwark against the Slav by the nations of Western Europe, and while as regards the United States there can be little chance of hostility between us and Russia, there is always the chance of hostility between us and Japan, or Oriental Asia under the lead of Japan."

The outbreak of the war gave Roosevelt renewed opportunity to exercise his anger against Wilson. Had Roosevelt been able to view himself and Wilson objectively, he would have recognized that there wasn't all that much separating them on domestic issues; of course, had Roosevelt possessed such objectivity, he would have had to admit that his animus toward the president was motivated principally by jealousy. The onset of the war came as a relief, in one respect, for it reminded him—and others—of the very real and deep differences that divided the two men regarding international affairs.

Needless to say, this reminder rendered Roosevelt no more generous toward his rival. "Wilson is almost as much of a prize jackass as Bryan," he muttered privately. (Bryan, meanwhile, was "a third-rate revivalist preacher . . . and not a wholly sincere revivalist preacher at that.") With the world going up in flames, the president and other "preposterous little fools" advocated arbitration treaties as the universal remedy to bad behavior. "It seems incredible that at the moment when the experience of Luxembourg and Belgium shows the utter worthlessness of treaties of this kind, our sapient jacks should officially proclaim to the world their belief in the unlimited power of bits of paper with names put on them."

Roosevelt was more circumspect in his public statements, but barely. During the autumn of 1914 he wrote a series of articles that ran syndicated in various newspapers across the country; these articles, together with some from the *Outlook* and other magazines, he compiled and polished and published at the beginning of 1915 as *America and the World War.*

Therein Roosevelt remarked, with substantial accuracy, that he had held his tongue and pen for a reasonable period in order to give the Wilson administration opportunity to formulate its reaction to the fighting. "But when so much time has passed, either without action or with only mischievous action, as gravely to compromise both the honor and the interest of the country, then it becomes a duty for self-respecting citizens to whom their country is dear to speak out." Already opportunities had slipped that would not return. The president should have registered America's strongest disapproval at Germany's violation of Belgian neutrality. "We should have interfered, at least to the extent of the most emphatic diplomatic protest and at the very outset—and then by whatever further action was necessary." Such vigorous action might have stopped the war in its tracks or at least prevented its expansion. It certainly would have warned the Germans against additional outrages.

The failure to protest over Belgium was the root of the present evil, but there were branches almost as rotten. Britain, for instance, had flouted international law by sinking at least one German vessel in neutral waters and by mining the North Sea; the Wilson administration should have stoutly protested this encroachment on neutral rights instead of following the "timid and spiritless" course of abject acquiescence. To suffer wrong in silence was to encourage its repetition.

In light of Britain's sins, Roosevelt wasn't ready to take sides between the belligerents. Indeed, he went as far as expressing admiration for certain aspects of German social organization—and Japanese, for balance and true broad-mindedness. "We should in all humility imitate not a little of the spirit so much in evidence among the Germans and the Japanese, the two nations which in modern times have shown the most practical type of patriotism, the greatest devotion to the common weal, the greatest success in developing their economic resources and abilities from within, and the greatest far-sightedness in safeguarding the country against possible disaster from without."

It was on this last point that Roosevelt especially condemned the Wilson administration. The president, he said, was so mesmerized by the notion that he might mediate between the warring parties that he wholly failed to understand the preconditions for effective mediation. Roosevelt granted that Wilson might indeed find himself invited to a postwar peace conference. "But under conditions as they are now the real importance of the President in such a peace conference will be comparable to the real importance of the drum-major when he walks at the head of a regiment." Small boys were impressed by drum-majors, but not adults. Meanwhile, the president refused to insist on the kind of military preparations that alone would render American participation at a peace conference effective. Such refusal was nothing less than "criminal."

Roosevelt raked Bryan and Navy Secretary Josephus Daniels for being incompetent and unfit to hold their crucial offices; but he saved his special bile for Wilson. "The President, unlike Mr. Bryan, uses good English and does not say things that are on their face ridiculous. Unfortunately, his cleverness of style and his entire refusal to face facts apparently make him believe that he really has dismissed and done away with ugly realities whenever he has uttered some pretty phrase about them." So desperate was Wilson to achieve peace that he had become blind to the righteousness that must underlie any lasting peace.

Wilson and the "ultrapacificists" and "peace prattlers" simply couldn't conceive that there were things more important than peace. War was not an unmitigated bane. "The storm that is raging in Europe at this moment is terrible and evil; but it is also grand and noble." This ultimate strife summoned forth the heroic in human nature.

> Untried men who live at ease will do well to remember that there is a certain sublimity even in Milton's defeated archangel, but none whatever in the spirits who kept neutral, who remained at peace, and dared side neither with hell nor with heaven. They will also do well to remember that when heroes have battled together, and have wrought good and evil, and when the time has come out of the contest to get all the good possible and to prevent as far as possible the evil from being made permanent, they will not be influenced much by the theory that soft and short-sighted outsiders have put themselves in better condition to stop war abroad by making themselves defenseless at home.

III

Roosevelt's readers may have been taken aback by his reference to the grand, noble, and sublime nature of war; reports from the Western front indicated that this war, at any rate, was brutal, confused, and demoralizing. It certainly was nothing like the one brief brush Roosevelt had had with war.

Yet after his rejection at the polls in 1912, Roosevelt had come to savor unpopularity; it made him feel more principled. Through the first autumn and winter of the world war he repeatedly referred to the fact that his was the voice crying in the wilderness. "In writing my articles, I have not been under the least illusion," he commented to Spring Rice, who was now the British ambassador in Washington and consequently was required not to agree with the nasty things Roosevelt was saying about the president. "I know that at the moment my own countrymen will not follow my advice and I do not know that they will ever profit much by it. I do know that it will be remembered against me personally and that my taking the action will be a harm to me, if I were ever again to wish to take any part in American public affairs."

Many of Roosevelt's friends thought so, too. The most blunt of them, William White, told him to put down his pen and button his lip. "I thoroughly agree with you about Bryan and Wilson," White said; but there was a time for everything, and now wasn't the time for attacking the administration. "We should all of us merge ourselves into the landscape." This held particularly true for Roosevelt. "Your cistern is dry on politics. If I were you I would discuss anything in the world except politics." Roosevelt should indulge his myriad other interests—literature, for example. "Hop on to Mr. Howells if you want to, for his disparagement of Dickens as a realist, or jump Chesterton's views of Browning." But leave politics alone. "Friend Bryan and friend Wilson will not last long at their present rate and I think you will be a lot stronger if you do not have their blood on your hands."

Roosevelt, however, was beyond such advice. He told White that he would dearly love to deal with topics other than politics: literature, as White suggested, or philosophy or other high-minded motifs. But he made his living from writing—he currently had a contract with the *Metropolitan* magazine—and politics and international affairs were what his editors demanded. He did promise, however, to tone down his attacks. "I shall do my best to avoid mentioning Wilson's and Bryan's names."

IV

His best wasn't very good. Had Roosevelt possessed the most apolitical of intentions, laying off Bryan and Wilson would have been difficult. Bryan and increasingly Wilson were obviously directing American policy; to criticize that policy was to criticize them. Besides, with Roosevelt public affairs had always been intensely personal. After thirty-five years at the game, he could hardly be expected to alter his approach now.

But above everything else, he was absolutely convinced that Wilson's approach was fundamentally and objectively evil. The war brought Roosevelt's moralism to the surface with a vengeance; as it did, he shed such ambivalence as he had earlier expressed regarding responsibility for the fighting. Germany was the aggressor; Germany must be opposed and punished. This was what Wilson, with his insistence on a sterile neutrality, refused to acknowledge. "More and more I come to the view that in a really tremendous world struggle, with a great moral issue involved, neutrality does not serve righteousness; for to be neutral between right and wrong is to serve wrong." At the moment neutrality might serve American ease and selfishness. "But it does not serve morality." Nor, in the long run, would it serve the national interest. The more Roosevelt thought about the situation, the more it galled him. "I can't express sufficiently my scorn and contempt for Wilson and Bryan."

Roosevelt resented the position Wilson had put patriots like himself in. "I am bitterly humiliated by what this Administration has done," he wrote to Spring Rice in February 1915. To another British friend, John St. Loe Strachey, he said, "My dear fellow, you & those like you are playing heroic parts; I admire and respect you; I bitterly regret that my own people are not at this time rising to the same level." By early 1915 it was becoming tragically evident that the war, far from being a limited conflict like those that had marked European politics for a century, was a struggle on the Napoleonic scale. Roosevelt simply couldn't bear that his country should not have a central role in the great struggle of the age. "It is a dreadful thing that this world-war should exist," he told Kermit. "But after all there is an element of splendid heroism in it, shown on both sides and by all of the nations involved." Because of the timidity of their leaders, however, Americans were missing out. "The attitude of Wilson and Bryan is contemptible."

Nor could he bear that he personally was missing out. Before leaving for his Brazilian expedition, Roosevelt had guessed that it would be his final real adventure. On returning, still enervated by fever and with the sight in his long-damaged left eye now completely gone, he had felt even more certain that the Amazon trip would have to suffice for his last hurrah. As late as February 1915 he lamented to his old family doctor, "I am practically through. I am not a man like you who keeps his youth almost to the end; and now I am pretty nearly done out. I would not say this except to my old friend who was also my old physical adviser, because it is rather poor business to speak about one's personal ailments; but the trouble is that I have rheumatism or gout and things of that kind to a degree that makes it impossible for me to take very much exercise; and then in turn the fact that I cannot exercise prevents my keeping in good condition."

Yet like the old warrior who rises from his pallet for one ultimate battle, Roosevelt saw the war as his crowning chance to do something heroic, something genuinely noteworthy. The war against Spain had been a mere skirmish, a stroll in the garden, compared to what was going on in France. The heroes of this war would far overshadow the standouts of that small contest. Besides, on his better days he remembered that for all his aches and pains, he was only fifty-seven—not exactly a youth but neither a decrepit graybeard.

Roosevelt envied those already in the fight, whether on the field or in the councils of war. "You and Jusserand are doing what is very fine, perhaps the finest thing that men can do," he told Spring Rice; "that is, you are rendering the utmost service to your country when your country most needs such service and when your country is engaged in a struggle in which your success is for the benefit of mankind." Americans—Unionists, rather—had rendered such service to mankind during the Civil War. But Americans were not rendering it now. "If I were willing to let myself grow cast down, I should be pretty well cast down at the fact that in this great crisis America, because of having unworthy leaders, has played an unworthy part."

V

Rather than be cast down, Roosevelt devoted himself to making America's part more worthy. German actions during the spring of 1915 seemed to provide the necessary assistance. In May a German submarine sank the British liner *Lusitania;* the death toll ran past one thousand, including almost two hundred Americans. Roosevelt judged the sinking of the *Lusitania* a clear casus belli; having already raped Belgium, the Germans were now murdering Americans. But to Roosevelt's enormous disgust—although not his especial surprise—Wilson thought otherwise. Asserting that there was such a thing as being too proud to fight, the president merely insisted on an apology, reparations, and a pledge of future good behavior from the German government. Berlin, disinclined to goad the Americans to full hostilities at this stage, complied, and the crisis passed.

Roosevelt could hardly contain his outrage. Noting that the president had delivered his too-proud-to-fight verdict to a gathering of naturalized citizens, he told his son Archie, "Wilson and Bryan are cordially supported by all the hyphenated Americans, by the solid flubdub and pacifist vote. Every soft creature, every coward and weakling, every man who can't look more than six inches ahead, every man whose god is money, or pleasure, or ease, and every man who has not got in him both the sterner virtues and the power of seeking after an ideal, is enthusiastically in favor of Wilson." Roosevelt attributed the deaths of the men, women, and children on the *Lusitania* to Wilson's "abject cowardice and weakness" in treating previous German violations. "He and Bryan are morally responsible for the loss of the lives of those American women and children. . . . They are both of them abject creatures and they won't go to war unless they are kicked into it."

Roosevelt told Arthur Lee he was "sick at heart" to see where Wilson was leading the country. He assured his friend that things would have been different had the election of 1912 turned out otherwise. "I would from the beginning, if I had been President, have taken a stand which would have made the Germans either absolutely alter all their conduct or else put them into war with us. If the United States had taken this stand, in my judgment we would now have been fighting beside you." Even if he hadn't been president, the United States still should have entered the war. "If we had done what we ought to have done after the sinking of *Lusitania,* I and my four boys would now be in an army getting ready to serve with you in Flanders or else to serve against Constantinople." (Roosevelt got into the habit of telling friends that if he had been president prior to the *Lusitania*'s sailing, when the German embassy took out an advertisement warning passengers against the dangers of booking passage, he would have handed the German ambassador his papers and told him to leave the country—aboard the *Lusitania*. This solution seems to have occurred to him after the fact.)

Under Wilson, Roosevelt said, America suffered from a fatal failure of leadership. "Our people lack imagination; they do not understand the conditions abroad; and above all they have been misled by the screaming and shrieking and bleating of the peace people until really good men and women have gotten so puzzle-headed that they advocate a course of national infamy." Roosevelt told Lee he had done his best to remedy the situation, but unfortunately without observable positive result. "I have spoken out as strongly and as clearly as possible; and I do not think it has had any effect beyond making people think that I am a truculent and bloodthirsty person, endeavoring futilely to thwart able, dignified, humane Mr. Wilson in his noble plan to bring peace everywhere by excellently written letters sent to persons who care nothing for any letter that is not backed up by force!"

VI

Lee had resigned his civilian position and enlisted in the army; Roosevelt said he had done the right thing. "I do not wonder that you feel that you are breathing a cleaner and manlier air now that you are again a soldier and not in politics." Roosevelt sought a similar dispensation himself. "I only wish I and my boys were beside you in the trenches." Roosevelt revealed to Lee that he was already planning to raise a unit modeled on the Rough Riders, but a division rather than a mere regiment. "I have the brigade commanders and regimental commanders picked."

This time around, however, Roosevelt intended to leave the heavy fighting to younger men, such as his sons. Not long before he wrote Lee he had injured himself in an embarrassing fashion. "The simple fact is that I tried to ride a horse that was too good for me. I might just as well admit that I am old and stiff; and while I can *sit* on a horse fairly well, I cannot mount him if he misbehaves. This horse threw me before I got my right foot into the stirrup, and I struck the ground a good deal as if I had been a walrus, and broke a couple of ribs in consequence."

Fortunately, there were the younger Roosevelts to uphold the family honor mounted and afoot. Roosevelt wasn't quite such a lonely voice as he sometimes made out: During the summer of 1915 others who thought as he did, including his old friend and superior officer Leonard Wood, organized a military training camp for prospective soldiers at Plattsburg, New York. Archie and Quentin were among the first to enroll in the student section of the camp; Ted signed on for the businessmen's cadre.

Their father, needless to say, heartily endorsed both the idea of the camp and his sons' participation in it. He proudly informed Kermit—back at work in South America—of his brothers' progress. Quentin's commanders said he was acquitting himself very well, and with more age and experience would make an excellent second lieutenant. Archie won a battalion second-lieutenancy and was asked to stay on to work with the businessmen. "Rather to my delight he was put over Ted!" their father told Kermit. "One Sunday the two regular officers over them, together with Archie and Ted, went to Montreal to look at some of the military preparations there. Archie with glee mentioned to me the fact that at the Club the two regular officers were both always addressed as 'Major,' he (Archie) as 'Captain,' and Ted as 'Mr. Roosevelt.' I shall tactfully and sympathetically question Ted about the matter day after tomorrow when I see him in camp." Roosevelt went on to say that Archie's superiors stated that he was fit to be captain in a volunteer regiment right now. He added, mixing the political with the paternal: "And if this infernal skunk in the White House can be kicked into war Captain Archie shall be."

VII

Roosevelt did his best to make the commission possible when he visited the Plattsburg camp two days later. He gave a rousing speech praising the work of the officers and men in preparing themselves for the possibility of war; he condemned those who seemed to think that fine phrases could substitute for decisive action. The speech got General Wood into trouble with his civilian superiors at the War Department; they wanted to know what he was doing providing a platform for such a scarcely veiled assault on the administration. Wood maintained a dignified silence, not wishing to criticize his friend and former commander in chief, with whom, in any event, he happened to agree. Roosevelt filled the silence by claiming entire responsibility for the affair.

The Plattsburg speech, coming at a moment of broader reevaluation of America's role vis-à-vis the war, brought Roosevelt back into the middle of the public arena. Scarcely a year remained before the next presidential election, and Roosevelt again attracted attention as a possible candidate. The Progressives almost certainly would nominate him if the new party didn't expire before then; more intriguingly, many Republicans looked to Roosevelt as their answer to Wilson and their ticket back into power. Taft was discredited, and uninterested besides; the other likely candidates generated far less excitement among them than Roosevelt alone on an off day. To be sure, he had committed a grave sin by bolting the party, but Jesus had preached acceptance of the prodigal son, and who were Republicans to gainsay the Savior?

Roosevelt's prospects drew additional strength from an unlikely source. In the spring of 1915 the former president defended himself in a libel suit. This was his third direct experience with libel law. The first had come in the Pulitzer case, which had been unsuccessful but instructive. The second case was equally instructive but more success-ful. For years he had ignored repeated allegations of drunkenness, but during the 1912 campaign he decided he'd had enough and deter-mined to teach the scandalmongers a lesson. *Iron Ore,* an obscure Michigan paper, happened to provide the most likely target. Roosevelt trotted out one witness after another to testify to his sobriety; the trial ended in a complete moral and political vindication. To underline his disdain for his detractors, he requested and received token damages of six cents.

His third brush with libel law, which commenced in early 1915, placed him in the unfamiliar position of defendant. During the cam-paign season the previous summer, Roosevelt had made some charac-teristically intemperate charges against William Barnes, alleging that the Republican boss and Democratic headman Charles Murphy were twins in New York corruption. Barnes had been called much worse in his day, but he hoped to use Roosevelt's loose and probably unprov-able claim as a weapon to discredit the Rough Rider once and for all.

Barnes's strategy, as it surfaced at trial, was to impugn Roosevelt's veracity by showing that the former president had, at numerous times throughout his career, trimmed and temporized in the service of his political ambitions. By one means or another Barnes's investigators managed to obtain sheaves of letters written by Roosevelt over the years that seemingly placed their author in a compromising position. The highlight of the trial was ten days that Roosevelt spent on the witness stand answering questions regarding these letters and related actions.

Barnes's strategy backfired brilliantly. Roosevelt parried every aspersion, rebutted each innuendo, and in sum stole the show from his antagonists. Former presidents aren't placed on the witness stand every day and compelled to answer for their conduct; accordingly, the trial attracted national attention. Roosevelt exploited the opportunity to defend himself not only against Barnes's charges but against many others that had been made over the years. His bravura performance left at least one of his enemies shaking his head at the whole idea of the lawsuit. "Of all the blundering lunatics I have ever known," this man told Joseph Bishop, "Barnes is the worst. Here we had Roosevelt, after his candidacy against Taft, dead and buried politically. We were rid of him for all time. Now Barnes has not only opened the door for him to come back, but he has pushed him through to the front of the stage and made him a greater popular idol than ever."

VIII

Roosevelt wasn't so sanguine, although he was certainly pleased, if utterly unsurprised, when the jury found in his favor. At about the time he was provoking Barnes, he had told former attorney general Charles Bonaparte that there was "no reasonable possibility" the bosses would let him win the Republican nomination in 1916. Speaking of their feelings toward him, he declared, "I have never seen greater bitterness." And of course there was his own self-respect to consider. "I personally cannot go back to the Republican party," he told Archie.

Roosevelt recognized that the Barnes trial may have improved his standing among the people at large, but if anything—and if possible—it additionally embittered the bosses. Consequently, he dismissed the talk of his nomination by the Republicans as either meaningless or malign. "If the Republicans are ever found to entertain the thought of nominating me next year," he told George Perkins in September 1915, "it will be because they know they will be defeated under me and intend that I shall receive the heaviest defeat that they can give me and that they nominate me with this purpose in view, thereby not only smashing the Progressives but definitely getting rid of me and enthroning standpattism in the Republican party."

All the same, and typically, Roosevelt refused to squelch talk of a Republican nomination. The ambition for leadership, never absent in him, had grown stronger with his belief that Wilson was taking the nation down the road of ignominy and perhaps defeat. In 1912 he had convinced himself that America required his hand at the helm; now, with the fate of world democracy hanging in the balance, conviction came even easier. Perhaps the bitter old guard would succeed in blocking his nomination; pessimism was the appropriate attitude. Even so, by keeping his name alive as a threat to the old guard's supremacy, he would win attention for the message he had to convey to the nation and to the world.

This message came in two parts, neither popular—which was another reason for his pessimism. The first part was military preparedness. This, of course, was a career theme for Roosevelt, who had started preaching preparedness in *The Naval War of 1812* and never stopped. For most of those thirty-five years he had focused on the navy, especially battleships. He still advocated strengthening the blue-water fleet, but he believed that the immediate need was for soldiers. He asked himself and his readers why Belgium and not Switzerland had been attacked. The Alps provided one reason, but the one that illustrated Roosevelt's point was that the Swiss had long ago made a commitment to military readiness. Universal military training was a cherished Swiss tradition; every male citizen was also a soldier. On progressive grounds alone, Roosevelt had been attracted to universal training, which instilled a communitarian ethic of public responsibility and service. It also served as a democratizing influence: Rich and poor boys alike slept in the same barracks, ate the same rations, marched through the same mud, and dug the same latrines. Now, with Europe convulsed by war, universal training served as Switzerland's shield. Any aggressor knew that tangling with the Swiss would be like tangling with a tiger. "This country needs something like the Swiss system of war training for its young men," Roosevelt concluded.

Roosevelt's calls for preparedness provoked strong reactions.

Critics contended that the erstwhile wielder of the big stick had merely dusted off his same old militaristic message. More than a few self-styled peace advocates argued that military preparations would constitute the first step on a slippery slope that inevitably would land American boys in those deadly trenches in France.

The second half of Roosevelt's message triggered even stronger reactions. Here Roosevelt preached nationalism—or, as he liked to put it, "real Americanism." Roosevelt had no patience, no tolerance even, for what a later generation would call multiculturalism. He insisted that those who came to America must forsake their emotional and cultural attachments to their native lands and embrace the culture and mores of their adopted country. To do otherwise, and for native-born Americans to allow them to do otherwise, would invite exactly the kind of particularist pandering the president was engaged in. Terrified of losing the German-American vote, Wilson—in Roosevelt's interpretation—was selling out American national interests. Roosevelt believed that in matters touching the nation's honor and security, there was no legitimate German-American position—any more than there was an Irish-American or English-American position, or for that matter a Democratic or Republican or Progressive position. There was only an American position. Roosevelt regularly railed against "hyphenated Americanism" and against all who admitted the existence of such. As he put it, he was "striving to make native-American, Irish-American, German-American, English-American, standpatter and Progressive, Republican and Democrat, all alike, remember that in the last analysis, when it comes to dealing with the safety of the nation, we should act as Americans and nothing else."

The campaign against hyphenated Americanism put Roosevelt in bad company, for it often came across as an attack on hyphenated Americans—that is, immigrants. Roosevelt had as little use for the anti-immigrant ravings of the American Protective Association and other nativist groups as he did for all demagoguery besides his own; but he was willing to risk guilt by association in what he judged to be the uncompromisably vital endeavor to rescue American honor from Germany and from Wilson.

Roosevelt saw the campaign against the hyphen as being even more important than the campaign for preparedness. "The overwhelming issue at this moment is whether or not we are a real nation, able to command unfaltering loyalty from all our citizens and to secure the respect of outside powers. We want to know whether it means something to be an American." Matters of preparedness were essential, to be sure. "But these must be taken as adjuncts to and included in the question of the large and real Americanism."

IX

Roosevelt's unyielding stance against hyphenated Americanism worried some of those who hoped to see him recapture the Republican nomination in 1916. He could make the same point, they urged, in a more positive way, and in the process not hand the crucial ethnic vote to the Democrats or to his more tactful Republican rivals.

Roosevelt refused to modulate his tone. He was as certain as he had ever been that he was right and his opponents wrong. "If the German-American vote is solid against me, because of the position I have taken, then, in my judgment, it shows that the German-Americans are solidly against this country." Roosevelt didn't actually believe that Americans of German descent were solidly against him, but if they were, that made it the more imperative to sound the alarm. "It renders it all the more necessary that I should, in the sharpest possible manner, wake up real Americans to their danger."

Roosevelt rejected the role of candidate, preferring to play the prophet. The "decent Americans who are of German descent," he reiterated, would stand beside him. "But the professional hyphenated German-Americans I shall smite with the sword of the Lord and of Gideon whenever I get the chance." Roosevelt realized that this posture might not make him popular, even when a majority came around to his way of thinking, as they surely would. "It is a very old experience that when men finally have to pay heed to a prophecy they relieve their feelings by stoning the prophet." Yet he was beyond worrying about such things. "This is of importance only from the prophet's standpoint; and in this particular case the prophet does not give a hang!"

This prophet was also a politician, however, for all his assertions of the opposite. "Abraham Lincoln on one occasion when told that a given course of action of his would not achieve results responded that at least he was keeping his conscience clear," Roosevelt wrote to Spring Rice. "I am afraid that that is all that I am doing." In fact, that wasn't all that he was doing—just as it hadn't been all that Lincoln, another instinctive politician, had been doing. Roosevelt understood that the source of such popularity as he commanded lay in the perception people had that he told only the truth, hard though that truth might be. Indeed, he was in the paradoxical position of being more attractive the more unpopular he became. Of course, there were limits to this strategy: If he alienated everyone, there wouldn't be anyone left to follow him. The trick was to make enough enemies to make just enough friends to win the nomination and then the presidency.

Roosevelt definitely wanted to be president. Obsessed as he was with Lincoln and the Civil War, he dearly wished to play a similar role during democracy's current crisis. He was absolutely certain that he would make a better wartime leader than Wilson, and better than any Republican available. Elihu Root was readying a run for the nomination; Roosevelt still resented Root's role in giving Taft the 1912 nomination and dismissed his former friend's character on that ground. As he told Cabot Lodge, "His action in the Chicago Convention was morally exactly as bad as the actions for which very many Tammany and small Republican politicians who have committed election offenses are now serving or have served terms in Sing Sing." Such a man could hardly be trusted with the nation's leadership. Former secretary of state Philander Knox had some strengths. "But Knox has been defending Hyphenated Americanism lately." And for all his experience of diplomacy, he lacked a "proper understanding" of foreign policy. A third candidate was Charles Evans Hughes. "I thoroughly dislike him," Roosevelt told Lodge. "He got me into the fight against Barnes; and then his memory proved conveniently short on the subject when the libel suit came up. He was very close with the *Evening Post* people; and I am not sure that he is all right about preparedness and defense and foreign policies generally."

Roosevelt realized that the eastern Republican bosses still opposed him, but he hoped that by promising to deliver the Progressive vote in the general election he might entice enough westerners, moderates, and zealous anti-Wilsonians to push him past the party panjandrums.

X

The key to this approach was the occupant of the White House. All Republicans and nearly all Progressives agreed that Wilson ought to be evicted, and if Roosevelt could demonstrate that he was the only man who could accomplish the eviction, the nomination might be his.

But by now Roosevelt could hardly think straight on the subject of Wilson, and political calculation hardly entered his conscious mind. He hadn't the slightest doubt that the president was leading America to dishonor and perdition; he granted him not the least credit for any but the basest motives. "*Your* country is passing through the flame and will come out cleansed, and refined to lofty nobleness," he told Spring Rice. "*Mine* is passing through the thick yellow mud-streak of 'safety first.'" At this critical hour, America found itself guided by "the men of little soul who desire only sordid ease." The country's prospect was to "eat the bitter bread of shame."

Roosevelt grew absolutely obsessed with Wilson. He continued to account him a coward in dealing with Germany, a fool for failing to ready the country for the war it would not be able to avoid much longer, and a blackguard for unconscionably catering to the ethnic vote. But Roosevelt went beyond this into depths of hatred he had never visited. When Wilson married Edith Gault, Roosevelt complained that the president hadn't shown sufficient respect to the memory of his deceased first wife. "The worthy gentleman's motto seems to be 'My wife is dead! Long live my wife!'" When Wilson finally responded to the criticism of Roosevelt and others and announced his intention that the United States should construct a navy second to none, Roosevelt—the lifetime advocate of a bigger fleet—unaccountably complained that the president was asking for too much. "I do not think that at this time it is necessary or advisable to do more than demand what I am demanding"— namely, a navy second to Britain's. Roosevelt conceded that Wilson, "with his adroit, unscrupulous cunning, his readiness to about-face, his timidity about any manly assertion of our rights, and his pandering to the feelings of those who love ease and the chance of material profit, and his lack of all conviction and willingness to follow every gust of popular opinion," might well win the support of the mass of

Americans. But that would simply indicate another failure of democracy. "This will no more make me think he is right than the election of Pierce and Buchanan makes me think the majority of the Americans were right in the decade that led up to the Civil War."

Roosevelt's supporters occasionally suggested that he was allowing his animus against the president to influence his judgment excessively. Or if he couldn't change his opinions, at least he might soften his phrasing.

Roosevelt denied that he spoke too strongly. "I have got to be emphatic to attract attention," he explained. "We are not in a rose-water parlor pink-tea crisis at present, and what I am trying to do is to get the American people to think about its position and to face its responsibilities." Roosevelt likened the current situation to the one he had confronted during the war with Spain. "In the Santiago crisis I now and then had to use very strong language, indeed, in order to attract the attention of the men and etch with instant effect upon their conscience just exactly what I expected them to do and to do quickly. . . . I was not really overstating the case; I was emphasizing it!" On another occasion Roosevelt referred again to the deficiencies of democracy, this time in terms of the people's inability to register subtlety and nuance. "You know at least as well as I do," he told Lodge, who hated Wilson almost as much as Roosevelt did but who nonetheless deemed some of Roosevelt's rhetoric counterproductive, "that the public cannot take in an etching. They want something along the lines of a circus poster. They do not wish fine details, and it is really not to be expected that they should see them. They want the broad strokes of the brush."

And in any event, Roosevelt felt himself past worrying about the popular reaction to his judgments. "I don't give a damn what my countrymen think of me in the present or the future," he told Arthur Lee. His mission precluded such mundane concerns. "What I am trying to do is make this country go right."

XI

But of course he *did* care what the people—as opposed to the party bosses and the self-appointed keepers of the public conscience—

thought. If he hoped to make America "go right," he had to win popular support. As the Republican convention neared, he thought he was faring as well as could be expected. "My own judgment is that among the rank and file of the Republican voters, and including the voters opposed to Mr. Wilson, there is very much more sentiment for me than for any other candidate."

Quite likely he was correct; unfortunately, as in 1912, the rank and file wouldn't decide the nomination. Roosevelt remained pessimistic about his chances of actually winning. "I think the convention at Chicago will be in the hands of a very sordid set of machine masters associated with rather well-meaning and rather timid citizens of the ordinary type without strong convictions." Under such circumstances, the odds against him grew.

He did his best to overcome those odds. In the weeks before the convention Roosevelt exhibited his customary coyness in signaling his availability for a draft. A group calling itself the Roosevelt Non-Partisan League was plumping him for the presidency, by means that included a four-page spread in the *Saturday Evening Post* that featured a large photograph of the hero on page one and accounts of his exploits on behalf of American security and world peace on the following pages. Roosevelt discreetly encouraged the efforts. In response to a letter from the organization's secretary inquiring about his intentions, he wrote, "As you know, I have refused to indorse the use of my name in the primaries, or in any way to enter into any factional contest which has for its object my nomination in Chicago in June. You know also that I have emphatically stated that it would be unwise to nominate me unless with full understanding that such nomination means the hearty indorsement of the principles for which I stand."

This was all the Roosevelt boosters needed. The next three weeks saw frantic maneuvering among those who had followed the Colonel into no-man's-land in 1912 and those who had cheered him, sometimes quietly, from behind the lines. Roosevelt gave the appearance of remaining above the fray, although he didn't hide the fact that he was trying to make up with some of his old Republican allies, including Elihu Root. At the same time, he conspicuously refrained from announcing what he would do in the event the Republicans nominated someone else. Neither his friends nor his foes required particular insight to interpret this as a threat to split the non-Democratic vote again, as in 1912, and deprive the G.O.P. nominee of the White House once more.

Roosevelt's positioning left the Progressives puzzled. He was their obvious, if not their only, candidate; yet he would not commit to run. Confusing the issue further was the fact that the Progressives were convening at the same time as the Republicans and in the same city. This, of course, was no accident; a bit of calculated confusion might serve the Progressive Party as much as it served Roosevelt. If the Progressive leaders could help arrange a joint nomination of Roosevelt with the Republicans, they and the rest of their wayward tribe might return in triumph to the party that nearly all of them knew they'd have to return to sooner or later. The coincidence of conventions was designed to facilitate the hotel room bargaining that might make a reunion possible.

But despite much finagling, many telephone calls, hundreds of cigars, and hogsheads of liquor, the hoped-for reconciliation failed to take place. A Roosevelt loyalist put the former president's name before the Republican convention, touching off a half-hour of cheers, applause, and foot-pounding; but when order returned the regulars demonstrated the same control that had guaranteed Taft the nomination four years earlier. Roosevelt had offered to speak to the convention; the party leaders refused him that forum. They rallied behind Hughes, who won the nomination without great difficulty.

Roosevelt responded to this latest failure with ill grace. He lambasted the "profound political immorality" of the convention and contended that Hughes had won because "nobody knew anything of his views on living subjects of the day" and because the German-Americans in the party had insisted on making him—Roosevelt—pay for his forthrightness. Typically egotistical, he asserted that the party leaders were "more intent upon disciplining me and teaching a lesson in party regularity and party supremacy than anything else." A good portion of the blame rested with Root, Roosevelt judged. During the fusion negotiations, Roosevelt had suggested that he would appoint Root secretary of state if elected. Root, who wasn't quite out of the running for the nomination himself, had declined the offer. Roosevelt groused afterward: "Root had a chance to be Warwick, but he threw it away because he wished to be King, which was impossible." In a letter to his sister Bamie, he ascribed his defeat to a failure of popular nerve. "The country wasn't in heroic mood!" Repeating an earlier image, he added, "We are passing through a thick streak of yellow in our national life."

Yet this time Roosevelt had the sense to keep his blaming to himself and to trusted correspondents. In public he took the defeat well. Between his hatred of Wilson, his conviction that the Democrats were leading the nation to disgrace, and his latter-day realization of the futility of third-party politics, he decided not to repeat the vain exercise of 1912. He declined the Progressive nomination, instead endorsing Hughes. In his letter of declination he asserted that the Wilson administration was "guilty of shortcomings more signal than those of any Administration since the days of Buchanan." Wilson and his associates had been tried and found wanting. "They have brought us to impotence abroad and to division and weakness at home. They have accustomed us to see the highest and most responsible offices of government filled by incompetent men, appointed only for reasons of partisan politics. They have dulled the moral sense of the people. They have taught us that peace, the peace of cowardice and dishonor and indifference to the welfare of others, is to be put above righteousness, above the stern and unflinching performance of duty." Under the circumstances, Roosevelt made clear, he had no choice but to support Hughes. He urged his fellow Progressives—and all American voters—to do likewise.

Part Five

FADING TO DUSK

CHAPTER THIRTY

The One They Left Behind
1916–18

A nd so Roosevelt returned to the party of his youth. The homecoming was less than joyous, on both sides. Hughes and the regulars were happy enough to have him inside the stockade shooting out, rather than outside shooting in, but many worried that if Hughes lost to Wilson this year, they'd have to contend with Roosevelt all over again in the future. For Roosevelt's part, his opinion of the regulars had improved only by comparison to the alternative. "The Republicans are a sordid crowd!" he expostulated to Corinne. "They are a trifle better than the corrupt and lunatic wild asses of the desert who seem most influential in Democratic counsels, under the lead of that astute, unprincipled and physically cowardly demagogue Wilson; but they are a sorry lot."

Neither group approached Roosevelt himself in rectitude or vision. "For six years I have been I believe emphatically right, emphatically the servant of the best interests of the American people." Lamentably, however, his work went unappreciated. "The American people have steadily grown to think less and less of me, and more definitely determined not to use me in any public position." It was enough to make one despair of democracy. "I despise Wilson," he told Bamie; "but I despise still more our foolish, foolish people who, partly from ignorance and partly from sheer timidity and partly from lack of imagination and of sensitive national feeling, support him." Referring to the Democratic gathering that had just renominated the president, Roosevelt concluded, "The St. Louis Convention was one of the most degrading spectacles we have ever seen."

But America and Roosevelt were stuck with democracy, and he resigned himself to playing by its rules. During the late summer and early autumn of 1916 he grudgingly campaigned for Hughes. "It is very galling to have to take any action which helps these scoundrels," he said of the Republicans who nominated Hughes. Yet help them he did, since the only other choice was that "dreadful creature" Wilson. He gave several speeches in the general vicinity of New York before heading for the upper Midwest, where he carried considerably more clout than the regular Republicans against whom he had been railing with such vigor for the last six years.

It was a delicate business stumping on behalf of a candidate for whom he felt absolutely no enthusiasm. "Hughes is not an attractive personality at best," Roosevelt told journalist John Leary. "Close contact does not make him more attractive, for he is a very selfish, very self-centered man." Moreover, he was wobbly on the issues, particularly the issue of most pressing concern to Roosevelt. With Wilson campaigning as the leader who had kept—and presumably would continue to keep—America out of war, Hughes would have required a political death wish to promise to plunge the country into the conflict; he had no such wish, and he didn't.

Roosevelt, of course, thought the United States should be in the war and had been saying as much for months. Consequently, he had to watch his words. "I need hardly tell you that it has been no light task for me in my speeches to avoid seeming to clash with Hughes and, at the same time, not to go back on any of the things for which I stand," he confided. He had long ago learned to rationalize in good causes; never, in his opinion, had he had a better cause than the present one. "This country owes it to its own soul to defeat Wilson." So he suppressed his qualms and acted the loyal Republican.

Indeed, he acted more vigorously than he had intended. Midway through the campaign he told Corinne he was being "worked to the limit" by the Hughes crew; he added that he found this wonderfully ironic, for these were the very people who had claimed just four months earlier that he had lost all his pulling power and that Hughes was the man the people now wanted. Yet the campaigning fortified him, as it usually did, and by the week of the election he pronounced himself in "first class shape."

The omens looked good as the country trudged to the polls. "I hope to heaven we beat Wilson, and I believe we shall do so," Roosevelt told Quentin on election day. Hughes and much of the nation believed the same thing as late as twenty-four hours after the polls closed. But as the returns trickled in during the few days after that, Wilson erased Hughes's advantage and edged ahead. The six-hundred-thousand-vote final margin for Wilson in the popular count wasn't breathtakingly tight, but the twenty-three-vote electoral margin could have been reversed by the swing of a couple of close states.

II

The Democratic victory occasioned the usual recriminations among the losers. Many Republican regulars blamed Roosevelt for refusing to curtail his attacks on ethnic politicking. Roosevelt naturally thought just the opposite. He argued that Hughes should have been more forthright, more like himself. A Republican victory, he said, "would have been a certainty if Hughes had had it in him to make a straight-from-the-shoulder fighting campaign." To his old friend William White of Kansas, Roosevelt boasted: "I was literally the only national leader who dared stand straight on Americanism, preparedness and the performance of international duty." With rather less foundation but equal assurance, the former president declared of his once and recent Republican allies: "Their one chance of winning was with me."

Roosevelt hated to think that the country would be stuck with Wilson for another four years. "Outside of Mr. Hughes and his immediate circle of friends," he said very believably, "I question if there was a man more keenly disappointed than I was." At the same time, the campaign and its outcome had reinstalled him as the most likely leader of his old party. Twice in a row the regulars had nominated a loser; while Taft's defeat could be ascribed to Roosevelt's defection, Hughes's couldn't. Doubtless the old guard would continue to hold his season of irregularity—not to mention his numerous earlier trespasses—against him, but the rank and file of the party would demand a winner, and Roosevelt looked like the closest thing the Republicans had to that. Meanwhile, he was the obvious man to lead the opposition to the Democratic administration. Summarizing the party's situation, and even more his own, he commented, "We did not elect Hughes and we are not responsible for Mr. Wilson."

III

Events soon made leading the opposition as problematic as backing Hughes had been. In January 1917 the German government announced a policy of unrestricted submarine warfare in the waters off the shores of its antagonists. Starved and nearly strangled by the British blockade, Berlin decided to gamble the outcome of the war on a final offensive that would crack the stalemate in northern France and force a peace settlement on German terms. The key to the success of the plan was the prevention of resupply of Allied positions along the front; the key to prevention of resupply was the severing of the Atlantic link between America and Britain. Hence the shoot-on-sight policy. The advance announcement was not merely a matter of good form, which by this time had pretty well gone by the boards among all the belligerents; Berlin hoped to hold American merchantmen in port by the mere threat of sinking.

The German announcement made American belligerence inevitable, although Wilson initially satisfied himself with breaking diplomatic relations. Roosevelt would have found this final procrastination incredible if he hadn't already decided that Wilson was capable of absolutely any infamy. "He is yellow all through in the presence of danger, either physically or morally," Roosevelt declared to Lodge. By all evidence, Wilson would accept the most egregious insult or injury to the nation. "Of course, it costs him nothing, if the insult or injury is to the country, because I don't believe he is capable of understanding what the words 'pride of country' mean." As for the country, it was in such a "Chinese condition of soul" that it continued to confuse the president's cowardice for wisdom.

Yet for all his distrust of the president, Roosevelt still hoped for the best. "Even the lily-livered skunk in the White House may not be able to prevent Germany from kicking us into war," he told Kermit.

With the war declaration he had been demanding so close, Roosevelt suspended his attacks on Wilson. He didn't wish to give the president any excuse for avoiding the right and necessary course. Moreover, it would have been political folly to snipe at Wilson while German submariners were fixing their periscopes on American vessels.

Roosevelt had an additional reason for holding his tongue: He was in the process of requesting a major favor from the Wilson administration, although he considered it nothing less than his due and nothing less than what the welfare of the country demanded. On the third day after the German announcement of submarine warfare, Roosevelt wrote to War Secretary Newton Baker requesting permission to raise a division of volunteers for deployment against Germany.

Baker responded politely but—from Roosevelt's viewpoint— unsatisfactorily. Roosevelt and Edith had planned a vacation to the West Indies; in his letter to Baker he said he would cancel the trip if the secretary believed that war was imminent. Baker replied that the former president and Mrs. Roosevelt should go ahead and set sail. Things were well under control, and the administration could handle any difficulties that arose.

Roosevelt canceled anyway upon learning of Wilson's decision to break relations. He reiterated his desire to raise a division. "I should of course strain every nerve to have it ready for efficient action at the earliest moment, so that it could be sent across with the first expeditionary force, if the Department were willing."

Baker replied this time by applauding Roosevelt's patriotism but saying that the raising of forces rested with Congress, which had not yet acted in the matter.

Roosevelt recognized a runaround. "If they will give me permission," he told Hiram Johnson, speaking of Baker and Wilson, "I can get into the trenches within six months with my division." He went on to say, however: "I anticipate heart-breaking experiences over it." So great was Roosevelt's desire to join the fight that he vowed to cease all criticism of the administration at once. "If President Wilson would give me a free hand, and send me to the front, I would support him as loyally as any man possibly could, behaving exactly as Thomas and Farragut behaved in the days of the Civil War."

Wilson could be forgiven for doubts on this score, perhaps considering Zachary Taylor from the Mexican War more likely as a role model for Roosevelt than Thomas or Farragut. The Democratic president certainly had to consider the possibility that Roosevelt would steam off to France at the head of his division and return an even greater hero than he had been on his arrival back from Cuba in 1898. Political calculations aside, there were sound, though not necessarily compelling, military reasons for insisting that whatever forces were raised should be raised under the direction of the regular army's officer corps. This wasn't 1898, and Germany wasn't Spain. Such was the position Baker took in turning Roosevelt down a second time.

Roosevelt wasn't satisfied with this answer, either. He pointed out that he was a retired commander in chief of the United States Army and therefore entirely eligible for any position of command to which he might be appointed. He also respectfully submitted that his record in the field qualified him to lead a division. Lest Baker have any doubts on the subject, Roosevelt supplied as references the names of his three immediate superiors from the Spanish war. Baker deflected this request as well.

Frustrated but not surprised, Roosevelt sought a way around the administration's blockade. In the weeks before the American war declaration, he went as far as to inquire of Jusserand and Spring Rice whether, in the event of American belligerence and continued administration intransigence, he might raise a division of American volunteers on Canadian soil and take them over to France himself. He recognized the extraordinary nature of his request and would not have mentioned it if he hadn't known the two European diplomats so long and so well. "Of course," he added, "I would not attempt to raise it so far as I can now see, unless this country went to war, because I gravely doubt the propriety of an ex-President of the United States attempting to go to war, unless his country is at war." (It was a measure of Roosevelt's desperation to reach the front that he only "gravely doubted" the propriety of an action that he almost certainly would have labeled treasonous had the shoe been on the other foot.) Roosevelt continued, in a rare understatement, "But if we were at war, I should be profoundly unhappy unless I got into the fighting line."

IV

Roosevelt's desire to get into the fighting line kept him quiet until the middle of March. By then, however, receiving no satisfaction from the administration and fearing that Wilson, who still hadn't requested a war declaration, was going to lie down before even this latest German outrage, he could contain himself no longer. "I am so utterly sick of the gush about 'supporting the President' that I shall write a brief and courteous, but unequivocal statement of our present condition . . ." he told Lodge. "Taft, Hughes, and even Root take part in the general idiot cry which aligns us behind the President, right or wrong—and he is 99 per cent wrong."

Roosevelt's notion of what was courteous doubtless differed from Wilson's. The only thing he held back was Wilson's name; otherwise his statement, delivered to the Union League Club of New York, was an artillery barrage against the administration's handling of the current crisis. "There is no question about 'going to war,'" he thundered. "Germany is already at war with us. The only question for us to decide is whether we shall make war nobly or ignobly." The president's recent decision to arm American merchantmen was a timid act that would have no effect. "Germany despises timidity as she despises all other forms of feebleness." Linking Wilson's failure to bolster American defenses to another recent move—his proposal to compensate Colombia $25 million for America's handling of the Panama case thirteen years before (a measure Roosevelt interpreted, as Wilson certainly expected, as a direct slap)—Roosevelt declared, "In the days when this Republic prized manhood, a favorite motto was 'Millions for defense but not a cent for tribute.' Apparently our present motto is, twenty-five millions for tribute but not a cent for defense." The time had come—indeed, the time had come long before—when America needed to stand up for its honor and its rights. "Let us face the accomplished fact, admit that Germany is at war with us, and in our turn wage war on Germany with all our energy and courage, and regain the right to look the whole world in the eyes without flinching."

Having done his best to spur the administration to action, Roosevelt still expected no imminent response. "I intend to go to Florida for some shark and devil-fish harpooning," he told Lodge disgustedly. "I can do absolutely nothing here."

Roosevelt's salvos doubtless had some effect, but Germany's torpedoes, which began sinking American vessels at a rapid rate, had more. Early in April, Wilson asked Congress for the war declaration

Roosevelt thought was long overdue. Congress granted the president his request.

V

Finally, Roosevelt thought, America was doing the heroic thing. And he would do the same—if only that wretched creature in the White House would let him. Up to this point his discussions with the administration about a volunteer division had been essentially hypothetical; now that the country was actually at war, a different set of calculations would come into play. With the nation's honor committed, the public would rally to the flag and would support all who were willing to serve. Wilson wouldn't dare stand in the way of a popular outpouring of patriotism.

Such were Roosevelt's hopes on the train to Washington a few days after the war declaration. Nothing besides sheer desperation to fight could have compelled him to make a personal appeal to the man he so hated and despised. He had long ago learned that political effectiveness required tactical trimming; he had appeased Platt and Hanna and others of their ilk when necessary to achieve his goals. But Wilson was another matter. Platt and Hanna he had come to respect, in a grudging way; they were principled, after their own lights. Not Wilson—that hypocrite, liar, coward. It took all of Roosevelt's moral self-discipline to propel himself through the door of the White House on the morning of April 10.

His return to the seat of power could only have intensified the feeling he had had ever since the war broke out in Europe: that at this moment of world peril, *he* should be the one leading the nation, not Wilson. *He* knew the kaiser; *he* understood what power was for. On this same visit to the capital he conferred with the French and British ambassadors: Jusserand, *his* old friend, and Spring Rice, *his* best man and onetime housemate. *He* knew these people, and they knew *him*. Who was this impostor, this pretender to the throne?

He was, of course, the president of the United States, the commander in chief and, consequently, the one who would determine whether

Roosevelt fulfilled his desire for a return to battle. So the old colonel swallowed his pride and with hat in hand went calling to ask for what only Wilson could give.

The meeting began awkwardly. "The President doesn't like Theodore Roosevelt and he was not one bit effusive in his greeting," recorded Wilson aide Thomas Brahany. But Roosevelt was on a mission, and he attacked the president's defenses with the full force of his exuberance—partly feigned, partly sincere.

"Mr. President," he declared, "what I have said and thought, and what others have said and thought, is all dust in a windy street, if we can now make your message good." The message Roosevelt referred to was Wilson's call for war, in which he had spoken of a struggle to make the world "safe for democracy." Roosevelt had never doubted his rival's facility with language; indeed, this was much of what made him distrust Wilson so. And now he had to concede the stirring character of this latest installment of the Wilsonian rhetoric. The question was—as it had always been with Wilson—would the language lead to action?

"Of course," Roosevelt continued (as he related it shortly afterward), "it amounts to nothing, if we cannot make it good. But, if we can translate it into fact, then it will rank as a great state paper, with the great state papers of Washington and Lincoln."

Wilson was no more immune to flattery than most public figures (including Roosevelt), and between further compliments—of the president's program for conscription, most notably—and personal charm, Roosevelt began to win the president over. "The interview lasted twenty-five minutes," Brahany noted, "and before it closed the President had thawed out and was laughing and 'talking back.' They had a real good visit."

Amid the laughing, Roosevelt reiterated his proposal to raise a division. He explained that it was imperative for the American entry into the war to have an immediate impact. "I told him we should hit at once and hit hard," he recounted. The next several months would be critical; American soldiers must get into the field as soon as possible. This was where the volunteers would come in. Roosevelt explained how he had already done much research and planning. The Allies had plenty of weapons; what they needed was men. A division of highly motivated volunteers, training with English and French rifles, could be ready for combat months before a larger expeditionary force of regular recruits. Nor would the volunteers steal resources from the regular army. "I explained that all necessary expense could be provided out of private funds. I also explained to him that I would not take a man the draft might get."

This part of the offer piqued Wilson's curiosity. "The fact that I proposed to use material that otherwise would be unavailable seemed new to him. He seemed interested and he asked many questions."

Wilson indeed *was* interested—although more in Roosevelt than in his military proposal. "Well, and how did the Colonel impress you?" asked secretary Joseph Tumulty, who himself had been thoroughly taken by Roosevelt. Roosevelt had clapped Tumulty on the back on the way out the door: "By Jove, Tumulty, you are a man after my own heart! Six children, eh? Well now, you get me across and I will put you on my staff, and you may tell Mrs. Tumulty that I will not allow them to place you at any point of danger." Tumulty offered his own opinion of Roosevelt to Wilson: "I told the President of the very favorable impression the Colonel had made upon me by his buoyancy, charm of manner, and his great good nature."

Wilson listened while his secretary rambled on, and then agreed. "Yes, he is a great big boy. I was, as formerly, charmed by his personality. There is a sweetness about him that is very compelling. You can't resist the man. I can easily understand why his followers are so fond of him."

Roosevelt realized that he had scored a personal triumph. But he wondered what that meant in the present circumstances. "If any other man than he had talked to me as he did I would feel assured," he said upon leaving the White House. "If I talked to another man as he talked to me it would mean that that man was going to get permission to fight. But I was talking to Mr. Wilson. His words may mean much; they may mean little."

VI

In fact they meant little, as soon became evident. Neither Wilson and his advisers nor the careerists at the War Department were about to let Roosevelt steal their show, which they all knew he probably would if allowed into the field. The regular military men had long memories. They recollected what a pain Roosevelt had been in 1898 with his entourage of reporters and his constant carping about the deficiencies of the regular regiments compared to his volunteers, and they wouldn't put up with the same sort of thing again if they didn't absolutely have to. In a reply to one of Roosevelt's letters, in which the former Rough Rider alluded to his record during the Spanish war, Newton Baker remarked dryly, "The military record to which you call my attention is, of course, a part of the permanent records of this Department and is available, in detail, for consideration."

Between them, Wilson and the generals stymied Roosevelt's desire to return to the battlefield. Roosevelt tried again and again, answering at length each objection the administration put forward. He pointed out that, military considerations apart, the swift arrival of volunteers at the front would have an immense and positive impact on the morale of the Allies. If the president doubted this, he should merely ask the Allies. The French in particular were clamoring for him. Clemenceau told Wilson that one American in particular could raise the spirits of French soldiers more than any other. "Send them Roosevelt," the French premier implored.

But Wilson stood firm. Although Congress authorized the president to raise volunteer divisions, it did not—despite Roosevelt's earnest efforts with congressional sympathizers—require him to do so.

Once more Roosevelt felt obliged to choke down his loathing of Wilson and "respectfully ask permission" to raise his unit.

And once more Wilson refused. "It would be very agreeable to me," the president announced, "to pay Mr. Roosevelt this compliment and the Allies the compliment of sending to their aid one of our most distinguished public men, an ex-President who has rendered many conspicuous public services and proved his gallantry in many striking ways. Politically, too, it would no doubt have a very fine effect and make a profound impression." But military necessity forbade such a course. To raise volunteers would "seriously interfere" with the creation of a large and effective regular army and would contribute "practically nothing" to the strength of the armies currently engaged against Germany.

VII

Roosevelt was left to gnash his teeth in fury at this final crushing of his hopes of returning to battle. (On sober second thought he had recognized that trying to take a division to France on his own, as he had suggested to Spring Rice and Jusserand, was a bad idea, and he let it drop.) "It is bitter to me to feel that I shall not be with you in the fighting," he told Frank McCoy, to whom he had offered the now illusory post of his chief of staff. He had no doubt that Wilson's claim of military necessity was a smoke screen. "I could have raised four divisions (or eight divisions—200,000 men) of the finest fighting men," he declared to a friend, "could have put the finest fighting edge on them, and could have got them into the fighting line at the earliest moment, long before we had even begun to prepare our army here." Once in action they would have made "a literally unequaled record."

It was this argument from national interest that Roosevelt stressed in complaining to others about Wilson's veto of his volunteers, but what really galled him was something far more personal. For Roosevelt, France offered a last chance for heroism. He wasn't exactly the suicidal type, although an observer of his risk-taking behavior over the course of his life might have been forgiven for thinking so. And yet the romantic notion of death in battle held an irresistible appeal for him—the more so as he felt old age coming on and the prospect of increasing enfeeblement. "I would literally, and gladly, give my life to command a brigade of regulars under Pershing," he wrote. He believed that overseas service might indeed finish him off. "It would have mattered very little whether or not I personally cracked—from pneumonia in the trenches, or shell fire, or exhaustion or anything else." But such an end would mark a glorious finish to a life lived as well as he had been able to live it. "If I should die tomorrow," he mused, "I would be more than content to have as my epitaph, and my only epitaph, 'Roosevelt to France.'"

He never forgave Wilson for denying him this opportunity. He took it as a personal injury and additional evidence of Wilson's disqualification to lead the country in its hour of danger. "I cannot overstate how bitterly I regret that the President refused my offer to raise troops," he wrote Clemenceau, who already shared Roosevelt's skepticism of Wilson and would come to share his disdain. Cautioning that this message was for the French leader's eyes alone, Roosevelt went on to criticize his own president in terms he himself would have judged intolerable, perhaps felonious, had the situation been reversed. "Of course the fundamental trouble with Mr. Wilson is that he is merely a rhetorician, vindictive and yet not physically brave; he cannot help believing that inasmuch as sonorous platitudes in certain crises win votes they can in other crises win battles."

VIII

Roosevelt's attitude couldn't help but strengthen Clemenceau for those moments bound to come when French interests would diverge from American; by that time Roosevelt's opposition to Wilson would again be open and forthright. For now he merely assassinated the president's character semiprivately, as in the letter to Clemenceau, who was hardly a close friend. Politics kept his voice down; so did a desire to see his sons well placed in the war he himself was being denied.

Roosevelt had enemies in the War Department but he also had allies, and he used every connection he had to get good assignments for his four sons. His task was facilitated by the fact that the kinds of posts he was seeking for them were not the ones every other influential parent had in mind. With their enthusiastic assent—in this regard, if not in all others, he had taught them well—he eschewed safe staff positions, aiming instead to place his boys precisely where he wanted to be: amid the fiercest fighting.

His efforts, combined with the boys' qualifications, succeeded. Ted and Archie joined General Pershing's expeditionary force, eventually serving in the same infantry regiment. Kermit's experiences in Africa and South America suited him for a more exotic assignment: with the British army fighting the Turks in Mesopotamia. Roosevelt had gone direct to the top for Kermit; he wrote British prime minister Lloyd George, declaring, "I pledge my honor that he will serve you honorably and efficiently." Quentin, the youngest and most forward-looking of the quartet, was fascinated by the military's newest weapon: He enlisted in the army's air squadron.

More than once while throwing his sons into death's way, Roosevelt shuddered slightly at what he was doing. A letter from Ted contained a parable in which a big bear showed his two small offspring the ways of the world; Roosevelt responded in similar language, although more ambivalently: "The big bear was not, down at the bottom of his heart, any too happy at striving to get the two little bears where the danger is; elderly bears whose teeth and claws are blunted by age can far better be spared." To Kermit he wrote, "I hate to feel that I am out of it, especially because I so strongly believe that where physical conditions will permit it is the old, the men whose life is behind them and who have drained the cup of joy and sorrow, of achievement and failure, who should be in the danger line, for the little sooner or the little later matters little to them." After the boys were well on their way to battle, he confided to Quentin: "My disappointment at not going myself was down at bottom chiefly reluctance to see you four, in whom my heart was wrapped, exposed to danger while I stayed at home in do-nothing ease and safety."

Yet Roosevelt knew his duty as a parent—or thought he did—as certainly as he had known his duty as a soldier. In the same letter to Quentin in which he described his fear for his sons, he went on to say, "But the feeling has now been completely swallowed in my immense pride in all four of you." Over and over during the months of fighting he told his sons how proud he was of them that they were taking a vital part in the great struggle of the epoch. To Archie he wrote, "I am more proud of you, and of the other three, than I can say. And every one who speaks to me of you boys does it with a look and in a tone that makes my heart swell." He described to Kermit the fine times they would have when the war was over. "You will come back; and how much there will be to tell, as we sit before the great fire place in the north room." To be sure, the war demanded sacrifices; that was in the nature of war. "It is a very hard thing on you four to go," he wrote Archie. But the alternative was worse. "It would be infinitely harder not to go, not to have risen level to the supreme crisis in the world's history, not to have won the right to stand with the mighty men of the mighty days."

IX

With his sons fairly launched on their careers in arms, Roosevelt felt no further reason to hold his tongue regarding the Wilson administration. Indeed, the participation of the boys in the war effort gave him additional cause for lambasting the failings of those offices and individuals charged with training, provisioning, and transporting the troops. In September 1917, Roosevelt diversified from being a writer principally of essays and articles for monthly magazines such as the *Outlook* and the *Metropolitan* to being an editorialist for a daily newspaper. The *Kansas City Star* had long been one of his favorite papers, not least since he had long been the *Star*'s favorite statesman. In June 1917 a chance meeting on a train between Roosevelt and a son-in-law of the *Star*'s editor and owner, William Nelson, set Roosevelt to calculating the advantages of writing for next-day publication, as contrasted to the next-month schedule of the *Metropolitan*. Subsequent discussions led to a September handshake that closed the deal. Working alternatively out of the *Star*'s New York office and his own study at Sagamore Hill, he delivered his editorials by hand or telegraph. They appeared, on average, about once a week and soon were syndicated across the country.

Long-winded and iron-bottomed, Roosevelt at first had difficulty confining himself to the five-hundred-word format of the editorial. He frequently found that before he had worked up a decent head of indignation, he had exhausted his handful of paragraphs. But eventually he acquired the knack and discovered that a few paragraphs could deliver a stinging blow.

Most of those blows were directed at Wilson and members of the Democratic administration, and anyone else Roosevelt judged insufficiently enthusiastic or efficient regarding the war. In his maiden contribution to the *Star* he mourned the first American army death in France, blaming it both on German brutality—the victim, a doctor, was killed in a bombing raid that destroyed his hospital—and on the American unpreparedness that allowed the Germans to conduct such raids with impunity. Roosevelt expressed his "fathomless contempt" for the "base or unthinking folly" of those Americans who explained away German atrocities, criticized America's allies, obstructed the war effort, or called for an inconclusive peace. In later articles Roosevelt's anger grew more pointed and specific. He charged that the Wilson administration had long had evidence that German money was being used to foment anti-Allied feeling in America, as well as for more direct forms of sabotage, but the administration had hidden its head in the sand of its fatuous neutrality. He asserted that the president's pledge to make the world safe for democracy was a "rhetorical sham" as long as the United States refused to declare war on Germany's allies Austria and Turkey. He assailed the "broomstick preparedness" that resulted from the past and continuing failures of the president and the War Department to ready the country for war. He railed at reports that the president was considering a peace settlement short of complete victory. "Germany has made herself the outlaw among nations, and with her we should negotiate only through the mouths of our cannon."

Roosevelt's written wrath sometimes got him into trouble. On occasion the *Star* felt obliged to run something less vitriolic in Roosevelt's accustomed slot, and at least once officials of the Wilson administration considered barring the *Star* from the mail on grounds that Roosevelt's column impeded the war effort. Had the author not been an ex-president and the most prominent member of the opposition party, and had he been just slightly more intemperate, he might even have been prosecuted under the wartime sedition law.

(That he wasn't was no accident. Wilson responded to suggestions that charges be brought against Roosevelt by explaining: "I really think the best way to treat Mr. Roosevelt is to take no notice of him. That breaks his heart and is the best punishment that can be administered." The president went on: "While what he says is outrageous in every particular, he does, I am afraid, keep within the limits of the law, for he is as careful as he is unscrupulous.")

If private, as opposed to published, opinions had been illegal, Roosevelt almost certainly would have felt the Justice Department's lash. "I fear to write anything of public interest," he explained in one letter to Kermit, "because I fear the censor might not let it pass." Yet his fear didn't hold him back for long. In correspondence with friends and close allies, he vented an outrage that was certainly seditious by contemporary loose standards. He labeled Wilson a "white rabbit" and a "wretched creature." The nation's problems were the president's fault. "Fundamentally our whole trouble in this country is due more to Wilson than any other one man," Roosevelt told William

White. Wilson had gained reelection on an utterly insincere he-kept-us-out-of-war platform. "He had no convictions in the matter. He has no convictions at all; although he has opinions and coldly malicious hatreds." This cynical ploy, and others like it, had maintained Wilson in office but hurt the country enormously. "The damage he did to our people morally and materially during the last three years will bear evil fruit for a generation to come." Since the election, the president had been guilty of "intolerable hypocrisy." Wilson said he wanted to fight, but he deliberately kept good men away from the front. "He was much more anxious to spite Leonard Wood and myself than he was to save the country." He tolerated, indeed encouraged, abysmal performance by his subordinates. "To have appointed Daniels and Baker originally was evil enough; to have kept them on during a great war was a criminal thing." Roosevelt liked this formulation, and repeated it to others, lambasting Wilson's "criminal folly" in failing to prepare for war prior to April 1917 and in failing to prosecute the war with necessary vigor since.

White and others among Roosevelt's friends cautioned him against excessive criticism of the president; Roosevelt insisted that criticism was exactly what was required. Overlooking the president's crimes would constitute "the gravest possible moral offense against this country." For emphasis he added,

> The greatest damage that can be done to the cause of decency in this country is to stand by Wilson in such a way as to imply that we approve or condone his utterly cynical disregard of considerations of patriotism and national efficiency and his eagerness to sacrifice anything if to do so will advance his own political interests. He has just one kind of ability; a most sinister and adroit power of appealing in his own interest to all that is foolish and base in our people. He not only appeals to base and foolish men; he appeals also to the Mr. Hyde who, even in many good and honorable men, lurks behind the Dr. Jekyll in their souls.

X

Roosevelt's (or Robert Louis Stevenson's) metaphor of the dual personality might have applied equally to Roosevelt himself during this period. While Wilson's handling of the war elicited the worst in Roosevelt, the former president's continuing concern for his sons and his pride in their military accomplishments reflected the best. He wrote almost daily to one or another of his boys, or to his son-in-law Dick Derby, also in France, or to his daughter Ethel about Dick, or to one of his three daughters-in-law about their husbands. And needless to say—although harder to document—he spent endless hours talking to Edith about their brood, reading and rereading with her each letter that found its way across the Atlantic, fearing, as the American forces got closer to the front, the telegram bearing the news they couldn't bear to think about but could never stop thinking about. In nice weather Roosevelt would take Edith out in the boat for a row on the bay, as he had done since they were teenagers. As a concession to advancing years, she now sat in a chair with a back that had been fixed in the boat; he rowed only two or three hours at a stretch, rather than the five or six (or twelve or fifteen when Edith hadn't been along) of his youth.

Roosevelt recognized that Edith had a harder time than he did dealing with the danger the boys faced. She had never been to war, nor did she accept so enthusiastically the idea that war was man's highest calling. He also realized that he didn't always help matters. Replying to Ted's wife Eleanor, who had sent a reminder of an earlier, more carefree time, Roosevelt said he had passed it along to Edith. "She instantly looked very pretty and felt very woebegone, and realized that she was mated to a dull-nerved, coarse-natured unappreciative and nonunderstanding boor—a jovial boor, which made it worse—and that life stretched before and behind in a straight, monotonous, dusty road of uncheered duty."

But if duty required sending one's sons off to fight, there were always the grandchildren to dispel the sense of foreboding, albeit only briefly. Roosevelt reveled more than ever in the presence of the little ones. Writing to Eleanor shortly after she and her trio had visited, he declared, "I miss the little family *very* much!—most of all the dainty, pretty, exceedingly efficient and exceedingly companionable little mother, but also the three blessed small people; Gracie and Teddy and Cornelius of the white head and the black heart. I can just see Gracie marshalling Teddy for the extraordinary effort to frighten at least one pig; and breakfast is a distinctly tame affair when I no longer have to guard against an affectionate, busy and officious Ted doctoring 'Grandfather's soup' with salt."

Roosevelt's letters to his sons contained news of the home front; they also contained advice on family and related matters. He cautioned Kermit against trying to find a way for Belle and little Kim to follow him to the Middle East. "You have no right to do more than provide for them and say good-bye to them here on this side. The British War Office must get no impression that you intend to try to go to war en famille." As Kermit well knew, Ted's wife Eleanor had traveled to France to work in the military hospitals there; but that was different, Roosevelt said, because Ted had not tried to pull any strings to get her the job. "This is war; it needs the sternest, most exclusive, and most business-like attention; and no officer (especially an officer of a foreign nationality who has been approved by favor) must try to get his wife near him on the campaign, or try to have her go over with him. He must devote himself solely to his grim work."

Other advice was more touching. Quentin was the only one of the children not yet married, but he had an intended, Flora Whitney. Roosevelt and Edith knew the young lady and approved of the match—Roosevelt, characteristically, with more enthusiasm than Edith. Consequently, the father worried when Quentin proved to be a sporadic correspondent. "Mother, the adamantine, has stopped writing to you because you have not written to her—or to any of us—for a long time. That will make no permanent difference to you; but I write about something that may make a permanent difference. Flora spoke to Ethel yesterday of the fact that you only wrote rarely to her. She made no complaint whatever. But she knows that some of her friends receive three or four letters a week from their lovers or husbands (Archie writes Gracie rather more often than this—exceedingly interesting letters)." Letters alone couldn't keep love alive, but a lack of letters could surely kill it. "If you wish to lose her, continue to be an infrequent correspondent. If however you wish to keep her write her letters—interesting letters, and love letters—at least three times a week. Write no matter how tired you are, no matter how inconvenient it is; write if you're smashed up in a hospital; write when you are doing your most dangerous stunts; write when your work is most irksome and disheartening; write all the time! Write enough letters to allow for half being lost." Roosevelt signed this, "Affectionately, A hardened and wary old father."

Quentin knew he had been remiss. "I have been a perfect pig about not writing more," he said, and vowed to do better. His efforts caused his relationship with Flora to flourish, to the point where Roosevelt—who wanted to see all his children married as happily as he was—urged the boy to tie the knot. "Why don't you write to Flora, and to her father and mother, asking if she won't come abroad and marry you? As for your getting killed, or ordinarily crippled, afterwards, why she would a thousand times rather have married you than not have married you under those conditions; and as for the extraordinary kinds of crippling, they are rare, and anyway we have to take certain chances in life. You and she have now passed your period of probation; you have been tried; you are absolutely sure of yourselves; and I would most heartily approve of your getting married at the earliest possible moment."

Quentin had to think this one over; meanwhile, his father had words of wisdom for his other sons. He warned Ted of the complications that could develop should Archie get assigned to his regiment. He cautioned Kermit, who wanted to leave the Middle East for France where the fighting was much heavier, against trying to transfer before the British made absolutely clear that they were fully satisfied with his performance. When Archie had trouble procuring shoes for his men, his father told him to pay for them himself—much as he had done in the Spanish war—and send the bill home.

But mostly he avowed his tremendous pride in them all. To Ted he wrote of his deep gratification at how well they were doing. "Until you are an old man you will never be able quite to understand the satisfaction I feel because each of my sons is doing and has done better than I was doing and had done at his age—and I had done well. And of course this is preeminently true of you. I don't mean that any of you will be President; as regards the extraordinary prizes the element of luck is *the* determining factor; but getting in the class of those who have to their credit worthy, and even distinguished, achievement—that's what I mean."

When Archie was wounded in action and received the Croix de Guerre for gallantry from the French government, his father told him how thrilled he was "to have a hero in the family." He was tickled to imagine the scene of the ceremony. "It must have been rather fine," Roosevelt told Kermit, "to see Archie, on the operating table, receive the cross; and imagine that iron-natured young Puritan's aspect when the French General kissed him on both cheeks!" In a more serious vein, Roosevelt related to Archie how his bravery had been feted on the home front. "At lunch Mother ordered in some madeira; all four of us filled the glasses and drank them off to you; then Mother, her eyes shining, her cheeks flushed, as pretty as a picture, and as spirited as any heroine of romance, dashed her glass on the floor, shivering it in pieces, saying 'that glass shall never be drunk out of again'; and the rest of us followed suit and broke our glasses too."

Not content with telling family and friends how he felt, Roosevelt informed Clemenceau himself of what his son had done, just in case the French premier didn't keep up on all the recipients of his government's honors. Roosevelt added, quite sincerely and believably, "I am prouder of his having received it than of my having been President!"

And yet the fact that Archie had been the first to be decorated didn't diminish in the slightest Roosevelt's pride in his other sons. He wrote to Kermit, apropos of nothing in particular, "Well, old side partner, your letters are perfectly delightful and surely you must know how my heart thrills with pride whenever I think of you. I don't believe in all the United States there is any father who has quite the same right that I have to be proud of his four sons."

XI

But the pride never came free, for the glory never did. On receiving the news of Archie's injuries and honors, Roosevelt wrote his son, "Of course tonight we are divided between pride and anxiety, beloved fellow." Even after it was apparent that Archie was out of danger, Roosevelt still felt the ambivalence. "It seems a strange thing to say, for I suppose one ought not to take pride in the fact that another who is very dear has been wounded, but I cannot help feeling pride that one of my boys has been severely wounded in fighting for civilization and humanity." To his son-in-law Dick Derby he declared, "In days such as these the only men about whom one can feel joy and pride are the men about whom one must also feel deep anxiety. The pride and the anxiety go hand in hand."

Both Roosevelt's pride and his anxiety were increased by growing evidence of his own mortality. In February 1918 he entered the hospital for surgery. The leg injury from his Amazon trip had never healed properly and lately had festered again. Meanwhile, his jungle fever had returned, and he had managed to contract an ear infection as well. Recalling his brush with septicemia in 1902, his doctors ordered the infected leg tissue cut away. After the operation was over, Roosevelt dismissed the procedure as "entirely trivial"—a judgment that differed from the doctors'. Yet Roosevelt himself conceded that the operation wouldn't have been trivial if it had been delayed much longer. He went on to tell Kermit, "I can quite honestly say that my only feeling was the deepest gratitude that it was not one of you boys, and a very earnest wish that it were possible for me to play my small part by taking it, instead of having some similar thing happen to one of you boys."

The possibility of nontrivial complications brought other thoughts to mind as well. "I have taken a somewhat sardonic amusement in the real panic that affected a great many people when for a moment it looked as if I might not pull through. They have been bitterly against me for the last three and a half years and have denounced me beyond measure." The prospect of his passing brought what Roosevelt perceived as a change of heart. "When they thought I might die they suddenly had an awful feeling that maybe I represented what down at the bottom of their hearts they really believed to be right, and that although they have followed Wilson they knew also, down at the bottom of their hearts, that they did so only because he pandered to the basest side of their nature, and gave them an excuse for following the easy path that led away from effort and hardship and risk and unpleasantness of every kind, and also incidentally from honor and duty."

XII

For better or worse, fate and able medical care deprived Roosevelt of this particular chance to best Wilson; he improved, slowly. At the end of February he declared himself "on the high road to recovery." A

few days later, even though his ear troubles rendered him deaf on the
left side and made him walk, as he put it, like a "lunatic duck," he
returned home.

His glimpse of the farther shore, now receding again, didn't
improve his opinion of Wilson. If anything, by reminding him how
thin was the thread that held a man—any man, including each of his
sons—to life, the experience intensified his animus against the president.

Increasingly, Roosevelt felt that Wilson's mishandling of the war
was placing his sons in greater danger than necessary. "The best are
paying with their blood for Wilson's cold selfishness and timidity and
longdrawn delays," the angry father declared. "Wilson is the criminal. . . . If this war goes wrong Wilson must bear the major share of
the responsibility." Nearly a year into belligerency, the president continued to allow incompetents to oversee the provisioning and reinforcement of American troops. "It is sickening to feel that this army,
including Ted and Archie, may be sacrificed without any adequate
reinforcement, because of the folly, and worse than folly, of our high
civilians at home, and of the fuddled elderly fools of the regular army
who were kept in high position by these same civilians during the first
year of the war." To Arthur Lee he declared, "There never was a more
heartsickening position than that which I am in. . . . My perpetual
nightmare is that the small body of American troops now at the front
in France, who include two of my sons in the infantry and one in the
aviation service, may be callously sacrificed by Wilson, through entirely
insufficient support being given them, either because he thinks on the
whole such sacrifice is the least disadvantageous way out of it for him,
or else from sheer administrative incapacity on his part." Personal
failings of the most serious kind also figured in the president's shockingly poor performance. "As he is physically timid he positively dis-
likes and resents the exhibition of soldierly valor by others. Even after
nominally going to war he never intended to do any fighting."

Yet though Roosevelt's paternal feelings intensified his anger at
Wilson and his frustration at being unable to affect the course of
events, they also afforded hope for the time after the war when the
dangers and annoyances of the present would be behind them. His
sons had carried his heart to the front, and they would bring it back
on their return. Repeating an earlier, and constant, theme, he wrote

Kermit: "I really don't mind being reduced to puttering round with the infinitely unimportant, because I am so very proud of the part that you boys have played. I should like to see all of you come home, and watch Mother's face as she greets you, and see you with your darling little wives and blessed babies—and then let nunc dimittis be sung over me at any moment! The flags and sword in the North Room will have as companions weapons that tell of far more, infinitely more, distinguished and dangerous and important service; and how glad I am!"

XIII

But they wouldn't all come home.

In May, Quentin wrote with great news: "I've gotten my first real excitement on the front, for I think I got a Boche." As it turned out, this downing couldn't be confirmed; but another, in July, was. Roosevelt could hardly contain his pride and joy in his youngest. "The last of the 'lion's brood' has been blooded!"

Quentin occupied a special spot in Roosevelt's heart. As a boy he had hardly been what his father envisioned in a son—and what Ted, for example, tried so hard to be. "I wish Quentin could hold his own better in a rough and tumble with other boys," Roosevelt worried to Archie when Quentin was ten. "He seems a little soft." And he was always up to some devilment. Roosevelt described having to steal time from his presidential duties to chide Quentin and accomplices for bombarding the portraits in the White House with spitballs. "I explained to them that they had behaved like boors; that it would have been a disgrace to have behaved so in any gentleman's house, but that it was a double disgrace in the house of the Nation." At least once Quentin was caught cutting school and lying to cover his absence. "I have had to give him a severe whipping—the first real whipping I have ever had to give one of my children." On good days Roosevelt called Quentin a "blessed rogue"; on other occasions a "regular alley-cat." In the latter mood, Roosevelt confessed that the boy caused Edith and himself "a great deal of concern."

But time took some of the wildness out of the boy—and much of the pudginess as well. "Quentin turned up last night," Roosevelt wrote at Christmas 1911. "He is half-an-inch taller than I am, and is in great shape. He is much less fat than he was, and seems to be turning out right in every way." He kept improving until the coming of the war, when his enlistment in the air corps caused his father to forgive any youthful indiscretions still on the books. Roosevelt had ridden in an airplane in 1910 and could appreciate what his son was feeling as he soared above the French countryside in search of the foe. The father had found fighting afoot to be intoxicating; fighting in the air must be even more so.

Aerial combat was indeed intoxicating—and deadly. Within a week of the receipt of Quentin's thrilling news of downing a German aircraft, an opposite and appalling report arrived at Sagamore Hill. The first inkling came indirectly, in fact accidentally. Roosevelt was sitting in his library in the late afternoon of July 16 when a reporter friend, Phil Thompson of the Associated Press, entered with a puzzled look on his face. He held a telegram addressed to the New York *Sun*, evidently from that paper's overseas bureau, for it carried the marks of official censorship. "Watch Sagamore Hill for [censored]," the cable read. Thompson asked the former president if he knew what it meant.

Roosevelt rose at once, went to the entrance of the library, looked into the hall, then turned back and quietly closed the door. "Something's happened to one of the boys," he said in a tight but controlled voice. He considered briefly which one it might be. Archie was recovering from his wound; it couldn't be him. Ted had taken a whiff of gas and been slightly shrapnelled; he, too, must still be on the sidelines. Kermit hadn't reached the front in his sector yet. It had to be Quentin. Roosevelt told Thompson not to say a word to anyone, especially Mrs. Roosevelt, until further news arrived.

All the rest of that day Roosevelt kept his grim surmise to himself. He changed his knickers and work shirt for his customary dinner jacket, and spent the evening chatting with Edith and reading. But he couldn't keep his mind on his book—and Edith apparently sensed his distraction, for she neglected to make her usual entry in her diary that night.

The next morning, shortly after breakfast, Thompson drove back up the hill from Oyster Bay. The reporter didn't have to say a word: Roosevelt could tell from his look that the news was bad. He took Thompson out to the piazza where they might speak alone. The reporter succinctly explained that Quentin's plane had engaged two German fighters and been shot down behind enemy lines.

Though he had been expecting it, the report still staggered the father. Yet his first thought was for Edith. "But—Mrs. Roosevelt!" he said, pacing back and forth across the piazza. "How am I going to break it to her?"

The worst of it was, he didn't know just what to tell Edith. Quentin was down—that was all the report said. He might have survived the crash—men did. There was still reason to hope.

Roosevelt gathered his emotions and went inside. For half an hour he and Edith consoled each other, seeking the scattered beams that shone through this cloud. Then he returned to the piazza and handed Thompson a statement for publication: "Quentin's mother and I are very glad that he got to the front and had a chance to render some service to his country, and show the stuff that was in him before his fate befell him."

For the next three days Roosevelt and Edith remained in the limbo of uncertainty. Eleanor sent word from Paris emphasizing that the rumors of Quentin's death were "absolutely unconfirmed." Dick Derby had it secondhand—or was it thirdhand?—that one of Quentin's airmates thought he had brought his plane to earth intact and been captured by the Germans.

As agonizing as not knowing was, it was nothing new to Edith. She had been rehearsing this moment ever since that day in 1898 when Theodore had gone off to war. She had relived the feeling any number of times during his presidency when she thought of Lincoln's assassination, and Garfield's, and McKinley's, and . . . Her fears had lifted somewhat when they left the White House, only to return redoubled when Theodore was shot in 1912. Now he was safe, but her sons were in danger—and Quentin in more than danger. Was he dead? Was he dying? It was more than a mother could bear.

But perhaps because she was a mother, perhaps because she had been anticipating these emotions for decades, she focused on her husband. As she emerged from the house on that first black morning, her eyes wet with tears, she took Thompson aside. "We must do everything we can to help him," she said. "The burden must not rest entirely on his shoulders."

XIV

The burden had never felt so heavy. Roosevelt had faced live fire in battle, but he had never fully understood what war exacted from those who stayed behind. The hero he had long ago fashioned in his mind, the hero he had patterned himself after, the hero he had made himself into—this hero was a man in control of his destiny, or as in control as man could be. At the moment of danger he acted—boldly, decisively, defiant of the odds.

Only now did he appreciate that there was another kind of heroism: the heroism of those who watched their loved ones march into battle, knowing that the lives they valued more than their own were at the mercy of forces utterly beyond their control. Only now did he realize what Edith had experienced every time he indulged his affinity for danger. He had laughed at danger, confident that he would win a glorious victory or die a glorious death. But to Edith, his danger was no laughing matter; rather, it was a dagger suspended over her heart. Where was the glory in that? Was it any wonder that she developed the stoic exterior he often teased her about?

Now it was his turn to be the stoic—or to try. After handing his statement to Thompson, Roosevelt spent most of the morning answering his mail. He got through it, but not without great difficulty. His secretary, to whom he dictated his replies, afterward described "his voice choking with emotion . . . and the tears streaming down his face."

Earlier he had promised to address the Republican state convention at Saratoga on July 18. Some supporters were talking of a Roosevelt run for governor in the autumn. Although it was all he could do to drive to the station and board the train, he determined to carry on. Isaac Hunt, who had known him since his first days in Albany, now nearly forty years ago, and who had been with him after Alice's death, recognized that same dull agony in his eyes. Roosevelt's prepared text was unremarkable; his delivery was lively by ordinary standards but subdued by his own. In the middle of his speech he put down his text and spoke from the heart. With an earnestness he had never felt before, he reaffirmed the romantic ideal he had spent his life striving after: "The finest, the bravest, the best of our young men have sprung eagerly forward to face death for the sake of a high ideal; and thereby they have brought home to us the great truth that life consists of more than easygoing pleasures, and more than hard, conscienceless, brutal striving after purely material success."

During the next forty-eight hours he continued about his business, deflecting questions about his future, deflecting everything but the essentials, listening and watching for the message that would rekindle his sputtering hopes or snuff them out.

Finally, the candle died. As he wrote to Kermit, the son to whom he was closest:

> On Tuesday the first rumors of Quentin's death came; the final and definite announcement that he was killed and not captured came yesterday, Saturday, afternoon. Ethel and Alice had come on; and poor, darling heartbroken Flora had been spending the night here. There is not much to say. No man could have died in finer or more gallant fashion; and our pride equals our sorrow—each is limited only by the other. It is dreadful that the young should die; I need hardly say to you, who know so intimately how I feel, that in hospital last winter my one constant thought was how I wished that by dying it were possible for me to save any one of you from death; but after all how infinitely better death is than life purchased on unworthy terms; and you four, and Dick, being what you are—and neither your mother nor I would for anything in the world have you other than you are—it was unthinkable that you should do anything, any of you, except exactly what you have done.

Again Roosevelt acknowledged that things were more trying for Edith. "It is hard for the women who weep—and hardest for those who weep but little—when word comes that henceforth they are to walk in the shadow." But it was a comfort and a support to him that she was as strong as she was. "Mother has been as wonderful as she always is in a great crisis. She has the heroic soul. Yesterday morning she went for a couple of hours row with me out on the still, glassy water towards the sound; there was a little haze, and it all soothed her poor bruised and aching spirit. Then we took a swim; and as we swam she spoke of the velvet touch of the water and turning to me smiled and said: 'there is left the wind on the heath, brother!'"

Roosevelt updated Kermit on Ted and Archie. Ted had recently been badly hit (Roosevelt had been wrong about his being on the sidelines); he was recovering, however, and Eleanor had gone to him. Archie's wounds were crippling, at least temporarily; his father thought he would heal more quickly at home. But both, thankfully, were out of the line of fire for the moment. Kermit himself was the only one unaccounted for. "I do not know where you are or what you are doing," his father wrote plaintively.

Yet across the miles and across the generation separating them, Roosevelt felt a bond that transcended the tie of father to son, basic though that was. He felt the bond of battle. "I do not think I could bear to send you my sons to face deadly peril if I had not myself twenty years ago eagerly faced a far smaller but similar risk. We are brothers, you and I!"

CHAPTER THIRTY-ONE

The Last Romantic
1918–19

Roosevelt never got over Quentin's death. Not since his beloved Alice had died thirty-five years earlier had anything caused him such grief. In public he put a stern face on his emotions, but those close to him could feel the anguish that made every action an effort. Edith told Kermit: "Quentin's death shook him greatly. I can see how constantly he thinks of him and not the merry happy silly recollections which I have but sad thoughts of what Quentin would have counted for in the future." James Amos, who as butler, bodyguard, and all-purpose "head man"—Roosevelt's term—had probably spent more time with his boss since 1901 than anyone besides Edith, saw a different person than he had known. "He did not weep or talk about it," Amos said. "But to me, who had been used to watch his every movement for years and who knew him so well, it was plain that he was a changed man. He kept his peace, but he was eating his heart out." Occasionally, when Roosevelt thought no one was around, Amos could hear him say softly: "Poor Quinikins!"

Corinne observed much the same thing. On the train coming back from Saratoga, she noticed that not even books—until now his assured escape and soul-soother—could hold his attention. Corinne had left him with a volume in hand before going to order dinner; on her return: "I stood behind him for a moment before making myself known to him again, and I could see that he was not reading, that his sombre eyes were fixed on the swiftly passing woodlands and the river, and that the book had not the power of distracting him from the all-embracing grief which enveloped him."

Roosevelt himself conceded how hard it was to carry on. "It is useless," he told his daughter-in-law Belle, "for me to pretend that it is not very bitter to see that good, gallant, tenderhearted boy, leave life at its crest, when it held Flora, and such happiness, and certainly an honorable and perhaps a distinguished career." To author Edith Wharton, a relative of Edith's and a woman who understood the power of words, he explained that this was a case where words failed. "There is no use of my writing about Quentin; for I should break down if I tried. His death is heartbreaking."

Roosevelt again granted that it was harder for Edith. She was "pretty well heart broken," he told Kermit. So was Flora, needless to say; but she was young and would recover. Not so Edith. "Mother, of course, will carry the wound green to her grave." Roosevelt took his wife to Maine, to escape the memories the old house held. "At home she sees Quentin in every room."

Roosevelt did too, but he saw something else besides. Beyond the agony of the moment, he saw the same shimmering vision that had lifted him out of his grief at his father's death, at Alice's death, and at assorted other emotional crises. The slowness of mail from the front meant that Quentin would speak to his father and mother from beyond the grave, when letters written before his death arrived at Oyster Bay. A different personality than Roosevelt's might have found such a situation too trying to bear; Roosevelt saw it as a celebration of life and a confirmation of the values he had clung to from boyhood. "When we reached here we found Quentin's last letters," he told Belle. "He was at the fighting front, very proud and happy—and singularly modest, with all his pride, and his pleasure at showing his metal. Of course that was a wonderful company of men, flying in the swift battle planes—not the ordinary observation or bombing planes—at the front; they were bound together in the close ties of men who know that most of them are going to die, and who face their fate high of heart and with a gallant defiance." Quentin had said that he would not for the world have been anywhere else. Two days before his death he had visited Eleanor in Paris. "She was so proud of him, and took him round as the young hero. He had his crowded hour of glorious life."

Roosevelt's heroic interpretation was confirmed by the homage that soon began pouring in for his son. "Quentin's death has had a most extraordinary effect on this nation," he wrote Kermit. Editors, public speakers, even foes of the former president lauded the young man who had given his life for liberty. "Quentin has become the symbol of the high and gallant souls whom we have sent to face death in the great war for right."

Roosevelt would have felt this way even had no one joined him in the feeling; he had been preparing, in various ways, for this moment his entire life. But the popular acclaim for Quentin made it that much easier to convince himself that whatever pain he felt personally at his youngest son's death, the glory that accompanied the death made it worthwhile. He declared that even if all four of his sons should have been killed by war's end, he wouldn't regret encouraging the boys to join the fighting. "Altho we were crushed by the blow," he said, including Edith in his conviction, "we would rather have it that way than not have had them go." (Yet even in speaking for Edith, he acknowledged one more time that her task was harder than his: "It's the woman who pays in a case like this. It's the mothers and wives who feel most deeply.") To James Bryce, who had lost a nephew to the conflict, he wrote, "It is very dreadful that the young should die and the old be left, especially when the young are those who above all others should be the leaders of the next generation. But they have died with high honor, and not in vain; for it is they, and those like them, who have saved the soul of the world."

II

As convinced as he was that Quentin and his comrades had saved the soul of the world from German militarism, Roosevelt was equally convinced that Woodrow Wilson was willing to sacrifice that soul to the president's private political agenda. Roosevelt wasn't quite so reductionist as to blame Wilson for Quentin's death, although at times he came close. But he was absolutely certain that the president had no conception of what the war was about or what the sacrifices of Quentin and the others signified. After Quentin's death, Roosevelt rededicated himself to alerting the American people to the true nature of the literally life-and-death issues their country faced, and to frustrate what he saw as Wilson's plan to sell American interests down the river of personal ambition.

The centerpiece of Wilson's planning was his fourteen-point package of peace terms, unveiled the previous January following criticism by the new rulers of Russia—Lenin and the Bolsheviks—of various secret treaties among the Allies. Roosevelt held no brief for the Bolsheviks; on the contrary, he declared that they seemed to have "absolutely ruined" Russia. But he largely blamed Wilson for their success, contending that the president's "shilly-shallying," his "delays and refusals to act," and "the way in which he has gratified his private malice at the expense of the country" had, by prolonging the war, encouraged the communist takeover.

Accordingly, Roosevelt was far from impressed by Wilson's rejoinder to Lenin. The slippery language made it difficult to tell exactly what the president proposed, but the fundamental premise was clear enough and was so thoroughly wrongheaded as to be almost inconceivable—except, again, that by now Roosevelt could conceive anything of Wilson. Quite obviously the president intended for the war to stop short of a German surrender. Not only did this reveal a shocking moral indifference to Germany's gross and brutal crime in starting the war, but it insulted the millions of Allied dead, now including many thousands of Americans and not least Quentin, who had given their lives to punish and right this wrong. Besides, it was strategically inane: To halt the war before Germany's capacity to wage another such conflict had been annihilated would simply invite repetition. "If construed in its probable sense," Roosevelt told Lodge, who agreed, "many and possibly most of these fourteen points are thoroly mischievous and if made the basis of a peace, such peace would represent not the unconditional surrender of Germany but the conditional surrender of the United States."

Yet Wilson's peace program had one thing to recommend it—it made patently obvious where the president stood. "I am glad Wilson has come out in the open; I fear Judas most when he can cloak his activities behind a treacherous make-believe of non-partisanship."

Roosevelt pounded Wilson throughout the late summer and early autumn of 1918. By now the full weight of American military power was being felt in France; Germany had gambled on winning the war before the Yanks arrived en masse, and lost. The war quite obviously was approaching an end; the only question involved the terms Germany would be required to accept. Wilson proposed his fourteen points as the basis for a cessation of hostilities, but the British and French governments held out for a more decisive conclusion.

Roosevelt sided with the Allies against his own president. Editorializing in the *Star* in late October, Roosevelt described Germany as "the outlaw among nations" and asserted that the sole way to deal with an outlaw was to capture, try, and punish him. One did not negotiate with outlaws, as the president was negotiating with Germany. Roosevelt realized that unconditional surrender might require more bloodshed, perhaps much more. This was a "sad and dreadful thing" to contemplate. "But it is a much worse thing to quit now and have the children now growing up obliged to do the job all over again, with ten times as much bloodshed and suffering, when their turn comes." The last time the world had had to deal with the likes of Kaiser Wilhelm was a century before, when another tyrant had trampled across Europe. That experience should provide the lesson for the present. "The surest way to secure a peace as lasting as that which followed the downfall of Napoleon is to overthrow the Prussianized Germany of the Hohenzollerns as Napoleon was overthrown."

Many influential Americans agreed with Roosevelt, as did the governments and most of the people of the Allies; the combined opposition compelled Wilson to change course and stiffen the terms he would require of Berlin. The reversal merely intensified Roosevelt's disdain. "The President suddenly made his, say, 800dth volte-face," he sneered. "A fortnight ago he believed he could step in as a Peace-God, make a negotiated peace with the Central Powers, and be humbly followed by the Allies and slavishly adored by our own people." But the uproar that Wilson's approach precipitated had proved the fatuousness of this view. "He promptly turned a somersault."

Yet he landed on his feet, and had another maneuver at the ready. The last weeks of the war coincided with the culmination of America's congressional campaign; Wilson called on voters to register their approval of his handling of the war by voting Democratic.

Roosevelt castigated Wilson's call as the most cynical form of narrow partisanship. "The President's appeal is a cruel insult to every

Republican father and mother whose sons have entered the Army or the Navy," he told a Republican ally. He added that it would be resented as well by Democratic parents who didn't want their sons' sacrifices devalued by such a transparent ploy.

Roosevelt linked arms with other Republicans in an effort to repudiate Wilson. "The Republicans, feeling rather hopeless, are turning towards me to act as their as leader in opposition," he explained to James Bryce. Roosevelt saw the regulars' discomfiture as a chance both to rebuke Wilson and to recapture the Republican Party. "We *must* make the Republican party the forward-looking party, and not let Wilson appear as the progressive champion. My motto is: anti-Romanoff; and anti-Bolshevist!"

Another motto was: Let bygones be bygones, when possible. Roosevelt made up with Taft, whom he had treated so shabbily and who, fortunately for the prospects of reconciliation, had a greater capacity for forgiveness than Roosevelt did. Together the only surviving Republican presidents urged voters to stand firm for unconditional surrender and a sensible and lasting peace settlement. "I do hope the mills of the Gods begin to grind some time as regards Wilson—but they are awfully slow about it," he told Brander Matthews. "I help them when I can!"

III

With Roosevelt's help, the political gods persuaded the American people to reject Wilson's call for a Democratic Congress. Local domestic issues had much to do with their decision, but whatever the reasons, the Republicans recaptured both houses of Congress. Their victory not only embarrassed the president but imperiled his plan for peace. This latter grew more important when, just days after the election, the Germans accepted an armistice.

Meanwhile, Roosevelt became the acknowledged leader of the Republican Party and the favorite for the presidential nomination a little over eighteen months hence. Talk of 1920 had taken second place to the war since American entry, but with the fighting now ended and the Democrats rebuffed, Roosevelt's name emerged once more.

Roosevelt did nothing to discourage the discussion. Not since leaving the White House had he been so well placed to claim the party's mantle. The regulars, in fighting off Roosevelt, had led the party to defeat twice in a row. Moreover, the events of the war had proved him a prophet against the noninterventionists and lukewarm patriots of both parties. And now the voters had spoken out against Wilson. If anyone had a mandate to speak for the American people, it was Roosevelt.

He didn't hesitate to do so, within the limits of tactical circumspection. He reminded Bryce, who had made a scholarly study of such questions, that in a system of parliamentary government any no-confidence vote comparable to that just delivered against Wilson would have turned him out of office and delivered control to the leader of the Republicans. Roosevelt didn't say explicitly that this meant him, but Bryce doubtless divined his meaning. In a letter to Arthur Lee, Roosevelt boasted how he personally had foiled Wilson's nefarious plan to force an incomplete and unworthy peace upon the American people—and upon Lee's Britain as well. "His success in browbeating our own people, the terror which he had impressed on the newspapers, the immense political funds which he used nominally for national, but really for party, purposes, and the natural tendency of good people to stand by the President in wartime made him convinced that he could induce the nation to follow him in another somersault." Wilson's call for a Democratic majority in the elections—designed to yield what Roosevelt called "a rubber-stamp Congress"—was the latest manifestation of Wilson's hubris. "This gave me my chance," Roosevelt explained, "and in the last week of the campaign we did the seemingly impossible."

Roosevelt continued to rebuke the president in the weeks after the election. He agreed with Lodge—who upon the Republican takeover of the Senate became chairman of the critical Foreign Relations Committee—that they should "show no mercy" to Wilson, although he cautioned against overplaying the Republican hand lest the public start to sympathize with the president. More questionably, Roosevelt made a concerted effort to undermine the president in the upcoming peace negotiations. "Wilson's one thought is to sit at the head of the peace table," Roosevelt ventured to Kermit, even as he did his utmost to deprive Wilson of that place. He wrote to Clemenceau and British foreign secretary Arthur Balfour reminding them of Wilson's rejection at the polls. "In any free country, except the United States," he explained to those Allied leaders, "the result of the Congressional elections on November 5th last would have meant Mr. Wilson's retirement from office and return to private life." (This wasn't quite right: The head of a defeated parliamentary government typically took his seat with the opposition.) "He demanded a vote of confidence. The people voted a want of confidence, by returning to each House of Congress a majority of the Republican Party of which I am one of the leaders." Having already made clear that he deemed Wilson's fourteen points an entirely unsatisfactory basis for a peace settlement, Roosevelt added crucially that the Republicans stood for "the unconditional surrender of Germany and for absolute loyalty to France and England in the peace negotiations."

This was an extraordinary tactic, patriotically dubious if not downright seditious. Had Roosevelt discovered anyone trying such a thing against him when he was president, he probably would have ordered that person arrested at once. He certainly would have condemned any such maneuver as the most vile elevation of partisan and personal ambition above the welfare of the country. Regardless of the outcome of the congressional contests, Wilson was still president of the United States; Republicans might differ with Democrats, but almost all Americans—including Roosevelt in his calmer moments—would have agreed that the two parties ought to confine their differences to American soil. To bring foreign governments into their quarrels was to step beyond the pale. Yet so deep and bitter was Roosevelt's hatred of Wilson—deeper and more bitter than ever since Quentin's death— that it blinded him to such fundamental patriotic principles.

Roosevelt simply couldn't bear that Wilson might win credit for the defeat of Germany. To Rudyard Kipling he denounced as "inconceivable folly" an apparent decision by British opinion leaders to promote the "the utterly baseless myth that Wilson by much patience got a reluctant people to go to war." Roosevelt retorted, "That is a simple lie; he did all he could to keep down the rising popular demand for war, and finally was swept off his legs by it, and hurried backwards into the conflict." With no little justice, Roosevelt believed that he himself had been more responsible for rallying the American people behind the war than Wilson had. He, not Wilson, ought to receive the credit.

IV

He might have, had his heart held out. In declining to enter the contest for New York governor in the days after Quentin's death, Roosevelt told his sister: "Corinne, I have only one fight left in me, and I think I should reserve my strength in case I am needed in 1920." Corinne, slightly alarmed at this intimation of mortality in her older brother, who had never appeared anything but a paragon of strength and purpose to her, asked if he were really ill. "No," he replied, "but I am not what I was and there is only one fight left in me."

He *was* really ill, though, as became apparent in the weeks after the 1918 elections. His malady was diagnosed this time as inflammatory rheumatism but was almost certainly related to the persistent infections that had dogged him since his Amazon trip. Quite likely he harbored parasites that were undetectable by contemporary medical tests. On the day the armistice was signed in France he returned to the hospital in New York. He remained there until Christmas Eve. Various medications, including morphine, treated his pain; despite both the pain and the painkillers, he managed to keep up his correspondence and see visitors.

Most important among the visitors were family members. Edith, of course, came in daily. Wounded Archie had been sent home from France to recuperate, prompting his father to write: "Of our four hawks one has come home, broken-winged, but his soul as high as ever." He added, "Never did four falcons fly with such daring speed at such formidable quarry." Quentin's fiancée Flora remained like one of the family. "Remember, Flora," Roosevelt told her, "that as long as I live I shall love you as if you were my own daughter." Various grandchildren dropped in when circumstances and physicians allowed.

Roosevelt was now sixty and felt every year. Yet he also felt that his age afforded him a right to a certain measure of infirmity. "I am glad to be sixty," he told Kermit, "for it somehow gives me the right to be titularly as old as I feel." To Corinne he declared, "Well, anyway, no matter what comes, I have kept the promise that I made to myself when I was twenty-one." "What promise, Theodore?" Corinne asked. "You made many promises to yourself, and I am sure have kept them all." He answered, "I promised myself that I would work up to the hilt until I was sixty, and I have done it. I have kept my promise, and now, even if I should be an invalid—I should not like to be an invalid—but even if I should be an invalid, or if I should die"—here he gave a snap of the fingers—"what difference would it make?"

On Christmas Eve his doctors discharged him to Sagamore Hill. The prognosis was that he would recover, if not rapidly and perhaps not completely. Christmas Day, the first since Quentin's death, was subdued, although the smallest grandchildren paid no attention to the memory of their missing uncle and, in their merriment, momentarily lifted their grandfather's spirits.

The first days of the new year brought a glimpse of his old energy. He wrote an editorial for the *Star* and touched up the proofs of an article for the *Metropolitan*. On January 5 he put in more than a full measure of work: eleven hours.

Late that evening, however, he told Edith he felt queer, as though his heart or breathing were about to stop. "I know it is not going to happen," he told her, "but it is such a strange feeling." A nurse and then a doctor checked his vital signs and reported nothing amiss. To ensure a restful sleep, the nurse administered an injection of morphine, and at midnight he went to bed. "James, will you please put out the light?" he asked Amos, standing the night watch.

He drifted off, his regular respiration in the silent house telling Amos that he was sleeping soundly. Edith dropped in once to check on him, then again before going to bed herself.

But at about four o'clock Amos was startled by sudden irregularities in the patient's breathing. It stopped, then started, then stopped again. At 4:15 it stopped and didn't resume. Amos quickly informed the nurse, who called Edith. She hurried to her husband's bedside. "Theodore, darling!" she said to the still form.

There was little more to say—and that little by Archie, who cabled his brothers across the ocean: "The old lion is dead."

V

Had the lion lived—had a coronary embolism not completed the work Quentin's death commenced—he might well have won the elec-

tion of 1920. It was probably for the better that he didn't. Not even
Roosevelt could have rescued the country from the wave of reaction
that set in after the war, and his failure to do so would have tested his
faith in democracy as never before. Roosevelt was a romantic in an era
when America responded to romance; but romance died on the killing
fields of the war—or, more precisely, at Paris, where the peace conference about to begin at the time of his death rendered all the carnage, in
the end, futile. Death came for Roosevelt at just the right moment:
when it was still possible to think that the war and the horrendous sacrifices it entailed had been for something noble and lasting.

Roosevelt often spoke of the importance of luck in his success; he
was usually thinking of his good luck at San Juan Hill or McKinley's
bad luck in Buffalo. But his greatest good luck was to come of age at
a time when America had a particular weakness for romantic heroes.
Had he been of his father's generation, the generation of the Civil War
and the still-raw West, when military heroes were a dozen a county
and cowboys were recognized for the marginal misfits they frequently
were, his peculiar flair would have fallen flat. Had he been of his sons'
generation, the lost generation of the Jazz Age, he would have
appeared woefully naive.

But Roosevelt arrived at just the right hour. The nation's supply of
heroes was dwindling with each decade farther from Appomattox; the
frontier was fading into mythic memory with each quarter-section
brought behind the fence and under the plow. The more rapidly the past
slipped away, the more anxious Americans grew to hold on to what was
left. Roosevelt gave them something to grasp. By his experience of war
and of the West, he symbolized those two essential characteristics of
the nation's identity; by his public rectitude and eagerness to take on
the bosses, he represented an era remembered for being cleaner and
more straightforward than the muddy present. One longtime Roosevelt
watcher observed, "You had to hate the Colonel a whole lot to keep
from loving him." Those who hated him often did so for the same reason the many more loved him: He called to mind America's better
days and Americans' better selves.

But romance had its limits. The frustrating fact for Roosevelt was
that, as much as Americans loved him, they didn't particularly heed
him, and he died having failed to accomplish the major continuing
task of his career: the reform of the Republican Party. For nearly forty

years, with time off for his Progressive sabbatical, he tried to reinject the spirit of Lincoln into the party of Lincoln. But he failed, and the party he bequeathed to Warren Harding looked (and acted, as soon became embarrassingly evident) far more like the party of Grant.

Yet if Roosevelt failed to change his party, he succeeded in changing the country. When he became president in 1901, the accepted scope of government remained not much larger than it had been under Lincoln—indeed, in certain areas, such as civil rights, the effective reach of the federal government was substantially smaller than it had been during the 1860s. Roosevelt, with his penchant for power and his belief that the moral and upstanding leader needn't worry excessively about procedural details, set in motion the expansion of federal authority that became one of the hallmarks of American politics during the twentieth century. Roosevelt established the principle that the people of the United States, acting through their government, have a right to regulate the private economy in the public interest. Under Roosevelt the exercise of this right took such forms as antitrust suits, consumer protection laws, maximum rates for railroads, and federal stewardship of natural resources. Under several of Roosevelt's successors, especially during the second half of the twentieth century, the principle would broaden greatly—doubtless into areas Roosevelt himself, with his stern sense of individual responsibility, would have repudiated had he lived so long. But he never would have denied, as certain of his successors did, that the people collectively, acting through government, have the right to ensure the beneficent operation of the private sector.

Roosevelt also set the standard for what would become another signature of twentieth-century America: an assumption of responsibility for international order. He was the first president to clearly grasp the potential uses of American power in the world beyond American shores. As in his wielding of power domestically, Roosevelt refused to be deflected by criticism that he trampled forms and precedents; it was enough for him to believe—to *know*—that he was in the right in building an isthmian canal, in declaring an American police power in the Western Hemisphere, in mediating a peace between Japan and Russia, in browbeating the kaiser into accepting French ascendancy in Morocco. Again, Roosevelt's successors would elaborate enormously upon the principle he established, until the United States found itself burdened with the defense of countries and governments all over the globe. Again, Roosevelt doubtless would have considered certain aspects of the elaboration dubious, to say the least. Following the frontier adage, "Don't draw unless you intend to shoot," he would have been stingy with the commitments his successors dispensed so freely. But he never would have questioned the assertion that enlightened countries like the United States have a special duty to enforce civilized behavior on countries not civilly inclined of their own.

As a group, the progressives of Roosevelt's generation tended to the technocratic. Given a social problem—and, in that age, they were given plenty—their first reaction was to propose a structural solution: a statute, a constitutional amendment, a regulatory board. Roosevelt certainly did his part toward enlarging the structures of government, from the Interstate Commerce Commission to the Bureau of Corporations and the Forest Service—not to mention his personal favorite, the Navy Department.

But he never placed great faith in institutions, which he realized were just as likely to evolve in the direction of Tammany Hall as along progressive lines. Instead, like any true romantic, he fastened his faith and hope in people. Ordinary people—the Bill Sewalls and Joe Murrays of America—were the touchstone of his democratic faith. Roosevelt fully exploited the constitutional powers of the presidency and, indeed, expanded those powers through their vigorous exercise, much as he had expanded his muscles through vigorous physical exercise. But he recognized that, whatever the Constitution said, it was only by marshaling public opinion that any president could work with lasting effect. Despite occasional moments of doubt, he passionately believed in the capacity of the ordinary people of America to act in the public welfare, once they were alerted to the true nature of that welfare.

He also believed that no one was better positioned to do the alerting than the president. Roosevelt didn't build the bully pulpit all by himself: Washington and Lincoln, his two special heroes, had drawn the design and laid the foundation. But he updated and expanded it, and he certainly made fuller use of it than anyone before him. And the path he wore up its steps served as a guide to all the presidents who came after him. He wouldn't have agreed with every passage those presidents preached—indeed, if anything could drive him to blasphemy, it was Woodrow Wilson's sermons from that very pulpit. But Wilson was merely the negative exception—in Roosevelt's jaundiced view—that proved the rule of the overriding obligation of the president to prod the conscience of the country.

VI

Roosevelt did just that, even from the grave. He was buried on January 8, 1919, in a hillside plot not far from his cherished Sagamore. Old friends, some of them also erstwhile foes, attended the simple service at the church in Oyster Bay and accompanied the oak casket through the snow of that winter morning to the grave site he and Edith had selected several years before.

Meanwhile, condolences and appreciations flooded in from across the country and around the world. Crowned heads, elected officials, editorialists, and assorted other admirers lauded a life well spent; even those rivals who weren't disappointed to see him go recognized that the country wouldn't witness his like again.

But as always, Roosevelt had the last word. Shortly before his death his publisher, Scribner's, had collected some two dozen of his recent editorials, essays, and speeches. This collection had appeared in book form at the end of 1918 and got lost amid all the other material relating to the war just over and the peace not yet begun. Roosevelt's death, however, drew fresh attention to the author, speaking now, as it were, from beyond the realm of partisanship or pedestrian ambition.

The book's most affecting passage was written with Quentin obviously in mind, but it served just as well as an epitaph for that valiant young man's father—and as a final affirmation of the romantic creed. "Only those are fit to live who do not fear to die," Roosevelt declared. "And none are fit to die who have shrunk from the joy of life and the duty of life. Both life and death are parts of the same Great Adventure." Everyone was called to the Great Adventure, each to serve in his or her own way. In time of war, some fought, while others watched and waited. Glory rewarded the former, often bitter sorrow—though tempered by pride—the latter.

Yet each showed the path to a brighter and more glorious future:

All of us who give service, and stand ready for sacrifice, are the torch-bearers. We run with the torches until we fall, content if we can pass them to the hands of other runners. The torches whose flame is brightest are borne by the gallant men at the front, and by the gallant women whose husbands and lovers, whose sons and brothers are at the front. These men are high of soul, as they face their fate on the shell-shattered earth, or in the skies above or in the waters beneath; and no less high of soul are the women with torn hearts and shining eyes; the girls whose boy-lovers have been struck down in their golden morning, and the mothers and wives to whom word has been brought that henceforth they must walk in the shadow.

These are the torch-bearers; these are they who have dared the Great Adventure.

SOURCES

———◯———

The principal sources for this work are the correspondence and published writings of Theodore Roosevelt. For the most part, selections from the writings have been taken from the Memorial Edition of *The Works of Theodore Roosevelt.* The correspondence comes from a variety of archival and published sources. The most important archival collections are the Theodore Roosevelt papers at the Library of Congress (abbreviated as LC below) and the Theodore Roosevelt Collection at Harvard University (TRC). These collections have formed the basis for several published collections of letters, of which the most significant is *The Letters of Theodore Roosevelt,* edited by Elting E. Morison and John M. Blum (M). In the interest of accessibility, citations below list published collections when possible; where a letter appears in more than one published collection, the earliest is usually cited.

The notes indicate most published works by author; full citations appear in the bibliography.

ABBREVIATIONS OF SOURCES

ARLP: Alice Roosevelt Longworth Papers, Library of Congress.
BHP: Benjamin Harrison Papers, Library of Congress.
BLC: Joseph Bucklin Bishop, ed., TR's *Letters to His Children,* in *Works,*
   v. 21.
BR: *William Barnes against Theodore Roosevelt* (Supreme Court, Appellate Division-Fourth Department, New York, 1917)

C: Anna Roosevelt Cowles, *Letters from Theodore Roosevelt to Anna Roosevelt Cowles,* 1870–1918, 1924.

CSC: *Theodore Roosevelt: United States Civil Service Commissioner* (letters), 1940.

DBY: *Theodore Roosevelt's Diaries of Boyhood and Youth,* 1928.

FDRL: Franklin D. Roosevelt Library.

GCP: Grover Cleveland Papers, Library of Congress.

JBB: Joseph Bucklin Bishop, *Theodore Roosevelt and His Time, Shown in His Own Letters,* 1920; later published as vol. 23–24 of *Works.*

K: *Letters to Kermit from Theodore Roosevelt,* ed. by Will Irwin, 1946.

KBR: Kermit and Belle Roosevelt Papers, Library of Congress.

L: *Selections from the Correspondence of Theodore Roosevelt and Henry Cabot Lodge, 1884–1918,* ed. by Henry Cabot Lodge and Charles F. Redmond, 1925, 1971.

LC: Theodore Roosevelt papers, Library of Congress (most of this collection is available on microfilm).

LC addenda: Additional TR materials at the Library of Congress (not on microfilm).

LD: TR Legislative Diary, TRC.

LMHS: Henry Cabot Lodge Papers, Massachusetts Historical Society.

LSN: TR Law School Notebooks, Columbia University Law Library.

M: *The Letters of Theodore Roosevelt,* ed. by Elting Morison and John M. Blum, 1951–54. (When something other than a letter is cited from this collection, the reference is "Morison.")

PD: Private Diary, Roosevelt Papers, Library of Congress.

PD–1886 and PD–1898: TR diary fragments, chronologies, and excerpts of correspondence from 1886 and 1898: in TRC.

R: Corinne Roosevelt Robinson, *My Brother Theodore Roosevelt,* 1926. (When something other than a letter is cited, the reference is "Robinson.")

SH: Sagamore Hill National Historical Site: assorted papers.

TRB: Theodore Roosevelt Birthplace records, New York City.

TRBM: *The Letters of Theodore Roosevelt and Brander Matthews,* ed. by Lawrence J. Oliver, 1995.

TRC: Theodore Roosevelt Collection, Harvard College Library, Harvard University.

WHTP: William Howard Taft Papers, Library of Congress.

WWP: *The Papers of Woodrow Wilson,* ed. by Arthur S. Link, 1966–92.

ABBREVIATIONS OF PERSONAL NAMES

TR: Theodore Roosevelt
TR Sr.: Theodore Roosevelt, Sr.
MBR: Martha Bulloch Roosevelt
AR(C): Anna Roosevelt (Cowles)

ER: Elliott Roosevelt
CR(R): Corinne Roosevelt (Robinson)
AL(R): Alice Lee (Roosevelt)
EKR: Edith Kermit (Carow) Roosevelt
AR(L): Alice Roosevelt (Longworth)
TR Jr.: Theodore Roosevelt, Jr.
KR: Kermit Roosevelt
Arch. R: Archibald Roosevelt
Eth. R: Ethel Roosevelt
QR: Quentin Roosevelt
HCL: Henry Cabot Lodge

PROLOGUE: JULY 1918

Page x. "There is not one among us": to E. Robinson, Mar. 27, 1916, M.

ONE. A CHILD OF THE CIVIL WAR: 1858–65

Page 3. "Overturn": Hone 730.
Page 4. James: *Washington Square* 25.
Page 4. *Evening Post:* Apr. 15, 1854.
Page 5. Halliday: 195–96.
Page 5. Astor: Porter 2:939–40.
Page 6. Roosevelt fortune: Miller, *Chronicles,* 116–17; McCullough 27.
Page 6. "Hot corn": Spann 70.
Page 6. *Tribune:* Mar. 10, 1855.
Page 7. Hone 434.
Page 7. An English visitor: Lockwood 116.
Page 7. Police problems: Patterson 113–14.
Page 7. Prostitution: Lockwood 144–46.
Page 8. Hone 624.
Page 11. "that lovely Mrs. Roosevelt . . . five horrid boys": Robinson 3.
Page 12. "Father of all the fishes": Miller, *Chronicles* 147.
Page 12. "tired of changes": Robinson 3.
Page 13. "troublesome conscience": E. Morris 34.
Page 13. "How much": Robinson 5.
Page 14. "The men looked as hard": ibid. 22.
Page 14. The draft riots: Cook.
Page 15. British officer quoted: ibid. 77.
Page 16. O'Brien's death and battle at the steam works: TRB.
Page 16. "I really do not wonder": McCullough 58.
Page 17. "grind the southern troops": Robinson 17.
Page 18. "always afterward felt": ibid. 57.

Two. Foreign Ventures: 1865–73

Page 19. Corinne on TR's obsession: Putnam 48–49.

Page 19. *Alabama:* Delaney 147–64.

Page 20. Miller: *Chronicles* 160–61.

Page 21. Grant: LaFeber, *American Search* 61.

Page 21. Sumner's love life: Jones 199.

Page 21. We shall all gladly: McCullough 70.

Page 22. "so, so homesick": May 16, 1869, DBY.

Page 22. To Edith Carow, May 29, [1869], TRC. Here and below, the young
  TR's original spelling is preserved.

Page 23. "Met Jeff Davises": May 27, 1869, DBY.

Page 23. "We went to York": June 12, 1869, DBY.

Page 23. To Edith Carow, July 10, 1869, TRC.

Page 23. "I was sick": Sept. 24, 1869, DBY.

Page 23. "I was sick of the Asthma": Sept. 26, 1869, DBY.

Page 23. "verry sick": Oct. 10, 1869, DBY.

Page 23. "I had a miserable night": Oct. 12, 1869, DBY.

Page 23. "I was rubbed so hard": Oct. 15, 1869, DBY.

Page 23. "Conie was sick": Dec. 12, 1869, DBY.

Page 24. "As I was not well": Oct. 3, 1869, DBY.

Page 24. "I have had a good day": Aug. 11, 1869, DBY.

Page 24. "Papa and I": Sept. 4, 1869, DBY.

Page 24. Mount Vesuvius: to E. Carow, Jan. 1, 1870, TRC.

Page 24. As Corinne later: Robinson, 43–44.

Page 24. "We ran about": May 22, 1869, DBY.

Page 24. "We played in the house": Aug. 23, 1869, DBY.

Page 24. "We 3 children": Aug. 26, 1869, DBY.

Page 25. "Papa would not let me go": Jan. 17, 1870, DBY.

Page 25. "If you were to doubt": Dec. 29, 1869, DBY.

Page 25. To E. Carow, Jan. 28, 1870, TRC.

Page 25. *Autobiography* 18.

Page 26. Father's challenge: Robinson 50.

Page 27. TR on *Our Young Folks: Autobiography* 20–21.

Page 28. "The saying that the child": ibid. 34.

Page 29. Seal: ibid. 18.

Page 30. "foregoing ant": Robinson 2.

Page 30. Mice: to Corinne in TR to MBR, Apr. 28, 1868, R.

Page 30. "I could revel in . . . get some feathers": to MBR, Apr. 28, 1868, R.

Page 31. "reedy striplings": ibid. 36.

Page 33. "I gave up all the meals": Nov. 6, 1872, DBY.

Page 33. "As usual everybody combines": Nov. 23, 1872, DBY.

Page 33. "At eight o'clock . . . scotch terrier": Nov. 28, 1872, DBY.

Page 34. "To look out on the desert": Dec. 3, 1872, DBY.

Page 34. "I was proportionately delighted": Dec. 13, 1872, DBY.

Page 34. Theodore Sr.: Robinson 56.

Page 34. Corinne: ibid. 57.
Page 35. To A. Bulloch, Jan. 26 and Feb. 9, 1873, R.
Page 35. Tombs: Feb. 12, 1873, DBY.
Page 36. Corinne on Emerson: Robinson 63.
Page 36. "Smike suit": *Autobiography* 25.
Page 36. "The horses are all very good": Feb. 24, 1873, DBY.
Page 36. To Edith Carow, undated, R, 67–68.
Page 36. Jackal chase: Mar. 17, 1873, DBY.
Page 37. Wailing Wall: Feb. 28, 1873, DBY.
Page 37. Mosque of Omar: Feb. 27, 1873, DBY.
Page 37. Jordan River: Mar. 4, 1873, DBY.
Page 37. Baalbek: Mar. 14, 1873, DBY.
Page 37. Boys on donkey: H. Jessup to TR, undated, TRB.
Page 38. Constantinople: Apr. 11, 1873, DBY.
Page 38. Viennese monotony: May 11, 1873, DBY.
Page 40. "Mrs. Field Mouse's Dinner Party ": Robinson 72–76.
Page 40. "I really feel that": Putnam 104.
Page 40. "Excuse my writing": to TR Sr., June 29, 1873, M.
Page 40. "Picture to yourself": to MBR, July 13, 1873, Putnam 107.
Page 41. "wits," "ringleader," "Suddenly an idea": Robinson 71–72, 80.
Page 41. "Teedie woke up": ibid. 81.
Page 42. Boxing match: to TR Sr., June 15, 1873, M.
Page 42. Pinned the younger Minkwitz: to TR Sr., no date given, Putnam 111.
Page 42. To AR, Sept. 21, 1873, R.
Page 43. Impressions of Germans: *Autobiography* 26–27.

THREE. OYSTER BAY: 1873–76

Page 45. *Herald* in Lockwood 242.
Page 46. "falling on my head": to A. Fisher, Feb. 5, 1876, M.
Page 46. Corinne on Oyster Bay: Robinson 89.
Page 47. "sporting calendar": entries for Aug. 21 and Nov. 1, 1875, DBY.
Page 48. "He had queer things alive": TRB.
Page 48. To AR, June 20, 1875, M.
Page 48. "I worked": *Autobiography* 27.
Page 49. "We have to talk french": to T. Watkins, July 7, [1867 or 1868], TRC.
Page 49. "With me, reading is a disease": F. Wood 359.
Page 49. Cutler: Putnam 127.
Page 51. Dancing school: to S. West, Feb. 21, 1868, TRC.
Page 51. To MBR, Apr. 13, 1874, C.
Page 51. "Saturday evening . . . 'till eleven o'clock": Putnam 121–22.
Page 51. To AR, Aug. 29, 1875, Putnam 121.
Page 52. "for your namesake": to Edith Carow, Aug. 6, 1875, S. Morris 47.

Page 52. "How horribly near": to AR, June 28, 1875, TRC.
Page 52. To AR, July 25, 1875, M.
Page 53. To A. Minkwitz Fisher, Feb. 5, 1876, M.

FOUR. ANXIOUS UNDERCLASSMAN: 1876–77

Page 54. To MBR, Sept. 29, 1876, M.
Page 55. To AR, Sept. 30, 1876, TRC.
Page 56. Eliot described and quoted: James, *Eliot* 2:3 and Fleming 63, 70.
Page 58. "We ask but time to drift": Pringle 32.
Page 58. Harvard style: Putnam 131.
Page 59. Elliott as social leader: Robinson 94.
Page 59. "very fair": to MBR, Sept. 29, 1876, M.
Page 59. "As I am decidedly discontented": to MBR, Oct. 6, 1876, M.
Page 60. "I am very glad . . . as soon as possible": to AR, Oct. 15, 1876, M.
Page 60. "out of the eleven . . . not to drink and smoke": to TR Sr., Oct. 22, 1876, M.
Page 60. To MBR, Oct. 23, 1876, M.
Page 61. To CR, Dec. 14, 1876, M.
Page 61. "I am sorry to say . . . more scrubby set than ours": to MBR, Nov. 19, 1876, M.
Page 61. Welling: Putnam 143–44.
Page 62. "I remembered a book": F. Wood 361.
Page 63. To TR Sr., Nov. 5, 1876, TRC.
Page 64. To MBR, Oct. 23, 1876, M.
Page 64. Roosevelt's courses (and instructors) are listed in Wilhelm 107–11; his grades are reproduced in Morison 1:25–26.
Page 64. "He told me . . . of becoming a scientist": *Autobiography* 30–31.
Page 66. To CR, Nov. 26, 1876, M.
Page 66. "quite pleasant . . . perfectly convenient": to CR, Dec. 14, 1876, M.
Page 66. Corinne: Robinson 96.
Page 66. "prettiest": to CR, Jan. 14, 1877, Putnam 168–69.
Page 66. "looked as pretty as a picture" and "My two weeks": to ER, Jan. 1, 1877, FDRL.
Page 66. To AR, Jan. 22, 1877, M.
Page 67. "On Wednesday . . . specimen of humanity": to CR, Feb. 5, 1877, M.
Page 67. Recollections of TR: Parsons 28; E. Morris 77; McCullough 207–10; Wilhelm 35; Thayer 21.
Page 68. "Please send": to AR, Oct. 15, 1876, M.
Page 69. To TR Sr. and MBR, Feb. 11, 1877, M.
Page 69. "I do not go": ibid.
Page 69. "The Summer Birds": reproduced in part in Robinson 101.
Page 70. Entry for July 16, 1877, DBY.
Page 70. To H. Minot, July 11, 1877, M.
Page 70. From E. Carow, May 19, 1877, TRC.

Page 70. To CR, June 3, 1877, M.

Page 71. Missed rendezvous: Robinson 94–95; Sept. 22, 1877, DBY (Robinson seems to have misdated her recollection).

Page 71. To AR, Nov. 9, 1877, M.

Page 72. "My respect": to CR, Oct. [no day given], 1877, R.

Page 72. "Some of the boys": to CR, Nov. [no day given], 1877, R.

Page 72. "The work": Oct. 8, 1877, DBY.

Page 72. "One of my studies": to AR, Oct. 14, 1877, M.

Page 73. To CR, Feb. 5, 1877, M.

Page 73. TR Sr.: quoted in TR to MBR , Mar. 24, 1878, M.

Page 74. "seeing the world": Boston *Saturday Evening Gazette,* Nov. 9, 1879, in Putnam 130–31.

Page 74. To AR, Oct. 15, 1876, M.

Page 74. "Cornelius has distinguished ": entry for Oct. 24, 1878, PD.

Page 74. "Thank Heaven": Apr. 18, 1878, PD.

Page 74. To MBR, Oct. 29, 1876, M.

FIVE. A MAN OF HIS OWN: 1877–78

Page 78. Conkling and Curtis: Josephson 244–48.

Page 79. To TR Sr., Dec. 8, 1877, M.

Page 79. To AR, Dec. 16, 1877, C.

Page 80. "Dear Father . . . shot gun": entries for Dec. 21, 23, 25, 1877, PD.

Page 80. Corinne: Robinson 104.

Page 80. Elliott: E. Morris 94.

Page 81. To MBR, Feb. 28, 1878, M.

Page 81. "My dear Father": Feb. 9, 1878, PD.

Page 81. "He has just been buried": Feb. 12, 1878.

Page 82. Re mother and father: *Autobiography* 10–17.

Page 82. To MBR, Oct. 29, 1876, C.

Page 83. To TR Sr., Oct. 22, 1876, M.

Page 83. To H. Minot, Feb. 20, 1878, M.

Page 84. "It seems impossible . . . long for you": Feb. 19, 22, 24, Mar. 3, 7, 9, 10, 11, 12, 15, 17, 19, 21, 24, Apr. 11, May 26, June 19, July 7, 1878, PD.

Page 85. "It seems brutal . . . brave Christian gentleman": Mar. 5, 6, May 7, June 30, Sept. 1, 1878, PD.

Page 86. To MBR, Feb. 28, 1878, M.

Page 88. "a thin, pale youngster": Sewall 2.

Page 89. "I don't think . . . great success": Sept. 14, 16, 21, 24, 1878, PD.

Page 90. "Funnily enough": to MBR, Oct. 8, 1878, M.

Page 90. "the A.D. men": Oct. 15, 1878, PD.

Page 91. Thayer 19–20.

Page 92. "My studies . . . are reading": to MBR, Oct. 8, 1878, M.

Page 92. "I have hitherto . . . not very good": ibid.

Page 92. Boxing match: Wister 4–5; Thayer 23.
Page 93. "Don't mention it": *Globe,* Mar. 23, 1879.

Six. First Love: 1878–81

Page 94. To CR, Nov. 10, 1878, M.
Page 94. "a very sweet pretty girl": Oct. 19, 1878, PD.
Page 95. To AL, Dec. 6, 1878, M.
Page 95. From AL, Dec. 8, 1878, TRC.
Page 95. Mrs. Bacon: Pringle 42.
Page 95. "Those two young ladies": June 17, 1879, PD.
Page 96. To AR, May 20, 1879, TRC.
Page 96. "It was the one thing": Apr. 22, 1879, PD.
Page 96. From AL, Feb. 13, 1879, TRC.
Page 97. "Pretty uncomfortable": Mar. 7, 1879, PD.
Page 97. "I have never seen . . . Charley Brown": Mar. 9, 1879, PD.
Page 97. "I have never passed": Mar. 14, 1879, PD.
Page 97. To MBR, Mar. 10, 1879, Putnam 161.
Page 97. To AR, Apr. 20, 1879, M.
Page 97. To MBR, Apr. 27, 1879, M.
Page 98. To CR, Aug. 22, 1879, M.
Page 98. To CR, May 5, 1879, M.
Page 98. "The senior year": to AR, Sept. 29, 1879, M.
Page 98. Wister 14–15.
Page 99. To MBR, Jan. 11, 1880, M.
Page 99. "Pretty Annie Murray . . . most charming": Jan. 4, 15, Apr. 3, 11,
   Aug. 5, Sept. 30, Nov. 8, 1879, PD.
Page 99. "It appears": June 19, 1879, PD.
Page 100. "My conscience": Apr. 26, 1879, PD.
Page 100. "Truly . . . good time I am having": Dec. 21, 22, 31, 1878; May 8,
   1879, PD.
Page 100. To MBR, June 22, 1879, TRC.
Page 100. "I doubt": June 28, 1879, PD.
Page 100. "I don't know . . . lovely time": Sept. 8, 14, 1879, PD.
Page 101. To MBR, Sept. 14, 1879, TRC.
Page 101. "My life . . . every minute I live": Sept. 21, 24, 1879, PD.
Page 101. To MBR, Nov. 29, 1879, TRC.
Page 101. "It is perfectly lovely": Dec. 28, 1879, PD.
Page 101. "At last": Jan. 25, 1880, PD.
Page 102. "When I look back": Jan. 30, 1880, PD.
Page 102. "I am so happy": to AL, Jan. 28, 1880, TRC.
Page 102. Edith: S. Morris 58–59.
Page 103. To AL, June 8, 1880, TRC.
Page 103. "Alice studied": Apr. 26, 1880, PD.
Page 103. "Since I have been engaged . . . little wife": Mar. 25, 1880, PD.

Page 104. "I have certainly lived": May 5, 1880, PD.

Page 104. "I miss Alice": July 14, 1880, PD.

Page 104. From AL, June 9, 1880, TRC.

Page 105. "I jump involuntarily . . . all your money": B. Cook, 1:34–35.

Page 105. "Very embarrassing": to CR, July 24, 1880, M.

Page 106. "Doctor": Hagedorn, *Boys' Life* 64.

Page 106. "We have had . . . Miss Costigan": to AR, Aug. 22, 1880, M; to MBR, Aug. 25, 1880, Putnam 203.

Page 107. "very good fun . . . good sized cows": to CR, Sept. 12, 1880, M.

Page 108. Totals: Sept. 24, 1880, PD.

Page 108. From AL, July 13, 1880, TRC.

Page 108. To AL, Aug. 15, 1880, TRC.

Page 108. "The trip . . . my true-love": Sept. 25, 30, Oct. 2, 1880, PD.

Page 108. From AL, Oct. 16, 1880, TRC.

Page 109. "I have been spending money": Oct. 6, 1880, PD.

Page 109. To ER, Nov. 28, 1880, TRC.

Page 109. "It almost frightens me": Oct. 17, 1880, PD.

Page 109. To AL, Oct. 17, 1880, TRC.

Page 109. From AL, Oct. 6, 1880, TRC.

Page 109. Edith dancing: Ethel Roosevelt Derby in Putnam 210.

Page 109. "the most absolutely ideal time": to Elliott Roosevelt, Nov. 21, 1880, FDRL.

Page 109. "We breakfast . . . Keats poems": to MBR, Oct. 31, 1880, M.

Page 110. "It is impossible . . . last forever": Nov. 1, 4, 10, 1880, PD.

Page 110. "Blackstone Oct 7th . . . apprehension of such violence": entries for Oct. 7, 8, 12, Dec. 20, 1880, LSN.

Page 112. "the pertinacity": Putnam 219.

Page 112. To ER, Dec. 6, 1880, TRC.

Page 112. "Thus ends": Dec. 31, 1880, PD.

Page 113. "I have had no one": to ALR, Mar. 28, 1881, TRC.

Page 113. "There is no pretty": to ALR, Apr. 6, 1881, TRC.

Page 113. From ALR, Apr. 4, [1881], TRC.

Page 113. "It is not necessary": entry for Mar. 11, 1881, LSN.

Page 114. "The *caveat emptor* side": *Autobiography* 66.

Page 114. "We had a beautiful passage . . . awfully sick": to R. Lee, May 22, 1881, M.

Page 114. "Confound a European": May 18, 1881, PD.

Page 115. "Alice is the best": May 25, 1881, PD.

Page 115. Irish countryside: to MBR, May 24, 1881, C.

Page 115. Kissing: to MBR, June 5, 1881, TRC.

Page 115. "The two innocents": to CR, June 13, 1881. M.

Page 115. "an excellent traveller . . . any language but English": to CR, June 16, 1881, M.

Page 116. Jungfrau: July 25, 1881, PD.

Page 116. "I was anxious": to AR, Aug. 5, 1881, C.

Page 116. To Sewall, Sept. 5, 1881, LC addenda.

Page 116. "The mountain is so steep . . . than on the Jungfrau": to AR, Aug. 5, 1881, C.
Page 117. "The scenery . . . little giblets": to AR, Aug. 21, 1881, C.
Page 118. "how the people . . . but I can't": to CR, Aug. 24, 1881, M.
Page 118. "I never have sympathized": to MBR, June 5, 1881, TRC.
Page 118. "Our stay in Paris . . . in his hands!": to AR, Sept. 5, 1881, C.
Page 118. To Sewall, Sept. 5, 1881, LC addenda.
Page 119. "Of course, had I been": to MBR, Sept. 14, 1881, C.
Page 119. Wister 24.
Page 120. *The Naval History of the War of 1812: Works* 7:34, 126, 226, 417.

SEVEN. CRASHING THE PARTY: 1881–83

Page 123. Re Joe Murray: *Autobiography* 70–72.
Page 125. "Just heard . . . wish their country well": July 5, 6, 1881, PD.
Page 125. "Some of the teaching": *Autobiography* 66.
Page 125. "Idiot has congenital trouble": entry for Oct. 21, 1880, LSN.
Page 126. Emlen at Morton Hall: Hagedorn interviews, TRB.
Page 126. "The men I knew": *Autobiography* 68–69
Page 127. "I thought I would interest": Lawrence Abbott 39.
Page 128. "Most of my friends": Oct. 26, 1881, PD.
Page 128. "Dear Sir": Nov. 1, 1881, M.
Page 128. Choate et al.: Thayer 30.
Page 128. Run-in with Fisher: Murray interview, TRC.
Page 129. "Too True": to C. Washburn, Nov. 10, 1881, M.
Page 129. "it is a dreadful misfortune": *Autobiography* 67.
Page 130. "a society man and dude": Hunt: Hagedorn interviews, TRB.
Page 130. "All of a sudden": Putnam 251.
Page 130. Milholland recollections, TRB.
Page 130. "The chairman": Feb. 14, 1882, LD.
Page 131. "bad enough . . . balloon": Jan. 7, Feb. 21, Mar. 1, 1882, LD.
Page 131. "They are a stupid . . . unintelligent brute": Jan. 12, 1882, LD.
Page 131. Re Bogan: Jan. 7, 1882, LD.
Page 132. "In most other . . . might have been put": *Autobiography* 78–79.
Page 132. "He and I": ibid. 80.
Page 133. "evil and heart-sickening . . . Albany correspondent": Talcott Williams in F. Wood 8.
Page 134. "There is no more disgraceful": Klein, 284.
Page 136. "It is sheer nonsense": to H. Hull, Oct. 24, 1882, M.
Page 136. Westbrook: Klein 289.
Page 137. "We have a right": speech, Apr. 6, 1882, *Works,* 16:8–13.
Page 137. To ALR, Apr. 6, 1882, TRC.
Page 137. "Mr. Roosevelt . . . blowing of the wind": clips in JBB 15–17.
Page 137. *World,* ibid., 16.
Page 138. "I believe": *Autobiography* 93–94.

Page 139. "'Every party . . . lawful owners": Putnam 269.

Page 139. "How that man . . . wasn't anything to get": ibid.

Page 139. Trap: Pringle 73.

Page 140. "I was by no means . . . favor it": *Autobiography* 92.

Page 140. "I cannot believe . . . leprosy": New York *Daily Tribune,* June 1, 1882, Putnam 271.

Page 140. "He really got what he deserved": G. Spinney with Hagedorn, TRB.

Page 141. Hunt interview, TRB.

Page 141. "It really was not much": to J. Roosevelt, Jan. 28, 1881 [probably 1882], TRC.

Page 141. To MBR, Feb. 20, 1883, TRC.

Page 141. Hunt interview, TRB.

Page 141. Spinney interview, TRB.

Page 142. "To Young New York": Pringle 72.

Page 142. "I am really glad": to ALR, Oct. 14, 1881, TRC.

Page 142. "I so longed for you": to ALR, Nov. 5, 1881, TRC.

Page 142. "Every day": to AR, Sept. 15, 1882, M.

Page 143. "I hardly know": ibid.

Page 143. To MBR, July 5, 1882, TRC.

Page 144. "the deplorable lack": New York *Times,* Oct. 9, 1882, quoted in Morison 1:57.

Page 145. To O'Neill, Nov. 12, 1882, M.

Page 145. "I went in": to L. Van Allen, Dec. 15, 1882, M.

Page 145. To ALR, Dec. 31, 1882, TRC.

Page 147. "I have to say": address, Mar. 2, 1883, *Works* 16:19–21.

Page 147. To ALR, Mar. 6, 1883, TRC.

Page 148. "It would be farcical . . . sodden lump of the Democracy": address, Mar. 9, 1883, *Works* 16:22–29.

Page 149. "There is an increasing suspicion . . . ridiculous in both roles": Putnam 288–90.

Page 149. "Immediately after": to TR Jr., Oct. 20, 1903, M.

Page 150. "Like most young men": *Autobiography* 103.

Page 151. "Under the direction": to CRR, July 1, 1883, M.

Page 151. "This place": to MBR, July 8, 1883, M.

Page 151. "a typical frontier town": to MBR, Sept. 7, 1883, TRC.

Page 152. "This town": Dickinson Press, undated, in Hagedorn, *Bad Lands* 65.

Page 153. "It is a very desolate place": to ALR, Sept. 8, 1883, TRC.

Page 154. General description of TR's trip: Hagedorn, *Bad Lands* 3ff.

Page 154. "frightful ground . . . cow's milk tastes of it": to ALR, Sept. 8, 1883, TRC.

Page 155. "I want to congratulate you": Lang 111.

Page 155. "I have been out a week": to ALR, Sept. 14, 1883, TRC.

Page 155. Lincoln Lang: Hagedorn, *Bad Lands* 27.

Page 155. "I am now feeling very well": to AR, Sept. 17, 1883, TRC.

Page 156. "I have definitely decided . . . disappoint him": Lang 116.

Page 157. Fourteen thousand, Merrifield and Ferris: Hagedorn, *Bad Lands* 43.
Page 157. Ferris: ibid. 45.
Page 158. "Hurrah!": to ALR, Sept. 20, 1883, TRC.
Page 158. "The more I have looked . . . you may be sure": to ALR, Sept. 23, 1883, TRC.
Page 159. G. Lang: Lang 119.

EIGHT. THE LIGHT THAT FAILED: 1883–86

Page 160. To John and Nannie Roosevelt, Sept. 4, 1881, TRC.
Page 160. Alice's surgery: see Teague.
Page 160. "You must not dirty your new clothes": from ALR, Oct. 8, 1881, TRC.
Page 161. "Darling Wifie . . . with you again": to ALR, Jan. 22 and Feb. 6, 1884, M.
Page 161. "when you get 'crampy'": to ALR, Feb. 6, 1884, TRC.
Page 161. From ALR, Feb. 11, 1884, TRC.
Page 161. Anna Gracie and Alice's response: written recollection by Anna B. Gracie, Mar. 25, 1884, TRC.
Page 162. Elliott: Pringle, 51.
Page 163. "Alice Hathaway Lee": Feb. 16, 1884, PD.
Page 164. Photograph to Anna Gracie: Anna Gracie recollection, Mar. 25, 1884, TRC.
Page 164. Hunt interview, TRC.
Page 165. "I shall come back": to A. White, Feb. 18, 1884, M.
Page 168. "There!": Pringle 80.
Page 168. To Lodge, May 5 and 26, 1884, L.
Page 169. "The fight . . . like to see them": to AR, June 8, 1884, M.
Page 172. "I have been having . . . at night now!": to AR, June 17, 1884, M.
Page 173. "For the last week . . . winding canyons": to AR, June 23, 1884, M.
Page 173. "I wear . . . face anything": to AR, Aug. 17, 1884, C.
Page 173. Re Lebo and supplies: Aug. 16, 1884, PD.
Page 174. "Lebo is a chatty . . . chaparajos": Aug. 23 and 28, 1884, PD.
Page 174. "One day": to AR, Aug. 24, 1884, C.
Page 174. "I saw Merrifield": to AR, Sept. 20, 1884, M.
Page 176. White: letter in *New York Times,* Oct. 20, 1884.
Page 176. "Certainly the Independents": to Lodge, June 18, 1884, L.
Page 176. "A man cannot act . . . in the future": interview in Boston *Herald,* July 20, 1884, *Works* 16:71–72.
Page 177. Lee: Wister 26.
Page 177. "Most of my friends": to Lodge, July 28, 1884, L.
Page 177. "At midnight": to editor of Boston *Journal,* Oct. 21, 1884, ibid. 77–78.
Page 178. Young Republican Club address, Oct. 18, 1884, *Works* 16:73–75.
Page 178. To Lodge, Nov. 7 and 11, 1884, L.

Page 179. "Of course": to Lodge, Nov. 7, 1884, L.
Page 180. To Sewall, July 6, 1884, LC addenda.
Page 181. "Why there's nothing . . . beavered down seventeen": *Autobiography* 117.
Page 184. "Four-Eyes . . . senseless": ibid. 146–47.
Page 185. "furious blizzard" and "absolute surprise": Apr. 1, 1886, PD–1886.
Page 185. To CRR, Apr. 12, 1886, M.
Page 186. *Bad Lands Cowboy:* Collins 47–48.
Page 187. *Hunting Trips of a Ranchman: Works* 1:4, 8, 15, 244–45, 289–90.
Page 188. $20,000: Partnership contract, May 17, 1884, TRC.
Page 189. "Tomorrow . . . cowboy work pretty well": to Lodge, May 15 and June 5, 1885, L.
Page 189. "the Apotheosis . . . to the Democracy": to Lodge, Mar. 8, 1885, L.
Page 190. "I really have not": to W. Hubbell, June 8, 1885, M.
Page 191. To F. Smith Dana, Oct. 21, 1886, M.
Page 192. "There is need . . . take off his head": reported in New York *Times,* Oct. 16 and 30, 1886, in *Works* 16:115–18, 124–25.
Page 192. To Lodge, Nov. 1, 1886, L.

NINE. FROM THE LITTLE MISSOURI TO THE POTOMAC: 1886–89

Page 194. "He never": ARL in Longworth 4.
Page 195. "I utterly disbelieve": to AR, Sept. 20, 1886, TRC.
Page 196. "Eight years ago": ibid.
Page 197. *Bismarck Tribune:* July 8, 1886, PD–1886.
Page 199. "One of my earliest memories": ARL in Longworth, Mrs. L 42.
Page 199. From Edith Carow, June 2, 1886, TRC.
Page 200. "my usual restless": to AR, May 15, 1886, C.
Page 200. "if I did not miss": to AR, June 19, 1886, C.
Page 201. "savagely irritated . . . no plea against it": to AR, Sept. 20, 1886, TRC.
Page 201. Corinne's reaction: S. Morris 92, 532.
Page 202. "Theodore is the only person": ibid., 93.
Page 202. "If you wish . . . Oct. 6, '86": to AR, Sept. 20, 1886, TRC.
Page 202. Bamie to Edith, Oct. 23, 1886, S. Morris 92–93.
Page 203. West Roosevelt: N. Roosevelt 23.
Page 203. To Lodge, Nov. 22, 1886, L.
Page 205. Sewall: Hagedorn, *Bad Lands* 425.
Page 206. "Although it is a lot of money": from EKR, Nov. 14, 1887, TRC.
Page 206. "idyllic": to AR, Jan. 3, 1887, M.
Page 208. Lang 250–51.
Page 209. To Sewall, Apr. 7, 1887, LC addenda.
Page 209. To AR, Apr. 16, 1887, M.
Page 210. Sewall 93.
Page 212. "I feel a little . . . get rid of": to Lodge, Feb. 7 and Mar. 27, 1886, L.
Page 212. "I wonder . . . finish it": to Lodge, June 7 and 19, 1886, L.

Page 213. "I sent . . . good deal": to Lodge, Aug. 10 and 20, 1886, L.

Page 213. *Thomas Hart Benton: Works* 8:3, 5–6, 16–17, 194, 197, 199, 269.

Page 214. "utter surprise . . . mugwumps": to Lodge, Feb. 15, 1887 and Apr. 15, 1888, L.

Page 214. *The Nation,* Mar. 29, 1888.

Page 214. "The work . . . with him": to Lodge, Sept. 5, 1887, L.

Page 214. "I should like": to J. Van Duzer, Jan. 15, 1888, M.

Page 215. "magnum opus": to Lodge, Feb. 15, 1887, L.

Page 215. *The Winning of the West: Works* 10:xli–xlii.

Page 216. To AR, Sept. 13, 1887, M; to AR, Sept. 18, 1887, S. Morris 112.

Page 216. To CRR, Sept. 20, 1887, M.

Page 216. "great fun": to Lodge, Mar. 15, 1888, L.

Page 216. "I have not the least idea": to Lodge, Apr. 15, 1888. L.

Page 217. To AR, July 8 and Aug. 8, 1888, M.

Page 217. To AR, Aug. 5, 1888, M.

Page 217. To AR, Aug. 22, 1888, M.

Page 218. Willis interview, TRB.

Page 218. "immense fun": to Lodge, Oct. 19, 1888, L.

Page 218. To Spring Rice, Nov. 18, 1888, M.

Page 219. Harrison and Quay: McClure 2:572–73; Gibbons 1:269.

Page 219. "You are certainly . . . decent man should": to Lodge, Mar. 25, 1889, L.

Page 220. "Do come": to Lodge, Apr. [no day given] 1889, L.

Page 220. From Lodge, Mar. 29, 1889, L.

Page 222. To Spring Rice, Apr. 14, 1889, M.

Page 223. "about as thorough paced . . . hit him a clip": to Lodge, June 24, July 11 and 17, 1889, L.

Page 223. "I have made . . . I mean business": to Lodge, June 29, 1889, L.

Page 224. To Parkman, July 13, 1889, M.

Page 224. "The spoils system . . . Washington and Madison": speech of Feb. 23, 1889, *Works* 16:145–50.

Page 225. "As well might he . . . ten years behind him": *Century,* Feb. 1890, *Works* 16:158–74.

Page 225. "utter recklessness": *Atlantic Monthly,* Feb. 1891, *Works* 16:177–89.

Page 226. Contra W. H. S.: to Charles Lane, Dec. 13, 1889, reprinted in *Civil Service Record,* Jan. 1890, *Works* 16:151–57.

Page 227. To Lodge, July 1 and Oct. 8, 1889, L.

Page 228. Adams 320.

Page 229. By and about Reed: McCall 167–68, 248; Robinson 255–57, 261–62; Dunn, *Harrison to Harding* 1:71.

Page 230. "Beyond question": speech of Mar. 6, 1891, *Works* 16:190–98.

Page 231. "I have the very highest regard": address of Dec. 13, 1888, *Works* 16:133–41.

Page 232. *The Winning of the West: Works* 10:3, 78, 96, 130. ck this

Page 233. *Atlantic Monthly,* Nov. 1889.

Page 234. From EKR, Aug. 15, 1889, TRC.
Page 235. To Lodge, Aug. 28, 1889, L.
Page 235. From EKR, Aug. 15, 1889, TRC.

TEN. STRATEGIC ALLIANCES: 1890–95

Page 236. To A. T. Mahan, May 12, 1890, M.
Page 237. *Atlantic Monthly,* Oct. 1890, *Works* 14:306–16.
Page 239. "I have felt . . . Southwest": to Lodge, Nov. 10, 1890, L.
Page 240. To Putnam, Jan. 13, 1890, M.
Page 240. "the little runt": to AR, July 2, 1891, TRC.
Page 240. "He has never given us": to Lodge, July 22, 1891, L.
Page 241. "As for their praise": to Lodge, June 29, 1891, L.
Page 241. "The very fact": to Lodge, July 22, 1891, L.
Page 241. "Each morning . . . missionary work": to Lodge, Aug. 23, 1890, L.
Page 242. "On Wednesday": to Lodge, June 19, 1891, L.
Page 243. "Come home": from EKR, undated [1891], TRC.
Page 243. "Please think of me": from EKR, undated [1891], TRC.
Page 243. "The children want you": from EKR, undated [1892], TRC.
Page 243. "I have rarely . . . and so does Edith": to G. Carow, Oct. 18, 1890, M.
Page 245. "I think the dear old boy": to CRR, July 1, 1883, M.
Page 245. "I honestly believe": to MBR, July 8, 1883, M.
Page 245. "I do hate his Hempstead life": to AR, June 24, 1888, M.
Page 245. "Anna, sweet though she is": to AR, Apr. 30, 1890, TRC.
Page 245. "darling Anna": to AR, May 2, 1890, TRC.
Page 246. "I hate to think . . . public scandal greater": to AR, Apr. 30 and May 2, 1890, TRC.
Page 247. "The last hideous revelation": to AR, Jan. 25, 1891, TRC.
Page 247. "From what you say": to AR, Mar. [no day given], 1891, TRC.
Page 247. "We believe Elliott . . . on the stand": to AR, June 14, 1891, TRC.
Page 247. "I hate the idea": to AR, May 10, 1891, TRC.
Page 247. "How glad I am": to AR, June 17, 1891, TRC.
Page 247. "K.M. has demanded": to AR, July 8, 1891, TRC.
Page 247. "Cosgrove has seen the baby": to AR, July 12, 1891, TRC.
Page 248. "Tell him": to AR, June 7, 1891, TRC.
Page 248. "He is evidently a maniac": to AR, June 17, 1891, TRC.
Page 248. "If he is not utterly irresponsible": to AR, June 20, 1891, TRC.
Page 248. "This morning I had a dreadful letter": to AR, Aug. 22, 1891, TRC.
Page 248. "I regard it": to AR, Mar. [no day], 1891, TRC.
Page 248. "It is no less criminal than foolish": to AR, June 17, 1891, TRC.
Page 248. "It is dreadful": to AR, July 2, 1891, TRC.
Page 249. "I come on but one condition": to AR, June 7, 1891, TRC.
Page 249. "Won! . . . no one can say": to AR, Jan. 21, 1892 [misdated 1891], TRC.

Page 250. From EKR, undated [1890], TRC.

Page 250. Edith's inheritance: S. Morris 139.

Page 251. "It is safe to state": *The Independent,* Aug. 11, 1892, *Works* 16:208–26.

Page 251. To Lodge, Sept. 25, 1892, L.

Page 252. "the Farmers' Alliance . . . against most immigrants!": ibid.

Page 252. "There is astonishingly . . . safe with either": to Sternberg, Oct. 16, 1892, TRC.

Page 252. "I don't know . . . Alliance cranks": to Lodge, Oct. 11, 1892, L.

Page 252. "Frankly": to Lodge, July 27, 1892, L.

Page 253. "When I leave . . . my own party": to W. Foulke, Dec. 5, 1892, M.

Page 254. To Schurz, Dec. 29, 1892 and Jan. 5, 1893, M.

Page 255. "I will stay": to Schurz, Mar. 28, 1893, M.

Page 256. Adams 338.

Page 256. To AR, Dec. 17, 1893, C.

Page 257. "horrified": to EKR, Aug. 25, 1894, TRC.

Page 258. To Matthews, June 8, 1893, M.

Page 259. "I do wish Corinne . . . instead of Anna": to AR, July 29, 1894, TRC.

Page 259. EKR to Gertrude Carow, Aug. 10, 1894, TRC.

Page 259. "more overcome": CRR to AR, Aug. 15, 1894, quoted in B. Cook 88.

Page 259. "He would have been in a straight jacket . . . into man's body and soul": to AR, Aug. 18, 1894, TRC.

Page 260. "I promptly vetoed . . . bright youth": ibid.; Mrs. Evans and revolver: to AR, Aug. 25, 1894, TRC.

Page 261. To AR, May 15, 1886, M.

Page 261. "We have come out . . . best of all": to AR, July 22, 1894, M.

Page 262. To Lodge, Sept. 2, 1894, L.

Page 262. *The Nation,* Mar. 28, 1895.

Page 263. "Dear Sir": [to Turner], Apr. 2, 1895, M.

Page 263. "I think you . . . haven't even touched": to Turner, Feb. 10, 1894 and Apr. 10, 1895, M.

Page 264. To AR, June 24, 1894, M.

Page 265. Reed: Morgan 477.

Page 265. "Washington is just . . . narrow minded enough": to AR, Feb. 11, 1894, C.

Page 266. "It is curious": to Lodge, Oct. 11, 1894, L.

Page 266. "High attainments": to E. Porritt, Jan. 26, 1895, CSC.

Page 267. "The last four weeks . . . realize my feelings": to Lodge, Oct. 24, 1894, M.

Page 268. EKR to AR, Sept. 28, 1894, S. Morris 153.

Page 269. "I was very strongly . . . twelvemonth longer": to Schurz, Dec. 26, 1894, M.

Page 269. To Riis, Jan. 3, 1895, LC.

Page 270. To Quigg, Mar. 26, 1895, M.

Page 270. "I do not know . . . very puzzling!": to Lodge, Apr. 3, 1895, L.
Page 271. "I hated to leave . . . 'taking chances'": to AR, Apr. 14, 1895, C.

ELEVEN. ON THE BEAT: 1895–96

Page 274. Re Riis: *Autobiography* 203–4.
Page 275. Croker: Brands, *Reckless Decade* 110.
Page 276. "hopelessly vicious . . . iniquity": New York *Daily Tribune,* May 13, 1895.
Page 276. Williams: Jeffers, *Commissioner* 11.
Page 277. "I am getting": to AR, June 2, 1895, C.
Page 277. "My queer, strong, able colleague": to AR, June 23, 1895, M.
Page 278. "Where in blazes does": typescript by Avery Andrews, TRB; other details of ramble: Jeffers, *Commissioner* 105–8.
Page 278. "What, no mother?": ibid. 104–5
Page 279. "Tickets received": Garrison recollections, TRB.
Page 279. Packing crates: Sheffield recollections, TRB.
Page 280. "great fun": to AR, June 23, 1895, M.
Page 280. "A Bagdad Night": *Commercial Advertiser,* June 7, 1895.
Page 280. "Sing, heavenly Muse": *World,* May 17, 1895.
Page 280. Sash and pink shirt: Pringle 136.
Page 281. "probably the smallest ear": World, May 17, 1895.
Page 281. TR bags the beer drinker: Pringle 139.
Page 281. "Officer . . . 9:30 o'clock": *Commercial Advertiser,* June 7, 1895.
Page 283. "I do not deal . . . taint of corruption": statement to press, printed in New York *Sun,* June 20, 1895, *Works* 16:259–60.
Page 284. TR's costume: Pringle 137.
Page 284. "The position of Senator Hill . . . prohibited by law": *Forum,* Sept. 1895, *Works* 16:261–70.
Page 285. "absorbingly interesting": to AR, June 2, 1895, C.
Page 285. From EKR, undated [1896], TRC.
Page 286. "anti-suffragist": Rixey 285.
Page 287. Lodge to ARC: ibid. 89.
Page 287. "You need not . . . you may be sure": to Lodge, May 18, 1895, L.
Page 288. Lodge on Monroe Doctrine: *North American Review,* June 1895.
Page 288. To Lodge, June 5, 1895, L.
Page 289. Cleveland on "twenty-inch gun": Nevins 634.
Page 289. "I am very much pleased . . . take Canada": to Lodge, Dec. 20, 1895, L.
Page 289. To ARC, Jan. 19, 1896, C.
Page 289. "The antics . . . needs a war": to Lodge, Dec. 27, 1895, L.
Page 289. "If there is a muss . . . big enough": to W. Cowles, Dec. 22, 1895, M.
Page 290. To Harvard *Crimson,* Jan. 2, 1896, M.

Page 291. To Lodge, July 20, 1895, L.

Page 292. "I have undoubtedly . . . lightning striking": to Lodge, Aug. 27 and Sept. [no day given], 1895, L.

Page 293. "Nothing ever done": to Lodge, Dec. 2, 1895, L.

Page 293. "We got along": to Lodge, Jan. 19, 1896, L.

Page 294. "I shall not break": to Lodge, Jan. 19, 1896, L.

Page 294. "We are having?": to ARC, Jan. 26, 1896, C.

Page 296. From Lodge, Feb. 27, 1896, LMHS.

Page 296. Lodge and Hanna: Kohlsaat 37.

Page 297. "There are in this country": speech at Utica, Sept. 29, 1896, *Works* 16:392–93.

Page 297. *Review of Reviews,* Sept. 1896, *Works* 16:351ff.

Page 299. "Messrs. Bryan, Altgeld . . . of the mob": speech of Oct. 15, 1896, *Works* 16:394–413; speech of Sept. 29, 1896, *Works* 16:392–93.

TWELVE. THE COCKPIT OF EMPIRE: 1896–98

Page 302. "You may easily imagine": to ARC, Nov. 8, 1896, C.

Page 302. "I have to contend": to ARC, June 28, 1896, C.

Page 303. "I don't wish": to M. Storer, Dec. 5, 1896, M.

Page 304. From Lodge, Dec. 2, 1896, L.

Page 304. Platt 541.

Page 305. From Lodge, Dec. 7, 1896, L.

Page 305. "Of course I should . . . dragged into this": to Lodge, Dec. 9, 17 and 26, 1896, L.

Page 306. "I want him . . . a success": to Lodge, Mar. 22, 1897, L.

Page 307. "Sinbad has": to Lodge, Apr. 6, 1897, L.

Page 307. To ARC, Apr. 11, 1897, C.

Page 307. To White, Apr. 16, 1897, M.

Page 307. To Spring Rice, May 29, 1897, M.

Page 308. "Never again": to J. Long, Apr. 26, 1897, M.

Page 308. "I think . . . in the head": to Rice, May 29, 1897, M.

Page 308. "Adams not Herodotus . . . harmlessness": to J. Hay, May 3, 1897, M.

Page 309. "This letter . . . dozen new battleships": to A. T. Mahan, May 3, 1897, M.

Page 310. "There are [sic] at Hawaii . . . point of completion": to W. McKinley, Apr. 22, 1897, M.

Page 310. "It seems . . . in Cuba": to McKinley, Apr. 26, 1897, M.

Page 312. "I doubt . . . our action": to ARC, Jan. 2, 1897, C.

Page 313. "Long is just a dear . . . charge of the Department": to Lodge, Sept. 24, 1897, L.

Page 314. "He had previously . . . difficulty that arises": to Lodge, Sept. 15, 1897, L.

Page 315. "We can get ready . . . satisfactory talk": ibid.

Page 315. "I gave him a paper . . . there will be a war": to Lodge, Sept. 21, 1897, L.

Page 317. Address to Naval War College: *Works* 15: 240–59.

Page 317. "hot-weather secretary": to J. Long, Sept. 17, 1897, LC.

Page 318. "little Kaiser . . . fair share": to Spring Rice, Aug. 13, 1897, M.

Page 320. "I have been flying about the country": to J. Wilson, Aug. 2, 1897, LC.

Page 320. "I belong": to C. Sulloway, Oct. 28, 1897, LC.

Page 320. "I never": to J. Long, Sept. 10, 1897, M.

Page 320. "Think of it . . . was needed": to Lodge, Sept. 11, 1897, M.

Page 321. "try in every way . . . handle them": to W. Kimball, Sept. 18, 1897, M.

Page 321. To Remington, Sept. 15, 1897, M.

Page 321. "Oh Lord!": to C. Boutelle, Sept. 16, 1897, M.

Page 322. de Lome: Morgan, *Road to Empire* 41.

Page 323. "bitterly angry . . . interfering": to W. Kimball, Dec. 17, 1897, M.

Page 323. "I wish": to R. Wainwright, Dec. 23, 1897, M.

Page 323. To Long, Jan. 14, 1898, M.

Page 324. To Sternberg, Jan. 17, 1898, M.

Page 324. "by an accident": to Long, Feb. 16, 1898, M.

Page 325. "The Maine was sunk": to B. Diblee, Feb. 16, 1898, M.

Page 325. "If ever . . . outset of the war": to Long, Feb. 16, 1898, M.

Page 326. To Dewey, Feb. 25, 1898, Trask 81.

Page 326. L. Wood xvii-xviii.

Page 326. Long: *New American Navy* 174; *Journal* 169–70.

Page 327. "The President . . . the country": to D. Robinson, Mar. 6, 1898, M.

Page 327. McKinley and Wood: L. Wood xv-xvi.

Page 328. To Cowles, Mar. 30, 1898, M.

Page 328. McKinley: "In the name": Morgan, *Road to Empire* 59.

Page 329. "The President still feebly": Apr. 16, 1898, PD–1898.

Page 329. "I don't think anybody knows anything": to W. Chanler, Apr. 12, 1898, LC.

THIRTEEN. THE HERO IN HIS ELEMENT: 1898

Page 333. To Robinson, Apr. 2, 1898, M.

Page 333. To Sewall, Apr. 23, 1898, LC addenda.

Page 334. "My usefulness . . . all its bearings": to A. Lambert, Apr. 1, 1898, M.

Page 334. "I suppose": to J. Hay, Sept. 1, 1898, LC.

Page 335. "It was my one chance": recounted in Butt, *Letters* 146.

Page 335. "Edith's eyes": to Emily Carow, Mar. 1, 1918, TRC.

Page 335. To ARC, Mar. 7, 1898, M.

Page 336. "We have been very much worried": to Emily Carow, Mar. 18, 1898, TRC.

Page 336. "I shall give . . . right thing for him": to A. Lambert, Mar. 29, 1898, M.
Page 337. To CRR, May 5, 1898, M.
Page 338. "They were a splendid set": *The Rough Riders: Works* 13:13.
Page 339. "perhaps the best quarter-back . . . an Englishman": ibid. 10.
Page 339. "stirring up everything": to L. Wood, May 4, 1898, LC.
Page 339. "We are working . . . enjoying it nevertheless": to Lodge, May 19, 1898, L.
Page 340. "Do not make peace": ibid.
Page 340. "We most earnestly . . . Navy Department": to Lodge, May 25, 1898, L.
Page 341. "I really doubt . . . regular regiment": ibid.
Page 341. "one of the best fellows": to R. Wolcott, Apr. 16, 1898, LC.
Page 342. "wonderful": May 26, 1898, PD–1898.
Page 342. "the ideal man . . . at a gallop": to Lodge, May 25, 1898, L.
Page 342. "The men can go in . . . Good night, sir!": Pringle 186–87.
Page 343. "If they begin . . . faith to them": to Lodge, May 25, 1898, L.
Page 343. "Help him out . . . as I ever was in battle": Pringle 187–88.
Page 344. "We were all": to Roosevelt children, May [actually June] 6, 1898, BLC.
Page 344. "4 lovely days": June 3, 1898, PD–1898.
Page 344. To CRR, June 7, 1898, M.
Page 344. *Rough Riders* 42.
Page 345. "No words could describe": to Lodge, June 10, 1898, L.
Page 345. "I ran": *Rough Riders* 46.
Page 345. "If the authorities . . . disease": to ARC, June 12, 1898, C.
Page 345. "I cannot speak . . . incompetence": to Lodge, June 12, 1898, L.
Page 346. "It is a great": to CRR, June 15, 1898, M.
Page 346. Re landing (and quotes): Trask 213–14.
Page 347. "Five hundred": *Rough Riders* 57.
Page 347. Wheeler: Millis 274.
Page 348. "We marched fast": *Rough Riders* 59.
Page 348. "I shall never forget . . . ammunition left": V. Jones 111–12.
Page 349. "Yesterday we struck . . . for the children": to CRR, June 25, 1898 [appended to June 15], M.
Page 350. "They plucked . . . the fallen": to CRR, June 27, 1898 [with June 15], M.
Page 350. "The mismanagement . . . into the fight": to Lodge, June 27, 1898, L.
Page 350. "Damn Strategy!": Trask 227–28.
Page 351. "Why, Colonel": *Autobiography* 302–3.
Page 351. R. Davis 176.
Page 351. To Lodge, June 27, 1898, L.
Page 352. "It was a very lovely": *Rough Riders* 89.
Page 353. "The Mauser bullets": ibid. 92.
Page 354. "Are you afraid": ibid. 96.
Page 354. "If you don't . . . please": R. Davis 214.

Page 356. "On the other hand . . . Rough Riders": ibid. 217.
Page 356. "just reveling": with entry for July 5, 1898, PD–1898.
Page 356. "I think I earned . . . hard fought battle": to Lodge, July 10 and 19, 1898, L.
Page 357. "San Juan was the great day": interview with H. Hagedorn, Aug. 18, 1918, Pringle 181.

FOURTEEN. GUNPOWDER GOVERNOR: 1898–99

Page 359. "Not since . . . panic struck": to Lodge, July 5 and 7, 1898, L.
Page 359. "Well, the fight . . . Probably I did": to Lodge, July 19, 1898, L.
Page 359. "The misery": to CRR, July 19, 1898, M.
Page 360. "a grim and fearful . . . is terrible": to AR, July 18, 1898, Kerr 35–36.
Page 360. "If the army . . . I earned it": to Lodge, July 31, 1898, L.
Page 360. Letter to Shafter and round-robin: *Rough Riders* 168–70.
Page 361. To Alger, July 23, 1898, M; from Alger, undated, *Democratic Campaign Book* 70.
Page 361. From Lodge, July 4, 6 and probably 12, 1898, L.
Page 362. "Do not think": to J. Childs, July 27, 1898, M.
Page 362. "Of course . . . street sweepers": to Lodge, July 31, 1898, L.
Page 363. "How are you": with entry for Aug. 15, 1898, PD–1898.
Page 363. Depew 161–62.
Page 364. Odell recollections, TRB.
Page 365. "Apparently . . . responsibilities": to Lodge, Sept. 19, 1898, L.
Page 366. "There comes a time . . . new career": address, Oct. 5, 1898, *Works* 16:441–50.
Page 367. "I have heard . . . on the wrist": New York *Daily Tribune*, Oct. 19, 1898.
Page 367. "My friends": Depew 162.
Page 367. "a failure and a hindrance": Odell recollections, TRB.
Page 367. "Taking it . . . pleasant campaign": to Lodge, Oct. 16, 1898, L.
Page 367. To Schurz, Oct. 14, 1898, M.
Page 368. To Sewall, Oct. 6, 1898, LC addenda.
Page 368. "This gave me my chance": *Autobiography* 311.
Page 368. "The Trojan distrust": to F. Holls, Apr. 12, 1899, LC.
Page 369. "I have played it . . . another office": to Rice, Nov. 25, 1898, LC.
Page 370. Odell recollections, TRB.
Page 370. "This produced an explosion": *Autobiography* 326.
Page 371. "She takes such an interest": Rixey 131.
Page 372. "If I didn't earn it . . . I want it": to Lodge, Dec. 6, 1898, L.
Page 373. $1,000: publication agreement with *Scribner's*, TRC.
Page 373. "This will stand": *Scribner's* clip in ARL.
Page 374. Review reprinted in Dunne 13–18.
Page 376. To Dunne, Nov. 28, 1899, M.

Page 376. From Dunne, Jan. 10, 1900, LC.

Page 376. "Well, I oughtn't": Ellis 146.

Page 376. To Bryce, Nov. 25, 1898, M.

Page 377. "I want a man of backbone": to J. O'Grady, Jan. 17, 1899, LC.

Page 377. "So far as politics": to A. Shaw, Jan. 31, 1899, LC.

Page 377. "I can conscientiously say": to J. Bulloch, Oct. 17, 1899, LC.

Page 377. To Sewall, July 8, 1899, LC addenda.

Page 378. "the champion . . . modern times": to S. Rogers, Feb. 1, 1899, M.

Page 379. From Platt, May 6, 1899, BR.

Page 379. To Platt, May 8, 1899, M.

Page 380. Edith on Alice: S. Morris 197.

Page 381. "My stepmother . . . I hated": *Mrs. L* 5, 16–18, 40–42.

Page 382. "He said this morning": from EKR, May 2, 1898, TRC.

Page 382. "a solemn, cunning mite . . . every day": to Emily Carow, Mar. 20, 1899, M.

Page 382. "Last night": from EKR, June 27, 1898, TRC.

Page 383. To Spring Rice, Feb. 14, 1899, M.

Page 383. "a hideous building": *Mrs. L* 54.

Page 383. To Emily Carow, Mar. 20, 1899, M.

Page 383. "I am working under high pressure": to F. Holls, Sept. 9, 1899, LC.

Page 384. Annexation debate: Brands, *Bound to Empire* 27–30.

Page 385. "You and your comrades . . . against civilization": address, Feb. 3, 1899, *Works* 16:470–72.

Page 386. "a speech admirable . . . shown ourselves weaklings": address, Feb. 13, 1899, ibid. 473–78.

FIFTEEN. ON THEIR HEADS: 1899–1901

Page 389. Hunt interview with Hagedorn, TRB.

Page 389. "I always tell them . . . machine of my own": to A. Shaw, Jan. 31, 1899, LC.

Page 389. To Lodge, July 1, 1899, L.

Page 390. "very absorbing": to J. Bulloch, Oct. 17, 1899, LC.

Page 391. From Lodge, Dec. 7, 1899, L.

Page 391. "I really do not see": to G. Lyman, Dec. 29, 1899, M.

Page 392. "That is a job": ibid.

Page 392. Hunt interview, TRB.

Page 392. "Personally both Platt . . . by a friend": to Bishop, Apr. 11, 1900, M.

Page 393. To Platt, Feb. 1, 1900, M.

Page 394. To Hanna, Apr. 3, 1900, M.

Page 394. Payn: Platt 374.

Page 395. "We will have this war": Dunn, *Gridiron Nights* 72.

Page 395. McKinley's backbone: Dunn, *Harrison to Harding* 1:235; Kohlsaat 77.

Page 396. TR and Hanna: Beer 196.

Page 396. "The last position": to A. Elliott, May 16, 1900, LC.

Page 396. "It is quite on the cards": to J. B. Matthews, Apr. 30, 1900, M.

Page 396. "I do not think": to H. Kohlsaat, May 26, 1900, M.

Page 396. "If you will remain away": Odell recollections, TRB.

Page 396. "I believe": to Lodge, Apr. 17, 1900, L.

Page 396. "Then you will be nominated": Odell recollections, TRB.

Page 397. "Gentlemen": Leech 535.

Page 397. Hanna: Dunn, *Harrison to Harding* 1:335.

Page 398. "It was simply impossible . . . could stop it": to S. Low, June 23, 1900, M.

Page 399. Platt and TR's veil: Kohlsaat 89.

Page 399. "I believe it all . . . such a fashion": to Lodge, June 25, 1900, L.

Page 399. "It was horridly painful": to G. LaFarge, June 28, 1900, LC.

Page 399. "It certainly is odd . . . think well of me": to Lodge, June 25, 1900, L.

Page 400. To Hanna, June 27, 1900, M.

Page 400. Address, June 21, 1900, *Works* 16:525–29.

Page 401. "The simple truth . . . such an oligarchy": to E. Wolcott (officially accepting the vice presidential nomination), Sept. 15, 1900, ibid. 546–60.

Page 402. Address, Sept. 7, 1900, ibid. 530–45.

Page 403. "It seemed": to A. Moot, July 10, 1900, M.

Page 403. "What a thorough-paced hypocrite": to Lodge, Oct. 14, 1900, L.

Page 403. "every force of ignorance": to J. Bulloch, Nov. 9, 1900, M.

Page 403. "I cannot express": to AL, July 14, 1900, M.

Page 403. "I ate it": campaign account, TRB.

Page 404. "I am delighted . . . who did most": to Lodge, Nov. 9, 1900, L.

Page 404. "Even to live . . . you will forgive me": to Lodge, Jan. 30 and Feb. 2, 1900, M.

Page 404. Edith re Cuba and with Parker: S. Morris 203–4.

Page 405. "We started soon . . . dogs and the knife": to TR Jr., Jan. 14, 1901, BLC.

Page 406. "There is a strong disposition": to G. Cabot, Aug. 6, 1900, LC.

Page 407. "neither of which": to W. Chanler, Mar. 8, 1901, M.

Page 407. "Show them to no one": to C. Gunther's Sons, Apr. 23, 1901, M.

Page 407. "My experience": to P. Stewart, Apr. 6, 1901, M.

Page 407. To Taft, Apr. 26, 1901, M.

Page 407. To ARC, June 19, 1901, M.

Page 408. "I have very ugly feelings": to Taft, Apr. 26, 1901, M.

Page 408. From Lodge, June 29, 1900, L.

Page 409. "Our speeches": from Lodge, June 17, 1901, L.

Page 409. "My own view . . . intend to shoot'": to Lodge, Mar. 27, 1901, L.

Page 409. "the absolute innocuousness": to A. Sartoris, Nov. 23, 1900, LC.

Page 409. "He is perfectly cordial . . . overimpulsive": to B. and M. Storer, Apr. 17, 1901, M.

Page 410. Reed on war: Dunn, *Harrison to Harding* 1:235.

Page 410. "I have been amply rewarded . . . ahead of the deal": to H. Nelson, Apr. 8, 1901, M.

Page 410. To Wood, Apr. 17, 1901, M.

Page 411. To Taft, July 15, 1901, M.

Page 411. "I have been greatly astonished": to Lodge, Aug. 20, 1901, L.

Page 411. "Stunned amazement . . . natural thing": to Lodge, Sept. 9, 1901, L.

Page 412. "It's mighty lonesome": Leech 600.

Page 412. "Things are now progressing": to A. Whitney, Sept. 9, 1901, LC.

Page 412. "Thank Heaven": to L. Cannon, Sept. 10, 1901, LC.

Page 413. "We should war": to Lodge, Sept. 9, 1901, L.

Page 413. "with a light heart": to R. Proctor, Sept. 10, 1901, LC.

Page 414. "I felt at once": *Autobiography* 395.

Page 414. From Cortelyou: Thayer 154.

Page 414. "I'm not going to go": S. Morris 212.

SIXTEEN. SUDDENLY IN THE SADDLE: 1901

Page 418. To Sewall, Apr. 24, 1900, LC addenda.

Page 418. To Lodge, Sept. 23, 1901, L.

Page 418. "to continue absolutely unbroken": JBB 173.

Page 419. Adams: Adams 417.

Page 419. "cave dwellers": *Mrs. L* 52.

Page 420. "I declined . . . prohibition": *Autobiography* 405.

Page 421. "I get real enjoyment": to S. Bulloch, Nov. 1, 1901, LC.

Page 421. Kohlsaat 105.

Page 422. Editorial quotes: Sullivan 3:133–35.

Page 423. "No one could possibly be": to J. Strachey, Nov. 20, 1901, LC.

Page 423. "The idiot": to C. Guild, Oct. 28, 1901, M.

Page 423. "melancholy": to Washington, Nov. 2, 1901, LC.

Page 424. "I never thought": to J. Strachey, Nov. 20, 1901, LC.

Page 424. To Spooner, Sept. 30, 1901, M.

Page 424. To Aldrich, Nov. 18, 1901, M.

Page 424. To O. Platt, Nov. 15, 1901, M.

Page 425. To Hoar, Nov. 14, 1901, LC.

Page 425. From Hay, Sept. 15, 1901, LC.

Page 426. From Lodge, Oct. 17 and 19, 1901, L.

Page 426. Annual message, Dec. 3, 1901, *Works* 17:93–160.

Page 429. From Lodge, Dec. 3, 1901, L.

Page 430. *Journal, Evening Post, Courant: Literary Digest,* Dec. 14, 1901.

Page 430. Dunne: Harbaugh 154–56.

Page 431. "I play with the children": to Alice Roosevelt, Nov. 29, 1901, M.

Page 431. To TR Jr., Oct. 19, 1901, M.

Page 431. "Pray do not . . . playing later": to E. Peabody, Jan. 4, 1902, M.

Page 431. Edith: S. Morris 221.

Page 432. TR and pistol: Dunn, *Harrison to Harding* 1:361.

Page 433. "Edith is too sweet": to S. Leavitt, Oct. 7, 1901, M.

Page 433. To Hay, Oct. 5, 1901, M.

Page 433. "so young and pretty . . . I have done pretty well": to TR Jr., Oct. 19, 1901, M.

SEVENTEEN. HAND TO HAND WITH THE COAL KINGS: 1902

Page 434. Morgan and TR: JBB 211–12.

Page 438. "If a corporation . . . afford it": *Autobiography* 493.

Page 438. "the reactionaries . . . of a plutocracy": ibid., 483–84.

Page 440. "He possesses . . . ends of government": to Lodge, July 10, 1902, L.

Page 440. "He is distinctly": to A. Moses, May 16, 1900, LC.

Page 440. "a statesman of the national type . . . in public life": to Lodge, July 10, 1902, L.

Page 442. To Holmes, Aug. 19, 1902, M.

Page 442. To Knox, May 6, 1902, M.

Page 442. "I am sorry . . . obey the law": to J. Wilson, June 3, 1902, LC.

Page 443. "merely a brave peacock": Apr. 17, 1898, PD–1898.

Page 443. "a perfect curse": to H. Kohlsaat, Mar. 24, 1902, M.

Page 443. "Of course General Miles'": to O. Villard, Mar. 22, 1902, M.

Page 444. To Lodge, Sept. 3, 1903, L.

Page 444. "I am not sure": to C. Davis, Aug. 24, 1903, LC.

Page 445. Smith and major: Karnow 191.

Page 445. To Sternberg, July 19, 1902, M.

Page 446. Speech of May 30, 1902, JBB 220.

Page 446. "cruelty infinitely worse . . . in the Philippines": address of May 30, 1902, ibid. 220–21.

Page 447. To Ireland, July 23, 1902, LC.

Page 447. "I am pained . . . people will listen": to E. Philbin, July 16, 1902, M.

Page 447. "the most bitter indignation": to W. Comerford, July 16, 1902, LC.

Page 447. "We have been endeavoring": to H. Gabriele, July 14, 1902, LC.

Page 447. "a lecherous lot": Kohlsaat 111.

Page 448. Taft: Brands, *Bound to Empire,* 99.

Page 448. To Taft, July 31, 1902, M.

Page 448. "the hurly burly": to [J.] P. Morgan, Sept. 18, 1899, LC.

Page 449. "one of the bruises": to A. Gardner, Sept. 25, 1902, LC.

Page 450. To Bishop, Sept. 25, 1902, LC.

Page 450. "As I lead": to H. Putnam, Oct. 6, 1902, M.

Page 453. "My rule": F. Wood 464.

Page 453. To Hanna, Sept. 27, 1902, M.

Page 453. From Low, Oct. 2, 1902, LC.

Page 453. From Lodge, Sept. 27, 1902, L.

Page 453. "vital need": to A. Shaw, Oct. 1, 1902, LC.

Page 453. To Crane, Oct. 22, 1902, M.

Page 454. Meeting with Mitchell and operators: Sullivan 2:430–33

Page 455. "If it wasn't for the high office": F. Wood 109.

Page 456. To Cleveland, Oct. 5, 1902, M.

Page 456. To Hanna, Oct. 3, 1902, M.

Page 456. To Shaw, Oct. 1, 1902, LC.

Page 457. Baer and editorial reaction: Sullivan 2:426–27.

Page 457. "painful fogginess": to S. McKelway, Oct. 7, 1902, LC.

Page 457. To Riis, Oct. 8, 1902, LC.

Page 457. To ARC, Oct. 16, 1902, LC.

Page 458. "In this present crisis . . . of labor unions": to Bacon, Oct. 7, 1902, M.

Page 458. "I suppose Mitchell": to O. Villard, Oct. 9, 1902, M.

Page 459. "paying no heed": *Autobiography* 542.

Page 459. "I do not know": to Crane, Oct. 22, 1902, M.

Page 460. "This seemed reasonable": ibid.

Page 460. To Lodge, Oct. 17, 1902, L.

Page 460. "cleared tremendously": to J. Bishop, Oct. 16, 1902, LC.

Page 460. "I at last grasped . . . I ever dealt with": to Lodge, Oct. 17, 1902, L.

Page 461. To Cleveland, Oct. 15, 1902, GCP.

Page 462. "a great personal triumph" and "knight errantry": Gould 71.

Page 462. To Bishop, Oct. 18, 1902, M.

Page 462. "Every strike . . . just passed": to J. Woodard, Oct. 19, 1902, M.

EIGHTEEN. THE KAISER AND THE CANAL: 1902–3

Page 463. "well contented": to W. Roosevelt, Nov. 6, 1902, M.

Page 464. To Hay, Apr. 2, 1905, M.

Page 465. To Sternberg, July 12, 1901, M.

Page 465. To Spring Rice, July 3, 1901, M.

Page 465. "It seems to me . . . clash with us": to G. Meyer, Apr. 12, 1901, M.

Page 466. To Lodge, Mar. 27, 1901, L.

Page 467. "that Germany intended to seize . . . undertake arbitration myself": to W. Thayer, Aug. 21, 1916, M.

Page 469. To Spring Rice, Nov. 1, 1905, M.

Page 469. To White, Aug. 14, 1906, M.

Page 470. German decision to arbitrate: The most recent and careful study—by Mitchell—concludes that it was indeed concern at losing British support rather than fear of the American fleet that prompted Berlin's backdown.

Page 470. "very satisfactory": to L. Abbott, Dec. 27, 1902, LC.

Page 470. "some real advantages": to J. Clarkson, Dec. 25, 1902, LC.

Page 470. "Of course complications": to C. Smith, Dec. 26, 1902, LC.

Page 471. "We have sustained the Hague court": to Abbott, Dec. 27, 1902, LC.

Page 471. To Muir, May 19, 1903, M.

Page 471. To Hay, Aug. 9, 1903, M.

Page 473. "The Medora President": to J. and S. Ferris, Nov. 10, 1904, LC.

Page 476. To Lodge, June 6, 1903, M.

Page 476. "Let them sweat": Barry 275.

Page 476. "as lovely a summer . . . kind of a summer together": to CRR, Sept. 23, 1903, M.

Page 477. "Grant La Farge . . . wind and tide": to Lodge, Sept. 30, 1903, L.

Page 478. "It stands by itself . . . a most unpleasant aspect": to W. Draper, Sept. 19, 1903, LC.

Page 478. "foolish extremists . . . disaffected elements": to Lodge, Sept. 30, 1903, M (Lodge discreetly deleted the remarks on Reed from his own published version of this letter).

Page 478. Reed on "purchase of Malays": Dunn, *Harrison to Harding* 1:297.

Page 482. "I do not think . . . such proceeding": to Hay, Aug. 19, 1903, M.

Page 483. "I shall be back . . . those Bogota people": to Hay, Sept. 15, 1903, M.

Page 483. To Hanna, Oct. 5, 1903, LC.

Page 483. "As yet the people . . . I do not know": to Shaw, Oct. 7, 1903, M.

Page 484. Bunau-Varilla 310–12.

Page 485. "He had no assurances . . . make such guess": to J. Bigelow, Jan. 6, 1904, M.

Page 486. To Shaw, Nov. 6, 1903, M.

Page 486. To Spring Rice, Nov. 9, 1903, M.

Page 486. To Abbott, Nov. 12, 1903, LC.

Page 487. "By every law": to O. Gresham, Nov. 30, 1903, M.

Page 487. Hearst: LaFeber, *Panama Canal* 39.

Page 487. *Evening Post,* Dec. 3, 1903, Peck 704.

Page 487. "Nothing could be more wicked . . . laws of righteousness": to O. Gresham, Nov. 30, 1903, M.

Page 487. To Lee, Dec. 7, 1903, M.

Page 488. To TR Jr., Nov. 15, 1903, M.

Page 488. To KR, Nov. 15, 1903, LC.

Page 488. Knox: Butler 1:318.

Page 488. Root: Jessup 1:404–5.

NINETEEN. THE LIFE OF THE PARTY: 1904

Page 489. To Scott, Oct. 9, 1904, M.

Page 490. Annual message to Congress, Dec. 7, 1903, *Works,* 17:196–249.

Page 492. "old man" and "Teddy": Kohlsaat 103.

Page 493. "Good luck": to Hanna, May 29, 1902, LC.

Page 494. From Hanna, May 23, 1903, LC.

Page 494. To Lodge, May 27, 1903, L.

Page 494. To Hanna, May 25, 1903, M; "Hurrah": Beer 282.

Page 494. From Hanna, May 26, 1903, LC.

Page 494. To Lodge, May 27, 1903, L.

Page 495. To Hanna, May 29, 1903. LC.

Page 496. "Among the causes . . . burning alive": to Knox, July 24, 1903, M.

Page 496. "In a certain proportion . . . of which I speak": to Durbin, Aug. 6, 1903, M.

Page 499. "I have been greatly puzzled . . . in the South": to Schurz, Dec. 24, 1903, M.

Page 500. To Root, Feb. 16, 1904, M; from Hanna, undated, quoted ibid.

Page 501. "Poor Hanna": to G. Dodge, Feb. 14, 1904, LC.

Page 501. "veritable tragedy": to CRR, Feb. 17, 1904, LC.

Page 501. "Thank Heaven": to H. White, Feb. 17, 1904, LC.

Page 501. "He was a big man": to Root, Feb. 16, 1904, M.

Page 502. Root: Jessup 1:416.

Page 502. To Bliss, May 6, 1904, M.

Page 503. "If I am to run . . . the republican party": to Meyer, June 17, 1904, M.

Page 504. "I am sure": to C. Mellen, Jan. 27, 1904, LC.

Page 504. To TR Jr., May 14, 1904, M.

Page 505. "We want either Perdicaris alive": JBB 1:370.

Page 505. Hay: Thayer, *Hay* 2:383.

Page 506. "fundamentally ours . . . or abandon": to J. Cannon, Sept. 12, 1904, *Works* 18:498–537.

Page 506. To Cortelyou, Aug. 12, 1904, M.

Page 507. "I see hundreds of men . . . personal conversations": Dunn, *Harrison to Harding* 1:419.

Page 508. TR and Kohlsaat: Kohlsaat 151.

Page 508. "When we get hold . . . as the title": to Baker, Aug. 27, 1904, M.

Page 509. "What an insincere": to E. Crumpacker, Oct. 12, 1904, M.

Page 509. "They are scandalously": to W. Reid, Sept. 29, 1904, LC.

Page 509. "I used to think": to Cortelyou, Oct. 29, 1904, M.

Page 510. To Cortelyou, Oct. 26, 1904, M.

Page 510. "attack Parker": to W. Moody, Sept. 29, 1904, LC.

Page 510. "an aggressive fight": to W. Reid, Sept. 29, 1904, LC.

Page 510. Parker, "blackmail," and TR, "monstrous . . . the man making them": Pringle 355–56.

Page 511. To KR, Oct. 23, 1904, LC.

Page 511. Standard Oil money: Pringle, 357–58.

Page 512. "very much concerned": to J. Bishop, Aug. 13, 1904, LC.

Page 512. *Sun,* Aug. 11, 1904.

Page 512. "A candidate can never tell": to J. Strachey, Oct. 13, 1904, LC.

Page 512. "I shall be confident": to R. Thorndike, Oct. 22, 1904, LC.

Page 512. To KR, Oct. 26, 1904, M.

Page 512. "Good Heavens": to F. Doubleday, Nov. 1, 1904, M.

Page 513. "I haven't an idea": to O. Platt, Nov. 3, 1904, LC.

Page 513. "Parker is": to KR, Nov. 3, 1904, M.

Page 513. To Lodge, Nov. 9 [dated Nov. 8 in M and LC] and 10, 1904, L.

TWENTY. THE LOGIC OF POWER: 1904–5

Page 514. "The wise custom": Washington *Post,* Nov. 9, 1904.

Page 514. To Crane, Nov. 12, 1904, M.

Page 514. From Lodge, Nov. 9, 1904, L.

Page 514. Edith to Wister: Hagedorn, *Roosevelt Family* 272–73.

Page 515. Kohlsaat 138.

Page 516. "Carl Schurz . . . to defeat me": to Wister, Nov. 19, 1904, M;

Page 516. "lying scoundrels": to F. Rawle, Apr. 27, 1901, LC.

Page 517. To KR, Nov. 10, 1904, M.

Page 517. To Wister, Nov. 19, 1904, M.

Page 519. "deliberate falsification . . . malicious inventions": to E. Haskell, Dec. 10, 1904, M.

Page 519. Alice: S. Morris, 273.

Page 520. "I meant to warn you": EKR to AR, undated, ARL.

Page 520. "If you have debts": EKR to AR, Aug. 2, 1904, TRC.

Page 520. "I feel quite repentant": EKR to AR, [Aug. 3, 1904], TRC.

Page 521. To TR Jr., Jan. 20, 1903, M.

Page 521. "Well, Franklin": Lash 141.

Page 521. "I can be president": Gould 104.

Page 521. "Alice came in" to "the entire nation": Rixey 146, 181–82, 188.

Page 524. "idiotic jealousy": to J. Strachey, Jan. 9, 1905, LC.

Page 524. "Santo Domingo . . . is inevitable": to TR Jr., Feb. 10, 1904, M.

Page 525. To Bishop, Feb. 23, 1904, M.

Page 525. "If I acted . . . purposes and motives": to C. Eliot, Apr. 4, 1904 [unsent], M.

Page 526. "It is our duty": to W. Hale, Feb. 26, 1904, M.

Page 526. "Brutal wrongdoing": to Root, May 20, 1904, M.

Page 526. To Root, June 7, 1904, M.

Page 527. "It looks to me . . . behave decently": to Hay, Aug. 30 and Sept. 2, 1904, M.

Page 527. "Chronic wrongdoing . . . good use of it": message to Congress, Dec. 6, 1904, *Works* 17:299–300.

Page 528. To Reid, Feb. 11, 1904, LC.

Page 528. To TR Jr., Feb. 10, 1904, M.

Page 529. "I believe . . . or a Slav peril": to Rice, Mar. 19, 1904, M; "No one can": to TR Jr., Mar. 5, 1904, LC.

Page 531. "The Japs interest me . . . the great nations": to Rice, June 13, 1904, M.

Page 532. "The situation . . . truthfulness is low": to Meyer, Dec. 26, 1904, M.

Page 532. "The summing up": to Spring Rice, Dec. 27, 1904, M.

Page 533. To Lodge, June 5, 1905, L.

Page 533. To KR, June 14, 1905, LC.

Page 534. "Doubtless Japan . . . policy led her": to S. Low, June 14, 1905, LC.

Page 534. "so as to convince even the most doubting": memo to Russian ambassador, June 15, 1905, LC.

Page 534. "not in the least": memo for Japanese government, June 15, 1905, LC.

Page 534. To Lodge, June 16, 1905, L.

Page 535. To C. Hay, July 1, 1905, M.

Page 535. To Spring Rice, July 24, 1905, M.

Page 536. "Of course . . . fine reputation": to Lodge, July 11, 1905, M (Lodge's version omits TR's criticism of Hay).

Page 536. "In Elihu Root": to Spring Rice, July 24, 1905, M.

Page 537. To Taft, July 29, 1905, M.

Page 537. To Spring Rice, July 24, 1905, M.

Page 538. To Czar Nicholas in message to Witte, Aug. 21, 1905, LC.

Page 538. To Sternberg, Aug. 21, 1905, M.

Page 538. To Kaneko, Aug. 22, 1905, M.

Page 538. "If Japan": to H. Durand, Aug. 23, 1905, M.

Page 538. To Witte in telegram to H. Peirce, Aug. 23, 1905, M.

Page 539. "She has won . . . not be deaf": to Kaneko, Aug. 23, 1905, M.

Page 539. "I feel . . . to make it": to William II, Aug. 27, 1905, M.

Page 539. To KR, Aug. 25, 1905, M.

Page 540. To Rockhill, Aug. 29, 1905, M.

Page 540. "Tell Baron Komura": to Peirce, Aug. 29, 1905, M.

Page 540. Message to Japanese emperor in message to Komura, Aug. 30, 1905, LC.

Page 540. To Nicholas, Aug. 31, 1905, M.

Page 540. To William II, Aug. 30, 1905, LC.

Page 540. "I think the Japanese government": to J. O'Laughlin, Aug. 31, 1905, LC.

Page 540. To Lee, Sept. 1, 1905, LC.

Page 540. To Spring Rice, Sept. 1, 1905, LC.

Twenty-one. Square Dealing: 1905–6

Page 541. To Wood, Mar. 9, 1905, M.

Page 541. To Spring Rice, Feb. 27, 1905, M.

Page 541. To Trevelyan, Mar. 9, 1905, M.

Page 542. Holmes: Holmes 63–64.

Page 543. "In the vast . . . on the other": annual message, Dec. 6, 1904, Works 17:250–310.

Page 544. To Baker, Nov. 13, 1905, M.

Page 545. "I have had . . . not a blessing": to Baker, Nov. 20 and 28, 1905, M.

Page 546. To Abbott, Dec. 19, 1905, M.

Page 547. To Anna Lodge, Mar. 11, 1906, M.

Page 547. "The rate bill fight": to KR, Mar. 19, 1906, LC.

Page 547. "The Republican leaders . . . most of the Democrats": to KR, Apr. 1, 1906, M.

Page 547. "one of the foulest": to KR, Jan. 10, 1909, TRC.

Page 548. "As for the Tillman incident": to C. Hanks, May 18, 1905, LC.

Page 548. To Allison, May 5, 1906, M.

Page 548. "The rate bill went through": to ARC, May 20, 1905, C.

Page 548. Sinclair: Sullivan, 2:480.

Page 549. To Wilson, Mar. 12, 1906, M.

Page 549. "I wish he had left out": to F. Doubleday, Mar. 22, 1906, LC.

Page 549. To Sinclair, Mar. 15, 1906, M.

Page 550. "I was not very much impressed": to G. McCabe, June 16, 1906, LC.

Page 550. "The information . . . before Congress": to Wadsworth, May 31, 1906, M.

Page 550. "The misdeeds . . . I have asked": to Wadsworth, June 8, 1906, M.

Page 550. "a thorough . . . I have in view": to Wadsworth, June 15, 1906, M.

Page 551. "We may have long and ugly fighting": to KR, June 17, 1906, LC.

Page 551. To Beveridge, June 30, 1906, M.

Page 551. "If I were . . . my second term": to J. Sleicher, Aug. 11, 1906, M.

Page 552. "No, God Almighty": Butt, *Taft and Roosevelt* 1:334.

Page 552. Cannon: Moore 219

Page 553. "mucker play": to KR, Oct. 9, 1905, LC.

Page 553. "I want to take up": to G. Gray, Oct. 6, 1905, M.

Page 553. "I am perfectly willing": to E. Brandegee, Mar. 7, 1906, M.

Page 553. "honorable obligation": in TR to N. M. Butler, Oct. 11, 1905, LC.

Page 553. "Believe me": to Camp (telegram), Oct. 11, 1905, LC.

Page 553. "I can not tell you": to Camp (letter), Oct. 11, 1905, LC.

Page 554. "In many cases": to G. Foss, Feb. 1, 1906, M.

Page 554. "I am not satisfied . . . at the Naval Academy": to C. Bonaparte, Feb. 17, 1906, M.

Page 555. "which is the one": to L. Shaw, Sept. 11, 1906, M.

Page 555. To Wilson, Sept. 12, 1906, M.

Page 555. To Sternberg, Sept. 6, 1905, M.

Page 556. "There is not . . . foolish and fantastic": to C. Stillings, Aug. 27, 1906, M.

Page 557. "observe and adhere . . . tu soot himself": Sullivan, 3:178–81, 189.

Page 558. To J. B. Matthews, Dec. 16, 1906, M.

Page 558. "Of course he's insane": Brough 156.

Page 559. "Alice is really in love": S. Morris 303.

Page 559. "Longworth . . . well with politicians": to J. Strachey, Feb. 12, 1906, M.

Page 560. Hoover: S. Morris, 305–7.

Page 560. "I am inclined . . . after Ted": to Eliot, Sept. 29, 1905, M.

Page 561. "There is not leeway . . . retrieve it": to TR Jr., Feb. 23, 1906, M.

Page 561. "general disorder": from V. Arnold, May 9, 1906, SH.

Page 562. "Mrs. Roosevelt . . . keep them": to V. Arnold, May 10, 1906, M.
Page 563. To B. Storer, Dec. 19, 1903, M.
Page 563. "certain chivalric feeling": Sullivan 3:123.
Page 563. "Considerate married men": ibid. 124.
Page 564. Jusserand jaunt: Thayer 262–63.
Page 565. "I have had to temporarily": to TR Jr., Jan. 20, 1903, M.
Page 565. "I am sorry to say": to M. Donovan, Dec. 13, 1904, M.
Page 565. "Gracious me!": to KR, Dec. 11, 1904, LC.
Page 565. "I eat too much": to KR, Feb. 19, 1904, LC.
Page 565. "old and fat": to W. Rainsford, Feb. 12, 1904, LC.
Page 565. To Lodge, Aug. 6, 1906, L.
Page 566. To KR, June 9, 1906, M.

TWENTY-TWO. NEITHER WAR NOR QUITE PEACE: 1906–7

Page 567. "President Roosevelt": Sullivan 3:189.
Page 568. To Butler, Feb. 4, 1902, M.
Page 568. Palma: Collin 529.
Page 569. "If I am forced": to W. Reid, Sept. 24, 1906, LC.
Page 569. "Just at the moment": to H. White, Sept. 13, 1906, LC.
Page 569. "I have just been notified . . . misrule and anarchy": to Trevelyan,
    Sept. 9, 1906, M.
Page 570. "Simply say": to Taft, Sept. 21, 1906, M.
Page 570. To Palma in telegram to Taft, Sept. 25, 1906, M.
Page 571. "I am inclined . . . guerrilla warfare": to Taft, Sept. 25, 1906, M.
Page 571. "shiver at the consequences": from Taft, Sept. 26, 1906, LC.
Page 571. "With Taft in Havana": to C. Bonaparte, Sept. 19, 1906, LC.
Page 571. "It is undoubtedly": to Taft, Sept. 26, 1906 (second of three), M.
Page 572. "Avoid the use . . . of the landing": to Taft, Sept. 26, 1906 (first of
    three), M.
Page 572. "This as I say": ibid.
Page 573. "While I am a Jeffersonian": to W. Potter, Apr. 23, 1906, M.
Page 573. "You know . . . is demanded": to Taft, Sept. 17, 1906, M.
Page 573. "If it becomes . . . initiative themselves": ibid.
Page 575. "She is bound . . . other quarters: Wilhelm in Sternberg to TR, Apr. 5,
    1905, LC.
Page 575. "A word from you": from Sternberg, Apr. 25, 1905, LC.
Page 575. "He would have to choose": from Sternberg, May, 13, 1905, LC.
Page 575. To Taft, Apr. 20, 1905, M.
Page 576. "It really did look . . . for the sake of France": to W. Reid, Apr. 28,
    1906, M.
Page 576. To Sternberg, June 25, 1905, M.
Page 577. "The two Governments": in TR to Reid, Apr. 28, 1906, M.
Page 577. "He seems to have a brain . . . here as Ambassador": ibid.
Page 578. To Edward, Apr. 25, 1906, LC.

Page 580. To KR, Oct. 27, 1906, M.

Page 580. "gravest concern . . . movements like this": to Kaneko, Oct. 26, 1906, M.

Page 580. "In the Japanese matter . . . as a citizen": to L. Abbott, Jan. 3, 1907, M.

Page 581. "McCall and Olney": to W. Lawrence, Feb. 6, 1907, M.

Page 582. "violent extremists . . . becoming a fact": to Gillett, Mar. 11, 1907, M.

Page 583. "It therefore appears": ibid.

Page 583. To Carnegie, Feb. 17, 1907, M.

Page 584. "I hunted faithfully": to KR, Nov. 4, 1906, LC.

Page 585. "All the forenoon": to KR, Nov. 14, 1906, M.

Page 585. "perfection": to E. Root, Nov. 14, 1906, LC.

Page 585. "It gives me great pride": to TR Jr., Nov. 14 [undated in LC], 1906, BLC.

Page 585. "a great sight . . . here and there through it": to TR Jr., Nov. 20, 1906, BLC.

Page 586. "I kept thinking . . . civilization lasts": to KR, Nov. 20, 1906, M.

Page 588. "When the discipline . . . I have punished: to C. Guild, Nov. 7, 1906, M.

Page 588. "I have been amazed . . . disapproval of it": to S. McBee, Nov. 27, 1906, M.

Page 589. "I have been really . . . of their race": to Baker, Mar. 30, 1907, M.

Page 590. Gridiron dinner: Dunn, *Gridiron Nights* 178–88; Foraker, 2:254–58; Washington *Post,* Jan. 29, 1907.

Twenty-three. Heir Apparenting: 1907

Page 593. "hit your case": Pringle, *Taft* 1:21.

Page 593. "How is the horse?": Thompson 245.

Page 593. "a huge pan": Manners 7.

Page 594. To Taft, May 22, 1903, M.

Page 594. To TR Jr., Feb. 6, 1904, M.

Page 595. To Anna Lodge, Feb. 19, 1886, M.

Page 595. "You cannot know . . . admire you": to Taft, Apr. 22 and May 22, 1903, M.

Page 596. "You beloved individual": to Taft, Aug. 2, 1906, M.

Page 597. "I know no man . . . unscrupulous corporate wealth": to Taft, July 26, 1907, M.

Page 597. To White, July 30, 1907, M.

Page 598. To KR, Apr. 23, 1907, M.

Page 598. To Taft, Sept. 19, 1907, M.

Page 599. Speech at Provincetown, Mass., Aug. 20, 1907, *Works* 18:90–101.

Page 600. To Reid, Nov. 14, 1907, LC.

Page 601. "the usual paroxysm": to KR, Oct. 27, 1907, LC; "Whether I can do . . . perplexing": to A. Lambert, Nov. 1, 1907, M.

Page 602. "those conservative . . . real prosperity": to Cortelyou (for publication), Oct. 25, 1907, M.

Page 603. "a general industrial smashup": to C. Bonaparte, Nov. 4, 1907, M.

Page 603. "I answered": ibid.

Page 604. To Watson, Nov. 12, 1907, M.

Page 604. "I am doing everything . . . is to endure": to D. Robinson, Nov. 16, 1907, M; "hydrophobia": to KR, Nov. 14, 1907, LC.

Page 605. "If we check it": to CRR, Oct. 29, 1907, LC.

Page 606. "Our people . . . trouble with Japan": to S. Bigelow, July 26, 1907, LC.

Page 606. To Kaneko, May 23, 1907, M.

Page 606. To Lodge, July 10, 1907, L.

Page 607. To Root, July 13, 1907, M; to Lodge, July 10, 1907, L.

Page 609. "I have almost as much trouble": to A. Carnegie, July 15, 1907, LC.

Page 609. "blind to every consideration": to J. Bell, July 23, 1907, LC.

Page 609. "downright cowardice": to W. Reid, July 26, 1907, LC.

Page 609. "if he were actuated . . . physical coward": to T. Newberry, July 30, 1907, M; to Lodge, Sept. 2, 1907, L; to Root, July 13 and 31, 1907, M.

Page 609. To Root, July 31, 1907, M.

Page 609. "I decline . . . material well-being": to Sternberg, July 16, 1907, M.

Page 610. "My prime purpose . . . fully achieved": *Autobiography* 624.

Page 610. "This cruise . . . not entirely approve": to Newberry, Aug. 10, 1907, M.

Page 610. From Sternberg, July 14, 1907, LC.

Page 611. To Sternberg, July 16, 1907, M.

Page 611. "Nothing that has been done . . . anything that comes": to Root, July 26, 1907, M.

Page 611. "My own judgment": to Root, July 23, 1907, M.

Page 612. "The fleet is . . . fleet was there": to C. Tower, Nov. 19, 1907, M.

Page 612. "Our relations": to L. Abbott, Sept. 13, 1907, M.

Page 612. "There was no further difficulty": *Autobiography* 628.

Page 613. "Did you ever see": Reckner 23.

TWENTY-FOUR. THE BREATHLESS END OF A ROUSING RUN: 1908–9

Page 614. To Wilhelm, Apr. 4, 1908, M.

Page 615. "exercise the most careful watch . . . peculiar conditions": to C. Sperry, Mar. 21, 1908, M.

Page 615. "The Philippines form . . . under duress": to Taft, Aug. 21, 1907, M.

Page 617. To Watson, Dec. 21, 1907, M.

Page 618. "It was time . . . marrow of their being": to Bonaparte, Jan. 2, 1908, M.

Page 618. Message to Congress, Jan. 31, 1908, Morison 1572ff.

Page 619. From Butler, Feb. 4, 1908, LC.

Page 620. "I have interfered": to D. Gray, Dec. 22, 1907, LC.

Page 620. To CRR, Dec. 25, 1907, LC.

Page 620. "You regret . . . fight in New York": to Butler, Feb. 6, 1908, M.

Page 623. TR on Pinchot: to A. Carnegie, Feb. 15, 1904, LC.

Page 624. "the utmost care . . . it may desire": memo, Mar. 2, 1907, LC.

Page 624. "We are prone . . . national life": annual message, Dec. 3, 1907, *Works* 17:481ff.

Page 625. Muir and Pinchot: Cutright 230.

Page 625. "one of the most": ibid.

Page 626. "There has never been . . . low morality": to Abbott, May 29, 1908, M.

Page 626. To Taft, Jan. 6, 1908, M.

Page 626. "false and malicious . . . something injurious": to W. Foulke, Feb. 7, 1908, M.

Page 626. Account of convention: New York *Daily Tribune,* June 18, 1908.

Page 627. "any danger of a stampede": to ARC, June 17, 1980, LC.

Page 627. "some lively work": to W. Reid, June 19, 1908, LC.

Page 627. "splendidly": to ARC, June 22, 1908, C.

Page 627. "The demonstration": *Tribune,* June 18, 1908.

Page 627. To A. Lodge, June 19, 1908, M.

Page 628. To Trevelyan, June 19, 1908, M.

Page 629. "a man . . . in the office": ibid.

Page 629. "the honest wageworker . . . from the railroads": to C. Kohrs, Sept. 9, 1908, M.

Page 630. "the cheapest faker": to W. Kent, Sept. 28, 1908, M.

Page 630. "Bryan gave me . . . the Bryanites": to Taft, Sept. 14, 1908, M.

Page 630. "I believe . . . the need arose": to Taft, July 17 and Sept. 11, 1908, M; to Taft, Sept. 16, 1908, LC.

Page 630. To Longworth, Sept. 21, 1908, M.

Page 631. To Abbott, Sept. 22, 1908, M.

Page 631. "I don't think . . . men would stop": to KR, Oct. 24, 1908, M.

Page 631. "Skinning skunks": to W. Foulke, Oct. 30, 1908, M.

Page 631. "What curious changes . . . for which I stood": to C. Moore, Sept. 11, 1908, LC.

Page 631. To Hitchcock, Sept. 11, 1908, LC.

Page 631. To Taft, Oct. 6, 1908, LC.

Page 632. "The result": to J. Clarkson, Nov. 4, 1908, LC.

Page 632. "Naturally I am": to E. Martin, Nov. 6, 1908, LC.

Page 632. To Trevelyan, Nov. 6, 1908, M.

Page 632. "the hated Black Cabinet" to "criminal class": Pringle 483–84.

Page 633. *World,* Dec. 8, 1908.

Page 633. To Stimson, Dec. 9, 1908, M.

Page 633. "unfortunately": to L. Abbott, Dec. 15, 1908, M.

Page 634. To Ethel Roosevelt, Nov. 8, 1908, M.
Page 634. To KR, Jan. 14, 1909, M.
Page 634. Butt, *Letters* 294–95.
Page 635. Re London: to M. Sullivan, Sept. 9, 1908, M.
Page 635. Re cherub: to S. Young, Sept. 15, 1908, M.
Page 635. Re Carpenter: to G. Buell, Aug. 18, 1908, M.
Page 635. To TR Jr., Feb. 6, 1909, M.
Page 636. To A. Lee, Feb. 7, 1909, M.
Page 636. To CRR and D. Robinson, Feb. 21, 1909, M.
Page 636. To AR, Feb. 23, 1909, LC.
Page 637. "This is the first battle fleet": quoted in *Autobiography* 634.
Page 637. "the apotheosis": New York *Times,* Feb. 23, 1909.

TWENTY-FIVE. LIONS AND LESSER ROYALTY: 1909–10

Page 641. Edith in Butt, *Letters* 323.
Page 642. "He told me": Butt, *Taft and Roosevelt* 29.
Page 642. "If it were not": S. Morris 348.
Page 643. "I have never shot": to F. Selous, Feb. 7, 1909, LC.
Page 643. "I quite appreciate": to Selous, Aug. 9, 1908, LC.
Page 643. "People have told me": to R. Cunninghame, Jan. 31, 1909, LC.
Page 643. "Except for actual food": to R. Wingate, Sept. 14, 1908, LC.
Page 644. "I have been a little worried": to E. Buxton, Aug. 1, 1908, LC.
Page 644. "I fairly dream of the trip": to Selous, Sept. 12, 1908, LC.
Page 644. "I shall be absolutely soft": to R. Cunninghame, Jan. 31, 1909, LC.
Page 644. "Hurrah for Africa": to E. Root, Sept. 9, 1908, LC.
Page 645. Butt, *Letters* 203.
Page 646. Akeley foreword to *African Game Trails: Works* 5:xi.
Page 646. "I speak of Africa . . . through time everlasting": ibid. xxv-xxvii.
Page 648. "The natives . . . made for use": ibid. 35–36.
Page 649. "out-of-the-way regions": ibid. 6.
Page 649. "The Wakamba": ibid. 37.
Page 649. "It is a white man's country": ibid. 31–32.
Page 650. "There could be no": ibid. 40.
Page 650. "To an American . . . the native negro": ibid. 10.
Page 651. "Every time Mr. Roosevelt": Sullivan 3:155.
Page 651. "certain facts . . . soundness of heart": *African Game Trails* 13–14.
Page 652. "We rode up": ibid. 72–73.
Page 653. "Watching the game . . . blood and guts": ibid. 195–96.
Page 653. "Around the dead rhino . . . red relief": ibid. 93–94.
Page 654. "I slipped it": ibid. 184.
Page 654. "Kermit and I . . . faithful black followers": ibid. 449.
Page 655. "My tent": to ARC, June 21, 1909, C.
Page 655. "After returning": to ARC, May 19, 1909, C.

Page 656. From Bullock, Aug. 31, 1905, LC.

Page 656. "Do you remember . . . a rabbit": to CRR, June 21, 1909, M.

Page 656. "Kermit has become": to ARC, Dec. 17, 1909, C.

Page 657. "My coming here . . . every standpoint advisable": to R. Bridges, July 17, 1909, M.

Page 657. To Carnegie, June 1, 1909, M.

Page 658. "I want to go home!": to Carnegie, Feb. 18, 1910, M.

Page 659. To EKR, Nov. 12, 1909, S. Morris 351–52.

Page 660. To E. Alexander, Mar. 17, 1910, M.

Page 660. To TR Jr., Mar. 21, 1910, M.

Page 660. "every kind of muss": to A. Lee, Apr. 5, 1910, LC.

Page 660. "a pretty good Imperialist": to A. Lee, Oct. 6, 1909, M.

Page 661. "an elegant row": to Lodge, Apr. 6, 1910, L.

Page 661. To A. Lambert, Apr. 21, 1910, LC.

Page 661. "a most interesting time . . . on the backs": to Lodge, May 14, 1910, L.

Page 661. "a perfect whirl": to R. Kerens, May 3, 1910, LC.

Page 662. "Peace is generally good . . . virile virtues": address at Christiana, Norway, May 5, 1910, *Works* 18:410–15.

Page 662. "soul-harrowing business": to W. Reid, Apr. 5, 1910, LC.

Page 662. "Literally every minute": to B. Herman, Apr. 6, 1910, LC.

Page 662. To Lee, Apr. 13, 1910, LC.

Page 663. "In the long run . . . day and generation": lecture at Oxford, June 7, 1910, *Works* 14:65–106.

TWENTY-SIX. RETIREMENT RUINED: 1910–11

Page 664. From Taft, Nov. 7, 1908, LC.

Page 665. "You are the only man": to Taft, Nov. 10, 1908, M.

Page 665. "Abraham Lincoln": Gould 290.

Page 666. From Lodge, Nov. 30, 1909; Jan. 15, 1910, L.

Page 667. From Pinchot, Dec. 31, 1909, Pinchot 498–500.

Page 667. "There is a constantly growing": from Lodge, Jan. 15, 1910, L.

Page 667. To Pinchot, Mar. 1, 1910, Pinchot 501.

Page 668. "I am absolutely . . . responsibility": to Lodge, Mar. 4 and 28, 1910, L.

Page 669. "People easily . . . appreciate the fact": to Lodge and Anna Lodge, Sept. 10, 1909, L.

Page 669. "a flat failure": to C. Whitney, Sept. 11, 1908, LC.

Page 669. "When he reached the bridge . . . than when he left": Butt, *Taft and Roosevelt* 1:396–400; description of welcome: ibid. and Manners 163–64.

Page 671. To Taft, June 20, 1910, M.

Page 671. TR and Taft meeting: Butt, *Taft and Roosevelt* 1:417–31.

Page 672. To Pinchot, June 28, 1910, M.

Page 673. To Lee, July 19, 1910, M.

Page 674. To Garfield, July 19, 1910, LC.

Page 674. "I am not taking sides": to J. Ashton, July 22, 1910, LC.

Page 674. To Longworth, July 22, 1910, M.

Page 674. Butler: Rixey 176.

Page 675. To Lee, Sept. 16, 1910, M.

Page 675. To AR, Aug. 16, 1910, M.

Page 675. Speech of Aug. 31, 1910, *Works* 19:10–30.

Page 677. "I answered": to Lodge, Aug. 17, 1910, M.

Page 678. "swaying from side to side" and other details: Manners 180–81.

Page 678. "Taft and Norton . . . I have called": to Lodge, Sept. 21, 1910, M.

Page 678. To Lodge, Aug. 8, 1908, L.

Page 679. "By George . . . some trophies": New York *Tribune,* Sept. 27, 1910; "from all responsibility": to F. Dingley, Aug. 18, 1910, LC.

Page 679. "Is Teddy . . . elephant": *Tribune,* Sept. 27, 1910.

Page 680. "the credit": address of Sept. 27, 1910, *Works* 19:31–37.

Page 680. "overwhelming": to TR Jr., Oct. 3, 1910, LC.

Page 680. "The Tower of Siloam . . . if it does not": to White, Nov. 11, 1910, M.

Page 680. To Parsons, Nov. 11, 1910, LC.

Page 681. "Win or lose": to White, Nov. 11, 1910, M.

Page 681. To TR Jr., Dec. 5, 1910, M.

Page 682. To TR Jr., Jan. 22, 1911, M.

Page 683. From La Follette, Jan. 19, 1911, LC.

Page 683. "in any factional spirit": to F. Dingley, Aug. 18, 1910, LC.

Page 683. "I think well of La Follette": to TR Jr., Nov. 21, 1910, LC.

Page 684. To La Follette, Jan. 3, 1911, M.

Page 684. *Outlook,* various issues from January to April 1911, in *Works* 19:81–160.

Page 686. To Taft, Apr. 1, 1911, M.

Page 686. To Lodge, Aug. 22, 1911, M (In deference to young Grace, Lodge omitted her grandfather's candid comments from the version he published).

Page 686. To Wister, May 23, 1911, M.

Page 686. "distinct additions": to C. Hughes, Oct. 3, 19 , LC.

Page 686. To ARC, July 28, 1911, M.

Page 687. To Eleanor A. Roosevelt, July 30, 1911, M.

Page 687. To Peabody, May 5, 1911, M.

Page 687. To Lee, Sept. 25, 1911, M.

Page 687. To F. Delamere, Sept. 22, 1910, LC.

Page 688. To Taft, Mar. 14, 1911, M.

Page 688. "Taft is stronger": to Lee, June 27, 1911, M.

Page 689. "I shall do whatever": to Spring Rice, Aug. 22, 1911, M.

Page 689. "I feel that my nomination": to F. Shotwell, May 19, 1911, LC.
Page 689. "academic": to O. K. Davis, June 30, 1911, LC.
Page 689. "I think all danger": to Lee, June 27, 1911, M.
Page 689. "I do not think": to Spring Rice, Aug. 22, 1911, M.
Page 689. "Neither you": to C. Jackman, Oct. 24, 1911, LC.
Page 689. To White, Oct. 24, 1911, M.
Page 689. "not of the slightest consequence": to G. Pinchot, Nov. 11, 1910, LC.
Page 690. To Johnson, Oct. 27, 1911, M.

Twenty-seven. To the Barricades Once More: 1912

Page 691. "Twenty or even ten . . . right code to hold": to J. Rose, July 20, 1911, M.
Page 692. "much improved": to KR, Dec. 1, 1906, LC.
Page 692. "It immensely amused me . . . honest dealing": to Rice, Aug. 22, 1911, M.
Page 694. "frightful pain": to CRR, Oct. 2, 1911, TRB.
Page 694. "hardly talk": to KR, Oct. 5, 1911, TRC.
Page 694. "very frail and wasted": to E. Peabody, Oct. 24, 1911, LC.
Page 694. To TR Jr., Oct. 30, 1911, M.
Page 694. "exceedingly narrow escape": to S. Young, Oct. 6, 1911, LC.
Page 695. Butt on lunch: Butt, *Taft and Roosevelt* 829–32.
Page 697. To Garfield, Nov. 24, 1911, M.
Page 697. From Garfield, Nov. 27, 1911, LC.
Page 697. To Parsons, Dec. 6, 1911, M.
Page 698. "Frequently when asked": to E. Martin, Feb. 8, 1912, M.
Page 698. "I am really sorry . . . against La Follette": to C. Willard, Dec. 11, 1911, M.
Page 699. "He lacks": to B. Wheeler, Dec. 21, 1911, M.
Page 699. To A. Willson, Feb. 14, 1912, M.
Page 699. "Those who will not read": to F. Munsey, Jan. 16, 1912, M.
Page 699. "Why!": to G. Daniels, Dec. 15, 1911, LC.
Page 699. "I am not . . . could not shirk": to W. Howland, Dec. 23, 1911, M.
Page 700. To Lindsey, Jan. 7, 1912, LC.
Page 700. To H. Hadley, Jan. 23, 1912, M.
Page 700. To Root, Feb. 14, 1912, M.
Page 701. "It seems to me . . . honor bound to do so": to C. Osborn, Jan. 18, 1912, M.
Page 702. To Cowles, Jan. 22, 1912, M.
Page 702. "The situation changes": to R. Bass, Jan. 23, 1912, LC.
Page 702. From W. Glasscock et al., Feb. 10, 1912, *Works* 19:198–99.
Page 703. "My hat is in the ring": Pringle 556.
Page 703. Speech at Columbus, Feb. 21, 1912, *Works* 19:163–97.
Page 704. Grant to J. Rhodes, Mar. 22, 1912, Morison 8:1456–61.

Page 705. "I will accept": to W. Glasscock et al., Feb. 24, 1912, *Works* 19:198–99.

Page 706. Root: Jessup 2:180–81.

Page 706. From Lodge, Feb. 28, 1912, L.

Page 707. "Roosevelt was my closest friend": Pringle, *Taft* 2:781–82.

Page 707. To Lodge, Mar. 1, 1912, L.

Page 707. To Root, Feb. 14, 1912, M.

Page 708. From White, Mar. 2, 1912, LC.

Page 708. Criticism of TR: Mowry 218–21.

Page 709. "Such extremists": Pringle, *Taft* 2:766.

Page 709. "Mr. Taft's position . . . cannot turn back": address, Mar. 20, 1912, *Works* 19:200ff.

Page 709. "I do not think": to W. Stubbs, Mar. 8, 1912, LC.

Page 709. To Ferguson, Mar. 26, 1912, LC.

Page 710. To KR, Mar. 9, 1912, TRC.

Page 710. Speeches of Mar. 30 and May 4, 1912, *Works* 19:272–82.

Page 711. "There is not one state": speech at Omaha, Apr. 17, 1912, LC.

Page 711. Mudslinging: Pringle, *Taft* 2:783; Mowry 234–35.

Page 712. "to wreck the Progressive cause": to T. Thorson, Mar. 26, 1912, LC.

Page 713. "Evidently, Taft": to W. Nelson, May 28, 1912, M.

Page 714. "The saturnalia": Mowry 240.

Page 714. Address, June 17, 1912, *Works* 19:285–317.

Page 716. TR and Micah: John O'Leary recollections, TRB.

Page 717. "I'll name the compromise candidate": Harbaugh 405–6.

Page 717. "eighty per cent": to A. Hart, July 10, 1912, LC.

Page 717. "I shall accept": to J. Hammond, June 25, 1912, LC.

Page 717. "My feeling": to W. Foulke, July 1, 1912, M.

Page 718. "a general smashup": to H. R. Haggard, June 28, 1912, M.

Page 718. "excellent man": to C. Osborn, July 5, 1912, M.

Page 718. "good man . . . over forty years": to H. Plunkett, Aug. 3, 1912, M; "The Democratic platform . . . as ever before": to H. Smith, July 13, 1912, LC.

Page 719. "To see good old Oscar Straus": Kohlsaat 194.

Page 719. "At Three o'Clock": Sullivan, 4:511.

Page 719. "fairly religious fervor": to KR, July 13, 1912, TRC.

Page 719. "The time is ripe": address, Aug. 6, 1912, *Works* 19:358–411.

Page 721. "As I did not cough blood": to KR, Oct. 19, 1912, TRC.

Page 721. Address, Oct. 14, 1912, *Works* 19:441–52; "He stopped and glared": Davis memo, Oct. 15, 1912, LC addenda.

Page 722. "The Colonel was feeling very good": Davis memo.

Page 723. To EKR, Oct. 14, 1912, M.

Page 723. "That sedate and determined woman": S. Morris 388.

Page 723. To ARC, Oct. 19, 1912, C.

Page 723. Statement, Oct. 16, 1912, *Works* 19:453.

Page 724. Speech, Nov. 2, 1912, *Works* 19:464–72.

TWENTY-EIGHT. THE RIVER OF DOUBT: 1913–14

Page 725. "Well, we have gone down": to KR, Nov. 5, 1912, TRC.
Page 725. "I had expected . . . unscrupulous demagogues": to Lee, Nov. 5, 1912, M.
Page 725. "proud to have made the fight": to H. Halbert, Nov. 8, 1912, LC.
Page 725. "the next four years": to M. Hale, Nov. 8, 1912, LC.
Page 725. "You may be sure": to J. Hackett, Nov. 8, 1912, LC.
Page 726. "a real misfortune": to G. Miller, Nov. 8, 1912, LC.
Page 726. "As things were . . . Progressive leader": to Lee, Nov. 5, 1912, M.
Page 727. "The Progressive Party": to T. Robinson, Oct. 29, 1912, TRB.
Page 727. "I only wish": to E. Watkins, Nov. 13, 1912, LC.
Page 727. Address, Dec. 10, 1912, Works 19:473–81.
Page 728. To G. Pinchot, Nov. 11, 1912, M.
Page 728. To A. Pinchot, Dec. 5, 1912, M.
Page 728. To Johnson, Jan. 28, 1913, M.
Page 729. "It is for the Taft Republicans": to J. Yeiser, Dec. 7, 1912, LC.
Page 729. "unwelcome guests": to W. Chanler, Apr. 1, 1913, M.
Page 729. "It is imperatively necessary": to R. Vessey et al., Jan. 22, 1913, M.
Page 729. "I shall fight": to H. Johnson, Jan. 28, 1913, M.
Page 729. To Lee, Dec. 31, 1912, M.
Page 729. To E. Carow, Jan. 4, 1913, M.
Page 731. "just the happy middle": to KR, Jan. 21, 1913, TRC.
Page 731. To Lodge, Feb. 27, 1913, L.
Page 731. Address, Dec. 27, 1912, Works 14:3–28.
Page 734. To Madero, Nov. 8, 1912, LC.
Page 734. "What it has seemed . . . advising Mr. Wilson": to G. Raine, Mar. 4, 1913, M.
Page 735. "Well!" to H. White, May 2, 1913, M.
Page 735. To Lodge, Sept. 9, 1913, M (This letter is not in the Lodge edition; by this stage of the editing process, Lodge himself was sick, and though he—an inveterate Wilson hater—might have included this letter, his coeditor chose not to).
Page 736. To N. Longworth, Feb. 13, 1912, M.
Page 737. "a tin pin": S. Morris 393–94.
Page 737. "just when everything" and "Ted and Eleanor": ibid. 396–97.
Page 740. "I never saw cooler": Through the Brazilian Wilderness: Works, 6:24–26.
Page 742. "There was one": K. Roosevelt 46–48.
Page 743. "It is not ideal": Works 6:307.
Page 745. "This jungle fever": to F. Butterworth, July 2, 1914, LC.
Page 745. To Wood, June 26, 1914, LC.
Page 745. "The call of duty": to R. Robins, June 26, 1914, LC.
Page 745. "Even as it is": to J. Shaffer, July 2, 1914, LC.
Page 745. "I would welcome": to D. Heard, June 26, 1914, M.

Page 745. "If necessary": to C. Hamlin, July 24, 1914, M.

Page 746. "Where either . . . common sense": to H. Johnson, July 30, 1914, M.

Twenty-nine. The Irregular's Return: 1914–16

Page 747. To Arch. R, Nov. 7, 1914, LC.

Page 747. "It will be": to Eth. R, Nov. 4, 1914, M.

Page 747. "The people are tired": to E. Earl, Nov. 12, 1914, LC.

Page 747. To White, Nov. 7, 1914, M.

Page 748. "The average American . . . tired of us all": to M. Lissner, Nov. 16, 1914, M; "the stomach vote": to Arch. R, Nov. 7, 1914, LC.

Page 748. To Eth. R, Nov. 26, 1914, M.

Page 748. "I simply do not know the facts": to G. Viereck, Aug. 8, 1914, LC.

Page 748. To Lee, Aug. 22, 1914, M.

Page 749. To Eleanor A. Roosevelt, Mar. 20, 1917, M.

Page 749. To Lee, Aug. 22, 1914, M.

Page 750. "Wilson is almost . . . names put on them": ibid.; "third-rate revivalist": to T. Bowlker, June 26, 1914, LC.

Page 750. *America and the World War: Works* 20:191–216.

Page 752. To Spring Rice, Nov. 11, 1914, M.

Page 753. From White, Dec. 28, 1914, LC.

Page 753. To White, Jan. 4, 1915, M.

Page 754. "More and more . . . does not serve morality": to J. Strachey, Feb. 22, 1915, M.

Page 754. "I can't express": to J. Bishop, May 14, 1915, LC.

Page 754. To Spring Rice, Feb. 9, 1915, LC.

Page 754. To Strachey, Feb. 22, 1915, M.

Page 754. To KR, Nov. 11, 1914, TRC.

Page 754. "I am practically through": to P. Rixey, Feb. 22, 1915, M.

Page 755. To Spring Rice, Feb. 18, 1915, M.

Page 756. To Arch. R, May 19, 1915, M.

Page 756. TR re *Lusitania* and German ambassador: Wister 342.

Page 756. "sick at heart . . . ribs in consequence": to Lee, June 17, 1915, M.

Page 758. To KR, Aug. 28, 1915, M.

Page 760. "Of all the blundering lunatics": Bishop 2:367–68.

Page 760. "no reasonable possiblity": to C. Bonaparte, July 24, 1914, LC.

Page 760. "I have never seen": to E. Roberts, Aug. 7, 1914, LC.

Page 760. "I personally": to Arch. R, Nov. 7, 1914, LC.

Page 760. To Perkins, Sept. 3, 1915, M.

Page 761. "This country needs": *America and the World War* 104.

Page 762. "striving to make": to G. Pinchot, Feb. 8, 1916, M.

Page 762. "The overwhelming issue": to C. Bonaparte, Dec. 31, 1915, M.

Page 763. "If the German-American vote . . . to their danger": to G. Pinchot, Feb. 8, 1916, M.

Page 763. "decent Americans . . . give a hang!": to W. Knox, Dec. 21, 1915, M.

Page 763. "Abraham Lincoln": to Spring Rice, Oct. 25, 1915, LC.

Page 764. "His action . . . foreign policies generally": to Lodge, Nov. 27, 1915, L; and Dec. 7, 1915, M.

Page 765. "*Your* country": to Spring Rice, July 16, 1916, LC.

Page 765. "The worthy gentleman's": to C. Bull, Feb. 4, 1916, M.

Page 765. "I do not think": to J. Graves, Feb. 9, 1916, M.

Page 765. "with his adroit . . . the Civil War": to Lodge, Feb. 4, 1916, L.

Page 766. "I have got to be emphatic . . . emphasizing it!": to W. Straight, Jan. 13, 1916, M.

Page 766. To Lodge, Feb. 4, 1916, LC.

Page 766. To Lee, Feb. 18, 1916, M.

Page 767. "My own judgment . . . strong convictions": to C. Washburn, May 6, 1916, M.

Page 767. "As you know": to G. Emerson, May 11, 1916, M.

Page 768. "profound political immorality . . . subjects of the day": to J. Bryce, June 19, 1916, M.

Page 768. "more intent": to I. Russell, June 16, 1916, M.

Page 768. "Root had a chance": to F. Laughlin, June 8, 1916, M.

Page 769. To ARC, June 16, 1916, C.

Page 769. To Progressive national committee, June 22, 1916, *Works* 19:564ff.

THIRTY. THE ONE THEY LEFT BEHIND: 1916–18

Page 773. "The Republicans are . . . any public position": to CRR, July 21, 1916, M.

Page 773. To ARC, July 23, 1916, C.

Page 774. "It is very galling": to R. Bass, July 28, 1916, M.

Page 774. "dreadful creature": to W. Sewall, Apr. 7, 1916, LC addenda.

Page 774. "Hughes is not an attractive personality": Leary 53.

Page 774. "I need hardly . . . defeat Wilson": to J. Garfield, Sept. 28, 1916, M.

Page 774. To CRR, Oct. 5, 1916, R.

Page 774. "first class shape . . . fighting campaign": to QR, Nov. 7, 1916, M.

Page 775. To White, Jan. 1, 1917, M.

Page 775. "Their one chance": to B. Wheeler, Nov. 29, 1916, M.

Page 775. "Outside of Mr. Hughes": to W. Willcox, Nov. 29, 1916, M.

Page 776. "We did not elect Hughes": Leary, 61.

Page 776. To Lodge, Feb. 20, 1917, M.

Page 776. "Chinese condition": to G. Perkins, Feb. 28, 1917, LC.

Page 776. To KR, Mar. 1, 1917, TRC.

Page 777. To Baker, Feb. 7, 1917, M.

Page 777. To Johnson, Feb. 17, 1917, M.

Page 778. To Jusserand, Feb. 16, 1917, M.

Page 779. To Lodge, Mar. 18, 1917, L.

Page 779. Speech of Mar. 20, 1917, Morison 8:1163n.

Page 779. To Lodge, Mar. 18, 1917, L.

Page 781. TR and Wilson meeting: to J. O'Laughlin, Apr. 13, 1917, M; Brahany diary, Apr. 10, 1917, WWP; Leary 95–98; Tumulty 285–88.

Page 783. From Baker, Mar. 26, 1917, LC.

Page 783. "Send them Roosevelt": Morison 8:1201n.

Page 783. "respectfully ask permission": to W. Wilson, May 18, 1917, LC.

Page 783. Wilson: statement of May 18, 1917, WWP.

Page 784. To McCoy, June 22, 1917, LC addenda.

Page 784. "I could have raised": to A. Gardner, June 6, 1917, M; "literally unequaled record": to F. McCoy, June 8, 1917, Frank McCoy Papers, Library of Congress.

Page 784. "I would literally . . . or anything else": to A. Gardner, June 6, 1917, M; "if I should die": to J. Scott, Feb. 1, 1918, LC.

Page 784. To Clemenceau, June 6, 1917, M.

Page 785. To Lloyd George, June 20, 1917, TRC.

Page 786. To TR Jr., May 30, 1917, M.

Page 786. To KR, May 31, 1917, TRC.

Page 786. To QR, Sept. 1, 1917, M.

Page 786. To KR, Sept. 16, 1917, TRC.

Page 786. To Arch. R, Sept. 1 and 8, 1917, M.

Page 787. *Kansas City Star,* Sept. 17 and 23, Oct. 4, 18, 23, reprinted in *Roosevelt in the Kansas City Star.*

Page 788. Wilson: Wilson to J. Tumulty, c. Dec. 18, 1917, WWP.

Page 788. "I fear": to KR, Oct. 30, 1917, KBR.

Page 788. "white rabbit . . . wretched creature": to KR, Sept. 16, 1917, KBR.

Page 788. "Fundamentally our whole trouble . . . Jekyl in their souls": to White, Aug. 3, 1917, M.

Page 789. "criminal folly": to KR, Nov. 9, 1917, KBR.

Page 790. To Eleanor A. Roosevelt, Aug. 23, 1917, M.

Page 790. To Eleanor A. Roosevelt, June 27, 1917, M.

Page 791. To KR, July 3, 1917, M.

Page 791. To QR, Dec. 24, 1917, M.

Page 792. From QR, Dec. 16, 1917, SH.

Page 792. To QR, Mar. 17, 1918, M.

Page 792. To TR Jr., Sept. 13, 1917, M.

Page 792. To Arch. R, Mar. 13, 1918, M; "It must have been rather fine": to KR, Mar. 17, 1918, KBR.

Page 793. To Clemenceau, Mar. 22, 1918, M.

Page 793. To KR, Feb. 18, 1918, M.

Page 793. To Arch. R, Mar. 13, 1918, M.

Page 793. "It seems a strange thing": to H. Bordeaux, May 27, 1918, M.

Page 793. To R. Derby, July 1, 1918, M.

Page 794. "entirely trivial . . . honor and duty": to KR, Feb. 18, 1918, M.

Page 794. "on the high road": to J. Connolly, Feb. 28, 1918, LC.

Page 795. "lunatic duck": to Eleanor A. Roosevelt, Feb. 28, 1918, TRC.

Page 795. "The best are paying": to KR, Apr. 8, 1918, KBR.

Page 795. "Wilson is the criminal": to KR, Dec. 10, 1917, TRC.

Page 795. "It is sickening": to KR, Feb. 18, 1918, LC.

Page 795. To A. Lee, Feb. 21, 1918, LC.

Page 795. "As he is physically timid": to KR, May 22, 1918, KBR.

Page 796. To KR, Apr. 21, 1918, KBR.

Page 796. "I've gotten my first": from QR, May 18, 1918, SH.

Page 796. "The last of the 'lion's brood'": to KR, July 13, 1918, TRC.

Page 796. "I wish Quentin": to Arch. R, Feb. 23, 1908, LC addenda.

Page 796. "I explained": to Arch. R, Apr. 11, 1908, LC addenda.

Page 796. "I have had": to Arch. R, Jan. 10, 1909, LC addenda.

Page 796. "blessed rogue": to Arch. R, Feb. 28, 1909, LC addenda.

Page 796. "regular alley-cat . . . great deal of concern": to Arch. R, Jan. 16, 1909, LC addenda.

Page 796. "Quentin turned up": to Arch. R, Dec. 23, 1911, LC addenda.

Page 797. Account of news of Quentin's downing and Saratoga speech: Hagedorn, *Roosevelt Family* 412–13; also S. Morris 422–24.

Page 800. "On Tuesday . . . you and I!": to KR, July 21, 1918, KBR.

THIRTY-ONE. THE LAST ROMANTIC: 1918–19

Page 802. EKR to KR: Oct. 29, 1918, S. Morris 428.

Page 802. Amos 160–61.

Page 802. Corinne: Robinson 346.

Page 803. To BWR: Aug. 11, 1918, M.

Page 803. To E. Wharton: Aug. 15, 1918, M.

Page 803. "There is no use": to KR, Aug. 4, 1918, TRC.

Page 803. "pretty well heart broken": to BWR and KR, Aug. 22, 1918, TRC.

Page 803. "Mother, of course": to KR, Aug. 10, 1918, TRC.

Page 803. "At home": to KR, July 28, 1918, TRC.

Page 803. To BWR: Aug. 11, 1918, M.

Page 804. "Quentin's death": to KR, July 28, 1918, TRC.

Page 804. "Quentin has become": to KR, Aug. 18, 1918, TRC.

Page 804. "Altho we were crushed": to W. Chanler, Oct. 25, 1918, M.

Page 804. To Bryce: Aug. 7, 1918, M.

Page 805. "absolutely ruined": to KR, Mar. 11, 1918, M.

Page 805. "shilly-shallying . . . expense of the country": to Lodge, Nov. 13, 1917, M.

Page 805. To Lodge: Oct. 24, 1918, M; Oct. 25, 1918, L.

Page 806. *Kansas City Star,* Oct. 26, 1918, *Roosevelt in Star.*

Page 806. "The President suddenly": to KR, Oct. 13, 1918, KBR.

Page 806. "A fortnight ago . . . somersault": to KR, Oct. 20, 1918, LC.

Page 806. "The President's appeal": to H. Timken, Nov. 2, 1918, M.

Page 807. To Bryce: Mar. 25, 1918, TRC.

Page 807. "We *must*": to Sen. France, Sept. 1, 1918, TRC.

Page 807. To Matthews: Sept. 13, 1918, TRBM.

Page 808. To A. Lee: Nov. 19, 1918, M.

Page 808. "show no mercy": to Lodge, Dec. 6, 1918, M (Lodge's coeditor chose to omit this phrase from Lodge's published correspondence with Roosevelt).

Page 808. To KR: Nov. 3, 1918, KBR.

Page 809. To Clemenceau: Dec. 10, 1918, LC; to Balfour, Dec. 10, 1918, LC.

Page 809. To R. Kipling: Nov. 23, 1918, M.

Page 810. "Corinne": Robinson 346–47.

Page 810. "Of our four hawks": to Belle and KR, Sept. 8, 1918, TRC.

Page 810. To Flora Whitney: Aug. 13, 1918 [erroneously dated 1919], TRC.

Page 810. "I am glad to be sixty": to KR, Oct. 27, 1918, TRC.

Page 810. TR and Corinne: Robinson, 362–63.

Page 811. TR's death: Amos 155–58, S. Morris 433–34.

Page 812. "You had to hate": Irvin Cobb in Harbaugh 490.

Page 815. "Only those . . . the same Great Adventure": *The Great Adventure: Works* 21:263–67.

SELECTED BIBLIOGRAPHY

L est a very long book be even longer, the following list is restricted to those titles cited in the notes—which is to say, in nearly all cases, titles from which a direct quotation has been taken—and a few others that have been especially useful in preparing this book. Any comprehensive bibliography of Roosevelt's life and career would include at least twenty times as many works as appear here.

Abbott, Lawrence F. *Impressions of Theodore Roosevelt,* 1919.
Abbott, Lyman. *Reminiscences,* 1915.
Adams, Henry. *The Education of Henry Adams,* 1961 ed.
Alexander, DeAlva Stanwood. *A Political History of the State of New York,* 1906.
Allen, Frederick Lewis. *The Great Pierpont Morgan,* 1948, 1965.
Amos, James E. *Theodore Roosevelt: Hero to His Valet,* 1927.
Bailey, Thomas A. *Theodore Roosevelt and the Japanese-American Crises,* 1934.
Bailyn, Bernard, et al. *Glimpses of the Harvard Past,* 1986.
Barry, David S. *Forty Years in Washington,* 1924.
Beale, Howard K. *Theodore Roosevelt and the Rise of America to World Power,* 1956.
Beer, Thomas. *Hanna,* 1929.
Berman, Jay Stuart. *Police Administration and Progressive Reform: Theodore Roosevelt as Police Commissioner of New York,* 1987.
Bishop, Joseph Bucklin. *Theodore Roosevelt and His Time, Shown in His Own Letters,* 1920; later published as vols. 23–24 of Roosevelt's *Works* (the latter cited here).
Blum, John Morton. *The Republican Roosevelt,* 1970 ed.
Brace, Charles Loring. *The Dangerous Classes of New York.* 1872, 1973.
Brands, H. W. *Bound to Empire: The United States and the Philippines,* 1992.

———. *The Reckless Decade: America in the 1890s,* 1995.

Breen, Matthew P. *Thirty Years of New York Politics,* 1899.

Brough, James. *Princess Alice,* 1975.

Bunau-Varilla, Philippe. *Panama,* 1914.

Burroughs, John. *Camping and Tramping with Roosevelt,* 1907.

Burton, David H. *Theodore Roosevelt: Confident Imperialist,* 1968.

Butler, Nicholas Murray. *Across the Busy Years,* 1939–40.

Butt, Archie. *The Letters of Archie Butt, Personal Aide to President Roosevelt,* 1924.

———. *Taft and Roosevelt: The Intimate Letters of Archie Butt, Military Aide,* 1930.

Callow, Alexander B., Jr. *The Tweed Ring,* 1965.

Cheney, Albert Loren. *Personal Memoirs of the Home Life of the Late Theodore Roosevelt as Soldier, Governor, Vice President, and President, in Relation to Oyster Bay,* 1919.

Chessman, G. Wallace. *Governor Theodore Roosevelt,* 1965.

Chidsey, Donald Barr. *The Gentleman from New York: A Life of Roscoe Conkling,* 1935.

Collin, Richard H. *Theodore Roosevelt's Caribbean,* 1990.

Collins, Michael L. *That Damned Cowboy: Theodore Roosevelt and the American West, 1883–1898,* 1989.

Cook, Adrian. *The Armies of the Streets: The New York City Draft Riots of 1863,* 1974.

Cook, Blanche Wiesen. *Eleanor Roosevelt,* vol. 1, 1992.

Cooper, John Milton, Jr. *The Warrior and the Priest: Woodrow Wilson and Theodore Roosevelt,* 1983.

Costas, Graham A. *An Army for Empire: The United States Army in the Spanish-American War,* 1994.

Cutright, Paul Russell. *Theodore Roosevelt: The Making of a Conservationist,* 1985.

Dalton, Kathleen. "The Early Life of Theodore Roosevelt," Johns Hopkins University dissertation, 1979.

Daniels, Josephus. *Editor in Politics,* 1941.

Davis, Oscar King. *Released for Publication,* 1925.

Davis, Richard Harding. *The Cuban and Porto Rican Campaigns,* 1898.

Delaney, Norman C. "The End of the Alabama," in Sears.

Democratic National Committee. *National Democratic Campaign Book: Presidential Election 1900,* 1900.

Dennett, Tyler. *Roosevelt and the Russo-Japanese War,* 1925.

Depew, Chauncey M. *My Memories of Eighty Years,* 1922.

Dunn, Arthur Wallace. *From Harrison to Harding,* 1922, 1971.

———. *Gridiron Nights,* 1915.

Dunne, Finley Peter. *Mr. Dooley's Philosophy,* 1900.

Ellis, Elmer. *Mr. Dooley's America: A Life of Finley Peter Dunne,* 1941.

Felsenthal, Carol. *Alice Roosevelt Longworth,* 1988.

Fleming, Donald. "Eliot's New Broom," in Bailyn.

Foraker, Joseph Benson. *Notes of a Busy Life*, 1916.

Friedel, Frank. *The Splendid Little War*, 1958.

Gable, John A. *The Bull Moose Years*, 1978.

Gardner, Joseph L. *Departing Glory: Theodore Roosevelt as Ex-President.* 1973.

Garraty, John Arthur. *Henry Cabot Lodge*, 1953.

Gibbons, Herbert Adams. *John Wanamaker*, 1926.

Gordon, John Steele. *The Scarlet Woman of Wall Street*, 1988.

Gould, Lewis L. *The Presidency of Theodore Roosevelt*, 1991.

Hagedorn, Hermann, *The Boys' Life of Theodore Roosevelt*, 1918.

———. *Leonard Wood*, 1931.

———. *The Roosevelt Family of Sagamore Hill*, 1954.

———. *Roosevelt in the Bad Lands*, 1930.

Harbaugh, William Henry. *The Life and Times of Theodore Roosevelt*, 1961, 1975.

Harlan, Louis R. *Booker T. Washington*, 1972–83.

Holmes, Oliver Wendell Jr., and Frederick Pollock. *Holmes-Pollock Letters*, ed. by Mark DeWolfe Howe, 1961 ed.

Hone, Philip. *The Diary of Philip Hone*, ed. by Allan Nevins, 1936.

Iglehart, Ferdinand C. *Theodore Roosevelt: The Man as I Knew Him*, 1919.

James, Henry. *Charles W. Eliot*, 1930.

James, Henry. *Washington Square*, 1971 ed.

Jeffers, H. Paul. *Colonel Roosevelt*, 1996.

———. *Commissioner Roosevelt*, 1994.

Jessup, Philip C. *Elihu Root*, 1938.

Jones, Howard. *The Course of American Diplomacy*, 1985.

Jones, Virgil Carrington. *Roosevelt's Rough Riders*, 1971.

Josephson, Matthew. *The Politicos*, 1938.

Karnow, Stanley. *In Our Image: America's Empire in the Philippines*, 1989.

Kennan, George. *Campaigning in Cuba*, 1899, 1971.

Kerr, Joan Peterson, ed. *A Bully Father*, 1995.

Klein, Maury. *The Life and Legend of Jay Gould*, 1986.

Kohlsaat, H. H. *From McKinley to Harding*, 1923.

LaFeber, Walter. *The American Search for Opportunity, 1865–1913*, 1993.

———. *The Panama Canal*, 1978.

Lang, Lincoln A. *Ranching with Roosevelt*, 1926.

Lash, Joseph P. *Eleanor and Franklin*, 1971.

Leary, John J. Jr. *Talks with T.R.*, 1920.

Leech, Margaret. *In the Days of McKinley*, 1959.

Lockwood, Charles. *Manhattan Moves Uptown*, 1976.

Long, John Davis. *America of Yesterday, as Reflected in the Journal of John Davis Long*, ed. by Lawrence Shaw Mayo, 1923.

———. *The New American Navy*, 1903.

Longworth, Alice Roosevelt. *Crowded Hours*, 1933.

———. *Mrs. L: Conversations with Alice Roosevelt Longworth*, ed. by Michael Teague, 1981.

Looker, Earle. *The White House Gang*, 1929.

Lorant, Stefan. *The Life and Times of Theodore Roosevelt*, 1959.

Manners, William. *TR and Will*, 1969.

Marshall, Logan. *The Life of Theodore Roosevelt*, 1910.

McCall, Samuel W. *Thomas B. Reed*, 1914.

McClure, A. K. *Old Time Notes of Pennsylvania*, 1905.

McCullough, David. *Mornings on Horseback*, New York, 1981. (Unless otherwise indicated, this is the "McCullough" cited in the notes.)

———. *The Path Between the Seas*, 1977.

Miller, Nathan. *The Roosevelt Chronicles*, 1979.

———. *Theodore Roosevelt*, 1992.

Millis, Walter. *The Martial Spirit*, 1931, 1989.

Mitchell, Nancy. "The Height of the German Challenge: The Venezuela Blockade, 1902–3," *Diplomatic History*, Spring 1996.

Moore, J. Hampton. *Roosevelt and the Old Guard*, 1925.

Morgan, H. Wayne. *America's Road to Empire*, 1965.

———. *From Hayes to McKinley*, 1969.

Morris, Edmund. *The Rise of Theodore Roosevelt*, 1979.

Morris, Sylvia Jukes. *Edith Kermit Roosevelt*, 1980.

Mowry, George E. *The Era of Theodore Roosevelt*, 1958.

———. *Theodore Roosevelt and the Progressive Movement*, 1946.

Naylor, Natalie A., Douglas Brinkley and John Allen Gable. *Theodore Roosevelt: Many-Sided American*, 1992.

Nevins, Allan. *Grover Cleveland*, 1964.

Ornig, Joseph R. *My Last Chance to be a Boy: Theodore Roosevelt's South American Expedition of 1913–1914*, 1994.

Parsons, Frances Theodora. *Perchance Some Day*, 1951.

Patterson, Jerry E. *The City of New York*, 1978.

Peck, Harry Thurston. *Twenty Years of the Republic, 1885–1905*, 1920.

Peirce, Clyde. *The Roosevelt Panama Libel Cases*, 1959.

Pinchot, Gifford. *Breaking New Ground*, 1947, 1972.

Platt, Thomas Collier. *The Autobiography of Thomas Collier Platt*, ed. by Louis J. Lang, 1910.

Porter, Kenneth Wiggins. *John Jacob Astor*, 1931.

Pringle, Henry F. *Theodore Roosevelt*, 1931 ("Pringle" in the notes).

———. *The Life and Times of William Howard Taft*, 1939.

Putnam, Carleton. *Theodore Roosevelt: The Formative Years*, 1958.

Reckner, James R. *Teddy Roosevelt's Great White Fleet*, 1988.

Rice, Cecil Spring. *The Letters and Friendships of Sir Cecil Spring Rice*, ed. by Stephen Gwynn, 1929.

Riis, Jacob. *The Making of an American*, 1935.

———. *Theodore Roosevelt the Citizen*, 1904.

Rixey, Lilian. *Bamie: Theodore Roosevelt's Remarkable Sister*, 1963.

Robinson, Corinne Roosevelt. *My Brother Theodore Roosevelt*, 1926.

Robinson, William A. *Thomas B. Reed*, 1930.

Roosevelt, Kermit. *The Happy Hunting Grounds*, 1921.

Roosevelt, Nicholas. *Theodore Roosevelt: The Man as I Knew Him*, 1967.

Roosevelt, Theodore. *Addresses and Presidential Messages*, 1904.

———. *African and European Addresses*, 1910.

———. *Presidential Messages and State Papers*, 1904.

———. *Public Papers of Theodore Roosevelt, Governor*, 1889–1900.

———. *Roosevelt in the Kansas City Star*, 1921.

———. *The Works of Theodore Roosevelt* (Memorial Edition), 1923–26.

Roosevelt, Theodore, Jr. *All in the Family*, 1929.

Sears, Stephen W., ed., *The Civil War*, 1991.

Sewall, William Wingate. *Bill Sewall's Story of T.R.*, 1919.

Sinclair, Andrew. *Corsair: The Life of J. Pierpont Morgan*, 1981.

Spann, Edward K. *The New Metropolis: New York City, 1840–1857*, 1981.

Street, Julian. *The Most Interesting American*, 1916.

Strong, George Templeton. *The Diary of George Templeton Strong*, 1952 ed.

Sullivan, Mark. *Our Times: The United States, 1900–1925*, 1926–37.

Teague, Michael. "Theodore Roosevelt and Alice Hathaway Lee: A New Perspective," *Harvard Library Bulletin*, Summer 1985.

Thayer, William Roscoe. *The Life and Letters of John Hay*, 1915.

———. *Theodore Roosevelt: An Intimate Biography*, 1919 ("Thayer" in the notes).

Thompson, Charles Willis. *Presidents I've Known and Two Near Presidents*, 1929.

Trask, David F. *The War with Spain in 1898*, 1981.

Tumulty, Joseph P. *Woodrow Wilson as I Knew Him*. 1921.

Turk, Richard W. *The Ambiguous Relationship: Theodore Roosevelt and Alfred Thayer Mahan*, 1987.

Viereck, George Sylvester. *Roosevelt: A Study in Ambivalence*, 1919.

Vivian, James F. *The Romance of My Life: Theodore Roosevelt's Speeches in Dakota*, 1989.

Watson, James E. *As I Knew Them*. 1936.

Weaver, John D. *The Brownsville Raid*, 1973 ed.

White, William Allen. *Autobiography*, 1946.

Wilhelm, Donald. *Theodore Roosevelt as an Undergraduate*, 1910.

Wister, Owen. *Roosevelt: The Story of a Friendship*, 1930.

Wood, Frederick S. *Roosevelt as We Knew Him*, 1927.

Wood, Leonard. "Roosevelt: Soldier, Statesman, and Friend": intro. to Roosevelt, *The Rough Riders and Men of Action*, 1926 ed.

ACKNOWLEDGMENTS

The author has received the help of archivists, librarians, and colleagues too numerous to mention. But he would like to extend special thanks to John Gable, executive director of the Theodore Roosevelt Association; Wallace Dailey, curator of the Theodore Roosevelt Collection at Harvard University; Kathleen Young Sheedy of the Sagamore Hill National Historical Site; Whitney Bagnall of the Columbia University Law Library; Lewis Gould of the University of Texas at Austin; and Alex Mintz and the Program in Foreign Policy Decision-making of Texas A&M University. Also thanks to Steve Fraser, Susan Rabiner, and James Hornfischer.

INDEX